Emergence of Communication and Language

T0205681

Caroline Lyon, Chrystopher L. Nehaniv
and Angelo Cangelosi (Eds)

Emergence of Communication and Language

 Springer

Caroline Lyon
School of Computer Science
University of Hertfordshire
Hatfield, UK

Chrystopher L. Nehaniv
School of Computer Science
University of Hertfordshire
Hatfield, UK

Angelo Cangelosi
School of Computing
Communications and Electronics
University of Plymouth
Plymouth, UK

British Library Cataloguing in Publication Data
A catalogue record for this book is available from the British Library

ISBN-13: 978-1-84996-610-8   e-ISBN-13: 978-1-84628-779-4

9 8 7 6 5 4 3 2 1

Springer Science+Business Media

springer.com

TABLE OF CONTENTS

LIST OF CONTRIBUTORS

Tony Belpaeme
School of Computing, Communications and Electronics, University of Plymouth, UK

Joris Bleys
Artificial Intelligence Laboratory, Vrije Universiteit Brussel, Belgium

Joanna J. Bryson
Department of Computer Science, University of Bath, UK

Ivana Čače
Cognitive Artificial Intelligence (CKI), Universiteit Utrecht, The Netherlands

Stephen J. Cowley
School of Psychology, University of Hertfordshire, UK
University of KwaZulu-Natal, South Africa

Bob Dickerson
School of Computer Science, University of Hertfordshire, UK

W. Tecumseh Fitch
School of Psychology, Centre for Social Learning and Cognitive Evolution, University of St Andrews, UK

Anna Fedor
Collegium Budapest (Institute for Advanced Study), Hungary
Institute of Biology, Eötvös University, Budapest, Hungary

Jonathan Ginzburg
Department of Computer Science, King's College, London, UK

Takashi Hashimoto
School of Knowledge Science, Japan Advanced Institute of Science and Technology (JAIST), Japan

Ferenc Huszár
Collegium Budapest (Institute for Advanced Study), Hungary

Péter Ittzés
Collegium Budapest (Institute for Advanced Study), Hungary

Simon Kirby
Language Evolution and Computation Research Unit, University of Edinburgh, UK

Zoran Macura
Department of Computer Science, King's College, London, UK

Davide Marocco
Institute of Cognitive Science and Technologies, CNR, Rome, Italy

Akira Masumi
School of Knowledge Science, Japan Advanced Institute of Science and Technology (JAIST), Japan

Bjorn Merker
Gamla Kyrkv. 44, SE-14171 Segeltorp, Sweden

Marco Mirolli
Institute of Cognitive Sciences and Technologies, National Research Council, Rome, Italy

Makoto Nakamura
School of Information Science, Japan Advanced Institute of Science and Technology (JAIST), Japan

Stefano Nolfi
Institute of Cognitive Science and Technologies, CNR, Rome, Italy

Kazuo Okanoya
RIKEN Brain Science Institute, Japan

Gergő Orbán
Collegium Budapest (Institute for Advanced Study), Hungary

Pierre-Yves Oudeyer
SONY Computer Science Laboratory, Paris, France

Domenico Parisi
Institute of Cognitive Sciences and Technologies, National Research Council, Rome, Italy

Irene M. Pepperberg
Department of Psychology, Brandeis University, Waltham, USA
Department of Psychology, Harvard University, Cambridge, USA

Graham R. S. Ritchie
Language Evolution and Computation Research Unit, University of Edinburgh, UK

Rachel Rosenstock
Linguistics Department, Gallaudet University, Washington DC, USA

Andrew D. M. Smith
Language Evolution and Computation Research Unit, University of Edinburgh, UK

Luc Steels
SONY Computer Science Laboratory, Paris, France
Artificial Intelligence Laboratory, Vrije Universiteit Brussel, Belgium

Eörs Szathmáry
Collegium Budapest (Institute for Advanced Study), Hungary
Institute of Biology, Eötvös University, Budapest, Hungary
Parmenides Center for the Study of Thinking, München, Germany

Zoltán Szatmáry
Collegium Budapest (Institute for Advanced Study), Hungary

Szabolcs Számadó
Collegium Budapest (Institute for Advanced Study), Hungary
Institute of Biology, Eötvös University, Budapest, Hungary

Satoshi Tojo
School of Information Science, Japan Advanced Institute of Science and Technology
(JAIST), Japan

Máté Varga
Collegium Budapest (Institute for Advanced Study), Hungary,
Institute of Biology, Eötvös University, Budapest, Hungary

Alison Wray
Centre for Language and Communication Research, Cardiff University, UK

István Zachár
Collegium Budapest (Institute for Advanced Study), Hungary
Institute of Biology, Eötvös University, Budapest, Hungary

1
Introduction

Current Work and Open Problems: A Road-Map for Research into the Emergence of Communication and Language

Chrystopher L. Nehaniv, Caroline Lyon, and Angelo Cangelosi

1.1. Introduction

This book brings together work on the emergence of communication and language from researchers working in a broad array of scientific paradigms in North America, Europe, Japan and Africa.

We hope that its multi-disciplinary approach will encourage cross-fertilization and promote further advances in this active research field. The volume draws on diverse disciplines, including linguistics, psychology, neuroscience, ethology, anthropology, robotics, and computer science. Computational simulations of the emergence of phenomena associated with communication and language play a key role in illuminating some of the most significant issues, and the renewed scientific interest in language emergence has benefited greatly from research in Artificial Intelligence and Cognitive Science.

The book starts with this road map chapter by the editors, pointing to the ways in which disparate disciplines can inform and stimulate each other. It examines the role of simulations as a novel way to express theories in science, and their contribution to the development of a new approach to the study of the emergence of communication and language. We will also discuss and collect the most promising directions and grand challenge problems for future research.

The present volume, is organized into three parts: I. Empirical Investigations on Human Language, II. Synthesis and Simulation of Communication and Language in Artificial Systems, and III. Insights from Animal Communication. The aims are to provide a common interdisciplinary forum for research into the emergence and evolution of communication and language, to disseminate the latest work on theoretical, empirical and modelling investigations, to help set the agenda for future research and identify the most promising theoretical and methodological issues in the area.

1.2. The Interdisciplinary Investigation of the Emergence of Communication and Language

The renewed scientific interest in the emergence and evolution of linguistic communication has become one of the most important research issues in Artificial Intelligence and Cognitive Science. This volume therefore focuses on the latest empirical and modelling research on the evolutionary factors that affect the acquisition, self-organization and origins of linguistic communication systems and their pre-cursors in communication. This requires consideration of both language-specific abilities (e.g. speech, semantics and syntax) and other cognitive, sensorimotor and social abilities (e.g. category learning, action and embodiment, social networks). From the viewpoint of cognitive and evolutionary continuity (Griffin 1976; Maynard Smith and Szathmáry 1995), it is also fruitful to examine the emergence of communicative systems in non-human animals in order to better understand the context surrounding the advent of human language and its pre-cursors. One should also consider constellations of potential mechanisms and properties known from the animal world that may be necessary or sufficient for various aspects of linguistic communication to arise (e.g. Hauser (1996); Fitch (this volume), Pepperberg (this volume)).

For communicative systems in animals, some key questions relate to the origin, persistence and evolution of signalling channels in the sensory ecology of various species; transitions from signalling to communication; the relationships between information, utility, and representational capacity of communicative signals; the origin and possible roles of complexity in communication systems, and the roles of social interaction in the emergence of these systems. For lingustic communication, key questions relate to the the emergence of symbol grounding; deixis, gesture, and reference; predication; negation; syntactic categories; and compositionality among other issues in the context of embodied, social interaction and evolution.

This is a field characterized by an interdisciplinary and multi-methodological approach. The methodologies adopted cover a wide range, from animal and human experiments, to brain studies and to computational and robotic modelling of linguistic behaviour. For example, computational models of language evolution and emergence involve artificial intelligence methods (e.g. artificial neural networks, evolutionary computation, rule-based systems) and techniques for the simulation of behaviour (artificial life, multi-agent systems, adaptive behaviour and robotics). This interaction creates the opportunity and need for the most influential researchers in the field to present their latest work and to discuss the agenda for future studies.

The use of computational models for simulating the evolution of language has made a significant contribution to the renewed interest in language evolution research. In fact, up to ten years ago, very few researchers were directly interested in the origins and evolution of language, and publications on new language evolution studies were uncommon. This was partly the result of the famous ban in the 19th century by the Société Linguistique de Paris on research and publication on language origins to quell rampant, unfounded speculation on the topic. The development of the first language evolution models in the early 1990s enabled some of the main difficulties in such a scientific field to be addressed. Previously theories of language origins and evolution not only were difficult or impossible to test empirically but they tended to be stated in vague and general terms and were unable to generate specific empirical predictions. This had been partially due to the problem of the objective scarcity of empirical evidence. It is this very problematic aspect of the study of language evolution which computer simulations can help us to overcome. Computer simulations embody theories of the empirical phenomena that are simulated (Cangelosi and Parisi 2002). They are scientific theories expressed as computer programs. The program incorporates a set of hypotheses on the causes, mechanisms, and processes underlying the simulated phenomena and, when the program runs, the results are the empirical predictions derived from the theory incorporated in the simulation. All this contributes to the development of a new approach to the study of the origins and evolution of language.

In the last decade or so, there has been an explosion of interest in the modelling and understanding of language origins. The employment of simulation and robotic agent-based, artificial neural network, and evolutionary techniques has provided new methods for formulating hypotheses, validating mechanisms, and selecting between alternative theories on the emergence of linguistic and language-like phenomena in controlled experimental settings that meet the scientific criteria of reproducibility. Recent work on the emergence and evolution of human language and more simple communication systems has been increasingly interdisciplinary, involving collaborations between linguists, philosophers, biologists, cognitive scientists, roboticists, mathematical and computational modellers – see e.g. research papers (MacLennan 1992; Steels 1995; Hashimoto and Ikegami 1995; Arita and Koyama 1998; Billard and Dautenhahn 1999; Kirby 1999; Nehaniv 2000; Cangelosi 2001; Steels 2003) and interdisciplinary collections (Wray 2002; Cangelosi and Parisi 2002; Christiansen and Kirby 2003). The unifying aim is to gain deeper insight into issues surrounding the emergence and evolution of communication and language.

Of course the bases of simulations lie in empirical studies, which provide the starting points to inspire computational models. We therefore begin the volume with Part I reporting on recent empirical investigations illuminating the emergence of communication and language in humans. This is followed by the most substantial part of the book, a range of chapters on simulations of aspects of the emergence of communication and language in artificial systems. To conclude, Part III focuses on recent research on animal communication, which gives further insight into some of the issues and open problems addressed earlier.

1.2.1. Empirical Investigations on Human Language

The first part leads with the chapter *Evolving Meaning: The Roles of Kin Selection, Allomothering and Paternal Care in Language Evolution* by

W. Tecumseh Fitch, showing how the evolution of propositional semantics could be related to hominid life history and other observable factors. He reviews several bodies of comparative data, not discussed in previous studies. Acknowledging the need for an approach to language evolution that includes separate components such as vocal imitation, syntactic ability, and the capacities underlying honest, complex propositional meanings, Fitch reviews relevant comparative and evolutionary evidence. The latter capacity for propositonal semantics is considered as a critical component of language, and, due to its apparent uniqueness, the one whose evolution is the most difficult to explain. He argues that kin selection drove the evolution of rich semantic communication bringing to bear comparative evidence on this problem from hominid life history, and the long period of dependency in childhood, the flexible extractive foraging techniques typical of both modern humans and chimpanzees, and the evolution of parental care by males that typifies humans but not other great apes.

The work of Alison Wray on *'Needs-only' Analysis in Linguistic Ontogeny and Phylogeny* questions the requirement for the full systematicity of language structures that is pre-supposed in traditional linguistics. Based on empirical investigations into actual language usage, she argues that effective communication is often achieved by formulaic processes. Indeed, utterances are often processed as groups of words or higher level chunks, rather than at the level of individual items, in a 'needs only' analysis. Language models that only partially systematize structures may thus provide a more faithful description of natural language processing. (In the second part of this book, related ideas enter in the work of Steels and of Kirby in synthetic models of language origins and evolution via self-organizing processes.)

The chapter *Clues from Information Theory Indicating a Phased Emergence of Grammar* by Caroline Lyon, Chrystopher L. Nehaniv and Bob Dickerson also supports this approach, demonstrating that present-day human language is characterized by an underlying local sequential statistical structure. This gives clues to a possible phased emergence of grammar by partially systematizing such local sequential dependencies. The work by Lyon et al., using information-theoretic tools to analyse a corpus of 100 million words, would not have been possible in past decades and provides an example of how technical advances have enabled new approaches in this field. A computer is to the linguist what a telescope is to the astronomer. Further support for the hypothesis that local sequential processing underlies the production and perception of speech comes from neurobiological evidence. Moreover, observations that homophones are apparently ubiquitous and used without confusion in human language also suggests that language processing may be largely based on local sequential context.

A different type of empirical study on *Emergence of a Communication System: International Sign* comes from Rachel Rosenstock, who presents an account of the actual emergence of a new international communication system for the deaf: International Sign (IS), used widely in the Deaf Community at international events. Presently, deaf speakers have their own natural (national) sign languages (SL) and this is a second language. She reports on how an initial prescriptive approach to creating IS has been modified by natural processes of language change and presents evidence on how the lexicon and syntactic structures have developed. This present study is one of the first to research extensively the origin of both the IS lexicon and grammatical structures. Her findings suggest that IS, with its still comparatively limited vocabulary, is both influenced by natural SLs and relies more heavily on iconic, universal structures, as well as on role play. This work shows how IS continues to develop from a simplistic iconic system into a conventionalized system with increasingly complex rules.

The chapter *Distributed Language: Biomechanics, Functions, and the Origins of Talk* by psychologist Stephen J. Cowley reports on investigations into communication between pre-linguistic infants and carers, focusing on the underlying distributed and embodied nature of human language. Evidence is framed that, in development, language emerges under dual control by adult and child as they transform each other's agency already in the early stages of language acquisition. Drawing from field studies of caregiver-child interaction in different cultures, Cowley describes the roles of cultural selection, norm-based behavioural, affective, and body kinetic factors leading to the emergence of language use in children in their ongoing negotiated interactions with adults. The issue of symbol grounding is also discussed in this light, as are suggestions for understanding the emergence of language via multi-agent modelling simulations using interaction between humans and humanoid robots.

These chapters throw into relief the need to examine real language, with implications for modelling and simulation as discussed below.

1.2.2. Synthesis and Simulation of Communication and Language in Artificial Systems

This central part of the book presents a range of new simulations, computational and robotic models.

Presenting *The Recruitment Theory of Language Origins*, Luc Steels argues that language users try out and recruit strategies from various neural or cognitive mechanisms which may in themselves serve a wide range of purposes independent of language (such as perspective transformation, discrimination, and reduction of computational complexity in cognitive processing) and could have evolved separately from language. This theory is supported by the results of computational and robotic experiments described in his chapter. They illustrate how recruitment of particular simulated cognitive functionalities leads to improved communicative success in robotic and software simulation settings, giving rise to self-organized vowel system discrimination, shared vocabularies, perspective marking, and predicate-argument structure.

In the chapter *In silico Evolutionary Developmental Neurobiology and the Origin of Natural Language* by Eörs Szathmáry, Zoltán Szatmáry, Péter Ittzés, Gergő Orbán, István Zachár, Ferenc Huszár, Anna Fedor, Máté Varga, and Szabolcs Számadó, the authors first survey evidence that part of our genetic endowment contributes to language skills, but discuss that it is impossible to determine at present exactly how genes affect the language faculty. They present in outline their detailed computational model for the bases of human cognitive faculties from a biological perspective. From this they suggest how aspects of their model could be used as a basis for simulating the emergence of primitive communication and language. The authors complement experimental biological studies with a computational modelling approach to simulate the evolution of neural networks under selection for language-related skills. Their agents are shown to evolve the capacity for phenotypic variability suitable for developing communicative capacities, resembling in some aspects those of the human brain.

In their chapter *Communication in Natural and Artificial Organisms: Experiments in Evolutionary Robotics*, Davide Marocco and Stefano Nolfi describe experiments with simulated robots in which primitive bi-directional communication emerges in evolving groups of initially non-communicating agents. Communication about aspects of the external environment, as well as synchronized communication forms such as 'duetting', are seen to evolve in the simulated robotic examples in which the robots use communication to solve a collective navigation task. The authors find analogies with features of certain animal communication systems that could be prerequisites for human language.

The chapter *From Vocal Replication to Shared Combinatorial Speech Codes: A Small Step for Evolution, a Big Step for Language* by Pierre-Yves Oudeyer presents simulations of self-organizing processes that could account for the origins of phonological and phonotactic patterns in a shared, combinatorial signalling system with structural regularity and diversity in a population of agents. From this he argues that the step from vocal replication to human speech systems might have been rather small.

Takashi Hashimoto and Akira Masumi have a different approach. They note a remarkable phenomenon in certain artificial neural networks, where chaotic systems enter into phases of stability under certain conditions. Their chapter *Learning and Transition of Symbols: Towards a Dynamical Model of a Symbolic Individual* describes the construction of dynamical systems for which they propose correspondences of symbolic activities to the behaviour of the systems: mapping symbols to attractors, symbol manipulations to transitions among attractors, and manipulation rules to transition sequences. These dynamical transitions are shown to be inducible by certain external inputs. The authors argue that such models could help explain the development of some cognitive faculties in biological networks, and in particular the emergence of symbol processing capabilities.

In *Language Change among 'Memoryless Learners' Simulated in Language Dynamics Equations* Makoto Nakamura, Takashi Hashimoto and Satoshi Tojo also start from a theoretical position, based on nativist assumptions, and develop language dynamics equations to simulate the emergence of a dominant grammar among users of multiple languages. They improve on earlier work in this field by introducing more realistic conditions for modelling language similarity and language contact, and discuss how their work could be used to model the emergence of creoles.

The Evolution of Meaning-Space Structure through Iterated Learning by Simon Kirby investigates a model that extends his previous work on iterated learning. This emphasizes the impact of transmissional properties of language on its persistence, change, and systematization over generations. He examines the dynamics of the emergence of mixed compositional and holistic languages as shaped by the influence of a transmissional bottleneck on syntactic and semantic structures. As a result of undergoing repeated cycles of transmission, language changes some its properties. While previous work examined the impact of the transmission bottleneck on syntactic aspects of language, this chapter allows linguistic agents flexibility and choice in how they construct the semantics of linguistic expressions. This approach shows how semantics might evolve culturally in tandem with syntax, and how communicative contexts could impact the evolution of meaning structure.

Domenico Parisi and Marco Mirolli's chapter *The Emergence of Language: How to Simulate It* explores the modelling of an evolutionary sequence of events, relating linguistic ability to bipedalism and other landmark factors. Bipedalism and the advent of the need to predict the effect of actions of the hands for manipulating the environment, due to increased behavioural repertoire, are discussed. Further transitions are considered in imitative capacity and the ability to predict the results of imitating the behaviour of others, as well as the imitation of their communicative behaviour. This leads to a consideration of the role of mirror-neurons, cf. (Arbib 2002), in the evolution of language.

In *Lexical Acquisition with and without Metacommunication* Jonathan Ginzburg and Zoran Macura report on results of language games between synthetic agents, and the light this throws on the emergence of meta-communicative interaction with its important role in human language. In these meta-communicative interactions, the agents are able to acknowledge understanding or request clarification. Simulations show that convergence of the lexicon improves in a qualitatively significant way once agents in the population are endowed with the capacity for requesting clarification.

Ivana Čače and Joanna Bryson develop a model of interacting synthetic agents showing how advantages of sharing information can arise in *Agent Based Modelling of Communication Costs: Why Information Can be Free*. This chapter describes a model that demonstrates that sharing knowledge in a foraging environment can be adaptive even when sharing knowledge costs the speaker in terms of foraging opportunities. This is found even when initially the majority of the population consists of free-riders, who take information from those that share it but do not themselves communicate any information. The population is able to take advantage of the increased carrying capacity of the environment that results from the spread of knowledge, and the free riders are reliably out-competed by the speakers.

In *Language Change and the Inference of Meaning*, Andrew D. M. Smith presents the results of simulating processes of language change through generations in which there is indeterminacy of meaning that individuals ascribe to a given word. Partial disambiguation of the meaning of words can be learned through multiple contexts of use. Although uncertainty inherent in the inference of meanings leads to conceptual and lexical variation in this model, this variation leads to representational flexibility and proves sufficiently stable to explain both how a language can become shared between individuals with different semantic representations, and how it can change rapidly while remaining a tool for successful communication.

In their chapter *Language, Perceptual Categories and their Interaction: Insights from Computational Modelling*, Tony Belpaeme and Joris Bleys study how language might affect the acquisition of perceptual categories, taking colour as a case study. They compare models of synthetic agents acquiring colour categories, in which language plays different roles. The authors demonstrate how categories can become coordinated under the influence of language. They also show that, depending on how strictly linguistic utterances are interpreted, coordination of the individuals' categories is not always a prerequisite for successful communication.

1.2.3. Insights from Animal Communication

In addition to many other animal communication systems touched upon in various chapters, the final part of this book presents studies on avian communication, and the light this throws on possible routes for the emergence of human language. The communication systems of birds can be extremely complex, but evidently differ from humans in their very limited semantic range. However, their structural and expressive scope is not yet fully understood.

In her chapter, *Emergence of Linguistic Communication: Studies on Grey Parrots*, Irene M. Pepperberg gives a comprehensive account of the communication skills of Grey Parrots, which find parallels with some human abilities. Although phylogenetically remote from humans, they may have been subject to similar evolutionary pressures that affected the evolution of complex communication systems. Many studies on the evolution of communication systems concentrate on the primate lineage, ignoring the concept of parallel lines of evolution. She shows that for certain tasks, Grey Parrots demonstrate processing abilities comparable to 5–6 year-old humans. They can learn very simple vocal syntactic patterns and referential elements of human communication, but only through social interaction and in a manner that proceeds in ways similar to that in humans (where language use is functional, and other people serve not only as models but also as rivals). Pepperberg argues that, given this kind of vocal learning in birds, the effects of social interaction on such learning, and of birds' complex cognitive abilities, the avian line must be considered in seeking to understand the evolutionary contingencies that affect the evolution of complex communication systems.

Unlike these examples from parrots, vocal learning and complex communicative signalling, but without referential communication, is possible in other avian species. In *A Possible Role for Selective Masking in the Evolution of Complex, Learned Communication Systems*, Graham R. S. Ritchie and

Simon Kirby report on the song behaviour of the domesticated Bengalese finch, which differs markedly from that of its feral ancestor, still common in the wild. They present a model in which increased song complexity and increased influence from early learning could evolve spontaneously as a result of domestication, and they argue that this could illuminate the evolution of reliance on vocal learning in other species, including humans.

In *The Natural History of Human Language: Bridging the Gaps without Magic* by Bjorn Merker and Kazuo Okanoya and *Neural Substrates for String-Context Mutual Segmentation: A Path to Human Language* by Okanoya and Merker the authors investigate vocal imitation and complex sequence learning as observed in songbirds. They present a possible origin of human language: that the human ancestor was a singing ape (as Darwin once suggested). While examples of vocal learning are common in birds, whale and human song provide rare mammalian examples of the phenomenon. In their two chapters they first propose that linguistic structures are products of particular biological requisites together with historical processes. They examine the ability of birds to learn vocal strings, the sequence complexity of song-bouts, and its relation to human language. They go on to examine a number of neural, behavioural and learning mechanisms that serve necessary or facilitating roles in the initiation of the historical processes. They consider the neural substrates for complex vocal imitation, and contextual string segmentation in bird species, arguing that a shared repertoire of many distinct songs-strings could become a vehicle for semantic communication if the repertoire became differentiated according to specific environmental, behavioral, or social contexts.

1.3. Evaluating and Validating Synthetic Models

Simulations of the evolution of language have progressed very quickly in recent years with good reason (Cangelosi and Parisi 2002). The advantages of working in a virtual laboratory include the ability to carry out experiments that would be empirically impossible in the real world, as well as those that are prohibited for ethical reasons (e.g. lesioning). Simulations are used as tools for testing theories by generating predictions that can be empirically investigated (e.g. Belpaeme and Bleys, this volume). They can throw light on the nature of language as a complex system, enabling different interacting parameters to be varied for multiple experiments (e.g. Hashimoto and Masumi, this volume).

However, issues arise in placing the constructive methodology of simulation and modelling in the general framework of valid scientific method. In classical terms a scientific theory should in principle be falsifiable: if it could not conceivably be falsified it does not warrant the label 'scientific' (Popper 1959)[1]

---

[1] Informal accounts can be found at http://en.wikipedia.org/wiki/Karl_Popper and http://en.wikipedia.org/wiki/Falsifiability

Well-known examples are the theories of Newtonian physics: these are properly called 'scientific' since one can imagine experiments where their predictions could be shown to be false – as they were by the theory of relativity. Scientific theories must in principle be open to a contrary example. However, showing that a falsifiable theory has some counterexamples to its predictions is not necessarily useful unless one can produce an alternative theory which explains more. Comparing the predictions of two theories with experimental results, allows one to locate areas where one or the other has superior predictive power.

Though the work we have described here is carried out in a scientific framework, models may not be falsifiable in the same way as classical theories. To elucidate this, consider a simple model, such as the plan of the London Underground, often considered an example of excellent design. The plan has a purpose, which is to show underground routes to passengers; it does not aim to reflect the real underground layout. Information about lines, stations and junctions has been *abstracted*, then presented and displayed in a diagrammatic form. It would not be a valid criticism to complain that distances between stations were not to scale, since this was not part of the requirement. We may want the model to be fit for its purpose rather than a reflection of reality.

Cognitive scientists and neurophysiologists typically are interested primarily in theories and models that realistically reflect what occurs in human cognition. In contrast, it is worth noting that researchers in artificial intelligence, artificial life, and robotics might, with different purposes, seek to understand the various other possible methods of communication and language in artificial systems in addition to those that happen to be realized in humans or animals. For these researchers, the demonstration of the effectness of potential mechanisms is often the main focus of study. Any theory and mechanism leading to the realization of communication and language-like phenomena might potentially be useful in engineering applications, regardless of how real animals and humans with their particular evolutionary history and neural organization might achieve them. After all, there is nothing like a wheel in a biological system.

It is worth noting that modelling and simulation can have beneficial side effects. Many neural network approaches that purported to model the human brain have fallen far short of this aim, but have generated a wealth of effective practical data processors. Genetic algorithms that are inspired by theories such as the random mutation and neutral drift of genotypes have produced some very effective searching tools, whether or not these theories continue to hold sway.

Understanding communication and language as they could be (rather than only as they are in extant humans and animals) is a new and fascinating area opened up by the possibilities of constructive studies using artificial media including robots and computational modelling. Alternative possible mechanisms in agents, robots and other potentially communicating systems are being actively studied in artificial environments, often independently of whether they model human cognition.

However, understanding the origin, maintenance, evolution and transformations of human language remains the main focus of anthropologists, psychologists, linguists, and cognitive scientists in this interdisciplinary field. These simulation tools and new experimental media can be used for building models of human language and animal communication and for validating explanations by exhibiting the emergence of phenomena in question (or finding gaps in these explanations). Often a computational model can be used to demonstrate that a particular minimal set of assumptions can (or cannot) parsimoniously generate essential aspects of a phenomenon being studied, and by adding and removing features and assumptions one can study their relative importance by the effects of this on the behaviour of the model.

In a similar way, simulations described in this volume and elsewhere are based on abstractions that model some factors and ignore others in the emergence of communication and language. Parameters of the models are abstracted from real, empirical observations and the selection of abstracted features will give a model its particular characteristics. They address many different issues, since, as Tecumseh Fitch observes "The first step ... is to recognize the complexity of language and and acknowledge that no single cause, factor, function or explanation can explain 'Language' as a whole". The selection of features to abstract is an informed decision by the researcher, varying widely and usually based on highly simplified assumptions.

The question we have to answer is how these diverse models should be evaluated. Since they are based on abstracted features, a subset of the totality of characteristics, we know before we start that it will be possible to falsify the model by focusing on features that have not been used. Different criteria are needed to evaluate simulations and models. Some can be tested by examining empirical predictions that are generated, comparing them with empirical observations as well with the predictions of other models, cf. for instance Nowak's model of the evolution of word meanings (Lyon et al., this volume). Others can be tested for internal consistency on theoretical grounds. For instance, Elman's well known recurrent neural network model of language processing has not been scaled up from a toy language: internal inconsistencies would arise (Elman 1991; Bengio 1996).

Many simulations and models in this field of language evolution do not immediately appear to be amenable to scientific scrutiny. For instance, though the experiments can be repeated, they aim *post hoc* to explain developments in a past that can never be revisited. The first open research question is the methodological one of how we can develop principled methods of evaluating and validating simulations and models. Issues of consistency with other bodies of knowledge, internal consistency, fitness for purpose and rationale for choice of abstractions will need to be addressed, as will the competition with alternative explanations and models. Meanwhile, researchers in the field will carry on using these fruitful approaches. Perhaps there is a parallel with the status of the transfinite set theory of Cantor, now generally accepted, when it was first proposed and criticized: Recall the comment of mathematician Hilbert "No one shall expel us from the paradise that Cantor has created" (Giaquinto 2002)[2]. The lack of rigorous foundations did not prevent the pioneering work of those with insights that would later be justified.

1.4. Open Problems in the Emergence of Communication

Considerations of the emergence and evolution of communication in living systems lead to several open problems in the emergence of communication centred on several issues that are at present little understood, including:

(1) origin and evolution of signalling channels
(2) transition from signalling to communication
(3) sources of representation in signals
(4) complexity of communication systems
(5) roles of social interaction in learned communication systems

This area is a much broader field than linguistic communication, but provides essential background for understanding the advent of the latter. Human communication and language are special cases of animal signalling and cognition. For introduction to this vast field and further background, see for instance (Griffin 1976; Smith 1977; Griffin 1992; Hauser 1996; Dusenbery 1992; Krebs and Davies 1984; Bekoff and Jamieson 1996; Bradbury and Vehrencamp 1998).

1.4.1. Transition from Signalling to True Communication

Evolutionary communication theorists distinguish *'true communication'*, in which in a statistical sense both sender and receiver benefit, from other forms of signalling such as manipulation, incidental movements revealing intentions, camouflage, etc. e.g. (Bradbury and Vehrencamp 1998). This usage of the term *communication* in the literature on behavioural ecology contrasts with the Shannon information-theoretic notion of communication which presupposes only a channel from sender to receiver, usually sprinkled with noise, over which the sender can transmit a signal which on average lowers the uncertainty of the receiver concerning which signal was actually sent (Shannon and Weaver 1963 [1949]). In general the first type of ('true') communication is a very special case of Shannon communication. Empirically and rigorously establishing potential mutual benefit to both partners in a putative communication (on average, for either individual in the interaction or for members of the evolving populations to which they belong) is operationally difficult – if not practically impossible – in many cases in the natural setting of intra- or inter-species animal interaction. In constructed computational examples involving artificial evolving populations,

---

[2] For an informal overview see http://en.wikipedia.org/wiki/Georg_Cantor

some of these issues become susceptible to rigorous study (e.g. via synthetic ethology (MacLennan 1992)).

1.4.2. The Advent of and Evolutionary Change in Signalling Channels

Where do extant signalling channels come from? That is, what is their evolutionary origin, and what is responsible for their continued persistence over evolutionary time in particular species?

This is a problem for which computational methods of evolution in artificial systems will allow the systematic exploration of the impact and relative importance of various contributing factors in various contextual settings.

1.4.3. Meaning and Representation in Signals

What is the evolutionary origin in signalling channels of information that potentially carries meaning? The information in sensory and communication channels used by particular organisms is not necessarily accessible or meaningful to other organisms. Human ears do not benefit from information carried in the ultrasonic calls of bats, infrasonic signals of elephants, nor the electric field changes perceived by electric fish. The colours of flowers are perceived differently by insects and carry information relevant (to the plant) for pollination and (to the insect) for feeding. Smells that we may have no or only partial access to may be of great interest to dogs and cats. Meaningful information is not universal but specific to particular species (von Uexküll (1985) [1909], Nehaniv (1999)). How can signalling channels evolve which carry information that is meaningful for particular organisms? Information in most of these examples is not representational in the same way that human language is. It is not generally compositional, nor propositional. Instead, smells, visual perceptions of flowers, polarization of light (perceived by bees, ants, wasps, cuttlefish, etc.), alarm calls, or a neural signal for the eye to blink when something approaches it, at same time indicate for a particular organism both *what is the case* and *what action to take* (Millikan's *pushmi-pullyu representations* (Millikan 2004)). Such signals have both these properties and are more fundamental and primitive than the highly derived representations in human language in which these functions have become separated in a manner that seems unusual in nature. The information channels and the information conveyed in them are useful to an organism for selecting action and thus meaningful in an agent-specific sense (Nehaniv 1999).

These questions are related to the deep question, What is representation? One suggestion is that representation could be defined using the information flow (a generalization of mutual information) from the environment or from another agent at one end of a Shannon channel via signals to, at the other end, an organism's action selection, where the latter is modelled as a random variable, see (Klyubin et al. 2006).

1.4.4. Complexity of Communication Systems

Communication systems exist that are of various degrees of complexity. The calls of vervet monkeys are associated with particular classes of their predators and trigger appropriate defensive behaviours for these predator types, but are quite limited in number and apparently have no further structure (Seyferth and Cheney 1986). On the other hand, communication systems can be complex apparently without carrying complex compositional meanings as shown by many examples of birdsong. The sexually selected songs of birds may be syntactically extremely complex apparently without being associated to any apparent complexity of meaning. What are the sources of the complexity in communication systems? Is a complex syntactic system a prerequisite for a communication system such as human language, or something that can grow gradually in complexity of messages conveyed? What is the significance of the differences in avian communication systems as compared with human language? The example of bird vocalizations provides a non-human set of communication systems for comparison that may lead to insight into the role that various factors played in the emergence of human language. In this volume, the contributions of Pepperberg, Merker and Okanoya, Okanoya and Merker, Ritchie and Kirby, as well as that of Fitch not only touch on but dance around this open question.

1.4.5. Social Interaction

The role of social interaction seems essential in the ontogeny of functional communicative capacity with learned communicative systems, although not all types of social interaction need result in this (e.g. Pepperberg; Fitch; Cowley – this volume). How can this be modelled or synthesized in artificial examples? Processes of self-organization guide convergence to common vocabularies, conceptual spaces, and grammars (e.g. Steels; Nakamura et al.; Belpaeme and Bleys; Smith; Kirby; this volume) as well as the continuing evolution of these aspects of communicative systems. What roles do different type of social interaction play in the transmission of learned communicative systems? Can we gain a comprehensive understanding of all these roles?

1.5. Open Problems in the Evolution of Linguistic Communication

The remainder of this chapter surveys some specific open problems that present grand challenges to those working in constructive aspects of the emergence of *linguistic* communication, addressing various language-like properties in computational agent and robotic models. This is not intended to be an exhaustive survey. Many important research articles and researchers could not be mentioned here. The discussion is instead indicative of current research activity (and inactivity) as regards a set of fundamental problems in the area.

We will discuss the following completely or largely open areas:

(1) deixis, gesture, and reference;
(2) predication;
(3) negation;
(4) emergence of syntactic categories
(5) compositionality

The emergence and modelling of these phenomena are discussed in the context of embodied, social interaction and evolution (cultural or otherwise). Ideally, mechanisms based on sensorimotor and experiential grounding in bottom-up, agent-centered models involving populations of agents will help yield deep understanding of the emergence of the above phenomena.

One area is conspicuously missing from the above list:

(0) grounding and shared vocabularies

and will also be discussed briefly below. This area has not been included in the list of current grand challenges since there has been substantial progress in it. However grounding and shared vocabularies will need to be integrated with the answers to the grand challenge problem areas (1–5) to yield grounded and shared language-like communication systems with much more complex types of structure with grounded meaning.

1.6. What is Meaning and What is Language For?

We regard linguistic and language-like communication as the capacity of an agent to influence the world around by the systematic use of signals mediated by their reception by other agents in its environment. Thus, language is regarded as a means for the agent to 'manipulate' the world around for its own benefit, similar to other traits of biological organisms (cf. the discussion of the transition to language from a biological viewpoint in (Maynard Smith and Szathmáry 1995)). As Wittgenstein (1949) [published Wittgenstein (1968)] taught us, the *meaning* of any signalling behaviour, such as in language, arises in how it is used by the agent to manipulate its environment (including other agents) in its interactions with other agents. This can be related to the utility to an agent (in a statistical sense) of information in a signalling channel (see (Nehaniv 1999; Nehaniv et al. 1999, 2002)). According to the insights of Peirce (1839–1914) [republished in (Peirce 1995)], the relationship between signs and significations is mediated by an interpretant, and the mapping between signs and what they signify is a *process* that depends on the particular agents involved and on their situated contexts. The ideas just presented follow the discussion of (Nehaniv 1999, 2000). The Wittgensteinian-Peircian viewpoint outlined by (Parisi et al. 2002) is similar.

In particular, these realizations lead to a tremendous amount freedom in the emergence of language-like phenomena that has often been ignored and oversimplified by naively, often unconsciously, applying constraints on simulation models. This freedom and the related lack of constraints is illustrated by several corollaries. Understanding the emergence of meaning and language requires the generative synthesis of the phenomena in question beginning with the following:

1. Meaning is always agent-specific.
2. There is no privileged set or pre-existing space of possible meaning, containing ideal concepts.
3. There is no unique and no pre-existing syntactic structure on possible meanings.
4. If meanings, spaces of meaning, or syntax in meaning space do arise, they will be agent-specific as well.
5. The mappings between signs and meaning are mediated by interpreted signals between agents, and these mappings are also agent-specific and depend on the context of the interaction.

See (Nehaniv 1999, 2000) for further discussion of these points.

Note that none of the above discussion refers to truth values or truth conditions, which reflect highly derived properties of human linguistic behaviour (Nehaniv 2000), and thus should not be the starting point for an attempt to understand meaning, communication, and language. The highly refined formal tools mathematics and logic – including truth values, predicate logic, context-free grammars, denotational semantics, etc. – have allowed scientists to achieve precision and thus escape from ambiguities and dependence on context and specific agents. But specific agents and context are inherent to the emergence of language, while these tools are based on abstractions and refinements from human language. Any explanation of the emergence of language that uses them as primitives to derive the phenomena that they are based on thus puts the proverbial cart before the horse (Nehaniv 2000; Millikan 2004).

This is not to say that these tools and formalisms should never be used. In computational modelling this clearly would not be possible, simply due to the use of computers. No simulation or robotic study in the emergence and evolution of linguistic communication has been able to proceed successfully without simplifying some (or sometimes all) of the above complexity away. If agents are endowed with some of these language-like capacities, it is important to keep track of which ones. If new phenomena then emerge, one has an argument that the built-in capacities provide scaffolding for the new phenomena. For instance, the work of Kirby (1999) and (this volume) shows that, in populations of agents *with the capacity to use and derive context-free grammars*, processes of self-organization resulting from attempts to learn grammar based on induction from the evidence of grammar-generated utterances of other agents lead over generations to increasingly compositional grammars. His work does not show how it is that context-free grammars nor the capacity for compositionality could first emerge (since these are given at the start).

1.6.1. Symbol Grounding and Shared Vocabularies

Different aspects of *symbol grounding* (Harnad 1990) and the self-organization and maintenance of *shared vocabularies* are increasingly well-studied and coming to be understood, especially for vocabularies to identify or name objects (selecting one target of reference from an environment) or label situations (MacLennan 1992; Steels 1995, 1998; Billard and Dautenhahn 1999; Baillie and Nehaniv 2001; Cangelosi 2001; Parisi et al. 2002). Less work has been done on the grounding of shared vocabularies with more complexity, e.g. in which various parts of speech exist (labelling for example actions or actions on objects, or with compositional syntax), although the work of Cangelosi and collaborators has moved in this direction (e.g. (Parisi et al. 2002; Cangelosi and Riga, in press; Cangelosi et al. 2006)). For example, Cangelosi and Riga (in press) and Cangelosi et al. (2006) present a model of the acquisition of names of actions in embodied ontogenetic robots. Agents ground the names of basic action primitives (e.g. close_left_arm, close_right_arm) through direct imitation of an expert teacher. Subsequently, they learn new action categories though linguistic instructions. The teacher produces new sentences of the type: "grab is close_left_arm and close_right_arm". Through an internal re-enactment of the motor grounding of the basic terms (Barsalou 1999), the robot is able to transfer the grounding from basic action names to higher-order actions. After learning, robots give a motor demonstration of the indirectly-grounded action name grab by grabbing objects in front of them. This model, in addition to demonstrating the grounding of vocabularies of action names, proposes an important learning mechanism for symbolic productivity, i.e. the generation of new symbols and meaning through language.

1.6.2. From Deixis, Gesture, and Manipulation to Reference

Deixis and gesture, in challenge area (1) are clearly related to the emergence of reference, but just how this occurs needs elucidation. Pointing, deictic gaze, joint attention, and gesture play important roles in the development of intersubjectivity and language in humans (cf. Kita (2003)).

Pointing, since it can be directed at many things and since it directs others' attention at them, could have provided for a kind "ur-pronominalization" in the emergence of linguistic communication. That is, pointing provides for a variable or variables that can be bound to objects and persons in the environment, giving at least a degree of shared reference via shared attention.

Rizzolatti and Arbib (1998) present a hypothesis on the emergence of language based on mirror-neurons in primates and humans. These neurons in the premotor cortex fire both when carrying out and when seeing an action performed. It is argued that this provides a substrate on which shared meaning can arise, as similar affordant gestures (e.g. manipulations such as grasping a fruit) are immediately understood by a conspecific interaction partner. Gestural language is then hypothesized to have developed and eventually to have given way to vocal language. Hurford (2004) acknowledges a possible role for mirror neurons in understanding the possible emergence of language, but surveys many gaps that remain in such an explanation, such as the well-known arbitrariness of the sign in regard to its reference.

Millikan (2004) has a more general notion of reference that relates to utility of information in internal states or signalling channels. A more general notion of gesture regards gesture as the signalling of such useful information. This is similar to the viewpoints on the meaning of signals in (Nehaniv 1999, 2000; Wittgenstein 1968).

The issues discussed in this section relate closely to the grounding of symbols and the emergence of shared systems of communication. Despite progress in these fields, constructive studies linking deixis and gesture to these problem areas remain to be carried out constructively in robotic and simulation models (but see (Baillie and Nehaniv 2001; Baillie et al. 2004) for some first work in this direction).

1.6.3. Predication

For detailed analysis of predication and its complex structure in human language from the viewpoint of linguistics, see (Napoli 1989). In human language, a rudimentary function of noun phrases is to pick out objects of reference from the environment (possibly even absent ones). Adjectives constrain the selection by imposing conditions on which object might be referred to.

One formal view of reference (implicit e.g. in (Steels 2005) and classical box-world natural language processing systems) is that instances of lexical items such as a noun ("ball") or adjective ("red") are understood as predicating properties of object variables. Selection of referents is determined by solving constraints on such predicates over a space of objects in the environment. For example, $ball(X)$ and $red(Y)$, restricts the reference to a red ball if X must equal Y, as it must in the phrase "the red ball". Similarly verbs provide another class of predicates which might take multiple semantic role arguments expressed in a given syntactic subcategorization frame that resolves variable references (Steels 2005).

As mentioned above, predicate logic and first-order logic are abstractions from the predicate structure of natural language. With the approach just described, predication itself is a primitive and therefore does not emerge. However, *a transition from reference to predication* is suggested by an association that tends to identify referential variables in one-place referential predicates (like $red(X)$), or by grammatical rules that force the identification of variables in the referential predicates.

Scenario for the emergence of predication. Early on, proto-words or gestural signs could have their referents *associated* in a general, non-specific way merely by co-occurring close together in time. We elaborate a suggestion on the earliest source of predication: it may be a highly derived form of *topic-comment* structure, which is itself founded on association (Nehaniv 2000). For instance, deictic gesture serves to select a target of joint attention (*topic*), and then another gesture or utterance near to it on time serves to communicate content that was associated to the topic as *comment*. Eventually ritualization of such communicative practice produces grammaticalization of a topic-comment construction. Predication then arises via grammaticalization of the special case in which not only an association between topic and comment occurs, but the comment gives to the topic a labelling category: "This - food", a property label: "This – bad", or a semantic action-role: "This – eat". Thus there is a progression in the emergence of predication from association and topic-comment via ritualization to grammaticalization of predication.

Ritualization is well-known in animal communication systems (Smith 1977, 1996; Bradbury and Vehrencamp 1998) and one instance of it is grammaticalization, a well-recognized process in human language change (e.g. (Bybee et al. 1994)). A clear path for research into this open area would be to proceed to validate this proposed scenario by building computational or robotic realizations and showing whether and how the transitions

$$\text{association} \rightarrow \text{topic-comment} \rightarrow \text{predication}$$

could occur (ideally including *grounded referencing*). This should shed light on the details of the emergence of predication and the mechanisms required for this to occur.

If this could be done, more complex predication and modification could then be addressed. In more complex human language, both predicates and modifiers occur. Predicates tend to mark more highly salient assertions, while modifiers tend to act in the background to tune reference via constraints (Nehaniv 1987).

Let us again remark about the low relevance of truth values here. In early language as in animal communication systems, the emphasis could often have been on manipulation of and influence in the environment via signalling to others (cf. Maynard Smith and Szathmáry (1995); Millikan (2004); Nehaniv et al. (2002)), rather than on propositional assertions. In such cases truth values of predicates on objects were a later invention and abstraction of humans. While propositional semantics are certainly important in the evolution of human language, it must be remembered that they are not a starting point but a result of long evolutionary process which began with much more prevelant and primitive types of representation.

1.6.4. Negation: A Small Research Programme

It seems little has been done on emergence of negation in constructive evolution of language models. A discussion of negation of speech acts and within speech acts occurs in (Searle 1980/1969). A comprehensive book on negation is (Horn 2001).

Early scenarios for negation. (The material in this subsection is modified from text by Donna Jo Napoli (Napoli, pers. comm.).) Predicates used by early humans likely indicated actions such as "come", "hide", "be quiet", "run", or referenced objects, such as "food", "water". Negation can operate on nouns as well as on verbs, or other parts of speech, and is, of course, a predicate in itself.[3] Letting others know there is nothing in the cave, for example, was probably a pretty important early message. So one would expect "nothing" or "no living thing" to be an early negation.

Non-verbal, facial and manual gestures may have played an important role in early negation. When hunting, when trying to be quiet for any reason, people have always used their faces and hands. We all recognize the hush gesture. We know to raise our eyebrows to ask *yes/no*. This sort of thing is extremely common around the world. In Australia, many tribes used to have sign languages just for hunting. They also had sign languages for the deaf and for other things, too – such as to use with widows. The first negation was likely to have been either facial or gestural – perhaps a head shake or lowered brows (as in American Sign Language (Neidle et al. 2001)), or protruded lips. Also, early negation was likely simultaneous with whatever was being negated, whether spoken words or other gestures. So shake your head and say "buffalo" - or shake you head and say "swim/enter water" or shake your head and gesture "walk" (whatever that gesture might be for those peoples) – and you're getting across the messages "there are no buffaloes" – "don't go in the water" – "don't walk".

Computational scenarios for emergence of negation. We now give several ideas for constructivist approaches to negation:

1. It seems straightforward to use inhibition in artificial neural networks to suppress the behaviour in the presence of a negation signal N. Suppression of all action could yield compliance (by inaction) with commands such as "don't touch that". This could be realized in many existing models.

2. A research scenario into the use of more specific negation could employ artificial neural network models of agents using linguistic signalling such as those of Cangelosi (2001), which can have a noun-verb distinction (see below) that they exhibit in language games. We propose that these be extended by the introduction of tasks into the language games that sometimes involve negation: When the new signal N co-occurs with a previously learned linguistic signal S the language game task requires choosing a *different* object/property ("(proto)noun"/"(proto)adjective") or action ("(proto)verb"), respectively, than would be for the signal S. Tasks without the signal N must also be carried out by the agents and require the original interpretation of S. That is, the agents could carry commands such as "pull cup",

---

[3] Or a modifier, where modification plays a role, e.g. specifying a constraint on reference within consituent syntactic structure, and is then generally less marked than predication.

"not-pull [e.g. push] cup", "pull not-cup" (i.e. pull an object other than the cup), , or even "not-pull not-cup" (e.g. pushing a ball would be a correct response). The meaning of the negation signal N would be grounded in the language game tasks these agents have to perform. Demonstrating that evolving populations of neural network agents could learn this task would establish a basis for specific negation of constituents of simple linguistic utterances. Alternatively, one could do the same kind of study using agents such as in the work of Steels (2003).

3. We note that in many human sign languages such as American Sign Language (ASL), the scope of negation can be given over syntactic subunits by non-manual gestures. In ASL non-manual marking (furrowing of the eyebrows and side-to-side headshake) may spread over the domain of syntactic constituents, and moreover such spread is obligatory in the absence of a manual marker (Neidle et al. 2001). (This property agrees well with the likely simultaneity in the early negation described in Napoli's scenario above.) Thus in constructivist studies of the emergence of language, it would be very interesting to investigate the scope of negation. For example, in neural network agent models, the use of a negative signal would have presumably to involve the persistence in the network of internal states over the scope of the negated constituent. Synthetic neural imaging techniques like those of Cangelosi and Parisi (2004) could be useful here.

1.6.5. Syntactic Categories

In artificial neural network models, Cangelosi and Parisi (2004) and Cangelosi (2001) have shown the grounded emergence of rudimentary (proto)-nouns and -verbs: nouns, as linguistic signals that co-vary with sensory stimuli, and verbs, as linguistic signals that co-vary with actions (largely independent of sensory stimuli). They have suggested that this could be extended to (proto)adjectives, that select a referent within a noun category using some intrinsic property, and to non-adjectival modifiers, such as location indicators (e.g. left, right, above), that reflect more temporary properties which are not intrinsic to the object but depend on the relationship of object to speakers and the environment. This remains to be done, as does increasing the complexity of syntactic categories which the approach can generate (e.g. to verbs with a patient and recipient role, as "give the apple to Mary").

The same artificial life and neural network approach to modelling the emergence of proto-syntactic categories has been used to investigate the relationship between syntactic structure and sensorimotor categories. Cangelosi and Parisi (2004) apply synthetic brain imaging techniques on the neural network of language-speaking agents to demonstrate that nouns produce more activity in a sensory processing hidden layer. Instead, verbs produce more activity in the layer where sensory information is integrated with proprioceptive input. Such findings are qualitatively compared with human brain imaging data that indicate that nouns activate more the posterior areas of the brain related to sensory and associative processing while verbs activate more the anterior motor areas. These functional similarities suggest a strict evolutionary correlation between the organization of sensorimotor knowledge in the neural network of the agents and the corresponding organization of proto-syntactic structure in the lexicon emerging during evolution (Cangelosi 2004).

Steels (2005) and (this volume) also considers the emergence of shared semantic and syntactic frames based on grammaticalization driven by computational needs of disambiguation.[4]

This issue of emergence of syntactic categories, which are restricted in the types of semantic environments where they can occur (as in the work of Parisi et al. (2002)), and in their signal contexts, and in the types of arguments they can take (if any), leads to the next grand challenge, the achievement of full-blown compositional syntax in a grounded communication system.

1.6.6. Compositionality

The emergence of lexical items that take arguments (such as transitive verbs that take a noun-phrase as object) is called compositionality. This has syntactic and semantic aspects, and accounts for much of the combinatorial richness of human language. There have also been a growing number of studies on the emergence of various aspects of syntax (e.g. (Kirby 1999; Cangelosi 2001; Steels 2005)). While there has also been some pioneering work on syntactic categories (e.g. Cangelosi and Parisi (2004); Parisi et al. (2002)), and grounded compositionality (Steels 1998), many aspects of compositionality in linguistic communication remain completely open for constructive modellers to begin to explain.

Segmentation and pauses in modern human speech, e.g. arising from the need to breath or the temporal nature of cognitive processes, combined with local context have been shown information-theoretically to improve the disambiguation of speech, suggesting that sequential process of smaller sequential units may help provide the basis for syntax in language evolution and language processing (Lyon et al. (2003)).

Cangelosi (2001) showed the emergence of verbs for actions that take target objects references in neural network agents that can manipulate simple objects in the environment in an evolutionary simulation, but non-compositional communicative signals could also evolve.

Assuming a fixed and syntactically structured meaning space, and a capacity to use and learn context-free grammars, Kirby (1999, 2001), as mentioned above, has shown that grammars with high degrees of compositionality arise and are easier to transmit over the course of generations of learning in such agents starting from agents using non-compositional 'holistic' grammars (i.e. with a different utterance for each meaning). Extending this work to agent-centered spaces of meaning grounded in interaction and language games remains to be achieved.

---

[4] For many more details and computational modelling, see the Fluid Construction Grammar website of his research group at http://arti.vub.ac.be/FCG/.

Steels (2005) argues that the purpose of compositional grammar is to reduce the number of variables in a decoded meaning structure in order to cope with compuational complexity in interpretation. He constructs agents in simulation studies that apply this principle and are able to converge on shared grammars by reinforcing and modifying syntatic and semantic role-structural frames (to propagate referential constraints) based on communicative success and failure. The same structures are used for parsing and for production.

Recursive composition structure is possible if the expansion of argument can non-trivially include the same argument type (as with clauses embedded in other clauses). When this occurs, in principle the language becomes unbounded in size.

1.7. Conclusions

Numerous challenges face the interdisciplinary endeavour of understanding the emergence of communication and language. Not least of these problems is to clarify and make rigorous the role of models in this field.

For communication, grand challenges include understanding (1) origin and evolution of signalling channels, (2) the possible transitions from signalling to communication, (3) sources of meaning and representation in signals, (4) the role of complexity of communication systems, and (5) the roles of social interaction in learned communication systems.

While (1) and (2) can be approached with standard Darwinian thinking, (3) is likely the most difficult question since it will require not only a rigorous definition of represenation, preferrably based in Shannon information-theory, but development of an evolutionary theory of agent-specific relevant information that makes use of this concept of representation (some hints toward these goals are contained in (Nehaniv 1999; Millikan 2004; Klyubin et al. 2006). Challenge (4) is being illuminated by examining animal communication systems, especially avian ones (as in part III of this volume).

For linguistic communication, our list of grand challenge areas identified five challenges beyond symbol grounding and the emergence of shared systems of tokens communicating meaning: (1) the role of deixis, gesture, and manipulation in the grounding and emergence of reference, (2) predication, (3) negation, (4) syntactic categories, and (5) full syntax – compositionality and recursive structure.

Challenges (2), on predication, and (3), on negation, have been the most neglected by the evolution of language community. We hope this chapter stimulates discussion on these issues and promotes research into those areas.

The problem of predication (2) is argued to be related to associative processes and to topic-comment structures, as pre-cursors. Predicates as they exist today in human languages are seen as a highly derived special case of related processes.

Computational scenarios for studying the emergence of predication and of negation have been proposed and discussed in order to encourage investigations into their emergence.

Other immediate work to be done to meet these grand challenges includes: (4) emergence of syntactic categories needs to be investigated without assuming an underlying categorization on some pre-existing space of meanings in grounded language games. (5) compositionality (and recursion) needs to be modelled to emerge in a setting of grounded meaning without the assumption of an underlying grammatical ability, such as the capacity to learn and use context-free grammars.

Acknowledgments. The first author thanks Prof. Donna Jo Napoli (Swarthmore College, Linguistics) for many ideas relevant to the early negation and for discussing some thoughts on early predication and the view of foregrounded negation as an instance of predication. Sections 1.4, 1.5, and 1.6 of the present chapter extend (Nehaniv 2005).

The original idea for this book came from the successful Second International Symposium on the Emergence and Evolution of Linguistic Communication (EELC'05) held at the University of Hertfordshire, Hatfield, near London, in April 2005. It was part of the Artificial Intelligence and Simulation of Behaviour (AISB-2005) Convention, whose overall theme was "Social Intelligence and Interaction in Animals, Robots and Agents". Grants from the British Academy and the Engineering and Physical Research Council in support of this workshop are gratefully acknowledged.

EELC'05 followed the First International Workshop on the Emergence and Evolution of Linguistic Communication (EELC'04), held in Kanazawa (Japan) in May/June 2004 under the auspices of the Japanese Society for Artificial Intelligence (JSAI), the Japanese counterpart of AISB. The second EELC Symposium aimed to continue the philosophy of this series and its international tradition. This is particularly relevant because European, American, and Japanese scientists have played a major role in the development of computational models of language evolution. The Third Symposium on the Emergence and Evolution of Linguistic Communication is scheduled to be held in 2006 in Rome, Italy.

We are also grateful to Helen Callaghan, Catherine Brett, and the staff at Springer for their support and assistance in putting together this volume.

Bibliography

M. A. Arbib. The mirror system, imitation, and the evolution of language. In K. Dautenhahn and C. L. Nehaniv, editors, *Imitation in Animals and Artifacts*, pages 229–280. MIT Press, 2002.

T. Arita and Y. Koyama. Evolution of linguistic diversity in a simple communication system. *Artificial Life*, 4(1):109–124, 1998.

J. Baillie and C. L. Nehaniv. Deixis and the development of naming in asynchronously interacting connectionist agents. In *First International Workshop on Epigenetic Robotics*, pages 123–129. Lund University Cognitive Studies, vol. 85, 2001.

J. Baillie, C. L. Nehaniv, P. Quick, A. Egri-Nagy, and S. Warren. Deixis, interaction topology, and the emergence of naming. In *First International Workshop on the Emergence and Evolution of Linguistic Communication*, pages 33–40. Japanese Society for Artificial Intelligence, 2004.

L. W. Barsalou. Perceptual symbol systems. *Behavioral and Brain Sciences*, 22:577–609, 1999.

M. Bekoff and D. Jamieson. *Readings in Animal Cognition*. MIT Press, 1996.

Y. Bengio. *Neural Networks for Speech and Sequence Recognition*. ITP, 1996.

A. Billard and K. Dautenhahn. Experiments in learning by imitation - grounding and use of communication in robotic agents. *Adaptive Behavior*, 7(3/4), 1999.

J. W. Bradbury and S. L. Vehrencamp. *Principles of Animal Communication*. Sinauer, 1998.

J. Bybee, R. Perkins, and W. Pagliuca. *The Evolution of Grammar: Tense, Aspect, and Modality in the Languages of the World*. University of Chicago Press, 1994.

A. Cangelosi. Evolution of communication using signals, symbols, and words. *IEEE Transactions on Evolutionary Computation*, 5(2):93–101, 2001.

A. Cangelosi. The sensorimotor bases of linguistic structure: Experiments with grounded adaptive agents. In *Proceedings of the Eighth International Conference on the Simulation of Adaptive Behaviour: From Animals to Animats 8*, pages 487–496. MIT Press, 2004.

A. Cangelosi, E. Hourdakis, and vadim Tikhanoff. Language acquisition and symbol grounding transfer with neural networks and cognitive robots. In *Proceedings of IEEE World Congress on Computational Intelligence*. IEEE Press, 2006.

A. Cangelosi and D. Parisi, editors. *Simulating the Evolution of Language*. Springer Verlag, 2002.

A. Cangelosi and D. Parisi. The processing of verbs and nouns in neural networks: Insights from synthetic brain imaging. *Brain and Language*, 89(2):401–408, 2004.

A. Cangelosi and T. Riga. An embodied model for sensorimotor grounding and grounding transfer: Experiments with epigenetic robots. *Cognitive Science*, in press.

M. H. Christiansen and S. Kirby, editors. *Language and Evolution*. Oxford, 2003.

D. B. Dusenbery. *Sensory Ecology: How Organisms Acquire and Respond to Information*. W. H. Freeman and Company, New York, 1992.

J. L. Elman. Distributed representations, simple recurrent networks and grammatical structure. *Machine Learning*, pages 195–223, 1991.

M. Giaquinto. *The Search for Certainty: A Philosophical Account of Foundations of Mathematics*. Oxford University Press, 2002.

D. R. Griffin. *Animal Minds*. Chicago, 1992.

D. R. Griffin. *The Question of Animal Awareness: Evolutionary Continuity of Mental Experience*. The Rockefeller University Press, 1976.

S. Harnad. The symbol grounding problem. *Physica D*, 42, 1990.

T. Hashimoto and T. Ikegami. Evolution of symbolic grammar system. In F. Morán, A. Moreno, J. J. Merolo, and P. Chacón, editors, *Advances in Artificial Life (3rd European Conference on Artificial Life, Granada, Spain, June 1995)*, volume Lecture Notes in Artificial Intelligence, 929, 1995.

M. D. Hauser. *Tne Evolution of Communication*. MIT Press, Cambridge, MA, 1996.

L. R. Horn. *A Natural History of Negation*. CSLI Pubilications (The David Hume Series: Philosophy and Cognitive Science Reissues), 2001.

J. Hurford. Language beyond our grasp: What mirror neurons can, and cannot, do for the evolution of language. In K. Oller and U. Griebel, editors, *Evolution of Communication Systems: A Comparative Approach*, pages 297–313. MIT Press, Cambridge, MA, 2004. On-line at http://www.ling.ed.ac.uk/~jim/mirror//kl.s.ps.

S. Kirby. Learning, bottlenecks, and infinity: a working model of the evolution of syntactic communication. In K. Dautenhahn and C. L. Nehaniv, editors, *Proceedings of the AISB'99 Symposium on Imitation in Animals and Artifacts*, pages 55–63. Society of the Study of Artificial Intelligence and the Simulation of Behaviour, 1999.

S. Kirby. Spontaneous evolution of linguistic structure: an iterated learning model of the emergence of regularity and irregularity. *IEEE Transactions on Evolutionary Computation*, 5(2):102–110, 2001.

S. Kita, editor. *Pointing: Where Language, Culture and Cognition Meet*. Lawrence Erlbaum Associates, Inc, 2003.

A. Klyubin, D. Polani, and C. L. Nehaniv. Representations of space and time in the maximization of information flow in the perception-action loop. (submitted for journal publication), 2006.

J. R. Krebs and N. B. Davies, editors. *Behavioural Ecology*. Sinauer Associates, Sunderland, MA, 1984.

C. Lyon, C. L. Nehaniv, and B. Dickerson. The segmentation of speech and its implications for the emergence of language structure. *Evolution of Communication*, 4(2): 161–182, 2003.

B. MacLennan. Synthetic ethology: An approach to the study of communication. In *Artificial Life II*. Addison Wesley, 1992.

J. Maynard Smith and E. Szathmáry. *The Major Transitions in Evolution*. W.H. Freeman, 1995.

R. G. Millikan. *Varieties of Meaning – The 2002 Jean Nicod Lectures*. MIT Press, 2004.

D. J. Napoli. *Predication Theory: A Case Study for Indexing Theory*, volume 50. Cambridge Univ. Press, 1989.

D. J. Napoli. email correspondence, February 2005, pers. comm.

C. L. Nehaniv. Predication and modification in Chinese and universal grammar. Honors Thesis in Linguistics, University of Michigan, 1987.

C. L. Nehaniv. Meaning for observers and agents. In *IEEE International Symposium on Intelligent Control/Intelligent Systems and Semiotics (ISIC/ISAS'99)*, pages 435–440, 1999.

C. L. Nehaniv. The making of meaning in societies: Semiotic & information-theoretic background to the evolution of communication. In *Starting from Society*, pages 73–84. Society for the Study of Artificial Intelligence and Adaptive Behaviour, 2000. On-line at http://homepages.feis.herts.ac.uk/˜nehaniv/sfsn.ps.

C. L. Nehaniv. Open problems in the emergence and evolution of linguistic communication: A road-map for research. In A. Cangelosi and C. L. Nehaniv, editors, *Seconnd International Symposium on the Emergence and Evolution of Linguistic Communication*. Society for the Study of Artificial Intelligence and Adaptive Behaviour, 2005.

C. L. Nehaniv, K. Dautenhahn, and M. J. Loomes. Constructive biology and approaches to temporal grounding in post-reactive robotics. In *Sensor Fusion and Decentralized Control in Robotics Systems II (September 19–20, 1999, Boston, Massachusetts), Proceedings of SPIE Vol. 3839*, pages 156–167, 1999.

C. L. Nehaniv, D. Polani, K. Dautenhahn, R. te Boekhorst, and L. C. namero. Meaningful information, sensor evolution, and the temporal horizon of embodied organisms. In *Artificial Life VIII*, pages 345–349. MIT Press, 2002.

C. Neidle, J. Kegl, D. MacLaughlin, B. Bahan, and R. G. Lee. *The Syntax of American Sign Language: Functional Categories and Hierarchical Structure*. MIT Press, 2001.

D. Parisi, A. Cangelosi, and I. Falcetta. Verbs, nouns and simulated language games. *Italian Journal of Linguistics*, 14(1):99–114, 2002.

C. S. Peirce. *Collected Papers, Volume 2: Elements of Logic*. Harvard, 1995.

K. Popper. *The Logic of Scientific Discovery.* Basic Books, New York, 1959.

G. Rizzolatti and M. A. Arbib. Language within our grasp. *Trends in Neurosciences,* 21 (5):188–194, 1998.

J. R. Searle. *Speech Acts: An Essay in the Philosophy of Language.* Cambridge University Press, 1980/1969).

R. Seyferth and D. L. Cheney. Vocal development in vervet monkeys. *Animal Beahviour,* 34:1640–1658, 1986.

C. E. Shannon and W. Weaver. *The Mathematical Theory of Communication.* University of Illinois Press, 1963.

W. J. Smith. *The Behavior of Communicating: An Ethological Approach.* Harvard, 1977.

W. J. Smith. Communication and expectations: A social process and the operations it depends upon and influences. In M. Bekoff and D. Jamieson, editors, *Readings in Animal Cognition,* pages 243–255. MIT Press, 1996.

L. Steels. The origins of syntax in visually grounded robotic agents. *Artificial Intelligence,* 103:1–24, 1998.

L. Steels. A self-organizing spatial vocabulary. *Artificial Life,* 2:315–332, 1995.

L. Steels. What triggers the emergence of grammar? In A. Cangelosi and C. L. Nehaniv, editors, *Second International Symposium on the Emergence and Evolution of Linguistic Communication.* Society for the Study of Artificial Intelligence and Adaptive Behaviour, 2005.

L. Steels. Evolving grounded communication for robots. *Trends in Cognitive Science,* 7 (7):308–312, 2003.

J. von Uexküll. Environment [*umwelt*] and inner world of animals. In G. M. Burghardt, editor, *Foundations of Comparative Ethology,* pages 222–245. Van Nostrand Reinhold, New York, 1985.

L. Wittgenstein. *Philosophical Investigations (Philosophische Untersuchungen)* – German with English translation by G.E.M. Anscombe. Basil Blackwell, 3rd edition, 1968.

A. Wray, editor. *The Transition to Language.* Oxford, 2002.

Part 1
Empirical Investigations
on Human Language

2
Evolving Meaning: The Roles of Kin Selection, Allomothering and Paternal Care in Language Evolution

W. Tecumseh Fitch

2.1. Introduction: The Componential Approach to Language

Many contemporary scholars agree that future theories of language evolution need to take a componential approach to language that breaks human language into separate mechanistic components such as vocal imitation, syntactic abilities, and propositional semantics. In this chapter, I discuss the evolution of the last component – the abilities and proclivities underlying honest, complex, propositional meanings. This is both a critical component of language, and one whose evolution is the hardest to explain, precisely because of its apparent uniqueness. Nonetheless, I argue, the comparative approach has important insights to offer in this domain. I briefly discuss the hypothesis that kin selection played an important, but neglected, role in driving the evolution of rich semantic communication. I then review several bodies of comparative data not addressed in previous discussions. In particular, I discuss three related issues: 1) hominid life history, and our extremely long period of dependent childhood, 2) the flexible extractive foraging techniques typical of both modern humans and chimpanzees, and thus presumably present in our last common ancestor, and 3) the evolution of male parental care that typifies humans but not other great apes. I argue that these three factors combine to provide a unique selective regime that drove our ability and propensity to express semantically-complex concepts. I also discuss why sexual selection is unlikely to be adequate, by itself, to drive all elements of language evolution (and particularly semantics), but discuss the role that the evolution of male parental care might have played in "equalizing" the sexes, such that traits originally evolved in one or the other came, today, to be expressed equally in both.

The first step in devising adequate theories of language phylogeny and function is to recognize the complexity of language and acknowledge that no single cause, factor, function or explanation can explain "Language" as a whole. Despite a persistent tendency of theorists to highlight one factor in the belief that the rest will just "follow naturally", the search for single causes in language evolution has a long history of failure. An adequate explanation will require theorists to break down language into relevant components, highlighting and clarifying the specific mechanism(s) under discussion. Only after such fractionation can hypotheses about function or phylogeny be intelligently stated and tested, and only after progress has been made in this vein can we hope to combine the results in a model that encompasses the evolution language as a whole. There is no reason to believe that this eventual unification will ascribe the same causes or timing to each component of language, and many reasons to believe the contrary. Different components of language might have evolved at different times in hominid evolution, or under different selective regimes, reducing attempts to state precisely when "Language" evolved into mere terminological debates about what "the key" factor in language is. For these reasons, most theorists today accept the need for (at least) two stages in language evolution (Hauser, Chomsky & Fitch, 2002). Early hypothetical stage(s) before fully-modern human language can be termed protolanguage(s) (Arbib, 2005; Fitch, 2005b).

Acknowledging the methodological imperative to fractionate language is obviously simply a starting point for an adequate theory of language evolution. "Carving nature at the joints" to achieve a proper fractionation will be a non-trivial endeavour. Elsewhere I have argued for a basic fractionation into at least three components, each representing novelties required in human language evolution. This fractionation is either explicit or implied in most contemporary theories of language evolution (Fitch, 2005b). I have termed these components, for convenience, signal, syntax, and semantics. The most obvious requirement for externalizing language is a flexible, shared **signal** complex enough to convey novel thoughts. Because the dual desiderata of flexibility and conventionality (that the signals be shared by at least two communicators) entail an ability to learn signals (rather than having innate signals, as in honeybees or vervet monkeys), shared complex signals require a mechanism for vocal or manual imitation. In particular, the evolution of speech requires a mechanism for complex **vocal learning** which is not present in our nearest cousins, the chimpanzees, and indeed does not appear to be possessed by any nonhuman primate (Janik & Slater, 1997). Because the data against complex vocal learning in chimpanzees is very robust, complex vocal imitation is in some sense the most obvious mechanism that *must* have evolved at some point during hominid evolution. The fact that apes have richer gestural imitation abilities that may have paved the way to spoken language, does not explain this basic necessity away. I have shown elsewhere that peripheral anatomy of the vocal tract or larynx is not the crucial factor keeping chimpanzees or other mammals from vocal imitation (Fitch, 2000; Fitch, 2002; Fitch & Reby, 2001). The basic limitations that keep most mammals, and all nonhuman primates, from imitating complex vocalizations are therefore likely to be neural.

Fortunately, selective pressures potentially capable of driving the evolution of vocal learning are not hard to come by. Vocal learning has evolved multiple times in parallel in at least six lineages (among mammals in humans, cetaceans, and seals, and among birds in hummingbirds, parrots, and songbirds). Simple vocal learning is also present in bats, and perhaps other clades. In the majority of these species, vocal learning supports complex songs produced by males only, and these are produced during the breeding season. Since Darwin, such songs have been believed to result from sexual selection (Darwin, 1871). Thus, from a comparative viewpoint sexual selection is a plausible default assumption for the evolution of complex vocal imitation as seen in animal "song" (Fitch, 2005c, 2006). However, it should be noted that there are other possibilities, and that we need to keep an open mind about the selective pressures that drove the evolution of human vocal imitation. In particular, sexually-selected mechanisms in mammals are typically expressed only (or preferentially) in males, and typically appear only at puberty (when they become useful). In humans, of course, vocal abilities are basically equal among the sexes, and if anything, biased towards females (Henton, 1992; Hyde & Linn, 1988). More striking and obvious is the fact that vocal imitation develops long before puberty in humans, with auditory learning starting before birth and imitation already well developed at age two, at least a decade before sexual maturity. Thus, although sexual selection might provide an initial drive towards vocal imitation, it seems unable to fully explain its current pattern in humans. This idea that other selective forces can drive or influence song is consistent with the repeated evolution of female song in birds, and its shared distribution and early maturation in some other clades such as dolphins. However, with these caveats in mind, the repeated evolution of complex vocal learning in vertebrates suggests that the evolution of this capacity is not the major puzzle in understanding language evolution.

The evolution of **syntax** is much more of a challenge, for a number of reasons. First, from a purely methodological viewpoint, syntax is less clearly defined than the speech signal, and far more difficult to operationalize for behavioural testing in animals. At the simplest level, simple sequential grammars, which restrict the order of different call or song components, have been known in animal communication systems for many years (Balaban, 1988; Hailman & Ficken, 1987; Robinson, 1984). For instance in the "chick-a-dee" call of the black-capped chickadee *Parus atricapillus*, "chick" notes always precede "dee" notes, and the latter can be repeated without any clear limit. This constraint can be written as a simple formal grammar ("formal" meaning that no changes in meaning are implied by changes in structure), at the finite state level (Hailman & Ficken, 1987). Similarly, analyses of chimpanzee "sentences" in the plastic block language used by Premack (Premack, 1971), the gestural system studied by Terrace (Terrace, 1979), or analyses of humpback whale song (Payne, 2000; Payne & McVay, 1971) reveal rule-governed restrictions on symbol order that can be considered a simple form of syntax, again at a purely formal level. More recently, the presence or absence of a "boom" note in forest monkey calls has been shown to influence the interpretation of the following vocal output, which represents an addition of semantic interpretation of a "syntactic" aspect of the signal (Zuberbühler, 2002). Thus, there are abundant aspects of signal structure in animal communication systems that represent simple forms of grammar in either a purely formal sense, or in a few cases with added semantic implications.

Of course, human syntax goes far beyond simple restrictions on the order of elements. A core fact recognized by modern linguists is that human languages require grammatical systems that go beyond simple sequential ordering (grammars at the finite-state level) to include such factors as co-indexing and hierarchical embedding. A crucial part of the productivity of language, and its expressive power for representing thoughts, is that complex, hierarchically-structured *semantic* structures can be syntactically realized in the signaling system by various devices based on recursive embedding. For instance, any complex proposition *x* can be embedded in the sentence frame "I don't believe that *x*", and this can be further embedded in other similar frames *ad infinitum* (e.g. "Mary thinks that I don't believe that *x*"). Such embedding is crucial to all human languages. Unfortunately, though, this intuition is quite difficult to apply to animal communication systems (Fitch, 2005a). How can we ask a humpback whale whether its apparent embedding has this property, if the whale's song has no semantic meaning? One empirical approach is to back away from this difficult question to a more basic one: can animals recognize signals that are structured by rules powerful enough to capture such semantic embedding? Thus, Marc Hauser and I have developed an assay to probe for an animal subject's ability to recognize strings in a simple context-free grammar (Fitch & Hauser, 2004), finding that cotton-top tamarins are unable to master a very simple grammar at this level, despite their ability to master a closely-matched grammar at the finite-state level in the same test situation. Humans find this context-free grammar trivially easy to recognize. Because human languages require grammatical power above the finite-state level, animals who are limited to this level would be unable to perform the syntactic computations necessary for human language. If another species (e.g. songbirds or great apes) can be shown to achieve the context-free level, we could further probe their abilities regarding the "mildly context-sensitive" level of grammatical power thought to be required for human language (Joshi, Vijay-Shanker & Weir, 1991). Thus, studies of this sort provide one way to investigate the grammatical abilities of animals at a purely formal level without requiring any semantic content in the signals.

The most difficult remaining issue is thus that of **semantics**, or the ability to express complex flexible meanings via signals. Although animal communication systems such as honeybee dance or vervet alarm calls clearly have semantic content, the flexibility of these systems is strictly limited. Indeed, the vervet system is based on signals whose structure is innately determined rather than learned, and even the semantic content of these signals appears to be largely biologically determined, with learning required only to narrow down the range of meanings. Furthermore, monkeys do not appear able to represent others' minds, a key requirement of intentional, declarative semantics (Cheney & Seyfarth, 1990). A female monkey who watches food being hidden in a chamber does not make food calls when her young infant is subsequently released into it. More strikingly, when an infant is released into a cage where the mother has watched a predator hide, she does not increase her rate of alarm calling over baseline. Indeed, although recent data indicate that chimpanzees are able to follow gaze and under-stand that "seeing is knowing", this ability appears only in competitive situations and is never deployed in a cooperative, informative situation (Hare, Call, Agnetta & Tomasello, 2000; Hare, Call & Tomasello, 2001). Chimpanzee gestures are limited to imperative acts (e.g. reaching with outstretched hand to "beg" for food), and even basic declarative gestures (such as pointing, holding up objects for others to see, or even handing objects to others) are not observed in wild great apes (Tomasello & Call, 1997; Tomasello, Call, Nagell, Olguin & Carpenter, 1994). Together, such data on nonhuman primates suggests that the ability of humans to represent others as intentional mental beings, and particularly to be intentionally informative based on an understanding of what a conspecific does or does not know, may be unique to our species. This mechanism that underlies intentional, propositional semantics thus appears to represent another critical component to be explained in language evolution, and one of the most critical (Tomasello, 2003).

   In this paper I will address the functional and phylogenetic basis of this latter component of meaning in language: the intentionally informative, highly complex semantics of human language. The critical starting point is the comparative data just discussed, suggesting that our nearest cousins lack the ability (or, at least, the propensity) to communicate in an intentional, informative, propositional manner. As stressed above, my discussion is concerned only with the evolution of this crucial semantic communication component of language, and *not* with the evolution of language as a whole. I am particularly interested in understanding the forces that could lead to **displaced symbolic reference** – the ability to talk about past events, or future plans or goals. I have argued elsewhere that communication among kin played a crucial role in the evolution of these key semantic aspects of language. I will recap this argument briefly below. However, it is plausible (and even likely, in my opinion) that other aspects of language evolved under different selective regimes, and at different times, as suggested above. In particular, the comparative data render it likely that vocal imitation may have been driven by sexual selection, and may have preceded the evolution of meaningful language, as in Darwin's "musical protolanguage" hypothesis (Fitch, 2005c; Mithen, 2005). But if this is true, it raises the question of how an initially sexually-selected trait (a type that is almost invariably sexually dimorphic) became evenly distributed among the sexes, and came to develop long before maturity, in modern humans. The inverse question applies to the sharing of information among adults and young, which might be expected to be mainly expressed by females. I will argue that a role of males in parenting, an unusual facet of human biology, helps to explain this transformation and equalization.

2.2. Kin Communication and the Evolution of Meaning

I have previously suggested (Fitch, 2004) that kin selection provides a plausible but neglected selective regime relevant to a particular component of language: its capacity to convey complex propositional meaning. As already suggested above, attempts to explain this factor based only on sexual selection are unconvincing because of the early development and lack of sexual dimorphism in our abilities to communicate semantically.

The kin communication hypothesis is simple and relatively intuitive, making its neglect in previous discussions of language evolution somewhat puzzling. The hypothesis suggests that the selective force behind honest, semantic communication was the sharing of information among kin, and particularly between adults and their offspring or young relatives. This hypothesis solves a critical problem in the evolution of communication that has been extensively discussed outside the context of language evolution: the evolution of "honest" communication systems (Maynard Smith & Harper, 2003). What are the selective forces that favour the evolution of signals that convey useful information between individuals? This turns out to be a significant theoretical problem, because in many cases communication is appropriately seen as an "arms race" between signalers and receivers, where there are few or no incentives to emit honest signals, but many to exaggerate or bluff. Rather than a world of animals openly sharing information with one another, the modern picture is one of animals who selfishly emit signals when it benefits them to do so. In many cases of communication between adults (e.g., signals concerning courtship or territoriality) it will often benefit to mislead or exaggerate (Dawkins & Krebs, 1978). This in turn benefits receivers who are skeptical "mind readers", rather than gullibly accepting signals as valid (Krebs & Dawkins, 1984). The mechanisms by which "honesty" can be ensured (or at least partially encouraged) are rather limited (Fitch, 2002; Maynard Smith & Harper, 2003): signals may be automatically honest because of the signal production mechanism or similar constraints, or honesty can be guaranteed by handicaps. The handicap principle (Zahavi, 1975, 1977) suggests that *only* costly signals can be stable over evolutionary time, and more recent theoretical treatments further entail that handicap costs must vary with signaler quality (Grafen, 1990). Despite the intense theoretical and empirical interest in handicaps in recent years, it has long been clear that handicaps cannot account for honesty in human spoken language, because speech is an extremely low-cost signal (Zahavi, 1993). While certain information may be conveyed honestly by default in speech, physical constraints are clearly inadequate to drive semantics (Fitch, 2002). So what options are left?

The alternative to "guaranteeing" honesty in a Machiavellian world with some aspect of the signal itself is provided by situations in which it is in both communicators' best interest to communicate honestly ("best interest" in terms of increasing their long-term inclusive fitness). Specifically, if it is in the signaller's interest to share information honestly, and the receiver's to accept this information unskeptically, honest communication systems can evolve without any signal-internal guarantees necessary. Such conditions are provided neatly by kin selection if communication is preferentially directed towards kin (that is, honest signals are preferentially emitted in the presence of kin rather than others). In such a situation, the system need only satisfy Hamilton's inequality $C < Br$ (the Cost of signaling to the signaller is less than the Benefit obtained by the recipient, diluted by the fraction of relatedness r, a number between zero and one) to be evolutionarily favored. Given that vocal signals, and speech in particular, are low cost signals, this is not a particularly stringent requirement. Thus, kin selection on kin communication systems can easily drive the evolution of meaningful signals, neatly avoiding the dual traps of Machiavellian deceit and Zahavian handicaps. Once a communication capable of honestly conveying complex concepts has evolved via kin selection, it can then be utilized among non-related individuals via reciprocal altruism (Trivers, 1971), allowing the type of carefully-meted-out information among unrelated adults that we see in humans today. See (Fitch, 2004) for a more detailed and rigorous exploration of these ideas.

In the remainder of this paper I will outline some new arguments based on hominoid life history, ape foraging tactics, as well as human mating and childcare practices that I see as providing additional support for this "kin communication" or "mother tongue" hypothesis. The first issue addresses the question of why kin selection has not led to language in many more species. The second issue, not unrelated, is what specific aspects of human social behaviour could have licensed the transition from a hypothetical sexually selected "songlike" communication, expressed preferentially in males, to the sexually-egalitarian distribution of language abilities (and musical abilities, incidentally) that we see in modern humans. An understanding of both of these questions, I suggest, requires us to delve deeper into some well-known aspects of human biology that have rarely been integrated into discussions of language evolution.

First, given that kin selection is a ubiquitous force among group living animals, one might be justifiably skeptical about its *specific* significance in human communication. Put bluntly, if kin communication is enough to drive honest meaning, why haven't honeybees, songbirds, ground squirrels and many other species evolved language? There are two parts to the answer. First, most obviously, communication of complex thoughts requires a shared signaling system of comparable complexity. The lack of signal learning in most species means that, for most animals, such a system is unavailable (as discussed earlier). Only in species in which the mechanisms underlying complex signal learning are present already, in at least rudimentary form, can kin selection begin to drive complex symbolic communication. As already discussed, there are various phylogenetic routes to the evolution of learned signaling systems, but one of these must have already been taken to allow entry into this selective regime. From this viewpoint, the question becomes more limited to those species that have a system of vocal learning. Why don't songbirds, parrots, seals or cetaceans use their complex vocally-learned signals to transmit complex thoughts as humans do?

This brings us to the second part of the answer, the component more relevant in the context of this paper. The value of a complex communication system depends on the existence of complex thoughts which are worth conveying. That is, there must be some way in which successfully conveying thoughts would actually increase inclusive fitness. If cognitive representations are quite limited, this will provide an intrinsic limit on the concepts communicated, and thus on the value of communication. This is clearly relevant to species like honeybees, which are short-lived and have little relevant information to share with their sisters other than the location of food, water and nest sites. It is less obvious that this limit applies to birds, some of which have complex cognition rivaling that of nonhuman primates (Emery & Clayton, 2004) and thus might in principle have plenty to talk about. However, the period of parental care in songbirds is generally very short, so there is a time limit typically of a few months, and generally of less than a year, in which valuable knowledge acquired over a parents' lifetime might be imparted to its children (the upper end would be species with "helpers at the nest" with a contact time of less than two years). This is also the case for pinnipeds such as phocid seals, which generally have very short periods of maternal care (including the shortest of all mammals in the hooded seal *Cystophora cristata*). Finally, for marine mammals such as dolphins or killer whales, which are both intelligent and can have long term associations with their young, it is not clear that a mother's knowledge, if transferred to her young, could greatly increase her offspring's survivorship. The limited foraging demands involved in catching fish may not provide an adequate selective basis for a rich system to convey learned knowledge (alternatively it remains possible that some cetaceans do have undiscovered abilities in this direction).

In the next section I will argue, based on comparative data from other great apes, that the situation in our prehuman ancestors differed significantly from that of these other animals. The starting point will be the evolution of hominids *sensu strictu* starting with our divergence from chimpanzees about 7–8 million years ago. This was the time of our **last common ancestor** with chimpanzees, the LCA. The LCA was an African ape, probably confined to the forests stretching across the middle of Africa. We have essentially no fossil record for this species, although new fossils from this time period give considerable hope for future discoveries (Brunet et al., 2005). In order to reconstruct the lifeways of the LCA we thus need to turn to the comparative method, focussing particularly on the great apes. In the interest of brevity I will use the colloquial term "chimp" below to refer to both chimpanzees and bonobos, and will use their full names only when it is necessary to distinguish them. The discussion is based on data reviewed in (Aiello & Key, 2002; Boesch & Boesch-Achermann, 2000; Diamond, 1992; Goodall, 1986).

2.3. The Ape's Impasse: The Hominoid Mother's Dilemma

Primates are rather unusual mammals from a reproductive viewpoint. In sharp contrast to the large litters of puppies, kittens, piglets, or mice borne to most mammalian mothers, most primate mothers have just one child at a time (though twins are normal in a few species). Furthermore, this one child has an unusually long period of dependence on its mother: in most monkeys the infant is completely dependent for a year, and then still associates with its mother in a protective, affiliative relationship for years after that. But even by primate standards, apes are extreme (I use the term "hominoid" to refer to humans + apes, reserving the traditional term "hominid" to refer only to humans and their post-LCA ancestors). A chimpanzee infant is completely dependent on its mother for transportation and milk for at least two years, and more typically four, and the typical inter-birth interval for chimpanzees is between 5 and 6 years (Boesch & Boesch-Achermann, 2000). In the same period of time, a rhesus macaque female can already have grandchildren. The combination of low reproductive rates, long interbirth intervals and a lengthy childhood (including a longer period to sexual maturity – 10 years to sexual maturity for a female chimp) puts apes at a reproductive disadvantage relative to virtually all mammals their size (only elephants or whales have similarly long reproductive times: interbirth intervals of 3–4 years for African elephants and 2–3 years for humpback whales). With these powerful forces restricting her total lifetime reproduction, a female ape can meet her reproductive potential in only one way: survival – both of herself and of her offspring. Thus it is not surprising that apes (like whales and elephants) are also very long-lived, and very solicitous parents. Only by living a long time, and making sure that each of her precious children in turn live a long time, can the reproductive equation be balanced. Increasing any of the factors on one side (interbirth interval, gestation time, infant dependent period, or time till sexual maturity) decreases reproductive potential, and only a compensatory increase in the mother's own longevity can counteract them. In particular, the long period of childhood dependence means a long interbirth interval, and there seems to be no way around this impasse. This dilemma applies to all apes, including humans.

One of the many ways in which the *scala natura* caricature of evolution has clouded our vision is in the relationship between apes and monkeys. Because monkeys (which in the current context means Old World monkeys, cercopithecids) are supposedly lower on the great chain of being, there is a tendency to assume that they were dominant earlier in evolution. But the available paleontological evidence suggests that this prejudice gets the facts almost backwards. About 15 MYA, dryopithecine apes (ancestors of living great apes and humans) were widespread throughout Africa and Asia, while monkeys were quite rare. But the situation changed abruptly around the Miocene/Pliocene border, perhaps due to the climate changes and breakup of the once ubiquitous gallery forests into a mosaic of forest and grassland. The fossil record does not typically allow us to reconstruct what happened in detail, but in cases where it is adequate (e.g. Pleistocene East Asia), monkeys succeeded during periods of ecological instability, while apes disappeared, or were relegated to patches of stable rainforest (Jablonski, 1998). Today, the result of this difference is clear: monkeys dominate, and modern apes are confined to pockets of isolated forest. Monkeys, with their high reproductive rates, have taken over in most of the areas where apes once dominated. Indeed, apes today can be thought of as relict populations of a once-dominant clade, the last hangers-on in the most stable and welcoming environments. The monkeys' victory cannot be due to greater intelligence, more efficient food use, or direct physical competition – in all of these respects apes clearly outclass monkeys. Apes (sometimes literally) "eat monkeys for lunch".

So why are monkeys so successful today, and how did they displace the once-dominant apes? The only clear advantage is their much higher reproductive potential, particularly in situations of climatic change where high intelligence and large body size can no longer necessarily assure a long life.

There is, of course, one group of apes that somehow evaded the ape's impasse: the line leading to humans. But although we might, out of habit, think that it was our use of tools and our high intelligence that allowed us this demographic victory, the fossil record makes us think again: our first assured hominid fossils have brains no larger than a chimp, and no remains of material culture more sophisticated than those of a chimp (Cameron, 2004). But they had already moved into the drier, more variable mosaic environment that no other apes were able to occupy successfully. They were already bipedal, but it is not clear why this should have proved demographically advantageous. But if we examine modern humans today, we have another advantage over our ape cousins: our unusual system of shared child care gives modern humans a much higher reproductive potential than either a chimp, gorilla or orangutan. A human mother outreproduces any chimpanzee female through the simple expedient of having babies faster (Lovejoy, 1981). According to simple demographics, by having babies every 2–3 years instead of every 5–6 years, we humans (and this includes hunter gatherer mothers, not just supermarket-fed Western mothers) have found a way out of the ape's impasse. And the rest, we might say, is history. But if this solution is so easy, why haven't other apes done the same thing? Why don't chimp mothers simply wean earlier? The answer has become quite clear with recent studies of chimpanzee demographics (Boesch & Boesch-Achermann, 2000). Earlier weaning means poor survival of the young, and ends up leaving them smaller and less able to compete with other chimps whose mothers have fed them up to their full potential body weight.

It is revealing to look at the situation from a chimpanzee mother's perspective (Pusey, Williams & Goodall, 1997). Your infant will ride on your back and nurse, deriving all of its protection and nutriment from you for its first year, much like a human infant. However, your infant will continue to nurse consistently till age two, when solid food becomes an appreciable component of its diet, and will continue nursing periodically until between four and six years old. At age four, although it can locomote by itself, the child will still need to ride on your back for long voyages, and it is still mainly dependent on food you share with it. Weaning at this point could be disastrous – if conditions change suddenly and no food is available for your child, it still lacks the reserves and intelligence to survive on its own. From the child's viewpoint, none of this is very different from the human situation. The big difference is that, because she has weaned her child from breast milk much earlier, the human mother has already given birth to another child, and is raising two (or more) children in parallel. In a situation of superabundant, reliable food (e.g. the situation a grazing animal in a huge grassland faces with its offspring) this is clearly an excellent solution. Unfortunately, this is not the situation that faces chimps, or that faced our hominid forebears: although fruiting trees may present pockets of superabundance, they can be interspersed with long periods of want. At such times, difficult learned skills such as nutcracking, termite fishing, or exploitation of unpredictable food resources encountered only rarely, may provide the main source of rich nutrition (Boesch & Boesch-Achermann, 2000), and mean the difference between starvation and survival. There is no easy way that a chimp mother could double her child's food intake until that child is also competent at such complex foraging skills. The value of potentially sharing knowledge with offspring is, so to speak, "built in" to the chimp/human lineage by our reproductive biology and the resultant demographics, as well as the fact that we are generalist foragers dependent upon complex, learned extractive foraging techniques for survival. With the increased importance of cooperative foraging techniques (including scavenging, hunting, fishing and complex food processing) in our own lineage, these advantages would be even greater, giving a positive feedback loop between semantic communication and complex foraging.

Summarizing, an unusual combination of very slow reproduction, and uniquely extended childcare, with reliance on complex, learned foraging, characterized the LCA of the chimp/human lineage *before* we evolved language. I suggest that this situation (which is not speculation, but is based upon the actual observed behaviour and demographics of living apes and humans) provided an important precondition for the evolution of symbolic reference and intentional semantic communication in the hominid lineage. With some appropriate learned signalling system in place, such a situation would provide an excellent driving force for the honest, low-cost communication of complex concepts that we seek to explain. As already suggested above, there are several (independent) ways to evolve a complex learned signaling system, including sexual selection (Darwin's "singing ape" hypothesis) or various other possibilities (see Fitch, 2006). Combined with such a signaling system, we can perceive a definite, quite unusual, Darwinian advantage that our ancestors would have derived from the intentional sharing of ideas with other individuals. Although I have focused on mother/infant communication, it is clear that sharing of information among other kin (e.g. by grandmothers or siblings) would also increase the communicators' inclusive fitness. Thus a critical factor in explaining why kin selection drove the evolution of language in humans (but not other mammals known to have complex, shared signaling systems) is the long period of dependence combined with a crucial reliance on regionally-variable, complex, learned extractive foraging techniques: factors that characterize both chimpanzees and humans.

But what about fathers? The situation described so far inverts the difficulty already discussed that faces hypotheses based on sexual selection: predicting male-specific traits. By this model, we might expect human females to produce linguistic utterances and males to simply comprehend them (allowing male offspring to understand their mothers). At best we might expect intentionally informative male speech to be directed at siblings at an early age, but adult males should mainly produce meaningless songlike utterances. So there is still potentially a gap to be bridged between the predictions based on kin communication, and empirical reality. Why do adult males have meaningful language? Can the comparative database, or even fossils, help to clarify this apparent contradiction?

2.4. Male Parental Care in Humans and Other Vertebrates

Returning to the ape mother's dilemma, enter the male of the species. From the viewpoint of a female ape, adult males are basically a waste of resources, useful as sperm donors and little else. Males eat a lot, are often behaviourally dominant and can displace her or her child from food, but provide little or nothing in terms of childcare. Male primates and males of many other mammal groups may even kill the current crop of offspring to speed mothers' readiness to mate and produce new offspring. While male chimps preferentially hunt for meat, they mainly eat it themselves, partitioning it among the other (mostly male) hunters. Because a mother carrying a dependent child is not much use in the acrobatics required to catch a monkey during chimpanzee hunting, all she can hope for is a few scraps of meat for herself, obtained by tolerated theft from the hunter, and little or no meat for her child (Boesch & Boesch-Achermann, 2000). Thus, although potentially a rich source of additional nutrition, the meat caught by male chimpanzees contributes little or nothing to a mother's needs. The best we can say for male chimpanzees is that they provide a degree of protection, both from predators like leopards that can be a significant source of mortality for young chimps, and from the potentially infanticidal males of neighboring groups. These defensive advantages accrue to all members of the group. But from the viewpoint of feeding any particular baby, a mother chimp can forget about the males – unless there were some way to entice a male to contribute more specifically to her particular child. Thus, one crucial factor in human evolution that helped to solve the hominid mother's dilemma was the evolution of male parental care.

The importance of male paternal care in modern humans has long been known, and there are numerous empirical data supporting a critical role for an involved father in increasing infant survival in many cultures. Given the lack of such evidence in our nearest cousins (chimpanzees and bonobos), this appears to be a critical biological change in our species. Unfortunately, the fact that human males have an unusual potential for parental care has been over-extrapolated into a wide range of more dubious precepts about human behaviour, often including moral undertones, and the resulting complex has been repeatedly (and rightly) challenged in recent years. A caricature of a particularly long-standing model ties together two suspect ideas, of "man the hunter" and the nuclear family, and runs along the lines that, first men started hunting, providing a potential bonanza of protein and fat for building bigger, healthier babies, and second, women traded sex for meat to craft the monogamous nuclear family that we know today. Despite several grains of truth to this picture, it is clearly overly simplistic, and contradicted in numerous ways by the facts. In order to extract the grains of truth and leave behind the dross, we need to clearly distinguish several distinct issues and focus on the empirical basis and logical consistency for each of them. In particular we need to distinguish male paternal care (a social relationship between males and young who are often, but not necessarily, his offspring), pair-bonding (often termed behavioural monogamy – a social relationship between adult males and females) and sexual monogamy (indexed imperfectly by mating behaviour, but which ultimately boils down to the genetic facts about paternity: which adult males are the fathers of which young). Although these traits are often linked together in various ways, none of these links are inevitable. This means that the "prototypical" nuclear family, where there is a pair-bond and sexual monogamy between the parents, and the male devotes all of his paternal behaviour towards his mate's offspring, is simply one extreme of a continuum, a restricted region of a more complex space of possibilities.

The "nuclear family" model has been empirically challenged from several directions. Perhaps the most scandalous to modern sensibilities is the high number of children in Western "monogamous" societies who turn out genetically to be the progeny of extra-marital affairs. But similar levels of "extra pair copulations" are seen in many behaviourally monogamous species with solicitous paternal care (e.g. many birds), so for a biologist this comes as no surprise (Dewsbury, 1988). Another challenge comes from anthropology, where the range of socially-condoned human mating systems is wide, and often highly variable even within cultures. For example, the majority of the world's traditional cultures condone polygyny (though typically within strict limits that demand paternal care for all offspring). This fact squarely challenges the notion of social monogamy as "normal" human behaviour, but indeed emphasizes the cultural importance placed on male parental care in humans. The role of the father in childcare also varies considerably between cultures, and the benefits fathers provide to infants are not necessarily even measurable empirically in some cultures (Strassmann, 2003) (though in others, e.g. the Ache, they are large and undeniable (Hill & Hurtado, 1996)). Finally, increasing attention has been called in recent years to the role of alloparents – grandparents, siblings, uncles and aunts – in human childrearing. The most well-known version of this hypothesis, the "grandmother hypothesis" (Hawkes, O'Connell, Jones, Alvarez & Charnovs, 1998), suggests that post-menopausal grandmothers played a crucial alloparenting role in human evolution. Although sometimes seen as an alternative to hypotheses based on paternal care, most of the biological arguments put forth in support of the grandmother hypothesis actually carry through to all forms of allomothering, including paternal care, and these ideas are not mutually exclusive (Hrdy et al., 2004). Given that *females* other than the mother provide "aunting" of various sorts in a wide variety of primates, the thread that runs though all of this, and that remains to be explained, is the increasing role of *male* parental care since our split with other apes.

Do humans, as a species, exhibit male parental care? The answer to this question is certainly yes. The degree to which human males help care for children is quite striking to anyone who has spent time watching adult males of most other primate species. Not only are human males expected to help care for children in all cultures, but in many polygynous cultures the male's ability to care for his multiple wives and their children is a prerequisite for legal polygyny. Even in cultures where the mating system leads to low paternity certainty, men help care for their sister's offspring. This of course does not mean that *all* fathers care for *all* of their children: human males seem to pursue mixed strategies in this regard. As discussed below, there is a good correlation between a monogamous mating system and paternal care among birds and mammals, so the existence of male paternal care in humans certainly suggests a degree of monogamy in our species. Furthermore, most males who have fathered extra-marital offspring nonetheless act as industrious fathers to their own (well, mostly their own) offspring. Thus, imperfect sexual monogamy is no barrier to the evolution of male parental care, and new genetic data on monogamous mating systems in nonhuman animals reveal them to be strikingly similar, in many cases, to the mating systems of humans (Dewsbury, 1988).

The changes in mechanisms underlying male social behaviour that underwrite paternal behaviour in our species are still poorly understood, but recent advances in understanding the genetic, neural, and behavioural bases of paternal care and pair bonding in other mammals suggests the possibility of major breakthroughs in the near future (Insel, 1997). Monogamous male prairie voles show a much more female-like expression of neuropeptide receptors (particular vasopressin 1a receptors) in their brains than closely related, but polygynous, meadow voles. Within the same species, males' variation in receptor densities is correlated with paternal care, and experimental upregulation of gene expression leads to enhanced attention to their offspring (Hammock, Lim, Nair & Young, 2005; Lim et al., 2004). These results suggest that rather subtle shifts in gene regulation can have important effects on these types of behaviours, and it should soon be clear whether similar genetic mechanisms are involved in humans. In any case, from a phylogenetic perspective, the realization that shifts in social behaviour can drive changes in the male brain towards a loss of sexual dimorphism suggests one possible route to derive a sexually-egalitarian distribution of traits that were once sexually dimorphic. A cognitive mechanism that originally evolved in a context of sexual selection, and was strongly sexually dimorphic, can end up being expressed in both sexes equally under a new selection regime favouring male parental care. This provides one way in which traits such as vocal imitation (posited by Darwin and many others to originally be preferentially expressed in males), or information sharing with offspring (predicted by the kin selection model to be preferentially expressed in females) could end up being more or less equally expressed in both sexes.

Returning again to the female ape's reproductive dilemma, our own hominid line found a way around the demographic impasse, a solution that was novel for apes but common among vertebrates: increased reliance on allomaternal, including male paternal, care (Hrdy et al., 2004). Although some authors have therefore seen a monogamous protoype of the paternal "nuclear family" at the beginning of hominid evolution (e.g. Lovejoy, 1981), there is no reason that male parental care necessarily entailed strict monogamous pairing. Once interbirth interval decreases, it is in everyone's benefit to help the weanling survive (including not only the presumptive father, but also relatives like the mother's mother, or her brother (O'Connell, Hawkes & Blurton Jones, 1999)). A simple shift in a chimpanzee male's propensity to share meat with their previous consortship partners, and their own presumptive children, would be enough to start the ball rolling to the increased reproductive potential seen in modern humans. Again, these considerations reflect behavioural patterns observed in modern chimpanzees today, not imagined fairytales. Furthermore, such a shift to paternal care and restricted mating in the direction of sexual monogamy has evolved repeatedly among mammals, including most prominently the closest cousins to the great apes, the gibbons and siamang, all of which are behaviourally monogamous with some male parental care (probably with the occasional smattering of adultery). The same pattern has also evolved in the callitrichids (marmosets and tamarins) in which the solicitous support of fathers has made it possible for females to habitually give birth to twins, thus doubling at one stroke the reproductive output of a normal primate. Finally, behavioural monogamy, with paternal care, has evolved convergently in owl monkeys, *Aotus*. It is not surprising that monogamy has independently evolved multiple times among primates since primates are unusual among mammals in having such low reproductive potential in the first place. The trick for females is to somehow entice males to share parental care; the hurdle for males is high paternity certainty, and a tip in the balance of the trade-off between investing in current children vs. seeking additional matings from other fertile females.

2.5. Behavioural Monogamy and Paternity Certainty

In the free-for-all mating system that characterizes chimpanzees and bonobos, paternity is very uncertain, and male chimps typically have no way to know which child is their own. Furthermore, because female chimps emigrate out of the group, a male can't care for his sister's offspring either (unlike some human cultures, with high paternity uncertainty, where a sister's offspring are the target of male care). In highly polygynous apes like gorillas, the structure of the mating system itself guarantees that there will be other bachelor males in the vicinity, offering continual threat of "illicit" copulation and competition to the harem-holding males. In either case, the only way to reliably induce males to care for their children is to offer some degree of paternity certainty, and this requires a novel mating system: behavioural monogamy, often dependent on pair bonding.

Although uncommon in mammals, behavioural monogamy has evolved in parallel in many mammal clades, including various primates, most canids, and some rodents (Kleiman, 1977; Reichard & Boesch, 2003; Wickler & Seibt, 1981) as well as in some invertebrates (Wickler & Seibt, 1981). It is the main mating system in birds, with over 90% of bird species showing monogamy. In many species, there is a good overlap between monogamy and paternal care

(Clutton-Brock, 1991; Kleiman, 1977), though other factors certainly play a role (Reichard & Boesch, 2003). This, of course, makes perfect sense from an evolutionary viewpoint: a monogamous mating system (where a male and female pair off and stay together for the entire mating period) offers high paternity certainty. There is a point at which the evolutionary balance tips, and it becomes more beneficial for a male to help care for his own children and to help ensure their survival, than to abandon the mother after she is pregnant to seek another potential mate. This situation will often apply particularly in species with a short synchronized breeding system, where all females are fertile simultaneously (one reason that monogamy is so common in birds), in solitary species where mates are hard to find, or in areas where each female has a large home range and a male cannot defend multiple females effectively (Brotherton & Komers, 2003). None of these appear to be the case for humans, or for other apes: the spatial factors do not seem to apply, and we do not have the population-wide breeding season that many birds have. In contrast, female primates generally announce their own *private* breeding season – the oestrous period – to all comers. This can create intense competition for breeding among males, which in chimpanzees and bonobo typically results in multiple males (and often the entire group) mating with a fertile female, with concomitantly low paternity certainty. However, there is another strategy, even in chimpanzees, called "consortship", where a male and a female disappear alone into the woods together during her oestrus period (Goodall, 1986). A similar potential strategy was probably present in the LCA, already offering a path to monogamy for the hominid line. By being more willing to enter into such consortships, thereby granting paternity certainty to her mate, a female ape could tilt the balance towards male parental care.

Are humans behaviourally monogamous? One does not need to be particularly perceptive about our species to realize that, in any strict sense, the answer is "no". Despite the cultural imposition of legal monogamy in most widespread modern cultures, adultery is common (even in the face of extreme punishment). In most of the world's traditional cultures, polygyny is accepted: a man may have more than one wife. Thus, the notion that humans are biologically monogamous seems almost laughably naïve or Eurocentric, given the frequent exceptions to monogamy in both Western and other cultures. However, from a comparative perspective, it is now clear that many monogamous species have similar deviations from strict or pure *genetic monogamy* (where all offspring produced are from the pair) despite clear behavioural or *social monogamy* (where males and females pair off socially beyond the mating period) (Reichard & Boesch, 2003). "Monogamy" turns out to be a rather diverse phenomenon, with a wide range of combinations of social, mating and genetic monogamy possible. In many "monogamous" species, DNA paternity tests have revealed a heretofore unexpected amount of hanky-panky - demurely termed "extra-pair copulation" by biologists. Furthermore, many other species practice serial or sequential monogamy, with pairs mating and raising children, but then choosing new mates in future reproductive seasons. Thus, our mistake was to think monogamy is an all-or-nothing package, and biologists now realize that a fairly high amount of adultery is compatible with a behaviourally monogamous social system. By the definitions currently used by biologists, many human cultures, and most human sexual relationships, are typically socially monogamous, but genetic monogamy is less pervasive. But even social monogamy is quite rare in mammals (around 5% of all species), and demands an explanation (Clutton-Brock, 1991). Given the selective forces already discussed, what were the *mechanisms* that led humans away from the free-for-all system of chimps to the pair-bonding and partial monogamy seen in modern humans?

The factors that drove this change in our reproductive strategy have been discussed extensively and include most prominently the **concealed ovulation** of human females. There are many hypotheses for the precise function of concealed ovulation (for a light-hearted overview see (Diamond, 1992)), but one effect is clear - it tips the balance towards monogamy. Most primates copulate only while the female is in oestrous, and therefore fertile. A male who can either outcompete other males, or lure the female into solitary consortship, need only do so during this brief and obvious oestrus period in order to ensure his paternity. But human females do not advertise their fertility (even to themselves), but rather physiologically conceal it quite effectively, and therefore a much more extended period of exclusive copulation is necessary for males to achieve any paternity certainty. In the limit, well-concealed fertility "establishes mathematical parity between males restricted to a single mate and those practicing complete promiscuity" (p. 346 Lovejoy, 1981). It is important to note that most apes are more like humans than chimps: bonobos and chimpanzees are unique among apes in their redolent oestrous swellings and highly promiscuous mating patterns. It is thus likely the LCA was more like humans, orangutans or gorillas, with a relatively understated oestrus with little swelling or other obvious competition-inciting cues to her fertility. Physiologically speaking, humans have gone in one direction from this starting point, to unusually "invisible" fertility, while chimps have gone in the other. The critical point is that, with concealed fertility, male *mating* success (the number of females mated with) is somewhat decoupled from *reproductive* success (the number of offspring generated that survive). Put concretely, even a human male who mates with a different woman every night for one month is not *guaranteed* higher reproductive success than a male who mates with one woman every night over the same period. Unless they have some way of knowing when their mates are fertile, the two men may each conceive a single child from this pattern of mating. Of course, a woman is typically fertile for more than one day, so if the hyper-promiscuous male could keep up this performance, he would eventually out-reproduce the monogamous male on average. But, again, reproductive success involves not simply conceiving offspring, but raising them to maturity, and the human system of male paternal care may give an important advantage to the second male if he stays to help raise the child that he now *knows* he has fathered. Alternatively, the male may simply be coerced into this behaviour by the effective "trick" of concealed ovulation, along with social sanctions from females and their kin (as argued for callitrichids (Dunbar, 1995). Either way, the final outcome – male parental care in our species – is what matters.

In conclusion, at some point in its evolution the human lineage diverged from the other apes in its reproductive behaviour by extending the duties of childcare beyond the mother, in a manner familiar among other vertebrates. Although numerous perceptive scholars have recognized these facts (Deacon, 1997; Diamond, 1992; Hawkes, 1998; Hrdy et al., 2004; Lovejoy, 1981; Mithen, 2005), it is still insufficiently appreciated, particularly among students of language evolution, just how momentous a change this represented. The observations made in this section are based upon solid behavioural and paleontological data. Apes do face a reproductive dilemma, apes other than humans were mostly replaced by monkeys, and humans did evolve increased male parental care at some point. The critical remaining question is whether these facts are causally related. There is obviously no fossil evidence of direct male parental care (although Lovejoy has suggested that bipedalism itself is an adaptation to food carrying, and thus some indicator of food provisioning (Lovejoy, 1981)). Thus the evolutionary timing of this behavioural change in our species remains open. There are only two clear indicators present in the fossil record that are compatible with an increase in monogamy, both of which rely on the observation that monogamous species typically show a reduction in sexual dimorphism relative to their polygynous relatives. The first is the reduction in canine size overall, and a near-loss of canine dimorphism between males and females. This change was already in place in australopithecines (Johanson & White, 1979), compatible with the hypothesis that some reproductive changes occurred early in hominid evolution, well before expanded brains and increased tool use. The second indicator is the much later reduction in body size sexual dimorphism, thought by many authors to have occurred rather abruptly with *Homo erectus* (Kappelman, 1996). At this point, clearly, humans had shifted to something like our current system. Although I personally find the arguments of Lovejoy and others convincing – that the reproductive changes occurred very early – from the viewpoint of language evolution it makes little difference when these permissive factors evolved, since few commentators suspect the small-brained australopithecines of having language. By the time human language evolution was presumably underway (with the genus *Homo*), humans were less dimorphic than other apes, and the comparative data strongly suggest that this reflects an increase in male paternal care, and the (admittedly imperfect) behavioural monogamy that goes with it.

2.6. Conclusions and Prospects

To recap the argument presented here, a key issue preceding the evolution of symbolic, semantic communication in humans was the demographic dilemma faced by all great ape species. Our whole clade is characterized by very slow reproduction and very extended childcare, and this led to our clade's nearly complete replacement by faster-reproducing monkeys in the Pliocene. By shortening our interbirth interval, humans (alone among apes) have evaded the dilemma. One component of this solution has been allomothering: mothers enlist other individuals to help with childcare, including their own kin (grandmothers and siblings) and more surprisingly (among mammals) the father of the child. The latter addition was achieved by far-reaching changes in male and female human biology, along with changes in the human mating system that function to provide increased paternity certainty, and a consequent evolutionary incentive for some human fathers to aid in the care of their children. A second core factor in my argument is the fact that both chimps and humans are generalists with complex, learned extractive foraging techniques that need to be mastered by youngsters before they can feed themselves, and long-term knowledge about the dangers and affordances of their environment – precisely the sorts of knowledge that language is useful to share. These factors constitute observable facts about apes and humans, and provide part of the known biological fabric for any theory of any aspect of human evolution. I have tried to show that they have particular relevance to an aspect of language that is both highly unusual (indeed, unique at the level of complexity seen in modern humans), and perhaps the most idiosyncratic characteristic of language as a whole: our use of vocal signals to convey elaborate propositional meanings. Together, these aspects of ape and human biology help to explain why some other species that have complex vocal learning have not evolved symbolic semantic communication. Birds do not face the hominoid reproductive dilemma; seals or cetaceans have neither the extended post-weaning childcare *nor* the necessity to learn complex extractive foraging techniques and exploit unpredictable food resources. These arguments also help to understand why species that have simple semantic communication systems, like honeybees, have not gone further on the road towards language: they don't have enough novel, complex concepts worth talking about to drive the evolution of a more complex and flexible system. Such a system would therefore provide no evolutionary advantage over a simpler, unlearned system like the dance language.

In the argument I have made here, the rarity of flexible semantic communication systems in the animal kingdom derives simply from the rarity of this combination of factors. No one of these factors is in itself unique; from a comparative viewpoint each factor by itself (kin communication, vocal imitation, slow reproduction, extended childcare, allomothering, tool use or flexible foraging) can be found in nonhuman species. It is only the combination of factors that appears to be unique to humans. However, the analysis here also directs our attention to several other groups of vertebrates which would seem to possess enough of the factors discussed above to warrant additional, open-minded investigation of their communication system. These include the corvids (the songbird family that includes crows, ravens, jays) and some odontocetes (toothed whales: dolphins, killer whales, sperm whales, etc). Both of these groups possess many of the characteristics argued here to be preconditions for the evolution of a language-like system (especially vocal learning, complex intelligence, and, in some corvids, both male and alloparental childcare). And in neither of these clades would it be safe to say that we fully understand the communication system of all species (or indeed of *any* one species, though the bottlenosed dolphin *Tursiops truncatus* probably comes closest, and shows no signs of flexbile semantic communication (Evans & Bastian, 1969)). Thus, although my primary goal here has been to synthesize the available comparative data, the hypotheses explored here also point the way to further comparative explorations of animal communication systems that might share certain key components of language, or provide examples of earlier stages of language evolution that currently remain conjectural. More generally, I hope that this discussion illustrates how an integrated comparative approach to understanding human evolution can provide important clues to the function, phylogeny and mechanisms involved in human language evolution.

Acknowledgments. I thank Gesche Westphal, Chrystopher Nehaniv and Caroline Lyon for comments on an earlier version of this manuscript.

References

Aiello, L. C., & Key, C. (2002). Energetic consequences of being a Homo erectus female. *Am J Hum Biol, 14*(5), 551–565.

Arbib, M. A. (2005). From monkey-like action recognition to human language: An evolutionary framework for neurolinguistics. *Behavioral and Brain Sciences, 28*, 105–167.

Balaban, E. (1988). Bird song syntax: learned intraspecific variation is meaningful. *Proceedings of the National Academy of Sciences, 85*, 3657–3660.

Boesch, C., & Boesch-Achermann, H. (2000). *The chimpanzees of the Tai forest*. Oxford: Oxford University Press.

Brotherton, P. N. M., & Komers, P. E. (2003). Mate guarding and the evolution of social monogamy in mammals. In U. H. Reichard & C. Boesch (Eds.), *Monogamy: mating strategies and partnerships in birds, humans and other mammals* (pp. 42–58). Cambridge: Cambridge University Press.

Brunet, M., Guy, F., Pilbeam, D., Lieberman, D. E., Likius, A., Leon, M. P. D., Zollikofer, C., & Vignaud, P. (2005). New material of the earliest hominid from the Upper Miocene of Chad. *Nature, 434*, 752–755.

Cameron, D. W. (2004). *Hominid adaptations and extinctions*. Sydney: University of New South Wales Press.

Cheney, D. L., & Seyfarth, R. M. (1990). Attending to behaviour versus attending to knowledge: Examining monkeys' attribution of mental states. *Animal Behaviour, 40*, 742–753.

Clutton-Brock, T. H. (1991). *The evolution of parental care*. Princeton: Princeton University Press.

Darwin, C. (1871). *The Descent of Man and Selection in Relation to Sex*. London: John Murray.

Dawkins, R., & Krebs, J. R. (1978). Animal signals: information or manipulation? In J. R. Krebs & N. B. Davies (Eds.), *Behavioural Ecology* (pp. 282–309). Oxford, England: Blackwell Scientific Publications.

Deacon, T. W. (1997). *The Symbolic Species: The co-evolution of language and the brain*. New York: Norton.

Dewsbury, D. A. (1988). The comparative psychology of monogamy. In R. A. Dienstbier & D. W. Leger (Eds.), *Nebraska symposium on motivation 1987: Comparative Perspectives in Modern Psychology* (pp. 1–50). Lincoln, Nebraska: University of Nebraska Press.

Diamond, J. (1992). *The third chimpanzee.* New York: HarperCollins.

Dunbar, R. I. M. (1995). The mating system of callitrichid primates: I. Conditions for the coevolution of pair bonding and twinning. *Animal Behaviour, 50,* 1057–1070.

Emery, N. J., & Clayton, N. S. (2004). The mentality of crows: Convergent evolution of intelligence in corvids and apes. *Science, 306,* 1903–1907.

Evans, W. E., & Bastian, J. R. (1969). Marine Mammal Communication: Social and Ecological Factors. In H. T. Andersen (Ed.), *The Biology of Marine Mammals* (pp. 425–475). New York: Academic Press.

Fitch, W. T. (2000). The phonetic potential of nonhuman vocal tracts: Comparative cineradiographic observations of vocalizing animals. *Phonetica, 57,* 205–218.

Fitch, W. T. (2002). Comparative Vocal Production and the Evolution of Speech: Reinterpreting the Descent of the Larynx. In A. Wray (Ed.), *The Transition to Language* (pp. 21–45). Oxford: Oxford University Press.

Fitch, W. T. (2004). Kin selection and "Mother Tongues": A neglected component in language evolution. In D. K. Oller & U. Griebel (Eds.), *Evolution of Communication Systems: A Comparative Approach* (pp. 275–296). Cambridge, Massachusetts: MIT Press.

Fitch, W. T. (2005a). Computation and Cognition: Four distinctions and their implications. In A. Cutler (Ed.), *Twenty-First Century Psycholinguistics: Four Cornerstones* (pp. 381–400). Mahwah, New Jersey: Lawrence Erlbaum.

Fitch, W. T. (2005b). The evolution of language: A comparative review. *Biology and Philosophy, 20,* 193–230.

Fitch, W. T. (2005c). The Evolution of Music in Comparative Perspective. *Annals of the New York Academy of Sciences, 1060.*

Fitch, W. T. (2006). The biology and evolution of music: A comparative perspective. *Cognition, 100,* 173–215.

Fitch, W. T., & Hauser, M. D. (2002). Unpacking "Honesty": Vertebrate Vocal Production and the Evolution of Acoustic Signals. In A. M. Simmons & R. F. Fay & A. N. Popper (Eds.), *Acoustic Communication* (Vol. 16, pp. 65–137). New York: Springer.

Fitch, W. T., & Hauser, M. D. (2004). Computational constraints on syntactic processing in a nonhuman primate. *Science, 303,* 377–380.

Fitch, W. T., & Reby, D. (2001). The descended larynx is not uniquely human. *Proceedings of the Royal Society, Biological Sciences, 268*(1477), 1669–1675.

Goodall, J. (1986). *The Chimpanzees of Gombe: Patterns of Behavior.* Cambridge, Massachusetts: Harvard University Press.

Grafen, A. (1990). Biological signals as handicaps. *Journal of Theoretical Biology, 144,* 517–546.

Hailman, J. P., & Ficken, M. S. (1987). Combinatorial animal communication with computable syntax: Chick-a-dee calling qualifies as 'language' by structural linguistics. *Animal Behaviour, 34,* 1899–1901.

Hammock, E. A., Lim, M. M., Nair, H. P., & Young, L. J. (2005). Association of vasopressin 1a receptor levels with a regulatory microsatellite and behavior. *Genes, Brain and Behavior, 4*(5), 289–301.

Hare, B., Call, J., Agnetta, B., & Tomasello, M. (2000). Chimpanzees know what conspecifics do and do not see. *Animal Behaviour, 59*(4), 771–785.

Hare, B., Call, J., & Tomasello, M. (2001). Do chimpanzees know what conspecifics know? *Anim Behav, 61*(1), 139–151.

Hauser, M., Chomsky, N., & Fitch, W. T. (2002). The Language Faculty: What is it, who has it, and how did it evolve? *Science, 298*, 1569–1579.

Hawkes, K., O'Connell, J. F., Jones, N. G., Alvarez, H., & Charnov, E. L. (1998). Grandmothering, menopause, and the evolution of human life histories. *Proceedings of the National Academy of Sciences, USA, 95*(3), 1336–1339.

Henton, C. (1992). The abnormality of male speech. In G. Wolf (Ed.), *New Departures in Linguistics* (pp. 27–59). New York: Garland Publishing.

Hill, K., & Hurtado, A. (1996). *Ache Life History: The Ecology and Demography of a Foraging People*. Hawthorne, NY: Aldine de Gruyter.

Hrdy, S. B. (2004). Comes the Child before Man: How Cooperative Breeding and Prolonged Postweaning Dependence Shaped Human Potentials. In B. Hewlett & M. Lamb (Eds.), *Hunter Gatherer Childhoods* (pp. 65–91).

Hyde, J. S., & Linn, M. C. (1988). Gender differences in verbal ability: a meta-analysis. *Psychological Bulletin, 104*, 53–69.

Insel, T. R. (1997). A neurobiological basis of social attachment. *American Journal of Psychiatry, 154*(6), 726–735.

Jablonski, N. G. (1998). The response of catarrhine primates to Pleistocene environmental fluctuations in East Asia. *Primates, 39*(1), 29–37.

Janik, V. M., & Slater, P. B. (1997). Vocal learning in mammals. *Advances in the study of behavior, 26*, 59–99.

Johanson, D. C., & White, T. D. (1979). A systematic assessment of early African hominids. *Science, 203*, 321–330.

Joshi, A. K., Vijay-Shanker, K., & Weir, D. (1991). The convergence of Mildly Context-Sensitive formalisms. In P. Sells & S. Shieber & T. Wasow (Eds.), *Processing of Linguistic Structure* (pp. 31–81). Cambridge, MA: The MIT Press.

Kappelman, J. (1996). The evolution of body mass and relative brain size in fossil hominids. *Journal of Human Evolution, 30*, 243–276.

Kleiman, D. G. (1977). Monogamy in mammals. *Quarterly Review of Biology, 52*, 39–69.

Krebs, J. R., & Dawkins, R. (1984). Animal signals: Mind reading and manipulation. In J. R. Krebs & N. B. Davies (Eds.), *Behavioural Ecology* (pp. 380–402). Sunderland, Massachusetts: Sinauer Associates.

Lim, M. M., Wang, Z., Olazabal, D. E., Ren, X., Terwilliger, E. F., & Young, L. J. (2004). Enhanced partner preference in a promiscuous species by manipulating the expression of a single gene. *Nature, 429*(6993), 754–757.

Lovejoy, C. O. (1981). The origin of man. *Science, 211*, 341–350.

Maynard Smith, J., & Harper, D. (2003). *Animal Signals*. Oxford: Oxford University Press.

Mithen, S. (2005). *The Singing Neanderthals: The Origins of Music, Language, Mind, and Body*. London: Weidenfeld & Nicolson.

O'Connell, J. F., Hawkes, K., & Blurton Jones, N. G. (1999). Grandmothering and the evolution of *Homo erectus*. *Journal of Human Evolution, 36*(5), 461–485.

Payne, K. (2000). The progressively changing songs of humpback whales: A window on the creative process in a wild animal. In N. L. Wallin & B. Merker & S. Brown (Eds.), *The Origins of Music* (pp. 135–150). Cambridge, Mass.: The MIT Press.

Payne, R., & McVay, S. (1971). Songs of humpback whales. *Science, 173*, 583–597.

Premack, D. (1971). Language in chimpanzee? *Science, 172*, 808–822.

Pusey, A., Williams, J. R., & Goodall, J. (1997). The influence of dominance rank on the reproductive success of female chimpanzees. *Science, 277*, 828–831.

Reichard, U. H., & Boesch, C. (Eds.). (2003). *Monogamy: mating strategies and partnerships in birds, humans and other mammals.* Cambridge: Cambridge University Press.

Robinson, J. G. (1984). Syntactic structures in the vocalizations of wedge-capped capuchin monkeys, *Cebus nigrivittatus. Behaviour, 90,* 46–79.

Strassmann, B. I. (2003). Social monogamy in a human society: Marriage and reproductive success among the Dogon. In U. H. Reichard & C. Boesch (Eds.), *Monogamy: mating strategies and partnerships in birds, humans and other mammals* (pp. 177–189). Cambridge: Cambridge University Press.

Terrace, H. S. (1979). *Nim.* New York: Knopf.

Tomasello, M. (2003). On the different origins of symbols and grammar. In M. Christiansen & S. Kirby (Eds.), *Language Evolution* (pp. 94–110). Oxford: Oxford University Press.

Tomasello, M., & Call, J. (1997). *Primate Cognition.* Oxford: Oxford University Press.

Tomasello, M., Call, J., Nagell, K., Olguin, R., & Carpenter, M. (1994). The learning and use of gestural signals by young chimpanzees: A trans-generational study. *Primates, 35,* 137–154.

Trivers, R. L. (1971). The evolution of reciprocal altruism. *Quarterly Review of Biology, 46,* 35–57.

Wickler, W., & Seibt, U. (1981). Monogamy in Crustacea and Man. *Zeitschrift für Tierpsychologie, 57,* 215–234.

Zahavi, A. (1975). Mate selection: a selection for a handicap. *Journal of Theoretical Biology, 53,* 205–214.

Zahavi, A. (1977). The cost of honesty (further remarks on the handicap principle). *Journal of Theoretical Biology, 67,* 603–605.

Zahavi, A. (1993). The fallacy of conventional signalling. *Proceedings of the Royal Society, London, 340,* 227–230.

Zuberbühler, K. (2002). A syntactic rule in forest monkey communication. *Animal Behaviour, 63,* 293–299.

3
'Needs only' Analysis in Linguistic Ontogeny and Phylogeny

Alison Wray

3.1. Introduction

Recently, linguists from several quarters have begun to unpack some of the assumptions and claims made in linguistics over the last 40 years, opening up new possibilities for synergies between linguistic theory and the variety of fields that engage with it. A key point of exploration is the relationship between external manifestations of language and the underlying mental model that produces and understands them. To what extent does it remain reasonable to argue that all humans 'know' certain things about language, even if they never demonstrate that knowledge? What is the status of knowledge that is only stimulated into expression by particular cultural input? Many have asked whether the human's linguistic behaviour can be explained with recourse to less innate knowledge than Chomskian models traditionally assume. But to what extent might it be appropriate, in addition, to move away from the quest to model full systematicity at all? This chapter proposes that models that generate an untidy and only partially rationalised product may a better match for reality than is often supposed. The implications for simulation work are extensive: a reformulation of target outcomes offers new possibilities for characterising starting states and processes.

Linguistics in the pre-Chomskian era was much more open to the exploration of what variation between languages means, and what might underlie such variation. Revisiting the writings of Jakobson, Jespersen, Firth, Bloomfield, Saussure and others can refresh our perceptions of language (e.g. Wray 2002a, chap. 1), particularly if we ourselves have been heavily influenced by the Chomskian tradition. We need to move towards a mature synergistic approach that can evaluate the various contributions made to linguistic research over the past century or more, scrutinise points of difference, and identify and examine common assumptions. This is beginning to happen. To some extent language-focussed AI research is fuelling this activity, but beyond that, it has much to gain from engaging with the moving tide of questions about language, many of which can be answered empirically. Amongst the issues that are being examined, not least in response to the difficult questions that must be addressed in language evolution research, are the uniformity of language and of fundamental linguistic knowledge, and what, precisely, is it is that is innate in relation to language.

Approaches to simulation vary, but all need to specify and manipulate a starting state and/or process in order to observe the effect on an end state. At least one of these elements must be defined by and/or evaluated relative to some external reference point, such as a current model of learning, the real world target of the simulation, etc. Pre-specifications of the starting state must be scrutinized, justified and where possible minimized, since they build in features that might otherwise have been explained as a product of the process. It follows that language simulators seek clear answers to questions about the phenomena they model: if, in a model of language evolution, starting state X undergoes process Y to become end state Z, what do linguists, psychologists and others consider reasonable definitions of X and Z such that versions of Y can be explored?

Simulating language makes heavy demands if we construe language as a complex dynamic system with many interacting parts. Simulation research to date demonstrates that even quite simple processes can result in a level of complexity in the end state that it was previously assumed must be subject to specification in the starting state. Such discoveries, however, do not in themselves guarantee that the simulation is a close match for the phenomena it models. Furthermore, linguists have tended to believe that language is fundamentally so complex that it is unlikely to render its secrets easily in simulation studies. Although much is being done to establish how the basic building blocks of language could emerge – sound systems, meaning, basic thematic and grammatical roles, etc. – it remains unclear whether it will ever be possible to write a program that can learn a language, or generate linguistic material, in a way comparable (in outcome and/or process) to that of a human.

With regard to this holy grail, one line of exploration is to establish whether the features of language that are held to be universal need to be pre-specified in a Universal grammar (UG), or whether they can emerge on the basis of input. The account developed here is consistent with the latter position, but I also propose that the individual's language knowledge may be more patchy than linguistic theory has generally assumed – if this is the case, it may be easier to model than we thought. I shall explore two main themes. Firstly, some of the complex features of language may be 'universal' only in a secondary sense – they are not actually bound to manifest, but if they do manifest, then they will always comply with particular constraints on form (see discussion of Subjacency, later). If so, then although they must still be explained, their place in models of language evolution or acquisition can be marginalized. Secondly, accounting for the presence in language of troublesome elements such as irregularity and semi-regularity may be less a question of how such features are generated than how and why they are tolerated. The theoretical model I shall describe accounts for complexity in a way that brings with it interesting opportunities for simulation studies.

3.2. All Languages are Equal (but are some more equal than others?)

The strong version of the uniformitarian position holds that since all languages are defined by the design of the human brain, which is the same for all modern humans, all languages must be equal in their complexity (see Newmeyer 2002). Those who take this position set a parameter for simulation studies: if the product is always of the same order, the starting state and process must, between them, account for that fact. As Newmeyer points out, in the absence of contrary evidence, some kind of uniformity in language capacity must be assumed to exist. However, a weaker version of the uniformitarian position is possible.

Newmeyer opens up the possibility that the uniformitarian view can, and should, accommodate certain observable tendencies in language, specifically, directionality in language change, e.g. from verb-final to verb-medial, increasing morphophonemic and phonological complexity, increasing grammaticalisation, reduction in deictic complexity, and reduction of marked structures. He summarises a number of studies, including Nettle's simulation work, that variously suggest influences on linguistic structure from culture, group size, and language contact. He observes that if there is, as considerable evidence suggests, variation in the extent to which certain linguistic features are expressed, this undermines the strong uniformitarian view that all languages are of equal complexity, but does not challenge the weaker version, that all humans possess equal underlying linguistic capabilities.

He concludes that "if grammar is tailored to the needs and properties of language users (to whatever degree), and language users now are not what they used to be, then it follows that grammar is probably not what it used to be" (p.369). It is significant that he specifies "needs and properties of language users" as a determining factor in how the language is shaped. If, as the evidence suggests, one feature that is variable under conditions of user "needs and properties" is grammatically expressed subordination, that will automatically impact on the opportunities for certain supposed realisations of UG to be expressed, such as Subjacency.[1] It follows that while we still have to account for shared underlying linguistic capacities in *Homo sapiens* we may not invoke as evolutionary pressures any features of language that are contingent on socio-cultural or other factors not extant in prehistoric times. Care must be taken, of course. While we can make some reasonable guesses about group size, inter-group contact, ecology and food availability in pre-modern or early modern

---

[1] The Subjacency condition constrains the 'movement' of constituents across bounding nodes in complex sentences (see for instance Carnie 2006: 48–9). The effect is to render ungrammatical such examples such as *What did you believe the claim that Maisie saw?* derived from, say, *You believe the claim that Maisie saw a ghost.* The Subjacency condition only affects sentences that contain complex clause structures and so will not manifest in a language that does not have such complexity.

man, we cannot be as sure about the precise circumstances at vital moments as we would need to be for a monogenetic account of language emergence – especially catastrophic monogenesis. Nevertheless, features of language that evidence suggests are only expressed in literate and/or complex societies can reasonably be dismissed as candidates for selection at an early stage in human prehistory. Grammatical subordination seems to be one such (Kalmár 1985; Mithun 1984; Ong 1982; see Newmeyer 2002 and Wray & Grace *in press* for interpretations of this evidence. Also see further discussion in section 3.4 below).

We are challenged, then, to accommodate in a model of language evolution the emergence not only of what humans *know* and what humans *do* with what they know, but also a mechanism by which the one is mapped onto the other. This challenge cannot be reduced to a version of the old competence-performance debate – it is more fundamental than a simple failure of our production mechanisms to keep pace with some finely honed underlying system. Indeed, the notion that there is a fully-specified underlying system can no longer be taken for granted. Different theoretical approaches accommodate a lesser level of specification in different ways, but one feature that is increasingly playing a role is the question of how the experience of individuals could enable them to handle a linguistic system that is not entirely systematic, without mastering it. The implications are considerable for simulation research, since mastery of the system has always been the most difficult thing to model.

3.3. Mapping Linguistic Knowledge

3.3.1. Intuition and Patterns of Use

Establishing what humans 'know' about language is not easy. Corpus linguistics has opened our eyes to a great many things previously not recognised about patterns in linguistic behaviour, and these are surprisingly different from what our intuitions predict. Sinclair (1991) views linguistic intuition as "highly specific, and not at all a good guide to what actually happens when the same people actually use the language" (p.4). Much continues to be written, from both sides, about just why our intuitions don't match our language use. Increasingly, linguists are looking for a way to model our knowledge of language that can account for the mismatch in some plausible way. By plausible, I mean that there should be predictive power to the model of the relationship, rather than simply writing off one or the other component as mysterious or uninteresting. I shall propose such a model later. There are several things that it needs to accommodate.

On the performance side, one is the lexical patterns that corpus linguistics reveals: "Grammars based on intuitive data will imply more freedom of combination than is in fact possible" (Stubbs 1993: 17). Another is the disproportionate recurrence of certain formulations of common messages, where other formulations are also possible (Wray 2002a). A third is the paucity of certain grammatical structures that are intrinsic to a basic grammatical theory. Meyer & Tao (2004) looked for gapping in the International Corpus of English (ICE). They found only 120 tokens in 17,629 examples of local coordination capable of supporting it (0.007%).

On the competence side, we can note that our intuitions do not seem to match linguistic theory. Linguistics lecturers know that it is not always easy to convince a syntax class that the 'official' allocation of asterisks (on unacceptable sentences) is correct, even though it is supposed to reflect universal innate knowledge. Outside of the university setting, it is even more of an issue: Chipere (2000) found that relatively uneducated native speakers of English were very poor at making grammaticality judgements on complex sentences that did and did not contravene UG constraints.

What does this signify? Do people 'know' things but have difficulty articulating their judgements? Do they have problems separating out strictly structural judgements from semantic and pragmatic variables? Or is it possible that they really don't *know* certain grammatical constraints? And if so, how should we define 'know' without raising questions of inegality at a fundamental level? Answering these questions impacts considerably on where simulation studies go in the next few years.

3.3.2. What does it Mean to 'Know' Something?

Let us assume, with Newmeyer, that every human is innately bound to adhere to the Subjacency condition, even if he or she never creates a sentence sufficiently complex to invoke it. Let us further assume that Subjacency did not arise as a response to some mental or communicative pressure that no longer exists (though this should be fully explored at some point). It follows that we have to explain our sensitivity to constraints such as those of the Subjacency condition as a spandrel. This does not get us off the hook – a spandrel of *what*, and why did precisely this sort of constraint arise? Our model of how language evolved may be freed up by not having to build in certain constraints at the primary level, but it must still produce the constraints at the secondary level, and, if Newmeyer is correct, across the board, in humans that do and do not have occasion to apply them. It is similar to the way in which a model of how human physiology evolved does not need to build in, at the primary level, the human's capacity to ride a bicycle, since bicycle riding played no part in our physiological evolution; yet, at the same time, any evolutionary model that does not culminate in a modern physiology that includes the capacity to ride a bicycle is clearly wrong.

The question is, therefore, what sorts of models of language evolution can, without introducing the full gamut of linguistic realisations found today, nevertheless predict that they will be *possible* today? And how does one avoid building in unprincipled preadaptations, that is, shaping the model in certain ways in anticipation of what will be needed later?

3.4. Evaluating Alternative Models of Linguistic Knowledge

Once the door is opened, there are many paths to explore. In what follows, I pursue one particular line, which entails three potentially independent, but also linkable, insights into how we might account for the phylogenetic (and, in passing, ontogenetic) acquisition of linguistic knowledge.

3.4.1. Culturally Based Insights About Language

Echoing Newmeyer, and in keeping with various observations made about the role of literacy in our perceptions of language (e.g. Givon 1979, Grace 1987, 2002a-c, 2003, Kalmár 1985, Ong 1982), Wray & Grace (in press) propose that the extent to which humans engage with the free manipulation of linguistic structure is influenced by cultural and demographic variables. Drawing on ideas from Chafe (1985), Kay (1977), Laycock (1979), Mithun (1984), Thurston (1987, 1989) and Trudgill (1989, 2002), we suggest that the default level at which humans exploit the creative potential of language is somewhat conservative. However, under certain sorts of conditions, such as prolonged contact with adult learners of the language, and social structures that create and sustain linguistically defined in- and out-groups, additional engagement with the mechanics of language becomes necessary. This augmented engagement serves explicitness and form-meaning predictability. Messages will become easier to interpret out of their temporal and/or sociocultural context, and it will be easier to create and understand novel messages.[2]

According to this model, there is a fluid range of potential experience for individuals in relation to the manipulation of their language. Those operating at the default level are those whose environment and way of life feature a large measure of predictability in daily behaviour and message content, such that their ability to understand, and produce, novel messages is rarely challenged to handle more than limited lexical variation within much-used message frames.

Under different sociocultural conditions, however, these same individuals will increase their engagement with the mechanisms of their language, to accommodate the greater need for explicitness in messages. To take a modern-day example, a specialist 'in-group' such as car mechanics may possess a highly contextualised code for discussing their work amongst themselves. This code will feature jargon that affords short-cuts in relation to customary reference – jargon that must be acquired as part of an apprenticeship, both for social and practical reasons. The code may simultaneously facilitate in-group communication, furnish its users with a means of preventing outsiders from understanding

---

[2] It should not be inferred that there is no scope for novelty without this augmentation. The default level is above the threshold at which new meaning can be expressed and understood. However, more adventurous combinations will, indeed, be possible with augmented engagement. How this works is further described later.

certain secret messages, and signal, through that exclusion, professional identity. However, the code is of little use when the mechanic has to discuss the state of a car with its non-specialist owner. Jargon must be glossed, and technical procedures explained rather than just named. In order to achieve an adequate level of effective communication, both mechanic and customer must have access to a code of common terms and ways of formulating them. This *lingua franca* will be most effective if its components are subject to transparency and regularity, so that meaning can be teased out where it is not available outright. For practical reasons, the *lingua franca* will also need to be transferable to other similar situations.

Under this account, individuals' linguistic capabilities, in terms of novelty of expression, are conservative by default, but easily stretched when necessary. This 'elastic' model can explain the contrast between what we evidently *can* do, and what we customarily *do* do. Unlike models that assume all individuals to be exercising the full range of linguistic potential all the time, there is no need here to account for the failure of that full potential to be realised in most instances of language in use. Rather, the potent variable is that which forces the individual, temporarily or more permanently, out of the default mode in which messages are expressed in the same way as last time, and in which the interpretation of input is filtered through pragmatic and contextual predictability first, and only further analysed if necessary.

3.4.2. Processing by Need, not Principle

The processing mechanism upon which I propose the elasticity to be based is *needs only analysis* (NOA) (Wray 2002a: 130–2), and I shall explain it first in relation to child language acquisition. The principle of NOA is simply that the individual does not break down input any further than is necessary to extract or create meaning. That is, there is no gratuitous analysis of form beyond the point where form-meaning mapping is sufficient for the present comprehension event, or for the construction of the presently required output. Over a period of time, an accumulation of event-specific comprehension and production requirements will lead to the identification of many small, recombinable items, plus rules for their combination. However, large units that never require such reduction will remain intact, and this will result in a mixed inventory of small and large items, as determined by the patterns in the input. In many cases a large unit will loosen up to permit limited morphological or lexical variation, creating a partially lexicalised frame.[3]

---

[3] For example, there is a formulaic frame *at the end of the [time period]*, which permits the generation of a finite set of nativelike phrases, including *at the end of the year; at the end of the day; at the end of the month*. Similarly, there is a formulaic frame that can be expressed as NP_1 *pull* + *TENSE* NP_2 + *POSSESSIVE leg*, giving a potentially infinite set of realisations that conform to the one pattern, including 'you're pulling my leg', 'John pulled Helen's leg', and so on. This frame requires a different noun phrase in each of the two NP slots (thus preventing 'I'm pulling my leg') and takes closed class variation for the verb tense and possessive form. The items *pull* and *leg* are fixed.

Once a reliable meaning can be associated with a particular unit, that unit will be subject to privileged retrieval for that meaning, both in comprehension and production. As a result, in comprehension, even if the unit is internally complex (e.g. *don't count your chickens; the thing is*) other logical but disfavoured interpretations of the unit will not be countenanced. Thus, under normal circumstances, *tear along the dotted line* will not be interpreted as an instruction to sprint along the middle of the road because another meaning is already associated with that complex unit. In production, other entirely grammatical formulations of the intended message will tend not to be produced (e.g. *rip along the marked trajectory*), because it is easier to retrieve a preformed unit than to construct one.[4]

In further illustrating how NOA works, it is useful to look at the extreme end. An idiom like *by and large* has reliable meaning at this three-word level, and so there is no impetus to break it down any further. As a result, we do not construe the meaning of 'large' with reference to its occurrence in this idiom, and we are not tempted to create novel meanings by changing items within the phrase, e.g. **by but large; *by and small.*

A slightly less fixed idiom like *from now on* will also be initially assigned a holistic meaning, but over time, input will reveal the potential to loosen the fixedness of *now* to permit certain other time-related items, e.g. *from then on, from Tuesday on, from that moment on,* but without loosening the constraints on the first and third words, since no evidence will arise from input to suggest that **till now on* or **from now off* are possible. It follows that intuitions about what 'sounds right' are closely attuned to experience of input and how that has affected the specification of looseness for a given lexical configuration.

Literate language users will encounter a broader range of messages, many decontextualised and explicit. As outlined earlier, explicitness is achieved by virtue of predictability and system. Learning to be literate is, as any teacher will verify, much more than learning to recognise and form letters on the page. It entails the mastery of the manipulation of language in the service of explicitness—that is, effective communication through the written medium relies on the writer's ability to present sufficient information on the page for the reader to access the writer's intended meaning or effect without recourse to the kind of interactive checking and negotiation that goes on in face to face interaction. What we read counts as input, and the desire to read and understand changes the 'needs' dimension of needs only analysis. We need to analyse more in order to cope with the new ideas and structures we encounter, and this influences what we know of the language and what we can do with it. In addition, general western-style education tends to encourage us to perceive the whole as a product

---

[4] NOA explains why our language use is different from our linguistic insight. The former is subject to NOA, while the latter can be marshalled to judgements about what is logically possible too. NOA can also explain why our judgements about what words mean and what they can combine with do not match how we use them (see Wray 2002a: 276–7).

of its parts, further influencing our belief that the way to learn a language is to master its smallest components. In adult language learners, this compulsion is, I have elsewhere concluded, virtually irresistible, even where it specifically interferes with effective communication (Wray 2004). In contrast, NOA predicts that children, being preliterate and uneducated, will overlook even quite explicit linguistic regularities, if those patterns do not map onto something they need for the extraction of meaning. In line with this prediction, Bergen (2001) found that child native speakers of Esperanto introduced irregularities into the perfectly regular system. This is something that would not be predicted by a model of language acquisition that entailed the principled pursuit of fully systematic patterns (see Wray & Grace *forthcoming* for a full exploration of these issues).

3.4.3. Cultural Inheritance

Needs only analysis naturally entails that we can inherit linguistic material that we have not ourselves analysed. This is comparable to being able to drive a car that you couldn't build or fix, though you might be able to dabble with more or fewer components, such as filling up the water reservoir, putting air in the tyres, replacing a light bulb, or changing the spark plugs. The analogy is useful here, since our ability to do such maintenance jobs on our cars is also determined by need. Leaving aside going to car maintenance classes or training as a mechanic – the equivalent of taking language classes in school – one will tend not learn how to change the plugs until the plugs need changing, and only then if there is no alternative to doing it oneself. In the same way, the extent to which we manipulate language depends on the situations we find ourselves in, and what the alternatives are. In ordinary educational settings we may learn to manipulate the language sufficiently to recognise and command different styles for different purposes. In a poetry class we would learn to analyse and create novel formulations that push at the boundaries of customary semantic (and in some cases grammatical) practice. A professional writer would learn to hone text to create subtle effects. And, at the most extreme end, someone who does cryptic crosswords crosses the boundary into the bizarre misanalysis of what appear to be normal linguistic formulations. This would be the equivalent of melting down a car tyre to extract the chemical components, perhaps.

That we can also duck out of analysis if the opportunity exists is exemplified by Rehbein's (1987) observation that Turkish guest workers in Germany did not raise their linguistic skills to meet their communicative need, but rather curtailed their communicative need (by avoiding certain situations) to match their existing linguistic skills. Many people demonstrate this choice when, on holiday in a foreign country, they prefer self-service shopping rather than transactions at the counter or market-stall.

One particular consequence of NOA is of significance here. It relates to the potential for the inherited language to carry material that is not – and in due course could not come – under the control of its current users. A regular formulation might easily not be analysed by its users, if the messages expressed by paradigmatic variation upon it happen never to be needed. Where users do not activate the compositional structure of a wordstring, they will be less likely to update it in the light of diachronic or other language change, or to correct phonologically conditioned errors. Additionally, there may be semantic drift as the meaning is no longer grounded through its component parts. Thus, over time, idiomatic expressions can become stranded as fossils, maintaining lexical and/or grammatical forms that are no longer active in the language (e.g. *curry favour; rather thee than me; director general*), or phonological indeterminacy (e.g. *streaks/streets ahead; off his own back/bat*). The more irregular an item becomes, the more it resists analysis, until the individual encountering it has no choice but to accept it holistically and assign a global meaning to it (e.g. *by and large*).

3.4.4. Corollaries for Modelling Language Evolution

From this local consequence, longer-term scenarios become logically possible, and these have a direct bearing in how language processing (in evolution or acquisition) is modelled. For clarity, it must be noted that while NOA is proposed to be an identical process in both the phylogenetic and ontogenetic acquisition of language, there is, of course a key difference, in that children apply NOA to input deriving from an existing linguistic system (albeit not a fully specified one), while language itself either emerged spontaneously, or evolved from something that was not itself language. The mechanisms by which language is acquired by the individual have been adequately covered above, so we shall focus now on NOA in language evolution.

One possible scenario for how irregularities arise under a rule-based system requires us to envisage some parent language starting out perfectly formed, with no irregularities. Although implausible in all but certain kinds of catastrophic account, this scenario is worth briefly considering because a good test of NOA would be the modelling of its effects on regular initial input. In models of linguistic knowledge that assume humans to seek a fully specified grammar that will work optimally on fully regular input, it is difficult to explain why, if a language was, at some point in the past, fully regular, it should ever have ceased to be so. In contrast, as demonstrated in sections 3.4.2 and 3.4.3 above, under NOA irregularity is predicted to emerge, even if the starting place is one of perfect regularity (Bergen 2001).

However, there may never have been perfect regularity from which human languages have strayed. An alternative scenario is that language has always been irregular, either entirely or at least at the edges. Various explanations might be offered for this, including some vagary in the fundamental operations of the human mind on linguistic material, and the accumulation of complexity under the gradual emergence of fully formed language out of precursor systems. NOA is consistent with all such scenarios, but also with one in which the building blocks of the languages we manipulate today are the – albeit much changed – descendents of forms extracted through *post hoc* rationalisation from a phonetically expressed holistic protolanguage (Wray 1998, 2000, 2002b).[5]

In that account, the emergence of language is preceded by the capacity to use 'large words' – that is, holistic sound- or gesture-strings – to express frequent manipulative messages. These messages might reasonably be envisaged to be more numerous than those in other animals, and to be the product of more intricate and controlled articulatory movements. But they are still holistic units associated with specific messages used to signal within a narrow functional range. Also pre-specified is semanticity, in the specific sense of a capacity to discern and interpret things in the world. This seems uncontroversial, since (a) such discernment is fundamental for survival in numerous species, and (b) there is no implication that what is discerned can be labelled, nor that individuals would, if they could label, share judgements about what to label (compare Steels & Kaplan 2002 experimenting with AIBO). The holistic units, of course, must have their own semantic representations, but, as with animal calls, these are grounded in observable action[6] and if not so-grounded they will cease to be viable. This gives the process of NOA, when it kicks in,[7] the scope to itself fuel the emergence of semantic categories, based mostly on existing perceptual preferences but partly on pure chance.

In modern first language acquisition, variation in the input is a product of the rule-based flexibility in a system that is being manipulated by those who already command it. As a result, the child has many clues about what can change and what can't and what the effect is on meaning. In contrast, in the evolutionary context, the dividing up of holistic forms with complex meanings will be down to coincidental repeated mappings of sub-forms and sub-meanings, supported by pragmatically-motivated contingencies such as hyper-correction and semantic fission[8] (Wray 1998, 2000, 2002b).

---

[5] The holistic protolanguage story as I have framed it to date has focussed on a phonetic realisation. However, as Arbib (2005) demonstrates, a gestured protolanguage is also plausible and, I think, presents no major problems to my overall thesis.

[6] Animals seem to vary in the extent to which their holistic cries for basic communicative functions are innate versus learned. In the case of the precursor of human language, the signals must, of course, be learned. This in itself will narrowly constrain the messages to certain kinds of groundable meanings.

[7] Kirby's (2001) bottleneck account goes some way to providing a rationale for the use of NOA, though we cannot avoid the need to explain how our ancestors became equipped to use it, nor why they had not applied analysis before.

[8] That is, pragmatics (or expediency) might fuel an assumption that two not quite identical forms that apparently mean the same probably are supposed to be identical (hypercorrection). In another case, it might be concluded that two non-identical forms apparently meaning the same must in fact mean different, but related things (semantic fission, or 'the splitting of the semantic space'). The first will precipitate the fixing of form-meaning pairs while the latter provides an impetus for the creation of new meanings to match forms, e.g. hyper- and hyponyms, restricted collocations etc. For instance if forms X and Y are both thought to mean, say, 'not fit to eat', the context may be over-interpreted, so that X is taken to be the term used with food A while Y is used with food B. If A and B

So much for words. What of grammar, though? Why is language grammar the way it is? Neither NOA theory nor the holistic protolanguage model as I have framed it to date directly explain why grammatical patterns are what they are. However, what we can now do is separate out the origination of a system from its perpetuation. NOA in child language acquisition acts on an existing system. It maintains and perpetuates the parts that work. Anything that has no productivity is not analysed and so ends up on the irregular periphery. NOA acts, in fact, as a filter that ensures a good mapping between what can be said and what needs to be said, while maintaining the cutting edge necessary to meet unexpected additional demands. Since the system extrapolated by an individual on the basis of NOA is a product of (a) mapping the material of actual input onto the communicative need of the individual and (b) the principle of economy (that is, the principle of linguistic analysis according to need), it also follows that the active grammar can be subject to reformulation in the minds of individuals, something that easily accounts for phenomena such as grammaticalization. Because there is no underlying template to demand that exemplars of this or that be found, such changes in a language's make up are, indeed, much easier to account for under NOA than in theories that attribute to humans a fully specified linguistic system.

This may explain how grammar is perpetuated and managed once it exists, but one must still ask how grammar arose. Once it is there, pass the parcel is all very well. But how did the parcel get wrapped up in the first place? If Newmeyer and others are right, we can exclude certain features of modern language grammars from consideration, because they are only encoded in response to later cultural conditions. But whatever a child can work out in the early years of acquisition must surely be fundamental to how the human mind works, and must have played a role in why all human languages have turned out to have certain common properties. NOA in language evolution places the burden entirely on independently evolved cognitive mechanisms, exapted to find a way of representing not only entities, properties and actions, but also relationships between them. The NOA account does not require latent specific language capabilities (though it can accommodate them). All it needs is independently evolved mechanisms for perception, thought and memory management. Whether such mechanisms can really account for language grammar is a question that many linguists who favour the 'general cognitive mechanisms' approach are presently engaged in answering.

3.4.5. Nicaraguan Sign Language and NOA

Since the proposed scenario considerably downplays the role of an underlying drive to find linguistic structure for its own sake, it is worth considering the

---

have different properties, what begins as a semantically-neutral collocational restriction will easily lead to new nuances of meaning, as we see in English with *rancid butter, sour milk, over-ripe cheese*. Modern examples are not an adequate parallel for *ab initio* semantic fission but they do indicate that we can handle it.

issue of creolisation, and in particular the case of Nicaraguan Sign Language (NSL) (e.g. Kegl 1994; Senghas 1995; Senghas & Coppola 2001). A favoured interpretation of the progression of NSL is that, as Bickerton (1988) suggests, children look for evidence of realisations of UG in their input, and if they fail to find any (as with pidgin input) they will impose UG, using default settings. Whilst it is still premature to judge whether the NSL data support Bickerton's proposal, it does seem to me that there are other factors involved, and that the emerging patterns are, so far, equally consistent with NOA (Wade 2004). As outlined earlier, NOA operates in response to communicative need. In fully formed languages the input of adults offers ample guidance for the child to establish the points of variation and the tendencies to fixedness that are characteristic of the language in use in the speech community. That is, the language can be relied on to furnish a means of expressing key concepts and relations that the human brain perceives and that the individual will want to use language to articulate. Beyond that, the child will presumably develop its preferences for semantic differentiation in tandem with a developing awareness of how its language varies to convey different meanings. Furthermore, the child may tend to trust that it will not be confronted by the need to say something that the adults around it cannot also say – a supposition which if not true in the first instance will soon become so.

In the case of an emerging language, however, things are different. If the child is unable to access an effective means for expressing basic concepts and relations, then either the child must remain mute (e.g. Schaller 1995) or it must establish a means of making good the shortfall of expressive material. NOA will be sufficient to propel the child into looking for an opportunity to extract manipulable parts, and relationships between them, from anything it has access to, be it spoken pidgin, home sign or an emerging language (Wade 2004). That is, communicative need will, if able to, drive the establishment of sufficient material to create exactly those meanings that are needed (and by default, but not design, some others).

However, it must be recognised that the process of establishing a database of such manipulable forms and structures will certainly be influenced and precipitated by any independently developing awareness on the part of the child of what language has the potential to do, such as would arise under exposure to secondary, culturally-based input – literacy, general education – or to a fully-fledged language. Although NSL evolved in the playground and school bus, it did so precisely because communication in the classroom was not based around signing, but around Spanish. That is, we should not overlook the role that the classroom might have played in determining the needs of the children to express certain kinds of messages in certain kinds of ways. In short, it is reasonable to conjecture that NSL has been – and continues to be – shaped by other kinds of input than the signing itself. The effect might be, generally, to guide the language towards the development of particular kinds of features, and/or to engage Spanish, or other languages in the environment such as ASL, as substrates. This renders NSL a good modern example of a pidgin, but not, perhaps, such a good example of the evolutionary emergence of language.

3.5. Conclusion: The Potential of the Short Cut Approach

Needs only analysis predicts that individuals might appear to command a range of complex linguistic functions while actually not having full command of them – though they would retain the capability to develop a fuller command of them should the need arise. Insofar as configurations can be used before they are analysed (if they ever are analysed), it remains possible that some – particularly those that require an arcane rule to generate them – might not be under the generative control of anyone other than linguists and pedants (Grace 2002a-c, 2003). This is in line with our undoubted ability to use foreign phrases appropriately without having a command of the grammar underlying them. However, it potentially extends well beyond this, to, at the extreme end, the possibility that judgements about relationships between elements (or gaps) in embedded clauses – as for the Subjacency constraint – are not innately specified, but rather are developed in the course of cultural linguistic training, on the basis of institutionalised *post hoc* rationalisation.

Two key components of the NOA model can be separated out in the context of computational systems. The first is the handling of unanalysed chunks. That a surprising amount of effective communication can be achieved entirely formulaically has been demonstrated by artificial systems such as TALK – a communication aid for non-speaking people (Todman et al. 1999a,b; Wray 2002c) and TESSA – a limited English-BSL translation system for the British Post Office (Wray et al. 2004). Both of these are based on the handling of predictable, holistically managed material, and each has a limited capacity to generate new messages, either through on-line editing (TALK) or partially lexicalised frames (TESSA). However, neither system has the second element of NOA: a dynamic learning component.

NOA with the dynamic component is most closely exemplified in the modelling of Kirby (2001, 2002), Dominey (2004), Vogt (2005) and others. Kirby (2001) found that holistic input will, when broken down, not necessarily resolve everything into consistent unit types or sizes. Islands of non-compositional material will remain. It might be tempting for such modellers to aim to find a set of parameters that removes this 'problem', since we have come to expect that full systematicity is the goal. But NOA suggests that this is not necessary. Not only does the input not need to be structured in order for structure to be extracted; neither does the output have to be fully structured for the process to be in some way representative of what humans do with language. An NOA based model will be adept at dealing with novel strings (albeit only after catch-up analysis), but, usefully, it will not overgenerate. Overgeneration is a consequence of over-specification relative to the target model. It is time that we expected a good model of language to be able simultaneously to handle novelty and predict the shortfall between what it is theoretically possible to say and what we actually do say (Pawley & Syder 1983).

Needs only analysis offers an alternative approach, which could have far-reaching consequences for language-focussed AI research. NOA minimises unnecessary actions, but enables the system to extract additional components when it needs to. A system that is fed a plausible approximation of contextualised normal human language will never need to identify the full complement of potential atomic units, assign them to categories and generalise about their potential to appear elsewhere. That is, the system will remain underspecified, and in that regard, unstable – or, to put it more positively, continually open to modification in response to new evidence. Such dynamism is attractive as a basic characteristic in a model of human behaviour.

As I hope I have shown, under NOA, the modelling of language acquisition and language evolution are essentially the same thing. Ontogeny does, in this case, recapitulate phylogeny, other than that in the evolutionary emergence of compositionality there was no pre-existing system to find, whereas for the modern child, there is system there, albeit not perfect or complete. The child proceeds in the same way as those first analysing ancestors would have done: identifying form-meaning mappings at the gross level, and seeking out patterns where communicative need made it expedient to do so. The speed with which patterns could be identified and exploited would have been minimal when the input was random. It follows that in the evolutionary context it would have taken a while for regularities to proliferate through hypercorrection, and for those regularities then to justify further extrapolations of pattern from the remnant random material. However, the time frame from having no patterns at all to having a part-system able to service a sustainable augmented level of mental and social activity[9] might well have been in the order only of a few generations, not hundreds, and we can still reasonably construe the emergence of modern human language in our species as a relatively swift event. Significantly, we are not bound to propose that language arose all at once, and then everything became stable. NOA offers a plausible vehicle for the continuing directional changes that Newmeyer (2002) reviews. It also draws in the secondary variables of culture and social organisation, to also play their part in the continuing evolution of language.

---

[9] In the NOA framework, the need to express particular novel messages causes analysis. The analysed material then, of course, provides additional opportunities for expression. But any language will find its own balance of form to expression, beyond which it cannot easily express novel messages. Thus, much as Whorf proposed, translation between culturally distant languages may not be easy. See, for instance, Everett (2005), and also the Bleeks' translations of folklore from the /Xam-ka!ei people of South Africa, e.g. *They shall sail along with their footprints, which they, always sailing along, are following. While they feel that they are the Stars which descend* (Bennun 2004: 25).

References

Arbib, M. A. 2005. From monkey-like action recognition to human language: an evolutionary framework for neurolinguistics. *Behavioral and Brain Sciences* 28: 105–167.

Bennun, N. 2004. *The broken string: the last words of an extinct people.* London: Penguin.

Bergen, B.K. 2001. Nativization processes in L1 Esperanto. *Journal of Child Language* 28: 575–595.

Bickerton, D. 1988. Creole languages and the bioprogram. In Newmeyer, F. (ed.) *Linguistics: the Cambridge Survey. II: Linguistic theory: extensions and implications.* Cambridge: Cambridge University Press, p. 268–284.

Carnie, A. 2006. Island constraints. In Brown, K. (ed.) *Encyclopedia of language and linguistics.* 2nd edition. Oxford: Elsevier, vol 6, p. 48–51.

Chafe, W. 1985. Linguistic differences produced by differences between speaking and writing. In Olson, D.R., Torrance, N. & Hildyard, A. (eds.) *Literacy, language and learning.* Cambridge: Cambridge University Press, 105–123.

Chipere, N. 2000. *Processing embedding in humans and connectionist models.* Unpublished PhD Thesis, University of Cambridge.

Dominey, P. 2004. From holophrases to abstract grammatical constructions in development and evolution. Paper presented at the Evolution of Language 5th International Conference, Leipzig, http://www.ling.ed.ac.uk/evolang/2004/abstracts/talks/dominey.pdf

Everett, D. 2005. Cultural constraints on grammar and cognition in Pirahã: another look at the design features of human language *Current Anthropology* 46 (4): 621–47.

Givon, T. 1979. *On understanding grammar.* New York: Academic Press.

Grace, G.W. 1987. *The linguistic construction of reality.* London: Croom Helm.

Grace, G. W. 2002a. Collateral damage from linguistics? 1: The post-Chomskyan paradigm and its underlying assumptions. *Ethnolinguistic Notes* 4, 21. *http://www2.hawaii.edu/~grace/elniv21.html*

Grace, G. W. 2002b. Collateral damage from linguistics? 2: the cultural evolution of language. *Ethnolinguistic Notes* 4, 22. *http://www2.hawaii.edu/~grace/elniv22.html*

Grace, G. W. 2002c. Collateral damage from linguistics? 3: The role of culture-centrism. *Ethnolinguistic Notes* 4, 23. *http://www2.hawaii.edu/~grace/elniv23.html*

Grace, G. W. 2003. Collateral damage from linguistics? 4: Do we really know what kind of language the language acquisition device prepares us to acquire? *Ethnolinguistic Notes* 4, 21. *http://www2.hawaii.edu/~grace/elniv24.html*

Kalmár, I. 1985. Are there really no primitive languages? In Olson, D.R., Torrance, N. & Hildyard, A. (eds.) *Literacy, language and learning.* Cambridge: Cambridge University Press, 148–166.

Kay, P. 1977. Language evolution and speech style. In Blount, B.G. & Sanches, M. (eds.) *Sociocultural dimensions of language change.* New York: Ac. Press, 21–33.

Kegl, J. 1994. The Nicaraguan Sign Language Project: an overview. *Signpost* 7 (1): 24–31

Kirby, S. 2001. Spontaneous evolution of linguistic structure: an iterated learning model of the emergence of regularity and irregularity. *IEEE Journal of Evolutionary Computation* 5 (2): 102–110.

Kirby, S. 2002. Learning, bottlenecks and the evolution of recursive syntax. In Briscoe, T. (ed.) *Linguistic evolution through language acquisition: formal and computational models.* Cambridge: Cambridge University Press.

Laycock, D. 1979. Multilingualism: linguistic boundaries and unsolved problems in Papua New Guinea. In Wurm, S.A. (ed.) *New Guinea and neighboring areas: a sociolinguistic laboratory.* The Hague: Mouton, 81–99.

Meyer, Charles, and Tao, Hongyin. 2004. Gapped Coordination Constructions in English Discourse and Grammar. Paper presented at the Fifth North American Symposium on Corpus Linguistics, Montclair State University, New Jersey. May 21–23, 2004.

Mithun, M. 1984. How to avoid subordination. *Proceedings of the tenth annual meeting of the Berkeley Linguistics Society,* 493–523.

Newmeyer, F.J. 2002. Uniformitarian assumptions and language evolution research. In Wray, A. (ed.) *The transition to language.* Oxford: Oxford Univ. Press, 359–375.

Ong, W.J. 1982. *Orality and literacy: the technologizing of the word.* London: Methuen.

Pawley, A. & Syder, F. H. 1983. Two puzzles for linguistic theory: nativelike selection and nativelike fluency. In Richards, J.C. &. Schmidt, R.W.(eds.) *Language and Communication.* New York: Longman, 191–226.

Rehbein, J. 1987. Multiple formulae: aspects of Turkish migrant workers' German in intercultural communication. In Knapp, K., Enninger, W. & Knapp-Potthoff, A. (eds.) *Analysing Intercultural Communication.* Berlin: Mouton, 215–248.

Schaller, S. 1991. *A man without words.* Berkeley, CA: University of California Press.

Senghas, A. 1995. Children's contribution to the birth of Nicaraguan Sign Language. PhD thesis, MIT; MIT Working Papers in Linguistics, No. SENG01.

Senghas, A. & Coppola, M. 2001. Children creating language: how Nicaraguan Sign Language acquired a spatial grammar. *Psychological Science* 12 (4): 323–328.

Sinclair, J. McH. 1991. *Corpus, Concordance, Collocation.* Oxford: Oxford University Press.

Steels, L. & Kaplan, F. 2002. AIBO's first words. *Evolution of Communication* 4 (1): 3–32.

Stubbs, M. 1993. British traditions in text analysis: from Firth to Sinclair. In Baker, M., Francis, G. & Tognini-Bonelli, E. (eds.) *Text and Technology: in honour of John Sinclair.* Philadelphia/Amsterdam: John Benjamins, 1–33.

Thurston, W. 1987. Processes of change in the languages of north-western New Britain. *Pacific Linguistics B99.* Canberra: The Australian National University.

Thurston, W.R. 1989. How exoteric languages build a lexicon: esoterogeny in West New Britain. In Harlow, R. & Hooper, R. (eds.) *VICAL 1: Oceanic languages. Papers from the Fifth International Conference on Austronesian Linguistics,* Auckland, New Zealand, January 1988. Auckland, NZ: Linguistic Society of New Zealand, 555–579.

Todman, J., Rankin, D. and File, P. 1999a. The use of stored text in computer-aided conversation: a single-case experiment. *Journal of Language and Social Psychology* 18 (3): 320–342.

Todman, J., Rankin, D. and File, P. 1999b Enjoyment and perceived competence in computer-aided conversations with new and familiar partners. *International Journal of Rehabilitation Research* 22: 153–154.

Trudgill, P. 1989. Contact and isolation in linguistic change. In Breivik, L.E. & Jahr, E.H. (eds.) *Language change: contributions to the study of its causes.* Berlin: Mouton de Gruyter, 227–237.

Trudgill, P. 2002. Linguistic and social typology. In Chambers, J.K., Schilling-Estes, N. & Trudgill, P. (eds.) *Handbook of linguistic variation and change.* Oxford: Blackwell, 707–728.

Vogt, P. 2005. On the acquisition and evolution of compositional languages: sparse input and the productive creativity of children. *Adaptive Behaviour* 13: 325–346.

Wade, N. 2004. Deaf children's *ad hoc* language evolves and instructs. *New York Times* Sept 24th.

Wray, A. 1998. Protolanguage as a holistic system for social interaction. *Language and Communication* 18: 47–67.

Wray, A. 2000. Holistic utterances in protolanguage: the link from primates to humans. In Knight, C., Studdert-Kennedy, M. & Hurford, J. (eds.) *The evolutionary emergence of language: social function and the origins of linguistic form*. Cambridge: Cambridge University Press, 285–302.

Wray, A. 2002a. *Formulaic language and the lexicon*. Cambridge: Cambridge University Press.

Wray, A. 2002b. Dual processing in protolanguage: performance without competence. In Wray, A. (ed.) *The transition to language*. Oxford: Oxford Univ. Press, 113–137.

Wray, A. 2002c. Formulaic language in computer-supported communication: theory meets reality. *Language Awareness* 11 (2): 114–131.

Wray, A. 2004. 'Here's one I prepared earlier': formulaic language learning on television. In Schmitt, N. (ed.). *The acquisition and use of formulaic sequences*. Amsterdam: John Benjamins, 249–268.

Wray, A., Cox, S., Lincoln, M. & Tryggvason, J. 2004. A formulaic approach to translation at the post office: reading the signs. *Language and Communication* 24: 59–75.

Wray, A. & Grace, G.W. *in press*. The consequences of talking to strangers: evolutionary corollaries of socio-cultural influences on linguistic form. *Lingua*.

4
Clues from Information Theory Indicating a Phased Emergence of Grammar

Caroline Lyon, Chrystopher L. Nehaniv, and Bob Dickerson

4.1. Introduction

In this chapter we present evidence that there is an underlying local sequential structure in present day language, and suggest that the components of such a structure could have been the basis of a more highly evolved hierarchical grammar. The primary local sequential structure is shown to have its own benefits, which indicate that there could be an intermediate stage in the evolution of grammar, before the advantages of a fully developed syntax were realised.

A consequence of having such a structure is that the consecutive segments that compose it have internal cohesion, so we expect local dependencies to be pronounced – part of the small world effect. The closest dependencies are between neighbouring elements of a sequence, with a few long distance dependencies, and we expect sequential processing to play a key role.

The evidence we present is primarily drawn from investigations into the underlying characteristics of present day language. Linguistic communication is based on the interaction between the production of speakers and the perception of hearers, and we show that the processing of heard speech is more efficient when, rather than being taken as a string of individual words, it is segmented in a sequential local structure. This is achieved through the application of information theoretic tools. We note that recent neurobiological research supports our case, showing the key role played by primitive sequential processing in language production and perception. We also draw on simple observations of the abundance of homophones in everyday speech, to illuminate human language processing. The fact that we usually have no trouble disambiguating homophones indicates that words are taken in their context rather than individually.

4.1.1. Overview of the Investigations

The core of the work described in this chapter is an investigation into the statistical characteristics of spoken and written language which can help explain why language was likely to evolve with a certain structure. We take a large corpus of written text and transcribed speech to see whether the efficiency of encoding and decoding the stream of language is improved by processing a short sequence of words rather than individual words. To do this we measure the entropy of the word sequence, comparing values when we take single words, pairs, triples and quadruples. A decline in entropy indicates an increase in predictability, an improvement in decoding efficiency. Our experiments show that entropy does indeed decline as sequences of up to three words are processed, and thus support the hypothesis that local sequential processing underlies communication through language.

We also measure the entropy with and without punctuation, to see whether communication is more efficient if the stream of words is broken into segments that usually correspond to syntactic components. Entropy indeed declines further with the inclusion of punctuation. As there is a strong correlation between punctuation and prosodic markers in speech (Fang and Huckvale, 1996; Taylor and Black, 1997) this decline indicates that there is an advantage in processing language in the segments that prosodic markers provide, since it is then easier to decode.

This suggests that there could be an intermediate stage in the development of a full hierarchical grammar. Processing a linear stream of words that is appropriately segmented is more efficient for the decoder than taking unsegmented, continuous strings of words. Such segments can then be the components of a hierarchical grammar.

Experiments have been carried out with the British National Corpus, BNC, (Visited March 2006), about 100 million words of text and transcribed speech from many different domains.

Earlier work was carried out on a small parsed corpus, in which the subject and predicate of sentences were marked. The corpus was mapped onto part-of-speech tags, and 'virtual tags' were inserted into the sequence to mark the subject and predicate boundaries. Again, it was found that the entropy of the corpus with these virtual tags was lower than that without these syntactic components being represented (Lyon and Brown, 1997), though the corpus in this case was too small for the results to be very significant.

Other recent work in this field has been done on a comparatively small corpus of 26,000 words of transcribed speech, annotated with prosodic markers (Lyon et al. 2003). However, using the large BNC corpus enables us to confirm and expand upon those results.

4.1.2. Related Work

Recent work on the small world phenomenon has investigated possible universal patterns of organization in complex systems (Ferrer i Cancho and Solé, 2001).

This effect, which is evident in natural language, picks up on the dominance of local dependencies, and research is continuing into how robust complex systems can emerge (see section 4.5.1).

Other work that supports our hypotheses includes neurobiological investigations with fMRI and PET (Lieberman, 2002). Furthermore, observations on the frequency of homophones in everyday speech, and the ability of speakers and hearers to disambiguate them without difficulty, lend further credence to our hypothesis, as discussed below.

Another related area of research is in the role of 'chunking' mechanisms in human perception, cognition and learning (Gobet et al. 2001), and associated computational models such as CHREST (Chunk Hierarchy and REtrieval STructures). A variant of this, MOSAIC, simulates the early acquisition of syntactic categories by children aged 2–3 years, and indicates that chunking mechanisms play a significant role.

Essentially, the chunking theory says that local sequences or combinations of information (chunks) form the basis of human memory and expertise. We learn these sequences throughout life. Evidence for their presence in child learning is found in the typical errors that children make. For example, mistakes like "her sit" can be explained because children have heard the sentence "did you see her sit". From the MOSAIC work, it appears that these empirical approaches better explain the patterns of child errors than do more formal, grammar-based approaches. MOSAIC is trained from actual utterances of mothers to their children, and performance is compared against what the children actually say. Results hold in several languages.

4.2. Background to this Work

4.2.1. Co-operative Communication

A number of different scenarios have been used to introduce hypotheses on the evolution of language. They have included a range of possibilities, such as "gossip, deceit, alliance building, or other social purposes" (Bickerton, 2002). In contrast, the work described here is based on those scenarios where producers and receivers are co-operating, sharing information. As Fitch (this volume) explains "it is in the signaller's interest to share information honestly, and the receiver's to accept this information unskeptically". A typical scenario for co-operative communication would be in group hunting or fishing situations, where deceit would be counter-productive. Even with Bickerton's manipulative communication scenario a degree of co-operation is required to enable understanding. We look at modes of communication that are most efficient for producers and receivers. To investigate this we take a large corpus of spoken and written language and apply an analytic tool from information theory, the entropy measure, to determine the efficiency of different modes of communication.

4.2.2. Entropy Indicators

The original concept of entropy was introduced in 1948 by Shannon (1993). Informally, it is related to predictability: the lower the entropy the better the predictability of a sequence of symbols. Shannon showed that the entropy of a sequence of letters declined as more information about adjacent letters is taken into account; it is easier to predict a letter if the previous ones are known. Entropy is represented as H, and we measure:

- H_0 : entropy with no statistical information, symbols equi-probable;
- H_1 : entropy from information on the probability of single symbols occurring;
- H_2 : entropy from information on the probability of 2 symbols occurring consecutively; and
- H_n : entropy from information on the probability of n symbols occurring consecutively.

H_n measures the uncertainty of a symbol, conditional on its $n - 1$ predecessors; we call H_n the *conditional entropy*.

For an introductory explanation of the concept of entropy, see Lyon et al. (2003), page 170. The derivation of the formula for calculating entropy is in Appendix B. For many years Automated Speech Recognition developers have used entropy metrics to measure performance (e.g. Jelinek, 1990).

4.2.3. Using Real Language

A significant amount of language analysis has not been done with real language. Well known examples include Elman's experiments with recurrent nets (1991), which use a 23 word vocabulary: 12 verbs, 10 nouns and a relative pronoun. Sentences like *boy sees boy* are considered grammatical, because there is number agreement between the subject and verb, though this sentence would be considered ungrammatical in real language because the determiners are missing. Elman himself is careful to say that this language is artificial, but this is not the case with many of his followers, who assert that it is a subset of natural language.

This artificial example consists almost exclusively of content words, but in fact many, sometimes most, of the words most people utter are function words. Though in any model we have to abstract out the features we consider most significant, a focus on content words alone introduces distortions if we are looking at human communication. We present evidence that there is a phrasal basis to language, a view also supported by Wray (this volume). This is not to say that there are not other essential characteristics of language. For instance, a key development in its evolution is the emergence of compositionality (Kirby, this volume), but word focused compositionality is compatible with a linearly structured phrasal basis.

4.3. The British National Corpus

The BNC corpus is composed of a representative collection of English texts; about 10% of the total is transcribed speech. As we want to investigate the processing of natural language, headlines, titles, captions and lists are excluded from our experiments. Including punctuation marks leads to a corpus of about 107 million symbols.

To carry out an analysis on strings of words it is necessary to reduce an unlimited number of words to a smaller set of symbols, and so words are mapped onto part-of-speech tags. As well as making the project computationally feasible, this approach is justified by evidence that implicit allocation of parts of speech occurs very early in language acquisition by infants, even before lexical access to word meanings (Morgan et al. 1996).

The BNC corpus has been tagged, with a tagset of 57 parts of speech and 4 punctuation markers. We have mapped these tags onto our own tagset of 32 classes, of which one class represents any punctuation mark (Appendix A). Tag sets can vary in size but our underlying aim is to group together words that function in a similar way, having similar neighbours. Thus, for example, lexical verbs can usually have the same type of predecessors and successors whether they are in the present or past tense:

We like swimming / We liked swimming

so in our tagset they are in one class. We believe we have not lost discrimination by moving to the smaller tagset, as is evidenced by structure detected in our experiments.

Another reason for mapping the BNC tagset onto our smaller set is that the entropy measures are more pronounced for the smaller set.

4.4. Experiments

We have run the following experiments. First, we have processed the whole corpus of 107 million parts of speech tags, with punctuation, and found H_1, H_2, H_3, H_4 and H_5 as shown in Table 4.1. We also ran experiments over each of the 10 directories in which the corpus material is placed to see if there was much variation. In fact, variations between the directories is small: the results cluster round the measure for the whole corpus. An example is shown in the lower part of Table 4.1.

We also process a comparable set of randomly generated numbers, in order to ensure that distortions do not occur because of under sampling. With 32 tags the number of possible sequences of 5 tags is 33,554,432. If too small a sample is used, the entropy appears lower than it should because not all the infrequent cases have occurred. A simple empirical test on sample size is through a random number sequence check. For a random sequence, the entropy should not decline

TABLE 4.1. Entropy measures for the BNC corpus, mapped onto 32 part-of-speech tags. 3-grams, 4-grams and 5-grams that span a punctuation mark are omitted. Figures in brackets are to be treated with caution.

Corpus	H_0	H_1	H_2	H_3	H_4	H_5
107 million words + punctuation 32 tags	5.0	4.19	3.27	2.94	2.84	(2.75)
107 million random words 32 tags	5.0	5.0	5.0	5.0	5.0	4.8
10 million words, subdirectory F 32 tags	5.0	4.18	3.25	2.91	(2.79)	
10 million random words 32 tags	5.0	5.0	5.0	5.0	4.93	3.05

as more of the information over preceding items is taken into account, since they are generated independently. Thus H for a sequence of random numbers in the range 0 to 31 should stay at 5.0. Sequences of random numbers were produced by the Unix random number generator. The results show that for the whole corpus we can be fully confident up to the H_4 figure, but H_5 should be treated with caution. For the 10 subdirectories, H_4 should be treated with caution, and H_5 far underestimates the entropy given the sample size and so is omitted.

Secondly, we process the whole BNC corpus, but omitting punctuation marks, as shown in Table 4.2. This time there are 31 tags. The number of words is reduced, as punctuation marks are counted as words.

4.4.1. Analysis of Results

The results in Table 4.1 show that entropy declines as processing is extended over 2 and then 3 consecutive part-of-speech tags. There is a small further decline when 4 consecutive tags are taken. The results for 5 consecutive tags are not considered fully reliable, in view of the random sequence check for 107 million symbols.

Compare these results with those in Table 4.2. This time there is one less tag symbol, so we expect unpredictability to decrease compared to that for the corpus tagged with 32 symbols, and entropy to be less. This is what we find for H_0 and for H_1. However, as we take words 2, 3 and 4 at a time we find that entropy is slightly greater than in the first case. This indicates that punctuation captures some of the structure of language, and by removing it we increase the

TABLE 4.2. Entropy measures for the BNC corpus, mapped onto 31 parts of speech tags, omitting punctuation. The figure in brackets should be treated with caution.

Corpus	H_0	H_1	H_2	H_3	H_4	H_5
94 million words, no punctuation 31 tags	4.95	4.16	3.29	3.14	3.07	(3.01)
94 million random words, 31 tags	4.95	4.95	4.95	4.95	4.95	4.72

uncertainty. Paraphrasing Shannon, we can say that a string of words between punctuation marks is a cohesive group with internal statistical influences, and consequently the sequences within such phrases, clauses or sentences are more restricted than those which bridge punctuation (Shannon, 1993, page 197).

These results indicate that a stream of language is easier to decode if words are taken in short sequences rather than as individual items, and supports the hypothesis that local sequential processing underlies communication through language.

4.5. Other Evidence for Local Processes

4.5.1. Computer Modelling and the Small World Effect

It is worth looking at syntactic models based on dependency grammar and related concepts. Dependency grammar assumes that syntactic structure consists of lexical nodes (words) and binary relations (dependencies) linking them. Though these models are word based, phrase structure emerges. A practical example is the Link Parser (Sleator et al. 2005) where you can parse your own texts on line and see how the constituent tree emerges. Now, it is reported (Ferrer i Cancho, 2004) that, in experiments in Czech, German and Romanian with a related system, about 70% of dependencies are between neighbouring words, 17% at a distance of 2 words, with fewer long range dependencies. This is one of the characteristics of the small world effect. A significant amount of syntactic knowledge is available from local information, before our grammatic capability is enhanced by the addition of long range dependencies associated with hierarchical structures.

This again suggests that an intermediate stage in the development of a fully fledged grammar could have been based on local syntactic constraints.

Returning to another computer model, Elman's recurrent networks, we note that they could have a useful role to play in modelling short strings of words, but there are inherent obstacles to modelling longer dependencies (Bengio, 1996; Hochreiter et al. 2001).

4.5.2. Neurobiological Evidence

Further evidence for concatenated linear segments as a basis for language structure is provided by the fact that primitive sequential processors in the basal ganglia play an essential role in language processing (Lieberman, 2000, 2002). Language processing is not confined to Broca's and Wernicke's neocortical areas. An overview of the evidence that language and motor abilities are connected is given in a special edition of *Science* (2004). In detail, Lieberman reports on the results of recent investigations with fMRI and PET that indirectly track activity in the brain. The subcortical neural processors that control the sequencing of motor movements, which include articulatory acts, also play a role in sequencing cognitive activities. In studies of patients with Parkinson's disease deficits in sequencing manual motor movements and linguistic sequencing in a sentence comprehension task were correlated (Lieberman, 2002, p.45). The basal ganglia play a part in sequencing elements that make up a component in speech production, and can interrupt it, such as switching a sequence at a clause boundary (ibid p.57).

The importance of sequential processing supports the hypothesis that local dependencies play a key role in language production and perception. These local dependencies provide the internal cohesion for segments of an utterance, or piece of text, at a sub-sentential level. And these segments, which are concatenated to create a linear structure, are usually grammatical fragments.

4.5.3. Evidence from Homophony

Any hypothesis on the evolution of language needs to explain why all languages seem to have homophones. In English some of the most frequently used words have more than one meaning such as *to / too / two*. Even young children are able to disambiguate them without difficulty. In an agglutinative language such as Finnish they are rarely used by children, but occur in adult speech (Warren, 2001).

We can classify homophones into two groups: those in which the homophonous forms have the same part of speech, and those in which they do not. In English and other languages the latter group is much the larger (Ke et al. 2002). They are frequently function words, and the fact that we disambiguate them so easily provides clues to our underlying language processing abilities. Homophones such as *there / their* or *no / know* have dependencies on neighbouring words, so usually only one is possible in a given context. In the case of homophones with different parts of speech these dependencies are primarily syntactic. Local context is the key factor: words are not taken alone, but in sequential segments.

4.5.4. An Unrealistic Model

Recently Nowak et al. have proposed that words in evolutionarily advanced language have a single meaning, that "the evolutionary optimum is reached if every word is associated with exactly one signal" (Nowak et al. 1999, page 151). It is also asserted that there is a "loss of communicative capacity that arises if individual sounds are linked to more than one meaning" (Nowak et al. 2002, page 613) and that lack of ambiguity is a mark of evolutionary fitness. While such models may be logically attractive, and could be the basis of a communication system for some artificial agents and engineering applications, in no way do they represent human language.

We might have expected that there would be an optimum number of phonemes that provide the basis for speech but in fact the number of phonemes in different languages varies from about 12 to over 100 (Maddieson, 1984). There is massive redundancy, and no need for homophones because of a shortage of phonemes.

However, if we accept the hypothesis that local sequential processing underlies our language capability then there is not a problem in accounting for the homophone phenomenon : they are disambiguated by the local context, and there is no reason why they should not have occurred.

4.6. Conclusion

When we look for clues to the evolution of language we can examine the state we are in now and reason about how we could have arrived at the present position. This may take the form of brain studies, but it can also include the sort of analysis of language that we are doing. Chomsky (1957) once famously claimed that "One's ability to produce and recognize grammatical structures is not based on notions of statistical approximation and the like". We do not suggest that statistics are consciously used in the production or perception of speech: but they contribute to a post hoc analysis, and can illuminate the way in which language processing is carried out. Investigations on large corpora can now be done that were not possible a few decades back – a computer is to a linguist what a telescope is to an astronomer.

When we look at language around us we see that much of it is not composed of syntactically correct sentences. Newspaper headlines, advertisements, titles of books and papers are often sub-sentential, as is much informal conversation. However, though these fragments are not complete sentences, they are typically grammatical: if the words in a headline are mixed up the meaning is lost. We argue that such grammatical fragments are also the underlying components of longer elements such as sentences. There are local dependencies between neighbouring words that produce cohesive segments, and these segments make up a linear structure.

The fact that there are significant local dependencies does not mean that there are not also long distance dependencies. Consider a sentence like

The pipe connections of the boiler are regularly checked.

As well as the linear phrasal structure we have number agreement between the head of the subject, the plural "connections" and the plural verb "are", although these words are at a distance. The noun preceding the verb is the singular "boiler", but this does not determine the number of the verb. The case we are making is that a full hierarchical grammar could have been preceded by an intermediate linear structure that has its own benefits.

In fact, this preliminary stage is still the basis for successful language processing applications, such as automated speech recognition, which typically treat language as having a regular grammar that can be processed using Markov models. Though a regular grammar is known to be inadequate, it can still produce acceptable results (Lambourne et al. 2004). Accuracy levels of around 95% are typical of current speech recognisers – which could be interpreted as an average error rate of one word in every sentence, assuming an average of

20 words a sentence. At this level of performance the constraints of a hierarchical grammar with long range dependencies are masked by the dominant local constraints.

Our experiments have indicated that utterances are processed in segments composed of a few words. These segments are either grammatical fragments or have a looser local sequential structure making the utterance easier to comprehend than unstructured strings of words. We suggest that these segments may serve as the building blocks out of which a hierarchical grammar is built.

Acknowledgments. We thank Peter Lane for helpful suggestions on this chapter.

References

Bell, T. C., Cleary, J. G., Witten, I. H., 1990. Text Compression. Prentice Hall.

Bengio, Y., 1996. Neural Networks for Speech and Sequence Recognition. ITP.

Bickerton, D., 2002. Foraging Versus Social Intelligence in the Evolution of Protolanguage. In: Wray, A. (Ed.), The Transition to Language. OUP, pp. 207–225.

BNC, Visited March 2006. The British National Corpus. The BNC Consortium, http://www.hcu.ox.ac.uk/BNC.

Chomsky, N., 1957. Syntactic Structures. The Hague: Mouton.

Elman, J. L., 1991. Distributed representations, simple recurrent networks and grammatical structure. Machine Learning, 195–223.

Fang, A. C., Huckvale, M., 1996. Synchronising Syntax with Speech Signals. In: Hazan, V. et al. (Ed.), Speech, Hearing and Language. University College London.

Ferrer i Cancho, R., Solé, R. V., 2001. The small world of human language. Proceedings of The Royal Society of London. Series B, Biological Sciences 268 (1482), 2261–2265.

Ferrer i Cancho, R., 2004. Patterns in syntactic dependency networks. Physical Review E 69, 051915.

Gobet, F., Lane, P. C. R., Croker, S., Cheng, P. C-H., Jones, G., Oliver, I., Pine, J. M., 2001. Chunking Mechanisms in Human Learning. Trends in Cognitive Sciences Vol.5 No. 6, 236–243.

Hochreiter, S., Bengio, Y., Frasconi, P., Schmidhuber, J., 2001. Gradient flow in recurrent nets: the difficuly of learning long term dependencies. In: Kremer, S. C., Kolen, J. F. (Eds.), A Field Guide to Dynamical Recurrent Neural Networks. IEEE Press.

Holden, C., 2004. The origin of speech. Science 303, 1316–1319.

Jelinek, F., 1990. Self-organized language modeling for speech recognition. In: Waibel, A., Lee, K. F. (Eds.), Readings in Speech Recognition. Morgan Kaufmann, pp. 450–503, IBM T. J. Watson Research Centre.

Ke, J., Wang, F., Coupe, C., 2002. The rise and fall of homophones: a window to language evolution. In: Proceedings of 4th International Conference on the Evolution of Language.

Lambourne, A., Hewitt, J., Lyon, C., Warren, S., 2004. Speech-based real time subtitling services. International Journal of Speech Technology 4, 251–349.

Lieberman, P., 2000. Human Language and our Reptilian Brain. Harvard University Press.

Lieberman, P., 2002. On the nature and evolution of the neural bases of human language. Yearbook of Physical Anthropology.

Lyon, C., Brown, S., 1997. Evaluating Parsing Schemes with Entropy Indicators. In: MOL5, 5th Meeting on the Mathematics of Language.

Lyon, C., Dickerson, B., Nehaniv, C. L., 2003. The segmentation of speech and its implications for the emergence of language structure. Evolution of Communication 4, no.2, 161–182.

Maddieson, I., 1984. Patterns of sounds. Cambridge University Press.

Morgan, J., Shi, R., Allopenna, P., 1996. Perceptual bases of rudimentary grammatical categories. In: Morgan, J., Demuth, K. (Eds.), Signal to Syntax. Lawrence Erlbaum.

Nowak, M. A., Komaraova, N. L., Niyogi, P., 2002. Computational and evolutionary aspects of language. Nature 417, 611–617.

Nowak, M. A., Plotkin, J. B., Krakauer, D. C., 1999. The evolutionary language game. J. Theoretical Biology 200, 147–162.

Shannon, C. E., 1993. Prediction and Entropy of Printed English (1951). In: Sloane, N. J. A., Wyner, A. D. (Eds.), Shannon: Collected Papers. IEEE Press.

Sleator, D., Temperly, D., Lafferty, J., 2005. Link Grammar. Carnegie Mellon University, http://www.link.cs.cmu.edu/link/, visited 17 Jan 2006.

Taylor, P., Black, A., 1997. Assigning phrase breaks from part-of-speech sequences. In: Eurospeech'97. Vol. 2.

Warren, S., 2001. Phonological acquisition and ambient language: a corpus based, cross-linguistic exploration. Ph.D. thesis, University of Hertfordshire, UK.

Appendix A

The tagset of the British National Corpus is mapped onto our tagset. Each of the BNC tags is mapped onto an integer, as shown below, so that functionally similar tags are grouped together.

Tag   Code for our mapping

AJ0   1
Adjective (general or positive) (e.g. good, old, beautiful)
AJC   1
Comparative adjective (e.g. better, older)
AJS   1
Superlative adjective (e.g. best, oldest)
AT0   2
Article (e.g. the, a, an, no)
AV0   3
General adverb: an adverb not subclassified as AVP or AVQ (see below) (e.g. often, well, longer (adv.), furthest.
AVP   3
Adverb particle (e.g. up, off, out)
AVQ   3
Wh-adverb (e.g. when, where, how, why, wherever)
CJC   4
Coordinating conjunction (e.g. and, or, but)

CJS   4
Subordinating conjunction (e.g. although, when)
CJT   4
The subordinating conjunction that
CRD   2
Cardinal number (e.g. one, 3, fifty-five, 3609)
DPS   5
Possessive determiner-pronoun (e.g. your, their, his)
DT0   2
General determiner-pronoun: i.e. a determiner-pronoun which is not a DTQ or an AT0.
DTQ   2
Wh-determiner-pronoun (e.g. which, what, whose, whichever)
EX0   6
Existential there, i.e. there occurring in the there is ... or there are ... construction
ITJ   7
Interjection or other isolate (e.g. oh, yes, mhm, wow)
NN0   8
Common noun, neutral for number (e.g. aircraft, data, committee)
NN1   9
Singular common noun (e.g. pencil, goose, time, revelation)
NN2   10
Plural common noun (e.g. pencils, geese, times, revelations)
NP0   11
Proper noun (e.g. London, Michael, Mars, IBM)
ORD   1
Ordinal numeral (e.g. first, sixth, 77th, last).
PNI   12
Indefinite pronoun (e.g. none, everything, one [as pronoun], nobody)
PNP   13
Personal pronoun (e.g. I, you, them, ours)
PNQ   14
Wh-pronoun (e.g. who, whoever, whom)
PNX   15
Reflexive pronoun (e.g. myself, yourself, itself, ourselves)
POS   16
The possessive or genitive marker 's or '
PRF   17
The preposition of
PRP   18
Preposition (except for of) (e.g. about, at, in, on, on behalf of, with)
PUL   0
Punctuation: left bracket - i.e. (or [

PUN   0

Punctuation: general separating mark - i.e. . , ! , : ; - or ?

PUQ   0

Punctuation: quotation mark - i.e. ' or "

PUR   0

Punctuation: right bracket - i.e.) or]

TO0   19

Infinitive marker to

UNC   7

Unclassified items which are not appropriately considered as items of the English lexicon.

VBB   20

The present tense forms of the verb BE, except for is, 's: i.e. am, are, 'm, 're and be [subjunctive or imperative]

VBD   20

The past tense forms of the verb BE: was and were

VBG   21

The -ing form of the verb BE: being

VBI   22

The infinitive form of the verb BE: be

VBN   23

The past participle form of the verb BE: been

VBZ   24

The -s form of the verb BE: is, 's

VDB   20

The finite base form of the verb DO: do

VDD   20

The past tense form of the verb DO: did

VDG   21

The -ing form of the verb DO: doing

VDI   22

The infinitive form of the verb DO: do

VDN   23

The past participle form of the verb DO: done

VDZ   24

The -s form of the verb DO: does, 's

VHB   20

The finite base form of the verb HAVE: have, 've

VHD   20

The past tense form of the verb HAVE: had, 'd

VHG   21

The -ing form of the verb HAVE: having

VHI   22

The infinitive form of the verb HAVE: have

VHN   23
The past participle form of the verb HAVE: had
VHZ   24
The -s form of the verb HAVE: has, 's
VM0   25
Modal auxiliary verb (e.g. will, would, can, could, 'll, 'd)
VVB   26
The finite base form of lexical verbs (e.g. forget, send, live, return) [Including the imperative and present subjunctive]
VVD   26
The past tense form of lexical verbs (e.g. forgot, sent, lived, returned)
VVG   27
The -ing form of lexical verbs (e.g. forgetting, sending, living, returning)
VVI   28
The infinitive form of lexical verbs (e.g. forget, send, live, return)
VVN   29
The past participle form of lexical verbs (e.g. forgotten, sent, lived, returned)
VVZ   30
The -s form of lexical verbs (e.g. forgets, sends, lives, returns)
XX0   31
The negative particle not or n't
ZZ0   7
Alphabetical symbols (e.g. A, a, B, b, c, d)

Appendix B

The Derivation of the Formula for Calculating Entropy

This is derived from Shannon's work on the entropy of symbol sequences. He produced a series of approximations to the entropy H of written English, taking letters as symbols, which successively take more account of the statistics of the language.

H_0 represents the average number of bits required to determine a symbol with no statistical information. H_1 is calculated with information on single symbol frequencies; H_2 uses information on the probability of 2 symbols occurring together; H_n, called the n-gram entropy, measures the amount of entropy with information extending over n adjacent symbols. As n increases from 0 to 3, the n-gram entropy declines: the degree of predictability is increased as information from more adjacent symbols is taken into account. If $n-1$ symbols are known, H_n is the conditional entropy of the next symbol, and is defined as follows.

b_i is a block of $n-1$ symbols, j is an arbitrary symbol following b_i
$p(b_i, j)$ is the probability of the n-gram consisting of b_i followed by j
$p_{b_i}(j)$ is the conditional probability of symbol j after block b_i, that is
$p(b_i, j) \div p(b_i)$

$$H_n = -\sum_{i,j} p(b_i, j) * \log_2 p_{b_i}(j)$$

$$= -\sum_{i,j} p(b_i, j) * \log_2 p(b_i, j) + \sum_{i,j} p(b_i, j) * \log_2 p(b_i)$$

$$= -\sum_{i,j} p(b_i, j) * \log_2 p(b_i, j) + \sum_{i} p(b_i) * \log_2 p(b_i)$$

since $\sum_{i,j} p(b_i, j) = \sum_i p(b_i)$.

N.B. This notation is derived from that used by Shannon. It differs from that used, for instance, by Bell et al. (1990).

5
Emergence of a Communication System: International Sign

Rachel Rosenstock

5.1. Introduction

International Sign (henceforth IS) is a communication system that is used widely in the international Deaf Community. The present study is one of the first to research extensively the origin of both the IS lexicon and grammatical structures. Findings demonstrate that IS is both influenced by naturally evolved sign languages used in grown deaf communities (henceforth SLs) and relies heavily on iconic, universal structures. This paper shows that IS continues to develop from a simplistic iconic system into a conventionalized system with increasingly complex rules.

Many hearing people still harbor the misconception that sign language is universal. However, to linguists and Deaf people alike, it is clear that the sign languages used in the different Deaf communities are as varied as the spoken languages of the world. While a Deaf person using American Sign Language (ASL) might be able to communicate on a very basic level with a Deaf person using German Sign Language or French Sign Language, it is impossible to establish communication on sophisticated matters. With an expanding international Deaf community, there is a growing need for communication across linguistic borders. Unlike in the hearing world, where one or the other spoken language has served as a lingua franca, the deaf community filled this gap by invention – they developed a linguistic system called International Sign (IS).

The present study aims to describe the historic context in which the current system and its predecessor developed. It discusses the changes the system has undergone as a result of specific needs within the international Deaf community and describes in detail the sources of the vocabulary and grammar as used today. In analyzing the structure of IS, the study shows the development from a simplistic iconic system to a conventionalized system with complex grammatical structures.

5.2. History of International Sign

The desire for international communication, or so many believe, found its answer in the "invention" of signed languages or in the inherent iconicity of the system. Even deaf people believed until the beginning of the 20th century that sign language was an ideal means of communication across borders. At what might have been the first international gathering of deaf people in 1850, the French deaf educator Ferdinand Berthier observed seeing various deaf people from all over Europe interacting with ease. He remarked that '[f]or centuries, scholars from every country have searched for the universal language and failed. Well, it exists all around you, and it is Sign Language!!' (quoted in Moody 2002:10).

In the early 1900s, deaf people started to recognize that communication with gestures alone did not suffice for the increasingly more sophisticated exchanges required on an international level (see Moody 2002). A proposal to form a committee on the creation of an international sign system was introduced by a Finnish deaf delegate at a conference for deaf education in 1911. It was accepted but never actualized (ibid:12). It was at the same conference, Moody believes, that international signs were, at least to a degree conventionalized. In the Deaf Community, with the founding of the WFD and CISS (International Committee of Sports for the Deaf), this necessity grew to a degree that the loosely established 'international' signs did not suffice for satisfying communication needs. The emergence of IS in its present form began in the late 1950s, when the World Federation of the Deaf (WFD) recognized this need. While interpersonal communication seemed to allow for the spontaneous creation of a system of gestures, signs and pantomime, conference settings such as WFD meetings, committee discussions and sports event planning boards required a more elaborate system. A committee was established that consisted of five deaf people from various European countries and the US (Moody 1989). As a result of their work, 1200 signs were published under the name 'GESTUNO'. (The British Deaf Association 1975). From this collection of signs, a partially conventional sign system has evolved which is used today at international conferences as a both mode of presentation and interpretation. Moody (see above) summarizes the process of developing the dictionary and the reactions by the Deaf Community following the publication: "The task was enormous, given the highly flexible and uncoded nature of International Sign, the uncontrolled natural evolution it had followed since the beginning of the 19th century, and the logistical problems involved in calling meetings of the commission (in spite of the fact that the members were all European and American). [...] Deaf people soon began complaining that the signs in the GESTUNO lexicon weren't iconic enough to be readily understood" (Moody 2002:16).

5.3. Evolution

Early literature on GESTUNO suggests that the Deaf Community presumed that a collection of 1200 signs would provide enough basis for a full-fledged communication system. This is expressed in the first publication of the GESTUNO dictionary: '[This is a] sign language which would be of assistance to deaf brethren throughout the world enabling them to understand each other at friendly gatherings and official conferences.' (The British Deaf Association 1975, Preface). These signs included in the dictionary were either loan signs from the national SLs used by the committee members, or highly iconic in nature. The assumption was that this collection was easy to learn by both the presenters or interpreters who would use GESTUNO, as well as by the audience at international gatherings. Reports by the first consumers of GESTUNO at an international conference in Bulgaria in 1976, however, are a testimony to the impossibility of expecting an adequate translation by providing interpreters with only a limited list of vocabulary. Moody (2002) describes how the hearing Bulgarian interpreters use spoken Bulgarian grammatical structures, combining them with the GESTUNO signs and Bulgarian SL when GESTUNO signs are not available. The audience reports that they cannot follow any of the presentations or interpretations in GESTUNO. In the following years, native signers, both hearing and deaf, were taking over interpreting at international events.

Moody observes that the vocabulary of IS interpreters can be traced to three main sources: borrowed signs of the native languages of participants of a given discourse, pantomime, and a more conventionalized pool of vocabulary that might vary from group to group but is perceived by its users to be understood universally (1989:94). Moody emphasizes the influence of the sign language of the host country of any given event on the vocabulary of IS there. This is empirically supported by a study on the origin of IS vocabulary conducted by Woll (1990). Her data was collected exclusively in the UK. Over 70% of all IS signs were labelled borrowings from BSL. Other IS signs seem less conventional. Moody (2002) describes them as 'mimed actions'; Locker McKee and Napier describe them as "more iconic, simpler in form" (2002:48). This lack of conventionalized vocabulary could be explained by the lack of native speakers and the use of IS in only a limited number of domains. The role of the invented signs published under the name 'GESTUNO' is not discussed in recent articles. Woll (1990) mentions 13-21% signs that are nonce signs (signs that are created only for the purpose of a specific context) and calls these international signs. Whether or not she includes GESTUNO signs in this category is unclear.

The source of IS grammar, on the other hand, is still widely debated. The few empirical studies of IS in recent years take very different perspectives on the issue. The ability of the interpreters to string together words, express relations between people and objects, and convey meaning beyond the isolated sign indicates that a grammatical system exists. Allsop et al. (1994) summarize the different proposed sources for the grammar of IS as follows:

- "Signers export a fairly complete version of their own Sign Language grammar (Webb/Supalla [1994, in Allsop et al. 1994]);
- Signers export those parts of their own Sign Language grammar 'felt' to be most universal (Moody [1979, in Allsop et al. 1994]);

- Signers use a grammar specifically belonging to International Sign (what Garretson calls 'natural order' [1990, in Allsop et al. 1994]) which is different from the grammar of their own Sign Language;
- Signer uses some combination of their own Sign Language grammar and some structures particular to International Sign."

Moody (1989) notes that the grammatical properties of natural sign languages are important in the formation of IS. But while Supalla and Webb (1994) claim that the entire grammar is included in the formation of IS, Moody singles out only the most salient and universal structures. "Signed phrases use space, modifications of movements of signs and grammatical facial expressions that have been described by linguists for different sign languages and that seem to be common among most or all sign languages." (1989:90). Garretson (1990) does not recognize the influence the native sign language of the user might have on the structure of his/her particular IS. He describes the communication system as a "zone of 'pure' or non-language stripped of grammar and artificial ... rules, the only syntax being one of natural order." Allsop et al. (1994) take a more moderate stand among these extreme views. Their notion is that the signer uses a combination of the grammar of their own sign language and structures that are particular for IS. In the present study, the make-up of IS vocabulary and structure as it is used today will be compared to possible sources.

5.4. Data

Three IS interpreter teams consisting of two interpreters each were filmed for this study. All participants were recruited during an international Deaf Community event and were filmed in their natural work environment. The teams were approached based on the topics of the lectures and the linguistic background of the presenters. Having worked at the event for three days prior to this taping, it can be assumed that the IS interpreters were more familiar with the vocabulary and more comfortable with the structures of IS than on the first day of the event. All participants are native signers of either British SL or American SL, except for one who acquired American SL later in life. Three are also fluent in Australian SL. Other information collected on the IS interpreters includes certification, experience as an interpreter, mode of acquisition of IS and frequency of use.

Of the six 45-minute videotapes of IS interpretation collected at the event, twelve 5-minute clips were randomly chosen and transcribed. The topics of these clips varied from strongly deaf-related topics such as deaf-blindness to comparisons of the economic situation for deaf entrepreneurs in developed and developing countries. All clips were glossed. The glosses were entered into an excel spreadsheet. Various factors were then transcribed. Handshapes for each sign were recorded and counted. Occurrences of finger spelling, numbers, proper nouns, and different types of verbs were counted. Grammatical facial expressions and other non-manual structures were also noted in the spreadsheet.

In the present study, an attempt was made to determine sources of the IS lexicon by a comparison to a variety of natural sign languages. The number of occurrences for each sign in the transcribed data was counted. A list of signs occurring five or more times was compiled. For a determination of the origin of these 162 signs, native signers of 15 SLs were consulted. They were asked to translate all 162 into their native SLs. These forms were compared with the IS form used by the interpreters. In order to determine the degree of universality of signs, the SLs included in this comparison were divided into different groups (henceforth language groups). The division was derived on the basis of descriptions of historical relations between SLs in Woll et al. (2001:25ff) as well as observations made in this study during the review of vocabulary provided by the informants. SLs were categorized into one of five groups: European SLs, ASL, BSL, Asian SLs, and Near Eastern SLs. Since the ASL, BSL and European SLs groups are historically strongly related, those three occurrences were grouped in one category (Western SLs). Asian and Middle Eastern SLs were grouped in another category (Eastern SLs). The categorizations made for the purpose of this study are shown below in Figure 5.1.

5.5. IS Vocabulary

As described above, the source of the IS lexicon has been the subject of many discussions. While the general assumption that the vocabulary is based mostly on GESTUNO is easy to disprove (see below), the origin of most IS signs has been said to stem from the local SL where IS is used. Moody (2002) suggests that IS interpreters intentionally adapt vocabulary from the local SL in the assumption that the audience will be most familiar with that particular set of signs. Woll (1990) finds that in her data of IS used in Great Britain, 70 to 80% of the signs were based on BSL. In Woll's study, interpreters also created nonce signs for the specific context of use, employing metonymic and metaphoric expressions to convey the content.

After determining these categories, the use of different form/meaning pairs was counted in all SLs. For example, the IS sign DIFFERENT, shown in Figure 5.2, is used in identical form with the same meaning in eight different SLs (namely British SL, Dutch SL, German SL, Thai SL, Swiss-German SL, Jamaican SL, ASL and Nigerian SL). Based on the categorization described above, the IS sign DIFFERENT occurs in the same form in four out of the five SL groups.

Lastly, signs that occurred in three or more unrelated language groups were labeled 'common'. Within this group, those signs occurring in over four of the five language groups and also in over 10 individual sign languages were labeled 'very common'. Examples are the IS signs HOUSE or OLYMPICS, shown below.

In this limited set of data (162 signs), most signs were labeled 'common'. Over 60% were found in three or more unrelated language groups. Only 2% were identified as unique to IS. The remaining 36% were identified as loans

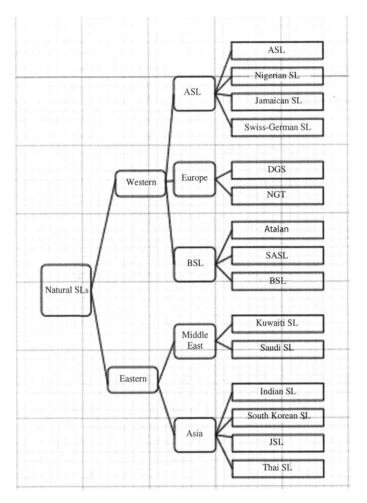

FIGURE 5.1. Language Groups.

from specific SLs or Sign Language groups. Original GESTUNO signs did occur in the current IS data. All GESTUNO signs, however, were iconic to a degree that they were counted into the category labeled 'common'.

5.5.1. GESTUNO

A comparison with the GESTUNO signs shows that most of the original signs were replaced by either more iconic signs or other loan vocabulary. Comparisons of the old GESTUNO signs and their new IS counterparts are shown in Figure 5.3. GESTUNO signs are above the gloss; the row beneath shows the forms used today.

FIGURE 5.2. IS sign DIFFERENT.

FIGURE 5.3. Comparison of GESTUNO (above) and IS Signs (below).

5.5.2. Signs Unique to IS

Only 2% percent of the signs included in this comparison were not found in natural SLs and thus labeled unique to IS. It is possible that these signs do occur in other natural SLs not included in this study.

5.5.3. Loans

Loans make up a significant part of the IS data. As described above, different categories were distinguished in order to examine the degree of distribution of a sign. 12% of the IS signs compared in this study are loans from a single SL (see Figure 5.4). 15% are loans that occur multiple times in SLs of the same language group. In 20% of the cases, the sign can be found in one Western and one Eastern SL. These are labeled 'Two Families'. The largest group of signs (53%) are shared by several of the Western SL families. Note that no loans are shared by Eastern families alone. This supports the notion that IS is based largely on Western SL structures.

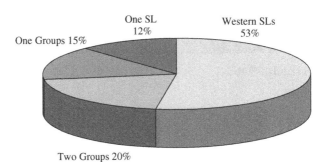

FIGURE 5.4. Sources of IS Loans.

Most loans can be traced back to several SLs within one or two language groups. In the figure below, the top row shows the IS signs for HAVE and GOVERNMENT. The screenshots below show the sign in a natural SL (Figure 5.5). HAVE is unique to the ASL language group. It occurs in ASL,

FIGURE 5.5. IS Loan Vocabulary.

Jamaican SL and Swiss German SL. GOVERNMENT is found in the BSL group, occurring in both Auslan and SASL.

5.5.4. Common Signs

This is the largest category of IS signs in this set of data. The most common signs, occurring in over 10 different SLs from four or five of the language groups, account for 24% of the total number of signs included in this study. 38% of the 162 signs are shared by three to five of the language groups in both Western and Eastern SLs. In the signs most common among all SLs, the degree of iconicity is striking. The Table 5.1 below shows the signs for HOUSE, OLYMPICS, BOOK, WRITE in three SLs from different language groups. The IS sign is shown on the left, followed by the examples from different SLs.

TABLE 5.1. Common Signs in IS.

IS Sign	Dutch SL	Australian SL	South Korean SL
HOUSE			
OLYMPICS			
BOOK			
WRITE			

5.5.5. Iconicity

As can be seen in the comparison of different sign languages above, iconicity plays an important role in the lexicon of IS. Woll (1990) has labeled 20-30% of all IS signs iconic or metaphoric in nature. The degree of iconic transparency a sign has for an IS consumer is highly dependent on the degree of shared cultural experience of the signer and addressee.

The signs used in the informants' natural SLs all use the same metaphors for knowledge and emotion (see Table 5.2). The location of the head represents knowledge; the chest has metaphoric meaning representing feeling (described for ASL in Taub 2001 and for BSL in Brennan 1990). Signs for the concept of 'increasing knowledge' are shown in the upper row. A depressed feeling is expressed in the signs in the row below. A non-signer was able to guess meanings related to knowledge and feeling.

TABLE 5.2. Universal Metaphors 'feel'/'know'.

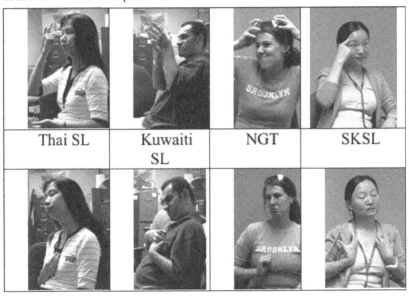

| Thai SL | Kuwaiti SL | NGT | SKSL |

IS makes use of the universality of these metaphors in several signs in combination with the morphemes {-SHRINK}/{-GROW}. The opening and closing movements of the morphemes {-SHRINK}/{-GROW} are used to represent increase and decrease. Without placement at a particular location, these morphemes are meaningless (Figure 5.6).

When placed at a location at the head, the morpheme {-GROW} expresses an increase in knowledge (MIND-GROW) (Figure 5.7). If the morpheme {-GROW} is placed on the chest or close to the heart, the meaning relates to emotional well-being. The morphemes {-GROW} and {-SHRINK} can also be placed by

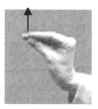

FIGURE 5.6. Iconic Morphemes.

the ears to symbolize hearing more or less. The diverse use of these iconic morphemes demonstrates the variability of the IS lexicon.

KNOW   MIND-GROW

FIGURE 5.7. Metaphoric Use of {-GROW}.

In the area of interrogatives, on the other hand, IS seems to be still very limited. Out of 99 interrogatives appearing in the present data, 97 are the sign glossed as WHAT (Figure 5.8). The remaining two are loan signs from ASL (HOW and WHY), are recognized as slips by the interpreter, and corrected with the additional use of the sign WHAT.

FIGURE 5.8. IS Interrogative WHAT.

This strongly suggests that IS only utilizes one interrogative. It is important to note, however, that the English source text includes a variety of different interrogatives. The examples below shows the English source text and a gloss of the IS translation.

(1) "How do you get financial resources?"
(2) MONEY GIVE GIVE-MONEY POINT WHAT
(3) "What are the sources available to you?"
(4) PRO-1 THINK WHAT WORK SELF WHAT
(5) "[...]who were stay-at-home moms [...]"
(6) PRO-1 WHAT

Overall, the IS lexicon shows a variety of highly iconic signs that are very common among all natural SLs, as well as loans specific to single SLs or SL groups. Only a very small number of signs is unique to IS. Generally, the interpreters seem to use the vocabulary in a flexible way, inventing nonce signs where necessary. The use of the one interrogative, on the other hand, suggests that the IS lexicon is limited in its expressiveness by the pragmatic constraints of broad accessibility.

5.6. IS Structure

This present analysis of structures found in interpreted IS confirms observations made in previous studies and reveals many new aspects. The assumption that IS makes use of many complex structures resembling those of natural SLs is confirmed on all linguistic levels.

Observations on the phonology of IS revealed structures that are as complex as those of natural SLs. The handshape inventory is varied and includes complex hand shapes. Phonotactic constraints match rules observed in natural SLs. These observations confirm the assumption by Moody (1989), Locker McKee and Napier (2002) and Webb and Suppalla (1994) that the most basic make-up of IS is similar to that of natural SLs. The fact that complex hand shapes are rarely used points to the pervasive attempt of the IS interpreter to simplify structures as much as possible.

The number system in IS shows the evolution from an entire iconic system to a more conventionalized one. Smaller numbers are often represented in an entirely iconic way with a one-to-one correspondence between the number of fingers and the number of items that is referenced. This is always true for the numbers between 1 and 10 and in some instances for numbers up to 20. For higher numbers, economic considerations control the structure. Digits are represented in the order of written Arabic numerals. This corresponds with observations for young SLs, specifically Katseff's (2004) work on the number system in Nicaraguan Sign Language (LSN). She observed that with increasing conventionality of the SL in general, number signs become more and more abstract, moving from a one-to-one representation to a representation of digits, and, in some cases, to a more complex and abstract structure (such as the numbers '6' to '10' in ASL). This last step of development was not observed in this IS data and is unlikely to occur, since IS prefers a high degree of iconicity.

The morphological system observed in this IS data is highly complex and in many ways comparable to that of natural SLs. As observed by Moody (1989) and Locker McKee and Napier (2002), IS makes use of space for grammatical purposes extensively. In the present study, the pronoun system and verb system were investigated comprehensively. IS has different forms for personal, possessive and reflexive pronouns. All pronouns use space iconically to indicate referents by directing the sign toward locations or people. Interestingly, the sign PRO-1 ("I"/ "me") seems to be used as the generic person in IS.

IS indicating verbs also use space for grammatical purposes. By directing signs toward an entity and moving toward another, the subject and object of a sign can be identified though spatial references. This phenomenon is described extensively for natural SLs (see Liddell 1980, Engberg-Pedersen 1984). Taub (2001) describes both the pronoun system and indicating verbs as very iconic structures that are common in many SLs. The fact, however, that both the pronoun system and the indicating verbs in IS seem to adhere to certain restrictions (hand shapes for the pronouns are lexicalized; only specific signs allow for the spatial reference of trajector and landmark, etc.) points to the complexity of the grammatical properties and a certain level of abstraction within the system.

IS has been researched most extensively on the syntactic level. Webb and Supalla's 1994 study on negation described grammatical facial expressions not only for negation, but also for topicalizations and rhetorical questions. Locker McKee and Napier (2002) observed the use of rhetorical questions and topic markers to divide the source message into smaller units that they hypothesized are easier to process. The present data confirms this function of both topicalization and rhetorical questions. These two grammatical markers are the most frequent in the data. Less frequent, but also occurring, are Wh-questions, relative clauses, yes/no questions and conditionals. The forms of facial expressions seem to correspond largely with the ones described by Liddell (1980) for ASL. Affirmatives and negations are frequently used to modify the meaning of manual signs. No lexical items are necessary to convey consent or disagreement with a proposition. The complexity of the grammatical facial expressions and the wide array of functions they fulfill in IS point to an underlying structure that is maximally accessible linking facial expressions to message content. Whether the forms of the facial expressions are indeed universal, or rather an influence from specific natural SLs, will have to be researched further.

On a discourse-pragmatic level, many structures were found that correspond to natural SLs structures. One of the most frequently described characteristics of IS that stands out to any observer is the extensive use of role play (see Moody 2002, Locker McKee and Napier 2002, Woll 1990, Rosenstock 2004). In several cases, actions are performed by assuming a role, rather than by description. This adds an element of personalization to the discourse that makes it easier for the members of the audience to envision the events. At other times, role play is used to re-enact dialogues or events or to demonstrate the relationship between two or more people. The techniques used for role play in IS are identical to those documented in natural SLs (see Liddell 2003).

Two structures that have not been described before in the IS literature were frequently employed by the IS interpreters in this study; these are tokens. Tokens are created when signers associate specific locations in space with different concepts. Tokens give interpreters a way to refer back to concepts without having to reiterate explanations. In some sequences, up to ten different tokens are introduced and re-accessed. Comparisons, contrasts, dichotomies of power and other relations can be expressed by specific placements of tokens based on iconic and metaphoric principles. While Moody (1989) and Locker McKee and Napier (2002) have described IS as placing persons in space, the complexity and multilayered nature of the tokens observed in this data suggest that IS interpreters assume that tokens are universally known and used.

On a discourse-pragmatic level, IS uses many techniques to convey information despite the lack of a conventionalized grammar and rich lexicon. The lack of signs for many concepts forces the IS interpreters to expand upon concepts in lengthy explanations. While this is useful in terms of the increased iconic value, these explanations are economically costly because they take a long time. Therefore, in many cases the interpreters limit the explanation of a concept to whatever is immediately necessary. This is illustrated with the introduction of the concept 'loan' in one context as a request for money and then, in another context, as the entire process of receiving money, working and paying it back. The lack of vocabulary also leads IS interpreters to repeat entire discourse sections. Often, the topic of a section is introduced in the beginning and repeated again at the end of an elaborate explanation. This technique might be used to compensate for the lack of syntactic connectors available to the interpreters. In many cases, the interpreter also has to omit information from the source text. A comparison of the ASL source text, English interpretation and IS output would give further insights into the choices the interpreter has to make in terms of expansions and omissions.

5.7. Conclusion

The analysis presented here shows an extremely complex grammatical system with a rather limited lexicon. As Haiman (1985:535) observes for taboo languages, systems with a limited vocabulary tend to have a more 'cumbersome' grammar and a higher degree of iconic motivation. This is true for IS. The temporal constraints of the discourse setting force the interpreters at times to choose time-saving strategies over iconic motivation. At other times, iconic structures are chosen despite the temporal constraints. The IS interpreters are constantly forced to consider the difficulties of an extended lag time or omissions versus ensuring the understanding of the audience by employing maximally iconic techniques. The iconic elements documented in IS resemble strongly those found in natural SLs (described by Taub 2001). The number of IS structures that resemble natural SLs indicate that there is a connection between the IS grammar and natural SL grammar. Webb and Suppalla (1994) speculated that the IS interpreters rely entirely on their native SL grammar in producing IS. A strong argument against this position can be made based on the existence of IS structures that differ from the native SL of the interpreter. A comparison of the native SLs of IS interpreters with their production of IS would provide reliable empirical evidence. The increased use of iconic structure (role play, tokens) in comparison to a natural SLs in the present data seems to suggest strongly that Webb and Supalla's position is not accurate.

Moody (1989) claims that IS interpreters use the most iconic structures of their own SL and superimpose them onto their production of IS. His position leaves unclear where other, more conventional parts of the IS grammar originate. If word order, for example, is assumed not to be iconic, Moody offers no explanation of the source of it in IS. Comparisons of the IS produced by natives of unrelated SLs, such as ASL and Japanese SL, will be required to provide more data to test this hypothesis.

Garretson's (1990) proposal of IS as a structure that is entirely iconic with no influence from a more conventionalized grammar can be rejected on the basis of data found in this study. IS shows several structures where convention is apparent. The use of a QUESTIONMARK sign to emphasize the structure of a sentence as a question only occurs at the end of a phrase, never at the beginning. Since there is no obvious iconic reason to use this particle at the end, this seems to be a conventionalized aspect of IS. The use of a similar particle in Kuwaiti SL is restricted to the beginning of a clause. This further supports the conventionality of the position of the QUESTIONMARK particle in IS. Another area where the sole use of universal, iconic structures is disproved is the SVO structure found both in Supalla and Webb's (1995) study and in this data. Goldin-Meadow and Mylander (1991) found the basic order of constituents in home sign systems to be agent-patient-action. If this is assumed to be a reflection of the maximally iconic structure, than the SVO (agent-action-patient) order found in this data suggests at least some degree of conventionality.

Lastly, Allsop et al. (1994) suggest the grammar of IS to be based on both universally common iconic structures and conventionalized rules. The findings in this study suggest that this is indeed the case. IS does have some conventional structures, as demonstrated above. Yet, the heavy reliance on tokens, surrogates, buoys, depicting verbs, indicating verbs indicates that the IS interpreter in the production of IS assumes a shared knowledge with the audience of all these structures. This suggests that these structures are universally available. This study demonstrates that IS relies on these very iconic structures to an extent far beyond what previous researchers have described.

Researchers in the past have attempted to classify IS as either a pidgin, a Creole or a koine. The complex grammatical structure and limited lexicon described for IS in the past and confirmed in this research rules out a classification as a pidgin. Koines, on the other hand, describe systems that are more complex in their grammatical properties and are often based on language dialects with a similar structural make-up. Koines are developed by neighboring communities that are in constant contact with each other. This is not the case for the community of users of IS. Similarly, creoles are more complex in their grammatical properties than pidgins and might be more similar to IS in that respect. Yet they are characterized by sociological processes that involve a generation of native speakers. This does not apply to IS which is a system with no native signers. Research on contact between two SLs (see Lucas and Valli 1992, Quinto-Pozos 2002) will likely help classify IS more adequately.

As this research has demonstrated, IS continues to evolve. Discourse strategies such as the use of tokens and role play show a level of sophistication similar to natural SLs. On the other hand, the restricted IS lexicon points to areas where IS will likely continue to develop. Future studies will have to show whether the current system suffices to fulfill the demands of international communication in the Deaf Community, whether it will be expanded or replaced by a natural SL.

References

Allsop, Lorna; Woll, Bencie; Brauti, John Martin. 1994. International Sign: The creation of an international deaf community and sign language. *Sign Language Research 1994*, ed. by Heleen Bos and Gertrude Schermer, 171–188. Hamburg: Signum Press.

Garretson, Mervin (ed.). 1990. *Eyes, hands, voices: Communication issues among deaf people*. Silver Spring, Maryland: National Association of the Deaf.

Goldin-Meadow, S., & Mylander, C. (1991). Levels of structure in a language developed without a language model. *Brain maturation and cognitive development: comparative and cross-cultural perspectives*, ed. by K. R. Gibson and A. C. Peterson, 315–344. Hawthorn, NY: Aldine Press.

Haiman, John (ed.). 1985. *Iconicity in Syntax: Proceedings of a Symposium on Iconicity in Syntax, Stanford, June 24–6, 1983*. Amsterdam: John Benjamins.

Katseff, Shira. 2004. *Number System in SLN (Nicaraguan Sign Language)*. GALA Lecture Series. Gallaudet University. 09/2004.

Liddell, Scott. 2003. *Grammar, Gesture and Meaning in ASL*. Cambridge: CUP.

Locker McKee, Rachel; Napier, Jemina. 1999. *International Sign Interpreting: What can we learn from it?* Unpublished manuscript.

Locker McKee, Rachel; Napier, Jemina. 2002. Interpreting into International Sign Pidgin: An analysis. *Sign Language & Linguistics* 5:1. 27–54.

Lucas, Ceil; Valli, Clayton. 1992. *Languages Contact Phenomena in the American Deaf Community*. San Diego: Academic Press.

Moody, Bill. 1989.*Communication International en Milieu Sourd. Le Pouvoir de Signes*, ed. by Alexis Karacostas; Couturier, Lysiane, 89–98. Paris: INJS.

Moody, Bill. 2002. International Sign: A Practitioner's Perspective. *Journal of Interpretation*. 1–47.

Quinto-Pozos, David. 2002. *Contact between Mexican Sign Language and American Sign Language in Two Texas Border Areas*. Ann Arbor, Michigan: UMI.

Rosenstock, Rachel. 2004. *International Sign, Investigating Structure and Comprehension*. Dissertation, unpublished.

Supalla, Ted; Webb, Rebecca. 1995. The grammar of international sign: A new look at pidgin languages. *Language, Gesture and Space*, ed. by Karen Emmorey; Judy Reilly, 333–352. Hillsdale: Erlbaum.

Taub, Sarah. 2001. *Language from the Body. Iconicity and Metaphor in ASL*. Washington DC: Gallaudet University Press.

The British Association of the Deaf. 1975. *GESTUNO. International sign language of the deaf*. Carlisle: British Deaf Association.

Webb, Rebecca; Supalla, Ted.1994. Negation in International Sign. *Perspectives on Sign Language Structure: Papers from the Fifth International Symposium on Sign Language Research* [Vol. 1], ed. by Inger Ahlgren; Brita Bergman; Mary Brennan, 173–186. Durham, England: ISLA

Woll, Bencie. 1990. International Perspectives on Sign Language Communication. *International Journal of Sign Linguistics* 1:2. 107–120

6
Distributed Language: Biomechanics, Functions, and the Origins of Talk

Stephen J. Cowley

6.1. Introduction

Emphasizing that word-forms are culturally selected, the paper takes a distributed view of language. This is used to frame evidence that, in ontogenesis, language emerges under dual control by adult and child. Since parties gear to each other's biomechanics, norm-based behaviour prompts affective processes that drive prepared learning. This, it is argued, explains early stages in learning to talk. Next, this approach to *external symbol grounding* (ESG) is contrasted with ones where a similar problem is treated as internal to the agent. Then, turning to synthetic models, I indicate how the ESG can be used to model either populations of agents or dyads who, using complex signals, transform each other's agency. Finally, I suggest that advances in understanding the emergence of language will follow if this kind of multi-agent modelling can be complemented by simulations using interaction between humans and robots or androids.

6.2. The Cultural Nature of Word-Forms

Until the middle of the last century, it was generally accepted that the verbal belonged to the domain of culture. Challenging this, Chomsky (1959) showed that learning encultured patterns could never, of itself, bring about mastery of a language. Instead, he proposed a dual research programme in Cartesian linguistics (1965a; 1965b). First, human language was to be redefined around a universal set of formal structures. Second, a logic would be developed to show how, using universals, a symbol processor could develop a grammar. With connectionism, neuroscience and the new robotics, however, symbol manipulating agents have ceased to be seen as providing anything more than one way of modelling complex processes. As views of organisms, brains and activity change, many have begun to ask if language too can be viewed as flexible, adaptive behaviour. In line with this, cultural selection is seen by many as the basis for verbal aspects of language.

While differing on much, Christiansen (1994), Deacon (1997), Clark (1997), Tomasello (1999) and Arbib (2002) think word-forms derive from cultural selection. Moreover, synthetic modelling (Steels 1997) shows how formal patterns can stabilize in a population (Kirby & Hurford 2002; Smith, 2005 & this volume). Models also show that users benefit if such patterns lead to convergence in perceptual categories (Steels & Belpaeme, 2005). This is consistent with primate biology and, intriguingly, Chomsky's recent work (Hauser et al, 2002). Below, I build on such views by examining how culturally selected processes impact on infants. Specifically, I sketch how, in coming to deal with adults, infants ground external symbols. This happens because, seeking efficient and rewarding interaction, they become sensitized to cultural patterns by using a trick of dual control. As discussed below, the trick depends on allowing their doings to be partly controlled by the caregiver's real-time activity. Gradually, without having to grasp why they act as they do, infants are led into a community's ways of life or, in other terms, its customs. In conforming to these, moreover, their agency is transformed. This happens as infants draw on meaningful cultural patterns that, used together with word-forms, alter their cognitive powers. First, they develop skills in assessing the likely affective reward of a vocalization-in-context or, as I will put it, become *self-implicating*. Then, by the end of the first year, they start to integrate bodily dynamics with syllabic patterns to manage caregiver actions. In so doing, as explained below, they become *self-regulating*. Due to how dual control alters infant agency, meaning gradually spreads as language is distributed in space and time.

Below I focus on two incidents involving infants who, at 3 and 9 months respectively, are learning to exploit adult vocalizations as background to behaviour. The examples come from work on how bodily dynamics –including language – enable infants to engage with caregivers (see, Cowley, 2004a; Cowley et al. 2004; Cowley, 2005; Spurrett & Cowley, 2004, Cowley, in press a). Then, having sketched how such events contribute to learning to talk, I propose new uses for modelling. Synthetic methods can be used both in examining how distributed cognitive processes impact on individual agency and, for populations, in gaining new perspectives on the evolutionary emergence of language-skills.

6.3. Cultural Selection: Implications for Language

Attributing the verbal to culture differs from appealing to cultural selection. This is, above all, because one can cease to identify a language with a code (see, Love, 2006; Cowley & Love, in press; Kravchenko, in press). By stressing, instead, how it contributes to social behaviour one can also deal with variability, heritability and competition. Given selection, certain patterns are favoured by the effects of cognitive dynamics or, simply, how persons integrate their activities. Language is thus an intrinsic part of behaviour which is organized in many time-scales. It is a distributed process shaped by both how communities act and, of course, how individuals use expression to connect what they do with how each other attends and feels. Below, applying the distributed perspective to developmental events, I argue cultural patterns both alter communication and help shape infant cognitive powers. Indeed, I aim to show how body-world interaction helps constitute new forms of agency. While based in real-time events, this draws on a complex selective history. Cultural patterns such as syllabic patterns or expressive moves are used against a background of historical constraints or norms that enable individuals to master the social and physical world. Instead of relying on what people say, infants can draw on human biomechanics which, hypothetically, arise from co-evolutionary processes. Language can thus be grounded in the real-time assessment and management of affect. By exploiting similarities between bodies, caregivers can integrate customs or *activities in which symbols play a part* with real-time vocalization, feeling, attention and expression. Language, on this view, arises in ways of life where affect-using agents co-ordinate actions in a social and physical setting. While infants initially make heavy use of micro-scale events, these gradually become interwoven with customary use of word-forms. This happens because, given adult[1] beliefs, certain patterns are repeatedly embodied, situated and thus manifestly *valued*.

Language is distributed across time, space and bodies. Far from being purely symbolic, the physical properties of human expression ensure that many cognitive functions build on how activity is co-ordinated. This opens up something resembling an infant's perspective on learning to talk. Even if we perceive it as symbolic, language is a hodge-podge of practices that, together with physical objects, shape what a baby feels and wants. By learning to react and respond to verbal, nonverbal and non-vocal events, an infant begins to understand and even make word-like vocalizations. In uttering 'more', for example, a baby acts in a self-regulating way by using circumstances in ways likely to correlate with a hoped-for effect. In contrast to the *code view*, which holds that we learn to talk by assigning meanings to signals, language is seen as arising when, in real-time, people integrate their social activities.[2] While the child finds its activity constrained by linguistic patterns and beliefs, these have very little impact on early behaviour. In engaging with other people, the child draws on a selection history that also involves affect and movements. What we call symbols –*the words that people actually speak* – are merely a culturally salient aspect of signalling. While symbolic patterns are favoured by selection (and the history of writing), bodily modalities, institutions and artefacts are all permeated by cultural processes. Language is, above all, a means for the real-time assessment and management of conspecific social activity. Emphasizing such functions,

---

[1] While lacking space to develop the argument, my view is that much human affective expression has strategic functions akin to those described by Ross and Dumouchel (2005).
[2] Especially in cultures with well established written traditions it is often assumed that infants 'acquire' a particular code by gaining control over a distinct set of word-forms and associated shared meanings. Related views dominate linguists working in, especially, what Matthews (1993) calls the American descriptivist tradition: while some appeal to innate systems that facilitate 'acquisition' others prefer to invoke general learning mechanisms (for discussion, see Cowley, 2001).

I sketch how dialogical biomechanics and, specifically, prosodically coupled bodily movements that function in time domains of much less than a second, grant a baby entry into human customs.[3] While constrained by words, much depends on bodily engagement between infants and caregivers. To distinguish full-bodied expression from its verbal aspect, I refer to human dialogue as *utterance-activity*.

Just as it is dubious to posit genes 'for' specific behaviours, verbal patterns (and functions) may derive from social biomechanics. Thus rather as it is naïve to explain traits by positing blueprints, vocalization and body language is irreducible to 'use' of verbal codes. Regularities often arise not from built-in functional systems but, rather, circumstances that prompt the rise of habits (based, presumably, on operant conditioning). Especially in micro-time domains associated with pitch, pace and rhythm, language (and visible movement) is run through with subtle patterns that are overlooked in models that highlight relations between verbal forms. We must therefore avoid models that, in Lyons' (1977) terms, begin by idealizing language around standardized, regularized and decon-textualized forms. As Linell (2005) argues, linguists over-rate the importance such sets of static forms because a 'written language bias' permeates our literate tradition. In fact, many aspects of language depend on attitudes that are manifest, not in word-forms, but the embodied, situated and cultural dynamics of talk. By turning to how verbal and nonverbal expression is integrated in utterance-activity, we begin to pursue how language integrates cognitive dynamics. Opening up changes across evolutionary, historical and developmental and real-time, one begins to discover analogies and homologies with signalling by primates, mammals and birds (Cowley, 1995; Hauser et al, 2002; Merker & Okanoya, 2005). Seen this way, moreover, one finds that aspects of meaning described by dictionaries are no more important than how speech exploits musical properties, relationships and, above all, repeated patterns in how utterance-activity permeates action. Rather than posit that language precedes thought (or vice versa), one can emphasize its 'supracommunicative' functions (Clark, 1997). Language is neither the product of quasi-linguistic modes of thought nor the only possible basis for sophisticated cognitive activity. While unique in that it prompts us to belief in word-forms, it is, above all, a mode of behaviour that enables us to develop artefacts which shape how human beings think, act and feel. Provided that we do not fall into the traps of what Sutton (2002) calls expressivism and lingualism, the roots of language can be traced to perceptual and behavioural abilities which, given our history, have been transformed by artefacts and technologies associated with written forms (e.g. Vygotsky, 1986; Hutchins, 1995a; Clark, 1997).

---

[3] Interindividual coupling is typically explored in terms of metaphors such as 'synchronization' (Condon, 1979) 'attunement' (Fogel, 1993) 'accommodation' (Giles, Coipland & Coulpland, 1991) and 'empathy' (Preston & de Waal, 2002). This is unfor-tunate because, as Cowley (1995; 1998; 2006) argues, its main functions arise because it evokes real-time response or, in terms developed in this paper, biobehaviour.

Language links brains, behaviour and culturally-based beliefs. It is distributed by connecting words, phrases, and meanings, with dialogical and neural activity. In real-time, talk unites what is said with speaking, acting and (apparent) feelings. While using syllabic patterns, it draws heavily on the micro- time scales used to integrate words with vocal and visible dynamics (Cowley, 1998; in press, b). Language thus connects words with affect and attitudes that play out through faces, whole bodies, arms, gaze and fluctuating voice dynamics. Although human beings refer, the interpersonal functions of language draw heavily on concurrent actions as well as qualitative, rhythmical and tonic patterning. Emotions, and relationships prompt us, in real-time, to re-enact cultural patterns. Neural processes are recruited to give bodies strategic control over their own situated, embodied joint activity.

6.3.1. Distributed Language, Distributed Mind

To regard language as grounded both in human customs and biomechanics has implications for how we conceptualize cognition. Instead of positing that 'mind' specifies input and output, the mental can be viewed as that which enables agents (especially, humans) to control adaptive and flexible behaviour. Minded activity thus connects causal processes that spread beyond the body with those which occur in brains (see, Clark, 1997). Today, many posit that human cognitive powers are embodied, situated, enactive, interactive and so on (see, Anderson, 2003). Adhering to this tradition, I regard human intelligence as, in Hutchins' (1995a) terms, 'culturally distributed' (see also Johnson, 2001). In his classic work, Hutchins shows how we use customs as, in both the US and Micronesian culture, sailors speak and act to fix a ship's position at sea. Navigating, of course, is irreducible to symbol manipulation. Rather, it emerges from the integration of training, practices based on belief in codes, and histori- cally specific use of artefacts that tap into the causal processes which enable us to reach a destination.[4]

In identifying patterns in the stars or looking though a telescope, distributed cognition enables the crew of a ship or the rowers of a canoe to get to port. Each individual sets off physical events based on the beliefs and artefacts of a culture. Micronesian sailors, for example, picture themselves as using the stars and ocean to keep a canoe still while awaiting a floating island (sic). In spite of relying on fictions, the strategy works. The myths of Micronesia permit them

---

[4] Even in air traffic control, pilots depend heavily on the myth that language functions as a shared code (Hutchins, 1995b). This belief enables them to use verbal patterns as carriers of Shannon-information. For example, a pilot may utter 'flaps zero' as a step in landing a plane: the basis of this, it transpires, lies in imposing additional information on the display of an air speed indicator. It depends on a network of beliefs and artefacts –not a shared code. The example recalls how Micronesian sailors impose information on the stars. They use this to adjust their rowing so that, with striking reliability, they make landfall by doing (what they call) waiting for a floating island.

to make landfall at their island destination. Physical features of the world are woven into old stories in ways that function pragmatically. Linguistic patterns connect history and perception with the senses and, of course, the strategies that shape social behaviour. Language too, I believe, sustains and is sustained by culturally-based fictions. Building on the work of Harris (1981; 1996; 1998), I treat identification of language and symbol-systems as like Micronesian belief in floating islands. In other words, while talk depends on a code-view where language is identified with systems (e.g. English, Zulu) that connect symbolic objects to the world perceived, this is no more than a useful picture. This language myth, like that of floating islands, enables us to use imagined units to many ends. Historically, it underpins the folk-view that language is essentially verbal and, remarkably, makes possible the development of writing systems. In what follows, however, I argue that the such code models are of little value in grasping how infants learn to talk. The problem is simple; babies neither discover nor come to believe in symbols. Rather, they rely on biomechanics and affect to gear their doings to caregiver expectations. Gradually, a dyad develops routines as intrinsically motivated infants use caregiver beliefs to discover ways of exploiting their cultural and physical environment. Language is ecologically special (Ross, in press) because our bodies enable us to lock on to historically specific cultural processes.

6.4. A Developmental View of Language Origins

Since cognition and language are distributed across space, time and bodily modalities, they have co-evolved. Developmentally, therefore, while our core cognitive powers are those of primates, characteristically *human* capacities co-emerge with language. As Vygotsky (1986) saw, utterance-activity transforms a human's cognitive powers. To come to terms with this, however, we must acknowledge how biomechanics integrate events shaped by the various time-scales of selection. It is, in other words, not enough to posit that action and world produce perceptual categories that map on to words. Rather, the resulting representations need to be brought under higher level control. If the infant's agency is to develop auto-regulatory resources, these must be prompted by co-ordinating with caregivers. Given dual control, the dynamics of utterance-activity gradually reshape perceptual representations. Pursuing similar thoughts, Steels and Belpaeme (2005) show how perceptual categories alter in synthetic agents with even rudimentary communication abilities. Since language is heterogeneous and culturally distributed, it can transform individual life history. Building on this, I sketch how caregiver biomechanics gradually change infant cognition. In real-time, vocal and visible expression shape social events where each individual strives to manage the other. Once we have seen how biomechanics help a child into language, I consider the relevance of this to synthetic models.

In code view of language, it is seen as a relatively closed system. Learning to talk is idealized as coming to identify and produce word-forms. Instead of explaining how this is done, too many choose to assume that children discover 'symbols'.[5] While the strategy may have its uses for modelling purposes, it sets up a necessary discontinuity between the biomechanics of value-laden human signalling and the rise of linguistic competence. To bridge the theoretical gap, one can posit that human signal-learning is supplemented by a special kind of symbol grounding (Harnad, 1991; Steels, 2002). By contrast, a distributed view of cognition emphasizes continuity with events beyond the skull. Babies do not need to match names to categories because, using affect, they have already learned to exploit the biomechanics of utterance-activity. From birth, indeed, they react to affective patterns in human voices and, using a limited range of vocal and other expressive patterns, excite response in caregivers. This depends on complex neural resources for intrinsic motivation that are dedicated to neither communication nor symbol-learning but discovering what the world has to offer. By examining how children enter social life, we find that they rely on locking on to cultural processes shaped around adult words, beliefs and deeds. Gradually, the child finds rewarding ways to integrate listening with responses to adult doings. Later, when familiar with custom-based routines, the baby begins acting to integrate signals with events. Instead of relying on causal flow, affect prompts us to take perspectives or, as Ross (in press) puts it, to use signals to partition the world. Humans are special because their language-saturated ecology leads to the rise of capacities that enable us to manage beliefs, feelings and appearances. Once equipped with higher-level control, a child can make use of local views of the world. Given its niche, it will follow a developmental trajectory where, first, it learns, to understand rudimentary talk and, later, words. Towards the end of the first year, having established a role in local customs, babies begin to use syllabic patterns (heard as words) to develop the self-conscious skills that co-develop with beliefs about language.

6.4.1. Human Biobehaviour and Utterance-Activity

Animals with a central nervous system use experience to adapt to their world. Above all, attention, reward and learning enable them to manage their activity. In their niche, many social processes are shaped by a trick that Wilson (1998) calls 'prepared learning'. For example, human newborns *prefer* aspects of vocalizations and the human face. Far from merely discriminating features (see, Legerstee, 2005), they respond to affective patterns based, most likely, in cultural selection. From birth, our behavioural ecology relies on expressive dynamics that reward infants who, to adult judgement, act appropriately. For example, there are cross cultural parallels in sounds and movements used to calm upset babies. Strikingly, some infant dynamics seem made to promote evaluative

---

[5] Deacon (1997) and Tomasello (1999; 2003) represent important exceptions to this general trend. However, as Cowley (2002) objects, they too assume that neural representations correspond to linguistic units. Indeed, Cowley (2004b) argues that it is only in order to save this picture that Tomasello is obliged to posit a 'social-cognitive adaptation'.

response. The biomechanics of well-timed tongue protrusions and other imitative expressions (Melzoff, 1981; Kugiumutzakis, 1999) relate to cultural values and ensure that, over time, each party will develop expectations for future events. Since interindividual behaviour shapes the brain's intrinsic motivation systems (Trevarthen, 1998; Trevarthen & Aitken, 2001; Tronick, 2003), it gradually readies an infant for language. Thus, where a caregiver treats tongue protrusion as a game, social activity will be reinforced by norms whose functions are prefigured by a specific individual history. Below I call such rewarded norm-based activity *biobehaviour*.

Adults talk to children from, at least, birth. Unless programmed to hear symbols, infant responses use the dynamics of utterance-activity. Biomechanics thus serve as a valuable tool for inducing gradual changes in infant behaviour. As in many species, prepared learning allows babies to make cognitive use of caregiver activity. Independently of words, gestural and prosodic events enable individuals to establish predictable affective routines. This happens as infant's biobehaviour sensitizes to norm-based expectations. Below this is illustrated by showing how a mother gets a 14 week baby to be quiet. While all parents sometimes silence infants, how this is done varies across cultures and relationships. It can be analysed into three stages:

• A baby is upset (U)
• A caregiver tries to control (C) the baby
• The baby falls silent (FS)

By classifying this as a UCFS routine, it becomes possible to describe any such encounter. While routines performing this function may universally begin with adult vocalizations accompanied by kinesis (e.g. rocking, shaking and touching), cultures and individuals use the modalities in different ways. Cowley et al. (2004) explored contrasts in South African settings. In this study the micro-timing of interactions was coded for 6 dyads classified as Zulu, Indian and White (mixing linguistic and official state classifications). In work based on frame-by-frame analysis, striking parallels and contrasts were found both within and across groups. An especially graphic example is that 14 week olds use biomechanics that exploit different bodily modalities (see also, Cowley, 2003). While mothers from Indian and White populations tend to silence an upset child by picking the baby up, hugging and soothing it, several Zulu mothers got their baby to *thula* (or fall silent) without exploiting touch at all. The isiZulu speakers sometimes explain this by saying that it is important that a baby learns to show *ukuhlonipha* (respect). An example is shown in Figure 6.1.

Mothers co-opt culturally specific patterns in getting their infants to *thula*. Instead of using kinectic contact, some accompanied dramatic hand movement with loud vocalizations. Given repetition, the dynamics prompt a baby at this stage of development to inhibit her crying. For Cowley (2005), therefore, Nokhukanya (pictured below) acts in a self-implicating fashion. Before describing this way of acting below, it is worthy of note that culture-specific dynamics are already of indexical value *for the baby*. Further, the baby's auto-inhibition anticipates a mother's affective reward (her expression of pleasure).

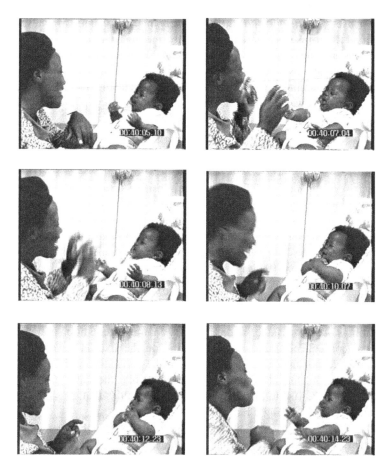

FIGURE 6.1. Urging Nokhukanya to *thula* (hold her tongue).

In using maternal dynamics to know exactly (to tens of milliseconds) when to *thula* Nokhukanya shows striking practical abilities. In spite of sensory under-development, she relies on micro-timing. Second, since her mother urges her to *thula*, the baby does *what* she wants. This has developmental importance because she meets her mother's expectations by using different perceptual pathways to monitor two different processes. In responding, she manages to solve both problems by acting in a single time-scale. Once habitual, this has important conse-quences. Not only does Nokhukanya gain a means of controlling her own body but using the skill also scaffolds her future maternal action. Events fall under dual control as the parties adjust to each other by drawing on both micro-movements and actions. While biobehaviour connects up with infant intrinsic motivations, the mother does what is *judged* to be appropriate (viz. getting the baby to *thula*). (Cowley, in press a) uses similar events to present *the gearing hypothesis*. He posits that much development arises as infant biobehaviour meshes with caregiver use of *cultural* dispositions to (over) interpret events. Mutual gearing prompts adults to use beliefs and desires to fine-tune interaction in ways that produce, among other things UCFS routines. While infants use biobehaviour and parents verbal patterns, common expectations emerge. Gradually, each develops strategies for regulating the other in real-time. Infants learn how micro-behaviour indexes affective reward, and adults become skilled in gauging how a baby feels. Before 4 months, babies use utterance-activity to assess a person's wants.

6.4.2. Talk, Biobehaviour and Gearing

In acting biomechanically, infants become sensitive to adult behaviour that is shaped by cultural norms. What babies do is thus reinforced by contingent events that come to underpin interactional routines. Based on dual control, social events differentiate the infant's internal motivation systems and, crucially, alter caregiver attitudes. While subtly motivated interindividual meshing is widely recognized (Trevarthen, 1998; Legerstee, 2005) and all concur that 3 month-olds respond differently to persons and things, the cognitive consequences of such co-ordination emerge only within a distributed framework. Indeed, if language is symbolic input and output, the coupling appears only contingently linked to saying things like "your father's coming".[6] By contrast, if cognition is distributed, functional consequences are seen as drawing on the speaker's words. This is because, while not understood by the baby, they shape how the mother acts and, by extension, her changing expectations. While the baby uses prepared learning, this gives rise to biobehaviour and expectations that, as shown below, are instrumental in guiding a baby into talk.

With a Western bias, primary intersubjectivity is usually associated with how infants co-ordinate play, set up mutually enjoyable events and, often, 'go solo' with vocalizations (see, Stern, 1977; Cowley, 2003). Instead of stressing how biobehaviour connects affect with cultural patterns, emphasis falls on infant biology. For similar reasons, others emphasize dynamics and attunement (Fogel, 1993) but not, surprisingly, how an infant's repertoire accommodates to culturally-specific norms. Indeed, the Zulu example brings out that the baby uses cultural events grounded in *local* values. The caregiver not only prompts the baby to *thula* (to hold her tongue) but, as Zulu speakers confirm, she rewards Nokhukanya for showing *ukuhlonipha* (respect). To act in accordance with cultural values, the baby needs only practical 'knowledge'. Yet by using how culture and affect shape parental wishes, this can become habitual. As the baby adjusts to adult expectations, she gains power over her mother. By using affect she can learn to act similarly or, in other settings, to expect sanctions. The baby uses caregiver beliefs that are specific to the history of a particular set of communities.

---

[6] In English translation, she says "no" (5 times), "I don't want it", "I'm going to get you", "Where's your father now", and "your father's coming".

Gearing provides both short-term reward and enables the infant to scaffold what a caregiver will do. Exerting a cognitive effect the baby may prompt a mother to think, 'My baby is good', 'she really understands' or, in audible imagination, 'she is afraid of her father'. UCFS routines thus embed behaviour in cultural norms. As these play out, the child's doings give rise to expected events. In kwaZulu Natal, strong effects arise when, at such moments, a baby *fails* to fall silent. If a caregiver hears lack of *ukuhlonipha*, she behaves differently from when hearing, say, signs of hunger. Drawing on the adult's belief in words, the dyad use coordination and conflict to bind affect with expectations. Co-ordination links culturally selected biomechanical and verbal patterns that mediate infant functionality. Gradually, culture transforms the child's affect-based expectations. Much depends on neither symbol processing nor pattern recognition but, rather, the soft assembly of biobehavioural control. While using operant conditioning and norms, infant activity falls under cultural influence. Given dual control, infants incorporate adult beliefs into habits (see, Spurrett and Cowley, 2004; Cowley, 2004b). In kwaZulu Natal, UCFS routines help infants use dynamics based on when a baby should show *ukuhlonipha*.

6.4.3. Gearing to the Physical World

Even at 3 months, a child is influenced by behaviour that involves *ukuhlonipha*, a central value in the baby's culture. Elsewhere, Cowley (2005) argues that infants who act as if drawing on maternal values are usefully viewed as 'self-implicating'. In other words, far from merely timing their movements to fit caregiver activity, the baby begins to carry out 'actions'. It develops biobehaviour that is time-locked with how adults tend to use local norms. Babies, therefore, draw on adult wants and beliefs to exert complex effects on future caregiver activity. These changes in how dyads act arise because, given its attractions (and genes), affect enables a baby to manipulate its carers. The selection history which allows infants to derive human functionality from utterance-activity is thus likely to be ancient.

Of course much infant behaviour depends, not on parents, but on the physical environment. While this has parallels with Piaget's concepts of accommodation and assimilation (1955), there are also contrasts in how gearing shapes relationships. First, when a baby accommodates to an object, assimilation is independent of feedback. By definition, the baby sensitizes to an object's situation-independent properties. In gearing, by contrast, situational aspects of caregiver response often matter more than the physical circumstances. In spite of the fact that adults use utterance-activity to influence infant attitudes, objects possess autonomy. Further, while assimilation drives neural change (or developing schema), adult gearing also uses cultural beliefs and attitudes. For a baby, gearing is less cognitively demanding than accommodation and assimilation. Piaget's mechanisms, however, do enable children to learn what to expect of objects. In Cowley's (2005) terms, they help infants become self-directing. As such, they begin to act in line with environmental prompts that result from past experience. Thus by the end of the first year, infants begin to show sensitivity not just to the physical environment but also to how their doings may strike caregivers. The next change in agency thus arises when social expectations begin to take on a central role in events. This permits the rise of triadic behaviour.

6.4.4. The Emergence of Triadic Behaviour

In Kenya, a Kispigis 9 month old child is affectionately called a monkey and, perhaps, relies as much on manual as vocal communication. In other cultures, babies of the same age are treated as more human. Thus, as illustrated below, mothers may attribute good understanding of what they can see and hear to 9 month olds. While surely mistaken, this fits with local emphasis on verbal intelligence. While all babies may be born with similar resources, they adjust to norms and affective patterns and, by so doing, develop a biobehavioural repertoire. As is described below, this enables them to use contingent dynamics in ways appropriate to how caregivers enact beliefs and values. In triadic behaviour, instead of merely linking to expectations, a baby begins to use her attitudes. In such circumstances, mutual gearing produces new outcomes. The following example (for details, see Cowley, in press a) was taken from an unpublished longditudinal study of three English speaking White South African dyads. Given the history of literacy in this community, weight is given to getting children to play games and, equally, to understand the words that parents actually speak. The example is of interest because it represents an early case of 'triadic' behaviour where baby Luke does *what his mother hopes he will do with a block*. Second, before fetching the object, he self-rewards by smiling to himself. Briefly, events are as follows. In the first slide, Luke lets fall a block he has been sucking. In the second, his mother attempts to get him to fetch it (she does so repeatedly over 9 seconds). Finally, in the third – 300 milliseconds before going to get the block – Luke self-rewards with an anticipatory smile - see Figure 6.2.

In that the adult gets the child to take a perspective on the scene, the event is triadic. Once Luke comes to see the block as something to be fetched, he goes and gets it. Thus, in the terms of Tomasello's (1993; 1999; 2003) influential work, the event can be *described* as intention-reading. Where we take this stance (Dennett, 1987), Luke indeed acts as his mother intends. Should we

FIGURE 6.2. Trying to get Luke to fetch a block.

then follow Tomasello by positing that the infant also engages in a cognitive process of intention-reading? At first sight, this may seem reasonable. Indeed, in the 6 seconds between the slides, the mother produces three variations on, "Do you want to fetch that?" She thus auto-prompts the thought that Luke grasps her 'intention' (and, perhaps, the word *fetch*). This, impression may be reinforced by a smile timed to occur before the baby moves off. Plainly, this is co-ordinated, self-initiated action. It raises a question that, significantly, permits two formulations. How does Luke understand what his mother wants? How does he decide to get the block?

Cowley (in press a) investigates the biomechanics in detail to present this as a classic case of mutual gearing. Lacking belief in words, the baby uses his mother's utterance-activity to decide 'what now?' Just as for the Zulu baby, maternal biomechanics enact, so to speak, *what she thinks*. In so doing, he gears micro-events with his mother's phenomenal experience. Thus, while she suggests getting the block in words and uses her body as an iconic representation of her hope, faster events prompt the baby to look, inhibit, engage socially, and improvise an action. By inhibiting action and then acting, the baby integrates brain-side events with attending and responding in a tens-of-milliseconds time scale. Using this rapid scale, the mother looks between block and baby (three times), smiles and, all the while, uses her body as an iconic background. By enacting her hope, she induces the baby to act. In gearing to her time-locked co-ordination, the baby sets up what may become a fetching routine. Luke does *what she wants him to do*. While relying on timing and the inhibition of stimuli, Luke also uses gaze, a desire for social activity, crawling, and skill in getting desired objects. Over 11 seconds, Luke brings the relevant schema together and, anticipating success, self-rewards with a smile. He then gets the block. For Cowley (in press), dual control enables the parties to reach a mutually-rewarding outcome. While this can be *described* as intention reading, the mother's behaviour is far too complex to be traced to a single intentional state. Rather, the baby uses past experience to fit its biobehaviour to the mother's real-time activity. *Contra* Tomasello (1999), then, the baby needs no socio-cultural adaptation (see also Cowley, 2004b). Instead, he uses a history of increasingly appropriate biobehaviour.

Luke's mother (misleadingly) experiences the baby as understanding. The event is thus another case where a capacity develops during events shaped by a belief-based cultural ecology. Triadic behaviour emerges from dual control that, in this setting, exploits (irrational) beliefs in verbal understanding. This deflationary view plays down the need for inner intentions. Instead, a history of coupled activity is posited to be sufficient for the baby to align to *the words actually spoken*. His actions answer "Do you want to fetch the block?" Just as for Nokhukanya, this new way of using his mother's attitudes and beliefs is likely to have long term effects. For example, she is likely to set up future opportunities for 'fetching'. These will help Luke to understand the routine without needing body-pointing or turn-taking. Gearing to utterance-activity, as with the small child, alters infant agency (Cowley, 2005). Instead of relying on the flow of events, Luke is becoming self-regulating. If fetching routines develop, his practical understanding can extend by making use of, among other things, skills in babbling. He may, for example, vocalize what, given the routine, his mother hears as [fe]. Indeed, this may trigger her to think he wants *her* to fetch. If she does so, the child will be pleased and begin to feel that [fe] can get him what he is looking (or pointing) at. When such a pattern emerges, the caregiver may draw on her belief in codes in adjusting her action in line with the assumption that the baby now 'knows' a symbol or word. Even if she is entirely mistaken, this will have significant consequences for subsequent events. This is because, in real-time, the syllable integrates vocalizing with perception-action schemata that use the caregiver's beliefs. Saying [fe] now gains new functionality –not because of infant understanding –but because of a caregiver's beliefs. Unwittingly, Luke makes opportunities to learn from her values. In learning to 'fetch', utterance-activity is a value-laden cognitive resource. It shapes triadic behaviour while bringing Luke to the edge of what his carers regard as knowledge of a language or code. By exploiting norms and biomechanics he has reached the threshold of acting ways that invite analysis around words and rules (see, Spurrett and Cowley, 2004; Cowley, 2004a).

6.5. Utterance-Activity and Agency

Culturally selected words and biomechanics permit adults to enact the norms used by agents with in-built biobehavioural powers. Thus parents develop nonverbal means of, for example, calming children, urging them to *thula,* and promoting social events. Equally, infants gear to such signals while using rewards to attune their intrinsic motivational systems. Utterance-activity thus transforms infant agency by giving babies new cognitive powers. Infants develop ways of exploiting their worlds – and talk – as they accomplish cognitive tasks. Initially, they are sensitive to affective dynamics. By the end of the first year, verbal patterns take on a cognitive role. From being helpless primates, infant agency moves through self-implicating, self-directing and self-regulating stages. By 12 months, adults sometimes do what they want and, when it suits them, understand a few utterance-types. This, of course, is just the beginning. Infants later develop more self-conscious aspects of human agency.

On the gearing hypothesis, words are not grounded in invariants. Rather, they connect categorical perception with both co-ordinated activity and caregiver beliefs. These reflect, among other things, how members of a culture think about language, cognition and communication. Learning to talk therefore begins with using biomechanics to advantage in a familiar setting. While initially managing without even sounds that resemble words, the infant later begins to exploit syllabic patterns. While a caregiver will hear these as words early on, a long time will pass before the infant comes to hear his or her own speaking this way. Eventually, however, it will do so and, by so doing, become ready to adopt the belief that talk reflects on a language or code that is, somehow, known to each member of a social community. Initially, however, biomechanical resources need only drive the asymmetrical motivation systems that shape joint activity. By gearing not only to biomechanics but also norm-based beliefs, infant behaviour can be *described* as reading intentions and, for this reason, elicits consistent forms of response. Further, babies learn to articulate syllables that can be co-opted into joint behaviour. Given adult beliefs, an infant has much to gain from using syllabic patterns.

6.6. Implications for Synthetic Models

To regard language and cognition as distributed highlights how parties manage social events. At root, human interaction is based on biomechanics that enable a baby's motivational systems to gear with events based in adult utterance-activity. Gradually, the baby's doings align with an adult's cultural values and beliefs. This opens up new issues for designers of synthetic models. First, instead of focusing on putative competences, attention can be given to modelling changes in cognitive-communicative powers. One can ask how agents develop dual control and, by so doing, develop increasingly symbol-focused routines. Potentially, there are several ways of pursuing such research. On the one hand, multi-agent models might be used to explore how less advanced agents develop norm-based activity. This, moreover, could be done with reference to events in various time-scales. On the other, sophisticated robotic agents could be used to examine if agency can be transformed by encounters with syllabic forms used against simulated customs.

6.6.1. External Symbol Grounding

Multi-agent models can be used to explore hypotheses about patterns that emerge from repeated interaction. In the evolution of language, these have been successful, among other things, in tracking the problem of symbol grounding (Harnad, 1991; MacDorman, 1999; Cangelosi et al. 2002). While variously construed, this conceptualization has been used to model agents that use categorical perception to develop symbol systems. Given its focus, grounding is regarded as linking environmental invariances *within* the agent. Using a series of encounters, representations come to index classes of object and, by so doing, change or 'warp' an agent's perceptual categories. Traditionally, building on the code-view, talk is also analysed as emanating from a symbol-processing agent. Accordingly, one view of symbol grounding applies to both physical objects and also to language (see, Steels, 2002). Seen against developmental evidence, however, this approach is found to depend on the code-view that language is essentially symbolic. While permitting interesting simulations, it throws little light on how human babies begin to engage with their linguistic environment.

If language is distributed, we ask how external symbols are grounded. Far from being a problem, this approach opens up new theoretical pathways. While we use symbols to refer, it is stressed that language is multiply constrained. Although using categorical perception, external signals exert other influences on social activity. To explore the origins of language, therefore, we can model how representational systems respond to changing biomechanics. Ecologically, this enables one to ask how joint behaviour gradually turns infants into self-regulating symbol users. The basis of external symbol grounding can thus be pursued with respect to at least two kinds of model. First, building on the tradition of evolutionary modelling, Cangelosi (in press) proposes to pursue population thinking. This enables him to ask how agents integrate movements with categories to develop use of shared symbols. Below, emphasizing life history, I conceptualize the process in dyadic terms. Echoing Steels (2002), I ask how supervised learning might transform an intrinsically motivated agent into the user of second order signals.

In appealing to external symbol grounding, so-called linguistic 'objects' are contrasted with those which a baby sucks, grasps and falls over. While experience with the latter may give rise to invariant-based categories only assessing and managing joint behaviour is likely to serve in grounding verbal patterns. Indeed, to become a self-regulating agent whose signalling fits cultural values, biomechanics have to be sensitive to recurrent affective stimuli. An agent that draws on such capacities will resemble Luke in being able to link a sound like *fe* (or *fetch*) with an aspect of social life. Talk is thus conceptualized as grounded in biomechanics that, as Anderson (2003) demands, can be traced to a physical grounding. Babies depend, above all, on how caregivers use utterance-activity to control and reward the doings of a responding body. Indeed, for an infant, symbols matter mainly because they give social events familiar properties.

In terms of behavioural ecology, there can be no objection to tracing language to biobehaviour. First, even rudimentary observation shows that human primates are highly sensitive to social norms. Second, given our hypersocial tendencies, dual control is a valuable resource in adjusting to the demands of others. Theoretically, gains accrue from asking how agents make increasing use of 'symbolic' resources. Not only do we turn to social strategies but the process is conceived of as using prepared learning and affective reward. Of course, this is incompatible with the code view that we learn to talk by assigning meanings to signals While children over the age of one will eventually adopt local beliefs about language, early rewards depend on *cultural* context. As agents develop appropriate ways of acting, intrinsic motivations are differentiated, dual control alters, and non-expert behaviour changes to fit a partner's demands. For example, as Nokhukanya develops a distress inhibiting strategy, she scaffolds how her mother gets her to *thula*. Further, while breaking with identification of language and symbol systems, we need not abandon the gains of synthetic modelling. First, in focusing on external signals, we retain the view that these depend on representations. Their basis is traced, in the first instance, to how affect encourages mutual gearing. Second, this leads to new use of the insight that interaction warps perceptual categories. Indeed, as babies gear to caregiver expectations, how they hear utterance-activity may also change. The cognitive dynamics of language thus link affect to how cultural patterns constrain what we do. Since (literally) dumb agents learn to talk, it is not surprising if the verbal is derived from social use of biomechanics. Indeed, if word-forms result from cultural selection, we should expect the processes to connect up with naturally-selected neural control of expression. Language is both affective and identifiable with the syllabic patterns we analyse as symbols.

In the human case, events within the child's brain give rise to mechanisms that control real-time social activity. As caregivers prompt babies to act, they use experience to come up with new ways of going on. Gradually, actions align to public symbols. Over developmental time, meaning spreads from the culture to a sub-set of child-based actions (events that adults interpret symbolically). The process is driven by motivated actions that enable an infant to gear with the adults' wants, hopes and beliefs and, by so doing, induce the latter to repeat similar events. Non-arbitrary (categorical) representations arise together with symbolically constrained caregiver actions. Given intrinsic motives and a capacity for some self-directed anticipatory learning (Christensen, 2004; Cowley, 2004a), a baby's doings become integrated with adult moves. The infant develops a system of sensorimotor control which functions in tandem with routine adult actions. Given practice, the necessary representations can mould later action where the infant's doings decouple from the adult's. Controlling schemata, therefore, can benefit from links with syllabic patterns. Where using, say, [fe], the action has three sets of roots: first, a neural representation integrates a perception-based action. Second, this is grounded in norm-based events and a routine. Third, these come to be connected with an identifiable syllable. For the child, [fe] functions as a symbol if and when its believed-in symbolic status prompts an adult to get what the child wants.

6.6.2. Simulating External Symbol Grounding?

Whereas Cangelosi (in press) makes suggestions about how multi-agent systems could be used to explore the population aspect of external symbol grounding, I focus on dyadic simulations. In principle, grounding could be simulated by assemblages of agents, robots or, given the achievements of Alex (Pepperberg, 2005 and this volume), human-parrot interaction. The best tool for simulating external symbol grounding, however, is likely to be robot technology. This is because, like cats and dogs, robots prompt humans to use talk in interaction while, unlike such animals, they could be designed to develop increasing sensitivity to utterance-activity. Cowley and Kanda (2005) find that even robot-like robots elicit context-changing behaviour from children. When placed in a Japanese classroom, such a machine elicits norm-based utterance-activity aimed at building relationships. For example, after the robot uses pseudo-learning to tell a secret, one child carries out a dance of joy before returning to give the robot affective reward.[7] Had the machine responded to such behaviour (ideally, by reciprocating), it would resemble a self-implicating three month old. Provided that the response used pattern-identification, such a robot could act to meet a child's expectations. Instead of implementing programmed behaviour, it would use cultural patterns to simulate *action*: it would enact a learned social function.

Such a simulation would be a step towards external symbol grounding. Indeed, this is why I stress that, for babies, symbols initially make aspects of the world familiar. They prompt them to learn about a social environment and, using routines, pick up what is salient. In exploiting related knowledge, even robot-like machines can produce responses that we find coherent. Of course, from an engineering point of view, this raises difficult problems. As the examples show, cultural norms exploit contingent patterns that develop through reinforcement. To develop such simulations, therefore, the focus must shift from physical invariances. The example involving Luke, indeed, suggests how machines might become sensitive to meaningful aspects of vocalization. By acting as if he understands 'do you want to fetch that?' he is using a strategy that could be in reach of robots. He relies on two processes to simultaneously participate in real-time activity while also using other-related skills (e.g. to follow gaze, to smile appropriately). Having inhibited other action, he eventually hits upon a way of acting towards a focal object that can be integrated with what both parties are doing. Were robots able to identify encultured encouragement while performing real-time social activity, they too could gear to another person's actions to perform under dual control.

In the case of learning to *thula* or to *fetch*, external symbol grounding depends on the emergence of biobehaviour. Equally, to scaffold a human expert, an agent's behaviour must draw on a synthesized motivational system which, depending on its inner state, can set off a range of responses. This is because, without unpredictability, human partners would not prompt others and thus bootstrap the development of routines. It is only because the baby is likely not to do what is required that its caregivers work at the process and provide rewards. If the process were automatic, therefore, the baby would not be able to develop ways of regulating its own doings. This, indeed, is why dual control matters to external symbol grounding. Ideally, to develop machines that use contingent patterns, they would look and move like humans. As MacDorman and Ishiguro report (2006), androids elicit human response in the right cultural and temporal scales. While not designed for relationships, experiments with gaze show remarkable results. Instead of gazing as we do at objects, human subjects use cultural patterns. To deal with hard questions, Japanese subjects tend to avert gaze downwards in responding to both humans and robots they believe to be under human control. This, however, did not occur if they believed it to be autonomous. This interaction is as different as the cultural pattern in Canada where, generally, asking the more difficult questions to humans elicits upwards gaze (MacDorman et al., 2005).

---

[7] The robot records the time spent interacting with each individual and is programmed in such a way that at different time thresholds (e.g. 50 hours), it tells a child a secret.

Affected as we are by appearance, we would be impressed by machines that return gaze with cultural appropriacy. Given a reward-system, such devices might even use gaze as does Luke's mother. Androids, it seems, may be an ideal test-bed for modelling how human infants learn to talk.

6.7. Conclusion

If verbal aspects of language are based in cultural selection, we need to rethink many issues in the language sciences. Rather as Chomsky persuaded cognitive scientists to drop learning models, we can stop pretending that human languages are 'like' computational symbol systems. This is because, unlike symbolic systems, language is grounded in how bodies exploit microtiming and affect. Indeed, in spite of the fact that the cognitive revolution was dependent on static models of language, there is nothing magical about quasi-linguistic symbols. Machines that use such principles provide just one way one of simulating complex systems. As argued above, if verbal patterns arise in cultural selection, language is bound to be hybrid. If they are to be replicated our belief in symbolic patterns must be connected with both local customs and human biomechanics. Thus both infants find themselves fitting their action to that of their caregivers by gradually adjusting their time-locked behaviour to how their communities interpret items such as 'ukuhlonipha' and 'fetch'. This is achieved, however, without the babies having any linguistic knowledge at all. They rely on linking perception and action in ways that ensure language is gradually insinuated into their perceived words. Dual control gradually enables them to use what happens between affect-sensitive human bodies to make sense of what happens in social space (or circumstances). Far from using one modality – or being non-modal – external language is grounded in affect or how cultural patterns use bodies.

Since language is distributed, dual control enables us to develop forms of biobehaviour that connect culture with an individual's behavioural strategies. This occurs as social events emerge under multi-agent control. Infants thus respond to caregiver utterance-activity from birth (or before). Initially, they rely on biases for recognizing patterns but soon they also use real-time rewards to adjust their activity. Gradually they develop adaptive biobehaviour which is sensitive to the verbal biomechanical norms used to control what babies do. At 14 weeks, therefore, a baby can use Zulu gestures to fall silent in accordance with his mother's wish. Already, utterance-activity is transforming the baby's agency. While this makes babies self-implicating, they also learn through assimilation and accommodation. As infants learn about the physical world, they become self-directing and, by the end of the first year, undergo a new phase shift. Given hard work by caregivers, they use self-directing powers to act triadically. This opens up decision-making which, if reinforced, permits the rise of self-regulating routines. In fact, this readies them for using syllabic patterns that caregivers hear as words. With further changes in agency, they later analyse their own behaviour and gradually come to present themselves as language users.

Once we take a distributed view of language and cognition, we see how utterance-activity transforms infants. Gradually, dual control and gearing give agents sensitivity to language-mediated norms. By focusing attention on how they ground external symbols, new space opens up for synthetic modelling. Whether focused on populations or dyads, directly grounded representations can link externally prompted action to culture-warped perception. The issue becomes how signal discrimination promotes strategic interaction. Potentially, multi-agent simulations might complement models using human-robot interaction. This is of interest since even robot-like robots can produce the norm-based human responses needed for self-organized dual control. Similar systems in androids might lead to interaction rituals with humans and, perhaps, artificial use of second-order signals. Such research could show how biomechanics sustain control systems that draw on culturally constrained cognition and communication. Indeed, agents might even simulate early stages of learning to talk by acting as if using words. If it is possible to develop such models, they would serve as evidence against identifying languages with the kinds of units that dominate alphabetic writing.[8] Whether or not symbols are basic to human language may turn out to be a question that can be addressed by empirical science.

References

Anderson, M. (2003). Embodied cognition: A field guide. *Artificial Intelligence*, 149(1): 91–130.

Arbib, M. (2002). The Grounding the mirror system hypothesis for the evolution of the language-ready brain. In Cangelosi, A. & Parisi, D. (eds.) *Simulating the Evolution of Language*. Springer: London, 229–254.

Cangelosi, A. (in press). Adaptive agent modelling of distributed language: investigations on the effects of cultural variation and internal action. To appear, *Language Sciences*.

Cangelosi, A. Greco, A. & Harnad, S. (2002) Symbol grounding and the symbolic theft hypothesis. In Cangelosi, A. & Parisi, D. (eds.) *Simulating the Evolution of Language*. Springer: London, pp 191–210.

Chomsky (1959). Review of Verbal Behavior. *Language* 35/1: 26–57.

Chomsky, N. (1965). *Aspects of a Theory of Syntax*. MIT Press: Cambridge MA.

Chomsky, N. (1965). *Cartesian Linguistics*. Harper and Row: New York.

Christiansen, M. (1994). Infinite languages, finite minds: Connectionism, learning and linguistic structure. Unpublished doctoral dissertation. Centre for Cognitive Science, University of Edinburgh, UK.

Christiansen, M., Dale R. Ellefson, M & Conway, C. (2002). The role of Sequential Learning in Language Evolution: Computational and Experimental Studies. In Cangelosi, A. & Parisi, D. (eds.) *Simulating the Evolution of Language*. Springer: London, pp. 149–164.

Christensen, W. (2004) Self-directedness, integration and higher cognition. *Language Sciences* 26(6): 661–692.

---

[8] If it proves impossible to develop such models, this would favour the view that language differs from anything else in biology or engineering.

Clark, A. (1997). *Being There: Putting Brain, Body and World Together Again*. MIT Press: Cambridge, MA.

Condon, W. (1979). An analysis of behavioral organization. In S. Weitz (Ed.) *Nonverbal Communication: Readings with Commentary*. Oxford: New York, pp. 149–167. [Originally published, 1976 *Sign Language Studies*, 13: 285–316.]

Cowley, S.J. (1995). Conversation, co-operation and vertebrate communication. *Semiotica*, 115: 27–52.

Cowley, S.J. (1998). Of timing, turn-taking and conversations. *Journal of Psycholinguistic Research*, 27/5: 541–571.

Cowley, S.J. (2001). The baby, the bathwater and the "language instinct" debate. *Language Sciences* 23: 69–91.

Cowley, S. J. (2002). Why brains matter: an integrational perspective on "The Symbolic Species". *Language Sciences*, 24: 73–95.

Cowley, S.J. (2003). Distributed cognition at three months: mother-infant dyads in kwaZulu Natal. *Alternation*, 10.2: 229–257.

Cowley, S.J. (2004a) Contextualizing bodies: human infants and distributed cognition. *Language Sciences*. 26/6: 565–591.

Cowley, S.J. (2004b). Simulating others: the basis of human cognition? *Language Sciences*, 26/3: 273–299.

Cowley, S., Moodley, S. & Fiori-Cowley, A. (2004). Grounding signs of culture: primary intersubjectivity in social semiosis. *Mind, Culture and Activity*, 11/2: 109–132.

Cowley, S.J. (2005). Languaging: How humans and bonobos lock on to human modes of life. *International Journal of Computational Cognition*, 3/1: 44–55.

Cowley, S.J. (in press a). The cradle of language: making sense of bodily connections. To appear in D. Moyal-Sharrock (ed.) *Perspicuous Presentations: Essays on Wittgenstein's Philosophy of Psychology*. Palgrave MacMillan: Basingstoke, UK., 2006.

Cowley, S.J. (in press b). Beyond symbols: how interaction enslaves distributed cognition. To appear in Thibault, P. & Prevignano, C. (Eds.), *Interaction Analysis and Language: Discussing the state-of-the-art*.

Cowley, S. J. (2006). Language and biosemiosis: a necessary unity? *Semiotica* 162(1/4), 417–444.

Cowley, S.J & Kanda, H. (2005). Friendly machines: Interaction-oriented robots today and tomorrow. *Alternation*, 12.1a: 79–106.

Cowley, S. J. & Love, N. (2006). Language and cognition, or, how to avoid the conduit metaphor. To appear in A. Duszak and U. Okulska (ed.) *Bridges and Walls in Metalinguistic Discourse*, Peter Lang: Frankfurt, pp. 135–154.

Deacon, T. (1997). *The Symbolic Species*. Penguin: Harmondsworth.

Dennett, D. (1987). *The Intentional Stance*. MIT Press: Cambridge MA.

Fogel, A. (1993). *Developing through Relationships: Origins of Communication, Self and Culture*. Harvester Wheatsheaf: London.

Giles, H., Coupland, J. and Coupland, N. (1991). *Contexts of Accommodation: Developments in Applied Sociolinguistics*. Cambridge: Cambridge University Press.

Harnad, S. (1991). The symbol grounding problem. *Physica D*, 42: 335–346.

Harris, R. (1981). *The Language Myth*. Duckworth: London.

Harris, R. (1996). *Signs, Language and Communication*. Routledge: London.

Harris, R. (1998). *Introduction to Integrational Linguistics*. Pergamon: Oxford.

Hauser, M., Chomsky, N. and Fitch, T. (2002). The faculty of language: What is it, who has it and how did it evolve? *Science*, 298: 1569–1579.

Hutchins, E. (1995a). *Cognition in the Wild*. MIT Press: Cambridge MA.

Hutchins, E. (1995b). How a cockpit remembers its speeds. *Cognitive Science* 19(3), 265–288.

Johnson, C. (2001). Distributed primate cognition: a review. *Animal Cognition*, 4: 167–183.

Kirby, S & Hurford, J. (2002). The emergence of Linguistic Structure: An Overview of the Iterated Learning Model. In Cangelosi, A. & Parisi, D. (eds.) *Simulating the Evolution of Language*. Springer: London, pp. 121–147.

Kravchenko, A. (in press). Essential properties of language, or why language is not a code. To appear in *Language Sciences*.

Kugiumutzakis, G. (1999). Genesis and development of mimesis in early imitation of facial and vocal models. In Nadel, J. & Butterworth, B. (eds.) Imitation in Infancy. Cambridge University Press: Cambridge, pp. 36–59.

Legerstee, M. (2005). *Infants' sense of People: Precursors to a Theory of Mind*. Cambridge University Press: Cambridge.

Linell, P. (2005). *The Written Language Bias in Linguistics: its Nature, Origins and Transformations*. Routledge: London.

Love, N. (2004). Cognition and the language myth. *Language Sciences,* 26(6), 525–544.

Lyons, J. (1977). *Semantics*. Volume 2. Cambridge University press: Cambridge.

MacDorman, K. F. (1997). How to ground symbols adaptively. In S. O'Nuallain, P. McKevitt & E. MacAogain (Eds.), *Readings in computation, content and consciousness*. Amsterdam: John Benjamins.

MacDorman, K. F. (1999). Grounding symbols through sensorimotor integration. *Journal of the Robotics Society of Japan, 17*(1), 20–24.

MacDorman, K. F., Tatani, K., Miyazaki, Y. & Koeda, M. (2000). Proto-symbol emergence. *Proceedings of IROS-2000: IEEE/RSJ International Conference on Intelligent Robots and Systems,* October 30 - November 5, Kagawa University, Takamatsu, Japan.

MacDorman, K. F., Chalodhorn, R. & Ishiguro, H. (2004). Learning to recognize and reproduce abstract actions from proprioception. *Third International Conference on Development and Learning: Developing Social Brains*. October 20–22, 2004. La Jolla, California.

MacDorman, K. F., Minato, T., Shimada, M., Itakura, S., Cowley, S. & Ishiguro, H. (2005). Assessing human likeness by eye contact in an android testbed. *Proceedings of the XXVII Annual Meeting of the Cognitive Science Society*.

MacDorman, K.F. & Ishiguro, H. (2006). The Uncanny Advantage of Using Androids in Cognitive Research, Interaction Studies, 7/3: 297–337.

Matthews, P., 1993. Grammatical Theory in the United States: From Bloomfield to Chomsky. Cambridge University Press: Cambridge.

Melzoff, A. (1981). Imitation, intermodal coordination and representation in early infancy. In Butterworth, G. (ed.) *Infancy and Epistemology*, Harvester Press: Brighton, pp. 85–114.

Merker, B. & Okanoya, K. (2005). *Contextual semanticization of songstring syntax: A possible path to human language.* Proceedings of Second International Symposium on the Emergence and Evolution of Linguistic Communication, University of Hertfordshire, April 2005, pp. 72–75.

Pepperberg, I. (2005). Grey parrots do not always "parrot": Roles of imitation and phonological awareness in the creation of new labels from existing vocalizations. *Proceedings of the Third International Symposium of Imitation in Animals and Artifacts*. Society for the Study of Artificial Intelligence and the Simulation of Behaviour Convention University of Hertfordshire, April 2005, pp. 97–104.

Piaget, J. (1955) *The Construction of Reality in the Child*. Trans. Cook, M. Routledge and Kegan Paul: London.

Preston, S. and de Waal, F. (2002). Empathy its proximate and ultimate beses. *Behavioral and Brain Sciences*, 25: 1–72.

Ross, D. (in press). H. Sapiens as ecologically special: what does language contribute? To appear in *Language Sciences*.

Ross, D & Dumouchel, P. (2004). *Emotions as Strategic Signals. Rationality and Society* 16: 251–286.

Smith. A, (2005). Stable communication through dynamic language. In Proceedings of the 2nd International Symposium on the Evolution and Emergence of Linguistic Communication, Society for the Study of Artificial Intelligence and the Simulation of Behaviour Convention University of Hertfordshire, April 2005, pp. 135–142.

Spurrett, D. and Cowley, D. (2004). How to do things without words: Infants, utterance-activity and distributed cognition. *Language Sciences*, 26(5), 443–466.

Steels, L. (1997). The synthetic modelling of language origins. *Evolution of Communication*, 1: 1–35.

Steels, L. (2002). Grounding symbols through evolutionary language games. In A. Cangelosi & D. Parisi (eds.) *Simulating the Evolution of Language*. Springer: London, pp. 211–226.

Steels, L & Belpaeme, T. (2005). Co-ordinating perceptually grounded categories through language: A case study for color. *Behavioral and Brain Sciences*, 28/4: 469–529.

Stern, D. (1977). *The First Relationship: Infant and Mother*. Harvard University Press: Cambridge MA.

Sutton, J. (2002). Cognitive conceptions of language and the development of autobiographical memory. *Language and Communication 22*, 375–390.

Tomasello, M. (1999). *The Cultural Origins of Human Cognition*. Harvard University Press:Cambridge MA.

Tomasello, M. (2003). *Constructing a Language: A Usage-Based Theory of Language Acquisition*. Harvard University Press: Cambridge MA

Trevarthen, (1998). The concept and foundations of infant intersubjectivity. In Braten, S. (ed.) *Intersubjective communication in early ontogeny*, Cambridge University Press: Cambridge, pp. 127–169.

Trevarthen, C. & Aitken, K. (2001). Infant intersubjectivity: research, theory and clinical applications. *Journal of Child Psychology and Psychiatry*, 42/1: 3–48.

Tronick, E. (2003). Things can still be done on the still face effect. *Infancy*, 4: 475–482.

Wilson, E. (1998). *Consilience: The Unity of Knowledge*. Knopf: New York.

Vygotsky, L. (1986). *Thought and Language*. MIT Press: Cambridge MA.

Part 2
Synthesis of Communication and Language in Artificial Systems

7
The Recruitment Theory of Language Origins

Luc Steels

7.1. Introduction

Tremendous progress has been made recently on the fascinating question of the origins and evolution of language (see e.g. (55), (7), (9), (31)). There is no widely accepted complete theory yet, but several proposals are on the table and observations and experiments are proceeding. This chapter focuses on the recruitment theory of language origins which we have been exploring for almost ten years now. This theory argues that language users recruit and try out different strategies for solving the task of communication and retain those that maximise communicative success and cognitive economy. Each strategy requires specific cognitive neural mechanisms, which in themselves serve a wide range of purposes and therefore may have evolved or could be learned independently of language. The application of a strategy has an impact on the properties of the emergent language and this fixates the use of the strategy in the population. Although neurological evidence can be used to show that certain cognitive neural mechanisms are common to linguistic and non-linguistic tasks, this only shows that recruitment has happened, not why. To show the latter, we need models demonstrating that the recruitment of a particular strategy and hence the mechanisms to carry out this strategy lead to a better communication system. This paper gives concrete examples of how such models can be built and shows the kinds of results that can be expected from them.

The recruitment theory is introduced (in section 7.3) against the background of the language as adaptation theory (section 7.2). Next possible methodologies for testing the recruitment theory are discussed (section 7.4) and three examples are given of computational and robotic experiments (sections 7.5–7.7). The chapter concludes with a discussion of issues for further research.

7.2. Language as an Adaptation

Recently Pinker (33) and Jackendoff (34) reiterated in their characteristically lucid style the theory that the "human language faculty is a complex adaptation that evolved by natural selection for communication" ((33), p. 16), in other words, that the interconnected areas of the brain involved in language form a highly specialised neural subsystem, a kind of organ, which is genetically determined and came into existence through Darwinian genetic evolution. Pinker contrasts this language-as-adaptation hypothesis with two alternatives: theories arguing that language is a manifestation of more general cognitive abilities which are in themselves adaptations (ascribed to Tomasello (51), and others.), and theories arguing that although there is a genetic basis for the language faculty, it has evolved by mechanisms other than natural selection (ascribed to Chomsky (10), and others.).

Pinker surveys three types of arguments in favor of the language-as-adaptation theory. Arguments of the first type are based on examining the structure of language. Human languages exhibit a number of non-trivial universal trends which could be a logical consequence of an innate language acquisition device (10), particularly because it is difficult to see how the intricate complexity of human language is so easily and routinely acquired by very young children based on apparently poor data (52), and because these same universal trends show up when new languages form, as in the case of creoles (3).

The second type of arguments surveyed by Pinker comes from molecular and population genetics. They rest on the identification of genes that have undergone selection in the human lineage, and have a clearly identified effect on language (49). The most prominent example in this respect is the FOXP2 gene which is linked to a specific constellation of language impairments identified in a particular multi-generational family (14). The third type of arguments in favor of the language-as-adaptation hypothesis is more recent and comes from mathematical and computational investigations which show "how a stable communication system might evolve from repeated pairwise interactions and, crucially, whether such systems have the major design features of human language" [(33), p. 16]. Computer simulations of the genetic evolution of communication systems ((21), (8), (7)) have indeed shown that certain features of human language, such as bi-directional (or Saussurean) use of signs, can emerge in evolutionary processes, if the competence for communicative success has a direct impact on fitness. This research is complemented by mathematical arguments based on evolutionary game theory, which attempt to show why compositionality or the expression of predicate-argument structure might have become part of the human phenotype if they functionally improve communication (32).

7.3. The Recruitment Theory

In this chapter, I introduce and discuss an alternative to the language-as-adaptation hypothesis: the recruitment theory of language origins. This theory hypothesises that the human language faculty is a dynamic configuration of brain mechanisms, which grows and adapts, like an organism, recruiting available cognitive/neural resources for optimally achieving the task of communication, i.e.

for maximising expressive power and communicative success while minimising cognitive effort in terms of processing and memory. The implied mechanisms are not specific for language and they are configured dynamically by each individual, and hence genetic evolution by natural selection is not seen as the causal force that explains the origins of language.

One example of recruitment, to be discussed later in more detail, concerns egocentric perspective transformation (computing what the world looks like from another viewpoint). This activity is normally carried out in the parietal-temporal-occipital junction (56) and used for a wide variety of non-linguistic tasks, such as prediction of the behavior of others or navigation (23). All human languages have ways to change and mark perspective (as in "your left" versus "my left"), which is only possible if speaker and hearer can conceptualize the scene from the listener's perspective, i.e. if they have recruited egocentric perspective transformation as part of their language system. Another example of a universal feature of human languages is that the emotional state of the speaker can be expressed by modulating the speech signal. For example, in case of anger, the speaker may increase rhythm and volume, use a higher pitch, a more agitated intonation pattern, etc. This requires that the neural subsystems involved in emotion (such as the amygdala) are somehow linked into the language system so that information on emotional states can influence speech production and that information from speech recognition can flow towards the brain areas involved with emotion. The recruitment theory argues that recruitment of these various brain functionalities is epigenetic, driven by the need to build a better, more expressive communication system as opposed to genetically pre-determined and evolved through biological selection.

Given that there are many conflicting constraints operating on language (e.g. less effort for the hearer may imply more effort for the speaker) and that there are obviously historical contingencies, we cannot expect that language users will ever arrive at an optimal communication system. On the contrary, there is overwhelming evidence from the historical development of all human languages that language users move around in the search space of possible solutions, sometimes optimising one aspect (for example dropping a complex case system) which then forces another solution with its own inconvenience (for example using a large number of verbal patterns with idiomatic prepositions - as in English). Consequently, language itself can be viewed as a complex adaptive system (40) that adapts to exploit the available physiological and cognitive resources of its community of users in order to handle their communicative challenges, but without ever reaching a stable state.

The recruitment theory resonates with several other proposals for the evolution of language. For example, the biologist Szathmáry has put forward the metaphor of a growing 'language amoeba', a pattern of neural activity that is essential for processing linguistic information and grows in the 'habitat' of a developing human brain with its characteristic connectivity pattern (50), and in this volume. Many researchers, including those who believe that some parts of the language faculty are innate, agree that a multitude of non-linguistic brain functions get recruited for language - if we take the language faculty in a broad sense, including conceptualization of what to say (17). And even Pinker, Jackendoff, et al., who argue for the innateness of many aspects of language, recognise that, at least initially, many of these mechanisms, such as the use of the vocal tract for speech or associative memories to store the lexicon, are pre-adaptations which have been recruited and then become genetically fine-tuned through a Baldwinian process of genetic assimilation, with possibly further extensions or alterations under the selectionist pressure of language (34), (7).

7.4. Methodology

In order to explore the recruitment theory, we can use several methods, analogous to the ones reviewed by Pinker (33):

(1) We can study what universal trends appear in human languages. However, rather than simply assuming that they are imposed by the innate language organ, we now try to show that they are emergent properties of solving the communication task, given the constraints of human embodiment, available cognitive mechanisms, properties of the real world, and the inherent difficulties of communication beween autonomous agents who do not have direct access to each other's mental states and need to interact about things in the real world as experienced through their sensori-motor system. If some properties of language are emergent in this sense, then they do not have to be genetically coded because they will spontaneously arise whenever human beings engage in building a communication system.

A particularly nice demonstration of this has come from recent investigations into the origins of vowel systems. It is well known that there are clear universal trends in human vowel systems (36) and those adopting the adaptationist view have argued that the features of the vocal tract that enable them, such as the lowering of the larynx (27), or even the distribution of vowels and vowel boundaries themselves (26), have genetically evolved under selectionist pressure for language. On the other hand, it has been shown that those same universal trends reflect constraints of human embodiment (both of the articulatory system and the auditory system) as well as optimality constraints on sound recognition and sound reproduction (28). Moreover recent simulations carried out in my group (13),(35) have shown that agents with similar embodiment constraints as human beings are able to autonomously self-organise vowel systems if they recruit a bi-directional associative memory to associate sound patterns with articulatory gestures. Even more interestingly, the emergent vowel systems have the same statistical distribution as observed in human languages (see figure 7.1 from (13)). So this is a clear example where a recruitment approach has yielded surprisingly powerful explanations for a universal trend in human languages. They are more plausible than nativist explanations because crucial features of the vocal

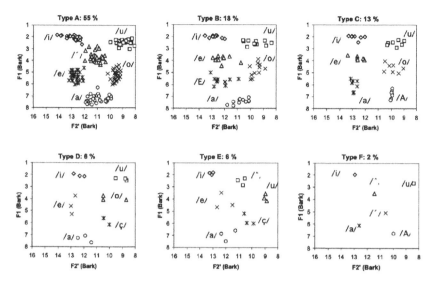

FIGURE 7.1. Results of experiments in the self-organisation of vowels. Systems with six vowels that emerged in the simulations are shown. Each diagram displays the vowel prototypes of all members of a population for the F1 (y-axis) and F2 (x-axis) formants in the Bark scale (non-linear frequency). Above the diagram, the frequency of each type of system is shown which has a similar distribution as natural vowel systems.

tract, such as a lowering of the larynx or the fine-grained control of the tongue, can just as well be explained through non-linguistic functional pressures, such as walking upright (1) or food manipulation before swallowing, and because detailed simulations of the Neanderthal vocal tract (with no lowered larynx and a more limited tongue flexibility) have shown that it is still possible to sustain a rich enough sound repertoire to build a language which is phonetically as complex as human languages today (5).

(2) Another source of support for the recruitment theory could come from evidence that similar brain areas are involved for dealing with linguistic and non-linguistic tasks, so that if there is a linguistic deficiency, there will be a related cognitive deficiency and vice-versa. This seems relatively easy. Whereas trying to find a gene that is unique for language or a brain impairment that exclusively affects language has proven to be like the search for a needle in a haystack, there exists overwhelming evidence of important correlations between linguistic and cognitive impairments. Brain imaging studies show that a verbal task always involves the activation of many other brain areas and that the areas supposedly genetically specialised for language are also active in non-linguistic tasks or that the functionalities of these areas can be taken over by others - possibly shifting from one hemisphere to another one. Even in the case of the FOXP2 gene, it is known that it is not uniquely relevant for language but plays an important

role in the development of many areas of the brain and leads to many other impairments if affected, particularly in the motor domain. So the function of the gene could be much more generic, such as regulation of postmigratory neuronal differentiation (15).

(3) We can also construct mathematical arguments why certain strategies would be adopted by a population, as long as they yield 'better' communication systems. This should be entirely feasible because before evolutionary game theory was adopted by biologists for studying genetic evolution, game theory was already widely used by economists for studying how (rational) agents come to adopt the best strategy for achieving a specific task and the mathematical arguments used in evolutionary game theory can be carried over almost directly to multi-agent systems with peer-to-peer imitation and learning instead of genetic transmission (29). Moreover techniques from complex systems science, such as network analysis, are beginning to yield proofs why particular microscopic behaviors of agents lead to global coherence (2).

(4) Finally, we can engage in the same sort of computational simulations as have been carried out to examine the genetic evolution of language. In other words, we can examine how a stable communication system might emerge from repeated pairwise interactions of agents - but now without any genetic coding of the strategies for doing so, nor of the language systems themselves. We can then examine whether such systems have the major design features of human language, such as bi-directional use of signs, compositionality, marking of predicate-argument structure, explicit marking of perspective, tense-aspect-mood systems, etc. Work in my group has almost entirely focused on this kind of effort and I will discuss some examples later.

It is important to realise that these mathematical and computational models are a necessary complement to neurobiological or psychological evidence. Brain imaging or brain impairments can help us to see that a particular area with a known function has been recruited for language, for example, it may show that the parietal-temporal-occipital junction is active both during navigation and during the parsing of sentences with perspective reversal. But this only demonstrates that recruitment took place, it does not show why. This can only be done by comparing communication systems that have recruited this capacity to those that have not. It is only when a particular strategy leads to more communicative success, greater expressive power and/or greater cognitive economy that the strategy can be expected to survive.

In the next sections of this chapter I give three examples to illustrate more concretely how we can investigate the recruitment theory through computational simulations and robotic experiments. The structure of the experiments is always the same: We focus on a particular feature of language, identify mechanisms and strategies that may give rise to this feature in an emergent communication system, set up experiments where agents endowed with these strategies play situated language games, and then test what difference the presence of this feature makes. The examples that follow examine quite different aspects of language:

the establishment of linguistic conventions, the expression of predicate-argument structure, and the marking of perspective.

7.5. The Naming Challenge

Clearly every human language has a way to name individual objects or more generally categories to identify classes of objects. Computer simulations have already been carried out to determine what strategy for tackling this naming challenge could have become innate through natural selection (21) or how a shared lexicon could arise through a simulation of genetic evolution (8). Although it is conceivable that an optimal strategy for acquiring a lexicon might have become genetically innate, it is highly unlikely that specific lexicons are genetically coded in the case of human languages, which clearly have language-specific lexicons of several tens of thousands of words which are continuously changing. The recruitment theory argues instead that each agent should autonomously discover strategies that allows him to successfully build up and negotiate a shared lexicon in peer-to-peer interaction and that the emerging lexicon is a temporal cultural consensus which is culturally transmitted. Various computer simulations (starting from (22) and (54)) have shown that the latter is entirely feasible and strategies have been found (by human designers) that are sufficiently robust to use them on situated embodied robot agents building up a common lexicon for perceptually grounded categories (41). Research is also proceeding on how agents could discover such strategies themselves in an epigenetic recruitment process.

Here are some results of these experiments. They are based on the so called Naming Game (38) which is played by agents from a population taking turns being speaker and hearer. In each game, the speaker chooses a topic (usually from a subset of the possible objects which constitutes a context) and then looks up a word to name this topic. The hearer only gets the name and then has to guess which topic was intended. The game is a success if the hearer points to the topic that was originally chosen by the speaker. The game can fail for a variety of reasons and agents then repair their lexicons after a failure: The speaker can invent a new word if he has no way yet to name the topic, the hearer can adopt an unknown word because the speaker corrects a wrong choice in case of failure, and speaker and hearer can change their opinion about which word is most common for naming an object.

One mechanism that can be recruited for this game is a bi-directional memory which has weights between objects and their names, bounded between 0.0 and 1.0. This kind of memory is clearly very generic and can be used for storing all sorts of information (24). Given this type of memory, many strategies are still possible:

1. If there are multiple choices (more than one name for the same object or more than one object for the same name), which one should be preferred?
2. Should a new word be invented each time the speaker fails to find a word?

3. Should the hearer always adopt an unknown word from the speaker, and if a new association is added to the lexicon, what should the initial weight be?
4. If the game succeeded, what should be the change in the association that was used by speaker and/or hearer?
5. If the game succeeds, should speaker or hearer do anything to the weights of competing associations, i.e. those with the same name but associated with another object, or conversely those with the same object but with another name?
6. If the game failed, what should be the change to the association that was used, if any?

Figure 7.2 (top) shows what happens with a strategy where agents always choose the association with the highest weight, initialise new associations with 0.5, use lateral inhibition in case of success, meaning that the weight of the used association is increased by 0.1 and the competitors decreased by 0.2, and decrease the used association in case of failure by 0.1. For a population of 10 agents who have to agree on names for 10 objects, this leads remarkably quickly to almost total success after about 1000 interactions (that is roughly 200 per agent) and to an optimal lexicon with one name for every object. Figure 7.2 (bottom) compares this strategy with a few others, focusing on the size of the lexicon, which impacts the time it takes for agents to reach consensus and the amount of memory they need to store a lexicon. Adoption means that there is no lateral inhibition and no decrease on failure. Enforcement means that there is an increase in case of success but no decrease of competitors and no decrease on failure. Lateral inhibition means that there is both enforcement and lateral inhibition but no decrease on failure. And finally damping means that there is not only enforcement and lateral inhibition but also a decrease on failure. All strategies lead to successful communication, but we see that only for the two last cases, inventory size is optimal. Many more experiments of this kind have been conducted, testing robustness against errors in signal transmission or feedback, flux in the population, increased homonymy, etc. (39).

It becomes even more interesting when agents do not have to name individual objects with proper names but perceptual categories for discriminating the topic from other objects in the context, so that there is no longer certainty and direct feedback about the meaning (as in Quine's famous Gavagai example). Simulations carried out in my laboratory have shown that it is entirely possible to set up a semiotic dynamics where agents self-organise from scratch a shared vocabulary and a shared set of perceptual categories by adopting weights for both the categorical repertoire and the lexicon in the process (46). It is particularly interesting that agents only arrive at a shared concept repertoire if concept development co-evolves with language development (see figure 7.3 from (46). If agents develop concepts using discrimination games prior to language games the concept repertoires are adequate for discrimination but not shared).

We learn from these experiments that (1) a variety of strategies for the naming challenge are effective but some are better than others, for example because they lead to a smaller lexicon, (2) when the agents apply these strategies they arrive

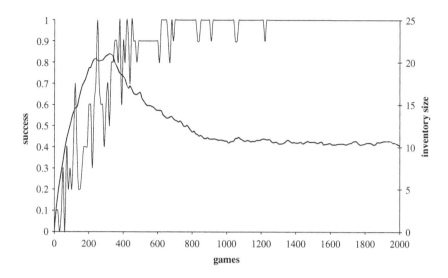

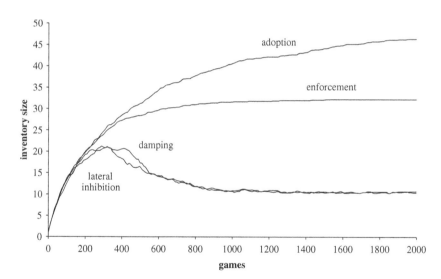

FIGURE 7.2. Top: Evolution of communicative success and lexicon size over 2000 language games by a population of 10 agents naming 10 objects. Success quickly increases and the lexicon becomes optimal. Bottom: evolution in lexicon size for four different strategies. From top to bottom: adoption, enforcement, damping, lateral inhibition. Only the latter two strategies lead to an optimal lexicon.

at a shared lexicon through self-organisation and this lexicon is maintained even if there is an in- and outflux in the population, and (3) the key mechanism that had to be recruited is a bi-directional associative memory, even though there are still many possible strategies on how it should be used.

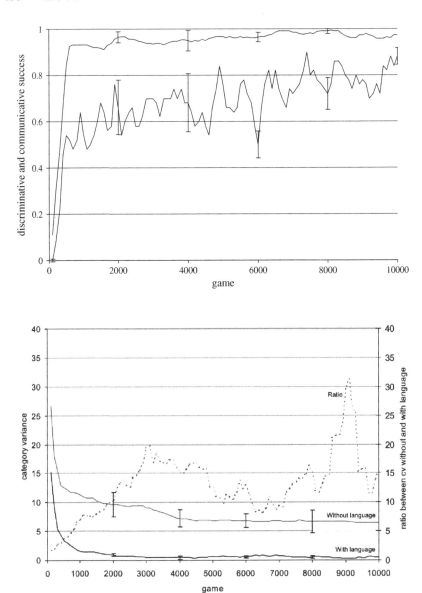

FIGURE 7.3. The top figure shows discriminative (top curve) and communicative (bottom curve) success in a population building up concept repertoires and language conventions at the same time. Bottom: Ratio of category variance between the concept repertoires in a population of agents and category variance with (bottom) and without (top) language. When there is no coordination through language, the individual concept repertoires do not converge.

7.6. Expressing Predicate-Argument Structure

We now look at a second example: the marking of predicate-argument structure, i.e. who is doing what to whom. Marking predicate-argument structure is clearly a strong universal tendency in human languages, although many different ways have evolved to do so. Some languages (like Latin or Russian) use a complex system of cases and morphosyntax, others (like Chinese or Japanese) use a system of particles, still others (like English) mainly rely on verbal Subject-DirectObject-IndirectObject patterns with additional prepositions (4). There is moreover a general tendency that specific predicate argument relations are not expressed with ad hoc markers. Human languages have universally developed a more abstract intermediary layer in which a specific predicate-argument structure is first categorised in terms of more abstract frames, such as physical-transfer+agent+object+recipient, and these abstract roles are mapped onto a system of abstract markings (like nominative/ accusative/ dative or subject/ direct-object/ indirect-object), so that there is a tremendous reduction in terms of the number of markers that are required (16), (19).

We have been carrying out various experiments to explore the expression of predicate-argument structure, using embodied agents which perceive the world through digital cameras. Agents are given access to real world scenes such as the ones shown in figure 7.4, in which puppets enact common events like the movement of people and objects, actions such as push' or pull', give' or take', etc. The recorded visual images are processed by each agent using a battery of machine vision algorithms that segment objects based on color and movement, track objects in real-time, and compute a stream of low-level features indicating which objects are touching, in which direction objects are moving, etc. These low-level features are input to an event-recognition system that uses an inventory of hierarchical event structures and matches them against the data streaming in from low-level vision, as described in detail in (45). Using the world models resulting from these perceptual processes, agents then engage in description games, where the speaker describes one of the events in the most recent scene and the game is a success if the hearer agrees that this event indeed occurred. As before, the population starts without any pre-programmed language.

FIGURE 7.4. Typical action sequence used in our case grammar experiments. The scenes are enacted with puppets and evoke typical interactions between animate agents and physical objects. A game succeeds if the hearer agrees that the event described by the speaker occurred in the most recent scene. In this case "Jill pushes the block from the table" might be a possible description.

We have explored the hypothesis that agents mark predicate-argument structure because it reduces complexity in semantic interpretation (44). Interpreting a meaning structure M_h with respect to a world model W_h with d possible objects is a function of the maximum number of possible assignments for a given meaning M_h with m variables, and hence the number of possible interpretations is equal to $O(d^m)$. Searching through this set to find the assignment(s) that are compatible with W_h is therefore exponential in the number of variables and hence, reducing the number of variables by communicating which ones are equal is the most effective way to drastically reduce the complexity of semantic interpretation. This suggests the following strategy: Before the speaker renders a sentence, he may re-enter it into his own language system, parsing and interpreting the sentence to simulate how the hearer would process it (which is possible because every agent develops both the competence for being speaker and for being hearer). The speaker can thus compare what he originally wanted to express with what would be interpreted, and hence detect complexities in semantic interpretation that could be eliminated by introducing grammar. The hearer goes through a similar process: He first tries to interpret the sentence as well as possible, given his own perception of the scene, and then attempts to pick up which clues were added by the speaker to make the semantic interpretation process more efficient in the future. The precise implementation of the required mechanisms (particularly for grammatical processing) is too complex to describe in detail here (see (43)). But our experiments show convincingly that a shared system of case' markers effectively arises when agents use this strategy (figure 7.5 - top).

Next we endowed agents with an additional mechanism: The ability to establish an analogy between two events. This is a well-established generic cognitive component with wide applicability in a variety of tasks. When agents need to mark predicate-argument structure, they can first try to find whether a convention to express an analogous event already exists. If so, the predicate-argument structures can be generalised as playing a common semantic role and the implicated words and markers can be categorised as belonging to the same parts of speech, thus giving rise to a new grammatical construction which can from now on be applied to other analogous events. As a side effect of using analogy, agents build up semantic and syntactic categories, similar to the way this is done in memory-based language learners (12). As results in figure 7.5(bottom) show, this strategy drastically reduces the number of markers, which not only leads to a reduction of memory and processing time in rule matching, but also helps agents to reach a consensus more quickly and achieve communicative success for situations never encountered before.

We learn from these experiments that (1) the marking of predicate-argument structure can be explained as the outcome of strategies that attempt to reduce the computational complexity of semantic interpretation, (2) when agents apply these strategies, they arrive at shared grammatical systems, such as a grammar of case, in a process of cultural negotiation similar to the way lexicons have been shown to self-organise, (3) the recruitment of analogy for re-using existing structures

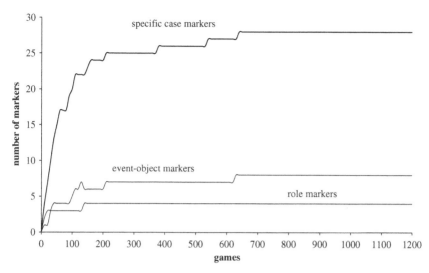

FIGURE 7.5. The graph compares two strategies for marking predicate-argument structure in description games played by a population of agents about dynamical real world scenes: The top thick line shows the number of specific case markers without recruiting analogy and the two bottom lines show the specific case markers as well as the more generic role markers when analogy is recruited. The same series of scenes was considered in both cases. The recruitment of analogy clearly results in great economy with respect to the number of markers.

automatically leads to an intermediary layer of abstract semantic and syntactic categories, which becomes progressively coordinated among the agents.

7.7. Perspective Marking

Another clear universal tendency of human speakers is to use not only their own perspective but also that of the hearer in order to conceptualise a scene, and to mark explicitly from what perspective the scene is viewed. For example, in English one can make a distinction between: "your left" and "my left" to mark whether the position is seen as left from the hearer's perspective or from the speaker's own perspective. German uses prepositions like "herein" and "hinein" depending on whether the required direction of movement is towards the speaker or away from the speaker, similar to English "come" and "go". We now look at experiments with autonomously moving robots designed to explain why this universal tendency might occur (48).

The robot agents in these experiments are even more sophisticated than those used in the earlier predicate-argument experiments[1]. They are capable of

---

[1] They are the Sony dog-like AIBO entertainment robots running programs designed specifically for these experiments.

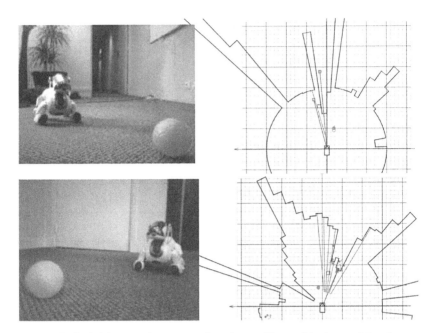

FIGURE 7.6. The left images shows two robots (top and bottom) both perceiving the same orange ball but from different points of view. The right figures show the analog self-lefted world models built up in real time by each robot. The position of the robot is indicated by the rectangle below in the middle. The black lines indicate estimated positions of surrounding obstacles. Dots indicate estimated positions of the ball and the other robot.

autonomous locomotion and vision-based obstacle avoidance, and maintain a real-time analog model of their immediate surroundings based on visual input (see figure 7.6 (left)). Using this vision-based world model, the robots are able to detect and track other robots as well as orange balls using standard image processing algorithms (see figure 7.6 (right)). Furthermore, the robots have been endowed with mechanisms to segment the flow of data into distinct events and they have a short term memory in which they can store a number of past events. The robots play again description games, describing to each other the most recent event. The language game is a success if, according to the hearer, the description given by the speaker not only fits with the scene as perceived by him but is also distinctive with respect to previous scenes.

Agents need to recruit on the one hand the same sort of strategies as discussed earlier. They acquire categories in the form of discrimination trees (as in (47)), although other mechanisms for categorisation (e.g. Radial Basis Function networks or Nearest Neighbour Classification) would work equally well. They also use again a bi-directional associative memory with lateral inhibition and damping (as in the Naming Game experiment discussed in section 7.5). To support compositional coding (where more than one word can be used to cover

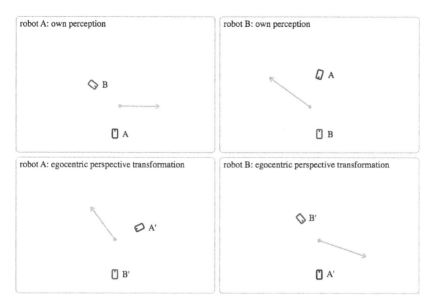

FIGURE 7.7. The left images illustrated the world models computed by the speaker (top) and the hearer (bottom). The self-position (the rectangle below in the middle), the estimated position of the other robot (the other rectangle), the ball's begin and end position, as well as the ball trajectory are shown. The right images show the world models of speaker (top) and hearer (bottom) after egocentric perspective transformation, so that they now illustrate how one robot hypothesises the perception of the world by the other.

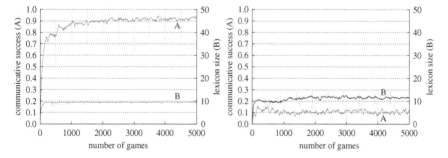

FIGURE 7.8. The graphs show communicative success (A - upper curve) and the size of lexical inventories (B - lower curve) over 5 runs for 5000 language games each. The left graphs show the case where agents share the same perception of the world and the right graphs where they have each a different viewpoint. We see a dramatic drop in communicative success. The lexicon is no longer converging in the latter case.

the meaning) agents use a pattern decomposition system that combines partial matches from multi-word sentences (53).

Figure 7.8 shows the results when a population of ten agents applies these strategies in a series of 5000 peer to peer language games. We have first done an experiment where both agents use exactly the same perception of the world in the game. This allows us to establish whether the proposed mechanisms indeed work. Figure 7.8 (left) shows that this is indeed the case. Communicative success rises to hover around 90%, despite the fact that none of the agents had any categories or words to start with. Residual communicative error is due to perceptual problems (for example one robot may fail to see where the other robot is) and not to incompatibilities of linguistic inventories or conflicting ways of conceptualising the world. Figure 7.8 (left) shows that the size of the lexicon stabilises to about 50 words, reached when they are sufficient to cope with the communicative challenges in this particular setting.

We next do an experiment where agents are truely embodied and hence have different perceptual views on the same scene. Figure 7.8 (right) shows that there is only 10% success. The communication system does not really come off the ground. This clearly shows that if situated embodied agents want to be successful in describing the movement of objects in the space around them, they will have to recruit additional mechanisms.

We now endow agents with the capacity of egocentric perspective transformation, which is a well established quasi-universal mechanism in human cognition (18). Egocentric perspective transformation allows agents to reconstruct a scene from the viewpoint of another agent. It requires that they first detect where the other agent is located (according to their own perception of the world) and then perform a geometric transformation of their own world model (see the example in figure 7.7 (right)). Inevitably, an agent's reconstruction of how another agent sees the world will never be completely accurate, and may even be grossly incorrect due to unavoidable misperceptions both of the other robot's position and of the real world itself. The sensory values obtained by the robots should not be interpreted as exact measures (which would be impossible on physical robots using real world perception) but at best as reasonable estimates. This type of inaccuracies is precisely what a viable communication system must be able to cope with and robotic models are therefore a very good way to seriously test and compare strategies and the mechanisms that implement them.

Figure 7.9 (left) shows that agents clearly increase communicative success when they recruit egocentric perspective transformations for conceptualisation. Even without explicitly marking perspective, success dramatically increases because agents try out what makes sense, first from their own perspective and then from the other's perspective. Here as in all our other experiments, agents use an inferential coding strategy which means that part of the meaning can be inferred or gleaned from the shared situation (37). The lexicon is almost the same size as in the first experiment and communicative success is steadily around 80%. In the next experimental run figure 7.9 (right), agents not only use egocentric perspective transformation for conceptualisation but also mark perspective when necessary, i.e. the adopted perspective (self or other) is part of the meanings they convey. We see that communicative success is similar. The size of the lexicon is bigger but beginning to settle to a more optimal level thanks to the compositional coding of perspective. It now takes longer to reach

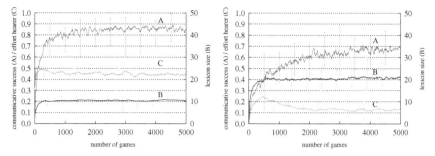

FIGURE 7.9. Communicative success (A) and lexical inventory size (B) for different world perception with egocentric perspective transformation without explicit marking (left), and with egocentric perspective transformation and the marking of perspective (right). The right graph shows not only communicative success and inventory size but also the decreased effort (C) involved in perspective transformation.

convergence but after a few thousand more games the same level of performance is reached.

Figure 7.9 (right) also shows the gain in cognitive economy. Curve C shows the amount of effort involved in computing different perspectives. In the experiment where no perspective is marked, agents always need to take the other perspective to check which perspective the speaker might have used. When perspective is marked, agents can optimise this computation and only do it when perspective reversal is explicitly signalled. We therefore see a decrease in effort (and hence increase in cognitive economy). We conclude that embodied and situated agents, which have different viewpoints on a scene, can reach significantly more success in communication when they recruit egocentric perspective transformation for conceptualising the scene and even more success if they also mark explicitly the adopted perspective in their language so that they know whether to apply perspective transformation or not. This justifies the adoption of this strategy and hence explains why it is universally found in human languages.

7.8. Discussion

The present chapter discussed the recruitment theory of language origins. This theory argues that human brains are capable of dynamically recruiting various cognitive mechanisms and configuring them into strategies for handling the challenges of communication in particular environments. The configurations are retained if they increase communicative success and expressive power while minimising the effort involved (processing time, memory resources, etc.). Each strategy has an impact on the emergent language and hence it gets culturally fixated. We discussed a number of very concrete experiments with computer simulations and robotic models that attempt to substantiate the recruitment theory. Each experiment focuses on a specific universal feature of language and tries to show that it is the consequence of the recruitment of a particular strategy and the cognitive mechanisms that can implement this strategy. If the adoption of the strategy leads to a better' communication system, then we have a functional explanation why a human language may have this particular feature.

The experiments reported here all compare different strategies and mechanisms. They show that communication systems with similar features as in human natural languages can emerge from the collective behaviors of individuals and that the adoption of some strategies leads to better communication systems compared to others. But these experiments do not yet attack the problem of how the recruitment process itself might work in individuals, nor how individual recruitment processes are influenced by solutions already adopted by others. Computational simulations and robotic experiments on this issue are progressing and they rest on earlier work in genetic programming (25), classifier systems (20), and other forms of adaptive machine learning in multiagent systems. Research can rely partly on a strong tradition in ethology to study behavioral decision-making in animals, which often appears to reach remarkably optimal performance (30).

As mentioned earlier, researchers in favor of innate linguistic structure split between adaptationists (such as Pinker and others) who claim that it is the (communicative) function of language which acts as the selectionist drive because it directly influences fitness and hence the spreading of genes, and non-adaptationists (such as Chomsky, Gould, and others (17)). The latter claim that language does not appear to be 'designed' well or primarily for communication and hence that other factors must have played a role to genetically shape the language organ. Similarly there are researchers who are generally in favor of the language-as-a-complex-adaptive-system view but do not take communicative function to be the main force that guides the process of (cultural) selection. One example is the work of Kirby and collaborators (6). Instead of communicative function, they take the challenge of cultural transmission (how a language system can be learned by the next generation) as the main driver for the emergence of linguistic structure and they have obtained a number of significant results using their iterated learning framework, including the selection of compositional versus holistic coding. The recruitment theory argues that communicative function, as well as the sensori-motor embodiment and the real world environments and ecologies constraining the behavior of a population, shape language. Learning still plays a significant role in the sense that conventions which are not learnable cannot be picked up by the hearer and hence will not propagate in the population, but learning is incorporated as part of peer-to-peer interactions instead of transmission from one generation to the next.

The recruitment theory is at this point still a research program instead of a fully complete and established theory. Many features of language remain to be investigated and much more research is needed on cognitive mechanisms. The experiments briefly reported here are very difficult to do, requiring a team working over several years. However, they yield very clear and solid results, thus establishing a growing body of functional explanations for human language.

Much more research is needed on the neurological basis for the recruitment theory. It requires taking the opposite view from what is now common in brain science. Rather than looking to see what is unique for language (genes or neural subsystems) we need to find out what is common between linguistic and non-linguistic tasks.

Acknowledgement. The research reported here is currently funded by the Sony Computer Science Laboratory in Paris with additional funding from the EU FET-ECAgents project IST-1940. Many researchers have participated in the experiments reported here, most of them as part of their Ph.D. thesis projects at the Artificial Intelligence Laboratory of the University of Brussels (VUB): Paul Vogt and Edwin de Jong participated in the early discoveries of the naming game, Frederic Kaplan, Angus McIntyre and Joris Van Looveren were key collaborators for the early 'Talking Heads experiments', which continued with a focus on the co-development of conceptual and linguistic repertoires by Tony Belpaeme and Joris Bleys. Pierre-Yves Oudeyer and Bart de Boer have successfully explored the emergence of sound repertoires through imitation games. Nicolas Neubauer and Joachim De Beule collaborated on the development of the Fluid Construction Grammar formalism and the predicate-argument experiments. Martin Loetsch and Benjamin Bergen played key roles in the perspective reversal experiments.

References

1. Aiello, L. C. (1996) Terrestriality, bipedalism and the origin of language. Runciman, W.G. , J. Maynard-Smith, and R.I.M. Dunbar (eds.) Evolution of Social Behaviour Patterns in Primates and Man, Oxford: Oxford University Press. p. 269–89.
2. Baronchelli, A., Felici, M., Caglioti, E., Loreto, V., and Steels, L. (2006) Sharp Transition towards Shared Vocabularies in Multi-Agent Systems. Submitted.
3. Bickerton, D. (1984) The language bioprogram hypothesis. Behavioral and Brain Sciences 7, 17–388.
4. Blake, B.J. (1994) Case. Cambridge University Press, Cambridge UK.
5. Boe, L-J., Heim, J.-L., Honda, K. and Maeda, S. (2002) The potential Neandertal vowel space was as large as that of modern humans. Journal of Phonetics, 30(3): 46584.
6. Brighton, H. and S. Kirby (2001) The survival of the smallest: stability conditions for the cultural evolution of compositional language. In J. Kelemen and P. Sosik (Eds.) Advances in Artificial Life. pp592601 Berlin: Springer-Verlag
7. Briscoe, T. (ed.) (2002) Linguistic Evolution through Language Acquisition: Formal and Computational Models. Cambridge University Press, Cambridge, UK.
8. Cangelosi A., D. Parisi (1998). The emergence of a "language" in an evolving population of neural networks. Connection Science, 10(2), 83–9
9. Cangelosi, A. and D. Parisi (eds.) (2001) Simulating the Evolution of Language. Springer-Verlag, Berlin.
10. Chomsky, N. (1988). Language and Problems of Knowledge. Cambridge, MA: MIT Press.
11. Croft, W. (2001) Radical Construction Grammar: syntactic theory in typological perspective. Oxford University Press, Oxford.

12. Daelemans W. (2002) A comparison of analogical modeling to memorybased language processing.- In: Skousen R. (ed) Analogical modeling. Amsterdam, Benjamins, 2002, p. 157–179
13. De Boer, B. (2000) Self organization in vowel systems. Journal of Phonetics 28 (4): 441465.
14. Enard et al (2002) Molecular evolution of FOXP2, a gene involved in speech and language', Nature 418, 869–872.
15. Ferland, R.J., T. J. Cherry, P. O. Preware, E. E. Morrisey, and C. A. Walsh (2003) Characterization of FOXP2 and FOXP1 mRNA and Protein in the Developing and Mature Brain. The Journal of Comparative Neurology 460:266279 (2003)
16. Fillmore, Charles J. (1976): Frame semantics and the nature of language; in Annals of the New York Academy of Sciences: Conference on the Origin and Development of Language and Speech, Volume 280 (pp. 20–32)
17. Fitch, W. Tecumseh, M. D. Hauser and N. Chomsky (2006) The Evolution of the Language Faculty: Clarifications and Implications. Cognition (in press).
18. Flavell, J.H., 1992. Perspectives of perspective taking. In: Beilin, H., Pufall, P. (Eds.), Piagets Theory: Prospects and Possibilities. Erlbaum, Hillsdale, N.J.
19. Goldberg, A.E. (1995) Constructions.: A Construction Grammar Approach to Argument Structure. University of Chicago Press, Chicago.
20. Holland, J.H. (1992) Adaptation in Natural and Artificial Systems. MIT Press, Cambridge, Massachusetts.
21. Hurford, J. (1989) Biological evolution of the Saussurean sign as a component of the language acquisition device. Lingua 77, 187–222.
22. Hutchins, E. and B. Hazlehurst (1995) How to invent a lexicon: The development of shared symbols in interaction. In N. Gilbert and R. Conte (eds.) Artificial societies: The computer simulation of social life (p. 157–189). UCL Press, London.
23. Iachini, T. and R. Logie (2003) The Role of Perspective in Locating Position in a Real-World, Unfamiliar Environment, Appl. Cognit. Psychol. 17: 904.
24. Kosko, B. (1988) Bidirectional Associative Memories. IEEE Transactions on Systems, Man, and Cybernetics, 18, pp. 49–60, 1988
25. Koza, J. (1992) Genetic Programming: On the Programming of Computers by Means of Natural Selection. The MIT Press, Cambridge MA.
26. Kuhl, P. K., Meltzoff, A. N. (1997). Evolution, nativism, and learning in the development of language and speech. In M. Gopnik (Ed.), The inheritance and innateness of grammars (pp. 7–44). New York: Oxford University Press.
27. Lieberman, P. (1975) On the Origins of Language. Macmillan, New York.
28. Lindblom, B., P. MacNeilage, and M. Studdert-Kennedy (1984) Selforganizing processes and the explanation of phonological universals. In: B. Butterworth, B. Comrie and O. Dahl (eds.), Explanations for Language Universals, 181203. Berlin: Walter de Gruyter.
29. Matsen, F.A., and M.A. Nowak (2004) Win-stay, lose-shift in language learning from peers. PNAS, Vol 101(52) 18053–18–57.
30. McFarland, D.J. (1977) Decision making in animals. Nature 269: 15–21.
31. Minett, J. W. and Wang, W. S-Y. (2005) Language Acquisition, Change and Emergence: Essays in Evolutionary Linguistics. City University of Hong Kong Press: Hong Kong.
32. Nowak, M.A., N. Komarova, P. Niyogi (2001) Evolution of universal grammar. Science, 291:114–118, 2001

33. Pinker, S. (2004) Language as an Adaptation to the Cognitive Niche. In: Christiansen, M.H. and S. Kirby (eds) Language Evolution: The States of the Art. Oxford University Press, Oxford. Chapter 2.

34. Pinker, S. and R. Jackendoff (2005) The Faculty of Language: What's Special about it? Cognition, in press.

35. Oudeyer, P-Y. (2005) The Self-Organization of Speech Sounds, Journal of Theoretical Biology, Volume 233, Issue 3, pp. 435449

36. Schwartz, J. L., Boe, L. J., Vall'ee N. and C. Abry (1997) Major trends in vowel system inventories. Journal of Phonetics 25, pp. 233253

37. Sperber, D. and Wilson, D. (1995) Relevance, communication, and cognition. Blackwell Pub., London.

38. Steels, L. (1995) A Self-organizing Spatial Vocabulary. Artificial Life 2(3), pp. 319–332.

39. Steels, L. and F. Kaplan (1998) Stochasticity as a source of innovation in language games. In C. Adami and R. Belew and H. Kitano and C. Taylor, editors, Artificial Life VI. Los Angeles: MIT Press.

40. Steels, L. (2000) Language as a complex adaptive system. Lecture Notes in Computer Science. Parallel Problem Solving from Nature - PPSN-VI. Volume Editor(s): Schoenauer et al., Springer-Verlag, Berlin.

41. Steels, L. (2003) Evolving grounded communication for robots. Trends in Cognitive Science. Volume 7, Issue 7, July 2003, pp. 308–312.

42. Steels, L. (2003) Intelligence with representation. Philosophical Transactions Royal Society: Mathematical, Physical and Engineering Sciences, 361(1811):23812395

43. Steels, L. (2004) Constructivist Development of Grounded Construction Grammars Scott, D., Daelemans, W. and Walker M. (eds) (2004) Proceedings Annual Meeting Association for Computational Linguistic Conference. Barcelona. p. 9–19.

44. Steels, L. (2005) What triggers the emergence of grammar? A. Cangelosi and C.L. Nehaniv (ed.) (2005) Proceedings of the AISB 2005 conference. EELC satellite workshop. University of Herfortshire, Hatfield, UK.

45. Steels, L. and J-C. Baillie (2003) Shared Grounding of Event Descriptions by Autonomous Robots. Journal of Robotics and Autonomous Systems 43, 2003, 163–173.

46. Steels, L. and T. Belpaeme (2005) Coordinating Perceptually Grounded Categories through Language. A Case Study for Colour. Behavioral and Brain Sciences. 24(6).

47. Steels, L., F. Kaplan, A McIntyre and J. Van Looveren (2002) Crucial factors in the origins of word-meaning. In Wray, A., editor, The Transition to Language, Oxford University Press. Oxford, UK, 2002.

48. Steels, L., M. Loetzsch and B. Bergen (2005) Explaining Language Universals: A Case Study on Perspective Marking. [submitted].

49. Stromswold, K. (2001) The Heritability of Language: a Review and Metaanalysis of Twin, Adoption, and Linkage Studies. Language, 77(4), p. 647–723.

50. Szathmary, E. (2001) Origin of the human language faculty: the language amoeba hypothesis. In: J. Trabant and S. Ward (eds) New Essays on the Origins of Language. Trends in Linguistics, Studies and Monographs Vol. 133. p. 41–55.

51. Tomasello, M. (1999). The cultural origins of human cognition. Harvard University Press, Cambridge, MA.

52. Thornton, R. and K. Wexler (1999) Principle B, VP Ellipsis, and Interpretation in Child Grammar. The MIT Press, Cambridge MA.

53. Van Looveren, J. (1999) Multiple word naming games. In Proceedings of the 11th Belgium-Netherlands Conference on Artificial Intelligence. Universiteit Maastricht, Maastricht, the Netherlands, 1999.

54. Werner, G. and M. Dyer (1991) "Evolution of Communication in Artificial Organisms", in Langton, C. et al. (ed.) Artificial Life II. Addison- Wesley Pub. Co. Redwood City, p. 659–687

55. Wray, A., ed. (2002) The Transition to Language, Oxford University Press. Oxford, UK, 2002.

56. Zacks, J., B. Rypma, J.D.E. Gabrieli, B. Tversky, G. H. Glover (1999) Imagined transformations of bodies: an fMRI investigation. Neuropsychologia 37 (1999) 1029–1040.

8
In silico Evolutionary Developmental Neurobiology and the Origin of Natural Language

Eörs Szathmáry, Zoltán Szatmáry, Péter Ittzés, Gergő Orbán, István Zachár, Ferenc Huszár, Anna Fedor, Máté Varga, Szabolcs Számadó

8.1. Introduction

It is justified to assume that part of our genetic endowment contributes to our language skills, yet it is impossible to tell at this moment exactly how genes affect the language faculty. We complement experimental biological studies by an *in silico* approach in that we simulate the evolution of neuronal networks under selection for language-related skills. At the heart of this project is the Evolutionary Neurogenetic Algorithm (ENGA) that is deliberately biomimetic. The design of the system was inspired by important biological phenomena such as brain ontogenesis, neuron morphologies, and indirect genetic encoding. Neuronal networks were selected and were allowed to reproduce as a function of their performance in the given task. The selected neuronal networks in all scenarios were able to solve the communication problem they had to face. The most striking feature of the model is that it works with highly indirect genetic encoding—just as brains do.

Natural language is a unique communication and cultural inheritance system. In its practically unlimited hereditary potential it is similar to the genetic and the immune systems. The underlying principle is also similar in that all these systems are generative: they achieve unlimited capacity by the combination of limited primitives. The origin of natural language is the last of the major evolutionary transitions (Maynard Smith & Szathmáry, 1995). Although later in society important transitions did happen in the way of storing, transmitting and using inherited information, they were not made possible or accompanied by relevant genetic changes in the biology of our species. In contrast, language has a genetic background, but it is an open question how a set of genes affect our language faculty. It is fair to say that with respect to their capacity to deal with the complexity of language, even so-called 'linguistically trained' animals are very far from us. Language has certain design features, such as symbolic reference, compositionality, recursion, and cultural transmission (Hockett, 1960). Understanding language origins and change is difficult because it involves three interwoven timescales and processes: individual learning, cultural transmission and biological evolution. These cannot be neatly separated from one another (Christiansen & Kirby, 2003). The fact that a population uses some useful language that is culturally transmitted changes the fitness landscape of the population genetic processes.

The origin of language is an unsolved problem; some have even called it the 'hardest problem of science' (Christiansen & Kirby, 2003). It is very hard because physiological and genetic experimentation on humans and even apes is very limited. The uniqueness of language prohibits, strictly speaking, application of the comparative method, so infinitely useful in other branches of biology. This limitation of the approaches calls for other types of investigation. We believe that simulations of various kinds are indispensable elements of a successful research programme. Yet a vast range of computational approaches have not brought spectacular success (Elman et al., 1996). This is attributable, we believe, to the utterly artificial nature of many of the systems involved, such as connectionist networks using back-propagation, for example (see (Marcus, 1998) for a detailed criticism).

The only system we know that has apparently solved the 'language problem' is biological evolution. Therefore, our research project is deliberately biomimetic as strongly as it can be, given the limitations prevailing in computability and basic knowledge. The strategy hence is to expose simulated agents to selective challenges in such a way that communication should possibly arise as a means to enhance the performance of the agents in synergistic collaborative tasks. The agents must therefore have simulated evolvable nervous systems (we aim at a 'toy' cortex, see below), which are under partial (again biomimetic) genetic control. If this research line turns out to be successful, it leads to the evolutionary emergence of communicating agents, possibly endowed with a faculty to master key components of language such as recursion, symbolism, compositionality, and cultural transmission. We now give justification for such an approach based on a brief survey of our current understanding of the biology of natural language.

Language needs certain prerequisites (Premack, 2004). There are some obvious prerequisites of language that are not especially relevant to our approach. For example, apes do not have a descended larynx or cortical control of their vocalizations. Undoubtedly, these traits must have evolved in the human lineage, but we do not think that they are indispensable for language as such. One could have a functional language with a smaller number of phonemes, and sign language (Senghas et al., 2004) (and Rosenstock in this volume) does not need either vocalization or auditory analysis. Thus, we are mostly concerned with the neuronal implementation of linguistic operations, irrespective of the modality. It seems difficult to imagine the origin of language without capacities for teaching (which differs from learning), imitation, and some theory of mind (Premack, 2004). Apes are limited in all these capacities. It is fair to assume that these traits have undergone significant evolution because they were evolving together with language in the hominine lineage. We conclude that in any selective scenario, capacities for teaching, imitation and some theory of mind must be rewarded, because an innate capacity for these renders language emergence more likely.

On the neurobiological side we must call attention to the fact that some textbooks, e.g. Kandel et al. (2000) still give a distorted image of the neurobiological basis of language. It would be very simple to have the Wernicke and Broca areas of the left hemisphere for semantics and syntax, respectively. But the localization of language components in the brain is extremely plastic, both between and within individuals (Neville & Bavelier, 1998; Müller et al., 1999).

Surprisingly, if a removal of the left hemisphere happens early enough, the patient can nearly completely retain his/her capacity to acquire language. This is of course in sharp contrast to the idea of anatomical modularity. It also puts severe limitation on the idea that it is only the afferent channels that changed in the evolution of the human brain: modality independence and the enormous brain plasticity in the localization of language favour the idea that whatever has changed in the brain that has rendered it capable of linguistic processing must be a very widespread property of the neuronal networks in the brain (Szathmáry, 2001). Components of language get localized somewhere in any particular brain in the most 'convenient' parts available. Language is just a certain activity pattern of the brain that finds its habitat like an amoeba in a medium. The metaphor 'language amoeba' expresses the plasticity of language but it also calls attention to the fact that a large part of the human brain is apparently a potential habitat for it, but no such habitat seems to exist in non-human ape brains (Szathmáry, 2001). The biomimetic approach offers a test of these ideas.

A dogma concerning the histological uniformity of homologous brain areas in different primate species has also been around for some time. Recent investigations do not support such a claim (DeFelipe et al., 2002). In fact the primary visual cortex shows marked cytoarchitectonic variation (Preuss, 2000), even between chimps and man. It is therefore not at all excluded that some of the species-specific differences in brain networks are genetically determined, and that some of these are crucial for our language capacity. But, as discussed above, these language-critical features must be a rather widespread network property.

A key feature of brain development is that there is something akin to selection in populations going on (Changeux, 1983): there is a vast overproduction of synapses and neurons, out of which at least half are eliminated under sensory influence. We suspect that it is practically impossible to obtain a linguistically proficient neuronal network without pruning (Jeffery & Reid, 1997; Johnston, 2001). This is a testable prediction of the biomimetic approach.

Pruning does not merely mean that some of the connection weights are set to zero: it also means that they remain zero for the rest of the lifetime of the network. Genes affect language through the development of the brain. One could thus say that the origin of language is to a large extent an exercise in the linguistically relevant developmental genetics of the human brain (Szathmáry, 2001).

The close genetic similarity between humans and chimps strongly suggests that the majority of changes relevant to the human condition are likely to have resulted from changes in gene regulation rather than from widespread changes of downstream structural genes. Recent genetic and genomic evidence corroborates this view. In contrast to other organs, genes expressed in the human brain seem almost always up-regulated relative to the homologous genes in chimp brains (Caceres et al., 2003). The functional consequences of this consistent pattern await further analysis.

We know something about genetic changes more directly relevant to language. The FOXP2 gene was discovered to have mutated in an English-speaking family (Gopnik 1990, 1999). It has a pleiotropic effect: it causes orofacial dyspraxia, but it also affects the morphology of language: affected patients must learn or form the past tense of verbs or the plurals of nouns case by case, and even after practice they do so differently from unaffected humans (see (Marcus & Fisher 2003) for review). The gene has been under positive selection (Enard et al., 2002) in the past, which shows that there are genetically influenced important traits of language other than recursion (Pinker & Jackendoff, 2005), contrary to some opinions (Hauser et al., 2002). There is a known human language, apparently with no recursion (Everett et al., 2005). It would be good to know how these particular people (speaking the Pirahã language in the Amazon) manage recursion in other domains, such as object manipulation. Apes are very bad at recursion both in the theory of mind or 'action grammar' (Greenfield, 1991).

It does seem that the capacity to handle recursion is different from species to species. Although the relevant experiment must be conducted with chimps as well, it has been demonstrated that tamarin monkeys are insensitive to auditory patterns defined by more general phrase structure grammar, whereas they discover violations of input conforming to finite state grammar (Fitch & Hauser, 2004). Human adults are sensitive to both violations. Needless to say it would be very interesting to know the relevant sensitivities in apes and human children (preferably before they can talk fluently). It will be interesting to see what kind of experiment can produce consistent patterns in such a capacity in evolving neuronal networks, and then reverse engineer proficient networks to discover evolved mechanisms for this capacity.

We share the view that language is a complex, genetically influenced system for communication that has been under positive selection in the human lineage (Pinker & Jackendoff, 2005). The task of the modeller is then to try to model intermediate stages of a hypothetical scenario and, ultimately, to re-enact critical steps of the transition from protolanguage (Bickerton, 1992) to language. It cannot be denied that language is also a means for representation (Bickerton, 1992). This is probably most obvious for abstract concepts, for which the generative properties of language may lead to the emergence of a clear concept itself. This is well demonstrated for arithmetics: for instance, an Amazonian indigenous group lacks words for numbers greater than 5; hence they are unable to perform exact calculations in the range of larger numbers, but they have approximate arithmetics (Pica et al., 2004).

We mentioned before that the fact that language changes while the genetic background also changes (which must have been true especially for the initial phases of language evolution), the processes and timescales are interwoven. This opens up the possibility for genetic assimilation (the Baldwin effect). Some changes that each individual must learn at first can become hard-wired in the brain later. Some have endorsed (Pinker & Bloom, 2004), while others have doubted (Deacon, 1997) the importance of this mechanism in language evolution. Deacon's argument against it was that linguistic structures change so fast that there is no chance for the genetic system to assimilate any grammatical rule. This is likely to be true but not very important. There are linguistic operations, performed by neuronal computations, related to compositionality and recursion that must have appeared sometime in evolution. Whatever the explicit grammatical rules are, such operations must be executed.

Hence a much more likely scenario for the importance of genetic assimilation proposes that many operations must have first been learned, and those individuals whose brain was genetically preconditioned to a better (faster, more accurate) performance of these operations had a selective advantage (Szathmáry, 2001). Learning was important in rendering the fitness landscape more climbable (Hinton & Nowlan, 1987). This view is consonant with Rapoport's (1990) view of brain evolution. This thesis is also open for experimental test.

The uniqueness of language poses special problems, and the limits of experimentation on primates (including humans) renders progress slow. Increasing knowledge of the genetic background of various cognitive deficiencies suggests how genes affect the structure and function of certain parts of the human brain, and lends credence to our earlier hypothesis that some genetic changes have influenced development of the human brain in such a way that it became more ready to perform language-related operations. Experimental evidence for the plasticity of the human brain suggests that this influence can be poorly localized, thus the traits in question are likely to be a widespread modification of our neuronal networks.

The origin of the eye, once considered one of the hardest problems in evolution, now looks almost trivial compared to that of the origin of human language. What makes the former such an easy one? We think there are at least four reasons:

- the anatomy and physiology of the eye is relatively well understood;
- there are many eye forms, which can be considered close to plausible intermediate stages in evolution (additionally, the vertebrate eye has a close analogue in cephalopods);
- although apparently related to an ancestral light-sensitive spot, eyes with various anatomical and physiological structures evolved about forty times; and
- the genetics of eye development is now becoming understood.

Compare this to the following list:

- our knowledge of the "language organ" is fairly limited;
- there seems to be no extant intermediate between "protolanguage" (broadly understood as limited vocabulary without syntax) and human language;
- even much simpler protolanguage evolved a few times only (candidate species where protolanguage could be used in the wild include bottle-nosed dolphins, grey parrots and chimps), and natural language evolved only once; and
- the genetics of human language is poorly known.

It may seem, then, almost impossible to say something useful about the origin of natural language. There are at least five sources of scientific input that can nevertheless, contribute to an enhanced understanding of this conundrum:

- The spread of elements of vocabulary and language rules can be analysed using the armamentarium of population biology.
- Better understanding of primate communication and social life greatly contributes to narrowing the evolutionary and intellectual gap between our ancestors and us.
- The anatomy, physiology and genetics of specific language impairment (SLI) do widen our knowledge of the biological foundations of language.
- New, non-invasive brain analysis methods (such as PET and fMRI) reveal a surprisingly dynamical neural foundation for human language.
- Linguistic theories come up with operations of which the biological rendering seems more straightforward.

Previously one of us argued that increased understanding in the relevant areas points in the direction of a "language amoeba" in the human brain [11]. The language amoeba is the neural activity pattern that essentially contributes to processing of linguistic information, including syntax. It is a dynamical manifestation of Chomsky's language organ, as it were. It finds its "habitat" in the developing human brain, whereas the brains of other primates apparently cannot sustain it. Why? Since the gap between other primates and us is not really wide, the genetic and correlated functional changes could not have been too numerous. What were the critical changes? We argued that an appropriate and rather widespread connectivity pattern of the immature human brain renders it a habitat for the emerging language amoeba. The required change presumably does not imply too many altered (probably regulatory) genes.

Worden (1995) in an insightful paper was able to deduce a "speed limit for evolution", which seems surprisingly uniform despite the fact that the relative contributions of component processes (mutation, recombination, selection and drift) are allowed to vary. He argues that the number of genes *specifically* associated with the "language organ" must be rather limited, which prompts one to think that it was not the number of genes, but their identity (i.e. mainly regulatory effects on the development of the human brain) that was peculiar during the evolution of natural language.

8.2. Biological Motivation

8.2.1. On the Genetic Background of Language

There is no disagreement that specific language impairment (SLI) is real. It is more contested how closely it is limited to, or rooted in, a specific grammatical impairment. The famous Gopnik (1990, 1999) case has been very stimulating because of its characterization as "feature-blind" dysphasia and its obvious genetic background (a single dominant allele). Whether other cognitive skills are also, or even primarily, affected, has been debated ever since (Vargha-Kadem et al., 1998). More evidence with other linguistic groups is accumulating, though (Dalalakis, 1990; Rose & Royle, 1999; Tomblin & Pandich 1999). A study (Van der Lely et al., 1998), sadly without genetics, claims to demonstrate that grammatically limited SLI does exist in "children" (although only one child is analysed in the paper!).

It is worth calling attention to the fact that the genetics of human cognitive skills is a notoriously difficult problem. One common reason is that usually the clinical characterizations are not sufficient as descriptions of phenotypes (Flint, 1999). A consensus seems to emerge that the genes involved are so-called "liability genes" that, when present in the right allelic form, significantly enhance the probability of developing the respective cognitive skills.

Even if some of our linguistic endowment is innate, there may not be genetic variation for the trait in normal people, just as normal people have ten fingers. In contrast, our linguistic capacity may be like height: whereas all people have height, there are quantitative differences in normal people. To be sure, children as well as adults differ in their linguistic skills; the question is how much this variation is accounted for by genes.

Surveying many studies Stromswold (2001) concluded that twin concordance rates have been significantly higher for monozygotic twins than for dizygotic twins. Twins are concordant for a trait if both express the trait or neither expresses it. Twins are discordant for a trait if one exhibits the trait and the other does not. If the concordance rate for language disorders is significantly greater for monozygotic than dizygotic twins, this suggests that genetic factors play a role in language disorders such as dyslexia and specific language impairment (SLI). The concordance rates for written and spoken language disorders are similar. For both written-language and spoken-language disorders, mean and overall concordance rates were approximately 30 percentage higher for monozygotic twins than for dizygotic twins, with genetic factors accounting for between one-half and two-thirds of the written and spoken language abilities of language-impaired people. In studies of normal twins, depending on the aspect of language being tested, between one-quarter and one-half of the variance in linguistic performance was attributable to genetic factors. People have been tested on phonological short-term memory, articulation, vocabulary, and morphosyntactic tasks. It seems that different genes may be responsible for the variance in different components and language and that some genetic effects may be language-specific.

The sum of all genetic effects is usually not much greater than 50% for various aspects of cognition (Stromswold, 2001). Most individual genes are expected to have small effects. Candidate genes affect functions including the cholinergic receptor, episodic memory, dopamine degradation, forebrain development, axonal growth cone guidance, and the serotonin receptor. It is a great problem that cognitive skills are likely to have been at least in part inadequately parsed, thus so-called intermediate phenotypes with a clearer genetic background should be sought. By this token schizophrenia as such does not exist; rather, different genes may go wrong and the symptoms such as hallucinations are emergent outcomes (Goldberg & Weinberger, 2004). The situation may be similar to that of geotaxis in *Drosophila*, where the individual involvement of different genes that collectively determine this capacity is counterintuitive (Toma et al., 2002).

Researchers have called attention to the fact that not only FoxP2, but also FoxP1 is expressed in functionally similar brain regions in songbirds and humans that are involved in sensorimotor integration and skilled motor control (Teramitsu et al., 2004). Moreover, differential expression of FoxP2 in avian vocal learners is correlated with vocal plasticity (Haesler et al., 2004). Mice, like man, have also two copies of the Foxp2 gene. If only one of them is affected in mice, the pups are severely affected in the ultrasonic vocalization upon separation from their mother. This suggests a role of this gene is social communication across different species. The Purkinje cells in the cerebellum are affected in the pups (Shu et al., 2005). Determination of the expression pattern in the developing mouse and human brain is consonant with these investigations: regions include the cortical plate, basal ganglia, thalamus, inferior olives and cerebellum. Impairments in sequencing of movement and procedural learning thus may be behind the linguistic symptoms in humans (Lai et al., 2003).

We think a key issue is the biologically motivated dissection of the language faculty. Put differently, what are the intermediate phenotypes composing language? This question cannot be answered, we believe, without an appropriate formulation of aspects of language. Thus linguistic theories must ultimately be biologically constrained. A good start in this direction may be Luc Steels' fluid construction grammar (Steels & DeBeule, 2006; DeBeule & Steels, 2005).

8.2.2. Localization of Language

Analyses of neural activity during the performance of cognitive tasks have become a growth industry. Their sensitivity has increased over the years. These methods are increasingly applied to the recording of brain activity during linguistic performance.

The recognition that neural localization of language can be plastic is now widely known (Nobre et al., 1997; Neville & Bavelier, 1998; Musso et al., 1999). Studies of brain injury revealed that damage to the left hemisphere before a critical period is not for life: the right hemisphere can take over the necessary functions (Müller et al., 1999). This does not contradict the finding that in normal people Broca's area does seem specialized for syntax (Embick et al., 2000).

It thus seems that the common left-hemisphere localization of language is just the most likely outcome when there is no genetic or epigenetic disturbance. What is more, cortical and subcortical areas both contribute to processing of language; reward systems and motor control provided by basal ganglia and the cerebellum seem to be critical components of our language faculty (Lieberman, 2002). PET studies have revealed a truly shocking feature of language development: the localization of linguistic processing shifts during normal ontogenesis. The outcome in "normal" people is also highly variable.

Analysis of a particularly interesting genetic syndrome, called Williams syndrome, also reveals surprisingly dynamical manifestations during ontogenesis. Whereas affected children seem to be bad at language and good with numbers, adults perform the other way round (Paterson et al., 1999). The classical characterization of the disease was based on adult performance.

The conclusions that we can draw from brain studies are the following:

- Localization of language is not fully genetically determined: even large injuries can be tolerated before a critical period.
- Language localization to certain brain areas is a highly plastic process, both in its development and its end result.
- It does seem that a surprisingly large part of the brain can sustain language: there are (traditionally recognized) areas that seem to be most commonly associated with language, but by no means are they exclusive, either at the individual or the population level, during either normal or impaired ontogenesis.
- Whereas a large part of the human brain can sustain language, no such region exists in apes.
- Language processing has a distributed character.

8.2.3. Brain Developmental Genetics and Plasticity

It is instructive too look at the evolutionary patterns of the sensory neocortex in mammals (Krubitzer & Kass, 2005). Auditory, somatosensory and visual fields (continuous brain tissue regions) have changed in location and size in different species. Fields can change in absolute and relative size, and in number. Connections of cortical fields can also change. Such alterations can be elicited by manipulation of either the peripheral morphology or activity, or that of the expression level of certain genes. Phenotypic within-species variation can be extremely broad; little is known about the relative magnitude of the genetic part of this variation, however. A good example of genetic influence is the variation in the cortical area map of inbred mice, reflecting strain identity (Airey et al., 2005).

Evolution of the vertebrate brain has produced an increase in cortical size, and an elaboration of the cortical circuit diagram (Hill & Walsh, 2005). Importantly, cortical layers II and IIIb, IIIc of the chimp differ from layers IIa, IIb and IIIa, IIIb and IIIc, respectively, in humans.

Despite the high overall similarity of the chimp and human genome, there are about 35 million nucleotide differences, and about 5 million indels, and several chromosomal rearrangements (Li & Saunders, 2005). In agreement with some expectations (Szathmáry, 2001), it seems that protein evolution by amino acid substitutions has *not* predominantly contributed significantly to the establishment of brain-specific human adaptations (Nielsen et al., 2005). In contrast to protein sequences, accelerated brain evolution in humans is more strongly reflected by an increase in gene expression levels, although a small subset of neural genes have been under positive selection. For example, the FOXP2 gene has undergone a selective sweep. Importantly, genes causing microcephaly have also been targets of positive selection, and the same genes are implicated in the formation of the upper (II and III) cortical layers also (Li & Saunders, 2005).

A tentative conclusion, based on "rewired" ferrets and three-eyed frogs, is that layers form independently of patterned input, but also that instructive electrical signals play a crucial role in fine network development, also affecting intracortical connections (Sur & Learney, 2001).

The high plasticity of the brain is consonant with the finding that the transcriptomes of the prefrontal cortex, Broca's area, the anterior cingulate cortex, and the primary visual cortex differ less within individuals than each of these regions differ between individuals. Yet, the methods are not sensitive enough to detect differential expression of certain cells within a given region; it is therefore possible that gene expression changes in certain cells may have been involved in language acquisition. The overall gene expression patterns are very similar within the human and the chimpanzee brain. Transcriptome data are consistent with the assertion that when human-specific cognitive abilities arose, they largely recruited pre-existing brain structures that already carried the appropriate cytoarchitecture as well as underlying molecular functions for the novel functions (Khaitovich et al., 2004).

Genetically determined patterning of parts of the brain follows mechanisms well-known from conventional developmental studies. For example, during the formation of the retionotopic map, axons from the retinal ganglion cells find their targets in the tectum as a result of matching between two receptor/ligand pairs (Schmitt et al., 2006), both expressed according to (altogether four) gradients, (two in the eye and two in the tectum).

8.2.4. Brain Epigenesis and Gene-Language Coevolution

It has to be admitted that on the whole we do not understand how the brain works. Nevertheless, some crucial elements seem to emerge. One is that development of the normal brain is enormously plastic, even though the power of genetic factors is obvious. One classic example is that in the same brain areas of identical twins the two hemispheres of the same individual resemble each other more closely than the same hemispheres in the two people (Changeux, 1983).

Another insight is that a tremendous amount of variation and selection is going on during brain ontogenesis. This is a Darwinian-type process, no doubt.

As the psychologist William James recognized a long time ago, natural selection of heritable variation is the only known force that can lead to adaptations, so let's apply it to brain ontogenesis and problem-solving as well (James thought that even learning is a result of selection of variation within the brain). There are several expositions that all regard the brain, one way or the other, as a "Darwin machine" (Calvin & Bickerton 2000). Here we stick to the formulation by Changeux (1983), because we think this is the most relevant to the language problem. According to this view, the functional microanatomy of the adult cortex is the result of the vastly surplus initial stock of synapses and their selective elimination according to functional criteria (performance).

We have just learnt in the previous section that a very large part of the human brain can process linguistic information, including syntactical operations. This means that there is no fixed macro-anatomical structure that is exclusively dedicated to language, but the micro-anatomical structure *must* be appropriate, otherwise it could not sustain language. This further suggests that there is some *statistical connectivity feature* of a large part of the human brain that renders is suitable for linguistic processing. From the selectionist perspective there are three options: the initial variation in synaptic connectivity is novel; the means of selection on functional criteria is novel; or both. Maybe both component processes are different in the relevant human brain areas, and we do not dare to speculate about their relative importance.

This idea must be seen in close connection to the one presented by Rapoport (1990) about the coevolution of brain and cognition. The traditional view is the so-called bottom-up mechanism: that a genetic change of some neural structure is subjected to selection and, based on its performance, it either does spread or it does not. There is, however, a so-called top-down mechanism, which could have more significantly contributed to the evolution of human cognitive skills, including, especially we argue, language. The crucial idea is as follows:

- Due to the plasticity in brain development, enhanced demands on a certain brain region lead to less synaptic pruning (a known mechanism).
- Less synaptic pruning is assumed to lead to more elaborate (and more adaptive) performance.
- Any genetic change contributing to the growth of the brain area thus affected will be favoured by natural selection.

There are two important connections that must be pointed out. First (observed by Rapoport himself), the top-down mechanism is a more detailed exposition of the late Allan Wilson's idea (Wyles, Kunkel & Wilson, 1983). Thus an increased brain, due to its more complex performance, alters the selective environment (in social animals composed of conspecifics to a great extent), which selects for an even larger brain, and so on. Second, and perhaps more important, this mechanism is also a neat example of a Baldwin effect (or genetic assimilation), when "learning guides evolution". As Deacon (1997) pointed out, it is trickier to apply the idea of genetic assimilation to language than usually thought.

The reason for this is that the performed behaviour must be sufficiently long lasting and uniform in the population. It is thus hard to imagine how specific grammatical rules, for example, could have been genetically assimilated. This point is well taken, but here we speak of a different thing: the genetic assimilation of a general processing mechanism that is performed by virtue of the connectivity of the underlying neural structures.

Our claim is that the most important, and largely novel, faculty selected for was the ability of the networks to process syntactical operations on symbols that are part of a semantically interwoven network. The specific hypothesis is that linguistically competent areas of the human brain have a statistical connectivity pattern that renders them especially suitable for syntactical operations. In conclusion, we think that

- The origin of human language required genetic changes in the mechanism of the epigenesis in large parts of the brain.
- This change affected statistical connectivity patterns and dynamical development of the neural networks involved.
- Due to the selectionist plasticity of brain epigenesis, coevolution of language and the brain resulted in the genetic assimilation of syntactical processing ability as such.

An intriguing possible example of gene-culture coevolution has recently been raised by Bufill and Carbonell (2004). They call attention to a number of facts. First, human brain size did not increase in the past 150,000 years, and it did even decrease somewhat in the last 35,000 years. Second, a new allele of the gene for apolipoprotein E originated sometime between 220,000 and 150,000 years ago. This allele improves synaptic repair (Teter et al., 2002). The original form entails a greater risk of Alzheimer disease and a more rapid, age-related decline in general (Raber et al., 2000). More importantly, ApoE4 impairs hippocampal plasticity and interferes with environmental stimulation of synaptogenesis and memory in transgenic mice (Levi et al., 2003). Interestingly, the ancestral allele decreases fertility in men (Gerdes et al., 1996). The facts taken together indicate, but do not prove, a role in enhanced synaptogenesis in a period when syntactically complex language is thought to have originated. More evidence like this would be welcome in the future, since one such case can at best be suggestive.

8.2.5. The Origin of Language: A Difficult Transition?

Some major transitions in evolution (such as the origin of multicellular organisms or that of social animals) occurred a number of times, whereas others (the origin of the genetic code, or language) seem to have been unique events (Maynard Smith & Szathmáry, 1995). One must be cautious with the word 'unique', however. Due to a lack of the 'true' phylogeny of all extinct and extant organisms, one can give it only an operational definition (Szathmáry, 2003). If all the extant and fossil species, which possess traits due to a particular transition, share a last common ancestor after that transition, then the transition is said to be unique.

Obviously, it is quite possible that there have been independent "trials", as it were, but we do not have comparative or fossil evidence for them. What factors can lead to "true" uniqueness of a transition? A) The transition is variation-limited. This means that the set of requisite genetic alterations has a very low probability. "Constraints" operate here in a broad sense. B) The transition is selection-limited. This means that there is something special in the selective environment that can favour the fixation of otherwise not really rare variants. Abiotic and biotic factors can both contribute to this limitation. For example (Maynard Smith, 1998), a single mutation in the haemoglobin gene can confer on the coded protein a greater affinity for oxygen: yet such a mutation got fixed in some animals living at high altitudes only (such as the lama or the barred goose, the latter migrating over the Himalayas at an altitude of 9000 m).

There are interesting sub-cases for both types of limitation. For (A), one can always enquire about the time-scale. "Not enough time" means that given a short evolutionary time horizon, the requisite variations have a very low probability indeed, but this could change with a widened horizon. An interesting sub-case of (B) is "pre-emption", meaning that the traits resulting from the transitions act via a selective overkill, and sweep through the biota so quickly that further evolutionary trials are competitively suppressed. The genetic code could be a case in point.

It is hard to assess at the moment why language is unique. Even the "not enough time" case could apply, which would be amusing. But pre-emption, due to the subsequent cultural evolution that language has triggered, may render further trials very difficult indeed. Let us point out, however, yet another consideration that indicates that language could be variation-limited in a deeper sense.

The habitat of the language amoeba is a large, appropriately connected neural network: most of the information processing within the network elaborates on information coming from other parts of the network. There is a special type of processing likely to be required: that of hierarchically embedded syntactic structures. We see the following difficulties (Szathmáry, 2001):

- Neural networks contain a large number of cycles: syntactic structures of language are tree-like. It seems difficult not to process large trees without getting into loops.
- Overproduction of initial synapses or decreased pruning, both implied in the origin of language, may easily lead to "solipsist" network dynamics, with two consequences: (i) the activity of the network is detached more than optimally from external sources of information; (ii) exaggerated internal processing leads to too much "internal talking": linguistic processing for its own sake.

8.2.6. What Can a Modeller Do?

Motivated by the surveyed observation, the modeller also would like to get a handle on the language problem. Clearly, purely linguistic modelling or the application of unnatural neural algorithms is not enlightening for a biologist. Experimentation is fine, except that there are severe (and understandable) practical and ethical constraints on physiological and genetic experiments of primates, including humans. Hence *in vivo* experiments and field observations should be complemented by an *in silico* approach. Such an approach should ideally be based on the distillation of available biological knowledge, as presented above. The modelling framework must be flexible enough to accommodate the necessary genetic and neural details; with the complication that 'necessary' depends on the actual tasks and cannot always be set in advance. Such a flexible approach cannot be based on an elegant but limited analytic model: rather, a flexible simulation platform is needed, which will be presented in the next section.

8.3. Evolutionary Neurogenetic Algorithm (ENGA)

We have developed a software framework called Evolutionary Neurogenetic Algorithm (ENGA in short) which offers researchers a fine control over biological detail in their simulations. Our original intent was to create software with much potential for variability. That is, we wanted a piece of software which is general enough to allow for a wide range of experimentation but appears as a coherent system and does not fall apart into a loosest of unrelated pieces of code. This required careful specification and design; especially in partitioning it into modules and the specification of interfaces in a programme that has grown to about 90,000 lines of C++ code. In such a short communication it is impossible to acknowledge all researchers of all important input fields to this paper. We have been especially influenced by evolutionary robotics, such as the work by Baldassare et al., (2003), and by the evolutionary approach to neuronal networks with indirect encoding by Rolls and Stringer (2000). Our model is a recombinant of these approaches, with some key new elements, such as topographical network architecture.

The software is organized into packages that are built upon each other, i.e. there is a dependency hierarchy between them. This gives the architecture a layered nature so that lower modules do not know about the existence of higher modules. The most important packages and their dependencies are shown in Figure 8.1. Layered design allows easy modifiability of higher levels without the need to modify lower levels. Moreover, each layer exposes an interface that can be used by any client, even those deviating from the original purpose of simulating evolution of embodied communicating agents. The genetic module for example can be used in any evolutionary computation, not only those evolving artificial neural networks. We may as well talk about a multilevel software framework consisting of several modules that can be used individually or in combination with others to produce various kinds of evolutionary and neural computation related simulations. In the following sections individual packages are described in more detail.

Below we provide a brief enumeration of the supposedly most important properties of neuronal networks, genetic codes and development processes. This enumeration is far from complete but we have taken it into account when designing our system.

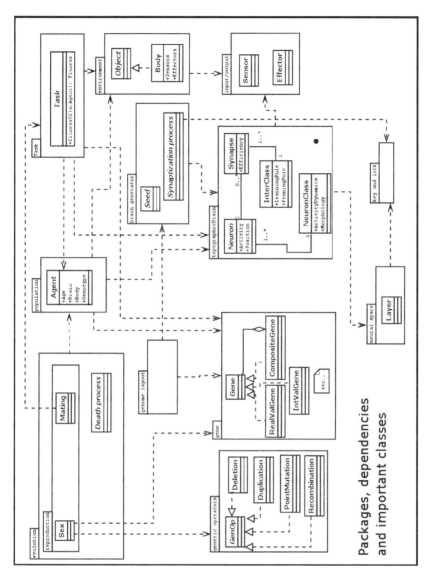

FIGURE 8.1. Architecture of the programme. Modularity of the different components is apparent.

8.3.1. Population and Agents

There is a population of agents. Agents have a genotype, a brain and a body. Bodies contain sensors and effectors and as such they provide the necessary input and output facilities for brains. Bodies reside in a simulated or real physical environment.

Death and reproduction processes. There is a death process operating in the population. It takes out members from the population forever. Parallel to the death process a reproduction process is going on, replenishing the population by allowing some members of the population to reproduce. It is the responsibility of the reproduction process to stabilize the size of the population (this is necessary because of finite computing resources). The reproduction process may include a mating process (if the reproduction is sexual), selecting pairs from the population.

Lifecycle of agents. Following the initialization of the population agents start their lifecycle. It begins with the birth phase in which a body and a brain are generated. Only brain generation is affected by the agent's genotype. Brain ontogenesis consists of two steps: neurogenesis and synaptogenesis. The actual life of an agent can be separated into two parts: childhood and adulthood. Learning takes place during both ages, but pruning is present only during childhood and only adult members of the population can reproduce. The separation between childhood and adulthood is dependent on the actual simulation and may be absent.

Tasks. In each simulation there is a task defined. Agents gain a so-called score (fitness) value according to their proficiency in the task. This fitness value can be used by death and reproduction processes (see Death-and-reproduction). Tasks can be solitary or social, reflecting the number of agents required to solve them. In case of social tasks the fitness of an agent may depend on the performance of its fellows as well. In an attempt to simulate the beginnings of communication, one sets tasks in such a way that successful signal transmission between agents becomes a fitness component (see below).

8.3.2. Gene and Genetic Operator Package

These strongly interacting packages are presented together. In general, information stored in a genotype is used during phenotype creation, i.e. during ontogenesis. A crucial feature of the package is indirect encoding, which simply reflects the biological fact that are by several orders of magnitude more neurons than genes: hence to assume that each cell or synaptic weight would have an associated gene (direct encoding) is completely out of question.

Genotype-phenotype mapping. It is usually a nontrivial task and decisions involving this process can significantly influence the performance and capabilities of a simulation. If we design a coding system, which is not open-ended, evolution will stop at the boundary of the genetic space. One way to create an open-ended coding is to use a marker-based encoding scheme that was inspired by the structure of the real genetic code (Fullmer & Miikkulainen, 1992). The other promising way is to encode information of the network in a tree structure (Zhang & Mühlenbein, 1993). Trees also have the advantage of storing information in a semantically structured way. Since virtually all mechanisms that translate a genotype to a phenotype in an artificial system exploit the underlying semantics of the genetic data, it is rational to store the data directly in the format it will be used. For all these reasons, in our system we chose a hierarchical tree-based representation.

Gene package. It defines and realizes this data structure. Atomic genes, residing at the leaf nodes in the tree, contain actual numeric or other elements of data, whereas composite genes aggregate subgenes (atomic or other composite genes). The major purpose of composite genes is therefore the semantic structuring of data. There are several types of atomic genes (integer gene, real gene, Boolean gene, bitvector gene, etc.), all corresponding to a particular elementary data type to be stored. Composite genes are also subdivided into subtypes, such as list genes, structure genes and option genes. Structure genes aggregate semantically cohesive subgenes, one per semantic subcategory. List genes can contain arbitrarily many subgenes with the same semantic meaning, all of which are expressed during ontogenesis. Option genes also contain a multitude of semantically interchangeable subgenes, only one of them to be expressed during ontogenesis, others being silent.

Genetic operators. These operators (point mutation, deletion, duplication, and recombination) work on this tree structure and alter the values of the nodes or change the structure of the tree. Mutation of atomic genes provides a random walk over a fixed dimensional genetic space. Complementarily to that, duplication and deletion of subgenes in a list gene ensures open-ended behaviour of the system, and is able to scale up the search space, if it is required in a new situation. To reduce the negative effect of genetic linkage (Calabretta et al., 2003), the use of recombination is necessary. Interpretation of recombination on a tree structure is not straightforward though, and careful specification of the expected behaviour of the recombination operator is inevitable. Currently two different implementations of recombination exist.

All the above genetic operators may or may not be included into a particular simulation run, and an optimal combination of these genetic operators depends on the given task. In this paper we are using PointMutation, Duplication, Deletion, SubTreeRecombination (where only semantically meaningful sub-trees recombine), in this order.

8.3.3. Neuronal Networks

Although our ultimate purpose is to generate neuronal networks from genotypes, still the TopographicBrain package (all features described in this section) is designed and implemented to be completely independent from the Gene and Genetic Operator package while put into the same layer of architecture. The two packages are linked together on a higher layer.

Ontogenesis of the brain. Development of the brain is controlled by the genotype in a highly indirect manner. By indirect we mean that no part of the genotype corresponds to individual neurons and synapses, and that only gross statistical properties of the brain are encoded in the genes. Individual brains are sampled from this statistical description. The neurogenesis phase goes on as follows. Neurons are situated in a layered topographic neural space mimicking real cortical layers but low-level biological mechanisms shaping the cortex such as concentration gradient dependence in neurogenesis are not present in the simulation. Instead, neuron classes define a probability density function over the neural space from which individual neuron soma positions are sampled. Neurons possess morphologies, i.e. there is some function over neural space describing their dendritic arborization. This morphology is applied to each neuron relative to its sampled soma position. Synaptogenesis exploits two mechanisms, just as in biology: a long-range one (called projections) and a subsequent short-range one (lock-and-key mechanism). Each neuron class has an associated list of projections. Projections are probability density functions over neural space, used in the following way. They can be defined either in absolute coordinates or in coordinates relative to a neuron's soma. When a neuron's efferents are to be determined, putative synapse locations are sampled from its projections (determined by its neuron class). Neurons having dendritic arborization near these putative locations become candidate efferents. Then the short-range mechanism selects from competing candidates at each synapse location. The short range lock-and-key mechanisms mimic the receptor/ligand-based binding mechanisms present in real synaptogenesis. Locks and keys are strings of 30bits. Every candidate postsynaptic neuron's lock is matched to the presynaptic neuron's key. Binding probability is then a decreasing function of the Hamming distance between the key and the lock. The complete ontogenetic algorithm is depicted in Figure 8.2

Topographicity. Unlike the majority of approaches to evolve neural networks we maintain the full topographic information of our networks, that is, neurons are situated in a layered neural space. Topographical information in a neural network can have a number of advantages. First, the interpretation of the structure can be easier. Second, developmental processes can model biological processes of neuron and synapse growth more accurately. Models, which acknowledge spatial information in biological systems yield various scale-free and small-world network attributes like the ones that are common in brain structure (Sporns et al., 2004).

Neuron classes. Neurons are classified. Neurons belonging to the same class share the same functional and morphological properties, whereas neurons belonging to different classes may differ in these properties. These properties are under genetic control in a full-blown simulation, that is, their actual values can be read from the genotype of the agent. The properties are:

- Probability distribution of neuron soma positions over a layered neural space.
- Activity model (e.g. rate code, or spiking).
- Activity dynamics.
- Activity initialization.
- Morphology.
- Projections, synaptization keys and locks.

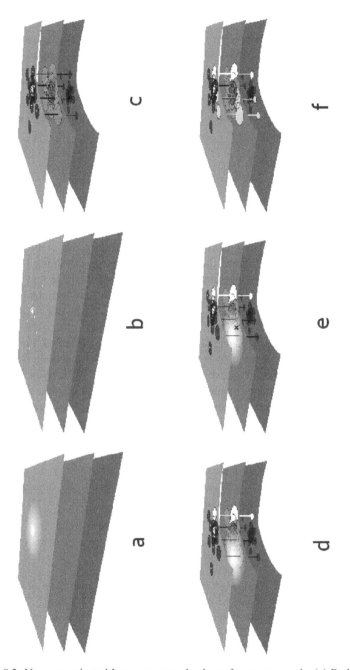

FIGURE 8.2. Neurogenesis and long-range mechanism of synaptogenesis. (a) Probability distribution of positions. (b) Sampled soma positions. (c) Morphology added to soma. (d) Projection (onto layer 2) from a presynaptic cell, marked with white. (e) Putative synapse location (X mark) is sampled from projection. (f) Candidate postsynaptic cells are determined.

Similarly, synapses belong to classes, too. We call them 'interclasses' because they represent functional properties that are shared by all synapses connecting a neuron belonging to a particular class A to a neuron belonging to class B (A and B can be in the same class). The properties inherent to interclasses are the following.

- Synapse model (e.g. weighted synapse with or without temporal delay)
- Synapse initialization.
- Learning rule.
- Pruning rule.

Neuron morphology. It has been suggested that more structured neuron morphology is required for more complex cortical functions (Elston et al., 2001). A more complex surface can facilitate more complex connection structure and if different neuron morphologies are encoded in the genome, the search process can change the network structure by changing morphology. Representation of neural networks in a topographic space allowed us to equip neurons with spatial dimensions. In our simulations neuron morphologies were only coarsely detailed and reduced to circles on each layer.

Potential for variation. Potential for variation arises within the boundaries of the core assumptions. For example, many kinds of activity models and dynamics can be imagined: rate code or spikes as activity model and summation of synaptic contributions fed through various transfer functions as activity dynamic. Of course, variations of core concepts are not necessarily compatible with each other. If, for example, a synapse model expects the presynaptic neuron activity to be rate coded then somehow it must be ensured that the presynaptic neuron class really defines its activity model as rate code. ENGA provides some mechanisms to enforce such compatibilities but eventually it is always the person designing the simulation who is responsible for the overall coherence.

8.4. Experiments: Testing ENGA

Once the modelling framework is ready, one should use it for investigations motivated by observations and questions in Sections 8.1 and 8.2. The ultimate goal of course is symbolic, grammatical language. Just as it is unlikely to have appeared in one jump in biology, one should not aim at seeing its emergence in the first *in silico* experiments either. We first test whether the agents can evolve the capacity to transmit and receives signals whose value (content) reflects on the environment, which in turn affects fitness.

Such a programme is necessarily under continuous development, testing, and application. One battles on several fronts simultaneously. It is natural to subject the algorithm to a number of simple tests that one can regard as benchmarks.

Other experiments qualify as genuine new research; and there is a grey zone in between. We first present a mere benchmark and then wander into the grey, and then possibly into the novelty zones in turn.

8.4.1. Mutual Information Maximization for a Single Neuron

We wanted to test ENGA's capabilities in solving well formed tasks that have a proven optimal solution, and see if the evolutionary search can come close to this optimum. The field of mutual information maximization in neural encoding of a stimulus (or stimuli) is a widely investigated one. Several studies have shown that information coming from various (auditory, visual, etc.) sources is encoded by living organism's neural system in such a way, that it minimizes information loss due to transcription of the original signal to the neural code. For example Laughlin reported that the large monopolar cell (LMC) in the visual system of the fly responds to contrast in a nearly optimal way, maximizing the mutual information between the contrast (the natural probability distribution of which is known) and the cell's membrane potential amplitude (Dubs, Laughlin & Srinivasan, 1981).

The encoding task we chose as a benchmarking test of ENGA's capabilities was deliberately simple, practically re-enacting the scenario described by Laughlin (see Appendix for parameter values). The search space of the genetic algorithm was reduced to parameters of the transfer function of a single neuron which received scalar input s from a predefined distribution. This distribution was a Gaussian with mean 0 and variance 5. There were 1000 agents in the population at every time-step, each having only one neuron. The activity of the neuron was described by a single scalar value. The activity dynamic to the neuron was input summation fed through a transfer function. There was no learning or pruning. The transfer function of the neuron of any agent could be either piecewise linear or a sigmoidal one (choice of transfer function type was under genetic control). Both transfer functions had a range between -1 and 1, and had two parameters under genetic control. Parameters of the trilinear function were the beginning and extent of the middle linear slope in the stimulus domain. The sigmoidal transfer function had its zero-crossing position and steepness coded by genetically determined parameters. Each agent's fitness was evaluated only once (immediately after ontogenesis) using the following protocol. One thousand samples were taken from the stimulus distribution and consecutively fed to the neuron as input. Before presenting an input, the neuron's activity was initialized and then updated (according to the activity dynamic using the particular transfer function) three times. After that the activity of the neuron was considered as the response to the presented stimulus, and stored together with the stimulus. After presentation of the last stimulus, mutual information was calculated on the stored stimulus-response pairs using a numeric, sample based calculus.

Under these conditions the fitness landscape was plotted in 3D as a function of the parameters for both types of transfer functions, and individual agents were indicated on the same plot as dots in their respective [parameter1, parameter2, fitness value] coordinates. We found that after a few hundred population dynamical updates, the overwhelming majority of the population gathered around the peak of the fitness landscape belonging to the sigmoidal transfer function (which allowed a higher fitness to be achieved than the trilinear). Thus, benchmarking of the algorithm was considered successful.

8.4.2. Games Setup

We have used simple 2×2 matrix games with one-way pre-play communication as test tasks: a coordination and a task-allocation game. There are two reasons we have chosen these games. First, because of their simplicity these scenarios are easy to implement. Second, these games are well studied in the economics literature, and it is shown both theoretically and empirically that (one-way) cost-free, pre-play communication (so called 'cheap talk') can resolve coordination problems in both coordination and task-allocation games (Cooper et al., 1992; Hurkens & Schlag, 1999). Thus it is reasonable to expect that our agents will evolve the use of signals under these scenarios.

List of games. To test further the flexibility of the neuronal architecture of our agents we have introduced two environments, which have an influence on the pay-off matrices. Accordingly we have three different scenarios:

1. Coordination game. Agents have to pick the same response, corresponding to the given environment to get high fitness. A pair of agents plays a coordination game in which they have to choose a given response conditional on the environment. (i) If both agents pick the correct response they both get a high reward; (ii) if only one of them picks the correct response then one gets a higher reward than the other; (iii) if both of them picks the wrong response then they both get low rewards.
2. Task-allocation game. Agents have to pick complementary responses to get high fitness. A pair of agents plays a task-allocation game in which they have to choose complementary responses to get high fitness. If they pick the same response they get low reward regardless of the environment.
3. Coordination or task-allocation depending on the environment. A pair of agents plays a coordination or a task-allocation game depending on the state of the environment. In case of $E(1)$ they play a task-allocation game, in case of $E(-1)$ they play a coordination

Steps of a game. Each game has the same plan:

1. A random partner is picked to play with the focal agent.
2. One of the agents out of the pair is picked as the signaller the other is the listener.

3. "Mother nature" picks the state of the environment (E(1) or E(−1)) with equal probability.
4. The signaller can see the state of the environment and gives signal that can have three states (S(1), S(0), or S(−1)).
5. The listener receives the signal.
6. Both agents make a decision (D(1), D(0), or D(−1)) independently from each other (i.e. they do not know what decision the other agent makes). Whether the listener takes the signal into account when making its decision depends on its brain activity.
7. Fitness of the agents determined by the state of the environment, and by their decisions according to the type of game they play (see Appendix for pay-off matrices).

Agent brains. Agents have five input/output neurons and they start with 10–30 interneurons (chosen from a uniform distribution) in this task. The input/output neurons are as follows:

1. Vision: this is the input neuron for the state of the environment, provided that the agent plays the role of the signaller. The listener receives a zero input on this neuron.
2. AudioIn: this is the input for the signal. The listener gets the value of the AudioOut neuron of the signaller. The signaller gets a zero input on this neuron.
3. AudioOut: this is the output neuron for the signal. The signaller receives the value of this neuron on the AudioIn input channel.
4. Decision: this is the output neuron for the decision. The value of this neuron determines the fitness gain of the given agent according to the pay-off matrix of the given game (see Appendix).

The connections between the input/output neurons and the interneurons are determined only indirectly by the genes and they are subject to all the developmental rules described in section 3.3. The genes coding for the number of interneurons are allowed to mutate during the simulations; as a result the number of interneurons, and of course their number of connections to the input/output neurons can vary from generation to generation.

Figure 8.6 depicts an agent with only with 2 interneurons which connects only the AudioIn and Decision input/output neurons. Conversely, Figure 8.7 depicts an agent with 15 interneurons with all the input/output neurons connected.

Steps of the Simulation. Agents engage in interactions according to the following scheme:

1. Each agent plays 100 games with randomly chosen partners. The environment is randomly chosen (E(1) or E(−1)).
2. Fitness values calculated according to the pay-off matrix of the given game (see Appendix).
3. Least fit 5 agents are killed.

4. Chance to reproduce is proportional to fitness. Two agents are picked because of sexual reproduction. The number of offspring is chosen from a Poisson distribution with a mean 5. Pairs of agents are picked to reproduce till 5 new agents born.
5. Return to step 1.

Parameter values are given in the Appendix.

8.4.3. Games Results

Our agents have achieved a better-than-random performance, in fact they have achieved maximum or near maximum fitness values in all scenarios (see Figure 8.3. and Figure 8.4; fitness of 1600 assuming 200 games played; higher than 1600 values are due to the fact that some agents played more than 200 games resulting from the randomness in choice of opponents) which suggests that they have managed to communicate sufficient amount of information to solve the task under question. Fitness values as a function of time are depicted for the task allocation and the coordination games in Figure 8.3 and 8.4, respectively. This suggestion turns out to be correct if we investigate the signals and decisions the agents make as a function of the environment. Figure 8.5. depicts these decisions as a function of time for one coordination game. As one can see agents roughly around the 250th turn settle down with the strategy E(1), S(1), DS(1), DL(1) and E(−1), S(−1), DS(−1), DL(−1) (where DS and DL denotes the decision of the signaller and listener respectively). The above strategy means that agents give S(1) when the environment is E(1), and both the listener and the signaller makes a decision D(1). Conversely, in the environment E(−1) the signaller gives S(−1) and both agent decides D(−1).

The topology of the evolved networks is noteworthy. Figure 8.6 and 8.7 depict an 'early', and an 'advanced' neuronal network taken at the 10th and at the 750th generation out of the population playing the coordination—task allocation game depending on the environment. As we can see selection had a profound effect on the topology. While the first network failed to make connections to the Decision neuron from the Vision neuron and thus is doomed to low fitness values, the later 'advanced' network utilizes both visual and audio input to determine the values of decision and signal outputs.

8.4.4. The Key Issue of Heritability

The central issue is whether one can find heritability of various traits of the simulated, evolved neuronal networks. If one maintains (as we do on the basis of biological evidence) that our language faculty has an innate basis, then it would be encouraging to see that various aspects of the communication ability of our evolved agents also have a genetic basis. Evidence cited in the Section 8.2 suggests that if our biomimetic, indirect encoding is successful; this should be the case. We have performed several different analyses of the networks, out of which we now present a few.

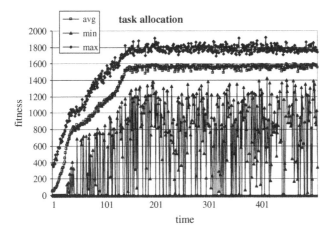

FIGURE 8.3. Highest, lowest and average fitness values as a function of time when agents played task allocation games. Fitness values are cumulative individual payoffs of all rounds of the game in the given generation.

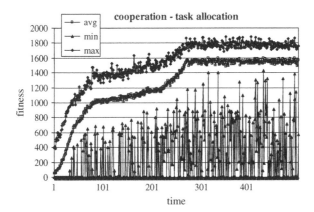

FIGURE 8.4. Highest, lowest and average fitness values as a function of time when agents played the coordination game. Fitness values are cumulative individual payoffs of all rounds of the game in the given generation.

Figure 8.8 compares structurally neuronal networks developed from unrelated genomes with those from a set of clones. Different, not closely related individuals were cloned (see Appendix for cloning), and their brains analysed. Because of indirect encoding (mimicking biological development), networks within a clone are expected to be different, but difference should be seen between clones as well. Figure 8.8 shows that indeed, clones characteristically differ from each other. Figure 8.9 shows that there is strong resemblance in the system between clonal offspring and their common founder, despite the fact that genomes have only a probabilistic influence of network development.

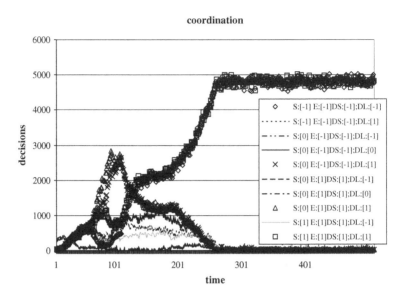

FIGURE 8.5. The decisions made by the agents during a coordination game as a function of time. Each data point represents the sum of the given type of decision made during the given turn. S(*), E(*), DS(*), DL(*) denotes the value of signal, the environment, the decision made by the signaller and the decision made by the receiver respectively. As one can see roughly after the 250th turn agents converged on a convention in which the signaller gives a signal corresponding to the environment and the listener heeds to this signal.

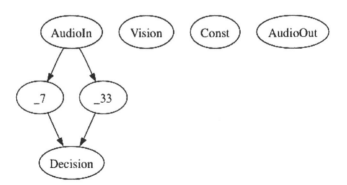

FIGURE 8.6. Topology of an early, incompetent neuronal network. Note that some of the input and output neurons are not even connected. Numbers indicate arbitrary neuronal identifiers. Input and output neurons are pre-defined, but their synapses develop. The Const neuron invariably gives output 1. Decision neuron takes the sum (S) of its inputs, and when $S \geq 1$, or $1 > S > 0$, or $S < 0$, it yields 1, S, and -1 as output, respectively. Const and Decision neurons are "written into" the network, but not their connections.

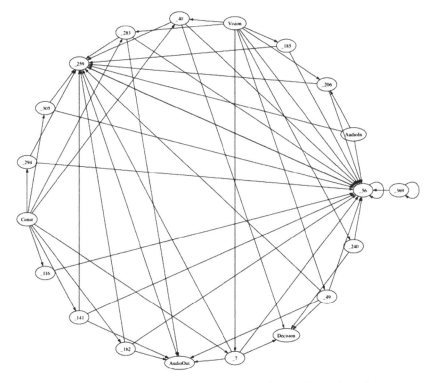

FIGURE 8.7. Topology of an evolved network. Conventions as in previous figure.

Heritability of the connections of the input/output neurons was calculated as described in the Appendix, section 5. The heritability values thus obtained are very high, as follows: h^2 (AudioIn) $= 0.8689$; h^2 (AudioOut) $= 0.8708$; h^2 (Const) $= 0.8696$; h^2 (Decision) $= 0.8123$; h^2 (Vision) $= 0.8428$. All values are highly significant. This is the final proof that ENGA works as we hoped: despite indirect encoding, there is hereditary variation between individual phenotypes on which simulated natural selection can act.

8.5. Discussion

The results of the games analysed in this paper suggest that the basic idea—the biomimetic approach—behind our neuro-genetic system is correct, and the highlighted design principles of the system are sufficient at least in this simple task. The other goal of the test was to prove that the developed software is working properly and is useful for scientific experimentation. The core of our neuro-genetic system is the stochastic ontogenetic process and the indirect tree-based coding behind it. Evolution of agents in these scenarios found the right solution in a relatively short period, and the length of the search time was

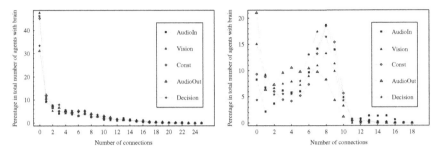

FIGURE 8.8. Frequency distribution of agents by the connection number of the five input/output neurons (AudioIn, AudioOut, Decision, Vision, Const). A sum of in and out connections (synapses) were counted on each input/output neuron in each brain (x axis). Symbols show the frequency of agents with the specific input/output neuron possessing exactly x connections in percentage of total number of agents with brain (i.e. those, that lacked neurons, or did not have any connections among them were considered as agents without brain, and were removed from the analysis). *Left* plot shows a totally random population of 2550 newborn agents, where agents without brain were removed, resulting in a total number of 1321 agents that possessed brains. *Right* plot shows a cloned population. 50 newborn agents (with brains, i.e. they all possess at least the five input/output neurons, and there is at least some connections among the neurons, thus the brain is not just present in the agent but is able to function as well) were cloned 50 times, hence a total of 2550 agents and 50 clone founders were present. Clones without brains were removed, resulting in a total number of 2497 agents with brain. Note that the brain topology does not change during the lifecycle of an agent after initial development, hence the age of the agents analysed is irrelevant.

proportional to the complexity of a particular game. The topology and size of the networks both changed in the simulations. It is important to emphasize that we have not taken advantage of any grossly unnatural (but sometimes very effective) algorithms such as back-propagation.

Our results show that indirect encoding and a genetically controlled but stochastic ontogenetic process together can provide an appropriate framework for evolving communicating agents in simple scenarios. Our next goal is to introduce our neuronal networks to more and more complicated selective scenarios, by which we hope to obtain better understanding of the evolution of, among other things, symbolic communication.

Explaining the evolution of human language is likely to remain a challenge for the coming decades. Currently, there is not a single theory that could sufficiently answer all the questions about uniqueness, selective pressure, and groundedness. Yet some theories do better than the average: these are the "tool making" (Greenfield, 1991) and "hunting" theories (Hewes, 1973). It might be a safe bet to say that some combination of these theories could provide a set of selective scenarios that would fit all of our criteria.

It is a striking fact that, although the different scenarios suggest all kinds of selective forces, none of these scenarios has been consistently implemented in a family of models. Given the limitations on experimentation on humans and

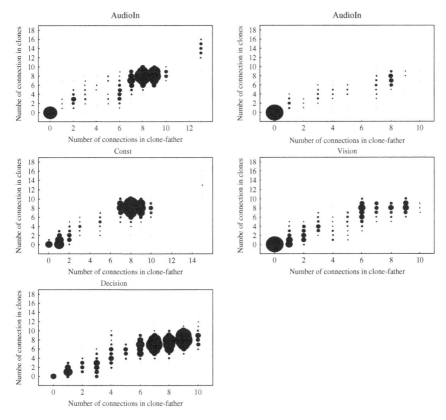

FIGURE 8.9. Scatter plots of agents by the connection number of the input/output neurons (AudioIn, AudioOut, Decision, Vision, and Const). Population consists of 50 clone founders, and 50 individuals for each founder (a total of 2550 agents). Agents without any neurons were removed, resulting 2497 agents with brain. A sum of in and out connections was counted on each input/output neuron in the brain of the founder (x axis), and in the brains of members in the clone-group (y axis). A disc shows that there is at least one clone member that has y number of connections on the actual input/output neuron where its founder had x connections on the same neuron. Radius of discs corresponds to the number of individuals with the same number of connections. Point distribution and bubble-size reveal a good correlation between a founder's brain and its clones' brains in case of all the five input/output neurons. Note that if the founder has zero connections on an input/output neuron, its clone members are distributed more closely to zero number of connection than in other cases (x ? 0).

chimps in all kinds of domains (neurobiology, genetics, etc.), one should really seriously consider implementing the different scenarios in various model-based settings. Ultimately, one should be able to re-enact the emergence of language in artificial worlds, many of which will probably involve robots (Steels, 2003). The reason for the latter statement is that embodiment offers a unique and probably indispensable way of grounding and somatosensory feedback (Nolfi & Floreano, 2002).

We cannot go into assessing the difficulties of such ambitious research projects, we just mention that the tasks that the agents will be subjected to imply a complicated fitness landscape, which is similar to climbing not a hill but a *staircase:* a good capacity for imitation is probably coevolving with the capacity of learning symbols (words), which then opens up the possibility for climbing to the first level of syntax (Jackendoff, 1992).

The only process that has solved the 'language problem' is evolution by natural selection. But there is no guarantee at all that just any kind of selection scenario, even if implemented *in silico,* will lead to the origin of such a faculty, partly due to the results of the analysis presented in this review, partly because of what is known as the 'no free lunches theorem' (Wolpert & Macready, 1997). Put simply, the latter says that the efficiency of an evolutionary search process is very much dependent on the problem. Putting constraints on the selective scenarios may constrain the search space to such an extent that simulated evolution will in fact be able to re-enact this fascinating evolutionary transition (Számadó & Szathmáry, 2006).

Acknowledgment. The authors thank Máté Lengyel, Luc Steels and Chrisantha Fernando for useful discussions. Partial support of this work has generously been provided by the National Office for Research and Technology (NAP 2005/KCKHA005) and the ECAGENTS project (http://ecagents.istc.cnr.it/). The ECAGENTS project is funded by the Future and Emerging Technologies programme (IST-FET) of the European Community under EU R&D contract IST-2003-1940. The information provided is the sole responsibility of the authors and does not reflect the Community's opinion. The Community is not responsible for any use that may be made of data appearing in this publication.

References

Airey, D.C., Robbins, A.I., Enzinger, K.M., Wu, F., Collins, C.E.: Variation in the cortical map of C57BL/6J and DBA/2J inbred mice predicts strain identity. BMC Neurosci. **6** (2005) 18

Baldassarre, G., Nolfi, S., Parisi, D.: Evolving mobile robots able to display collective behavior. Artif. Life **9** (2003) 255–267

Bickerton, D.: Language and Species. The Univ. of Chicago Press (1992)

Bufill, E., Carbonell, E.: Are symbolic behaviour and neuroplasticity an example of gene-culture coevolution (in Spanish)? Rev. Neurol. **39** (2004) 48–55

Caceres, M., Lachuer, J., Zapala, M.A., Redmond, J.C., Kudo, L., Geschwind, D.H., Lockhart, D.J., Preuss, T.M., Barlow, C.: Elevated gene expression levels distinguish human from non-human primate brains. Proc. Natl. Acad. Sci. USA **100** (2003) 13030–13035

Calabretta, R., Ferdinando, A.D., Wagner, G.P., Parisi, D.: What does it take to evolve behaviorally complex organisms? BioSystems **69** (2003) 245–262

Calvin, W.H., Bickerton, D.: Lingua ex Machina: Reconciling Darwin and Chomsky with the Human Brain. MIT Press, Cambridge (2000)

Changeux, J.-P.: L'Homme Neuronal. Librairie Arthème Fayard, Paris (1983)

Christiansen, M.H., Kirby, S.: Language evolution: consensus and controversies. Trends Cogn. Sci. **7** (2003) 300–307

Cooper, R., DeJong, D.V., Forshyte, R, Ross, T.W.: Communication in Coordination Games. Quart J Econ **107** (1992) 739–771

Dalalakis, J.E.: Morphological representation in specific language impairment: evidence from Greek word formation. Folia Phoniatr. Logop. 51 (1999) 20–35

Deacon, T.: The Symbolic Species. The coevolution of language and the brain. Norton, New York (1997)

De Beule, J., Steels, L.: Hierarchy in Fluid Construction Grammar. In Furbach U. (ed), Proceedings of KI-2005, Berlin: Springer-Verlag, Berlin (2005) 1–15

DeFelipe, J., Alonso-Nanclares, L., Arellano, J.I.: Microstructure of the neocortex: Comparative aspects. J. Neurocytol. 31 (2002) 299–316

Dubs, A., Laughlin, S.B., Srinivasan, M.V.: Single photon signals in fly photoreceptors and first order interneurones at behavioral threshold. J. Physiol. **317** (1981) 317–334

Elman, J.L., Bates, E., Johnson, M.H., Karmiloff-Smith, A., Parisi, D., Plunkett, K.: Rethinking Innateness. MIT Press, Cambridge (1996)

Elston, G.N., Benavides-Piccione, R., DeFelipe, J.: The Pyramidal Cell in Cognition: A Comparative Study in Human and Monkey. J. Neurosci.21 (2001) 1–5

Embick, D., Marantz, A., Miyashita, Y., O'Neil, W., Sakai, K.L.: A syntactic specialization for Broca's area. Proc. Natl. Acad. Sci. USA 97 (2000) 6150–6154

Enard, W., Przeworski, M., Fisher, S.E., Lai, C.S.L., Victor Wiebe, V., Kitano, T., Monaco, A.P. & Paabo, S.: Molecular evolution of FOXP2, a gene involved in speech and language. Nature **418** (2002) 869–872.

Everett, D.: Cultural Constraints on Pirahã Grammar. Curr.Anthropol. 46 (2005) 621–646

Fitch, W.T., Hauser, M.D.: Computational constraints on syntactic processing in nonhuman primates. Science 303 (2004) 377–380

Flint, J.: The genetic basis of cognition. Brain 122 (1999) 2015–2031

Fullmer, B., Miikkulainen, R.: Using marker-based genetic encoding of neural networks to evolve finite-state behaviour. In Varela, F. J., Bourgine, P. (eds): Toward a Practice of Autonomous Systems: Proceedings of the First European Conference on Artificial Life. MIT Press, Cambridge, MA (1992) 255–262

Gerdes, L.U., Gerdes, C., Hansen, P.S., Klausen, I.C., Faergman, O.: Are men carrying the apolipoprotein ε4– or ε2 allele less fertile than ε3 ε3 genotypes? Hum. Genet. **98** (1996) 239–242

Goldberg, T.E., Weinberger, D.R.: Genes and the parsing of cognitive processes. Trends Cogn. Sci. **8** (2004) 325–335

Gopnik, M.: Feature-blind grammar and dysphasia. Nature **344** (1990) 715

Gopnik, M.: Familial language impairment: more English evidence. Folia Phoniatr. Logop. **51** (1999) 5–19

Greenfield, P.M.: Language, tool use and the brain: the ontogeny and phylogeny of hierarchically organized sequential behaviour. Behav. Brain Sci. **14** (1991) 531–595

Haesler, S., Wada, K., Morrisey, E.E., Lints, T., Jarvis, E.D., Scharff, C.: FoxP2 expression in avian vocal learners and non-learners. J. Neurosci. **24** (2004) 3164–3175

Hauser, M.D., Chomsky, N. Fitch, W. T.: The faculty of language: What is it, who has it, and how did it evolve? Science 298 (2002) 1569–1579

Hewes, G.: Primate Communication and the Gestural Origin of Language. Current Anthropology. **14** (1973) 5–25

Hill, R.S. & Walsh, C.A.: Molecular insights into human brain evolution. Nature **437** (2005) 64–67

Hinton, G.E., Nowlan, S.J.: How learning can guide evolution. Complex Systems **1** (1987) 495–502

Hockett, C. F.: The origin of speech. Sci. Am. 203 (1960) 88–111

Hurkens S., Schlag, K.H. Communication, Coordination, and Efficiency in Evolutionary One-Population Models. Universitat Pompeu Fabra Department of Economics (1999) Working Paper No. 387

Jackendoff, R.S.: Languages of the Mind. MIT Press, Cambridge MA (1992)

Jeffery, K.J., Reid, I.C.: Modifiable neuronal connections: An overview for psychiatrists. Am. J. Psychiatry **154** (1997) 156–164

Johnston, M.V.: Developmental disorders of activity dependent neuronal plasticity. Ind. J. Pediat. **68** (2001) 423–426

Kandel, E.R., Schwartz, J.H. & Jessell, T.M.: Principles of Neural Science. Fourth Edition. McGraw-Hill, New York (2000)

Khaitovich, P., Muetzel, B., She, X., Lachmann, M., Hellmann, I., Dietzsch, J., Steigele, S., Do, H.H., Weiss, G., Enard, W., Heissig, F., Arendt, T., Nieselt-Struwe, K., Eichler, E.E., Paabo, S.: Regional patterns of gene expression in human and chimpanzee brains. Genome Res. **14** (2004) 1462–73

Krubitzer, L. & Kaas, J.: The evolution of the neocortex in mammals: how is phenotypic diversity generated? Curr. Op. Neurobiol. **15** (2005) 444–453

Lai, C.S.L., Gerelli, D., Monaco, A.P. Fisher, S.E., Copp, A.J.: FOXP2 expression during brain development coincides with adult sites of pathology in a severe speech and language disorder. Brain 126 (2003) 2455–2462

Levi, O., Jongen-Relo, A.L., Feldon, J., Roses, A.D., Michaelson, D.M.: ApoE4 impairs hippocampal plasticity isoform-specifically and blocks the environmental stimulation of synaptogenesis and memory. Neurobiol. Disease **13** (2003) 273–282

Li, W.-H., Saunders, M.A.: The chimpanzee and us. Nature **437** (2005) 50–51

Lieberman, P: On the nature and evolution of the neural bases of human language. Am. J. Phys. Anthropol. **35** (2002) 36–62

Marcus, G.F.: Rethinking eliminative connectionism. Cogn. Psychol. **37** (1998) 243–282

Marcus, G.F., Fisher, S. E.: FOXP2 in focus: what can genes tell us about speech and language. Trends Cogn. Sci. **7** (2003) 257–262

Maynard Smith, J.: Evolutionary Genetics. Oxford Univ. Press (1998)

Maynard Smith, J., Szathmáry, E. The Major Transitions in Evolution. Freeman, Oxford (1995)

Musso, M., Weiller, C., Kiebel, S., Müller, S.P., Bülau, P. Rijntjes, M.: Training-induced brain plasticity in aphasia. Brain **122** (1999) 1781–1790

Müller, R.-A., Rothermel, R.D., Behen, M.E., Muzik, O., Chakraborty, P.K. & Chugani, H.T.: Language organization in patients with early and late left-hemisphere lesion: a PET study. Neuropsychol. **37** (1999) 545–557

Neville, H. J., Bavelier, D.: Neural organization and plasticity of language. Curr. Op. Neurobiol. **8** (1998) 254–258

Nielsen, R., Bustamante, C., Clark, A.G., Glanowski, S., Sackton, T.B. et al.: A scan for positively selected genes in the genomes of humans and chimpanzees. PLoS Biol. **3**(6) (2005) e170

Nobre, A.C., Plunkett, K.: The neural system of language: structure and development. Curr. Op. Neurobiol. 7 (1997) 262–268

Nolfi, S., Floreano, D.: Synthesis of autonomous robots through evolution. Trends Cogn. Sci. 6 (2002) 31–37

Paterson, S.J., Brown, J.H., Gsödl, M.K., Johnson, M.H., Karmiloff-Smith, A.: Cognitive modularity and genetic disorders. Science 286 (1999) 2355–2357

Pica, P., Lemer, C., Izard, V., Dehaene, S.: Exact and approximate arithmetics in an Amazonian indigene group. Science 306 (2004) 499–503

Pinker, S., Bloom, P.: Natural language and natural selection. Behav. Brain Sci. 13 (1990) 707–784.

Pinker, S., Jackendoff, R.: The faculty of language: What's special about it? Cognition 95 (2005) 201–236

Premack, D.: Is language the key to human intelligence? Science303 (2004) 318–320

Preuss, T.M.: Taking the measure of diversity: Comparative alternatives to the model-animal paradigm in cortical neuroscience. Brain Behav. Evol. 55 (2000) 287–299

Raber, J., Wong, D., Yu, G., Buttini, M., Mahley, R.W., Pitas, R.E., Mucke, L.: Apolipoprotein E and cognitive performance. Nature 404 (2000) 353–353

Rapoport, S.I.: How did the human brain evolve? A proposal based on new evidence from in vivo brain imaging during attention and ideation. Brain Res. Bull. 50 (1990) 149–165

Rolls, E.T., Stringer, S.M.: On the design of neural networks in the brain by genetic evolution. Prog Neurobiol 61 (2000) 557–579

Rose, Y., Royle, P.: Uninflected structure in familial language impairment: evidence from French. Folia Phoniatr. Logop. 51 (1999) 70–90

Schmitt, A.M., Shi, J., Wolf, A. M., Lu, C.-C., King, L.A., Zou, Y.: Wnt-Ryk signalling mediates medial-lateral retinotectal topographic mapping. Nature 439 (2006) 31–37

Senghas, A., Kita S., Özyürek, A.: Children creating properties of language: Evidence from an emerging sign language in Nicaragua. Science 305 (2004) 1779–1782

Shu, W., Cho, J.Y., Jiang, Y., Zhang, M., Weisz, D., Elder, G.A., Schmeidler, J., De Gasperi, R., Sosa, M.A., Rabidou, D., Santucci, A.C., Perl, D., Morrisey, E., Buxbaum, J.D.: Altered ultrasonic vocalization in mice with a disruption in the Foxp2 gene. Proc Natl Acad Sci USA 102 (2005) 9643–9648

Sporns, O., Chialvo, D.R., Kaiser, M., Hilgetag, C.C.: Organization, development and function of complex brain networks. Trends Cogn. Sci. 8 (2004) 418–425

Steels, L.: Evolving grounded communication for robots. Trends Cogn. Sci. 7 (2003) 308–312

Steels, L., De Beule, J.: Unify and Merge in Fluid Construction Grammar. forthcoming, 2006.

Stromswold, K.: The heritability of language: a review and metaanalysis of twin, adoption, and linkage studies. Language 77 (2001) 647–723

Sur, M., Learney, C.A.: Development and plasticity of cortical areas and networks. Nat. Rev. Neurosci. 2 (2001) 251–262

Számadó, S., Szathmáry, E.: Language evolution: competing selective scenarios. Trends Ecol. Evol. Submitted (2006)

Szathmáry, E.: Origin of the human language faculty: the language amoeba hypothesis. In (J. Trabant & S. Ward, Eds.): New Essays on the Origin of Language. Mouton/de Gruyter, Berlin/New York (2001) 41–51.

Szathmáry, E.: Cultural processes: the latest major transition in evolution. In: L. Nadel (ed.) Encyclopedia of Cognitive Science Nature Publishing Group, Macmillan, London (2003)

Teramitsu, I., Kudo, L.C., London, S.E., Geschwind, D.H., White, S.A. Parallel FoxP1 and FoxP2 expression in songbird and human brain predicts functional interaction. J. Neurosci. 24 (2004) 3152–3163

Teter, B., Xu, P., Gilbert, J.R., Roses, A.D., Galasko, D., Cole, M.D.: Defective neuronal sprouting by human apolipoprotein E4 is a gain-of-negative function. J. Neurosci. Res. **68** (2002) 331–336

Toma, D.T. et al.: Identification of genes involved in *Drosophila melanogaster* geotaxis, a complex behavioral trait. Nat. Genet. **31** (2002) 349–353

Tomblin, J.B., Pandich, J.: Lessons from children with specific language impairment. Trends Cog. Sci. **3** (1999) 283–285

Van der Lely, H.J.K., Rosen, S., McClelland, A.: Evidence for a grammar-specific deficit in children. Curr. Biol. **8** (1998) 1253–125.

Vargha-Kadem, F., Watkins, K.E., Price, C.J., Ashburner, J., Alcock, K.J., Connelly, A., Frackowiak, R.S.J., Friston, K.J., Pembrey, M.E., Mishkin, M., Gadian, D.G. Passingham, R.E.: Neural basis of an inherited speech and language disorder. Proc. Natl. Acad. Sci. USA **95** (1998) 12695–12700

Wolpert, D.H., Macready, W.G.: No Free Lunch Theorems for Optimization, IEEE Transactions on Evolutionary Computation **1** (1997) 67–82

Worden, R.P.: A speed limit for evolution. J. theor. Biol. **176** (1995) 137–152

Wyles, J.S., Kunkel, J.G., Wilson, A.C.: Birds, behaviour, and anatomical evolution. Proc. Natl. Acad. Sci. USA **80** (1983) 4394–4397

Zhang, B., Mühlenbein, H.: Genetic programming of minimal neural nets using Occam's razor. Proc. of the Fifth Int. Conf. on Genetic Algorithms (1993) 342–349

Appendix

1. Parameter Settings for Benchmark (Encoding Task) Simulations

Population dynamics and games.

- Population size: 1000.
- Time steps: 1000
- Number of games played per time step per agent: 100
- Death process: least fit (2).
- Mating process: elitist
- Number of offspring: Poisson with Lambda=5.

Neurobiological parameters.

- Number of layers: fixed [1]
- Number of neuron classes: fixed [1]
- Number of neurons: fixed [1]
- Number of projections: not relevant, always one (fixed 1 weight) connection from input to the neuron and one from the neuron to the encoding output
- Rate coding

- Transfer functions: Trilinear (y value is within $[-1, 1]$, x value of begin and end of linear section varies, mutation rate = 0.02), Sigmoidal (y value is within $(-1, 1)$, x value of nullcrossing and steepness varies, mutation rate = 0.02)
- No learning rules.
- Brain update: 3

2. Parameter Settings for Game Simulations

Population dynamics and games.

- Population size: 100.
- Time steps: 500 (200 for the cloning test).
- Number of games played per time step per agent: 100.
- Death process: least fit (5).
- Mating process: roulette wheel.
- Number of offspring: Poisson with Lambda=5.

Neurobiological parameters.

- Number of layers: randomly chosen from the range $[1, 3]$ (mutation rate: 0.008).
- Number of neuron classes: randomly chosen from the range $[1, 3]$ (mutation rate: 0.2).
- Number of neurons: randomly chosen from the range $[10, 30]$ (mutation rate: 0.2).
- Number of projections: randomly chosen from the range $[1, 3]$ (mutation rate: 0.02).
- Rate coding with linear transfer function $[-1, 1]$.
- Hebbian learning rules.
- Reward matrix is same as the pay-off matrix of the given game (below).
- Brain update: 10 (same for listener and speaker).

3. Payoff Matrices

Here the payoff matrices indicate the scores in dyadic interactions, depending on the state of the environment and the value on the decision neuron.

Coordination game (first number denotes the fitness of the row player, the second the column player; D denotes decision, E denotes environment).

Environment: $E(-1)$

	$D(-1)$	$D(1)$	$D(0)$
$D(-1)$	8,8	2,1	2,0
$D(1)$	1,2	1,1	1,0
$D(0)$	0,2	0,1	0,0

Environment: E(1)

	D(−1)	D(1)	D(0)
D(−1)	1,1	1,2	1,0
D(1)	2,1	8,8	2,0
D(0)	0,1	0,2	0,0

Task allocation game (same in all environments).

	D(−1)	D(1)	D(0)
D(−1)	1,1	8,8	1,0
D(1)	8,8	1,1	1,0
D(0)	0,1	0,1	0,0

Coordination – task allocation game.
Environment: E(−1)

	D(−1)	D(1)	D(0)
D(−1)	8,8	2,1	2,0
D(1)	1,2	1,1	1,0
D(0)	0,2	0,1	0,0

Environment: E(1)

	D(−1)	D(1)	D(0)
D(−1)	1,1	8,8	1,0
D(1)	8,8	1,1	1,0
D(0)	0,1	0,1	0,0

4. Cloning

Test population.

- A test run was performed (population size: 100, time steps: 200), to select for agents that can solve the task allocation game.
- 50 agents (clone founders) with last-turn fitness larger than 500 were chosen to be cloned. Direct relations (fraternal and parental) were excluded.
- All the 50 clone founders were cloned 50 times (thus a total of 2500 clones and 50 clone founders were present).

Control population.

- 2550 unrelated agents were generated randomly, thus no relatives were present.
- Population was structured randomly resulting in 50 groups of 51 agents.

5. Brain Analysis and Heritability

- Brains of the 2550 agents were saved as connectivity vectors between neurons.
- Number of in-, and out connections were counted in case of the five special neurons (AudioIn, AudioOut, Vision, Decision, Const) as a characteristic property of brains.

- Sums of in-, and out connections (per neuron) were used in the calculations.
- Correlation between neuron connectivity of clone founder and its clones was analysed.
- Heritability for each input/output neuron was calculated using the following method:

Genetic variance equals the variance of mean clone values. Heritability is simply this value divided by the total phenotypic variance of the whole population (all individuals). Put differently, heritability is estimated as the intra-class correlation in one-way ANOVA.

9
Communication in Natural and Artificial Organisms: Experiments in Evolutionary Robotics

Davide Marocco and Stefano Nolfi

9.1. Introduction

In the field of ethological studies many efforts of researchers are devoted to understand how animals communicate and what is the role of communication from an evolutionary and functional point of view. Progress in this area might also have an impact on our understanding of human communication since animal and human communication systems share several features (Hauser, 1996). The social function played by human language, for instance, is one of the first traits that allows us to place language in the same evolutionary field as other animal communication systems. Moreover, recently also the idea of the uniqueness of human language regarding the representational fashion of the knowledge and the compositionality of signals is challenged by new findings in primate research that indicate that, in baboons, knowledge is representational, based on properties that have discrete values and, from a certain point of view, propositional (Seyfarth et al., 2005).

This type of research leads to new important discoveries on the structure and on the functional role of communication systems in modern animals (including humans). The evolutionary origins of communication and language, instead, still largely remain an open question (Christiansen & Kirby, 2003). Artificial experiments involving embodied and communicating agents that interact autonomously between themselves and with the environment represent a new promising method that might help us to answer this difficult question (Cangelosi & Parisi, 1998; Kirby, 2002; Steels, 2003; Wagner et al., 2003; Nolfi, 2005). The goal of this new research area is the attempt to identify the initial conditions and the required pre-requisites that might allow a population of embodied and communicating agents (consisting of robots or carefully simulated embodied agents) to develop a shared communication system that allows them to better coordinate and cooperate through an automated procedure and without human intervention.

9.2. Evolution of a Self-Organized Communication System

In the following sections we will present the results of an experiment in which a collection of simulated robots that are evolved for the ability to solve a collective navigation problem develop a communication system that allows them to cooperate better. Moreover, we will discuss the relation between the robots' communication system and related forms of communication observed in animals. We make particular reference to communication forms that convey information about the external environment and synchronized communication forms such us vocal duetting.

Robots are provided with simple sensory-motor systems that allow them to move, produce signals with varying intensities, and gather information from their physical and social environment (including signals produced by other agents). The chosen problem admits a variety of qualitatively different solutions and robots are selected on the basis of their ability to solve the collective navigation problem (and not on the basis of their communication abilities). Evolving robots are left free to determine the circumstances in which communication is used, the structure of the communication system (i.e. the number, the type and the "meaning" of signals), the communication modalities (i.e. the role played by communicating individuals and the social condition affecting the signal produced), and the relation between individual and social/communication abilities.

9.2.1. The Evolutionary Robotics Model

A group of four simulated robots placed in the same environment (i.e. an arena of 270×270 cm containing two target areas, Figure 9.1 Left) are evolved for the ability to solve a collective navigation problem. The evolutionary

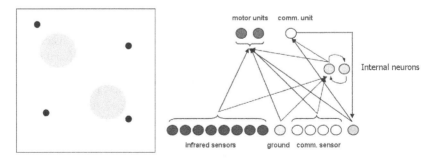

FIGURE 9.1. Left: The environment and the robots. The square represents the arena surrounded by walls. The two grey circles represent two target areas. The four black circles represent four robots. Right: The neural controller for evolving robots.

process is used to select the free parameters of the robot's controller (i.e. the synaptic weights, biases and time constants of a neural controller with a fixed architecture).

The robots have a circular body with a radius of 11 cm. The robots' neural controllers consist of neural networks with 14 sensory neurons that encode the activation states of the corresponding 8 infrared sensors, 1 ground sensor, 4 communicative sensors, and the activation state of the communication neuron at times t-1, i.e. each robot can hear its own emitted signal at the previous time step. These sensory neurons are directly connected to the three motor neurons that control the desired speed of the two wheels and the intensity of the communication signal produced by the robot. The neural controllers also include two internal neurons that receive connections from the sensory neurons and from themselves and send connections to the motor and communicating neurons (Figure 9.1 Right). For further details see the Appendix.

Robots of the team can communicate by producing signals and detecting the signals produced by other robots within a given range. The activation of the communication neurons (ranging between 0.0 and 1.0) encode the intensity of the signal produced. The four communication sensors encode the intensity of the signals produced (by robots located within a distance of 100 cm) from four corresponding orthogonal directions (i.e. frontal [315°–44°], rear [135°–224°], left [225°–314°], right [45°–134°]). This means, for example, that if a single robot B is within a distance of 100 cm with respect to robot A, one of the four communication sensors of robot A will be activated (on the basis of the intensity of the signal emitted by B) while the other three communication sensors will be not activated. Communication sensors encode the intensity of the signal produced by the nearest robot within the corresponding angular range.

Robots were evolved with the ability to find and remain in the two target areas by dividing themselves equally between the two areas. Each team of four robots was allowed to "live" for 20 trials, lasting 100 seconds (i.e. 1000 time steps of 100 ms each). At the beginning of each trial the position and the orientation of the robots was randomly assigned outside the target areas. The fitness of the team of robots consists of the sum of 0.25 scores for each robot located in a target area and a score of −1.00 for each extra robot (i.e. each robot exceeding the maximum number of two) located in a target area. The total fitness of a team is computed by summing the fitness gathered by the four robots in each time step.

The initial population consisted of 100 randomly generated genotypes that encoded the connection weights, the biases, and the time constants of 100 corresponding neural controllers. Each parameter was encoded with 8 bits and normalized in the range [−5.0, +5.0], in the case of connection weights and biases, and in the range [0.0, 1.0], in the case of time constants. Each genotype was translated into 4 identical neural controllers that were embodied in the four corresponding robots, i.e. teams were homogeneous and consisted of four identical robots. For a discussion about this point and alternative selection schemas see (Quinn, 2000, 2001; Quinn et al. 2003; Baldassarre et al., 2003). The 20 best genotypes of each generation were allowed to reproduce by generating five copies each, with 2% of their bits replaced with a new randomly selected value. The evolutionary process lasted 100 generations (i.e. the process of testing, selecting and reproducing robots is iterated 100 times). The experiment was replicated 10 times by creating 10 different initial populations.

9.2.2. Emergence of Communication

By analyzing the behavior of the best evolved team we can see that evolved robots are able to find and remain in the two target areas by dividing themselves equally between the two. In the example shown in Figure 9.2, robots 2 and 3 quickly reach two different empty target areas. Later on, robot 1 and then robot 0 approach and enter in the bottom-right target area. As soon as the third robot (i.e. robot 0) enters in the area, robot 1 leaves the bottom-right target area and, after exploring the environment for a while, enters and remains in the top-left target area.

To determine whether the possibility to signal and to use other robots' signals is exploited by evolving robots we tested the evolved team in three conditions: a "Normal" condition; a "Deprived" condition in which robots which had evolved in a normal condition were tested in a control condition in which the state of communication sensors was always set to a null value; and a "No-signal" conditions in which robots were evolved and tested with their communication sensors always set to a null value (see Figure 9.3). The fact that performance in the "Normal" condition is better and statistically different (p < 0.001) from the other two control conditions indicates that communication plays a role. The

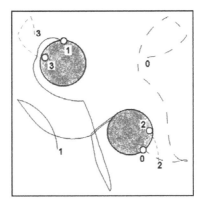

FIGURE 9.2. The behavior displayed by the team of evolved robots in one of the best replications. The square and the grey circles indicate the arena and the target area respectively. Lines inside the arena indicate the trajectory of the four robots during a trial. The numbers indicate the starting and ending position of the corresponding robot (the ending position is marked with a white circle).

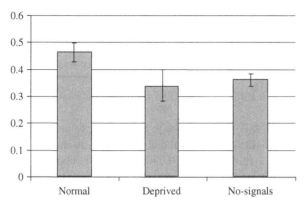

FIGURE 9.3. Average fitness of all teams of the last generations of 10 different replications of the experiment. Histograms represent the average fitness obtained by testing the robots in: a Normal condition (in the same condition in which they have been evolved), a Deprived condition in which robots are not allowed to detect other robots' signals and a No-signals condition in which they have been evolved and tested without the possibility of detecting other robots' signals. A fitness value of 1.0 cannot be reached in practice since robots have first to locate and reach the two target areas. In all cases, individuals have been tested for 1000 trials. Bars represent standard deviations.

performance of robots that are tested in the "Deprived" control condition are similar to those of robots evolved and tested in a "No-signal" control condition, see Figure 9.3. This indicates that evolved robots develop an effective individual behavior (i.e. a sensory-motor behavior shown by a single robot that allows the team to achieve a good performance in absence of communication) even if they have always been evaluated in a normal condition in which signals are available. This fact can be explained by considering that the social enhancement provided by communication is not always guaranteed. Indeed, the availability of the signals is subjected to the presence of other robots in the right environmental locations that, in turn, is influenced by unpredictable variables such us the initial positions and orientations of the robots.

9.3. The Evolved Communication System

By analyzing the team in the best replication of the experiment we observed that evolved individuals developed and relied on a non-trivial communication system. More specifically evolving robots display an ability to develop a sort of lexicon including five different signals, a perceptually grounded categorization of the physical and social world reflected by the different signals, an ability to appropriately modulate their motor behavior on the basis of the detected signals and an ability to appropriately modulate their signaling behavior on the basis of the detected signals.

More precisely, the five signals showed by the robots are the following:

- a signal **A** with an intensity value of 0.42 produced by robots located outside the target areas not interacting with other robots located inside or outside target areas;
- a signal **B** with a value of about 0.85 produced by robots located alone inside a target area;
- a signal **C**, an oscillatory signal with an average value of 0.57, produced by robots located inside a target area that also contains another robot;
- a signal **D** with a value of about 0.07 produced by robots outside target areas that are approaching a target area and are interacting with another robot located inside the target area;
- a signal **E**, an oscillatory signal with an average value of 0.33, emitted by robots located outside the target areas interacting with other robots also located outside target areas.

Robots receiving these five types of signals modify their motor and/or signaling behavior on the basis of the signal received and of other available sensory information. More specifically:

- robots located outside the target areas receiving signal **A** modify their signaling behavior by producing signal **E**;
- robots located outside target areas receiving signal **B** tend to modify their motor behavior (by approaching the robot emitting the signal and the corresponding target area) and their signaling behavior by producing signal **D**;
- robots located outside the target areas receiving the signal **C** (i.e. the signal produced by two robots located inside the target area) modify their motor behavior so as to move away from the signal source;
- robots located inside target areas receiving the signal **C** (i.e. the signal produced by two robots located inside the target area) modify their motor behavior so as to exit from the target area;
- robots located outside the target areas receiving signal **E** tend to modify their motor behavior to better explore the environment.

9.4. Functionality of Signals

To verify the functionality of the different signals we ran several tests on the best evolved team by manipulating the environment, the size of the group (i.e. the number of robots in the group) and the sensory system of the robots. In this section we will focus our analysis on the conditions in which signals are emitted and on the effects of signals on agents' behavior. In the next section, instead, we will analyze how agents dynamically affect each other during communicative interactions.

9.4.1. Functionality of Signals A and E

To verify the functionality of signals A and E, we measured the time elapsed until at least one robot of a team of four robots reaches one of the two target areas in a normal condition and in a control condition in which robots were not allowed to detect signals (i.e. in which the state of the four communication sensors of all robots were always set to a null value even when they are in contact with a robot that is emitting a signal). By testing the best evolved team of robots in the two conditions, we observed that the time needed to reach the first target area, on the average, is 5.922s and 6.478s in the case of the normal and the control condition, respectively. By testing the best teams in the other replications of the experiment similar results were observed in most of the cases (result not shown). Overall, these results indicate that robots exploit their signaling behavior to produce a form of coordinated exploration that increases their ability to quickly find the target areas. To identify the relative roles of the two signals we ran an additional test in which robots were allowed to produce and detect signal A but were not allowed to switch from signal A to E (they were forced to produce signal A even when they start to detect the signal A produced by other robots). The obtained result (i.e. an average time of 6.952s) indicates that the function of signal A is to trigger the production of signal E by robots located outside target area within a distance of 100cm. The function of signal of signal E, is to enhance robots' exploratory behavior.

9.4.2. Functionality of Signal B

To verify the functionality of signal B, we tested a team consisting of two robots placed in an environment including only a single target area (one of the robots was manually placed into the target area, while the other one was placed in a random position outside the area) in a normal condition and in a control condition in which robots were not allowed to detect signals (i.e. in which the state of the four communication sensors of both robots was always set to a null value). By testing the best evolved team of robots in the two conditions, we observed that the percentage of trials in which the robot placed outside was able to reach the target area within 100 seconds is 97.2% and 75.4% in the normal and control condition respectively. This demonstrates that robots detecting signal B modify their motor behavior so as to approach the source of the signal.

9.4.3. Functionality of Signal C

Robots located inside a target area produce signal B. However, two interacting robots located in the same target area reciprocally modulate their signaling behavior so to produce signal C (i.e. a highly varying signal with an average intensity of 0.57). Indeed, by placing two robots in a target area and by preventing the former from detecting the signal produced by the latter, we observed that the first robot produce the signal B. To verify whether signal C reduces the chances that more than two robots enter in the same target area, we tested a team consisting of three robots in an environment including only a single target area in a normal condition and in a "Deprived" control condition in which communication was disabled. At the beginning of each trial two robots are placed inside the target area and one robot is placed outside the target area with randomly selected positions and orientations. By testing the best evolved team of robots in the two conditions we observed that the percentage of trials in which the robot initially placed outside the target area erroneously joins the area is 2.3% and 82.6%, in the normal and control condition respectively.

To verify whether signal C increases the chances that a robot exit from a target area that contains more than two robots we tested a team of three robots in an environment including only a single target area in a normal condition and in a "Deprived" control condition in which communication was disabled. At the beginning of each trial, all the three robots were placed inside the target area with randomly selected positions and orientations. The percentage of times in which one of the three robots exit from the target area is 84.6% and 2.7% in normal and deprived conditions respectively.

9.5. On the Dynamics of Communicative Interactions

By observing the use of signals in their ecological context we noted that robots might rely on, at least, two different communication modalities, that we called mono-directional communication and bi-directional communication. In mono-directional communication forms, the motor behavior or the signal produced by one individual affects the behavior of a second individual but the behavior of the latter individual does not alter the behavior of the former. In bi-directional communication forms instead, the motor or signaling behavior of one individual affects the second individual and vice versa.

Moreover, by analyzing the functionality of the different signals coupled with the context in which they are used, we can see how evolved robots use the different communication modalities by selecting the modalities that are appropriate for each specific case. Indeed, in the experiment reported in this paper, evolved agents are able to use different communication modalities in different circumstances.

In this section we will analyze the communication modalities used by evolved robots. To simplify the analysis we will consider a simplified situation in which a group of two robots is placed in an arena that includes only a single target area. In section 9.5.1 we will describe mono-directional communication forms in which the signal produce by a robot affects the behavior of a second robot. In section 9.5.2 we will describe bi-directional communication forms in which the signaling behavior of each communication robot affects and is affected by the robot with which it communicate.

Figure 9.4 and Figure 9.5 show the typical motor and signaling behavior exhibited by two robots placed in an environment that contains only a single

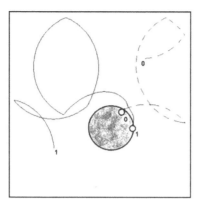

FIGURE 9.4. The behavior of two robots tested in an arena including a single target area. The dashed and full lines represent the trajectory of robot #0 and #1, respectively. The numbers indicate both the starting and ending positions of the corresponding robots.

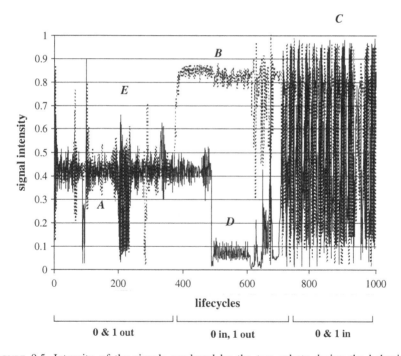

FIGURE 9.5. Intensity of the signals produced by the two robots during the behavior shown in Figure 9.4. Dashed and full lines indicate the intensity of the signals produced by robot #0 and #1, respectively. Letters (A, B, C, D and E) indicate the 5 classes of signals produced by the robots. The black lines in the bottom part of the figure indicate the three phases in which: (1) both robots are outside the target area, (2) robot #0 is inside and robot #1 is outside, and (3) both robots are inside the target area. The grey line in the bottom part of the figure indicates the phases in which the two robots are located within the signal range.

target area. Initially the two robots are both outside the target area and both produce a signal with an intensity of about 0.42 (signal A). As soon as the two robots get close enough to detect their signals, they produce a signal with a varying intensity and an average intensity of 0.33 (signal E) and they vary their motor trajectory by increasing their turning angle. After some time robot #0 reaches the target area and starts to produce a signal with an intensity of about 0.85 (signal B). Later on, once robot #1 returns close enough to robot #0 and detects the signal B produced by robot #0, it modifies its motor trajectory (by approaching robot #0) and its signaling behavior (by producing signal D, i.e. a signal with an almost null intensity, instead of signal A). When also robot #1 joins the area, the two robots start to produce a varying signal with an average intensity of about 0.57 (signal C) that reduces the probability that other robots will enter in the area and eventually, if an additional robot erroneously joins the area, increases the probability that one of the robots exits from the area.

9.5.1. Mono-Directional Communicative Interactions

As we said above, mono-directional communication occurs when the motor behavior or the signal produced by one individual affects the behavior of a second individual but the behavior of the latter individual does not alter the behavior of the former. In these forms of communication, the two robots play the role of the 'speaker' and of the 'hearer', respectively, and communication can be described as a form of information exchange (in which the 'hearer' may have access to information that is available to the 'speaker' but not to the 'hearer' by itself) or as a form of 'manipulation' (in which the 'speaker' alters the behavior of the 'hearer' in a way that is useful to the 'speaker' or both to the 'speaker' and the 'hearer').

Another important aspect that characterizes this type of communicative interaction is that they are 'static'. In mono-directional communication, in fact, the signal produced by an individual is only a function of the current state of the individual that remains the same until the individual's state changes.

In the case of our experiment, this kind of communicative interaction takes place in the situation in which a robot is located inside a target area and a second robot is located outside, within the communication range. In this case, in fact, the former robot has access to information (related to the location of the target area) to which the second robot does not have access. Thus, in this particular situation, communication should be mono-directional, since only the latter robot should change its behavior on the basis of the signal produced by the former and not vice versa. Indeed, in this situation evolved robots rely on a mono-directional communication form in which the former robot produces the signal B and the latter robot, that perceives the signal B, starts to follow the signal emitted by the former and switches its signaling behavior off by producing the signal D (i.e. a signal with an almost null intensity).

This communicative interaction thus can be described as an information exchange in which the former robot (the 'speaker') produces a signal that encodes information related to the location of the target area and the latter robot (the 'hearer') exploits this information to navigate toward the area. Or, alternatively, this interaction schema can be described as a form of manipulation in which the former robot (the 'speaker') 'manipulates' the motor behavior of the latter robot (the 'hearer') so as to drive the robot toward the target area.

The ability of the robots located outside the target area to switch their signaling behavior off (i.e. to produce the signal D) as soon as they detect the signal B plays an important function. Indeed, by testing a team of two robots, for 1000 trials, in an environment including a single target area in a normal condition and in a control condition in which robots were not able to switch between signal A and D, we observed that the percentage of trials in which both robots were able to reach the target area within 100 seconds drops from 97.2% to 0.12% in the normal and control conditions respectively.

Another situation in which mono-directional communication takes place is when two robots are both outside the target areas and are within communicative range. In this case, in fact, as in the situation described before, each of the two robots 'informs', or alternatively, 'manipulates' the other in order to modify the trajectory of the receiver, so to increase the chances that the two trajectories do not overlap. As a direct effect of this behavior, the exploratory ability of the entire group is enhanced (see section 9.4.1).

Mono-directional communication forms thus tend to be used when the signal emitted refers to the relation between one agent and the environment. Indeed, these communication forms are used to indicate whether the agent that emits the signal is located inside or outside a target area and what is its current location with respect to the hearer agent (or, according to the alternative interpretation, to manipulate the motor trajectory of the hearer agent).

These mono-directional communication forms are similar to that reported in animal communication involving signals that refer to the relation between the animal that emit the signal and the environmental characteristics detected by that agent. For example, various studies on animal communication, in particular on birds and primates, report that vocalization like animal calls, food calls or intergroup calls may provide information about events or objects external to the signaler (Hauser, 1996). One of the most famous research projects on this topic is presented by Seyfarth and colleagues (1980) which reports on the communication system shown by vervet monkeys. These monkeys are able to communicate to their conspecifics the type of predator (leopards, eagles and snakes) by producing different alarm calls for different type of predators. These alarm calls trigger in the conspecifics different motor responses that are appropriate to the specific type of predator. These alarm calls thus had a referential function. Starting from this pioneering work, several long distance calls have been discovered in other species that convey not only information about the emotional states of the emitter, as suggested by Lancaster (1968), but also information related to the characteristics of the external environment and of events occurring in the external environment (Marler et al., 1992, Hauser, 1998, Rendall et al., 1999).

From an analysis of the behavior exhibited by evolved robots we cannot conclude how this behavior should be described. It could be interpreted as a form of information-passing and information-exploitation in which the speaker "helps" the hearer (by providing to the hearer the relevant information) and hearer exploits the signals received (by triggering the appropriate motor behavior). Alternatively, it could be interpreted as a form of manipulation in which the speaker manipulates the hearer by exploiting its tendency to modify its behavior on the basis of specific detected sensory information (Krebs and Dawkins, 1984). More probably, it could be interpreted as a mixture of the two cases. For this reason in future work we plan to analyze the evolutionary origins of communication abilities. If the ability to produce the right signal precedes evolutionarily the ability to appropriately react to that signal, we can conclude that the final communication behavior can be described as a form of information-passing and information-exploitation. Otherwise, if the signaler exploits a pre-determined characteristic of the receiver to react to specific signals by producing a behavior that is useful to the signaler, we can conclude that these communication forms can be more properly described as a form of manipulation.

9.5.2. Bi-Directional Communicative Interactions

In bi-directional communication forms each robot plays both the role of the 'speaker' and of the 'hearer' (i.e. different roles cannot be identified) and the communicative interactions between the robots involved in the process is dynamic (i.e. it consists of a form of dialog in which the signals produced and the effect of the produced signals have affect the succeeding communicative interaction). As an example of a dynamic communication form we might consider the case of two individuals that alternatively play the role of the speaker and of the hearer by taking turns (Iizuka and Ikegami, 2003a, 2003b). Bi-directional and dynamical communication forms might lead to emergent properties (e.g. synchronization or shared attention) that result from the mutual interaction between two or more individuals and that cannot be explained by the sum of the individual contributions only (Di Paolo, 2000).

In the present experiment these types of communication forms take place when two robots are located in the same target area. In this situation, in fact, none of the two robots have access to the relevant information (i.e. the fact that the target area contains two robots). This information, however, can be generated through communication between the two robots on the basis of a bi-directional communicative interaction: the signal produced by one of the two robots affects the signal produced by the second robot, and vice versa. This bi-directional interaction allows the two robots to switch from signal B, that increases the chances that other robots will joint the area, to signal C, that decreases the chances that other robots will joint the area.

In this circumstance evolved robots also rely on a dynamical communication modality, since they produce signals that vary in time as a result of signals previously produced and detected by the two robots. More precisely, the signal

C tends to vary in time as a result of the following factors: (1) the intensity of the signal detected inhibits the intensity of the signal produced, (2) the intensity of the inhibition also depends on the direction of the detected signal, (3) the signal tends to be detected by constantly varying relative directions since robots located inside the target area turn on the spot. The production of an oscillatory signal, with an average intensity of 0.57, rather then a stable non-dynamical signal, plays an important functional role. Indeed, we observed that evolved robots rely on oscillatory signals in all the replications of the experiment. Moreover, we observed that stable signals do not allow the robots to reach the same level of performance. To ascertain whether the production of a stable signal could lead to the same functionality as the oscillatory signal we ran a test in which robots were forced to emit a stable signal when located in a target area that contained two robots. Robots were allowed to behave normally in all other cases. The test was repeated 10 times by using stable signals with 10 different intensities ranging from 0.1 to 1.0. The result of the test confirms that the oscillatory nature of the signal is functional, in fact the obtained performances in the test were always lower than the performance obtained by allowing robots to produce the oscillatory signal (data not shown).

Bi-directional communication takes place when two robots have to coordinate their motor and signaling behavior so to extract from the social and physical environment information which is not directly detectable by the sensory system of a single robot alone, but has to be built, in a sense, by the two robots together. Imagine two persons placed in two different rooms in the same house that have to remain for a certain amount of time in their respective rooms. They cannot see each other and they cannot talk to each other. How might one of the two persons be aware of the presence of the second in the other room? One possible way is to exchange some kind of signal, e.g. knocking the wall and wait for an answer. In this case, a signal followed by an answer is an indication of the presence of the other person. On the other hand, an unanswered signal is an indication of the absence of the other person. In this case, therefore, the two persons must actively participate to the 'creation' of the knowledge and, consequently, are forced to cooperate to achieve that knowledge. Thus, the communication signals refer more to agent-agent interactions then to external environmental characteristics.

Looking at the behavior of the two robots in the target area from this perspective may give a possible explanation of the oscillatory signal C. The two robots continuously send and receive signals, and consequently modulate in a coordinate fashion their signaling behavior, so as to stay in contact. This kind of behavior, in turn, modifies the communicative behavior of both robots that changes the emitted signal from B to C. At this point, it should be noted that signal C cannot be produced by a robot alone, being the product of the reciprocal modulation of the signals emitted and received by the two robots.

Analogous forms of bi-directional communication are well known in animal communication too, but the functionality of these forms of communication is still largely unexplained. From our point of view, the most interesting form of bi-directional communication is the *duet*, a form of communicative interaction that is presents in many species including insects, frogs, birds, primates, and great apes (Bailey, 2003; Farabaugh, 1982; Haimoff, 1986).

A duet can be defined as a cooperative and coordinated communicative behavior in which a pair of animals (it is mostly observed in monogamous couples) produce loud sounds, long calls or songs, in an interactive manner. The main characteristic of the duet is the synchronization of the emitting calls in which two animals concurrently act as speakers and the hearers.

The function of the duet is largely unknown, although some hypotheses have been made. The most important of them concern the joint territorial defense and the maintaining of the pair bond. Coming back to our experiment, one may note an interesting similarity between the possible function of duet in birds with the function of the bi-directional communicative interaction showed by two robots placed in the target area. Indeed, signal C, which is the product of this type of communication, is used by the two robots: (1) to maintain the two robots in the target area, and (2) to avoid another robot joining the area.

In more general terms, the results obtained in the evolutionary experiments indicate that bi-directional communication forms can be explained by the need to exploit social interactions to create and exchange important pieces of information that are not directly available but can be generated through social interactions.

9.6. Conclusion

In this paper we describe the results of evolutionary experiments with robots in which an effective communication system arises in a group of initially non-communicating agents evolved for the ability to solve a collective navigation problem. With the methodology chosen, we observed that agents developed an effective communication system based on five different signals that correspond to crucial features of the environment, of the agents/agents relations, and agents/environmental relations including the relative location of a target area and the number of agents contained in a target area. These categories, that have been autonomously discovered by the agents and that are grounded in agents' sensory-motor experiences and the effects of the signals associated with these categories constitute the 'meanings' of the signals produced and detected by the agents. Signals, therefore, do not only refer to the characteristics of the physical environment but also to those of the social environment constituted by the other agents and by their current state.

Interestingly, one can find analogies between the communication systems observed in our experiments and forms of animal communication described in the literature. For instance, signals that refer to agent/environment interactions are similar to alarm calls or food calls in birds and primates that provide information about objects or events that are external to the animal that emits the signal. Moreover, the function of coordinated oscillatory signals produced by two interacting robots is similar to the synchronized communicative interactions known as vocal duetting produced by several animals.

As pointed out by various studies, the fact that signals can have an external environmental referent, both in the animal domain and in simulation experiments, can be considered one of the most basic traits that a 'simple' communication system shares with more complex communication system like human language. In fact, by looking at the communication behavior not simply as a product of the emotional state of an animal (Lancaster, 1968) but as a way to convey, voluntarily or involuntarily, information about the external environment to other animals, one can claim that the referential use of vocalizations may represent an important prerequisite to the evolution of 'naming' (Hihara et al., 2003) and of more complex grounded syntactic categories (Cangelosi and Parisi, 2001; Marocco et al, 2003).

Furthermore the way in which agents mutually interact and reciprocally modify their behavior in bi-directional communication forms is another important aspect involved in any kind of communication act. In our experiment we have also been able to study this type of problem by observing that some forms of bi-directional communication emerged in artificial agents and present analogies with certain animal communication forms. In particular, the vocal duetting between two animals, that shares features with the two robots located in the target area, has been identified as one of the possible prerequisites for the evolution of language (Ujhelyi, 1996). This is one of the simplest forms of communication that involves strong mutual interactions between animals at the social level, allowing the differentiation of individuals in the group on the basis of the various bi-directional communicative interactions that take place between them.

References

Bailey, W. J. (2003). Insect duets: underlying mechanisms and their evolution. Physiological Entomology, 28: 157–174.

Baldassarre G., Nolfi S. & Parisi D. (2003). Evolving mobile robots able to display collective behaviour. Artificial Life, 9: 255–267.

Cangelosi A. & Parisi D. (1998). The emergence of a 'language' in an evolving population of neural networks. Connection Science, 10: 83–97.

Cangelosi A., Parisi D. (2001). How nouns and verbs differentially affect the behavior of artificial organisms. In J.D. Moore & K. Stenning (Eds.), Proceedings of the 23rd Annual Conference of the Cognitive Science Society, London: Lawrence Erlbaum Associates, 170–175.

Christiansen, M. H. & Kirby, S. (eds) (2003). Language Evolution, Oxford University Press.

Di Paolo E.A. (2000). Behavioural coordination, structural congruence and entrainment in a simulation of acoustically coupled agents. Adaptive Behaviour 8:1. 25–46.

Farabaugh S. M. (1982). The ecological and social significance of duetting. In D. E. Kroodsma & E. H. Miller, Acoustic Communication in Birds (Eds.), pp. 85–124. New York: Academic Press.

Haimoff E. H. (1986). Convergence in the duetting of monogamous old world Primates. J. Hum. Evol. 15: 767–782.

Hauser, M. D. (1996). The Evolution of Communication. MIT Press.

Hauser, M. D. (1998). Functional referents and acoustic similarity: field playback experiments with rhesus monkeys. Animal Behaviour, 55: 1647–1658.

Hihara S., Yamada H., Iriki A., Okanoya K. (2003). Spontaneous vocal differentiation of coo-calls for tools and food in Japanese monkeys. Neuroscience Research, 45 (4): 383–389.

Iizuka H. and Ikegami T. (2002). Simulating Turn-taking Behaviors with Coupled Dynamical Recognizers. In R. K. Standish, M. A. Bedau and H. A. Abbass (Eds.), MIT, Proceedings of Artificial Life VIII, Cambridge, MA: MIT Press.

Iizuka H. and Ikegami T. (2003). Adaptive Coupling and Intersubjectivity in Simulated Turn-Taking Behaviours. In Banzahf et al. (Eds.). Proceedings of ECAL 03, Dortmund: Springer Verlag.Iizuka H. & Ikegami T. (in press). Simulating autonomous coupling in discrimination of light frequencies. Connection Science.

Kirby S. (2002). Natural Language from Artificial Life. Artificial Life, 8(2):185–215.

Krebs, J. R. and Dawkins, R. (1984). Animal signals: mind-reading and manipulation. In J. R. Krebs and N. B. Davies, Behavioural ecology. An evolutionary approach (second ed.). Blackwell Scientific Publications, 380–405.

Lancaster J. B. (1968). Primate communication systems and the emergence of human language. In Jay P. J. (Eds.), Primates. New York: Holt, Rinehart & Winston, 439–457.

Marler P., Evans C.S. & Hauser M.D. (1992). Animal signals: moti-vational, referential, or both?. In Papousek H., Jurgens U. & Papousek M. (Eds), Nonverbal communication: comparative and developmental approaches. Cambridge: Cambridge University Press, 66–86

Marocco D., Cangelosi A. & Nolfi S. (2003). The emergence of communication in evolutionary robots. Philosophical Transactions of the Royal Society London - A, 361: 2397–2421.

Nolfi S. (2002). Evolving robots able to self-localize in the environment: The importance of viewing cognition as the result of processes occurring at different time scales. Connection Science (14) 3:231–244.

Nolfi S. (in press). Emergence of Communication in Embodied Agents: Co-Adapting Communicative and Non-Communicative Behaviours. Connection Science.

Nolfi S. & Marocco D. (2001). Evolving robots able to integrate sensory-motor information over time, Theory in Biosciences, 120: 287–310.

Quinn M. (2000). Evolving cooperative homogeneous multi-robot teams. In Proceedings of the IEEE/RSJ International Conference on Intelligent Robots and Systems (IROS 2000). IEEE Press.

Quinn M. (2001). Evolving communication without dedicated communication channels. In Kelemen, J. and Sosik, P. (Eds.) Advances in Artificial Life: Sixth European Conference on Artificial Life (ECAL 2001). Springer Verlag.

Quinn M., Smith L., Mayley G. & Husbands P. (2003). Evolving controllers for a homogeneous system of physical robots: Structured cooperation with minimal sensors. Philosophical Transactions of the Royal Society of London, Series A: Mathematical, Physical and Engineering Sciences 361, pp. 2321–2344.

Rendall D., Cheney D. L., Seyfarth R. M. and Owren, M. J. (1999). The meaning and function of grunt variants in baboons. Animal Behaviour, 57: 583–592.

Seyfarth R. M., Cheney D. L. & Marler P. (1980). Vervet monkey alarm calls: semantic communication in a free-ranging primate. Animal Behaviour, 28: 1070–1094.

Seyfarth R. M., Cheney D. L. & Bergman T. H. (2005). Primate social cognition and the origins of language. Trends in Cognitive Science. 9(6): 264–266.

Steels L. (1999). The Talking Heads Experiment, Antwerpen, Laboratorium. Limited Pre-edition.

Steels L. (2003) Evolving grounded communication for robots. Trends in Cognitive Science. 7(7): 308–312.

Steels L. and Kaplan F. (2001). AIBO's first words: The social learning of language and meaning. Evolution of Communication, 4: 3–32.

Steels L. & Vogt P. (1997) Grounding adaptive language games in robotic agents. In: P. Husband & I. Harvey (Eds.). Proceedings of the 4th European Conference on Artificial Life. Cambridge MA: MIT Press.

Ujhelyi, M. (1996). Is There Any Intermediate Stage Between Animal Communication and Language? Journal of Theoretical Biology, 180(1): 71–76.

Werner, G. M. & Dyer M. G. (1991). Evolution of communication in artificial organisms. In Langton, C. G., Taylor, C., Farmer, J. D., and Rasmussen, S. (Eds.) Proceedings of the Workshop on Artificial Life. pp: 659–687. Reading, MA, Addison-Wesley.

Wagner K., Reggia J. A., Uriagereka J., Wilkinson G. S. (2003). Progress in the simulation of emergent communication and language. Adaptive Behavior, 11(1): 37–69.

Appendix

Details of the Neural Controllers

The output of motor neurons was computed according to the logistic function (2), the output of sensory and internal neurons was computed according to function (3) and (4), respectively (for a detailed description of these activation functions and the relation with other related models see Nolfi, 2002).

$$A_j = t_j + \sum_i w_{ij} O_i \tag{1}$$

$$O_j = \frac{1}{1 + e^{-A_j}} \tag{2}$$

$$O_j = O_j^{(t-1)} \tau + I_j (1 - \tau_j) \tag{3}$$

$$O_j = O_j^{(t-1)} \tau + \left(1 + e^{-A_j}\right)^{-1} (1 - \tau_j) \tag{4}$$

With A_j being the activity of the jth neuron, t_j being the bias of the jth neuron, w_{ij} the weight of the incoming connections from the ith to the jth neuron, O_i the output of the ith neuron, $O_j^{(t-1)}$ being the output of the jth neuron at the previous time step, τ_j the time constant of the jth neuron, and I_j the intensity reading of the jth sensor.

10
From Vocal Replication to Shared Combinatorial Speech Codes: A Small Step for Evolution, A Big Step for Language

Pierre-Yves Oudeyer

10.1. Combinatorial Speech: A Pre-requisite for Language

Humans use spoken vocalizations, or their signed equivalent, as a physical support to carry language. This support is highly organized: vocalizations are built with the re-use of a small number of articulatory units, which are themselves discrete elements carved up by each linguistic community in the articulatory continuum. Moreover, the repertoires of these elementary units (the gestures, the phonemes, the morphemes) have a number of structural regularities: for example, while our vocal tract allows physically the production of hundreds of vowels, each language uses most often 5, and never more than 20 of them. Also, certain vowels are very frequent, like /a,e,i,o,u/, and some others are very rare, like /en/. All the speakers of a given linguistic community categorize the speech sounds in the same manner, and share the same repertoire of vocalizations. Speakers of different communities may have very different ways of categorizing sounds (for example, Chinese use tones to distinguish sounds), and repertoires of vocalizations. Such an organized physical support of language is crucial for the existence of language, and thus asking how it may have appeared in the biological and/or cultural history of humans is a fundamental questions. In particular, one can wonder how much the evolution of human speech codes relied on specific evolutionary innovations, and thus how difficult (or not) it was for speech to appear.

One possible answer, proposed by cognitive innatism (Mehler et al., 2000), is that speech does rely deeply on specific biological evolutions, and thus its structure is encoded precisely in the genes. There are two limits to this approach: 1) it does not explicitate what it means to have a speech structure encoded in the genes nor how these genes could have evolved 2) it does not explain why each linguistic community has a different speech code and how one specific speech code is "chosen" by a community. Another possible answer explains the structure of human speech as the optimal solution to efficient information transfer (in particular, perceptual distinctiveness between vocalizations) given the morpho-physiological properties of the vocal tract and the ear (Stevens, 1972; Lindblom, 1992). This approach also has a number of limits: 1) it does not explain how the optimization might be done in nature or culture; 2) like cognitive innatism, it does not explains why each linguistic community has a different speech code and how one specific speech code is "chosen" by a community.

Another answer, focused on the question of the origins of vowels systems, was proposed by de Boer (2001) and does not have these limits. He proposed a mechanism for explaining how a society of agents may come to agree on a vowel system. This mechanism is based on mutual imitations between agents and is called the "imitation game". He built a simulation in which agents were given a model of the vocal tract as well as a model of the ear. Agents played a game called the imitation game. Each of them had a repertoire of prototypes, which were associations between a motor program and its acoustic image. In a round of the game, one agent called the speaker, chose an item of its repertoire, and uttered it to the other agent, called the hearer. Then the hearer would search in its repertoire for the closest prototype to the speaker's sound, and produce it (he imitates). Then the speaker categorizes the utterance of the hearer and checks if the closest prototype in its repertoire is the one he used to produce its initial sound. He then tells the hearer whether it was "good" or "bad". All the items in the repertoires have scores that are used to promote items which lead to successful imitations and prune the other ones. In case of bad imitations, depending on the scores of the item used by the hearer, either this item is modified so as to match better the sound of the speaker, or a new item is created, as close as possible to the sound of the speaker.

This model is very interesting and was one of the first to demonstrate a process of cultural formation of shared vowel systems within a population of agents. This model also allowed us to understand how the interaction between learning mechanisms and morpho-physiological constraints could explain both the statistical regularities that we observe in the human vowel systems and their diversity. Finally, de Boer's model was also able to deal with phenomena of sound change, showing how repertoires of vowels could evolve with time. This model was then extended in (Oudeyer, 2005), which showed how similar results could be obtained concerning the formation of shared syllable systems with the prediction of regularities in syllable structures.

Nevertheless, if the "imitation game" is a good framework for studying the evolution of modern speech system, it is less clear to see how it can allow us to understand the evolutionary origins of speech. Indeed, the imitation game implies rather complex cognitive and behavioral capabilities for agents, and assumes implicitly the pre-existence of a linguistic context which is problematic if one wants to understand the origins of language. First of all, agents need to be able to play a game which is a protocol with partly arbitrary rules, involving successive turn-taking and asymmetric changing roles. Second, they need to understand that at a point in the game, one sound produced by the speaker should be imitated, and that this imitation will undergo evaluation from the speaker, which itself needs to understand that the sound produced by the hearer is intended to be an imitation and is not related to something else happening around. Finally, the speaker needs to be able to produce a feed-back signal associated with the quality of the imitation, and the hearer has to be able to understand the feedback, i.e. that from the point of view of the other, he did or did not manage to imitate successfully. Also, in the imitation game, there is a mechanism which explicitly forces the building of a repertoire of sounds which must be distinctive from each other, and there is an explicit pressure to invent new sounds. This clearly models a need to use these sounds in order to name efficiently a growing number of "things" in the environment, i.e. the pre-existence of a linguistic context.

So, because it implies a complex form of imitation involving both the understanding of the other's intentions and the interpretation of other's vocalization in terms of one's own repertoire of distinctive vocalizations, and because it involves the presence of a linguistic context, the "imitation game" of de Boer is more a model of the origins of particular languages than a model of the origins of the language capacity.

I will now present another model which might bring more light to this latter question. This model also involves a population of agents endowed with a vocal tract, a cochlea and an artificial brain, but what makes it special is that the neural system which is used is very basic and corresponds basically to the minimal kit necessary for analogic vocal replication. Vocal replication refers here to the capacity to reproduce precisely but in an holistic manner an acoustic/articulatory trajectory which is perceived. So, this is basically mimicry applied to the vocal domain (for a technical definition of mimicry, see (Nehaniv and Dautenhahn, 2002)). In general, the capacity for motor mimicry/copying might have appeared in evolution as a very basic form of imitation constituting the first kinds of social learning. For the vocal modality, and as present in a number of birds and whales species, vocal replication has been argued to be useful for the maintainance of social cohesion (Beecher and Brenowitz, 2005). What is interesting is that vocal replication/mimicry does not assume the understanding of intentions, and does not necessitate the existence of a repertoire of disctinctive and discrete vocal units serving as categories to cut a perceived trajectory into high-level segments. Moreover, in the model that I will present, on the one hand there is no explicit pressure for building such a repertoire of distinctive units, and on the other hand agents do not interact in an organized manner (there is no "game" or "protocol" of interaction). Yet, I will show that during the process of babbling and listening to vocalizations produced by nearby agents, a low-level and simple coupling of perception and production for vocal replication can spontaneously self-organize a shared repertoire of discrete combinatorial speech codes with structural regularities and diversity. This allows us to show that the minimal neural kit for vocal replication needs very few changes (even maybe no change at all) in order to generate a speech code which has the crucial properties of modern speech: in short, the evolutionary step from non-speech to speech may have been rather small.

10.2. Coupling Perception and Production in a Model of Vocal Replication

This model is based on the building of an artificial system, composed of agents endowed with working models of the vocal tract, of the cochlea and of some parts of the brain. Before going forward to the specificities of this vocal architecture, we will describe an outline of the minimal neural kit that allows us to achieve motor replication or mimicry. As stated above, motor mimicry involves the analogic and holistic replication by oneself of a movement performed by someone else. As shown by the computational literature (e.g. Morasso et al. (1998)), the most simple system which can do this is basically a neural machinery composed of three parts: one perceptual neural map encoding the movement into a perceptual trajectory, one motor neural map encoding motor trajectories and used to actually control the moving organs, and a set of connections which are typically hebbian synapses and whose purpose is to allow the transformation of the trajectory from one space to the other. Figure 10.1 presents a summary of this architecture. We can see that within this architecture, no mechanism of categorization is present and from a computational point of view, it amounts to mapping one continuous trajectory holistically from one space to the other. We will now instantiate this architecture in the context of vocal mimicry: the perceptual space will be acoustic, and the motor space will be articulatory.

10.2.1. Overview

Each agent has one ear which takes measures of the vocalizations that it perceives, which are then sent to its brain. It also has a vocal tract, whose shape is controllable and is used to produce sounds. Typically, the vocal tract and the ear define three spaces: the motor space (which will be for example 3-dimensional in

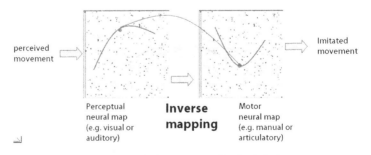

FIGURE 10.1. The minimal neural kit for motor replication/mimicry.

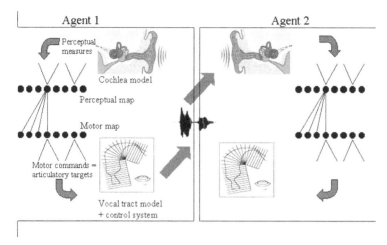

FIGURE 10.2. Architecture of the artificial system: agents are given an artificial ear, an artificial vocal tract, and an artificial "brain" which couples these two organs. Agents are themselves coupled through their common environment: they perceive the vocalizations of their neighbours.

the vowel simulations with tongue body position, tongue height and lip rounding); the acoustic space (which will be 4-dimensional in the vowel simulation with the first four formants) and the perceptual space (which corresponds to the information the ear sends to the brain, and will be 2-dimensional in the vowel simulations with the first formant and the second effective formant).

The ear and the vocal tract are connected to the brain, which is basically a set of interconnected artificial neurons. This set of artificial neurons is organized into two neural topological maps: one perceptual map and one motor map. Topological neural maps have been widely used for many models of cortical maps (Kohonen, 1982; Morasso et al., 1998) which are the neural devices that humans have to represent parts of the outside world (acoustic, visual, touch etc.). Figure 10.2 gives an overview of the architecture. We will now describe the technical details of the architecture.

10.2.2. Motor Neurons, Vocal Tract and Production of Vocalizations

A motor neuron j is characterized by a preferred vector v_j which determines the vocal tract configuration which is to be reached when it is activated and when the agent sends a GO signal to the motor neural map. This GO signal is sent at random times by the agent to the motor neural map. As a consequence, the agent produces vocalizations at random times, independently of any events.

When an agent produces a vocalization, the neurons which are activated are chosen randomly. Typically, 2, 3 or 4 neurons are chosen and activated in sequence. Each activation of a neuron specifies, through its preferred vector, a vocal tract configuration objective that a sub-system takes care of reaching by moving continuously the articulators. In this chapter, this sub-system is simply a linear interpolator, which produces 10 intermediate configurations between each articulatory objective, which is an approximation of a dynamic continuous vocalization and that we denote $ar_1, ar_2, \ldots, ar_N$. Figure 10.3 illustrates this process in the case of an abstract 2-dimensional articulatory space.

An artificial vocal tract is used to compute an acoustic image of the dynamic articulations. We have re-implemented the vocal tract model of vowel production designed by de Boer (2001). We use vowel production only because there exists this computationally efficient and rather accurate model, but one could do simulations with a vocal tract model which models consonants if efficient ones were available. This model is based on the three major vowel articulatory parameters (Ladefoged and Maddieson, 1996): lip rounding, tongue height and tongue position. The values within these dimensions are between 0 and 1, and a triplet of values $ar_i = (r, h, p)$ defines an articulatory configuration. The acoustic image of one articulatory configuration is a point in the 4-dimensional space defined by the first four formants, which are the frequencies of the peaks in the power spectrum, and is computed with the formula defined in (de Boer, 2001).

The preferred vector of each neuron in the motor map is updated each time the motor neurons are activated (which happens both when the agent produces a vocalization and when it hears a vocalization produced by another agent, as we will explain below). This update is made in two steps : 1) one computes which neuron m is most activated and takes the value v_m of its preferred vector ; 2) the preferred vectors of all neurons are modified with the formula:

$$v_{j,t+1} = v_{j,t} + 0.001 G_{j,t}(s)(v_m - v_{j,t})$$

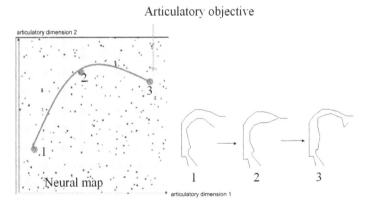

FIGURE 10.3. When an agent produces a vocalization, several motor neurons are activated in sequence. Each of them corresponds to an articulatory configuration which has to be reached from the current configuration. A sub-control system takes care of interpolating between the different configurations.

where $G_{j,t}(s)$ is the activation of neuron j at time t with the stimulus s (as we will detail later on) and $v_{j,t}$ denotes the value of v_j at time t. This law of adaptation of the preferred vectors has the consequence that the more a particular neuron is activated, the more the agent will produce articulations which are similar to the one coded by this neuron. This is because geometrically, when v_m is the preferred vector of the most active neuron, the preferred vectors of the neurons which are also highly activated are shifted a little bit towards v_m. The initial value of all the preferred vectors of the motor neurons is random and uniformly distributed. There are in this experiment 500 neurons in the motor neural map (above a certain number of neurons, which is about 150 in all the cases presented in the chapter, nothing changes if this number varies).

10.2.3. Ear, Perception of Vocalizations and Perceptual Neurons

We describe here the perceptual system of the agents, which is used when they perceive a vocalization. As explained in the previous paragraphs, this perceived vocalization takes the form of an acoustic trajectory, i.e. a sequence of points which approximate the continuous sounds. Here, these points are in the 4-D space whose dimensions are the first four formants of the acoustic signal. We then use a model of the cochlea, described in (Boe et al., 1995) and (de Boer, 2001), which transforms this 4-D acoustic representation in a 2-D perceptual representation that we know is close to the way humans represent vowels.

An agent gets as input to its perceptual neural system a trajectory of perceptual points. Each of these perceptual points is then presented in sequence to its perceptual neural map (this models a discretization of the acoustic signal by the ear due to its limited time resolution).

The neurons i in the perceptual map have a gaussian tuning function which allows us to compute the activation of the neurons upon the reception of an input stimulus. If we denote by $G_{i,t}$ the tuning function of neuron i at time t, s is a stimulus vector, then the form of the function is:

$$G_{i,t}(s) = \frac{1}{\sqrt{2\pi}\sigma} e^{-\frac{1}{2\sigma^2}(s \cdot v_{i,t})^2}$$

where the notation $v_1.v_2$ denotes the scalar product between vector v_1 and vector v_2, and $v_{i,t}$ defines the center of the gaussian at time t and is called the preferred vector of the neuron. This means that when a perceptual stimulus is sent to a neuron i, then this neuron will be activated maximally if the stimulus has the same value as $v_{i,t}$. The parameter σ determines the width of the gaussian, and so if it is large the neurons are broadly tuned (a value of 0.05, which is used in all simulations here, means that a neuron responds substantially to 10 percent of the input space).

When a neuron in the perceptual map is activated because of a stimulus, then its preferred vector is changed. The mathematical formula of the new tuning function is:

$$G_{i,t+1}(s) = \frac{1}{\sqrt{2\pi}\sigma} e^{-\frac{1}{2\sigma^2}(s - v_{i,t+1})^2}$$

where s is the input, and $v_{i,t+1}$ the preferred vector of neuron i after the processing of s:

$$v_{i,t+1} = v_{i,t} + 0.001 G_{i,t}(s)(s - v_{i,t})$$

This formula makes the distribution of preferred vectors evolve so as to approximate the distribution of sounds which are heard.

The initial value of the preferred vectors of all perceptual neurons follows a random and uniform distribution. There are 500 neurons in the perceptual map in the simulations presented in this chapter.

10.2.4. Connections Between the Perceptual Map and the Motor Map

Each neuron i in the perceptual map is connected unidirectionally to all the neurons j in the motor map. The connection between the perceptual neuron i and the motor neuron j is characterized by a weight $w_{i,j}$, which is used to compute the activation of neuron j when a stimulus s has been presented to the perceptual map, with the formula :

$$G_{j,t}(s) = \frac{1}{\sqrt{2\pi}\sigma} e^{-\frac{1}{\sigma^2} \sum_i w_{i,j} G_{i,t}(s)}$$

The weights $w_{i,j}$ are initially set to a small random value, and evolve so as to represent the correlation of activity between neurons. This is how agents will learn the perceptual/articulatory mapping. The learning rule is hebbian (Sejnowsky, 1977):

$$\delta w_{i,j} = c_2 (G_i - \langle G_i \rangle)(G_j - \langle G_j \rangle)$$

where G_i denotes the activation of neuron i and $\langle G_i \rangle$ the mean activation of neuron i over a certain time interval (correlation rule). c_2 denotes a small constant. This learning rule applies only when the motor neural map is already activated before the activations of the perceptual map have been propagated, i.e. when an agent hears a vocalization produced by itself. This amounts to learning the perceptual/motor mapping through vocal babbling.

Note that this means that the motor neurons can be activated either through the activation of the perceptual neurons when a vocalization is perceived, or by direct activation when the agent produces a vocalization (in this case, the activation of the chosen neuron is set to 1, and the activation of the other neurons is set to 0).

Because the connections are unidirectional, the propagation of activations only takes place from the perceptual to the articulatory map (this does not mean that a propagation in the other direction would change the dynamics of the system, but we did not study this variant).

This coupling between the motor map and the perceptual map has an important dynamical consequence: the agents will tend to produce more vocalizations composed of sounds that they have already heard. Said another way, when a vocalization is perceived by an agent, this increases the probability that the sounds that compose this vocalization will be re-used by the agent in its future vocalizations. It is interesting to note that this phenomenon of phonological attunement is observed in very young babies (Vihman, 1996).

10.2.5. Coupling of Agents

The agents are put in a world where they move randomly. At random times, a randomly chosen agent sends a GO signal and produces a vocalization. The agents which are close to it can perceive this vocalization. Here, we fix the number of agents who can hear the vocalization of another to 1 (we pick the closest one). This is a non-crucial parameter of the simulations, since basically nothing changes when we tune this parameter, except the speed of convergence of the system (and this speed is lowest when the parameter is 1). Typically, there are 20 agents in the system. This is also a non-crucial parameter of the simulation : nothing changes except the speed of convergence.

10.3. Dynamics

10.3.1. Crystallization

The present experiment used a population of 20 agents. Initially, as the preferred vectors of neurons are randomly and uniformly distributed across the space, the different targets that compose the vocalizations of agents are also randomly and uniformly distributed. Figure 10.4 shows the preferred vectors of the neurons of the perceptual map of two agents. We see that they cover the whole space uniformly. They are not organized.

The learning rule of the acoustic map is such that it evolves so as to approximate the distribution of sounds in the environment. All agents produce initially complex sounds composed of uniformly distributed targets. Hence, this situation is in equilibrium. Yet, this equilibrium is unstable, and fluctuations ensure that at some point, the symmetry of the distributions of the produced sounds breaks: from time to time, some sounds get produced a little more often than others, and these random fluctuations may be amplified through the positive feedback loop implied by the coupling between perception and production on the one hand, and the plasticity rules on the other hand. This leads to a multi-peaked

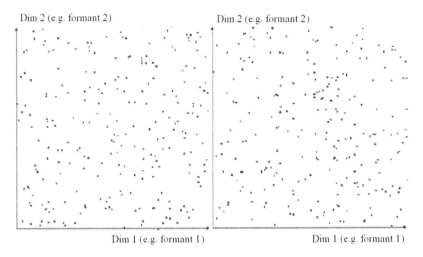

FIGURE 10.4. Perceptual neural maps of two agents at the beginning (the two agents are chosen randomly among a set of 20 agents). Units are arbitrary. Each of both square represents the perceptual map of one agent.

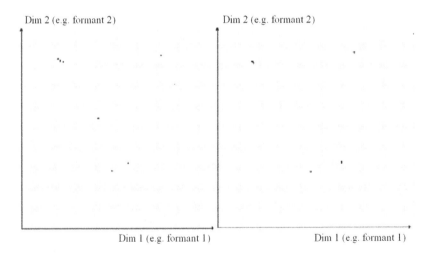

FIGURE 10.5. Neural maps of two agents after 2000 interactions, corresponding to the initial state of figure 10.4 The number of points that one can see is fewer than the number of neurons, since clusters of neurons have the same preferred vectors and this is represented by only one point.

distribution: agents get in a situation like that of Figure 10.5 which corresponds to Figure 10.4 after 2000 interactions in a population of 20 agents. Figure 10.5 shows that the distribution of preferred vectors is no longer uniform but clustered (the same phenomenon happens in the motor maps of the agents, so we represent here only the perceptual maps, as in the rest of the chapter). Yet, it is not so

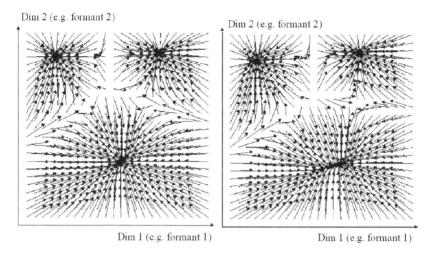

FIGURE 10.6. Representation of the distribution of preferred vectors shown in figure 10.5. The arrows indicate the direction of density increase. We see that the number of clusters is fewer that the number of points in the last figure. This is because in the previous figure, some points corresponded to clusters and other to single points. This figure allows to see that a combinatorial system based on three key articulatory configurations has been built.

easy to visualize the clusters with the representation in Figure 10.5, since there are a few neurons which have preferred vectors not belonging to these clusters. They are not statistically significant, but introduce noise into the representation. Furthermore, in the clusters, basically all points have the same value so that they appear as one point. Figure 10.6 shows better the clusters using a representation of the distribution of preferred vectors: the arrows show the direction of increase of their density. We see that there are now three well-defined attractors or categories, and that they are the same in the two agents represented (they are also the same in the 18 other agents in the simulation). This means that the targets the agents use now belong to one of several well-defined clusters. The continuum of possible targets has been broken, sound production is now discrete. Moreover, the number of clusters that appear is low, which automatically brings it about that targets are systematically re-used to build the complex sounds that agents produce: their vocalizations are now combinatorial. All the agents share the same speech code in any one simulation. Yet, in different simulations, the exact set of modes at the end is different. The number of modes also varies with exactly the same set of parameters. This is due to the inherent stochasticity of the process.

It is very important to note that this result of crystallization holds for any number of agents (experimentally), and in particular with only one agent which adapts to its own vocalizations. This means that the interaction with other agents (i.e. the social component) is not necessary for discreteness and combinatoriality to arise. But what is interesting is that when agents interact, they crystallize in the same state, with the same categories. To summarize, there are so far two results: on the one hand discreteness and compositionality arise thanks to the coupling between perception and production within agents, on the other hand shared systems of phonemic categories arise thanks to the coupling between perception and production across agents.

Finally, it has to be noted that a crucial parameter of the simulation is the parameter σ which defines the width of the tuning functions. All the results presented are with a value 0.05. In (Oudeyer, 2006), we present a study of what happens when we tune this parameter. This study shows that the simulation is quite robust to this parameter: indeed, there is a large zone of values in which we get a practical convergence of the system in a state where agents have a multi-peaked preferred vector distribution, as in the examples we presented. What changes is the mean number of these peaks in the distributions: for example, with $\sigma = 0.05$, we obtain between 3 and 10 clusters, and with $\sigma = 0.01$, we obtain between 6 and 15 clusters. If σ becomes too small, then the initial equilibrium of the system becomes stable and nothing changes: agents keep producing inarticulate and holistic vocalizations. If σ is too large, then the system converges to one cluster.

10.3.2. Structure

In the last paragraph, we showed that a system of combinatorial vocalizations self-organized, shared by the agents in the same simulation and different in agents of different simulations. We will now study the structure of these self-organized repertoires by focusing on the vowels that compose the complex dynamical vocalizations, and compare it to the structure of human vowel systems.

A series of 500 simulations was run with the same set of parameters, and each time the number of vowels as well as the structure of the system was checked. Each vowel system was classified according to the relative position of the vowels, as opposed to looking at the precise location of each of them. This is inspired by the work of Crothers (1978) on universals in vowel systems, and is identical to the type of classification performed in (de Boer, 2001). The first result shows that the distribution of vowel inventory sizes is very similar to that of human vowel systems (Ladefoged and Maddieson, 1996): experiments with the artificial system showed that there is a peak at 5 vowels, which is remarkable since 5 is neither the maximum nor the minimum number of vowels found in human languages. The prediction made by the model is even more accurate than the one provided by de Boer (2001) since his model predicted a peak at 4 vowels. Then the structure of the emergent vowel systems was compared to the structure of vowel systems in human languages as reported in (Schwartz et al., 1997). More precisely, the distributions of structures in the 500 emergent systems were compared to the distribution of structures in the 451 languages of the UPSID database (Maddieson, 1984). The results are shown in Figure 10.8. We see that the predictions are rather accurate, especially in the prediction of the most frequent system for each size of vowel system (less than 8). Figure 10.7 shows an instance of the most frequent system in both

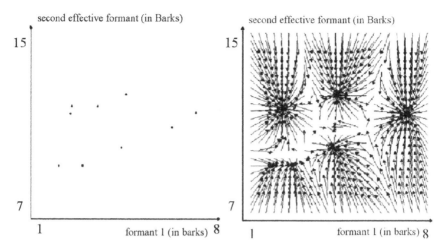

FIGURE 10.7. Neural map and associated attractor field of one agent after 2000 interactions with other 20 agents. The corresponding figures of other agents are nearly identical. The produced vowel system is here an instantiation the most frequent vowel system in human languages: /a, e, i, o, u/.

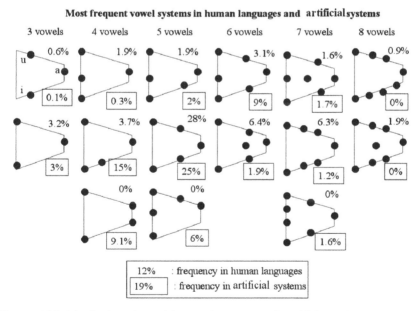

FIGURE 10.8. Distribution of vowel inventories structures in artificial and UPSID human vowel systems. This diagram uses the same notations than the one in (Schwartz et al., 1997). Note that here, the vertical axis is also F2, but oriented downwards.

emergent and human vowel systems. In spite of the predictions of one 4-vowel system and one 5-vowel system which appear frequently (9.1 and 6 percent of systems) in the simulations and never appear in UPSID languages, these results compare favourably to those obtained in (de Boer, 2001). Yet, like de Boer, we are not able to predict systems with many vowels (which are admittedly rare in human languages, but do exist). This is not very surprising since this model was designed to study the mechanisms which might have allowed the bootstrapping of speech, but not how these primitive speech systems might have been recruited later on for complex linguistic communication and thus undergo severe functional pressures for larger repertoires.

10.4. Conclusion

In this paper, we have shown that from a minimal neural kit for vocal replication, a shared combinatorial speech code with structural regularities and diversity could spontaneously self-organize in a population of agents. This result is conditioned by the value of the width of the tuning functions of neurons, which must be within a certain interval (but this interval is rather large). One needs to state that the capability of vocal replication is not diminished if this value gets out of this interval within certain limits. Yet, it is easy to see that from an evolutionary point of view, the transition from inarticulated speech to combinatorial and shared speech codes can be achieved just by tuning the width of these functions, which is admittedly a small modification. As a consequence, this allows us to understand that, in a scenario in which our ancestors passed through a stage where motor replication, and in particular vocal replication, was present and language still absent, the evolutionary step from vocal replication systems to modern human speech systems might have been rather small.

Acknowledgments. This research has been partially supported by the ECAGENTS project founded by the Future and Emerging Technologies programme (IST-FET) of the European Community under EU R&D contract IST-2003-1940

References

Beecher, M., Brenowitz, E., 2005. Functional aspects of song learning in songbirds. Trends in Ecology and Evolution 20, 143–149.

Boe, L., Schwartz, J., Valle, N., 1995. The prediction of vowel systems: perceptual contrast and stability. In: E., K. (Ed.), Fundamentals of Speech Synthesis and Recognition. Chichester:John Wiley, pp. 185–213.

Crothers, J., 1978. Typology and universals of vowels systems. Phonology 2, 93–152.

de Boer, B., 2001. The origins of vowel systems. Oxford Linguistics. Oxford University Press.

Kohonen, T., 1982. Self-organized formation of topologically correct feature maps. Biological Cybernetics 43 (1), 59–69.

Ladefoged, P., Maddieson, I., 1996. The Sounds of the World's Languages. Blackwell Publishers, Oxford.

Lindblom, B., 1992. Phonological units as adaptive emergents of lexical development. In: Ferguson, Menn, Stoel-Gammon (Eds.), Phonological Development: Models, Research, Implications. York Press, Timonnium, MD, pp. 565–604.

Maddieson, I., 1984. Patterns of sound. Cambridge university press.

Mehler, J., Christophe, A., Ramus, F., 2000. What we know about the initial state for language. In: Marantz, A., Miyashita, Y., O'Neil, W. (Eds.), Image, Language, Brain: Papers from the first Mind-Brain Articulation Project symposium. Cambridge, MA: MIT Press, pp. 51–75.

Morasso, P., Sanguinetti, V., Frisone, F., Perico, L., 1998. Coordinate-free sensorimotor processing: computing with population codes. Neural Networks 11, 1417–1428.

Nehaniv, C. L., Dautenhahn, K., 2002. The correspondence problem. In: Dautenhahn, K., Nehaniv, C. L. (Eds.), Imitation in Animals and Artifacts. MIT Press, pp. 41–61.

Oudeyer, P.-Y., 2005. How phonological structures can be culturally selected for learnability. Adaptive Behavior 13 (4), 269–280.

Oudeyer, P.-Y., 2006. Self-Organization in the Evolution of Speech. Studies in the Evolution of Language. Oxford University Press.

Schwartz, J., Bo, L., Valle, N., Abry, C., 1997. Major trends in vowel systems inventories. Journal of Phonetics 25, 255–286.

Sejnowsky, T., 1977. Storing covariance with non-linearly interacting neurons. Journal of mathematical biology 4, 303–312.

Stevens, K., 1972. The quantal nature of speech: evidence from articulatory-acoustic data. New-York: Mc Graw-Hill, pp. 51–66.

Vihman, M., 1996. Phonological Development: The Origins of Language in the Child. Oxford, UK: Blackwell Publishers.

11
Learning and Transition of Symbols: Towards a Dynamical Model of a Symbolic Individual

Takashi Hashimoto and Akira Masumi

11.1. Introduction

The remarkable feature of linguistic communications is the use of symbols for transmitting information and mutual understanding. Deacon (1997) pointed out that humans are symbolic species, namely, we show symbolic cognitive activities such as learning, formation, and manipulation of symbols. In research into the origin and the evolution of language, we should elucidate the emerging process of such symbolic cognitive activities.

Most agent models in simulation studies of language evolution presuppose symbol processing ability (Cangelosi and Parisi, 2002). For example, a computational model for the evolution of compositional syntax introduced in Kirby (2002) and in Kirby and Hurford (2002) can possess grammatical rules representing the correspondence of meanings and character strings that are considered as combinations of symbols. In a dynamical model for the evolution of prototypical category structure introduced in Hashimoto (2002a), agents can emit, receive and process sequences of words.

In order to understand the origin and the evolution of language, we should deal with the emerging process of such a symbol processing ability. To this end, we need a model of an agent that autonomously acquires the ability of symbolic cognitive activities for effectively studying the emergence and the evolution of linguistic communication with a constructive approach.

Mathematical and computational studies of symbol processing have been done in artificial intelligence and connectionism. The former has difficulty in the self-organisation and the emergence of symbols, since symbols and syntactic rules governing the symbol processing are usually given by hand. While the latter can acquire, in part, the symbolic representation from scratch without preparing explicit symbolic elements, it is not good at explicitly describing symbols and their processing rules, since symbols have a distributed representation in neural networks. Thus, a new approach for symbol formation has been required (Harnad, 1990), which integrates both artificial intelligence type and connectionism type methods[1].

A recent development is to view cognitive systems from the dynamic perspective. van Gelder (1998) argued that cognitive systems can be well understood by considering them as dynamical systems and has presented many examples of dynamic cognitive models (van Gelder and Port, 1995). This viewpoint is also proposed to describe dynamic aspects of brain activities using the framework of dynamical systems and chaos (Tsuda, 2001).

Chaos is deterministic but unpredictable – in spite of the fact that the time evolution of a system is fully described by deterministic equations, no one can predict its long term behaviour. The unpredictability is caused by the expansion of small differences in the nonlinear chaotic systems. This property is described as "sensitive dependence on initial conditions". Note that chaotic dynamics are not random but have certain structures temporally and geometrically. A geometrical structure of chaotic dynamics is often characterised by a "strange attractor", which is a limit set of orbits (attractor) having a fractal structure. Chaos can bring fertile spacio-temporal structures into existence. Attention has been paid to such interesting features of chaos as characterising brain functions (Skarda and Freeman, 1987; Tsuda, 2001), and actual chaotic dynamics are found in real neurons and brains (Aihara and Matsumoto, 1986; Freeman, 1987).

The purpose of the present study is to construct a model of an agent showing symbolic cognitive activities with a dynamical system. When we construct a model of a cognitive agent for linguistic communication, we take the dynamic viewpoint not only for the cognitive systems but also for language (van Gelder, 1998; Hashimoto, 2002a, 2002b). The dynamic view for language means that symbols are not mere correspondences of words to referents and section formation is not merely an assigning process of words to some objects.

The rest of this paper is organised as follows. In section 11.2 we discuss how symbolic systems are able to be interpreted in dynamical terms. Following the discussion, we introduce a model of dynamical systems for symbolic activities in section 11.3, based on the Hopfield model. In fact, the model is composed of coupled chaotic dynamical systems, called NZ maps. The simulation results of the model are shown in section 11.4. We discuss the results in section 11.5 and conclude this paper in section 11.6.

11.2. Symbol Systems as Dynamical Systems

To model the symbolic activities in the framework of dynamical systems, we consider features of symbols. In general, symbols are considered to represent

---

[1] Note that using a connectionist model does not necessarily mean that no symbolic element is involved. For example, in the simple recurrent network introduced by Elman (1995), sequences of words which are discrete representations are fed to the network as inputs.

or to signify something and are manipulated according to some rules such as a grammar in language or a deduction rule in calculation and formal thought.

Harnad (1990) summarised the features of symbol systems with the following definitions:

1. A symbol is a set of arbitrary physical tokens that are
2. manipulated on the basis of explicit rules
3. that are likewise physical tokens and strings tokens.
4. The rule-governed symbol-token manipulation is based purely on the form[2] of the symbol tokens, i.e. it is purely syntactic, and
5. consists of rulefully combining and recombining symbol tokens.
6. There are primitive atomic symbol tokens and
7. composite symbol-token strings.
8. The entire system and all its parts are all semantically interpretable: the syntax can be systematically assigned a meaning.

This definition describes an external system that can be interpreted as symbolic rather than internal symbolic activities. In order to construct an agent model showing symbolic activities, we construe this definition as internal cognitive processes. Further, to implement the agent model using a dynamical system, we interpret the processes through the concepts of dynamical systems.

The items 1, 6 and 8 imply that there are some entities that are accepted or interpreted as representing something such as objects, states of affairs, or abstract ideas by cognitive agents. To receive some physical tokens a cognitive process recalls some memorised concepts. In the terms of dynamical systems, some inputs to a dynamical system bring it to certain (dynamic) states. This representative function is thought of as being realised by a kind of memory that is usually modelled by attractors of the dynamical system.

The items 2, 3 and 4 state that the cognitive agent performs a process of successive recall of concepts (memories) and the successions are rule-governed. In dynamical terms, there are (spontaneous) transitions among attractors and a transition is rule-governed or, at least, ordered.

The items 5, 7 and 8 mean that a part of sets or some series of physical tokens, but not all sets and series, are accepted as an ordered combination of entities, not as independent entities, and receiving processes of such series induce retrieval processes of concepts. These activities are considered as evocations of ordered transitions among attractors by some input sequences in dynamical systems.

A chaotic neural network is a candidate to implement the above mentioned behaviour as a dynamical system. In chaotic neural networks, memories are realised as attractors of the system (Adachi and Aihara, 1997). In some chaotic dynamical systems, transitions among "attractor ruins"[3] have been found, called

---

[2] In Harnad's original article (1990), the term "shape" is used. We reword this as "form" for clarification.

[3] An attractor ruin is a region in a state space of a dynamical system, in which an orbit stays for a while like an attractor, but does not stay forever, and escapes from there.

"chaotic itinerancy" (Kaneko and Tsuda, 2003). Thus, we may be able to construct a system with plastically learnable symbolic activities by a chaotic dynamical system by introducing the following correspondences:

– symbols to attractors,
– symbol manipulations to transitions among attractors,
– manipulation rules, or regularities in manipulation, to order– the transition.

In the following we try to construct a dynamical system having the above mentioned properties corresponding to symbolic activities, that is, multiple attractors, transitions among the attractors, and order in transitions. We will enquire if the dynamical system introduced in the next section has actually such properties by computer simulations.

11.3. Model of Chaotic Neural Network

11.3.1. Coupled NZ Map

Nozawa (1992) derived a chaotic neural network model from the Hopfield model (Hopfield, 1984) by introducing small negative self-feedback connections and by discretising the time variable using the Euler method. The chaotic neural network model is called a coupled NZ map[4]. In a network model the elements described by a single NZ map interact through connections, therefore the elements are said to be "coupled" with each other in a neural network system. It is shown that this system chaotically itinerates among attractor ruins. Similar to the Hopfield model and other chaotic neural networks (Adachi and Aihara, 1997), the coupled NZ maps can be used as an associative memory device. Nozawa (1992) also demonstrated the high information processing ability of this system in solving a class of combinatorial optimisation problem and a nonlinear optimisation (Matsuo and Nozawa, 1997).

In this paper, we use the coupled NZ maps for a model representing the features of symbols discussed in the previous section. The coupled NZ map is given by the following equations[5]:

$$p_i(t+1) = F_{q_i(t)}\{p_i(t)\}, \tag{1}$$

$$q_i(t) = -\frac{1}{T_{ii}}\left\{\sum_{j \neq i}^{N} T_{ij}p_j(t) + I_i\right\}, \tag{2}$$

$$F_q(p) = rp + (1-r)\left[1 - \frac{1}{2}\left\{1 + \tanh\left(\frac{p-q}{2\beta}\right)\right\}\right], \tag{3}$$

---

[4] Because of the discretisation of the time variable, the model is represented by difference equations, that is, maps, while the original Hopfield model is represented by differential equations.

[5] Refer to Nozawa (1992) for the detailed derivation from the Hopfield model.

where the symbols in these equations are as follows:

- $p_i(t)$: the internal buffer of the ith neuron at time t, which develops according to the map, $F_{q_i(t)}$, defined by Eqn.(3)
- $q_i(t)$: the influence from the other neurons to the ith neuron as shown in Eqn.(2)
- T_{ij}: the synaptic connection between the ith and the jth neurons
- T_{ii}: the self-feedback connection of the ith neuron
- I_i : the threshold of the ith neuron
- N: the number of neurons
- r: the parameter related to the damping constant of the neurons
- β: the parameter related to the gain constant of the neurons[6]

In order to understand the basic properties of the NZ maps, let us look at the behaviour of a single NZ map, when there is no connection between the elements, $T_{ij} = 0$ for all i and $j \neq i$. Therefore, $q_i(t)$ in Eqn.(2) is constant $q_i = I_i/T_{ii} \equiv q$. Thus the single NZ map is described by

$$p(t+1) = rp + (1-r)\left[1 - \frac{1}{2}\left\{1 + \tanh\left(\frac{p-q}{2\beta}\right)\right\}\right]. \tag{4}$$

This map is a combination of a linear function p and a reversed sigmoid function with the combination coefficient r. The parameter r usually takes a value between 0 and 1, thus the map has three branches as shown in Figure 11.1. When an orbit comes to the middle branch, the expansion of small differences occurs

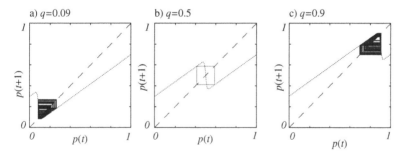

FIGURE 11.1. The shapes of the single NZ map, Eqn. (4), and their dynamics for different values of the control parameter a) $q = 0.09$, b) $q = 0.5$ and c) $q = 0.9$. The other parameters are $r = 0.7$ and $\beta = 0.006$. The horizontal and vertical axes are the value of the variable p at time t and $t+1$, respectively. The dotted lines are the shape of the map. The solid lines shows the dynamics (orbit) of the map (the cobweb plot). The dashed lines are the diagonals. If the orbit does not come to the middle branch which has steep negative slope, as in b), the dynamics are periodic. When the orbit comes to the middle branch, it shows chaotic motion as a) and c).

---

[6] As described later, the parameters T_{ii}, I_i, r and β are chosen for the system to show chaotic behaviour and T_{ij} is determined to store some memory patterns in the system.

and the dynamics comes to be chaotic, since the slope of this branch is steep. Because the variable q, which is the ratio of the threshold to the self-feedback connection, moves the threshold of the sigmoid function, the middle branch of the single NZ map moves with the value of q. Namely, the variable q plays a role of a control parameter to determine the shape and the nonlinearity of the single map. When q is 0 or 1, the map has a fixed point around $p = 0$ or $p = 1$, respectively. When $0 < q < 1$, the orbit shows chaotic behaviour. Examples of the map and the dynamics for different values of q are shown in Figure 11.1. In Figure 11.1a) and c), the dynamics are chaotic for $q = 0.09$ and 0.9, respectively, and in Figure 11.1b), period two dynamics are shown for $q = 0.5$.

In the coupled system, the control parameter q changes with time from the influences of other elements, as Eqn.(2) says. Even if the dynamics of some elements fall into fixed points, the values of q of such elements are changed by the other ones through the connections, and then the orbits can escape from the fixed points. Therefore, the coupled NZ maps consist of a variety of maps of all sorts of dynamical motions, that induces diverse dynamic behaviour of the system, such as fixed, periodic and chaotic motions and transitions among such states.

11.3.2. Embedding Patterns as Attractors

As mentioned above, we consider that symbols correspond to attractors of a dynamical system. Since the system introduced here is basically an associative memory model, we can embed several memory states as attractors of the dynamical system (Hopfield, 1984). To do this, the connection weights between elements should be appropriately set or learnt corresponding to patterns to be embedded, or memorised.

In order to embed a pattern represented by a N dimensional vector $V^s = (V^s_1, \cdots, V^s_N)$ with $V^s_i = 1$ ("ON") or 0 ("OFF"), where the index s indicates each embedded pattern, the following equation is used to determine the connection T_{ij} between the ith and the jth elements,

$$T_{ij} = \sum_s (2V^s_i - 1)(2V^s_j - 1). \tag{5}$$

11.3.3. Recalled Pattern

The coupled system behaving according to Eqns.(1)~(3) represents some patterns. We define a recalled pattern $\phi(t) = \{\phi_1(t), \cdots, \phi_N(t)\}$ by observing the values of $q_i(t)$ of all elements as

$$\phi_i(t) = \begin{cases} 1 & (q_i(t) \geq \bar{q}(t)), \\ 0 & (q_i(t) < \bar{q}(t)), \end{cases} \tag{6}$$

where

$$\bar{q}(t) = \lim_{t \to \infty} \frac{1}{tN} \sum_{t'=0}^{t-1} \sum_{i=1}^{N} q_i(t') \tag{7}$$

is the criterion to separate whether each element is "ON" ($\phi_i(t) = 1$) or "OFF" ($\phi_i(t) = 0$). This criterion is the spacio-temporal average of $q_i(t)$ (Nozawa, 1992). When a recalled pattern coincides with one of the embedded patterns, that is,

$$\phi(t) = V^s \qquad (8)$$

for some s, the embedded pattern, or memory, is retrieved.

11.4. Simulation Results

We embed three orthogonal patterns, shown in Figure 11.2 and named $C, F, 4$, respectively, in the system with $N = 16$ elements. Because of the symmetrical nature of the system, the reversed patterns of the embedded ones are also attractors. Such reversed patterns are labelled as $\bar{C}, \bar{F}$ and $\bar{4}$, respectively. All the patterns other than the embedded and their reversed patterns are treated in a lump and labelled as O. The parameters are $q = I_i/T_{ii} = 0.09, r = 0.7$, $\beta = 0.006$ throughout the experiments described in this paper. This parameter set means that each element alone keeps showing chaotic behaviour as depicted in Figure 11.1a). In the following experiments, we change the strength of the self-feedback connection, T_{ii}, of all the elements as a control parameter. Note that the ratio of T_{ii} to I_i is fixed.

11.4.1. Recall and Transition of Embedded Patterns

The system starts from a generic initial state. Then in a certain region the strength of the self-feedback connection, T_{ii}, causes the recall of one of the embedded or their reversed patterns after a certain time (Figure 11.3). The two graphs in Figure 11.3 have the same parameters but differ in their initial states. They converge to different patterns. The fact that different initial conditions end up with different converged attractors means that this system has multi-attractors.

When we raise the strength of the self-feedback connection from the convergence parameter region, the system itinerates among embedded patterns through non-memorised patterns as shown in Figure 11.4. Since there is no input to the system, the system autonomously changes its recalling patterns.

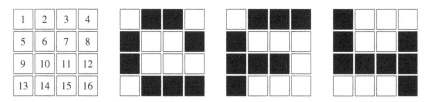

FIGURE 11.2. Schematic view of embedded patterns. The black and white boxes mean 1 ("ON") and 0 ("OFF"), respectively. The patterns are named as C, F and 4, respectively. The index for each element is arranged as the left most figure.

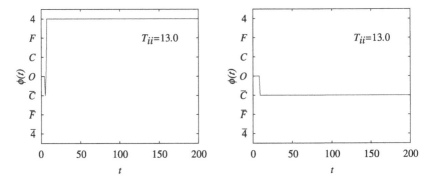

FIGURE 11.3. The time series of recalled patterns. The x and y axes are time t and the recalled patterns ϕ, respectively. The labels $C, F, 4$ are the embedded patterns and $\bar{C}, \bar{F}, \bar{4}$ are their reversed patterns, respectively. The label O means that the system is not in any embedded pattern. Two graphs starts from different initial conditions. The self-feedback connection is $T_{ii} = 13.0$ in the both graphs.

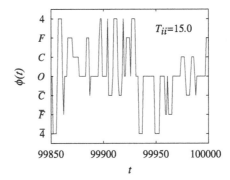

FIGURE 11.4. The time series of recalled patterns ϕ without input. The x axis is time. The self-feedback connection is $T_{ii} = 15.0$. This graph shows an itinerant motion among the embedded patterns.

11.4.2. Response to Input

We examine how the system reacts to external inputs. Among a great variety of ways to input signals, we consider, as the simplest cases, constant and periodic inputs and observe the response of the system to these inputs. The external input $S(t)$ is given in Eqn.(2) as

$$q_i(t) = -\frac{1}{T_{ii}} \left\{ \sum_{j \neq i}^{N} T_{ij} p_j(t) + S(t) + I_i \right\}. \tag{9}$$

In order to observe the dynamics of the system more precisely than just the sequence of recalled patterns, we introduce a distance measure of orbit $q_i(t)$ from the embedded patterns $V^{s'}$. The index s' is for the patterns both embedded and their reverses, that is, $C, F, 4$. and $\bar{C}, \bar{F}, \bar{4}$, while s in Eqn.(5) indicates only the embedded patters. The measure is defined as

$$Dist^{s'}(t) = \sqrt{\sum_{i=1}^{N}(V_i^{s'} - q_i(t))^2}. \qquad (10)$$

When any embedded and its reversed pattern is not definitely recalled, the orbit is categorised merely as O, as seen in Figures 11.3 and 11.4.

Constant Input. We give a constant input sequence $S(t) = 0.3$ at $t = 10000 \sim$ 20000 for the system with the self feedback connections $T_{ii} = 15.0$ for all the elements. While the system shows the itinerant motion when there is no input as in Figure 11.4, the constant input brings the system sometimes to become fixed to a pattern and sometimes to fluctuate among the patterns. Figure 11.5 (Left) shows the time series of $q_i(t)$ around the input when the system falls onto a fixed pattern. The elements fluctuate widely, they itinerate among attractors before the input is given, and are then stabilised by the input.

Figure 11.5 (Right) is a magnification of the dynamics of the system around the beginning of the input. Injecting the constant input causes the orbits showing chaotic dynamics to separate into two clusters. The dynamics are still chaotic but this is a transient state, and after 50 steps from the beginning of the input, the orbits of all elements enter stable periodic motions.

The elements are actually clustered hierarchically. Eight of 16 elements have higher values of $q_i(t)$ than the other ones as shown in Figure 11.6 (Left). The former elements, $i = 1, 6, 7, 8, 12, 14, 15, 16$ with numbering from top left to bottom right in Figure 11.2, correspond to "ON" elements of the pattern $\bar{F}$. They

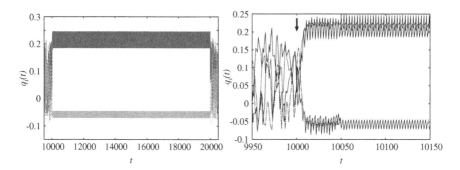

FIGURE 11.5. (Left) The time series of $q_i(t)$ when a fixed input $S(t) = 0.3$ in Eqn. (9) is given. The x axis is time. The self-feedback connection is $T_{ii} = 15.0$. The time series of 2 elements among 16 are drawn. (Right) The time series of $q_i(t)$ around the beginning of the input. The time series of 4 of 16 elements are depicted. The orbits, chaotically fluctuating before the input, promptly split into two clusters, when the input starts (indicated by the down arrow). Then, the dynamics are stabilised at a periodic state after 50 steps from the beginning of the input.

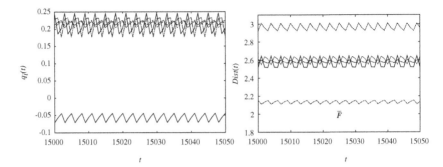

FIGURE 11.6. (Left) The time series of $q_i(t)$ around the mid of the inputting period when a fixed input $S(t) = 0.3$ is given. The x axis is time. The self-feedback connection is $T_{ii} = 15.0$. Note the change in scale of t on the x axis from Fig. 11.5 (Right). The time series of all 16 elements are superimposed, but only 5 lines are distinguishable. The elements form two clusters. The upper cluster consisting of 8 elements corresponds to a pattern, $\bar{F}$. The elements are subdivided into 4 clusters, each of which has two elements. The residual 8 elements in the lower cluster have the same values while the input is given. (Right) The time series of the distance measure from the embedded patterns, $Dist^s(t)$. The six orbits of the distance from all patterns are superimposed. The orbits periodically change, but the nearest pattern is fixed at $\bar{F}$.

form 4 sub-clusters consisting of two elements each. The residual 8 elements in the latter cluster, corresponding to "OFF" elements, synchronously oscillate while the input is given. Although the elements are not fixed by the dynamics of $q_i(t)$, the nearest pattern does not change. The time series of the distance measure, depicted in Figure 11.6 (Right), tells that the system stays at a state where the nearest pattern is $\bar{F}$.

As we mentioned, the system with a constant input sequence sometimes converges to various fixed patterns and sometimes itinerates among the embedded patterns and their reverses, in which case itinerant motion is not the same as one without an input sequence. This behavioural diversity depends on the timing of the input, since the system is in an itinerant motion as shown in Figure 11.4. This itinerant behaviour is considered as the internal dynamics of the system. The system differs in its response to stimuli according to its internal dynamics, even though the same stimulus is given.

Sinusoidal Input. We input a sinusoidal sequence,

$$S(t) = A\sin(2\pi\omega t), \tag{11}$$

at $t = 10000 \sim 20000 (A = 0.7, \omega = 0.001)$ to the same system as in the previous experiment, the self-feedback connections are $T_{ii} = 15.0$ for all the elements. A transition among the patterns is observed as shown in Figure 11.7.

For a closer observation, we draw the dynamics of the distance measure in Figure 11.8. This graph tells us that the change of the nearest patterns occurs with roughly the same intervals. The interval approximately matches with the cycle

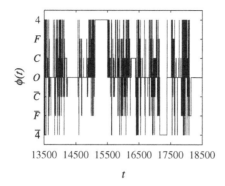

FIGURE 11.7. The time series of recalled patterns with a sinusoidal input sequence. The x axis is time. The self-feedback connection is $T_{ii} = 15.0$. This graph shows an itinerant motion among the patterns.

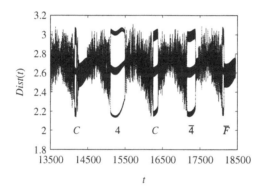

FIGURE 11.8. The time series of the distance measure from embedded patterns, $Dist^{s'}(t)$, when a sinusoidal input sequence is given. The x axis is time. The six orbits of the distance from all patterns are superimposed. The self-feedback connection is $T_{ii} = 15.0$. A transition among the nearest patterns with nearly the same intervals is observed.

of the sinusoidal input. The order of recalled patterns is not periodic. Further, we have not found clear statistical order in the transition among recalled patterns.

The change of the recalled pattern is certainly induced by the periodicity of the sine wave. This is clearly perceived from Figure 11.9. When the amplitude of the sine wave falls below zero, the clustering (synchronisation or recalling a pattern) is dissolved and the system enters a chaotic (itinerate) state. When the amplitude of the input become positive, the system starts to synchronise again and is attracted to a pattern. But a memory of the last recalled pattern (the time correlation between recalled patterns) is destroyed by the interleaved chaotic motion. Thus, there is no ordered transition and a transition rule among the patterns is not formed.

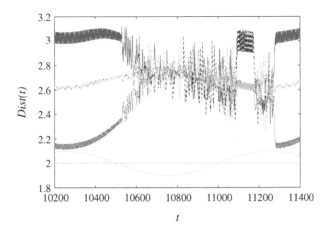

FIGURE 11.9. The time series of the distance measure from the embedded and reversed patterns, $Dist^{s}(t)$, with the sinusoidal input, $S(t) = A \sin(2\pi\omega t)$ (lower periodic line). The amplitude of the input is transformed appropriately. The straight line shows the zero level of the input.

Figure 11.9 shows the existence of intrinsic instability of the system, as well. The clustering is destroyed even though the amplitude of the input is large enough around $t = 11200$. This is the effect of internal chaotic dynamics.

11.5. Discussion

We have suggested correspondences between symbolic activities and dynamical systems such that symbols correspond to attractors, symbol manipulations to transitions among attractors, and regularities in symbol manipulation to the order of transitions. Let us examine how the simulation results of the coupled NZ maps conducted in this paper are concordant with these correspondences, and therefore appropriate as a model of a symbolic cognitive agent.

At first, some patterns are embedded in the system and they are retrieved as attractors. The embedded patterns are recalled when a constant input is given to the system. Namely, the patterns and input sequences are associated like memories and some patterns of perceptions. This representation is an important function of symbols. Further, embedding several patterns or having multi-attractors indicates that the system has the capacity to learn some number of symbols. The number of symbols is less than half of the system size N.

Concerning the second point, a dynamical system model of a symbolic cognitive agent is required to show, at least, transition among attractors. We can realise such behaviour in some parameter regions of the self-feedback connection T_{ii} as shown in Figure 11.4. The transition is evoked by the input sequence of an ordered change. Namely, our system also has a capacity for symbol manipulations.

However, the transitions among attractors are not orderly. We have not found regularities in the transitions, that is, no basis for syntax. In chaotic dynamical systems, in general, time correlation decays exponentially. The rapid decrease of the time correlation causes these disordered transitions. The low correlation seems to be brought about partly by the orthogonal embedded patterns created by hand. If so, system learning in a particular environment with some structure may overcome this inadequacy. Namely, the order in the external world might form a structural coupling with the internal structure of the agent. Thus, to examine the system's status as a model of a symbolic cognitive agent, it is important to investigate the behaviour of the system taught in a structured environment.

Let us further discuss the process of symbol formation or development of symbols based on the correspondences between symbolic activities and the behaviour of dynamical systems. Harnad (1990) summarises the developmental process of representation as a progress from iconic representation to categorical and to symbolic. The iconic representation is demonstrated by retrieving an attractor from an input. This is shown by our system.

The categorical representation can be translated in two ways. One is retrieving an attractor for different inputs, the other is grouping of attractors according to some features, such as dimension and nonlinearity. Our system shows the former behaviour. The dynamics of each element differ for different inputs but some dynamics are categorised into one pattern that is nearest. Namely, though precise internal states of the agent are not the same the representing symbol is the same for a class of inputs. To observe the latter interpretation, we need further investigation into the characteristics of attractors of the model.

The symbolic representation should show an orderly transition among attractors induced by an input sequence. As we found, this is not realised in the present system. If, however, we develop the system in a structured environment, the system may learn some symbols as attractors and show ordered transition among the attractors. Thus, we may be able to progress along the path of symbolic representation.

11.6. Conclusion

We have proposed a dynamical system model of a cognitive agent that can exhibit a part of symbolic behaviour using coupled chaotic maps, called NZ maps. We have shown that attractors of the dynamical system can represent symbols that can be embedded. The system can have internal dynamics and show symbol manipulation behaviour as transitions among the embedded attractors according to sequences of external input signals. However, the system did not show ordered transitions among symbols, that is, no basis for syntactically structured behaviour. Despite this drawback with the status quo, we conclude that the coupled NZ map system can be developed as a model of symbolic individuals, since we may overcome such insufficiency by further investigations, especially learning and developing in a particular structured environment.

Acknowledgements. This research is supported by JAIST research grant (grant for in-house research projects). We thank Caroline Lyon for her helpful comments and critical editing of the manuscript.

References

Adachi, M., Aihara, K.: Associative dynamics in a chaotic neural network. Neural Networks **10** (1997) 83–98

Aihara, K., Matsumoto, G.: Chaotic oscillations and bifurcations in squid giant axons. In Holden, A.V., ed.: Chaos. Princeton University Press (1986) 257–269

Cangelosi, A., Parisi, D., eds.: Simulating the Evolution of Language. Springer (2002)

Deacon, T.: The Symbolic Species: The Co-Evolution of Language and the Brain. W W Norton (1997)

Elman, J.L.: Language as a dynamical system. In Port, R., van Gelder, T., eds.: Mind as Motion: Dynamical Perspectives on Behavior and Cognition. MIT Press (1995) 195–225

Freeman, W.J.: Simulation of chaotic EEG patterns with a dynamic model of the olfactory system. Biological Cybernetics **56** (1987) 139–150

Harnad, S.: The symbol grounding problem. Physica D **42** (1990) 335–346

Hashimoto, T.: The constructive approach to the dynamical view of language. In Cangelosi, A., Parisi, D., eds.: Simulating the Evolution of Language. Springer (2002) 307–324

Hashimoto, T.: Language as dynamics, – a computational study of ontogenetic and glossogenetic loop. In Hurford, J.R., Fitch, T., eds.: Fourth International Conference on the Evolution of Language – Proceedings. (2002)

Hopfield, J.J.: Neurons with graded response have collective computational properties like those of two-state neurons. Proc. Natl. Acad. Sci. USA **81** (1984) 3088–3092

Kaneko, K., Tsuda, I.: Chaotic itinerancy. Chaos **13**(3) (2003) 926–936

Kirby, S.: Learning, bottlenecks and evolution of recursive syntax. In Briscoe, T., ed.: Linguistic Evolution through Language Acquisition. Cambridge University Press (2002) 173–203

Kirby, S., Hurford, J.R.: The emergence of linguistic structure: an overview of the iterated learning model. In Cangelosi, A., Parisi, D., eds.: Simulating the Evolution of Language. Springer (2002) 121–147

Matsuo, N., Nozawa, H.: Coupled maps and nonlinear optimization (in japanese). In: Proceedings of The Institute of Electrical Engineers of Japan (IEEJ). Volume IP-97-3. (1997)

Nozawa, H.: A neural network model as a globally coupled map and applications based on chaos. Chaos **2**(3) (1992) 377–386

Skarda, C.A., Freeman, W.J.: How brains make chaos in order to make sense of the world. Behavioral and Brain Sciences **10** (1987) 161–195

Tsuda, I.: Toward an interpretation of dynamic neural activity in terms of chaotic dynamical systems. Behavioral and Brain Sciences **24**(5) (2001) 793–847

van Gelder, T., Port, R., eds.: Mind as Motion: Dynamical Perspectives on Behavior and Cognition. MIT Press (1995)

van Gelder, T.: The dynamical hypothesis in cognitive science. Brain and Behavioural Sciences **10** (1998) 615–665

12
Language Change among 'Memoryless Learners' Simulated in Language Dynamics Equations

Makoto Nakamura, Takashi Hashimoto, and Satoshi Tojo

12.1. Introduction

In general, all human beings can learn any human language in their first language acquisition. One of the functions of language use is to communicate with others. In the work described here we investigate situations in which learners are exposed to more than one language. Our study leads us to suggest how creole languages could emerge. We make the assumption that the language learners come to acquire one of the languages that is optimal for communication, which would vary according to the environment. It is postulated that the most preferable language in the community would eventually survive and become dominant in competition with other languages, depending on how large a proportion of the people speak it. Accordingly, language change can be represented by population dynamics, examples of which include an agent-based model of language acquisition proposed by Briscoe et al. (2002) and a mathematical framework by Nowak et al. (2001), who elegantly presented an evolutionary dynamics of grammar acquisition in a differential equation, called the *language dynamics equation*.

One of the main factors of language change can be considered as the interaction between different language groups (Sebba, 1997). Introducing this factor to the language dynamics equation, we can provide a more realistic situation for language change than the existing language dynamics model. Thus, our purpose in this study is to develop a new formalism of language dynamics which deals with language contact among some number of different language speakers, and then to investigate the relationship between the language contact and language change.

For representing the first language acquisition, two extreme learning algorithms have been proposed, called *memoryless* and *batch* learning algorithms (Niyogi, 1998). Both memoryless and batch learners receive training examples as language input. While the batch learners guess a grammar after hearing a batch of language input, the memoryless learners do not need to store training examples for learning, changing their assumption of grammar whenever they receive an input that is inconsistent with their assumption. Komarova et al. (2001) adopted those two kinds of learners into their model, comparing conditions of the two models for the emergence of a dominant language. In this paper, introducing a new transition probability for a memoryless learner exposed to a variety of languages, we compare the behavior of the dynamics with that of Komarova et al. Thus far, we have revised the model of Nowak et al. (2001) in order to study the emergence of creole (Arends et al., 1994) in the context of population dynamics (Nakamura et al. 2003b). For the purpose of modeling the process of creolization, we claimed that infants during language acquisition had contact not only with their parents but also with other language speakers. To meet this condition, we revised the transition probability between languages to be sensitive to the distribution of languages in the population at each generation. A new control parameter, the *exposure rate*, is introduced to determine the degree of influence from other languages during acquisition. Namely, focusing on language learners, we have given a more precise environment of language acquisition than Nowak et al. (2001). In other words, introducing the exposure rate, we have regarded their model as a specific case of ours in language acquisition. Therefore, these revisions enable us to deal not only with the emergence of creole but also with other phenomena of language change. In this paper, we investigate the relationship between the exposure rate and the emergence of a dominant language. In addition, we suppose there is a special *communicative language* which has a higher similarity to some languages than others. We discuss the simulation results from the viewpoint of the language bioprogram hypothesis (Bickerton, 1984).

In Section 12.2, we propose a modified language dynamics equation and a new transition matrix for the memoryless learning algorithm. We describe our experiments in Section 12.3. We discuss the experimental results in Section 12.4. Finally, we conclude this paper in Section 12.5.

12.2. Learning Accuracy of Memoryless Learners

12.2.1. Outline of the Language Dynamics Equation

In this section, we explain the outline of the language dynamics equation proposed by Nowak et al. (2001). In their model, based on the principles of a universal grammar, the search space for candidate grammars is assumed to be finite, that is $\{G_1, \ldots, G_n\}$[1]. The language dynamics equation is given by the following differential equations:

$$\frac{dx_i}{dt} = \sum_{j=1}^{n} x_j f_j Q_{ji} - \phi x_i \ (i = 1, \ldots, n), \tag{1}$$

---

[1] In this chapter we take a grammar as equivalent to a language.

where

x_i : the proportion of the population that speak G_i, where $\sum_{j=1}^{n} x_j = 1$,

$Q = \{Q_{ij}\}$: the transition probability between grammars that a child of G_i speaker comes to acquire G_j,

f_i : fitness of G_i, which determines the number of children individuals reproduce, where $f_i = \sum_{j=1}^{n} (s_{ij} + s_{ji}) x_j / 2$,

$S = \{s_{ij}\}]$: the similarity between languages, which denotes the probability that a G_i speaker utters a sentence consistent with G_j, and

ϕ : the average fitness or *grammatical coherence* of the population, where $\phi = \sum_i x_i f_i$.

The language dynamics equations are mainly composed of (i) the similarity between languages given by the matrix $S = \{s_{ij}\}$ and (ii) the probability that children fail to acquire their parental languages by the matrix $Q = \{Q_{ij}\}$.

As a similarity matrix, in this paper, we mainly deal with a special case such that:

$$s_{ii} = 1, \quad s_{ij} = a \quad (i \neq j), \tag{2}$$

where $0 \leq a \leq 1$. In accordance, the transition probability comes to:

$$Q_{ii} = q, \quad Q_{ij} = \frac{1 - q}{n - 1} \quad (i \neq j), \tag{3}$$

where q is the probability of learning the correct grammar or the *learning accuracy* of grammar acquisition. The accuracy of language acquisition depends on the search space $\{G_1, \ldots, G_n\}$, the learning algorithm, and the number of input sentences, w, during language acquisition.

12.2.2. Modified Language Dynamics Equation

In a situation of language contact, a child may learn a language not only from his parents but also from other language speakers who speak a different language from his parental one. In order to incorporate this possibility in a language dynamics equation, we divide the language input into two categories; one is from the parents and the other is from other language speakers. We name the ratio of the latter to the former an *exposure rate* α. This α is subdivided into smaller ratios corresponding to the distribution of all language speakers. An example distribution of languages is shown in Figure 12.1. Suppose a child has parents who speak G_p, he receives input sentences from G_p on the percentage of the shaded part, $\alpha x_p + (1 - \alpha)$, and from non-parental languages G_j ($j \neq p$) on the percentage, αx_j.

Introducing the exposure rate α, we can represent the proportion of each language to which a child is exposed during the acquisition period. Hence,

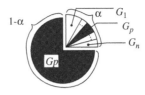

FIGURE 12.1. The exposure rate α.

assuming a total number of sentences for language acquisition, we can calculate the number of sentences the child hears for each language. We make the assumption that the language input is all in sentential form. Here, let us consider a probability of accepting with a grammar a sentence that a learner receives. If the learner presuming G_j hears a sentence only from one teacher speaking G_i, an element s_{ij} in the S matrix predefines the probability of accepting a sentence derived from G_i with G_j. In another case that the learner whose parents speak G_p is exposed to a number of languages, the learner presuming G_j accepts a sentence with such a probability, U_{pj}, that:

$$U_{pj} = \alpha \sum_{k=1}^{n} s_{kj} x_k + (1 - \alpha) s_{pj}. \tag{4}$$

For the special case where Eqn (2) is assumed, it is transformed to:

$$U_{pj} = \begin{cases} 1 - \alpha(1-a)(1-x_j) & (p = j) \\ a + \alpha(1-a)x_j & (p \neq j) \end{cases}. \tag{5}$$

When a learning algorithm is expanded to allow language learners to be exposed to a number of languages, the matrix $U = \{U_{ij}\}$ corresponds to $S = \{s_{ij}\}$ in terms of a probability of accepting a sentence with a learner's grammar. Then, the Q matrix depends on the U matrix and the U matrix on the distribution of languages in the population, $X = \{x_i\}$. Since the distribution of population changes in time, the Q matrix comes to include a time parameter t, that is, Q is redefined as $\overline{Q}(t) = \{\overline{Q}_{ij}(t)\}$. Thus, the new language dynamics equation is expressed by:

$$\frac{dx_i(t)}{dt} = \sum_{j=1}^{n} x_j(t) f_j(t) \overline{Q}_{j/i}(t) - \phi(t) x_i(t) \qquad (i = 1, \ldots, n). \tag{6}$$

We call it the *modified language dynamics equation*.

12.2.3. Memoryless Learning Algorithm

Niyogi (1998) presented two extreme learning algorithms called the batch learning algorithm and the memoryless learning algorithm, in which the former is considered as the most sophisticated algorithm within a range of reasonable possibilities, and the latter as the simplest mechanism. Because the memoryless learning algorithm is easy to remodel with our proposal, we will use it and compare the behavior of the dynamics with that of Komarova et al. (2001). In this section, we explain the learning accuracy of the memoryless learning algorithm, which is derived from a Markov process.

The memoryless learning algorithm describes the interaction between a child learner and language speakers, who are assumed to speak one language each. Namely, the learner hears a set of sentences in a particular language during the acquisition period. The learner starts presuming a grammar by randomly choosing one of the n grammars as an initial state. When the learner hears a sentence from the teacher, he tries to apply his temporary grammar to accept it. If the sentence is consistent with the learner's grammar, no action is taken; otherwise the learner changes his hypothesis about the grammar to the next one randomly picked up from the other grammars. This series of learning is repeated until the learner receives w sentences.

If we consider only one teacher (the learner's parent), the learner hears only one language. In this case, the algorithm is presented by the following expressions. Let us consider a probability distribution of grammar acquisition, denoted by $\boldsymbol{p}^{(w)} = (p_1, \ldots, p_n)^T$, where p_i represents a probability that the learner acquires the i-th grammar after hearing w sentences[2]. The initial probability distribution of the learner is uniform:

$$\boldsymbol{p}^{(0)} = (1/n, \ldots, 1/n)^T, \tag{7}$$

i.e., each of the grammars has the same chance to be picked at the initial state. If the teacher's grammar is G_k and the child hears a sentence from the teacher, the transition process from G_i to G_j in the child's mind is expressed by a Markov process with such a transition matrix $M(k)$ that:

$$M(k)_{ij} = \begin{cases} s_{ki} & (i = j) \\ \dfrac{1 - s_{ki}}{n - 1} & (i \neq j) \end{cases}. \tag{8}$$

After receiving w sentences, the child will acquire a grammar with a probability distribution $\boldsymbol{p}^{(w)}$. Therefore, the probability that a child of a G_i speaker acquires G_j after w sentences is expressed by:

$$Q_{ij} = [(\boldsymbol{p}^{(0)})^T M(i)^w]_j. \tag{9}$$

The transition probability of the memoryless learning algorithm depends on the S matrix. For instance, if the condition of Eqn (2) is satisfied, the off-diagonal

---

[2] A^T denotes the transposed matrix of A.

elements of the Q matrix are also equal to each other, and Eqn (3) holds. Therefore, $q = Q_{ii}$ $(i = 1, \ldots, n)$ is derived as follows:

$$q = 1 - \left(1 - \frac{1-a}{n-1}\right)^{w} \frac{n-1}{n}. \tag{10}$$

This is the learning accuracy of memoryless learners, the probability of learning the correct grammar.

Once a memoryless learner achieves his parental grammar, he will never change his hypothesis. Suppose there exist only two grammars, then the memoryless learner has two states in a Markov process, that is, a state for the hypothesis of his parental grammar, G_{parent}, and a state for the other grammar, G_{other}. The transition probability between the states is expressed by a Markov matrix $M = \{m_{ij}\}$ such that (See Figure 12.2(a) as the corresponding state transition diagram):

$$M = \begin{pmatrix} 1 & 0 \\ 1-a & a \end{pmatrix}, \tag{11}$$

where

m_{11}: the probability that a child who correctly guesses his parental grammar maintains the same grammar,

m_{12}: the probability that a child who correctly guesses his parental grammar changes his presumed grammar to another,

m_{21}: the probability that a child whose grammar is different from his parents' comes to presume his parental grammar, and

m_{22}: the probability that a child whose grammar is different from his parents' keeps the same grammar by accepting a sentence[3].

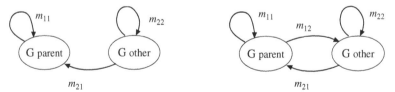

(a) The case in which a child hears sentences only from his parents

(b) The case in which a child hears sentences in a number of languages

FIGURE 12.2. Markov processes for the memoryless learning algorithm.

---

[3] If the memoryless learner is able to choose the refused grammar again with a uniform probability when he failed to accept the sentence, the Markov matrix is replaced by:

$$M = \begin{pmatrix} 1 & 0 \\ (1-a)/2 & a+(1-a)/2 \end{pmatrix}.$$

Komarova et al. (2001) have analyzed the language dynamics equation Eqn (1), and deduced the following results: (i) When the learning accuracy is high enough, most of the people use the same language, that is, there exists a dominant language. Otherwise, all languages appear at roughly similar frequencies. (ii) The learning accuracy is calculated from a learning algorithm. Receiving input sentences, a memoryless learner enhances his learning accuracy.

12.2.4. Memoryless Learners Exposed to a Number of Languages

We define a transition matrix, $\overline{Q}(t) = \{\overline{Q}_{ij}(t)\}$, of memoryless learners exposed to a number of languages during the acquisition period. For a child whose parents speak G_p, the transition matrix of a Markov process is defined by:

$$M(p)_{ij} = \begin{cases} U_{pi} & (i = j) \\ \dfrac{1 - U_{pi}}{n - 1} & (i \neq j) \end{cases}. \tag{12}$$

The learning accuracy is derived by substituting Eqn (12) for Eqn (9) instead of Eqn (8). Because U_{ij} varies according to the distribution of population of grammars, even in the special case where Eqn (2) is satisfied the learning accuracy of each grammar is different from each other[4]. In other words, there are n values of the learning accuracy for each grammar. The Markov matrix in Eqn (12) becomes equivalent to Eqn (8) at $\alpha = 0$. Thus, the transition probability with the exposure rate α is regarded as a natural extension of that of Komarova et al.

For a learner exposed to a variety of languages, the most important difference from a non-exposed learner is that even when the learner presumes his parental grammar G_p, a received sentence may not be accepted by the grammar with the probability $1 - U_{pp}$. In this case he chooses one of the non-parental grammars randomly with a uniform probability. In a two-grammars case, for example, the Markov matrix of this process is expressed by the following equation:

$$M(p) = \begin{pmatrix} U_{p1} & 1 - U_{p1} \\ 1 - U_{p2} & U_{p2} \end{pmatrix}. \tag{13}$$

We show in Figure 12.2(b) the corresponding state transition diagram of a memoryless learner exposed to a number of languages, which differs from Figure 12.2(a) in that for learners at a state G_p it is possible to move to another state.

---

[4] For example, suppose there are two grammars, G_1 and G_2, and the number of input sentences is $w = 1$. Then, the learning accuracy of G_1 is
$q_{11} = 1 - a/2 - \alpha(1 - a)(1 - x_1 + x_2)/2$, while
$q_{22} = 1 - a/2 - \alpha(1 - a)(1 + x_1 - x_2)/2$ for G_2. When $\alpha = 0$, $q_{11} = q_{22}$.

In the next section, we examine how a memoryless learner is influenced by a variety of languages, and how a dominant language appears dependent on the initial conditions. Especially, we will look into the relationship between the exposure rate and the occurrence of a dominant language.

12.3. Experiments

In this section, we show that the behavior of our model with the memoryless learning algorithm depends on the exposure rate α. We set the number of grammars, $n = 10$, throughout the experiments. Firstly, comparing the dynamics of the model with that of Komarova et al. (2001), we examine how the exposure rate α works in our model. Secondly, we observe the behavior of the dynamics, when we suppose there is a communicative language which has a higher similarity to some languages than others have. We take the term *communicative language* to mean a special language, the speakers of which can communicate with other language speakers more easily than speakers of those languages which are not termed *communicative*. This is reflected in the similarity between the special language and other languages.

12.3.1. Exposure and Learning Accuracy

In this section, we compare the behavior of our model with analytical solutions of Komarova et al. and with the behavior of their model by memoryless learners, which is equivalent to that of our model at $\alpha = 0$. We set the similarity between two languages, $a = 0.1$ in Eqn (2), and the number of input sentences w within the range from 10 to 50.

Komarova et al. (2001) have analytically solved Eqn (1) for which Eqn (2) and Eqn (3) are substituted. The solutions of the model are derived by setting an arbitrary initial condition of the distribution of population, affected by the learning accuracy. We show in Figure 12.3 the proportion of the population that speak the most prevalent grammar in the community, $\hat{x}$, versus the learning accuracy, q, by which children correctly acquire the grammar of their parents.

There are two types of solutions; one is that only one of the grammars attracts a certain proportion of the population whereas the others are given the rest divided equally. Which of the languages would be dominant depends on the initial condition. The other is that the solutions take the uniform distribution among grammars. Therefore, there are two thresholds, q_1 and q_2, in terms of the learning accuracy. When $q < q_1$, the population of each language would be uniform. When $q > q_2$, there would be one prevalent language in the community. Thus, q_1 is the necessary condition for the existence of a prevalent language and q_2 is the sufficient condition. When $q_1 < q < q_2$, the supremacy of one language depends on the initial distribution of the population.

Here, we examined our model with memoryless learners at $\alpha = 0$, which is equivalent to that of Komarova et al. Because the learning accuracy, q, depends

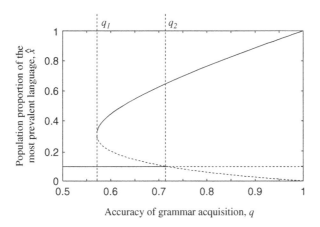

FIGURE 12.3. Analytical solutions of Eqn (1) with Eqn (2) and Eqn (3) ($n = 10, a = 0.1$).

on the number of input sentences, w, the $q - \hat{x}$ relation is discretely represented by integer numbers of w. At $\alpha = 0$, the relation must be identified with the analytical solutions, depicted in Figure 12.3. The result is shown in Figure 12.4(a), in which a cross ($\times$) denotes the $q - \hat{x}$ relation for a given w, and dotted lines are that of analytical solutions (copied from Figure 12.3). As the result, we observed that the $q - \hat{x}$ relation of the model with memoryless learners exactly corresponds to that of the analytical solutions.

Next, we experimented with different values of α in the memoryless learning by w. In our model, although the transition probability $\overline{Q}_{ij}(t)$ varies depending on the distribution of the population by language at each generation, the value of $\overline{Q}_{ij}(t)$ becomes stable as the distribution of the population approaches to the solution, and vice versa. Therefore, we can observe the $q - \hat{x}$ relation as well. We expected that because of the variable transition matrix $\overline{Q}(t)$, the $q - \hat{x}$ relation underwent a change from that of the base model along with the increase of α. However, as is shown in Figure 12.4(b) where $\alpha = 0.12$, the relation becomes the

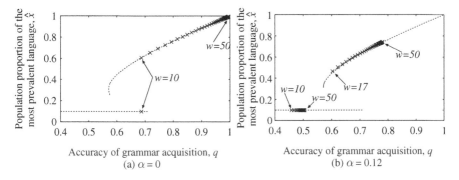

FIGURE 12.4. Solutions by memoryless learning ($a = 0.1, w = 10, \ldots, 50$).

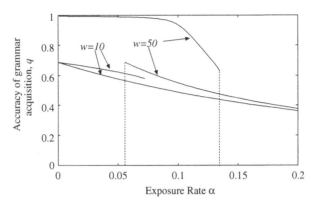

FIGURE 12.5. Exposure rate α versus learning accuracy q ($w = 10, 50$).

same as the one in Figure 12.3. Instead, we can easily observe that the increase of α produces a deterioration in q in regard to w. Additionally, the solutions of q seem to be separated into two groups. We drew the graph with several patterns of the initial distribution of population. As a result, some values of α seem to derive a bifurcation of q values which depend on the initial population distribution.

In order to observe the influence of α on q, we show $\alpha - q$ relation in Figure 12.5, where two lines are represented for each of $w = 10$ and 50. The number of q values is determined according to α. At $w = 50$, when α is between the dashed lines in the figure, there exist two solutions of q which depend on the initial distribution of population. Accordingly, two solutions of $\hat{x}$ are derived at $\alpha = 0.12$ and $w = 50$, as shown in Figure 12.4(b). Although the $\alpha - q$ relation varies along with w, the learning accuracy, q, monotonously decreases depending on α, in common with any w. Therefore, the increase of α produces a deterioration of q in regard to a common value of w.

In our model, q varies from generation to generation, while Komarova et al. gave a constant value to q fixed by a learning algorithm. We showed that q would be stable for given α and thus x also would be stable. Apparently $q - x$ relation is similar to that of the analytical solutions, regardless of the exposure rate. At this stage, we may well conclude that the increase of α would just decrease the accuracy of learning, and would not affect $q - x$ relation, when the algorithm is memoryless and the language similarity is uniform.

12.3.2. Communicative Language

In the previous section, assuming a set of languages with a uniform similarity matrix, we succeeded in observing the characteristic behaviors of our model. Toward the investigation of the model with the general case of a similarity matrix, that is non-uniform, we introduce a special communicative language, the speakers of which can communicate more easily with people speaking other languages than those who do not speak this communicative language can do.

In terms of similarity, the special language, say G_1, has a higher similarity with a subset of languages, say G_2 and G_3, than the rest. Namely, the S matrix is expressed by:

$$S = \begin{pmatrix} 1 & b & b & & \\ b & 1 & a & & a \\ b & a & 1 & & \\ & & & \ddots & \\ & a & & & 1 \end{pmatrix}, \qquad (14)$$

where $0 \le a < b \le 1$. We set $a = 0.1$ and $b = 0.5$ in the following experiments. Accordingly, languages are classified into three categories in terms of similarity. For simplicity, we call them LT_1, LT_2 and LT_3, which respectively contain the communicative language (G_1), the languages similar to G_1 (G_2 and G_3) and the others ($G_4 \ldots G_{10}$).

In order to observe how the exposure of children to a number of languages affects the most prevalent language, we draw diagrams of the proportion of the population that speak the most prevalent language, $\hat{x}$, versus the number of input sentences, w, at particular points of α (see Figure 12.6). Although the language which obtains the highest population depends on the initial distribution of the population, the proportion of the population speaking the most prevalent language is determined by its language type. For example, when the number of input sentences is $w_d = 8$ in Figure 12.6(a), only G_1 or one of the languages belonging to LT_3 can be the most prevalent language, while none of LT_2 can be predominant. When G_1 obtains the corresponding population speaking the most used language, that is $\hat{x}$, the rest of the languages $\{G_2, \ldots G_{10}\}$ share the rest of the population proportion, that is $1 - \hat{x}$.

In Figure 12.6(a), we can see that the greater the number of input sentences is, the higher the population proportion of the most prevalent language exists in stable generations. Although the most prevalent language is spoken by the

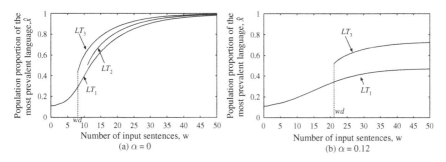

FIGURE 12.6. Number of input sentences, w, versus the proportion of the population that speak the most prevalent language, $\hat{x}$.

most of population, the proportion of the population depends on which of the language types the language belongs to. There are three kinds of $w - \hat{x}$ relation in the figure, which correspond to the type of the language (LT_i). Note that in Figure 12.6(a), $LT_1 < LT_2 < LT_3$. In the language dynamics equation, the more similar two languages are to each other, the easier it is for the population to flow out to each other. In this case, G_1 has two similar languages belonging to LT_2, while each of LT_2 is similar to only one language, that is G_1, and none of LT_3 has any similar language. Thus, LT_1 is the easiest for the population to flow out. This is because the highest proportion of the population speaking the most prevalent language G_1 in LT_1 is less than that of LT_2, and LT_2 is less than LT_3.

If w is smaller than a certain number, G_1 becomes the most prevalent at any initial distribution of population. Otherwise, one of the other languages might supersede G_1 depending on the initial condition. Here, we define a threshold w_d as the smallest number of input sentences in which a language other than G_1 could become the most prevalent language. When $\alpha = 0$, the threshold w_d is 8.

We show in Figure 12.6(b) a diagram of $\hat{x}$ versus w at $\alpha = 0.12$. The threshold w_d is boosted to 21, and none of LT_2 reaches enough of the population to become the most prevalent language at $w < 50$. As was mentioned in Section 12.3.1, the increase of the exposure rate makes the learning accuracy low. For the memoryless learning algorithm, the learning accuracy, q, increases with the number of input sentences, w. The increase of w keeps the same quality of learning accuracy in response to α. Accordingly, w_d increases along with the exposure rate α.

We suggested in Figure 12.6 that the larger the exposure rate α was, the greater the threshold w_d was. It is expected when language learners are exposed to a number of languages, one of the languages other than G_1 may stand out as long as the learners hear the proper quantity of language input. The minimum quantity is w_d in Figure 12.6. However, human beings have an acquisition period in which an appropriate grammar is estimated from their language input (Lenneberg, 1967). If the possible number of input sentences to be heard during the acquisition period was settled at a specific value, then we could draw a diagram concerned with the influence of the exposure rate, α, on the proportion of the population who speak the most prevalent language, $\hat{x}$. We show an example of the diagram for $w = 30$ in Figure 12.7.

We define α_d as the highest value of the exposure rate at which one of the languages other than G_1 could become the most prevalent depending on the initial distribution. When $w = 30$, $\alpha_d \simeq 0.128$. It is easily conceivable that the greater the number of the input sentences is, the larger the threshold α_d is.

Thus far, we have observed the smallest number of input sentences for the appearance of the most prevalent language other than G_1, that is w_d, at particular values of α. On the other hand, we saw the highest value of the exposure rate for the appearance of the most prevalent language other than G_1, that is α_d, at a particular number of input sentences. These two values have a functional relationship as shown in Figure 12.8. This figure represents the relationship between w and α for the most prevalent language other than

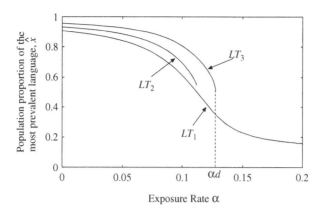

FIGURE 12.7. Influence of the exposure rate, α, on the population proportion of the most prevalent language, $\hat{x}$ ($w = 30$).

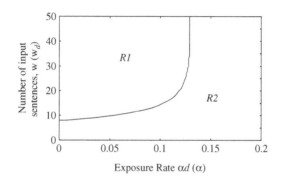

FIGURE 12.8. The relationship between two thresholds, α_d and w_d.

G_1. The necessary number of input sentences rapidly increases along with the exposure rate. Learners need to receive 222 sentences at $\alpha = 0.13$, though only 34 sentences at $\alpha = 0.129$.

This series of experiments shows that the communicative language may be the most prevalent, regardless of the exposure rate α or the number of input sentences w. We discuss the communicative language in the next section.

12.4. Discussion

12.4.1. Possibility of Language Change

In this paper, we consider the change of language as the transition of language users. In other words, the change of language is a phenomenon that the proportion of the population who speak a language at the final stable state exceeds that of the most used language at the initial state. Here, we discuss the possibility of language change, based on the experimental result shown in Figure 12.8.

The line in the diagram Figure 12.8 can be recognized as a boundary between the following two regions:

R1: All of the languages have a possibility of being predominant. The language change hardly occurs.

R2: Only the communicative language attracts a certain proportion of the population in any initial conditions. The language change is likely to occur.

Language learners developing under the condition of $R1$ hear enough language input to acquire their parental languages with high learning accuracy. One of the languages may predominate in the community, depending on the initial distribution of the population. In most cases, the language used by most speakers at the initial state tends to keep its predominance.

In the area of $R2$, the language used by most speakers is G_1, although the proportion of the population speaking G_1 after transition is quite low in comparison with that of the most prevalent languages in $R1$. Even if no one spoke G_1 at the initial state, G_1 eventually comes to be the most used language, and is considered the predominant language.

12.4.2. Communicative Language and the Bioprogram Hypothesis

In Section 12.3.2, we assumed that there is a communicative language G_1, which is more similar to two particular languages than the others. Let us consider what the language corresponds to in the real world. We suggest that it is considered as a language that Bickerton (1984) supposed in the *Language Bioprogram Hypothesis*. Kegl et al. (1999) briefly outline the features of the hypothesis as follows:

Bickerton proposed the Language Bioprogram Hypothesis. This hypothesis claims that a child exposed to nonoptimal or insufficient language input, such as a pidgin, will fall back on an innate language capacity to flesh out the acquisition process, subsequently creating a creole. This is argued to account for the striking similarities among creoles throughout the world.

Kegl et al. (1999)

The communicative language has something in common with the bioprogrammed language, the innate language in the passage above, with regard to the condition of emergence. It appears when learners are exposed to other languages so frequently that any dominant language does not appear, or when they are not given sufficient language input. The communicative language would emerge as a creole, since from the viewpoint of population dynamics, a creole is a language which no one spoke at the initial state but comes to obtain a significant population after generations (Nakamura et al., 2003a).

If we recognize that the communicative language is consistent with the language bioprogram hypothesis, does its reverse still keep true? Namely, are the bioprogrammed languages in the real world such as creoles more communicative with other languages than the others? We cannot examine in the real world whether the creoles are more similar to some particular languages or not. In order to answer the question, we further need to associate the languages given in our experiments with actual languages. Namely, if we introduced to some linguistic features into the equation, the *creole* which emerged in our experiments could be compared with actual ones.

12.4.3. Applicability of the Modified Language Dynamics Equation

Let us consider what further aspects of language could be modeled in our simulation. In both the models of Komarova et al. (2001) and ourselves, it is necessary to introduce a method of representing the similarity of languages. If we take some aspects of language in a real situation into the model, we need to abstract a similarity measure from the target languages. In other words, these models could be applied to whatever the underlying similarity of the target feature is calculated, and thus the model could be extended to investigate whether the emerging *creoles* resembled each other, as predicted by the bioprogram hypothesis.

12.5. Conclusion

Contact between different language groups has been considered as one of the main factors in language change. We modeled the language contact by introducing the *exposure rate* to the language dynamics equation proposed by Nowak et al. (2001). The exposure rate is the rate of influence of languages other than the parental one on language acquisition. We assess the accuracy of parental language acquisition in the memoryless learning algorithm. The exposure to other languages made it possible that the language learner refuted his presumed grammar even though he once acquired his parental grammar. We revised a new transition probability that changes in accordance with the distribution of users of each language, which is a different feature from Nowak et al. (2001).

As the experimental result showed, the emergence of a dominant language depends not only on the similarities between languages but also on the amount of contact between users of different languages. We compared our result with Komarova et al. (2001) in Section 12.3.1. First, when the similarity was uniform, we found that the introduction of the exposure rate only reduced the accuracy of the target language acquisition. And then, we confirmed that no dominant language emerges when the exposure rate is sufficiently high.

In the next experiment in Section 12.3.2, we assumed that there is a special language called the communicative language, the speakers of which can most easily communicate with users of other languages, among the multiple language communities. The result suggests the following conclusions. If language learners hear enough language input to estimate their parental language, one of the languages other than the communicative language would be dominant. However, when language learners are frequently exposed to a variety of languages, the communicative language attracts a significant proportion of the population regardless of the number of input sentences. This characteristic behavior suggests that a bioprogrammed language as hypothesized by Bickerton (1984) will develop. The experimental result shown in Figure 12.8 suggests that creole will emerge when language learners are exposed to a variety of languages at a certain rate.

Overall, we observed that language change is affected by the interaction between multiple languages in a rather convincing way through our experiments. Our contribution in this study can be of practical use in investigations into the relationship between the environment of language learning and language change.

Acknowledgment. We would like to thank Caroline Lyon, who is one of the editors, for reading the draft and making a number of helpful suggestions.

References

Arends, J., Muysken, P., Smith, N., eds.: Pidgins and Creoles. John Benjamins Publishing Co., Amsterdam (1994)

Bickerton, D.: The Language Bioprogram Hypothesis. Behavioral and Brain Sciences **7**(2) (1984) 173–222

Briscoe, E.J. Grammatical acquisition and linguistic selection. In Briscoe, T., ed.: Linguistic Evolution through Language Acquisition: Formal and Computational Models. Cambridge University Press (2002)

Kegl, J., Senghas, A., Coppola, M.: Creation through contact: Sign language emergence and sign language change in Nicaragua. In DeGraff, M., ed.: Language Creation and Language Change. The MIT Press, Cambridge, MA (1999)

Komarova, N.L., Niyogi, P., Nowak, M.A.: The evolutionary dynamics of grammar acquisition. Journal of Theoretical Biology **209**(1) (2001) 43–59

Lenneberg, E.H.: Biological Foundations of Language. John Wiley & Sons, Inc., New York (1967)

Nakamura, M., Hashimoto, T. and Tojo, S.: Creole viewed from population dynamics. Proc. of the Workshop on Language Evolution and Computation in ESSLLI, (2003a) 95–104

Nakamura, M., Hashimoto, T., Tojo, S.: The language dynamics equations of population-based transition – a scenario for creolization. In Arabnia, H.R., ed.: Proc. of the IC-AI'03, CSREA Press (2003b) 689–695

Niyogi, P.: The Informational Complexity of Learning. Kluwer, Boston (1998)

Nowak, M.A., Komarova, N.L., Niyogi, P.: Evolution of universal grammar. Science **291** (2001) 114–118

Sebba, M.: Contact Languages: Pidgins and Creoles. Macmillan, London (1997)

13
The Evolution of Meaning-Space Structure through Iterated Learning

Simon Kirby

13.1. Introduction

One of the most striking aspects of human linguistic communication is its extensive use of compositionality to convey meaning. When expressing a complex meaning, we tend to use signals whose structure reflects the structure of the meaning to some degree. This property is the foundation upon which the syntax of language is built. It is natural, therefore, that an evolutionary account of human language should contrast compositional communication with a non-compositional, holistic alternative where whole signals map onto whole meanings in an arbitrary, unstructured way. Indeed, Wray (1998) has argued that holistic communication (which is still in evidence in particular contexts today) can be seen as a living fossil of an earlier completely non-compositional protolanguage.

A compositional syntax has clear adaptive advantages — with it we are able to successfully communicate novel meanings (in the sense that we may never have witnessed signals for those meanings in the past). Despite this, research over the past decade has suggested that compositional syntax may have emerged not because of its utility to us, but rather because it ensures the successful transmission of language itself (see e.g. Kirby, 2000). It is suggested that the process of linguistic transmission, termed *iterated learning* (Kirby, 2002), is itself an adaptive system that operates on a timescale intermediate between individual learning and biological evolution. Computational models of this process (e.g. Kirby, 2000; Batali, 1998) have demonstrated that syntactic systems can emerge out of random holistic ones without biological evolution, at least for particular assumptions about learning, production and so on.

Further evidence for the argument that iterated learning can explain features of syntax has been provided by idealised computational (Brighton & Kirby, 2001) and mathematical (Brighton, 2002) models of iterated learning in general, showing that compositional languages have a stability advantage over holistic ones. These models compare two scenarios under a number of different parameters. They analyse completely holistic languages and completely compositional ones. The parameters that are varied relate to, on the one hand, the structure of the meaning space, and on the other, the number of training examples an individual is exposed to (also known as the *bottleneck* on linguistic transmission). The overall conclusion is that with highly structured meaning spaces and few training examples, compositional languages are more stable than holistic ones.

13.2. Problems

This foundational work on the cultural evolution of meaning-signal mappings through iterated learning, though important in demonstrating that language itself has significant adaptive dynamics, suffers from two significant drawbacks, which we will turn to below.

13.2.1. Stability Analysis

Early models such as Batali (1998) and Kirby (2000) involved populations of individual computational agents. These agents were equipped with: explicit internal representations of their languages (e.g. grammars, connection weights etc.); a set of meanings (provided by some world model) about which they wished to communicate; mechanisms for expressing signals for meanings using their linguistic representations; and algorithms for learning their language by observing meaning-signal pairs (e.g. grammar induction, back-propagation etc.).

Typically, these simulations initialise the population with no language, or a random pairing of meanings and signals and then allow the linguistic system to evolve through repeated encounters between speaking agents and learning agents.

There has been much work in building simulation models within this general iterated learning framework (e.g. Batali, 1998; Kirby, 2000; Tonkes, 2001; Kirby & Hurford, 2002; Brighton, 2002; K. Smith, 2003; Zuidema, 2003). The great advantage of this kind of modelling is that it allows the experimenter to demonstrate possible *routes* by which language can evolve from one qualitative state, such as holistic coding, to another, such as compositionality. The models show how fundamental features of language can emerge in a population over time given reasonable assumptions about how linguistic behaviour may be transmitted.

The emergence of compositionality in particular has received a lot of attention. However, it is important to note that other fundamental linguistic universals may well be explicable within this general framework. The central message is that wherever there is iterated learning, there is potential for adaptation of the system being transmitted to maximise its own transmissibility.

Models such as these tend to have a large range of parameters, and it is therefore reasonable to want to know the relationship between the emergent property and the parameter space of the model. Once we understand this, we can eventually hope to uncover theoretical principals that may apply to iterated learning *in general* rather than the specific model in question.

As mentioned above, two key parameters in the emergence of compositionality are: meaning-space structure (i.e. the set of things agents communicate about); and learning bottleneck[1] size (i.e. the number of training examples agents are exposed to).

Computational simulations indicate that it is important that there is some kind of learning bottleneck for there to be any interesting linguistic evolution. To put it simply, only when training data is sparse will language evolve to be compositional.

This parameter is relatively straightforward to experiment with, but meaning-space structure is far more difficult, and most of the simulations of iterated learning simply chose some kind of system of meaning representation and stick with it for all simulations.

The work of Brighton & Kirby (2001) and Brighton (2002) was an attempt to get round this problem by exploring a large range of possible meaning-spaces and examining what impact they would have in an iterated learning model.

In those papers — as in this one — a highly idealised notion of "meanings" is employed: meanings are simply feature vectors. A meaning-space is defined by the number of features F it has and the number of different values V over which each feature can vary. So, to communicate about a world where objects were either squares, circles or triangles, and could be coloured green, blue or red, agents would need a meaning-space with at least $F = 2$ and $V = 3$. A red triangle would thus be represented with the *colour* feature taking the *red* value and the *shape* feature taking the *triangle* value.

A reasonable strategy for thoroughly exploring the role of meaning-space structure might be to run many iterated learning simulations, each with a different meaning space, and determine the trajectory of the linguistic system in each instance. This proves computationally costly, so Brighton and Kirby instead looked at what would happen to either a completely compositional language or a completely holistic one for each meaning-space.

Firstly using a computational model, and then using a mathematical generalisation of this model, they were able to calculate how stable either language type was for all meaning spaces. Simplifying somewhat, the overall result was that compositional languages have a stability advantage over holistic ones for larger meaning spaces, especially where the number of features is high.

This kind of simplification of the iterated learning process is very useful but leads to the first of our two problems. Whereas a standard iterated learning simulation can demonstrate a trajectory, or route, from holism to compositionality, the Brighton and Kirby idealisation can only tell us about the relative stability of end-points of such a trajectory. In other words, we don't know

---

[1] See Hurford (2002) for discussion of why the term "bottleneck" is appropriate, and for an analysis of different types of bottleneck in language evolution.

whether there is a way to get to a stable compositional language from an unstable holistic one because we don't know anything about the languages in-between.

13.2.2. Fixed, Monolithic Meaning Space

A second problem with much research into iterated learning so far has been its reliance on a pre-existing meaning space provided for and shared by all agents in the simulation.[2] The work described in the previous section makes strong claims about the likelihood of the emergence of compositional syntax given a particular prior space of meanings. But, where does this meaning space come from? It is assumed that biological evolution somehow endows the agents with a representational scheme prior to language, and if those representations are of sufficient complexity, a compositional system of expressing them will follow naturally.

Furthermore most, if not all, models assume that there is a single, monolithic system for representing meanings. Everything the agents in the simulations want to talk about can be expressed in the same format, be that a feature vector of particular dimensionality, a predicate-logic representation, or a point on a real-number line etc. Equally, there is assumed to be one and only one meaning for representing every "object" in the agents' world. (The term "object" is used here by convention to stand-in for any communicatively relevant situation. In other words, an "object" is anything that an agent may wish to convey to another agent through language.)

As with the study of the relative stability of "end-points" in language evolution, a monolithic, fixed and shared meaning-space is a sensible idealisation to make. Modellers hold one aspect of the object of study constant — meanings — and allow another aspect — signals — to evolve through iterated learning. Much has been learned through these idealisations, but equally it is important to explore what happens if we relax these assumptions.

13.3. A Simple Model

In this paper I will set out a simple extension to the model in Brighton (2002) which allows us to look at what happens when agents have flexible meaning representations for objects. It turns out that this extension also allows us to move beyond a simple stability analysis of end-points of iterated learning and give us, for the first time, a complete view of the dynamics of iterated learning.

---

[2] This is not true of the extensive work on symbol grounding carried out by, for example, Steels & Vogt, 1997; Steels, 1998; A.D.M. Smith, 2003; Vogt, 2003.

13.3.1. Meanings

Language can be viewed as a system for mapping between two interfaces (see, e.g., Chomsky, 1995). On the one hand, there is an articulatory/perceptual interface, which handles input and output of signals. On the other, there is a conceptual/intentional interface, which relates linguistic representations to the things we actually communicate about. It is primarily the latter of these two that we are concerned with here.

In the model, there is a predefined set of things about which the agents wish to communicate — we will call this the *environment, E*. The conceptual/intentional interface C consists of a number of *meaning spaces* $M_{(F,V)} \in C$ onto which every object $o \in E$ in the environment is mapped. Each of these meaning spaces, in keeping with previous models is defined as a set of feature-vectors, such that each meaning space is defined by the number of features F it has (its *dimensionality*), and the number of values V each of these features can take (its *granularity*). (For simplicity we will assume that there are the same number of possible values each feature can take. So, in our earlier example in section 2.1, both the *shape* feature and the *colour* feature ranged over three possible values – *square, circle, triangle* and *green, blue, red* respectively.)

Throughout a simulation run, every object in the environment is paired with a particular point in every meaning space. For the simulation runs described here, this is set up completely randomly at the start of the run. Loosely speaking, we can think of this as giving an agent a number of different ways of conceiving an object. Note that each point in each meaning space can be mapped to zero, one or many objects in the environment. So, for example, there may be particular feature-vectors in particular meaning spaces that are *ambiguous* in that they map to more than one object in the environment.

The important point here is that agents are prompted to produce expressions for *objects in the environment* and not meanings themselves. Part of the task of the agent is to choose which of that object's meanings will be used to generate the linguistic expression. It is this that is the novel extension to previous work. Previously, only one meaning-space was available, so expressing an object and expressing a meaning were the same thing. Now that the latter is under the control of the agent the use of meanings can be learned and, ultimately, itself be subject to cultural evolution through iterated learning.

13.3.2. Learning

In this model I will follow Brighton (2002, 2003) in considering the task of learning a compositional system to be one of memorising signal elements that correspond to particular values on particular features. A single compositional utterance carries information about how to express each feature-value of the meaning expressed by that utterance.

If we consider just a single meaning space, then learning a perfect compositional system proceeds exactly as in Brighton (2002, 2003). The learner is exposed to a series of R meaning/signal pairs $(p_1, p_2, \ldots, p_R)$ each of which represents a point in the space $F \times V$. After this exposure, the learner is able to express at least as many meanings as are uniquely expressed in the training data. Note that this is likely to be less than R since meanings may be repeated.

Is this the best expressivity that the learner can expect to achieve after learning? Not if the learner is exposed to a compositional language. The learner may be able to express novel combinations of feature-values as long as each feature-value occurs somewhere in the training data.

Brighton (2003) gives the following simple approach to modelling the transmission of a compositional language. The first step is to construct a lookup table recording how each feature-value is to be expressed. This table, O, is an $F \times V$ matrix of signal elements. In fact, in this model the actual nature of those signal elements is irrelevant. This is based on the assumption that the learner can correctly generalise a compositional language from the minimum exposure. Brighton terms this the *assumption of optimal generalization*. (This idealises away from the task of decomposing the input signal into parts and identifying which parts of the signal correspond to which parts of the meaning. We should be aware that, in a more realistic scenario, more data is likely to be required and furthermore, segmentation errors are likely to occur.)

The benefit of this assumption is that we can simply treat each entry in the O matrix as a truth value:

$$O_{i,j} = \begin{cases} \textbf{true} & \text{if the } j\text{th value of the } i\text{th feature is observed} \\ \textbf{false} & \text{otherwise} \end{cases}$$

When the entry $O_{i,j}$ is true, this means that the sub-signal for the jth value of the ith feature has occurred at some point in the training data.

On receiving some meaning/signal pair $p = \langle m, s \rangle$ the matrix is updated so that each of the feature-values contained in m are logged in the O matrix. If $m = (v_1, v_2, \ldots, v_F)$, then:

$$O_{i,v_i} = \textbf{true} \text{ for } i = 1 \text{ to } F$$

So far, this is simply a restatement of Brighton's (2003) formalism. The novel feature here is just that there are multiple meaning-spaces, and therefore multiple O matrices to keep track of. To simplify matters for this paper, we will maintain the assumption that learners are given meaning-signal pairs. That is, learners are able to infer which point in which meaning-space a speaker is expressing. It is a topic of crucial and ongoing research, particularly by those researchers looking at symbol-grounding, to develop strategies to relax this assumption (e.g., Steels & Vogt, 1997; A.D.M. Smith, 2003).

So far, contra Brighton (2002, 2003), we have not looked at *holistic* languages. Holistic languages are those where meanings are unanalysed and each given distinct, idiosyncratic signals. Learners cannot, therefore, generalise beyond the data that they are given. However, we can simply equate a holistic language with a compositional language for a meaning-space with only one feature. The machinery described so far, is therefore sufficient to explore the difference between compositional and holistic language learning — we simply need to provide agents with the relevant meaning-spaces.

13.3.3. Language Production

We have specified an **environment** containing **objects** each of which are labelled with **feature-vectors** drawn from each of a set of **meaning-spaces**. We have set out a model of learning whereby sets of **meaning-signal pairs** given to a learning agent are transformed into **O matrices**, one for each meaning-space.

In order to complete a model of iterated learning, it is necessary to provide agents not just with a way of learning, but also a way of producing behaviour for future generations of agents to learn from.

Clearly, a particular meaning $m = (v_1, v_2, \ldots, v_F)$ can be expressed by an agent if, and only if, that agent has a way of expressing each feature-value using the language it has learned so far. In other words, iff $O_{1,v_1} \wedge O_{2,v_2} \wedge \ldots \wedge O_{F,v_F}$.

It is important to note, however, that the agents in this model are not prompted to express a *meaning*. Rather, they attempt to produce expressions for *objects* in the environment. This means that an agent may have a choice of potential meaning spaces to employ when signalling about any one object. An object is expressible, therefore, if *any* of the meanings associated with that object are expressible. If more than one meaning is expressible by an agent, a choice must be made. For the first simulations described below, that choice is simply made at random.

The goal of language production in this model is to produce a meaning-signal pair. However, learning as described in the previous section actually makes no use of signals because of the assumption of optimal generalisation. This means we can ignore the signal part of the signal-meaning pair. When a learning agent observes the behaviour of a speaker, the simulation need only note the set of meanings used.

13.3.4. Simulation Run

A simulation run consists of the following steps:

1. **Initialise environment.** Associate each object in the environment with a single random meaning in every meaning space.
2. **Initialise population.** In this simple model, the population consists of a single speaker, and a single learner. At the start of the simulation, the O matrices of the adult speaker are initialised with patterns of "true" and "false". The particular way in which they are filled depends on the experiment being run, and represents the initial language of the simulation. The learner's O matrices are filled uniformly with "false" because learners are born knowing no language.
3. **Production.** An object is picked randomly from the environment. A list of candidate meanings — one from each meaning space — is compiled for the

object. The O matrices of the speaker are used to determine which, if any, of these candidates the speaker can express. One of these is picked at random.

4. **Learning.** If the speaker has been able to find an expressible meaning, the learner takes that meaning and updates its own O matrix for that meaning space.

5. **Repeat.** Steps 3 and 4 are repeated R times (this defines the size of the learning bottleneck).

6. **Population update.** The adult speaker is deleted, the learner becomes the new speaker, and a new learner is created (with O matrices filled with "false" entries).

7. **Repeat.** Steps 3 to 6 are repeated indefinitely.

The relevant simulation parameters are: size of bottleneck, R; number of objects in the environment, N; the make-up of the conceptual/intentional system, C (i.e. the particular $\langle F, V \rangle$ values for each $M_{\langle F,V \rangle}$); and the initial language (i.e. the O matrices for each meaning space in C).

13.4. Results

This simulation model can be used to explore the dynamics of iterated learning given multiple meaning-spaces. Because, as mentioned earlier, holistic languages are identical to compositional languages for 1-dimensional meaning-spaces, it can also be used to examine how compositional communication can arise out of a prior holistic protolanguage.

13.4.1. Meaning Space Stability

As many previous models have shown, compositional languages are more stable than holistic ones through iterated learning with a bottleneck. We can track *expressivity* of the agents' languages in a simulation over generations given an initial completely expressive language that is compositional, and compare that with a simulation initialised with a completely expressive language that is holistic (table 13.1). Expressivity is defined simply as the proportion of all the objects in the environment that an agent is able to find an expression for.

Unsurprisingly, the holistic language cannot survive in the presence of a bottleneck. The size of the bottleneck affects the rate of decay of expressivity

TABLE 13.1. Expressivity over time for a simulation with $N = 100$, $R = 50$, $C = \{M_{\langle 8,2 \rangle}\}$ and a simulation with $N = 100$, $R = 50$, $C = \{M_{\langle 1,256 \rangle}\}$.

iteration	0	1	2	3	4	5	6	7	8
holistic	1	.45	.22	.13	.08	.02	.02	.02	0
comp.	1	1	1	1	1	1	1	1	1

TABLE 13.2. Rate of decay of expressivity in holistic meaning spaces varies with size of bottleneck.

iteration	0	50	100	150	200	250	300
R=100	1	0	0	0	0	0	0
R=200	1	.15	.1	.06	.06	.04	.02
R=300	1	.3	.21	.16	.16	.16	.12
R=400	1	.61	.43	.38	.34	.32	.31

in the holistic language (table 13.2). As in previous models, this demonstrates once again the crucial advantage a language gains from a compositional syntax.

13.4.2. Complete Holistic/Compositional Dynamics

Recall that one of the motives for this extension to previous work is to move beyond simple stability analysis to see the complete dynamics of the move from holism to compositionality. To do this, we can simply run simulations with two meaning spaces instead of one, such as: $C = \{M_{\langle 8,2 \rangle}, M_{\langle 1,256 \rangle}\}$.

A particular point in the space of possible languages can be described in terms of the proportion of objects that can be expressed using the compositional language, $M_{\langle 8,2 \rangle}$, and the proportion of objects that can be expressed using the holistic language, $M_{\langle 1,256 \rangle}$.

The complete dynamics for all points in holistic/compositional space is visible in the top graph in figure 13.1. The arrows show the magnitude and direction of change after one iteration of the model for that particular combination of holistic versus compositional expressivity. There is a single attractor at $(0,0)$. In other words, the inevitable end state is one where no objects are expressible either holistically or compositionally.

The reason for this is obvious: once a word is lost from the language, there is no way of getting it back. In fact, the agents rely on the expressivity of the language that is injected at the start of the simulation. To get round this, most iterated learning models allow agents to "invent" new expressions. To model this, a new parameter is added — the invention rate I. This gives the probability that, on failure to find any way of expressing an object, an agent will pick a meaning space at random and invent an expression for the relevant meaning in that space.

The bottom graph in figure 13.1 shows how an invention rate of $I = 0.1$ affects the dynamics of iterated learning. Now, the single attractor is the completely compositional language. This demonstrates that there is a clear route from all parts of the language space towards a completely compositional language, through intermediate mixed languages.

As has been shown before, the size of bottleneck is a crucial determinant of whether compositionality will replace holism. If the size of the bottleneck is increased, holistic utterances no longer have such a disadvantage and the movement to the left-hand side of these plots is removed. It is the fact that

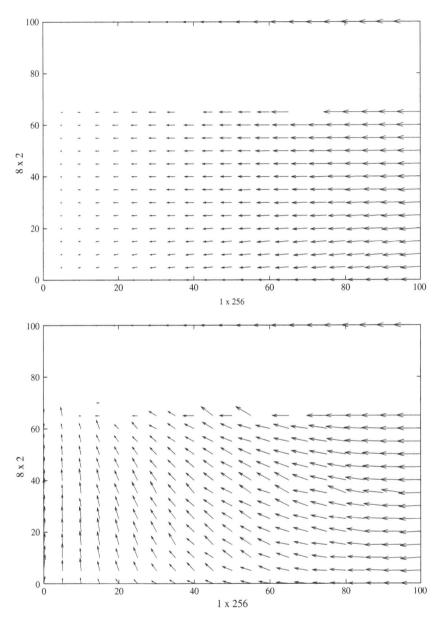

FIGURE 13.1. Complete dynamics for languages that are partially holistic and partially compositional, without invention (top graph) and with invention (bottom graph). Each point represents a language with a particular combination of holistic and compositional signals. Each arrow shows the direction and magnitude of movement in this space after a single instance of learning, and represents the average of 100 simulation runs. (The gaps in the graph result from points in this space that cannot be constructed for an environment of 100 objects.)

language must pass through a learning bottleneck as it is transmitted from generation to generation that causes it to adapt and causes idiosyncratic non-compositional expressions to die out.

13.4.3. The Evolution of Meaning Spaces

The second motivation for the current model was to see how iterated learning might result in adaptation of the meanings of expressions as well as the form of the expressions themselves. Previous models used a monolithic, fixed meaning space, but the current model allows for any number of meaning spaces to exist concurrently. An agent's learning experience (and hence, ultimately, its cultural inheritance) decide the structure of the meaning used to express an object in the environment.

The graph in figure 13.2 shows an example simulation run with $I = 0.1, N = 100, R = 50$ and the following conceptual system:

$$C = \{M_{\langle 1,256 \rangle}, M_{\langle 2,16 \rangle}, M_{\langle 3,6 \rangle}, M_{\langle 4,4 \rangle}, M_{\langle 5,3 \rangle}, M_{\langle 6,3 \rangle}, M_{\langle 7,3 \rangle}, M_{\langle 8,2 \rangle}\}$$

Table 13.3 shows the pattern of meaning space usage averaged over 100 simulations with these parameters measured at 50 generations. Despite being identical initially, agents end up using different systems of meaning for expressing objects in the environment in each simulation. In some runs, such as in figure 13.2, multiple meaning spaces remain partially expressive and stable. This means that agents may have different ways of expressing the same object. Real

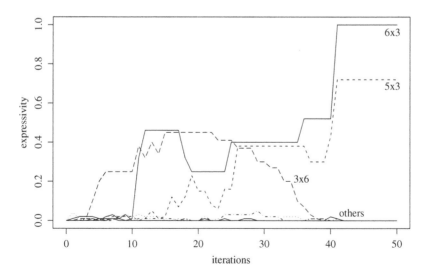

FIGURE 13.2. Competition between different meaning-spaces through cultural evolution in a single simulation run where agents have conceptual systems capable of representing each object in many different ways (see main text for details).

TABLE 13.3. Expressivity of the various meaning spaces at the end of simulation runs where agents have a complex conceptual system allowing flexibility in the way objects are expressed (average of 100 simulations).

features	1	2	3	4	5	6	7	8
values	256	16	6	4	3	3	3	2
average expressivity	0	0	0	.11	.29	.15	.03	.45

languages have different ways of carving up the world, and real speakers have different ways of expressing the same message. This simulation demonstrates a mechanism by which this can be acquired and can evolve culturally.

Are there any generalisations that can be made about the particular linguistic systems that emerge through this evolutionary process? A clear answer to this requires further research, but it may be that the meaning space adapts to structure in the environment. In the current model, the pairing between objects and points in meaning spaces is initialised randomly with uniform probability. A future version of the model will allow the experimenter to populate the environment with objects with non-uniform distribution in meaning space.

13.4.4. Uninformative Meaning Spaces and the Role of Context

In this model, there is a many-to-one mapping from objects in the environment onto meanings in any one meaning space. This means that the simulation can be set up in such a way that agents can produce expressions that are hugely ambiguous. Conceivably, a meaning space could be available that mapped all the objects in the environment onto one point. We can think of an agent using such a meaning space as expressing every object as "thing".

What happens in the iterated learning model when these "uninformative" meaning spaces are included? An experiment was run with the following parameters:

$$I = 0.1, N = 100, R = 50,$$

$$C = \{M_{\langle 1,256\rangle}, M_{\langle 8,2\rangle}, M_{\langle 2,2\rangle}\}$$

In this situation, the agents end up expressing all 100 of the objects in the environment using the two-by-two meaning space. To put it another way, they use two word sentences with a vocabulary of four words. This kind of language is very stable since it requires very little data to learn.

This seems a rather implausible result. In reality, language is used to communicate rather than merely label objects. To simplify somewhat, in a particular situation, a speaker may attempt to draw a hearer's attention towards one of a range of possible objects in the current context.[3] If all the objects in the context map to the same meaning in the language, then no expression could be possible that would successfully direct the hearer's attention. Only if the context size was minimised could an uninformative meaning space hope to discriminate the intended object from the others, but in the limit this essentially renders communication irrelevant. If there is only one possible object to talk about, then the hearer will already know what it is.

Contexts can be added to the simulation model relatively easily. Speakers are given a target object and a number of other objects that form the context. When choosing a meaning space to use to convey the target, speakers will reject meanings that fail to discriminate the target from one or more of the objects in the context.

Repeating the previous simulation with a context of 5 objects leads to the domination of the informative eight-by-two meaning space over the uninformative two-by-two one. This result demonstrates once again how iterated learning can result in language adapting over a cultural timescale to the particular constraints placed on its transmission.

13.5. Conclusions

In this paper I have shown how previous models of iterated learning which used monolithic meaning spaces can be extended to deal with a more flexible notion of meaning. By allowing agents choice over the semantics of linguistic expressions, we can see how meanings as well as signals evolve culturally.

This extension has allowed us to expand on earlier analyses of the relative stability of completely compositional versus completely holistic languages to look at the complete dynamics of a space of languages that are partially compositional. In addition, we can look at far more complex systems with ambiguity of meaning, varying degrees and types of compositionality and semantic structure, and examine how communicative contexts affect the way language is transmitted.

There is much work to be done in this area — I consider this model to be a preliminary investigation only. Many possible extensions of the model could be worth pursuing. For example, the results suggest a puzzle: why aren't all languages binary? The binary meaning spaces seem to be highly stable in the model, but nothing like this exists in natural language. What is needed is a more realistic treatment of semantics and also considerations of signal complexity. Natural language semantics does not take the form of fixed-length vectors, and there are plausible pressures to keep signals short.

Another interesting direction would be to combine this kind of idealised model with the mechanisms for collaborative meaning construction and grounding

---

[3] Recall that "object" here is merely a term of convenience. We might wish to gloss this with "communicative intention".

developed by those working with robotics models (e.g., Steels & Vogt, 1997; Steels, 1998; Vogt, 2003; Cangelosi, 2004). In this manner, we may begin to be able to relate abstract notions of expressivity, learnability and stability with the particular features of natural language semantics grounded in the real world and embodied in human agents.

The overarching conclusion of this line of work is that iterated learning is a surprisingly powerful adaptive system. The fact that language can only persist if it is repeatedly passed through a transmission bottleneck — the actual utterances that form the learning experience of children — has profound implications for its structure. This point has been made clear before in relation to the syntax of language. The model in this paper shows that the semantics of language are also likely to have been shaped by iterated learning.

References

Batali, J. Computational simulations of the emergence of grammar. In Hurford, J. R., Studdert-Kennedy, M. and Knight C.,editors, *Approaches to the Evolution of Language: Social and Cognitive Bases.* Cambridge: Cambridge University Press, 1998.

Brighton, H. Compositional Syntax from Cultural Transmission. *Artificial Life,* 8(1): 25–54, 2002.

Brighton, H. *Simplicity as a Driving Force in Linguistic Evolution.* PhD thesis, Theoretical and Applied Linguistics, The University of Edinburgh, 2003.

Brighton, H. and Kirby, S. The Survival of the Smallest: Stability Conditions for the Cultural Evolution of Compositional Language. In J. Kelemen and P. Sosk, editors, *ECAL01*, pages 592–601. Springer-Verlag, 2001.

Cangelosi, A. The sensorimotor bases of linguistic structure: Experiments with grounded adaptive agents. In S. Schaal et al., editor, *SAB04*, pages 487–496. Los Angeles: Cambridge MA, MIT Press, 2004.

Chomsky, N. *The Minimalist Program.* Cambridge, MA: MIT Press, 1995.

Hurford, J. Expression/induction models of language evolution: dimensions and issues. In Ted Briscoe, editor, *Linguistic Evolution through Language Acquisition: Formal and Computational Models.* Cambridge University Press, 2002.

Kirby, S. Syntax without Natural Selection: How compositionality emerges from vocabulary in a population of learners. In C. Knight, editor, *The Evolutionary Emergence of Language: Social Function and the Origins of Linguistic Form,* pages 303–323. Cambridge University Press, 2000.

Kirby, S. and Hurford, J. The Emergence of Linguistic Structure: An overview of the Iterated Learning Model. In Angelo Cangelosi and Domenico Parisi, editors, *Simulating the Evolution of Language,* pages 121–148. London: Springer Verlag, 2002.

Smith, A. D. M. Intelligent Meaning Creation in a Clumpy World Helps Communication. *Artificial Life,* 9(2):559–574, 2003.

Smith, K. *The Transmission of Language: models of biological and cultural evolution.* PhD thesis, Theoretical and Applied Linguistics, School of Philosophy, Psychology and Language Sciences, The University of Edinburgh, 2003.

Steels, L. The origins of syntax in visually grounded robotic agents. *Artificial Intelligence,* 103(1-2):133–156, 1998.

Steels, L. and Vogt, P. Grounding adaptive language games in robotic agents. In I. Harvey and P. Husbands, editors, *ECAL97.* Cambridge, MA: MIT Press, 1997.

Tonkes, B. *On the Origins of Linguistic Structure: Computational models of the evolution of language*. PhD thesis, School of Information Technology and Electrical Engineering, University of Queensland, Australia, 2001.

Vogt, P. Iterated Learning and Grounding: From Holistic to Compositional Languages. In Simon Kirby, editor, *Proceedings of Language Evolution and Computation Workshop/Course at ESSLLI*. Vienna, 2003.

Wray, A. Protolanguage as a holistic system for social interaction. *Language and Communication*, 18(1):47–67, 1998.

Zuidema, W. How the poverty of the stimulus solves the poverty of the stimulus. In Suzanna Becker, Sebastian Thrun, and Klaus Obermayer, editors, *Advances in Neural Information Processing Systems 15 (Proceedings of NIPS'02)*. Cambridge, MA: MIT Press., 2003.

14
The Emergence of Language: How to Simulate It

Domenico Parisi and Marco Mirolli

14.1. Introduction

The emergence of language in populations of primates that initially lacked language can be simulated with artificial organisms controlled by neural networks and living, evolving, and learning in artificial environments. Some simulations have already been done but most of the necessary work is a task for the future. We discuss language evolution under two topics: language is learned from others on the basis of genetically inherited predispositions, and language has important influences on human cognition. We propose an evolutionary sequence according to which bipedalism and the emergence of the hands represent a selective pressure for developing an ability to predict the consequences of one's actions, this ability is the basis for learning by imitating other individuals, and learning by imitating other individuals is applied to learning to imitate their communicative behaviour. The second topic includes the consequences of language for various aspects of human cognition, especially when language is used to talk to oneself.

14.2. The Starting Point and the End Point of Language Evolution

Everyone agrees that language is among the most important characteristics that distinguish human beings from other animals. Therefore, it would be an important scientific achievement to clearly understand and explain how language has emerged in human beings' evolutionary history. What we do know is that if we move sufficiently back in time we find ancestors of human beings that lacked language and that all modern humans, except for pathologies, have language. But because of the extreme complexity of human language and because language does not leave fossil traces, we only have speculative theories concerning how and when language has emerged and evolved. In this context, computer simulations can be of help. Simulations are computer programs and to express our hypotheses and theories as computer programs forces us to formulate our hypotheses and theories in a more explicit, detailed, and complete way than if they are just expressed in words because, otherwise, it would be impossible to translate them in a computer program. Furthermore, since a simulation's results are the empirical predictions which are derived from the theory incorporated in the simulation, hypotheses and theories expressed as simulations generate many detailed empirical predictions in a mechanical and, therefore, uncontroversial way. This allows us to make the best possible use of whatever empirical evidence we do have on the initial emergence and further evolution of human language. Of course, simulations simplify with respect to reality but this is true for all theories in science. Scientific theories let us better understand the extreme complexity of empirical phenomena because they abstract with respect to reality and try to capture the essential mechanisms and processes that lie behind the phenomena and explain them. The real problem is that simulations, and theories in general, should make the correct abstractions, that is, they should include the critical entities and factors that explain the phenomena of interest, and leave the rest out. But this can only be judged in each particular case.

If we want to simulate the historical process through which human language has first emerged in some proto-form and has then changed to reach its current form, we should have some idea of the initial state and of the terminal state of this evolutionary process. The initial state is some primate species, probably analogous but not necessarily identical to chimpanzees living today. Chimpanzees have a given body and a given brain, and they have given cognitive and social/communicative abilities. It is possible, however, that a communicative system which was clearly, even if to some limited extent, different from the communication systems of living chimpanzees, first made its appearance not when our evolutionary line first separated from their evolutionary line, that is, 5 or 6 million years ago, but some time later. During this interval some changes may have occurred in the human evolutionary line that may have played an important role in the first emergence of human language. For reasons that we will discuss later, one of these changes might have been bipedalism and the emergence of the hands with their great manipulative powers. In any case, our simulations should start with populations of "agents" that resemble living chimpanzees or modified forms of living chimpanzees which incorporate whatever changes have occurred in our evolutionary line that may have played a role in the first emergence of language.

With respect to the final state we can be somewhat more detailed since we are dealing with something which is very complex but can be directly observed: current human language. What are the most important aspects of human language that we should be able to simulate? This is a possible list (cf. also Hockett, 1960):

1. Human language is culturally learned. A human being is not born with language and language does not emerge as the result of a purely maturational process. Every child acquires a specific form of human language, i.e., an historical language such as English, Italian, or Chinese, which is the specific

language spoken in the particular environment in which the child happens to live and grow. Hence, language is learned from others, by imitating others.

2. Human language is learned by the child because the human genotype includes some information that makes the acquisition of language possible. This is suggested by a number of facts. Just to mention a few: nonhuman primates which are exposed to a human language do not acquire language, except in some very limited and special forms, while all normal children do acquire a language without any apparent effort; there seems to be a universal developmental program with which language is acquired by all children, with specific stages and specific timings for those stages; all human languages have shared characteristics. The genetic preparedness for language may include both predispositions that are not specific for language but are necessary for learning a language and may have played a role in the initial emergence of language, and predispositions that are specific for language.

3. Historical languages change constantly. The cultural transmission of language is accompanied by changes that may be the result of many different mechanisms, and this implies that language changes across successive generations. One of the sources of language change is the imperfectness of linguistic cultural transmission. Another is the fact that language changes as the result of the communicative interactions among individuals of the same generation. Furthermore, groups of individuals that interact with each other tend to develop a shared language which is different from the language of other groups because, even if the two groups descend from a single group speaking the same language, the changes tend to diverge.

4. Language is a complex communicative system with specific properties that make it different from animal communicative systems. Among these properties are its compositional and hierarchical structure, with phonemes making up words, words making up phrases, and phrases making up sentences.

5. Language has a crucial impact on human cognition, changing the way in which humans know and categorize the world, remember the past, and predict and plan the future.

6. Human language is used not only for communicating with others but also for communicating with oneself (thinking).

To simulate the evolutionary emergence of language and its subsequent changes is to start with a population of artificial organisms that resemble living apes and do not have language and gradually arrive to a population which has language with the six properties listed above. What we will do in this chapter is to discuss in somewhat more detail some of these properties of human language and how to simulate them. We will organize our discussion under two main headings: (1) language is learned from others on the basis of genetically inherited predispositions, and (2) human language influences human cognition. In some cases we will refer to simulations that have already been done but most of the work remains a task for the future.

14.3. Language is Learned from Others on the Basis of Genetically Inherited Predispositions

Although there are necessary species-specific genetic predispositions for learning a language, language is learned and is learned from others. The child acquires the specific language which is spoken in its environment by imitating the linguistic behaviour of other individuals. Therefore, one first requirement for simulating the evolutionary emergence of human language is to be able to construct artificial organisms that can learn from others. In many simulations a communication system emerges in a population of artificial organisms across a succession of generations but the communication system is entirely encoded in the organisms' inherited genotype and there is no individual learning. These can be simulations of the evolutionary emergence of animal communication systems but not of human language.

One important consideration is that human beings do not only learn language from others but they learn from others all sorts of behaviours and abilities. The communicative behaviour of other animals tends to be genetically inherited and their other behaviours tend to be either genetically inherited or learned by interacting with the non-social environment. Of course, there are exceptions (for a review of social learning and imitation in animals see Heyes, 1996) but learning from others as a general adaptive strategy appears to be typical of the human species.

Can we simulate learning from others? One possible simulation model is the following. The brain of our artificial organism is simulated with a neural network, a simplified model of the nervous system with units corresponding to neurons and connections between units corresponding to synapses between neurons. The basic neural network possessed by all organisms is a sensory-motor network which, in each cycle, maps sensory inputs, encoded as activation patterns in the network's sensory units, into movements, encoded as activation patterns in the network's motor units. The organisms live in a physical environment, which implies that the movements of their motor organs (including their phono-articulatory organs) cause changes in the environment that can be sensed by the sensory units of both their own neural network and the neural network of conspecifics.

One simple way of simulating imitation in neural networks is the following. Both the imitated individual and the imitating individual receive exactly the same input. They both produce an output in response to this input, and the output of the imitated individual (the model) is used by the imitating individual (the learner) as the teaching input of a standard back-propagation procedure, leading to changes in the connection weights of the learner's neural network that cause the learner's output to become progressively more similar to the model's output. In this way, after a number of input/output cycles, the learner will have learned to behave like the model (Denaro and Parisi, 1996). This way of implementing imitative learning in neural networks, however, suffers from a fundamental 'ecological' implausibility, being based on the direct comparison between the learner's motor output and the motor output of the imitated individual. This is implausible because real organisms have no access to the motor commands of other individuals but only to the consequences of their actions on the environment. We can solve this problem using a more sophisticated model of imitation. Imagine a more complex neural network which, in addition to the basic sensory-motor module, includes an additional set of units which, taken together, constitute a prediction module. On the basis of the current sensory input and the planned movements with which the neural network will respond to the input, the prediction module generates an activation pattern which corresponds to the activation pattern that will appear in the network's sensory units in the next cycle. This activation pattern is a prediction of the next sensory input. Neural networks can learn to predict their next sensory input using the backpropagation procedure, with the actual next sensory input, resulting from the actually executed movement, functioning as teaching input. The network compares its prediction with this teaching input and, on the basis of the discrepancy between the two (error), modifies the connection weights of its predictive module in such a way that in a succession of learning cycles the error goes to (almost) zero. The network has learned to make correct predictions.

After the prediction module has learned to make correct predictions, the sensory-motor module and the prediction module are connected together in such a way that when a sensory input arrives from outside to the sensory-motor module the sensory-motor module can learn to respond by generating a movement that reproduces the sensory input. In other words, the network learns to imitate sensory inputs. This is done by (a) generating a planned movement in response to the sensory input, (b) generating a prediction of the sensory input that will result from the planned movement, (c) comparing the predicted input with the actual input resulting after the planned movement has been executed, and (d) using the discrepancy between the two to change the connection weights of the sensory-motor module, while leaving unchanged the connection weights of the prediction module (which can already make correct predictions). To eliminate the discrepancy, the network will learn to generate movements that reproduce the sensory input which has caused the movement (Jordan and Rumelhart, 1992). If the sensory input is the result of the organism's own movements, the network will learn to imitate its own behavior (self-imitation). If the sensory input is caused by the behaviour of another individual, by reproducing with its behaviour this sensory input the network will learn to reproduce the other individual's behaviour (imitation).

This model of learning to predict and learning to imitate can be applied to the pre-linguistic development of the child in its first year of life (Parisi and Floreano, 1992). What happens to the child in the first year of its life which is relevant for language can be viewed as a succession of four stages. In Stage 1 (prediction), which covers the very first months of life, the child learns to predict the acoustic events that will result from its phono-articulatory movements. The child generates all sorts of phono-articulatory movements producing all sorts of sounds and, since it belongs to the human species and is a predicting animal, learns to anticipate which sound will result from which phono-articulatory movement. In stage 2 (self-imitation), at around 4–6 months, the child learns to imitate its own sounds. The child produces a sound, hears it, and reproduces it (babbling). In stage 3 (imitation), which covers the second semester of life, the process becomes social. Now the child pays attention to the sounds that are produced by other people and it learns to reproduce those sounds, that is, to produce sounds that resemble the sounds of the particular language which is spoken in the child's environment. Hence, the sounds produced by the child in the second semester of life tend to be different for children living in different linguistic communities. Finally, in Stage 4 (language), which starts at around 1 year of age, true language beings. Other individuals produce specific sounds in response to specific objects and the child learns to produce the same sounds that are produced by other individuals in response to the same objects. In other words, the sounds acquire a meaning for the child because the child notices that specific sounds systematically occur in its experience with specific objects. This is the beginning of language production and language comprehension. The child becomes able to produce one specific sound, not by imitating a heard sound, but in response to the object systematically paired in its experience with the sound (language production), and to respond to a specific sound not by imitating the sound but by executing the non-linguistic action normally evoked by the object systematically paired with that sound (language comprehension) (Mirolli and Parisi, 2005a).

What are the implications of this simulation model of the linguistic development which occurs during the child's first year of life? As already noted, human beings do not learn only the sounds of language and the meaning of these sounds by imitating other individuals. They learn all sorts of other behaviours and abilities by imitating other individuals. Therefore, one is led to formulate the following hypothesis. After the human evolutionary line has separated from the evolutionary line of living apes 5–6 million year ago, two genetic predispositions have been incorporated in the genotype of our evolutionary line: a predisposition to learn to predict the consequences of one's actions and a predisposition to apply this prediction ability to learning to behave like other individuals by imitating their behaviour.

It is an open question whether the ability to predict has evolved prior to the ability to imitate or the two abilities have evolved together. One important consideration is that the ability to predict can be adaptively useful also at the individual level, that is, independently of its usefulness for learning by imitating others. The ability to predict the effects of one's actions can be useful in hunting, in throwing objects, and in using and constructing artefacts. For example, in using an artefact it may be useful to be able to predict the changes that one's actions mediated by the artefact will cause in the environment. In constructing an artefact, it may be useful to be able to predict the changes that one's actions will cause in the artefact that one is constructing. However, even if some predictive ability may have initially emerged in our evolutionary line with these purely individual functions, it might also be that learning by imitating others has been a selective pressure for developing a more sophisticated ability to predict the results of one's actions. This hypothesis is suggested by our model of imitation which implies that the ability to predict the results of one's actions is a necessary component of learning by imitation, i.e., to make one's actions similar to the actions of others. (Consider that our model of imitation can be also applied to the imitation of artefacts, i.e., to making copies of existing artefacts.) In any case, by assuming that the incorporation of a tendency to learn to predict the consequences of one's actions in the human genotype has been a critical step in human evolution, we can explain in an economic way many different aspects of the human adaptive pattern: a general ability to generate more effective behaviours, the use, construction, and imitation of artefacts, and the tendency to learn by imitating others.

How and why has the tendency to learn to predict the consequences of one's actions been incorporated in the human genotype? We know that one of the first novelties that has appeared in the human evolutionary line after its separation from the chimpanzees' evolutionary line has been bipedalism and the consequent freeing of the hands for manipulation purposes. This has implied a great enlargement of our ancestors' repertoire of behaviours. With their hands free to manipulate objects, our ancestors of 2–4 million years ago became able to do many more different things and to cause many more different effects in the environment compared to their quadruped ancestors. The sheer increase in the number of different actions and of different effects of these actions has made the problem of choosing among the different actions more complex. We hypothesize that this has been a selective pressure for developing a tendency to pay attention to the consequences of each of these different actions and to learn to predict their consequences. Using simulations it can been shown that the behaviour of artificial organisms becomes more effective, in a variety of different ways, if they are able to predict the consequences of their actions (Nolfi et al., 1994; Parisi et al., 1990). This can be shown even if the artificial organisms have a very simple behavioural repertoire which includes only one type of action such as approaching food. We assume that the selective advantage of a tendency or ability to learn to predict the consequences of one's actions has become greater when, endowed with hands that can manipulate the environment, our ancestors' behavioural repertoire has become more extended.

Once a genetically inherited tendency/ability to learn to predict the consequences of one's actions has been encoded in the genotype of our ancestors, this tendency/ability has been recruited and exploited to develop two other tendencies/abilities: using and then constructing artefacts and imitating the behaviour of others. As we have already said, the influence may have not been only one-way but the adaptive significance of using and constructing artefacts and of imitating the behaviour of others may have represented a selective pressure to further develop the tendency/ability to predict the consequences of one's actions.

A well developed ability/tendency to learn by imitating others may have had a critical role in the emergence of a communication system such as human language which, unlike most animal communication systems, is culturally, not genetically, transmitted. Notice that learning to imitate the sounds produced by others appears to be easier than learning to imitate their other behaviours, for two reasons. The effects produced by phono-articulatory movements, i.e., the sounds that these movements create in the environment, depend almost uniquely on the phono-articulatory movements themselves, and on no other factor. This is not true for other types of movements, whose effects depend on both the movements themselves and other factors existing in the environment. For example, the effects of hitting a stone with another stone depend on the nature of the hitting movement (its direction and force) but also on the physical properties of the two stones. Hence, it may be easier to learn to predict the effects of one's phono-articulatory movements (sounds) than to predict the effects of other types of movements. The second reason why predicting the sounds resulting from phono-articulatory movements is easier is that sounds are very accessible (e.g., sounds can be perceived from a distance and they go around obstacles) and they are the same sounds for any number of individuals sufficiently close to the source of the sound, i.e., the individual who are produced the phono-articulatory movements. This is less true, for example, for the visual effects of hand movements which tend to be less accessible (they cannot be perceived from a distance and obstacles can make them non-accessible) and they may be somewhat different for individuals looking at the hands from different spatial locations.

This may be related to the question whether human language has originated in the acoustic/phono-articulatory form of today's language, or it first emerged in a gestural, visuo/motor, form and only some time later moved to an acoustic/phono-articulatory form (as proposed, for example, by Arbib, 2005, and Corballis, 2002). On the one hand, the hypothesis that language has evolved in the acoustic/phonoarticulatory form from the beginning is supported not only by the fact that today's natural medium of language is acoustic, but also by the fact that humans seem to inherit a species-specific set of predispositions to process and to produce linguistic sounds. As we have seen, this is shown, among other things, by the regular succession of stages in the phono-articulatory behaviour of the child in its first year of life. On the other hand, there is a growing body of evidence for a visuo-motor origin of human language. One kind of evidence is the easiness with which congenitally deaf children learn the sign languages of the deaf and in the emergence of gestural languages in communities of deaf people. Another is the importance of gestures in the very first phases of linguistic development (Volterra et al., 2005). Still another kind of evidence is the fact that the brain region which is devoted to the control of speech in humans – Broca's area – appears to be homologous to the brain region which controls the production and understanding of hand actions in monkeys – the F5 area, where mirror neurons have been found (Rizzolatti and Arbib, 1998). All these facts could be explained by a visuo-motor origin of language which has then moved to the acoustic/phono-articulatory form of present-day language because of the greater effectiveness of learning and using an acoustic/phono-articulatory language, without erasing the preceding visuo-motor evolutionary stage. This hypothesis is compatible with the important role played by the hands in the evolution of humans in the last 2–4 million years, that we have discussed above. On the other hand, one can also hypothesize that language was acoustic/phono-articulatory from its beginning and that gestural languages emerge as a generalization from the genetically inherited tendency to learn an acoustic/phono-articulatory language.

These issues could be decided, or at least illuminated, by doing simulations. For example, can we evolve artificial organisms that learn from others a language which is acoustic/phono-articulatory from its beginning? Will an artificial deaf individual belonging to a population of organisms with a genetically inherited tendency/ability to learn an acoustic/phono-articulatory language, be able to learn a visuo-motor language as easily as an individual without this genetically inherited tendency/ability? Or, for artificial organisms with very able hands, is it easier to first evolve a visuo-motor language and then move to an acoustic/phono-articulatory one because the acoustic/phono-articulatory language is more effective?

Language is culturally transmitted from one generation to the next but it also changes across a succession of generations, and what characterizes human language is not only that it is culturally transmitted but that it changes across successive generations with the typical speed of cultural evolution. Cultural evolution can be simulated in populations of artificial organisms if cultural transmission is selective and there are mechanisms that constantly introduce new variability (Denaro and Parisi, 1996; Hutchins and Hazlehurst, 1995; Mirolli and Parisi, 2004). One starts with a population of organisms with individually different linguistic behaviours, The different individuals are not all equally imitated by the individuals of the next generation; some potential models have more imitators than others. This is cultural selective reproduction. Furthermore, imitation is never perfect and one single individual can imitate many different "models" so that its linguistic behaviour is not identical to the linguistic behaviour of any of these models but is a novel recombination of parts of their different linguistic behaviours. The selective reproduction of linguistic behaviours and the constant addition of new linguistic behaviours cause language change across generations (Hare and Elman, 1995).

Not only language change but also the emergence of different historical languages can be simulated. Although linguistic behaviour is somewhat different in different individuals, in groups of individuals that descend from the same cultural ancestors and that imitate each other linguistic behaviours tend to be similar, constituting an historical language. If the group splits in two subgroups with little interaction between the two subgroups, the original mother-language gives origin to two different, even if historically related, daughter-languages.

14.4. Human Language Influences Human Cognition

Language first emerges in the child at around 1 year of age. It is approximately at this age that the child appears to be able to connect heard or pronounced sounds with specific objects and actions. We have assumed that the basic neural network that controls the behaviour of all organisms is a sensory-motor network that maps sensory inputs into motor outputs. The organism perceives something and it responds with some appropriate movement. We now assume that in the human brain there are two such networks and that from birth to 1 year these two networks are either anatomically or functionally separated (Figure 14.1a). One sensory-motor network, the non-linguistic network, maps non-linguistic sensory inputs into non-linguistic motor outputs. The connection weights and perhaps even the architecture of connections of this network change during the first year of life as the child learns to coordinate its movements and to respond to sensory inputs with the appropriate movements in reaching, touching, moving its eyes, etc. The other sensory-motor network, the linguistic network, maps linguistic (acoustic) sensory inputs into linguistic (phono-articulatory) motor outputs. As we have already seen, this second network learns during the first year of life to self-imitate and then imitate linguistic sounds. (For a model of the actual neural bases of human language which stresses the importance of the acoustic/phono-articulatory circuits in its evolution, see Lieberman, 2002).

At around 1 year the two networks become connected (Figure 14.1b). The child begins to learn the appropriate connection weights for the connections going from the non-linguistic network to the linguistic network and for the connections going from the linguistic network to the non-linguistic network. This is the beginning of language proper. Specific sounds produced by other individuals tend to be experienced by the child together with specific objects or specific actions and these systematic correspondences between linguistic sounds and non-linguistic objects and actions are incorporated in the weights of the connections linking the two networks. Given these weights, the child becomes increasingly able to respond with the appropriate motor outputs of its linguistic network (phono-articulatory movements) to sensory inputs to its non-linguistic network (naming a perceived object or action) and to respond with the appropriate motor outputs

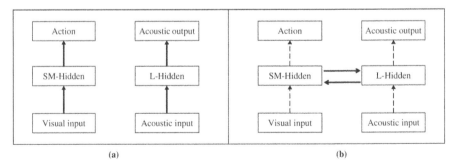

(a)   (b)

FIGURE 14.1. (a) The non-linguistic sensory-motor network and the linguistic sensory-motor network are anatomically or functionally separated until 1 year of a child's life. (b) At 1 year the two networks become connected when the child learns the weights of the connections going from the non-linguistic network to the linguistic network (language production) and of the connections going from the linguistic network to the non-linguistic network (language comprehension).

of its non-linguistic network (movements of the eyes, face, arms, hands, legs) to sensory inputs to its linguistic network (understanding linguistic sounds). In the model outlined here, language learning is learning the appropriate weights that go from the non-linguistic network to the linguistic network and from the linguistic network to the non-linguistic network. One general consequence of learning these weights is that much of an individual's cognitive activity can consist in going from sounds to meanings and from meaning to sounds. This can make the individual's cognitive activity more effective in a variety of ways.

Categorization. One of the influences of language on cognition concerns categorization. Different objects are put together in the organism's brain if these different objects are to be responded to by the organism with the same action. The different objects that are responded to with the same action constitute a category. In neural network terms, a sensory input is an activation pattern which is transformed in another activation pattern in the network's internal units by the connection weights of the connections linking the sensory input units to the internal units. Let us call the activation pattern in the internal units the internal representation of the sensory input. The ability to categorize consists in the possession of connections weights that tend to make more similar the internal representations of sensory inputs that must be responded to with the same action and to make more different the internal representations of sensory inputs that must be responded to with different actions (Di Ferdinando and Parisi, 2004; Harnad et al., 1995). The activation pattern of a set of units can be conceived as one point in a hyperspace with as many dimensions as the number of units and with the point's location in each dimension corresponding to the activation level of the corresponding unit. A category is a "cloud" of points in the hyperspace of the internal units that correspond to the internal representations of sensory inputs which must be responded to with the same action. A neural network which has "good" categories is a neural network whose "clouds" are small (inputs that must be responded to with the same action are internally represented in similar ways) and distant from each other (inputs that must be responded to with different actions are represented in different ways).

What is the effect of possessing a language on the organism's categories? As will be recalled, language begins when, at 1 year, the non-linguistic network is functionally linked to the linguistic network, and vice versa. Therefore, the internal representations of the non-linguistic network, which prepare the motor outputs with which the non-linguistic network will respond to its sensory inputs, tend to be influenced not only by the sensory inputs to the non-linguistic network but also by the linguistic network. What changes in the internal representations of the non-linguistic network as a consequence of this linking? The answer is that the non-linguistic network's categories tend to become better categories, that is, the "clouds" of its internal representations become smaller and more distant from each other (Mirolli and Parisi, 2005a; Mirolli and Parisi, 2006). Since an organism's categories influence the organism's behaviour by making it easier for the organism to select the appropriate action in response to sensory inputs, an organism endowed with language will have a more effective behaviour.

Learning of categories. The influence of language on categories may go well beyond the mere improvement of existing categorical representations. The categories that form inside an organism's neural network are in fact the result of the organism's experience with the world which allows the organism to learn the appropriate responses to the different sensory inputs. This experience can be long and costly. An individual that acquires a language also acquires the categories marked by the linguistic signals (Steels and Belpaeme, 2005). In this way the individual can exploit the experience of other individuals, both living and long dead, and acquire more easily more useful categories (Cangelosi and Harnad, 2000). This makes human cognition intrinsically social. Furthermore, it has been shown, both empirically (Nazzi and Gopnik, 2001) and by neural networks simulations (Lupyan, 2005; Schyns, 1991), that category learning itself can be improved by the aid of labels. Linguistic labelled categories can also have a negative side, however, since they may induce an unrealistic conception of reality as made up of clearly distinct class of entities, internally homogeneous and unchanging.

Selective Attention. Language can also be a mechanism for directing attention to specific portions of the input arriving from the environment and for articulating or analyzing complex sensory inputs. All organisms need selective attention mechanisms since all organisms live in environments that send to their sensory organs many different inputs at the same time, and the organism must select which of these inputs to process in order to generate a response, while ignoring all the other inputs. Language can be such a selective attention mechanism. When an individual sees a complex scene, a word originating from another individual which accompanies the perception of the complex scene can help the individual to isolate some particular component of the complex scene and to respond to this component, ignoring the other components. This is a consequence of the co-variation of specific sounds with specific non-linguistic inputs which gives linguistic sounds their meaning. Language can also help the individual to articulate a complex perceived scene into its elements. A sentence is a collection of linguistic sounds (words) each of which co-varies with a different component or aspect of a complex scene so that the sentence makes it easier for the individual that hears the sentence to isolate these different components and aspects and to respond more effectively.

Prediction and Planning. The capacity to predict and to plan can be deeply improved by language for two reasons. First, predictions can become more complex and articulated if they are linguistically labelled. Plans as sequences of actions for reaching some particular goal can also become more complex because the individual can work more effectively with linguistically labelled predictions and with linguistically labelled planned actions in response to these predictions. Finally, evaluations of linguistically labelled predicted effects of planned actions can be used to decide whether to actually execute those actions or not, making planning easier, more effective, and more "reasoned". Second, linguistically labelled predictions and plans can be shared and discussed with others, making the overall predicting and planning capacity of single individuals and of groups more effective.

Memory. Another example of the importance of language for cognition concerns short-term memory. One way of simulating short term memory with neural networks consists in copying the activation pattern of a network's internal units in a special set of memory units and then connecting the memory units to the internal units so as to allow the network to retrieve the memory trace (Elman, 1990). We can presume that both the non-linguistic network and the linguistic network (Fig. 14.1) have this type of short-term memory mechanism. However, the quantity of information, as measured by number of units and connections, contained in the non-linguistic network is probably much greater than the quantity of information contained in the linguistic network. This implies that it is generally easier to remember words than actual sensory-motor experience. This, in turn, has the consequence that an individual possessing language can work more easily with linguistic (sound) information and translate this information into the associated non-linguistic information when necessary. Delegating the memory function to the linguistic system can have the further advantage of leaving the sensory-motor system free to process other information useful for acting in the environment while linguistically remembering previous information. And, indeed, empirical evidence seems to confirm the importance of the linguistic system for human memory (Gruber and Goschke, 2004).

Talking to Oneself. A crucial characteristic of human language is that language can be used not only for communicating with others but also for communicating with oneself, i.e., for thinking, whereas we don't have evidence for this type of use of animal communication systems. Inputs to an individual's linguistic network can come from another individual's linguistic network but they can also come from the individual's own linguistic network: the individual talks to itself. If the sounds are actually (physically) produced by the individual's phono-articulatory movements and actually heard by the sensory units of the individual's linguistic network, we call these sounds, private speech; if the loop does not include the organism's peripheral motor and sensory organs but is more internal, we call them 'inner speech' (Mirolli and Parisi, 2006). Inner speech is faster than private speech and as a consequence can be more useful for certain purposes, but in both cases a number of interesting effects on the individual's cognitive activity can be observed.

One could think that using language to talk to oneself is a late development in human evolution and it presupposes an already complex language. However, in some simulations it has been shown that talking to oneself can be a selective pressure for the evolutionary emergence of a very simple communicative system if the linguistic signals are used by the individual to keep in memory some information which has been received from another individual (Mirolli and Parisi, 2005b). In these simulations the signals are genetically inherited and are not learned from others, so they are not linguistic signals, but the simulations can be a demonstration that using language for oneself can have advantages for the individual even if the language is very simple.

Using language to talk to oneself has a number of important consequences for human cognition. As we have seen, sensory-motor categories becomes better (smaller and more distant "clouds" of points in the space of sensory-motor internal representations) if they are linguistically labelled through the bi-directional connections linking the organism's non-linguistic network to its linguistic network. This is true not only when linguistic stimuli arrive from outside but also when they are self-generated by the organism. Hence, an organism with language can work with better sensory-motor categories even when it is all alone and is interacting with the non-social environment. Also the effects of language in directing an individual's attention and in articulating complex scenes can be internalized. Once an individual has experienced the positive effects of being guided by linguistic stimuli produced by other individuals, he or she can learn to linguistically stimulate him- or herself in the same way to produce the same effects. The use of linguistic self-stimulation is indeed very important in child development (Diaz and Berk, 1992) and can be considered as the beginning of *voluntary control* (Vygotsky, 1978).

14.5. Conclusion

The emergence of human language in the descendants of organisms that initially lacked language can be simulated with artificial organisms controlled by neural networks and living, evolving, and learning in artificial environments. The ideal simulation is a simulation in which we start with a population of organisms similar to living chimpanzees and therefore lacking language and have those organisms gradually evolve human language as we know it. Aspects of this ideal simulation have already been realized but most are a task for the future.

We have addressed two main topics in the evolutionary emergence of language. Human language is culturally learned from others on the basis of species-specific genetically inherited predispositions. We propose an evolutionary sequence for the human evolutionary line leading to human language: (1) bipedalism and the evolutionary emerge of hands for manipulating the environment; (2) the emergence of a tendency/ability to predict the effects one's actions on the environment due to the fact that the possession of hands greatly increases the size of one's behavioural repertoire and the number of different effects that can be caused in the environment by using the hands; (3) the use of this ability to predict the effects of one's actions in learning to imitate the behaviour of others by reproducing the effects of *their* behaviour; (4) the application of the ability to imitate others to imitating their communicative behaviour; (5) the transition from a visuo-motor to an acoustic-phonoarticulatory communicative behaviour. The other topic that we have addressed concerns the relation of language to cognition. One critical aspect of human language is that it has a number of consequences for human cognition and it can be used not only for communicating with others but also for communicating with oneself (thinking). We have examined some of these consequences and how they can be simulated: the improvement of one's sensory-motor categories, the learning of categories without directly experiencing them, the role of language as a mechanism for selective attention and for articulating complex sensory inputs, its role in generating better predictions and better plans by linguistically labelling them and, as a consequence, by becoming able to discuss them with other individuals, and, finally, the role of language in keeping more information in memory in linguistic rather than in sensory-motor form. An important aspect of language learning is language internalization, the transfer of social uses of language to individual uses, i.e., talking to oneself.

Acknowledgments. The research presented in this paper has been supported by the ECAGENTS project founded by the Future and Emerging Technologies program (IST-FET) of the European Community under EU R&D contract IST-2003-1940. The information provided is the sole responsibility of the authors and does not reflect the Community's opinion. The Community is not responsible for any use that may be made of data appearing in this publication.

References

Arbib, M.A.: From monkey-like action recognition to human language: An evolutionary framework for neurolinguistics. Behavioral and Brain Sciences, Vol. 28(2) (2005) 105–124

Cangelosi, A., Harnad, S.: The adaptive advantage of symbolic theft over sensori-motor toil: Grounding language in perceptual categories. Evolution of Communication, Vol. 4(1). (2000) 117–142

Corballis, M.C.: From Hand to Mouth: The Origins of Language. Princeton University Press, Princeton (2002)

Denaro, D., Parisi, D.: Cultural evolution in a population of neural networks. In Marinaro, M., Tagliaferri, R. (eds.) *Proceedings of the Vietri-96 Conference on Parallel Architectures and Neural Networks.* Springer, New York (1996) 100–111

Di Ferdinando, A., Parisi, D.: Internal representations of sensory input reflect the motor output with which organisms respond to the input. In Carsetti A. (ed.): Seeing, Thinking and Knowing. Kluwer, Dordrecht. (2004) 115–141

Diaz, R., Berk, L. (eds.): Private speech: From social interaction to self regulation. Erlbaum, New Jersey (1992)

Elman, J.L.: Finding structure in time. Cognitive Science, Vol. 14. (1990) 179–211

Gruber, O., Goschke, T.: Executive control emerging from dynamic interactions between brain systems mediating language, working memory and attentional processes. Acta Psychologica, Vol. 115. (2004) 105–121

Hare, M., Elman, J.L.: Learning and morphological change. Cognition, Vol. 56 (1995) 61–98

Harnad, S., Hanson, S.J., Lubin, J.: Learned categorical perception in neural nets: implications for symbol grounding. In Honavar and Uhr (eds.): Symbol processors and connectionist network models in artificial intelligence and cognitive modelling: steps toward principled integration. Academic Press, New York, NY (1995) 191–206

Heyes, C.M., Galef, B.G. Jr. (eds.): Social Learning and Imitation: the Roots of Culture. Academic Press, New York (1996)

Hockett, C.F.: Logical considerations in the study of animal communication. In Lanyon, W.E., Tavolga, W.N. (eds.): Animal Sounds and Communication. American Institute of Biological Sciences: Washington, D.C. (1960)

Hutchins, E., Hazlehurst, B.: How to invent a lexicon: the development of shared symbols in interaction. In Gilbert, N. and Conte, R. (eds.) Artificial Societies: the computer simulation of social life. UCL Press, London. (1995) 157–189

Jordan, M.I., Rumelhart, D.E.: Forward Models: Supervised Learning with a Distal Teacher, Cognitive Science, Vol. 16. (1992) 307–354

Lieberman, P.: On the nature and evolution of the neural bases of human language, Yearbook of Physical Anthropology, Vol. 45 (2002) 36–62

Lupyan, G.: Carving nature at its joints and carving joints into nature: How labels augment category representations. In Cangelosi, A., Bugmann, G., Borisyuk, R. (eds.) Modelling Language, Cognition and Action: Proceedings of the 9th Neural Computation and Psychology Workshop. World Scientific, Singapore (2005) 87–96

Mirolli, M., Parisi, D.: Language, altruism and docility: How cultural learning can favour language evolution. In Pollack, J.B., Bedau, M., Husbands, P., Ikegami, T., Watson, R.A. (eds.): Artificial Life IX: Proceedings of the Ninth International Conference on the Simulation and Synthesis of Living Systems. MIT Press, Cambridge, Mass. (2004) 182–187

Mirolli, M., Parisi, D.: Language as an Aid to Categorization: A Neural Network Model of Early Language Acquisition. In Cangelosi, A., Bugmann, G., Borisyuk, R. (eds.) Modelling Language, Cognition and Action: Proceedings of the 9th Neural Computation and Psychology Workshop. World Scientific, Singapore (2005a) 97–106

Mirolli, M., Parisi, D.: How can we explain the emergence of a language which benefits the hearer but not the speaker? Connection Science, Vol. 17(3–4). (2005b) 325–341

Mirolli, M., Parisi, D.: Talking to Oneself as a Selective Pressure for the Emergence of Language. In Cangelosi, A., Smith, K., Smith, A. (eds.) Proceedings of the 6th Evolution of Language Conference. World Scientific, Singapore (2006) 214–221

Nazzi, T., Gopnik, A.: Linguistic and cognitive abilities in infancy: When does language become a tool for categorization? Cognition, Vol. 80. (2001) 303–312

Nolfi S., Elman J.L., Parisi D.: Learning and evolution in neural networks. Adaptive Behavior, Vol. 3(1). (1994) 5–28

Parisi, D., Cecconi, F., Nolfi, S.: Econets: Neural networks that learn in an environment. Network, Vol. 1. (1990) 149–168

Parisi, D., Floreano, D.: Prediction and Imitation of Linguistic Sounds by Neural Networks. In Paoloni, A. (ed.): Proceedings of the First Workshop on Neural Networks and Speech Processing. Fondazione Bordoni, Roma (1992)

Rizzolatti, G., Arbib, M.A.: Language within our grasp. Trends in Neuroscience, Vol. 21. (1998) 188–194

Schyns, P.G.: A Modular Neural Network Model of Concept Acquisition. Cognitive Science, Vol. 15(4) (1991) 461–508

Steels, L., Belpaeme, T.: Coordinating Perceptually Grounded Categories through Language. A Case Study for Colour. Behavioral and Brain Sciences. Vol. 28(4). (2005) 469–529

Volterra, V., Caselli, M.C., Capirci, O., Pizzuto, E.: Gesture and the emergence and development of language. In Tomasello, M., Slobin, D.: Beyond Nature-Nurture. Essays in Honor of Elizabeth Bates. Lawrence Erlbaum Associates, New Jersey (2005) 3–40

Vygotsky, L.S.: Mind in society: The development of higher psychological processes. Harvard University Press, Cambridge, MA. (1978)

15
Lexical Acquisition with and without Metacommunication

Jonathan Ginzburg and Zoran Macura*

15.1. Introduction

A central concern of work on the evolution of language has been to offer an account for the emergence of syntactically complex structure, which underwrites a compositional semantics. In this chapter we consider the emergence of one class of utterances which illustrate that semantic expressiveness is not correlated with syntactic complexity, namely metacommunicative interaction (MCI) utterances. These are utterance acts in which conversationalists acknowledge understanding or request clarification. We offer a simple characterisation of the incremental change required for MCI to emerge from an MCI-less linguistic interaction system. This theoretical setting underpins and motivates the development of an ALife environment in which the lexicon dynamics of populations that possess and lack MCI capabilities are compared.

We ran a series of experiments whose initial state involved agents possessing distinct lexicons and whose end state was one in which all agents associated meanings with each word in a lexicon. The main effect demonstrated, one we dub the *Babel effect*, is that the convergence rate of a population that relies exclusively on introspection is intrinsically bounded and, moreover, this bound decreases with an increasing population. This bound seems to disappear once agents are endowed with clarification requests.

In natural language, semantic expressiveness is not correlated with syntactic complexity. A key feature of natural language, which provides a striking instance of *syntactically underdetermined* semantic complexity, is metacommunicative interaction (MCI)—utterance acts in which conversationalists acknowledge understanding or request clarification. (1b) exemplifies such a syntactically simple form which, nonetheless, in context can acquire a highly complex content:

(1) (a) A: Did Bo leave?
    (b) B: Bo?; ("Bo?" can mean in this context *Are you asking if Bo, of all people, left* or *Who were you referring to as Bo?*).

---

*The authors are listed in alphabetical order.

Indeed natural language possesses forms whose sole meaning concerns MCI, as exemplified by (2), a form whose sole use is to query an antecedently uttered polar interrogative whose subject has unclear reference:

(2) Do I like who?

The need to verify that mutual understanding among interlocutors has been achieved with respect to any given utterance—and engage in discussion of a clarification request if this is not the case—is one of the central organizing principles of conversation (Schegloff 1992; Clark 1996). However, hitherto there has been little work on the emergence of MCI meaning. Communicative interaction is fundamental to evolution of grammar work, since it is interactions among communicating agents that leads an initial 'agrammatical' system to evolve into a grammar (with possible, concomitant phylogenetic modification; see e.g. (Briscoe 2000; Kirby 2000). However, given an I-language[1] perspective, the communicative aspect as such is not internalized in the grammar (though see (Steels 1998)). Consequently, such models of evolution of grammar cannot explain the existence of forms whose meaning is intrinsically MCI oriented.

In this paper we offer a simple characterization of the incremental change required for MCI to emerge from an MCI-less communicative interaction system. We discuss the evolutionary background in which MCI might arise and become adaptive. Finally, we report on a series of experiments we ran using an ALife environment in which the lexicon dynamics of populations that possess and lack MCI capabilities are compared. These experiments reveal some clear differences in the lexicon dynamics of populations that acquire words solely by introspection contrasted with populations that learn using MCI or using a mixed strategy of introspection and MCI.

15.2. Metacommunicative Interaction and Evolution of Language

15.2.1. The Significance of MCI for a Linguistic Community

By metacommunicative interaction one means any interaction that comments about the communicative process underlying an utterance. More specifically, the commonest MCI utterances are: acknowledgements that an utterance has been understood, clarification requests (CRs) in which an unclear aspect of the utterance is queried, and corrections, where indications are provided of

---

[1] Following Chomsky (as clarified by Hurford), a distinction is sometimes made between 'I language' — language as represented in the brains of the population and 'E-language' — language that exists as utterances in the arena of use. Ginzburg and Sag (2000) dispute the dichotomy particularly given the need for a view of language that accommodates MCI.

erroneous assumptions concerning naming, concepts associated with predicates etc. Example (3) below, from the London Lund corpus, contains a CR (utterance (b)), a correction (utterance (d)), and an acknowledgement (utterance (e)):

(3) A(a): did you also scotch that other story which is something like was he
    wasn't he refused the chair in Oxford
    a(b): who
    A(c): Skeat, wasn't he refused
    a(d): that's Meak
    A(e): oh Meak, yes
    (London Lund S.1.9, p. 245)

What significance does MCI have for linguistic interaction within a community? MCI is redundant in so far as the communication channel, i.e. that which mediates between speaker and addressee, is perfect or close to that. The need for MCI arises when the communication channel is intrinsically liable to breakdown. If natural language resembled formal languages like first order predicate calculus (as often implicitly assumed in evolution of language work, see e.g. (Kirby 2000)), then problems with the communication channel would be restricted to actual physical problems with the speech signal (mishearing, mispronunciation, noise and the like), problems that affect just about any naturally occurring communicative interaction system. However, natural language diverges radically from first order predicate calculus in its context dependence. This manifests itself in (at least) three phenomena:

(4) (a) *indexicality*: words like 'I', 'you', 'here', 'now', that are resolved relative to the ongoing speech situation.
    (b) *anaphoricity*: words and phrases that are resolved relative to semantic values established by previous utterances (e.g. pronouns, non sentential utterances etc.).
    (c) *ambiguity*: words and phrases which possess multiple senses, one of which is utilised in a given context.

Moreover, even a language like first order predicate calculus used by agents who can reflect about intentions underlying communicative acts, will give rise to the sort of inferences that have come to be known as Gricean conversational implicatures (Grice 1989). These add an extra layer of uncertainty to the communicative process.

Given this, acknowledgements, CRs and corrections are a key communicative component for a linguistic community. They serve as devices for allaying worries about miscommunication (acknowledgements) or for reducing mismatches about the linguistic system among agents (CRs and corrections). That is, they serve as a device for ensuring a certain state of equilibrium or lack of divergence gets maintained within a linguistic community.

15.2.2. The Emergence of MCI: Basic Ingredients

Given the importance that MCI has for linguistic interaction, some fundamental questions that need to be answered are:

(5) (a) Under what circumstances does a linguistic interaction system without MCI evolve into one that has MCI?
    (b) What mechanisms are involved in such a development?
    (c) Why is the resulting interaction system maintained?

(5a,b) are questions to which we can offer only sketchy suggestions at present (see discussion in the following page); the main issue we will contend with is (5c). In order to address these issues, we need to fix what we mean by *an interaction system with MCI*. In the literature on the semantics and pragmatics of dialogue a number of interaction systems have been defined where in addition to the regular illocutionary acts (assertion, querying, commanding etc.), also additional grounding acts (e.g. acknowledgements) are available (see e.g. (Poesio and Traum 1997)) and also systems where clarification requests are available (see e.g. (Ginzburg and Sag 2000; Ginzburg and Cooper 2004)). Such systems assume that as a preliminary to the processing of an utterance u an addressee A checks whether she understands u. If she does, A optionally responds with an acknowledgement, and then reacts in the conventional way to the utterance (accepting/disputing an assertion, answering a query, and so on.). On the other hand, if A does not fully understand u, A poses a query that requests clarification concerning the unclear aspect of u (e.g. inability to resolve a referent, unfamiliarity with or mishearing of a word, etc.) using a number of predefined operations on utterances and utterance meanings.

Poesio and Traum (1997), Ginzburg and Sag(2000), Ginzburg and Cooper (2004) show how existing formal frameworks for grammatical/semantic processing of MCI-less natural language can be extended to process natural language that includes MCI utterances such as acknowledgements and CRs. To understand what is involved, though, one can restrict attention to much simpler systems. We mention two here discussed originally in (Ginzburg 2001).

The utt(erance) ack(nowledgement) Game. In this game, given an utterance u_0 consisting of a string (word$_1$ ... , word$_i$, ... , word$_n$) by the master, the novice may respond with the utterance u_1: word$_i$. In this context, this utterance is assigned content: *novice acknowledges that an utterance including the word word$_i$ happened.* This fact now becomes part of the novice's and master's common ground. What capabilities does playing *utt-ack* game require from the novice?

– Phonological imitation and segmentation module (can be played in one word mode, i.e. game does not require novice to have syntactically complex capabilities)
– Ability to form mutual beliefs

The reward for playing this game is shared interaction with the master. Who can play this game?

- Human neonates: the initial stage of speech consists largely in playing this game (Bates 1979; Ninio 1996)
- Chimps: (Greenfield and Rumbaugh 1993)

A Rudimentary Game with CRs: The **ack-huh?** *Game.* Given an utterance u_0, the responder may acknowledge the utterance or pose a simple CR querying the content of u_0? For instance:

(6) Master: You want the ball? Novice: (i)huh?/(ii)ball?

What additional capabilities does playing *ack-huh* require from the novice?

- Querying
- The ability to form questions querying the contents of antecedently uttered utterances
- No requirement for syntax

Who can play this game?

- Human neonates (from approx 20 months)
- **Not** chimps: (Greenfield and Rumbaugh 1993)

The key feature of these games is at the level of ontology, namely the possibility of reference to utterances and sub-utterances and their properties. In particular, agents capable of playing the *ack-huh?* game require a notion of synonymy between utterances (i.e. the ability to reformulate in a way that preserves content), otherwise any metacommunicative-oriented discussion will be circular. Thus, the simplest agent with the ability to *discuss* a CR is an agent who can communicate contents such as "I don't understand (previous-utterance)" and "What do you mean (previous-utterance)". Given an agent who can reflect and form questions about entities in the domain, this means that once 'say' and 'mean' predicates are in the language, then basic clarification requests can be expressed. Consequently, the emergence of metacommunicative interaction-oriented utterances that go beyond mere acknowledgement, as exemplified in the *ack-huh?* game, can be viewed as an instance of the problem of how vocabulary emerges to talk about a class of entities in a domain, given the need/desire to do so. We speculate that MCI has emerged as an interactional device that keeps members of a linguistic community from diverging too widely from each other's linguistic capabilities, say in terms of their basic vocabulary.

The plausibility of this speculation can be assessed by converting it into more concrete questions such as the following:

(7) (a) In a community with minor but random lexical differences where some people use clarification requests, whereas others do not, do the clarification request users gain an advantage?
    (b) Given a community A where clarification requests do not get expressed, and community B where they do, how do the two communities evolve with respect to vocabulary drift.

In the following sections we present some results obtained from an environment which simulates simple linguistic interactions with agents who are introspective or use CRs when encountering unknown words.

15.3. An ALife Simulation

15.3.1. Basic Properties

The approach we are following, along with many other researchers, employs computational simulations of a population of distributed, autonomous communicative agents endowed with some linguistic capacities. The agents interact via language games, and the outcome can give insight into the particular phenomena that is being investigated.

We are currently running artificial life simulations on a population of agents with dialogue capacities. The model is built using RePast (developed by Collier et al. 2003 and ROAD), a set of Java libraries that allow programmers to build simulation environments. The running of the simulation is divided into time steps or 'ticks', and at each tick some action occurs using the results of previous actions as its basis. Agents are created and placed in an environment in which they are able to wander around in search of 'food' resources. Agents are endowed with a vision capacity in order to see food resources as well as other agents. Upon meeting, the two agents enter a dialogue by playing a naming game where the speaker chooses a food resource in his field of vision, and sends a representation of it to the hearing agent, which in turn tries to interpret it.

15.3.2. Agents

In any multi-agent model the most basic component is the agent. The properties of this agent depend on what we want the agent to do. Since we are modelling a community of communicating agents in a spatial environment, each agent is endowed with the ability to walk, see and communicate. The environment consists of different food resources (i.e. plants) that the agents can see and talk about. An agent walks around the environment in a random fashion and this random probability is the same for every agent. An agent can also perceive other agents and plants that are close by. Agents can make syntactically simple utterances—essentially one consisting of a single word. Each agent's lexicon stores the 'meaning—representation' tuples for the different plants in the environment (e.g. plant-type—plant-word).

Communication is a two sided process involving an intrinsic asymmetry between speaker and addressee: when talking about a plant, the speaking agent necessarily has a lexical representation of the plant, which he sends to the hearing agent. There is no necessity, however, that the addressee agent is able to interpret this utterance. If unable to do so (meaning that the hearing agent doesn't have the word in her lexicon) the way that the agent tries to ground it depends on the agent's type.

Two types of communicative agents exist in the model; agents capable of making a clarification request (CR agents) and those incapable of doing so (introspective agents). A CR agent can resort to a clarification request upon hearing an unknown plant-word. The speaking agent answers this clarification request by giving the meaning-representation to the addressee, who is then able to store it in her lexicon.

An introspective agent, on the other hand tries to guess the meaning of an unknown plant-word instead of resorting to a clarification request. Upon hearing an unknown plant-word the agent looks around her and for each plant that she sees she increases the association score of the plant-word with the plants in her field of vision. This is stored in her temporary lexicon (of unknown plant-words) until she has sufficient information to pick a meaning for the unknown word (viz. associate a specific plant with the plant-word). When this happens the plant-word becomes part of the agent's permanent lexicon.

15.3.3. Simulation / Population Dynamics

Given a computational model of an individual agent we need to set out the ways in which a population of agents interacts. Before creating a population of agents, the environment is created containing different plants (which represent different meanings). The plants are distributed around the environment and they cover 2.28% of it.

The population in the simulations described here is made up of differing numbers of agents that are distributed randomly in the environment at the start. Agents form different communities each of whose members initially share a common lexicon. Agents can be either of the same or different type (CR or introspective) within the community. Apart from the differences in the initial lexicons and types between the agents, all other properties are the same.

Once the simulation starts the agents begin walking randomly in the environment. At every time step each agent moves to a random position, and looks for other agents (that fall into his field of vision). If he sees another agent then two of them will enter a dialogue where the 'seer' will be the speaker and the 'seen' the addressee. A dialogue is of the form:

– Agent 1 sees Agent 2 → `speaker` sees `addressee`.
– `speaker` looks around himself for a topic of conversation (a plant). If:

  • no plants in the field of vision, `speaker` sends *goodbye* to `addressee` and both of them walk off. Otherwise:
  • if plants in vision, `speaker` chooses a random plant as a topic for conversation.

– `speaker` sends the representation string for the chosen plant to the `addressee`.
– `addressee` tries to ground the plant-word via lexicon look up. There is no attempt to verify that the perceived meaning is same as the intended meaning.

– if **addressee** has the plant-word in her lexicon, the dialogue is considered *successful* and both agents continue walking.
– else if the **addressee** doesn't know the plant-word she resorts to CR or introspection (depending on her type) in order to acquire the meaning of the plant-word.

After the completion of the dialogue the agent continues walking in a random direction. This is then repeated until all agents acquire all the lexicon.

15.4. Results

This section describes different setups and experiment results for the model described in Sect. 15.3.3.

In order to test the questions raised in (7) the agents need to have minor but random lexical differences (here missing words), and clarification requesting (CR) and introspective capabilities.

The performance is based upon two behaviours which are collected at the end of the simulation run:

– *acquisition time*: the average time it takes the whole population to learn the whole lexicon.
– *convergence rate*: the percentage of *correctly* acquired meanings. Here an acquired meaning is *correct* if it is identical with the meaning associated with that word by the community who uses it at the start of the simulation. Note though that for one type of simulation, that involving a homogenous population of CR agents, this parameter has an entirely predictable value—100%. This is due to the fact that in the current set up each time an agent A makes a CR the original speaker explicitly provides A with the intended meaning associated with the unknown word. Thus at the end of such a simulation all the agents share a common lexicon with no divergence.

The initial conditions and model parameters affect the above behaviours in complex ways. To determine what consequences arise when a single parameter is manipulated there is a need to control all other parameters and keep them constant whilst only manipulating the parameter being investigated.

The three model parameters which we initially vary are:

– *meaning space*: the number of different meanings (plant-types) in the simulation.
– *population size*: the number of agents in the simulation.
– *acquisition threshold*: the number of times an agent has to hear an unknown word before she can acquire it. There are two types of acquisition threshold depending on the agent type:

- *CR threshold*: the number of times an agent has to hear an unknown plant-word before she can clarify it. For example if `CR-thres = 2` then an agent will only resort to a CR after hearing an unknown word for the second time.
- *Introspection threshold*: the number of times an agent has to associate an unknown plant-word with a plant-type in her field of vision before she can acquire the plant-word. For example if `Intr-thres = 4` then for every unknown plant-word that the agent hears, she has to see (associate) a plat-type four times with it before she is able to acquire the plant-word.

Each parameter has a default value throughout the experiments, unless it is being investigated. The default and investigative parameter values are shown in Table 15.1.

There are three types of experiments that we run where the different model parameters are tested. In the initial experiments (Sect. 15.4.1) the population is homogenous, either completely composed of CR agents or of introspective agents. In the second set of experiments (Sect. 15.4.2) the population is mixed, containing both CR and introspective agents in a 1:1 ratio. The final set of experiments (Sect. 15.4.3) is made up of populations of hybrid agents that can both ask a clarification request or introspect.

15.4.1. Homogenous Population Experiments

This section looks in detail at experiments with homogenous populations as described above. The results of these experiments serve as a benchmark for more complex population types. Manipulating the model parameters changes the behaviour of the simulation, where as stated above the performance of the populations will be judged on their *acquisition time* and *convergence rate*.

Meaning Space. In this set of experiments the parameter which is being manipulated is the meaning space. Increasing the meaning space involves increasing the differentiation among types of plants. The actual number of tokens remains constant. Increasing the meaning space causes the average acquisition time to go up polynomially (see Figure 15.1). This is the case for both CR and introspective populations, with CR performing slightly better. The reason for this is that an introspective agent has to associate an unknown

TABLE 15.1. Default and investigative parameter values.

Parameter	Default value	Investigative values
meaning space	5	3, 4, 5, 10, 20
population size	40	4 – 40
acquisition threshold	3	1 – 10, 20, 30, 40, 50

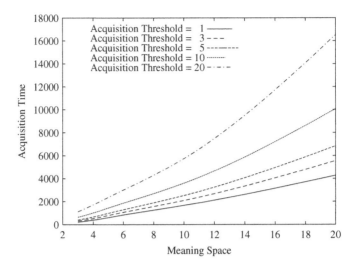

FIGURE 15.1. As the *meaning space* increases the *acquisition time* increases polynomially. Increasing the *acquisition threshold* causes the overall time to go up.

plant-word with the plants in her field of vision.[2] Sometimes it might happen that the addressee agent doesn't see any plants, or that she is looking at a different plant from the speaking agent, upon hearing an unknown plant-word. This increases the acquisition time, compared with a CR agent, who is given the meaning as soon as she requests clarification.

The convergence rate is always perfect in homogenous CR populations, thus we can only talk about the convergence rate in introspective populations for this set of experiments. The general trend here is that as the meaning space increases the convergence rate increases as well between 5 – 30% (depending on the inference threshold value) in the introspective population. The convergence rate increases for a meaning space up to a value of ten, then levels off afterwards (see Figure 15.2).

Population Size. The population size in these experiments increases from four agents up to forty agents whilst keeping the environment constant. The acquisition time decreases as the number of agents increases (see Figure 15.3). An explanation for this would appear to be that as more and more agents are placed in an environment of a constant size, the probability of seeing other agents at the next time step increases thus the probability of engaging in a dialogue also increases. Thus the time is dependant on the number of agents according to a power function $time = K * numAgents^{-a}$, where K and a are constants. This again holds for both CR and introspective populations. Here again the CR populations acquire their lexicons faster than the introspective populations.

---

[2] An agent's field of vision consists of a grid of fixed size originating from her location. Hence proximate agents have overlapping but not identical fields of vision.

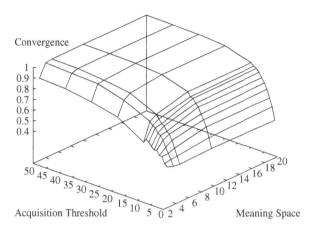

FIGURE 15.2. The relationship between *acquisition threshold, meaning space* and *convergence rate*: increasing the *acquisition threshold* causes the *convergence rate* to increase more than would be the case of increasing just the *meaning space*.

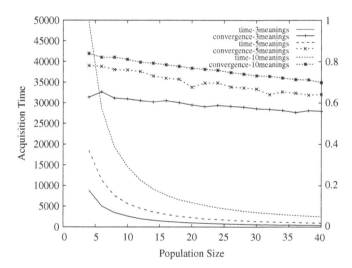

FIGURE 15.3. The relationship between *population size, acquisition time* and *convergence rate*. The smooth lines show the effect of increasing the *population size* on the *acquisition time* of the simulation. On the other hand the dotted lines represent the relationship between *population size* and *convergence rate*.

The convergence rate on the other hand decreases as the population size increases. The decrease in convergence rate is around 14% between a population size of four and forty. The reason for this might be termed the *Babel effect*. As the population increases the agents have more dialogues in a smaller part of the environment. So when an agent acquires a different meaning for a plant-word the agents around her are more likely to acquire this alternative meaning for an unknown plant-word causing the overall convergence rate to go down.

Acquisition Threshold. In these experiments the parameter that is changing is the number of times that an agent needs to hear a word before she is able to acquire it. For both types of populations the acquisition time increases linearly with the increasing acquisition threshold. As with the previous experiments the introspective populations are slower in acquiring the lexicon.

As for the convergence rate, it increases as the acquisition threshold increases. The reason is that an agent is given more chances to associate an unknown plant-word with the plants she sees as the threshold increases. Therefore she has more time to learn by observation, which improves the convergence rate. After a certain point the convergence rate starts to level off and even increasing the threshold values causes minimal change in the convergence rate. This can be seen in Figure 15.2.

15.4.2. Mixed Population Experiments

Now that we know how the parameters affect the simulation for homogeneous populations, we want to compare these results with the results of mixed populations of agents, containing both CR and introspective agents in a 1:1 ratio. In so doing, we want to keep the meaning space and the population constant and monitor how the manipulation of the acquisition thresholds affects the simulations. For the following experiments, the values for the meaning space and the population size used are as shown in Table 15.1.

In the CR community, the convergence rate increases from 90% to nearly 100%. On the other hand in the introspective community the convergence rate increases from 40% to 80%. This is shown in Figure 15.4(a). Increasing the CR threshold doesn't affect the convergence rate in any particular way as is shown in Figure 15.4(b). The convergence rate is much more dependent on the introspection threshold.

Comparing this result with the homogenous introspective population, the convergence rate is slightly better as shown in Figure 15.6. When averaging the overall convergence rate of both CR and introspective communities the convergence rate rises by quite a bit compared with the homogenous introspective population (see Figure 15.6).

The acquisition time doesn't seem to be affected for the differing population makeups. Only when calculating the overall average time (for both CR and introspective agents), do we see an improvement comparing it with the homogenous introspective population, but it is still higher than the homogenous CR populations (see Figure 15.7).

15.4.3. Hybrid Agent Experiments

In this final set of experiments the population is homogeneous, every agent has a capability of either using the CR strategy or the introspective strategy. Upon

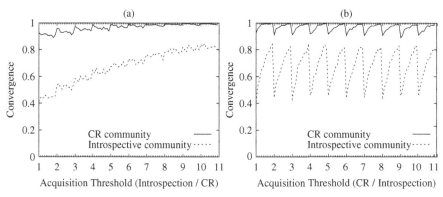

FIGURE 15.4. (a) A mixed population made up of a community of CR and a community of introspective agents (each containing 20 members) with differing *acquisition thresholds*. The x-axis shows different *acquisition threshold* make-ups, where the bigger line represents the introspection threshold and within each value there are 10 different CR threshold values (represented by the small lines on the x-axis). The upper curve represents the *convergence rate* of the CR community, while the lower curve represents the *convergence rate* of the introspective community. (b) This figure shows the same data as Fig. 15.4(a) but here the x-axis plots differing introspection threshold (small lines on the x-axis) values for the increasing CR threshold values.

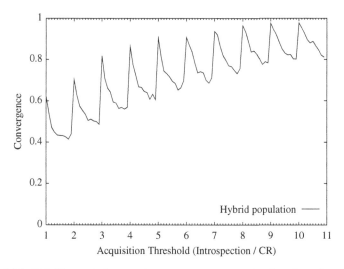

FIGURE 15.5. Hybrid population results: *convergence rate* is plotted against differing values for the *acquisition thresholds*, where for each introspection threshold value (represented on the x-axis with bigger gaps) CR threshold is being increased from 1 to 10 (represented by the smaller lines).

hearing an unknown plant-word the agent looks for plants close by. If she can see some plants, then she follows the introspective strategy, otherwise if there are no plants in her field of vision she resorts to a clarification request.

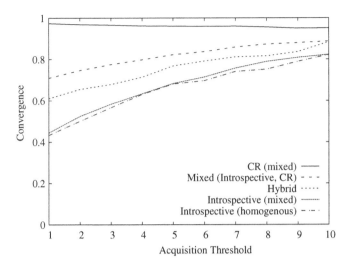

FIGURE 15.6. *Convergence rate* increases as the *acquisition threshold* increases for every population make-up except for *CR (mixed)* population for which it decreases slightly.

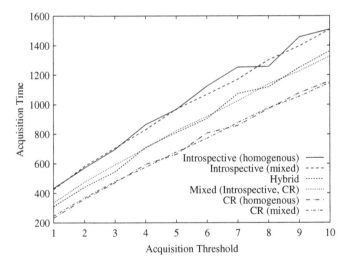

FIGURE 15.7. The comparison of *acquisition times* for the experiments on differing population make-ups. Changing the population from homogenous to mixed (either introspective or CR) doesn't affect the *acquisition time*. The overall acquisition time for a mixed population (average of *Introspective (mixed)* and *CR (mixed)*) is comparable with the acquisition time of the *Hybrid* population.

The results of these simulations are shown in Figure 15.5. The graph shows that as the introspection threshold increases so does the convergence rate. But the convergence rate also depends on the CR threshold, and as the CR threshold rises so the convergence rate falls. The reason for this is that as CR threshold rises, the agent will resort to clarification requests less frequently thus introspecting more often, a strategy which is more error prone. If the CR threshold value is low and the introspection threshold value high then the convergence rate outperforms all the other tested populations. The overall average convergence rate is still higher than the homogenous and mixed introspective populations (see Figure 15.6).

Timewise the hybrid population is comparable with the overall mixed population (as shown by Figure 15.7).

15.5. Discussion

Let us now sharpen our focus to concentrate on the key results that emerge from these simulations. Possibly the most fundamental result obtained here concerns the convergence rate of a homogeneous population of introspective agents. In particular, the notable convergence decrease as a population *increases* seems to point to an important phenomenon, which we dubbed the *Babel effect*. The Babel effect means that a population without CRs is in danger of arriving at a situation where apparently a single language is shared by the population, whereas in fact divergent meanings are associated with the same sounds.[3] Moreover, this dangerous situation could emerge in relatively quick time given that acquisition time decreases rapidly as the number of agents increase.

The counterpart to the Babel effect are the results concerning a population of hybrid agents, agents who use both introspection and CRs (the latter sort of as a last resort): such a population (as long as its members do not act recklessly, i.e. jump too quickly to conclusions about meanings) supports high rates of convergence.

15.6. Conclusions and Future Work

In this paper we have discussed how metacommunicative interaction (MCI) serves as a key component in the maintenance of a linguistic interaction system. We have outlined the basic components that need to emerge in order that an MCI-less linguistic system evolves into an MCI-containing system. This theoretical setting underpins and motivates the development of an ALife environment in which the lexicon dynamics of populations that possess and lack MCI capabilities are compared. The environment is one in which agents walk randomly and when proximate to one another engage in a brief conversational interaction concerning plants visible to the agents. We ran a series of experiments whose initial state involved agents possessing distinct lexicons and whose end state was

---

[3] Though there is some evidence that perhaps this is not so unusual a situation, see (Schober 2004).

one in which all agents associated meanings with each word in a lexicon. The experiments involved tracking two variables: acquisition time and convergence rate—the percentage of newly acquired words whose acquired meanings match the originally associated meanings. Several parameters were varied (size of meaning space, population size, acquisition threshold—the number of times an agent has to hear an unknown word before she can acquire it.) and results gathered across distinct types of populations: the essential contrast being between agents who can request clarification of unknown words as opposed to agents who acquire new meanings introspectively, by observing their environment. The overall results can be viewed in Figure 15.7 and Figure 15.6. The main effect demonstrated, one we dub the *Babel effect*, is that the convergence rate of population that relies exclusively on introspection is intrinsically bounded and, moreover, this bound decreases with an increasing population. This bound seems to disappear once agents are endowed with CRs.

While the Babel effect seems to be an interesting finding, confirming our initial theorizing, much work remains to butress it as a fundamental dividing line between MCI-ful and MCI-less populations. A significant simplification inherent in our simulation is the nature of linguistic interaction, which in our case involves syntactically unstructured messages. This intrinsically restricts the size and variation of the meaning space. An additional simplification is the built in success of responses to CRs. More open ended issues, whose role the simulation brings out, revolve around the influence of topography on lexicon dynamics (e.g. variety of plant types in the environment, ease of interaction between agents). An important future development to our simulation, obviously crucial for any evolutionary model, concerns mortality: as things stand, (for a single simulation run) agents are immortal and convergence rates are measured once all agents assign a meaning to each linguistic form. Limiting life span should reduce convergence and raise issues of generational variation.

Acknowledgments This work is supported by an EPSRC quota award to Macura and by grant RES-000-23-0065 from the Economic and Social Council of the United Kingdom to Ginzburg. We would like to thank two reviewers for EELC05 for their very helpful comments.

References

Bates, E.: The Emergence of Symbols. Academic Press (1979)
Briscoe, E. J.: Grammatical acquisition: Inductive bias and coevolution of language and the language acquisition device. Language, **76** (2000) (2):245–296
Clark, H.: Using Language. Cambridge University Press, Cambridge (1996)
Collier, N., Howe, T., and North, M.: Onward and Upward: The Transition to Repast 2.0, Proceedings of the First Annual North American Association for Computational Social and Organizational Science Conference, Electronic Proceedings, Pittsburgh, PA USA June (2003)
Ginzburg, J.: The emergence of metacommunicative meaning. Paper presented at the 13th Amsterdam Colloquium on Semantics and Logic, December (2001)

Ginzburg, J., Cooper R.: Clarification, ellipsis, and the nature of contextual updates. Linguistics and Philosophy, **27** (2004) (3):297–366

Ginzburg, J., Sag, I. A.: Interrogative Investigations: the form, meaning and use of English Interrogatives. Number 123 in CSLI Lecture Notes. CSLI Publications, Stanford: California (2000)

Greenfield, P., Rumbaugh, S. S.: Comparing communicative competence in child and chimp: The pragmatics of repetition. Journal of Child Language, **20** (1993) 1–26

Grice, H. P.: Studies in the Ways of Words. Reprinted from a 1957 article. Harvard University Press (1989)

Kirby, S.: Syntax without natural selection: How compositionality emerges from vocabulary in a population of learners. In The Evolutionary Emergence of Language: Social Function and the Origins of Linguistic Form. Cambridge University Press (2000) 303–323

Ninio, A., Snow, C.: Pragmatic Development. Westview (1996)

Poesio, M., Traum, D.: Conversational actions and discourse situations. Computational Intelligence, **13** (3) (1997)

Repast. Recursive porus agent simulation toolkit. http://repast.sourceforge.net

Schegloff, E.: Repair after the next turn: The last structurally provided defense of inter-subjectivity in conversation. American Journal of Sociology, **97** (1992) (5):1295–1345

Schober, M.: Just how aligned are interlocutors representations? Commentary on Pickering and Garrod. Behavioral and Brain Sciences, **27** (2004) 209–210

Steels, L.: The origins of ontologies and communication conventions in multi-agent systems. Autonomous Agents and Multi-Agent Systems, **1** (1998) (2):169–194

16
Agent Based Modelling of Communication Costs: Why Information Can Be Free

Ivana Čače and Joanna J. Bryson

16.1. Why We Have Language

What purposes, other than facilitating the sharing of information, can language have served? First, it may not have evolved to serve any purpose at all. It is possible that language is just a side effect of the large human brain — a spandrel or exaptation — that only became useful later. If language is adaptive, this does not necessarily mean that it is adaptive for the purpose of communication. For example Dennett (1996) and Chomsky (1980) have stressed the utility of language in thinking. Also, there are different ways to view communication. The purpose of language according to Dunbar (1993), is to replace grooming as a social bonding process and in this way to ensure the stability of large social groups.

Why would anyone think that communication might be a bad thing? Because communication is a form of altruism, it is a giving up of information to one's competitors. Remember, even friends are competitors in a biological sense, as they share the same food resources and mating opportunities. Consequently, many people find it unlikely that such altruism could evolve (Dessalles 2000; Marshall and Rowe 2003).

In this chapter we examine the costs and benefits of sharing information, using a simple spatial agent model. The information concerns the agents' food. The costs are for the signaling agent in terms of more competition over food, and the benefits are for the receiver in terms of access to more food. We will show that under some conditions agents that communicate do better — that is, have more offspring — than agents that do not. In the next section we will show how communication can be viewed in terms of costs and benefits. We will discuss some theories that fit in this framework and propose a slightly different approach. In the next section we will discuss communication in relation to parenting (kin-selection) and foraging abilities. We will then describe the experiment we used to show that communication is indeed a good thing.

16.2. The Signaling Framework

16.2.1. Introduction

The study of communication in terms of costs and benefits has originated in biology but has also been applied to the emergence of language. A scientifically effective way of looking at animal signals is in terms of mind-reading and manipulation (Krebs and Dawkins 1984). The signaling agent takes the role of manipulator while the receiving agent is the mind-reader. The manipulator sends some signal — intentionally or not — that will incite the mind-reader to some response. The mind-readers response might be costly to the mind-reader itself, to the manipulator or it could be advantageous to either or both.

When signaling is viewed in this way it can be formalized and then studied using for example game-theory or a simulation. Hopefully this will help explain some of the properties of signals found in nature. Animals will have evolved to maximize their gain and minimize their costs in their roles as signalers and receivers.

The honesty of the signal often determines the cost of/for the signal. Animals signal about themselves, most importantly their fitness or their intentions, or they signal about the environment. In a cooperative setting both signaler and receiver stand to gain from an accurate response to a honest signal. But in case of competition the signaler may gain more by manipulating the receiver to a response that may not be the most accurate for the given conditions. The signaler may try to pretend to be a fitter mate or a stronger adversary — or food instead of predator. So how does the receiver protect itself from being cheated? One solution, proposed first by Zahavi (1975), is to ensure signals are so costly, the weaker animals cannot afford to produce them. This is the so called "costly signaling" hypothesis and it has since been elaborated on by many others (Maynard-Smith and Harper 1995). This mechanism will obviously only work if the animal is signaling about itself. Other 'solutions' involve a penalty for lying or signals that are necessarily honest.

Formally the costs–and–benefits framework can be described as follows. Assume that not signaling has some effect on the signalers and receiver's fitness, the null hypothesis receiver n_r and the null hypothesis signaler n_s. Then signaling will be adaptive if, on average:

$$f_r > n_r \text{ and } c + f_s > n_s \tag{1}$$

Where f_r, f_s and c are defined as in Figure 16.1.

Altruism The costs–and–benefits framework can also be applied to the emergence of language. If language is simply perceived as signaling, the

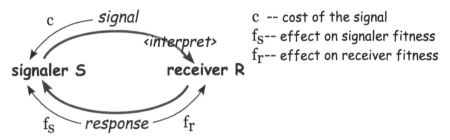

FIGURE 16.1. The signaling game has fitness effects for both the signaler and receiver. Signaling will be adaptive if S and R both benefit from it.

same question arises of how to keep it honest. Another problem occurs when language is taken to be primarily a tool for accurately sharing information. [1] If information is a resource then sharing it is altruistic behavior. The advantages of altruistic behavior to the group are evident, so long as it helps others more than it hurts the altruist. However, unless the behavior somehow increases the fitness of the altruistic individual it is not in itself adaptive, so it is unlikely to be selected. The two main mechanisms that are thought to underly apparent altruistic behavior are: reciprocal altruism and altruism in favor of kin.

Reciprocal altruism is possible if there are repeated interactions in which agents take turns in their roles as signallers and receivers. Over a longer period of time everyone involved could profit from these interactions. Reciprocal altruism presupposes a method of distinguishing between agents that will cooperate, or have cooperated in the past, and the 'free-riders' that will not. Cox et al. (1999) have shown that altruism will persist in an agent-based model if the agents are endowed with a memory that allows them to remember which other agents are likely to cooperate.

Cooperation among related individuals can exist even if it is not mutually beneficial. The success of an individual's *genes* depends on the individual's own reproductive success and that of others with the same genetic material. This notion has been been formalized by Hamilton (1964). Hamilton's rule relates the inclusive fitness (i.e. reproductive success) f of an altruistic act to c, its cost to the actor, and to the relatedness r of the recipients to the actor and the benefit b they have from it:

$$f = c + \sum (r \cdot b)$$

Note that kin selection implies that either the agent has control over its behavior and can distinguish between related and not related agents, or the altruistic

---

[1] Simple signaling too transfers information in the sense that it reduces the receiver's uncertainty about the signaler or the environment.

behavior is involuntary but will mostly be triggered when related agents are around to profit. The close presence of kin is is an important feature of so called viscous populations where individuals have limited mobility. Such populations are thought to facilitate cooperation and altruism[2] (Marshall and Rowe 2003; Hamilton 1964). When agents remain close to their place of origin they are more likely to be related to nearby individuals. Any altruism towards neighboring agents is likely to benefit kin. But at the same time competition between nearby individuals will be counteracting cooperation. Kin selection is also possible if the population structure is such that individuals mingle with others they are not related to. Only now the altruistic behavior will be voluntary and directed towards kin, and there will be some level of cognitive load. The agent will have to know somehow if it is related to another agent (and to what degree). This is a situation similar to reciprocal altruism, when agents have to keep track of which other agents are likely to cooperate.

16.2.2. Models

A number of theories have been brought forward to explain why we have language despite the opportunities it offers for cheating and despite it being the foundation of information sharing, a basically altruistic behavior. Because language is an example of conventional signaling, the signals themselves are necessarily cheap. If there is a price it will come from the content of the signal. The information being transferred might have cost the signaler time and energy to acquire. Sharing this information may have fitness effects, positive or negative, for the signaler and the receiver. We will now discuss some of the theories that have applied the framework described above to language and that do not rely on either kin-selection or reciprocal altruism.

The first entry in Table 16.1 is the costly signaling hypothesis mentioned earlier. From the receivers perspective, trust will pay off if the received information is worth more (on average) then the price of being cheated. Simon (1990) made a convincing case for cooperation and altruism as social learning. He has argued that the complexity of the environment people live in makes docility, that is receptivity to social influence, an adaptive strategy. "… the docile individual will often be unable to distinguish socially prescribed behavior that contributes to fitness from altruistic behavior." Human life history provides the perfect setting for social learning. Children are born with a undeveloped brain and require many years of nurture by adults during a time in their development in which they are very sensitive to learning. As adults too, we continue to live in social groups. This facilitates communication. In today's society information is important but the survival skills of early humans too included information about plant and animal food sources and how to make tools. After their childhood human beings

---

[2] Viscosity is also thought to facilitate reciprocal altruism because of repeated interactions among individuals. This is the first requirement for cooperation among agents that are not related.

TABLE 16.1. Different ways to ensure that communication benefits both signaler and receiver. The second column shows how this is achieved (based on variables in Figure 16.1).

variable	explanation
$\uparrow c$	S signals fitness to prospective mating partner. R cannot asses S's fitness, the signal will be honest if S cannot lie. One way to ensure this is if c of a signal indicating high quality is too high for a low quality individual.
$\uparrow f_r$	Over a longer period, the effects of acquiring useful information negates the effects of being cheated or manipulated (Simon 1990).
$\uparrow -f_s$	S signals its ability to fight to a competitor. R can choose to test S, if S lied it will run the risk of getting hurt more than a stronger individual (Lachmann and Bergstrom 2001).
$c + f_s > 0$	S tells R some fact K, this will cost it c. If K proves useful, S gains status: $\uparrow f_s$ (Dessalles 2000).

will continue to live in some form of social group. They will have to master social skills and survival skills for dealing with the outside world. The latter will include information about plant and animal food sources and how to make tools. Also hunter-gatherers (see section 16.2.3 below) may travel long distances, making it necessary to anticipate and communicate about expected travel conditions like shelters, food, water resources and weather.

On the signaling side there may be a cost to lying or a gain to producing accurate, useful information. We will give examples of both. We have already mentioned the model used by Lachmann and Bergstrom (2001) to show that a penalty for lying will incite honesty and make communication adaptive. They use a mathematical (game theoretic) model to describe the effects various cost functions have on the signaling-equilibrium between signaler and receiver. According to Lachmann and Bergstrom the results of their formal model are applicable to human language if there are socially imposed sanctions against liars. This requires that other group-members know and care about the accuracy of the information. If this is the case, the costs of lying will not only serve to favor honesty but will also select for the more careful and redundant signals that become possible through linguistic communication. Language may also facilitate social enforcement by making it easier to share information about others' reliability.

The possible gain from honesty can be explained as classic costly signaling if one assumes a cost to gathering and/or dispensing information. Dessalles (2000) uses a simulation of his model to show that "the evolution of language is at least conceivable in a context of political competition between coalitions". First he proposes a model in which communication has a cost. He then shows that there is no selective pressure for communication as reciprocal altruism in this model. Next he proposes a model in which there is also a *gain* to communicating successfully. Receivers rate the usability of the information. Agents that are known to supply others with high quality information gain status through coalitions. Coalitions are defined as "groups of individuals showing solidarity in action". In Dessalles' model there is competition between coalitions and individual fitness is tied in with the success of the coalition. Agents that supply useful information are readily joined by others. In a sense the individuals signal their fitness only now it is not determined by physical strength or speed, but by the ability to enter a successful coalition.

Does there have to be a Price? In the models discussed above there was always a presupposed cost to (honest) communication. Without abandoning the costs-benefits framework altogether, it is possible to find support for the idea that sharing knowledge may be useful if we take a more comprehensive view. Communication could offer advantages in the context of foraging and parenting, as we show in the next section. We have built a model to see *if* there is a cost to sharing knowledge, and found that this is not always the case. We challenge the hypothesis that compulsively sharing valuable knowledge is in itself not adaptive.

16.2.3. Food and Kin

Buckley and Steele (2002) have made an extensive survey and categorization of research in the area of the emergence of language and linked it to archaeological and palaeontological parameters that can aid in determining the plausibility of different hypotheses. This leads them to the conclusion of "life history strategy as the prime mover, and co-operative foraging and provisioning as the selective context for spoken language abilities."

They organize social models for the evolution of language into 3 groups: parenting strategy, status and rank, and co-operation. Each of these models, or rather models that emphasize on each of these three social contexts, entails certain conditions that can be can be compared to archaeological evidence. They find no reliable archaeological evidence for increase in group size, and therefore reject the third type of model. Furthermore, hominin fossil anatomy shows that the differences between male and female (in terms of body mass and canine size) became smaller. According to Buckley and Steele this "does not suggest that male-male competition for mates was a driver for the evolution of social communication strategies." Archaeological evidence does favor the first kind of model, which emphasizes the benefits of communication in the provisioning effort for child rearing. Increase in provisioning effort is tied in to the increase in hominin brain size and the subsequent prolonged immaturity in children. We will return to this shortly when we consider the role of communication in foraging. First we discuss the connection between communication and child-rearing.

Communication among Kin We have discussed the altruism in favor of kin above. An example of communication that can be viewed in this way is teaching. Communication among kin can also *facilitate* the development of communication abilities. The selective advantage that communication provides may not be enough to ensure that the inclination to communicate will spread through the population. The selective process will be frequency dependent, that is the benefits of communication will depend on the proportion of communicating individuals. When the trait first appears the proportion of the communicating individuals in the group is very small and therefore the advantages of communicating will be very small or rare. As a result the speed with which the trait spreads through the population could become so low, that it can easily be disrupted by random events.

Cavalli-Sforza and Feldman (1983) have shown that this bottleneck is removed if the communication occurs among close relatives or "if aggregation of communication occurs because of assortative mating or meeting". Cavalli-Sforza and Feldman assume that the ability to communicate — that is the combined ability to emit the signal and to understand what is being communicated — is hereditary. Communication is used to transmit some fitness enhancing skill, that all adult communicators have already acquired. If these conditions are met the communicators' offspring will have a sufficiently high fitness increase, due to contact with (at least one of) their parents, for the evolution of communication to take off. Communication with other family members or a preference for the company of others to communicate with, may speed up this process even more. This way the payoff of communication might be higher (if there is enough useful information to be communicated) for both adults and children. In this analytical model the adaptive pressure towards communication will persist, provided the relation between costs, benefits and the chances of meeting another communicator are favorable. For the process described above to work, the property in question need not be hereditary. Communication (cooperation, altruism) could very well be a learned trait, that is, the whole population has been born with the ability but only those who have been raised in a 'communicating environment' will display the actual behavior.

The Expensive Tissue Hypothesis Language is one of the things that sets us apart from the other primates, having a much larger brain is another one. The brain uses about 20–25% of the body's energy. Humans have approximately the same calorie-intake as chimpanzees, so how can we afford to feed our brain? The answer is that our intestine needs a lot less to uptake as many calories. The Expensive Tissue Hypothesis (Aiello and Wheeler 1995) states that the large human brain has been made possible by our small gut which was in turn made possible by a rich diet. Food of low digestibility requires relatively large guts while food of high digestibility (such as sugary fruits, protein and oil rich seeds and animal material) requires relatively smaller guts. This is true both in the general case (compare for example a cow with any given carnivore) as in the specific case among primates. The idea that language could have influenced diet was derived from one due to Steele (2004). Steele's idea was that language and a larger brain may have co-evolved. A large brain does not only offer many exiting possibilities in terms of cognitive functions, it also has a price. Because of the large brain children take a longer time to mature and place a high burden on those who provide for them. This would make it necessary to find new and more efficient ways of finding food. What if language is one of the factors that enabled us as a species to obtain this richer — but harder to get — food? Then having a larger brain could in turn have facilitated language.

16.3. Experiment

16.3.1. Agent Based Modeling

In this section we briefly introduce Agent Based Modeling (ABM) and describe our model. We will than move on to describing the experiment and the results. As a research tool, ABM is used in a variety of areas including: social science and economics (Epstein and Axtell1996; Cederman and Rao 2001), animal behavior (Hemelrijk 2000) and complex systems in general (Baray 1998; Esteva et al. 2001). ABM has also been applied before to the question of communication (Noble et al. 2002; Dessalles 2000). Because communication is a form of social interaction, examining this behavior is best done by simulating social interactions. ABM is the most suitable method for doing this.

Simulations and theoretical models are only tools to test the soundness of a hypothesis. We found that freely sharing information about food does not need to be costly. Our results signify something about the preconditions for the emergence of language. However, the use of models can only help clarify the mechanisms behind emergence of language, real-world data is needed to gain insight in the actual development undergone by early man. In other words we only describe a possibility. We do not make any claims about the evolutionary path from low level signaling to human language.

When we describe our model in the following section, it will become clear that we have not simulated any existing population. For example, the agents are presented with opportunities to feed at random, if there is more competition there will be less food. At this level of abstraction there is no distinction between collecting food or hunting for food.

16.3.2. Building the Model

The purpose of the model is to determine *if* communication about food is beneficial and to understand the mechanism that causes the costs and benefits in the context of honest communication about food. The model is intended to clarify rather than predict, so a simpler model is favored over a more complicated one. Other requirements are that it simulates communication and provides some way of measuring the effects it has on both the population as a whole and on individuals. That is, it needs to be suitable for comparing different behavioral *strategies*, communicating and not communicating. A number of simplifying assumptions have to be made in order to construct an abstract model with only a few factors, the influence of which can then be examined in turn. Bear in mind that the model should produce some kind of result within a reasonable amount of time when run on a computer, this has consequences for the choice of model. A model with a smaller number of agents runs faster but if the number drops below a certain threshold the agents may die out due to random population fluctuations. So the first crude constraint could be expressed as follows: the number of agents should be as small as possible but large enough to prevent arbitrary extinctions or other impairments. This entails a preference for a combination of model parameters that results in relatively small fluctuations in population size.

Our models were built in NetLogo (Wilensky 1999). NetLogo is a freely available multi-agent modeling environment, specifically designed for the ABM of natural and social phenomena. The NetLogo world consists of two kinds of programmable agents: an environment divided into patches and mobile agents called turtles. Patches can represent environmental change, such as growing food, while turtles are typically used to represent animals, including humans.

In the model we used in this experiment the environment consists of 101x101 patch square on a torus space, which is presented on screen as a square. This means that agents that walk of the edge of the square will reappear on the opposite edge.

The agents move round, eat and reproduce. At every time-step they lose a small amount of their energy and if their energy level drops under 0 they die. The environment 'grows food', that is at every time-step every patch is filled with a unit of food with probability P. These food-growth settings for the model we used were inspired by Wilensky (1998). For example, with a probability of 0.016 and a field size of 10201 ($101 \cdot 101$), around 163 food-units will be added to the environment. A patch can only contain one unit of food. To keep the model as simple as possible the agents reproduce a-sexually. When an agent reproduces its energy is divided between it and its offspring to keep the total energy constant, the new agent gets 20% of the parents' energy. Note that this means that if agents that have low energy levels are allowed to reproduce, their offspring (and maybe even they themselves) have a small survival chance. We have made the agents' probability of reproduction dependent on their energy, so as to give the weaker agents a better chance. With the progression of the agents with the better strategy slowed down, there is more time to study the system. New agents are instantiated on the same patch as their parent.

The agents have no cognitive architecture. After all we were testing the effects of communication and adding extra mechanisms to the model (e.g. perception, action selection) could cloud the main question. This does mean that intelligent walking patterns have to be simulated too. We accomplish this by generating a walking pattern that is found in foraging animals as well as in evolutionary optimized foraging agents (van Dartel et al. 2002). Prior to taking a step the agents make a random turn, then they take a step of length l (one unit is equivalent to the length of a patch) where:

$$l = (0.7/n)^{0.3}$$

n is a random value between 0 and 1, 0.7 is a normalizing factor. The value of 0.3 ensures that the agents' most frequent step length is 1.[3] This way viscousity is high and when communication is added to the model the impact of communication, in terms of more competition, is large. The density of the population has no impact on their mobility: any number of agents can be standing on the same patch.

These settings yield a stable model, that is, regardless of the *initial* values for the number of agents or the amount of food, the model will gravitate towards equilibrium values. Also, all else remaining equal, the number of agents depends on the amount of energy that is added to the environment. This means that adding more food will not serve to make the agents less 'needy' and decrease competition, it will only increase the number of agents the environment can sustain (the carrying capacity).

On top of this model the knowledge distribution and communication is modeled as follows. A second type of food is added to the environment. This 'special food' comes in 6 varieties and has twice the calorie value of the regular food. In order to collect any of the varieties, the agent needs specialized knowhow.

There are two ways to obtain the knowhow to eat one of the special food-types. Every agent has a small (5%) chance of knowing how to eat any one of the 6 items at birth. And, at every time-step, all the communicating agents pick one thing they know and tell all their neighbors. Agents are killed off when they have been around for more then 50 time-steps, to keep knowledge sparse. The knowhow itself is implemented as a 6-bit string. For example, an agent with string [0 1 0 0 1 0] knows two things. The pseudo-code for agents becomes:

```
take-credit
if (random energy) > 30 [offspring ]
set energy (energy - 1)
move
set age (age + 1)
if (breed = talker) [ communicate ]
```

At every time-step all the agents go through this routine, then the food in the environment is replenished (grown) as described earlier.

To prevent the special food from clogging up the environment when there is not enough knowhow among the agents to eat it, the regular food can overgrow the special food. The pseudo-code for the environment is:

---

[3] For larger values, up to 0.5, walking is even better optimized for foraging. The resulting pattern is one of random walk with a occasional large jump. Large jumps would significantly lower viscosity and competition and are therefore not desirable in this case.

for all patches:
fill patch with special food, with probability $P_{special}$
fill patch with regular food, with probability $P_{regular}$

A Priori Some things can be said about this model and models in general on forehand. Note that, as always in the agent based approach, only the agents and their environment are modeled. When the model is run, the complex behavior of the system emerges from the local interactions between the agents and between the agents and their environment. In this model the cost of communication is not given but emerges from the spatial interactions between the agents and their environment. If an agent shares food-information with its neighbors then it will have to deal with increased food competition. Both communication and competition take place locally. Small step size results in a viscous population as we discussed earlier. The question is which will be of greater influence: competition between nearby (possibly related) individuals or the positive effect of altruism towards nearby kin. In our model the costs of the communication are caused solely by competition. If the agents were to be more mobile communication would remain without consequences *for the individual communicating agent*. It would quickly leave the vicinity of the agents it had shared its knowhow with.

It would be tempting to make an analogy between evolution proper and the way in which our model evolves. This would also be wrong. Obviously the scale is wrong, both in terms of population size as well as in terms of time. But on a more fundamental level, any model that only models behavior and not genes is not a valid model of evolution. It only checks phenotypical properties for their evolutionary usefulness. It does not say anything about the genetic possibilities and dependencies (like the one between language, brain size and general cognitive abilities). The fake evolution in the model should be regarded as a *tool* for determining the usefulness of some agent trait in some context. If in the model, certain behavioral traits are made hereditary and after some length of time agents with particular traits have outnumbered agents with other behaviors, then the former behavior is *better within the model context*.

16.3.3. Getting Results

There are only two types of agents, a distinction based on their strategies. The agents' fitness depends on the amount of food they are able to collect, so the ratio between the two types of agents is a direct measure of the success of their strategies. The most straightforward way to decide which is the better strategy, communicating or not communicating, is to run the model several times and see which agents reproduce better.

Figure 16.2 shows the proportion of communicating agents in the population for running the model under nine different settings. When either type of agent had a clear advantage over the other, the model was run 3 times with the fitter agents initially making up around[4] 10% of the population. This way the fraction of the agent-type goes through values from 0.1 to 1. The results show no evidence that there can be a stable mixture of communicators and non-communicators. In the model with the smallest number of agents, 10% corresponds to around 30 agents. Should the number of agents fall below 20, the population will almost certainly die out. In the models where neither strategy provides a clear advantage we have run the model 4 times, twice for a ratio of 1 : 1 and twice for a ratio of 1 : 10. The models were run for a maximum of 5000 time-steps.

We have varied the stable number of agents by adding twice as much regular food, and the profitability of knowhow, by adding four times more special food. Note that with a higher agent density the agents have less probability of monopolizing knowhow about a particular type of food. These alternatives were run with and without communication, the two top rows in Figure 16.2. In a model without communication there is no difference between the two types of agents. The proportion of communicating agents will still vary, indicating the influence of chance in this kind of agent model.

The communicating agents have a clear advantage, and this advantage is larger if more food that requires knowhow is available. Querying the running model about the agents' knowhow per age category shows that both the agent types learn during their lifetime, but that the talker agents get a head start. The offspring of communicating agents on average know how to eat a little more then one type of food. The average sum of the knowhow of the offspring of silent agents is 0.3 ($6 \cdot 0.05$). This is a result of spatial interactions, the new talker agents are 'born', instantiated on the same spot as their talker parent. In a sense one could say the agents profit from parental investment. The parent may lose out on feeding opportunities but it does so in favor of its offspring. How much learning goes on in the rest of the agent's life depends on the number of communicators in the environment.

Now the next question is, without the parental investment, is communication still adaptive? The answer is no, as the bottom row in Figure 16.2 shows. If the new agent is born at a random location in the field, the benefit from having a talker parent disappears. The agent shares its knowhow with new cohabitants that are not related. However the speed with which the talkers die out is lower than the speed with which the non-communicating agents died out in the runs described above. This shows that the cost of honest signaling is not very high. Another way to remove parental investment is by increasing agent mobility. We also ran the model with the three different food settings for larger steps. The agents took steps of random length between 0 and 20 (units in patches), as well as between 0 and 10. The results from these runs are similar to those of the runs without communication.

Another metric is the number of agents the environment can support. The more the agents know the more food becomes available to them. It is no surprise

---

[4] When the model is set up, the new agents are randomly assigned a type, with a probability of 0.1.

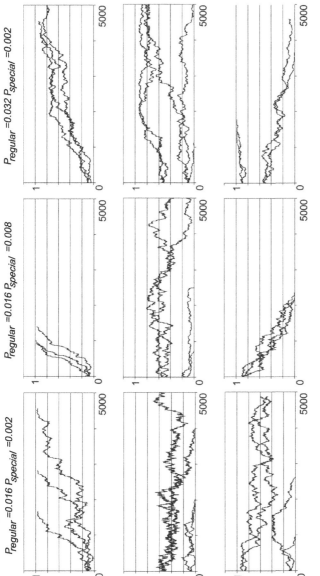

FIGURE 16.2. These graphs show the proportion of communicating agents, under different settings. Multiple lines in a single graph reflect multiple runs (see text). The top row shows what happens when the model is initialized with 10% communicating agents. In the middle row there are again two types of agents only now there is no difference between the two types. The bottom row shows the situation without parental investment.

TABLE 16.2. The carrying capacity (N) and spread of knowledge for communicating agents and 'silent' agents, for each of the nine model set-ups.

Conditions/food	Initial values			Special food ↑			Regular food ↑		
	N	talk	silent	N	talk	silent	N	talk	silent
no communication	316	0.3	0.3	352	0.3	0.3	700	0.3	0.3
with communication	370	1.5	0.7	531	2.0	0.6	745	2.1	1.3
no parental care	360	0.6	0.6	430	0.6	0.6	738	1.2	1.2

then, that as the communicating agents take over the population, knowhow spreads and the total agent population increases (a little). Table 16.2 shows the average number of agents and average knowhow per agent type (i.e. the number of food stuffs agents know about) for every one of the nine settings. With both communication and parental investment (middle row), there is a clear difference in knowhow between silent agents and agents that communicate. The spread of knowledge depends on the proportion of communicating agents, therefore the average number of agents and their knowledge will vary over time. The average knowhow was measured when half the population consisted of communicating agents.

The benefit of the parental investment in the form of communication, outweighs any costs that may result from communication towards 'strangers'. One possible explanation for the low cost would be that the agents form pockets of knowledge and that within these pockets communication is without consequences because all agents know the same things. It is true that only a small percentage (between 5% and 15%) of communications lead to agents acquiring new knowledge. But the effects even these seemingly ineffective communications have, both positive and negative, are apparent. When agents teach their surrounding kin new things the fitness effect is positive. If they share their knowhow with competing strangers, the effect is negative.

We have not fully quantified our results. That is we have not measured exactly how often agents meet their parent (or other related agents) compared to how often they meet other agents. Or how the ratio between interactions with strangers and interactions with kin changes during an agents lifetime. We have not examined which effect of communication dissolves sooner when the agents' mobility is increased: offspring benefit or increased competition. This is a valid question that has been under debate before (Marshall and Rowe 2003). The answer depends on very specific population properties and cannot be answered using a general model. In order to validate a model of these sorts of details we would need much more complete data on real-world communication. However, our model as it stands shows the important general characteristic we set out to test, whether communication could in fact be adaptive.

16.3.4. Conclusions

We found a model that supports honest, cost-free communication about food. The communication is cost-free in the sense that the cumulative effect of sharing knowhow is positive, even in the presence of free-riders who only benefit from the information without sharing their own know-how. Communication benefits the offspring of those that communicate. The agents' low mobility ensures they remain in the vicinity of their offspring for at least some time. Large steps disrupt both the positive (kin-selection) and the negative (increased competition) effects of communication.

One benefit of this freedom to communicate is that the cognitive load of recognizing individual agents and deliberating the possible effects of sharing knowledge with them is taken away. The positive effect of communication among kin will persist in any (agent) society where frequent interactions between parent and offspring are common during 'childhood'.

Our model shows that the positive effect of communication as parental investment is large enough to undo any kind of negative effect from random communication. These findings support the theory of language emergence in the parenting context, as brought forward by Buckley and Steele.

As we stated in our introduction, our results in no way challenge whether there are other selective forces that have affected the evolution of language, particularly language as we know it. But we have conclusively shown that arguments in favor of such mechanisms as selection for prestige cannot rely for evidence on free communication being non-adaptive. Communication may still have been the first selective advantage of language.

References

Aiello, L. C., Wheeler, P.: The expensive-tissue hypothesis: The brain and the digestive-system in human and primate evolution. Current Anthropology **36**(2) (1995) pp. 199–221

Baray, C.: Effects of Population Size upon Emergent Group Behavior. Complexity International **6** (1998)

Buckley, C., Steele, J.: Evolutionary ecology of spoken language: co-evolutionary hypotheses are testable. World Archaeology **34**(1) (2002) pp. 26–46

Cavalli-Sforza, L. L., Feldman M. W.: Paradox of the evolution of communication and of social interactivity. Proceedings of the National Academy of Sciences of the USA **80**(7) (1983) pp. 2017–21

Cederman L. -E., Rao, M. P.: Exploring the dynamics of the democratic peace. Journal of Conflict Resolution **45**(6) (2001) pp. 818–833

Chomsky, N.: Rules and Representations. Brain and Behavioral Sciences **3** (1980) pp. 1–61

Cox, S. J., Sluckin, T. J., Steele, J.: Group Size, Memory, and interaction Rate in the Evolution of cooperation. Current Anthropology **40**(3) (1999) pp. 369–377

van Dartel, M. F., Postma, E. O., van den Herik, H. J.: Universal properties of adaptive behaviour In Blockeel, H., Denecker, M. eds.: Proceedings of the 14th Belgium-Netherlands Conference on Artificial Intelligence (BNAIC 2002) Leuven, Belgium (2002) pp. 59–66

Dennett, D. C.: Kinds of minds: Towards an understanding of consciousness. Weidenfeld and Nicolson 1996

Dessalles, J. -L.: Language and hominid politics. In Knight, C., Studdert-Kennedy, M., Hurford, J., eds.: The Evolutionary Emergence of Language: Social Function and the Origins of Linguistic Form. Cambridge University Press, Cambridge, UK (2000) pp. 62–79

Dunbar, R. I. M.: Coevolution of neocortical size, group size and language in human. Behavioral and Brain Sciences. 16(4) (1993) pp. 681–735

Epstein, J. M., Axtell, R.: Growing Artificial Societies: Social Science from the Bottom Up. Brookings Institution Press, MIT Press Cambridge, MA (1996)

Esteva, M., Padget, J., Sierra, C.: Formalizing a language for institutions and norms. In Meyer, J. J., Tambe, M., eds.: Intelligent Agents VIII. Volume 2333 of Lecture Notes in Artificial Intelligence., Springer Verlag (2001) pp. 348–366

Gibson, K. R.: Social transmission of facts and skills in the human species: neural mechanisms. In Box, H. O., Gibson, K. R., eds.: Mammalian Social Learning, Comperative and Ecological Perspectives Cambridge University Press, Cambridge, UK, (1999) pp. 351–366

Hamilton, W. D.: The Genetical Evolution of Social Behaviour I Journal of Theoretical Biology 7(1) (1964) pp. 1–16

Hemelrijk, C. K.: Towards the integration of social dominance and spatial structure. Animal Behaviour 59(5) (2000) pp. 1035–48

Krebs, J. R., Dawkins, R.: Animal Signals: Mind-Reading and Manipulation. In Krebs, J. R., Davies, N. B., eds.: Behavioural ecology: An evolutionary approach (second ed.) Blackwell Scientific Publications, Oxford (1984) pp. 380–402

Lachmann, M., Számadó, S., Bergstrom C. T.: Cost and conflict in animal signals and human language. Proceedings of the National Academy of Sciences of the United States of America 98(23) (2001) pp. 13189–94

Marshall, J. A. R., Rowe, J. E.: Viscous Populations and Their Support for Reciprocal Cooperation. Artificial Life 9(3) (2003) pp. 327–334

Maynard-Smith, J., Harper, D.: Animal Signals: Models and Terminology. Journal of Theoretical Biology 177(1) (1995) pp. 305–311

Noble, J., Paolo, E. A. D., Bullock, S.: Adaptive Factors in the Evolution of Signaling Systems. In Cangelosi, A., Parisi, D., eds.: Simulating the Evolution of Language. London: Springer Verlag, London, UK, (2002) pp. 53–78

Simon, H. A.: A Mechanism for Social Selection and Successful Altruism. Science 250(4988) (1990) pp. 1665–68

James Steele, J.: What can archaeology contribute to solving the puzzle of language evolution? plenary talk at The Evolution of Language (April 2004)

Wilensky, U.: NetLogo Center for Connected Learning and Computer-Based Modeling, Northwestern University, Evanston, IL (1999)

Wilensky, U.: The NetLogo Rabbits-Grass-Weeds Model Center for Connected Learning and Computer-Based Modeling, Northwestern University, Evanston, IL (1998) http: //ccl.northwestern.edu/netlogo/models/RabbitsGrassWeeds

Zahavi, A.: Mate selection – A selection for a handicap. Journal of Theoretical Biology 53(1) (1975) pp. 205–214

Quine, W. v. O. (1960). *Word and object*. Cambridge, MA: MIT Press.

Siskind, J. M. (1996). A computational study of cross-situational techniques for learning word-to-meaning mappings. *Cognition, 61*, 39–91

Smith, A. D. M. (2003a). *Evolving communication through the inference of meaning.* PhD thesis, Philosophy, Psychology and Language Sciences, University of Edinburgh.

Smith, A. D. M. (2003b). Intelligent meaning creation in a clumpy world helps communication. *Artificial Life, 9*(2), 175–190

Smith, A. D. M. (2005a). The inferential transmission of language. *Adaptive Behavior,
13*(4), 311–324

Smith, A. D. M. (2005b). Mutual exclusivity: Communicative success despite conceptual
divergence. In M. Tallerman (Ed.), *Language origins: perspectives on evolution*
(pp. 372–388). Oxford: University Press

Smith, A. D. M., & Vogt, P. (2004). *Lexicon acquisition in an uncertain world.* (Paper
given at the 5th International Conference on the Evolution of Language, Leipzig)

Smith, K., Brighton, H., & Kirby, S. (2003). Complex systems in language evolution: the
cultural emergence of compositional structure. *Advances in Complex Systems, 6*(4),
537–558

Steels, L. (1996). Perceptually grounded meaning creation. In M. Tokro (Ed.), *Proceedings
of the International Conference on Multi-agent Systems.* Cambridge, MA: MIT Press.

Trask, R. L. (1996). *Historical linguistics.* London: Arnold

Vogt, P. (2003). Grounded lexicon formation without explicit reference transfer. In
W. Banzhaf, T. Christaller, J. Ziegler, P. Dittrich, & J. T. Kim (Eds.), *Advances
in Artificial Life: Proceedings of the 7th European Conference on Artificial Life*
(pp. 545–552). Heidelberg: Springer-Verlag

17
Language Change and the Inference of Meaning

Andrew D. M. Smith

17.1. Introduction

The natural state of living human languages is one of continuous gradual change, underpinned by variation in both form and meaning (Trask, 1996). Small differences in the contexts in which particular utterances are used, or changes in the way in which words are pronounced, accumulate over generations of use to such an extent that the language itself can become unrecognisable in only a few generations (Deutscher, 2005). In this paper, I explore the relationship between language change and the indeterminacy of meaning, using a computational model of iterated inferential communication. I use the term *inferential communication* in order to focus on the fact that, in communication, information is not transferred directly between communicants, but rather indirectly. In particular, the hearer must infer the meaning of the signal, both through pragmatic insights and by making use of the contexts in which the signal is heard. Uncertainty is inherent in the inferential process, and therefore it is not necessary that individuals in the same community infer the same meanings for signals. Differences in internal representations occur naturally as a product of the inferential communication process; over generations of such communication, these differences accumulate and may result in significant levels of language change.

In previous work, I have used inferential models of linguistic communication to investigate a number of different aspects of use, including the learning of conceptual structures and language in tandem (A. D. M. Smith, 2003b), and the effects of psychologically plausible constraints on lexical acquisition (A. D. M. Smith, 2005a, 2005b). In this study, I present computational experiments which I use to explore the processes of language change and variation across generations of language users. My previous inferential model of communication is extended and incorporated within a model of repeated cultural transmission with generational turnover (K. Smith, Brighton & Kirby, 2003).

The remainder of this paper is divided into five parts. In section 17.2, I describe the theoretical foundations on which the study is based, namely cultural transmission and the inference of meaning. In section 17.3, I describe the computational model in greater detail, including how simulated individuals create their own representations of meaning, how they use these representations in communication with each other, and how they infer the meanings of words across multiple contexts. In section 17.4, I discuss the different kinds of variation which occur in the model, and describe how these can be measured. In section 17.5, I present the experiments themselves, which demonstrate that conceptual and lexical variation can indeed result in remarkably rapid and significant change to the language, without harming the language's viability as a successful shared communication system within each individual generation. I then discuss why these results occur, and their relevance to natural processes of linguistic change. Finally, in section 17.6, I summarise the paper's main conclusions.

17.2. Theoretical Foundations

17.2.1. Cultural Transmission

The cognitive capacity to learn and use language is of course part of the human genetic endowment, but the particular languages we actually learn to use are not themselves stored in our genome. Instead, they exist in the communities in which we live, and are learnt culturally: we learn to speak only those languages which we hear used. Much recent research into language evolution has focused on the cultural nature of linguistic transmission, and this has resulted in a very useful paradigm, representing the external and internal manifestations of language as distinct phases in the life-cycle of a language. Figure 17.1 shows an idealisation of this framework: an individual uses their

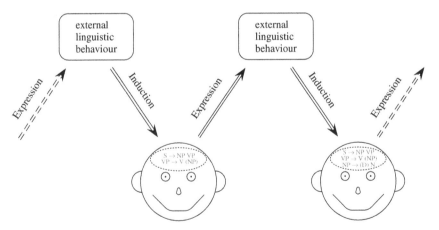

FIGURE 17.1. The expression/induction model of language as a dynamic and culturally transmitted system. Individuals *express* linguistic behaviour based on their internal representations; these internal representations are in turn *induced* in response to the linguistic behaviour encountered. Language therefore persists in two qualitatively different states: internal knowledge and external behaviour.

internal linguistic representations to express some *external* linguistic behaviour, and in turn induce these same *internal* linguistic representations (or grammars) in response to the linguistic behaviour (or primary linguistic data) which they encounter. Such models of linguistic change and evolution have been described as expression/induction (E/I) models (Hurford, 2002) and, more recently, as iterated learning models (K. Smith et al., 2003). The cultural nature of these models is captured in the fact that the linguistic input used by one individual to construct its grammar is itself the linguistic output of other individuals. Differences which occur between the internal grammars of individual members of the population, therefore, occur as a result of the dynamic cultural evolution of the language itself.

In recent years, E/I models have been used successfully to demonstrate the cultural emergence of a number of structural characteristics of language, most notably compositionality (Brighton, 2002) and recursion (Kirby, 2002). These properties arise through repeated cultural transmission if individuals are required to learn a language from a restricted set of data, through a so-called *transmission bottleneck*. There is a clear difference in the relative success of holistic rules of grammar, which relate a signal to an utterance idiosyncratically, and compositional rules, in which the meaning of the utterance is predictable from the meaning of its parts, and the way in which the parts are put together. Idiosyncratic structures can successfully pass through the bottleneck only if the specific signal-meaning pair which gives rise to the rule is encountered. Compositional rules, on the other hand, can be generalised more easily, are preferentially produced, and are therefore much more likely to pass through the bottleneck into the next generation (K. Smith et al., 2003). Indeed, idiosyncratic and irregular rules of language can only be maintained through frequency of use: it is no coincidence that, in all natural languages, the most irregular words are those which are used most frequently.

17.2.2. Meaning Inference

It is important to note, however, that all the specific models of cultural evolution mentioned in the previous section are characterised by a communicative process which involves the explicit conjunction of pairs of signals and predefined meanings. Unfortunately, it is clear that this conjunction necessarily leads to the development of syntactic structure which is identical to the predefined semantic structure, and which therefore weakens, to a very significant extent, the authors' claims for the emergence of the syntactic structure. In addition, the pre-definition of meaning structures means that there is no role for semantic variation in the model, despite its pivotal role in language change and evolution. The direct transfer of meaning in communication, moreover, has serious consequences for the validity of such models more generally, because there is no longer any meaningful role for the signals to play, and so they are redundant: what provides the motivation for language users to learn a complicated symbolic system of signals, which gives them no information that they do not already have, from the meanings which have been directly transferred to them? (A. D. M. Smith, 2003b, 2005b).

The inferential model presented here is motivated to a large extent by the desire to avoid this problem of signal redundancy, and by recognising that in natural language, meanings are of course *not* directly transferable (Quine, 1960). Simulated individuals in this model therefore have neither lexical nor conceptual structures at the start of a simulation, but merely the ability to develop their own representations based on the experiences and situations they face. Meanings and signals are not explicitly linked, and are instead associated with each other through a process of cross-situational inference, which allows variation of representation between individuals. Crucial to this model is the existence of an external world, which serves as the source from which meanings are inferred, and which, importantly, is separated from the individuals' internal representations of meaning. This is shown in Figure 17.2, where the external (or public) domain contains objects and situations which can be potentially accessed and manipulated by all individuals in the simulated world, and the internal (or private) domains are specific to each individual, containing representations and mappings created and developed by them alone, and accessible to them alone. Signals and their referents are therefore linked only *indirectly*; this linkage is mediated via separate associative mappings between themselves and each individual's internal meaning representations. The associative mappings are also specific to each individual, created through separate, discrete analyses of the co-occurrence of signals and potential referents over multiple situations.

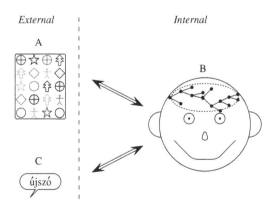

FIGURE 17.2. A model of communication which avoids the problem of signal redundancy. The model has three levels of representation: an external environment (A); an internal semantic representation (B); and a public set of signals (C). The mappings between A and B and between B and C, represented by the arrows, fall into the internal, private domain, whose boundary is shown by the dotted line.

17.3. The Inferential Model

The E/I models of cultural transmission described in this article, therefore, contain neither a predefined, structured meaning system, nor an explicit link between signals and meanings. Instead, the experiments are carried out using simulated language users who initially have neither conceptual nor lexical structures, but importantly have the ability to *create* their own conceptual representations and to *infer* meaning based on their experiences. The external world in the model is made up of a specific number of objects, which can be objectively described in terms of the values of their abstract features, real numbers generated within the range [0:1]. Individuals are each provided with dedicated sensory channels, which they can use to sense whether a particular feature value falls within two bounds. They can refine the sensitivity of these channels, and thereby create meanings which may allow them to distinguish objects from each other. Individuals can also create words which can be used to express these meanings and therefore to communicate about the objects. This model is based on that described initially by Steels (1996), in which two individuals (designated as a speaker and a hearer) play a series of language games, and has been extended in several ways. In the following sections, I describe the process through which individuals create meanings in response to their interactions with the external world, how they create and use signals to communicate to each other about situations in the world, and how they infer the meanings of signals they receive. Finally, I explain how the inferential model is incorporated into the iterated learning paradigm described above, which allows experiments exploring the nature and extent of language change over generations.

17.3.1. Meaning Creation

The individuals in the simulation explore their environment, and to try to discriminate the objects they find there from one another. In an exploratory episode, an individual investigates a random subset of objects, called the *context*, with the aim of distinguishing one particular, randomly-chosen *target* object within the context from all the other objects therein. The individual searches its sensory channels for a *distinctive category*, an internal semantic representation which accurately describes the target, but does not accurately describe any other object in the context. If the individual does not have such a category, then the exploratory episode fails, and the process of meaning creation is triggered. The individual chooses an existing category, and splits its sensitivity range in two equal parts, thereby creating two new categories, which are each a subset of the existing category. This process, repeated after each exploratory failure, results in the development of hierarchical, tree-shaped conceptual structures, in which semantic categories are represented by the nodes on the tree. Nodes nearer the tree root represent more general meanings; they have wider sensitivity ranges which therefore cover a larger proportion of the semantic space. Those nearer the leaves represent correspondingly more specific meanings, with narrower sensitivity ranges covering a smaller proportion of the space. There is no pre-definition of which categories should be created, and meaning creation is done by each individual separately, according to their own experiences. Many different representations of meaning structure are equally valid, as the goal of the conceptual structure is solely to provide categories which can be used to discriminate objects from each other, and indeed the individual basis of meaning creation leads to the creation of different, but typically equally successful, conceptual representations of the world.

17.3.2. Inferential Communication

Having found a successful distinctive category, the speaker tries to communicate this meaning to a hearer, by choosing a suitable signal from its lexicon. If no such signal exists, then the speaker creates a random string of letters, and uses this as the signal. In all cases, the signal is transmitted to the hearer, who does not know the speaker's meaning, but can observe the original context from which the distinctive category was derived. Importantly, however, neither the distinctive category nor the target object to which it refers are ever identified to the hearer.

Hurford (1989) explored the evolution of communication strategies in a population using dynamic communication matrices of transmission and reception behaviour, and demonstrated that bidirectional, Saussurean mappings between signals and meanings are essential for the development of viable communication systems. Oliphant and Batali (1997) then extended this model, showing that the best way to ensure continuing improvements in communicative accuracy is for speakers not to choose the signals they like to utter, but instead those the hearers like to hear. Their algorithm for signal choice, called obverter, is therefore based on the interpretation behaviour of the rest of the population. Unfortunately, however, calculating signal choice on this basis requires the speaker to have direct access to the internal representations of all the other individuals. In order to avoid this mind-reading, I use a modified version of the algorithm, in which the speaker chooses the signal which it would be most likely to interpret correctly, given the current context. and its own existing semantic categories (A. D. M. Smith, 2003a). Because the speaker cannot access the interpretative behaviour of the other individuals, signal choice is based on the speaker's own interpretative behaviour, and this method is therefore called *introspective obverter*.

As mentioned above, the hearer receives a signal, but neither information about the intended meaning, nor about which object the speaker is referring to. The meaning must be inferred from the information which can be gleaned from the context, and from the previous contexts in which this signal was encountered. The hearer uses its existing conceptual structures to try, in turn, to discriminate each object in the context from all the others, and thereby creates a list of possible meanings or *semantic hypotheses*. This list consists of every meaning in the hearer's current conceptual structure which could serve as a distinctive category for any single object in the context. In principle, each of these possible meanings is equally plausible, so each is stored in the hearer's internal lexicon, associated with the signal. The lexicon contains a count of the co-occurrence of each signal-meaning pair $< s, m >$, which is used to calculate the conditional probability $P(m|s)$ that, given s, m is associated with s:

$$P(m|s) = \frac{f(s, m)}{\sum_{i=1}^{n} f(s, i)},$$

where $f(s, m)$ is the number of times s has been associated with m (A. D. M. Smith, 2003b). The hearer simply chooses the meaning with the highest conditional probability for the signal it receives and assumes that this was the intended meaning. If two or more meanings have equal conditional probability, then one of them is chosen at random.

If the hearer's chosen meaning identifies the same object as the speaker's initial target object, then the communicative episode is deemed to be successful. There is therefore no requirement for the individuals to use (or even to have) the same internal meaning, only that they must identify the same external referent. Furthermore, neither individual receives any feedback about the communicative success of the episode. In *cross-situational inferential learning*, therefore, the learner relies solely on the co-occurrence of signals and referents across multiple contexts (A. D. M. Smith, 2005a). This is similar to Siskind (1996)'s proposal, but differs from it most fundamentally in that, in the model presented here, the set of possible meanings over which inferences are made is neither fixed nor predefined, but is instead dynamic, and in principle infinite.

Previous experiments using cross-situational inferential learning show that it is a sufficiently powerful technique for individuals to learn large lexicons, and that individuals with different conceptual structures can communicate with each other successfully. The time taken to learn a whole lexicon is primarily dependent on the size of the context in which each item is presented (A. D. M. Smith, 2003a; A. D. M. Smith & Vogt, 2004), while communicative success is closely related to the level of inter-individual meaning similarity (A. D. M. Smith, 2003b). However, if individuals have psychologically motivated interpretational biases to aid inference, such as mutual exclusivity (Markman, 1989), then even individuals with very dissimilar conceptual structures can communicate success-fully (A. D. M. Smith, 2005b). More broadly, experiments with this and similar models suggest that inferential learning may provide a unified account of the development of language on three different timescales: acquisition in the child; change in the language; and evolution in the species (A. D. M. Smith, 2005a).

17.3.3. Iterated Inference

In order to explore how languages change on a generational timescale, therefore, the inferential model is extended vertically into a traditional iterated learning model with generational turnover (K. Smith et al., 2003). When considering the structure of this model, it is helpful to consider the speaker as an adult, and the hearer as a child. Each generation consists of a number of exploratory episodes, in which both the adult and child explore the world individually, and create meanings to represent what they find, followed by a number of communicative episodes, in which the adult tries to communicate to the child. The child, in turn, tries to learn the adult's language, using cross-situational inferential learning. At the end of a generation, the adult is removed from the population, the child becomes an adult, and a new child is introduced. The language which was inferred in the previous generation by the child becomes the source of its own linguistic output in the subsequent generation. This process of generational turnover is then iterated a specified number of times.

17.4. Variation

Variability is one of the most fundamental features of language, and rather than treating variation as an unfortunate problem, it is a feature which must be taken account of in any realistic model of language use (Croft, 2000). Indeed variation, whether in the utterances which are expressed or in the linguistic representations which are induced, is the power driving language change and propelling the endless reworking of language (Deutscher, 2005). In the inferential model I have sketched above, there are two different kinds of linguistic variation, which I will call *conceptual* and *lexical*, and whose source and effects I will describe in the following sections. Figure 17.3 illustrates both of these with extracts from the conceptual and lexical structure of an adult and a child from the same generation of a representative simulation. Each individual has five sensory channels on which conceptual structures are built, but only one of these is shown for expository purposes.

17.4.1. Conceptual Variation

The independent creation of conceptual structure described in section 17.3.1 leads inevitably to variation in the conceptual representations which are created. This occurs both because an individual's response to a particular situation is not deterministic, but also because individuals encounter different experiences as they explore the world. It is helpful not only to record variation, however, but also to measure it, and this can be done by quantitative comparison of the tree structures. If $k(t, u)$ is the number of nodes which two trees t and u have in common, and $n(t)$ is the total number of nodes on t, then the similarity $\tau(t, u)$ between t and u is:

$$\tau(t, u) = \frac{2k(t, u)}{n(t) + n(u)}.$$

By averaging this tree-level measure of similarity across all sensory channels, we can produce a measure of overall conceptual, or meaning, similarity between individuals (A. D. M. Smith, 2003a). If a_{ij} identifies the tree on channel j for individual i, and each individual has c sensory channels on which they develop conceptual structure, then the meaning similarity $\sigma(a_1, a_2)$ between individuals a_1 and a_2 is:

$$\sigma(a_1, a_2) = \frac{1}{c} \left(\sum_{j=0}^{c-1} \tau(a_{1j}, a_{2j}) \right).$$

Conceptual variation can be seen in the upper part of Figure 17.3, which shows excerpts from the tree structures created by each individual. Nodes which have no equivalent in the other's conceptual structure are marked with dotted lines, and it is clear that, in this example, the child has created additional conceptual structure from three different nodes, in one case quite substantially.

17.4.2. Lexical Variation

The hallmark of cross-situational inferential learning is uncertainty in identifying the meanings of words, and it is no surprise that this uncertainty leads to significant variation in the particular lexical associations which are made by individuals. These lexical associations are determined firstly by the specific conceptual structures created by the individuals, and secondly by the particular contexts in which the words are heard. Lexical variation can be measured by considering whether two individuals have the same preferred word for a given meaning. An individual's preferred word for meaning m is the word in its lexicon which has the highest conditional probability in association with m, which does not have a higher conditional probability in association with a different meaning. In the lower part of Figure 17.3, preferred words are represented by the words attached to the appropriate nodes on the tree structure; empty nodes have no preferred word. If adult and child both have the same preferred word for a meaning, then we can say that the child has successfully learnt the word, or that the lexical item has succesfully *persisted* through the generation. Lexical persistence across the whole of an individual's lexicon is a useful measure of linguistic change, and can be measured both within and between generations: *intra-generational* lexical persistence is the proportion of the adult's lexicon learnt by the child, while *inter-generational* lexical persistence is the proportion of the language developed by the adult in the first generation of the simulation which is still intact in the language of the child after n generations.

Lexical items which do not persist can change in a number of different ways, as well as being lost altogether, but here I concentrate on generalisation, which plays a crucial role in many important processes of historical linguistic change such as grammaticalisation, namely the development of linguistic functional forms such as prepositions and case markers from earlier lexical forms such as nouns and verbs (Hopper & Traugott, 2003). A particular

A. Conceptual Variation

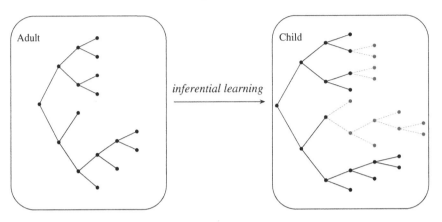

B. Conceptual and Lexical Variation

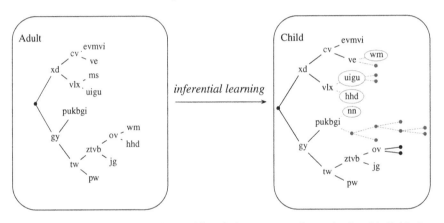

FIGURE 17.3. Extracts from the internal linguistic structures of two simulated individuals, showing both conceptual variation (A) and lexical variation (B). Conceptual structures are shown as hierarchical tree structures, on which each node represents a different meaning. Variations in conceptual structure (A) are marked with dotted lines. The words attached to the nodes represent the individual's preferred word for the meaning; empty nodes have no preferred word. Lexical variations (B) are marked with circles.

example of generalisation is given in Figure 17.3 by the words *wm* and *hhd*, which have not persisted into the child's language. Even though the child's conceptual representation contains the specific meanings which the adult had associated these words with, the child has associated them with nodes nearer the root of its conceptual tree; these nodes cover a larger area of the semantic space, are therefore more general, and so the words have been generalised.

17.5. Experimental Results

The experiments described here were performed with two aims in mind. Firstly, to verify whether results obtained previously with an inferential model in a single generation, briefly summarised in section 17.3.2, would remain valid in a multi-generational model. More importantly, to measure how languages themselves change over generations, and explore whether languages which are undergoing rapid language change over successive populations of users could still be communicatively viable.

17.5.1. Communicative Success and Meaning Similarity

Previous mono-generational inferential models have shown that levels of communicative success are closely correlated with levels of meaning similarity between individuals (A. D. M. Smith, 2003b). Figure 17.4 illustrates results from a typical multi-generational simulation, run across ten generations, each of which has 20,000 episodes. Analyses of communicative success and meaning similarity were calculated after every 1000 episodes: communicative success measures the proportion of successful communications over the previous 1000 episodes, while meaning similarity is measured as described in section 17.4.1.

Figure 17.4 shows clearly that levels of meaning similarity and communicative success remain very closely correlated, as in the mono-generational simulations. In each generation, the communicative success rate initially rises rapidly, as the child successfully learns the meanings of many words through cross-situational inference. As fewer words remain to be learnt, and these are used infrequently by the adult, the process of disambiguation takes much longer, and so the communicative success rate increases more slowly. Levels of communicative success and meaning similarity at the end of each generation were also measured, to check for the presence of any inter-generational trends, but we can clearly

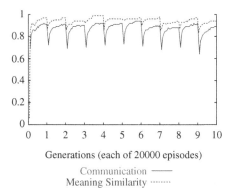

FIGURE 17.4. Communicative success and meaning similarity in an iterated inference model.

see that the levels of communicative success and meaning similarity achieved in each generation are very similar, and no significant inter-generational changes were discernible. Note that Vogt (2003), however, using a similar model of inferential learning which he calls 'selfish', has found an as yet unexplained inter-generational increase in communicative success.

17.5.2. Lexical Persistence

Having established that the multi-generational model was consistent with previous findings, I used the lexical persistence measure to explore the nature and extent of changes in the languages themselves. Figure 17.5 shows how inter- and intra-generational lexical persistence vary according to the *length* of each generation, which is measured simply in terms of the number of communicative episodes undertaken by the language users. We can see that this is proportional to the amount of the language which is successfully learnt by the child; the more exposure a child receives to a language, the higher the proportion which it will learn. Shorter generations (those containing 5000 episodes) result in intra-generational lexical persistence rates of between 60 and 70% at the end of each generation, but longer generations of 20,000 episodes produce lexical persistence rates of closer to 80%. We can confirm again that there are no significant differences between the levels of intra-generational lexical persistence obtained within specific different generations. On the other hand, it is equally clear that the rate of *inter-generational* lexical persistence shows a considerable relentless decline, so that only 10–20% of the original language remains after ten generations of iterated inferential learning, the exact proportion depending on the length of the generation. It is important to realise that this erosion of the original language is caused by two separate pressures on the language's ability to be learnt, which can be regarded as separate bottlenecks on the transmission of the language over generations.

Variation in conceptual structure first acts as a ceiling which restricts the potential for intra-generational lexical persistence: a word can only be learnt

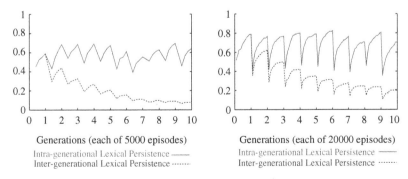

FIGURE 17.5. Inter-generational and intra-generation lexical persistence. Each generation consists of 5000 episodes (left) and 20,000 episodes (right).

if the child has constructed the meaning which the adult associates with it. Having passed through this first bottleneck, the imperfect nature of inferential learning causes lexical variation, and imposes further restrictions on the number of words which actually are learnt. This uncertainty also has implications for the *types* of words which are learnt, which I discuss below. The pressure exerted by these two bottlenecks is compounded over subsequent generations, and leads naturally to the significant cumulative erosion of the original language seen in Figure 17.5. Even after only a few generations of inferential learning, very little of the original language remains. This rapid language change, however, does not affect the communicative success rate, as we can see in Figure 17.4, and this leads to the important conclusion that inferential learning provides a plausible model for how language can, simultaneously, change very rapidly on an inter-generational timescale, and yet remain viable within each generation as a successful communication tool.

17.5.3. Generalisation and Stable Language Change

On investigating the make-up of the languages at the end of each generation in more detail, we find that there is a distinct pattern to the language change which occurs. Words referring to more specific meanings tend to disappear first, and only more general words tend to survive across multiple generations. As mentioned above, this finds an echo in natural language change, where words regularly progress from specific meanings to more general ones, as part of the *context-induced reinterpretation* (Heine & Kuteva, 2002) which characterises the process of grammaticalisation. For example, the Latin phrase *clara mente*, meaning 'with a clear mind', was reinterpreted to mean 'in a clear manner'. This reanalysis allowed it to be extended to non-psychological contexts, leading to modern French, where the morpheme *-ment* is a generalised derivational morpheme which can be applied to almost any adjective.

In the model discussed here, there are two clear reasons for the generalisation of words, which are both artefacts of the original design. The Steelsian method of conceptual construction ensures that there is a hierarchical order on the meanings which any individual creates: it is impossible as the model stands, for instance, to create a very specific meaning without having already created (and potentially used) its superordinate meaning higher up the tree. Because the existence of general meanings is a pre-requisite for the existence of specific meanings, it is much more likely that both individuals will share a general meaning than that they will share a specific meaning, and thus the general meaning is less likely to be excluded from being learnt by the conceptual variation bottleneck. Secondly, the model contains a hidden assumption of communicative practice which follows Grice (1975)'s philosophical model of conversation. Individuals will choose as distinctive categories meanings which are sufficiently distinctive to identify the target object, but which are not unduly specific. This is perfectly consistent with human behaviour (people do not generally describe an object as vermilion when red will do), but does also ensure that more general meanings are relatively more likely to be used in communication. The second bottleneck, on learning, is imposed by the inferential process itself, which works best when examples are encountered in multiple different contexts: words which occur frequently, therefore, are much more likely to be successfully learnt and to persist into the next generation.

17.6. Conclusions

The cultural nature of language transmission has in recent time become increasingly recognised, though its inferential nature is less widely acknowledged. Inferential communication provides a straightforward explanation for the existence of otherwise redundant signals, and also allows the construction of realistic models of dynamic language, in which uncertainty, variation and imperfect learning play crucial roles. In this article, I have briefly presented a model of language as a culturally transmitted system of communication, based on the creation and inference of meaning from experience. Individual meaning creation, and the uncertainty inherent in meaning inference lead to different degrees of variation in both conceptual and lexical structure. Conceptual variation and imperfect learning apply different bottlenecks on transmission, which result in rapid language change across generations. Despite such rapid language change, however, the language itself remains sufficiently stable within each generation to re-establish and maintain its utility as a successful communication system.

Acknowledgments. Andrew Smith was supported by AHRC research grant AR112105.

References

Brighton, H. (2002). Compositional syntax from cultural transmission. *Artificial Life, 8*(1), 25–54.

Croft, W. (2000). *Explaining language change: an evolutionary approach.* Harlow: Pearson.

Deutscher, G. (2005). *The unfolding of language: an evolutionary tour of mankind's greatest invention.* New York: Metropolitan Books.

Grice, H. P. (1975). Logic and conversation. In P. Cole & J. L. Morgan (Eds.), *Syntax and semantics* (Vol. 3, pp. 41–58). New York: Academic Press.

Heine, B., & Kuteva, T. (2002). *World lexicon of grammaticalization.* Cambridge: Cambridge University Press.

Hopper, P. J., & Traugott, E. C. (2003). *Grammaticalization* (2nd ed.). Cambridge: Cambridge University Press.

Hurford, J. R. (1989). Biological evolution of the Saussurean sign as a component of the language acquisition device. *Lingua, 77,* 187–222.

Hurford, J. R. (2002). Expression/induction models of language evolution: dimensions and issues. In E. Briscoe (Ed.), *Linguistic evolution through language acquisition: Formal and computational models* (pp. 301–344). Cambridge: Cambridge University Press.

Kirby, S. (2002). Learning, bottlenecks and the evolution of recursive syntax. In E. Briscoe (Ed.), *Linguistic evolution through language acquisition: Formal and computational models* (pp. 173–203). Cambridge: Cambridge University Press.

Markman, E. M. (1989). *Categorization and naming in children: problems of induction.* Cambridge. MA: MIT Press.

Oliphant, M., & Batali, J. (1997). Learning and the emergence of coordinated communication. *Center for Research on Language Newsletter, 11*(1).

Quine, W. v. O. (1960). *Word and object.* Cambridge, MA: MIT Press.

Siskind, J. M. (1996). A computational study of cross-situational techniques for learning word-to-meaning mappings. *Cognition, 61,* 39–91.

Smith, A. D. M. (2003a). *Evolving communication through the inference of meaning.* PhD thesis, Philosophy, Psychology and Language Sciences, University of Edinburgh.

Smith, A. D. M. (2003b). Intelligent meaning creation in a clumpy world helps communication. *Artificial Life, 9*(2), 175–190.

Smith, A. D. M. (2005a). The inferential transmission of language. *Adaptive Behavior, 13*(4), 311–324.

Smith, A. D. M. (2005b). Mutual exclusivity: Communicative success despite conceptual divergence. In M. Tallerman (Ed.), *Language origins: perspectives on evolution* (pp. 372–388). Oxford: University Press.

Smith, A. D. M., & Vogt, P. (2004). *Lexicon acquisition in an uncertain world.* (Paper given at the 5th International Conference on the Evolution of Language, Leipzig)

Smith, K., Brighton, H., & Kirby, S. (2003). Complex systems in language evolution: the cultural emergence of compositional structure. *Advances in Complex Systems, 6*(4), 537–558.

Steels, L. (1996). Perceptually grounded meaning creation. In M. Tokro (Ed.), *Proceedings of the International Conference on Multi-agent Systems.* Cambridge, MA: MIT Press.

Trask, R. L. (1996). *Historical linguistics.* London: Arnold.

Vogt, P. (2003). Grounded lexicon formation without explicit reference transfer. In W. Banzhaf, T. Christaller, J. Ziegler, P. Dittrich, & J. T. Kim (Eds.), Advances in Artificial Life: Proceedings of the 7th European Conference on Artificial Life (pp. 545–552). Heidelberg: Springer-Verlag.

18
Language, Perceptual Categories and their Interaction: Insights from Computational Modelling

Tony Belpaeme and Joris Bleys

18.1. Introduction

How do humans acquire perceptual categories? This question is far from being resolved. Specifically the balance between the influence of nature and nurture on perceptual categories remains the topic of heated debate. We present a computational model and take as case study colour categories to study two issues in perceptual category acquisition. The first issue is the effect of linguistic communication on categories during their acquisition: we demonstrate how categories can become coordinated under the influence of language. The second issue concerns the amount of coordination needed between the categories of individuals in order to achieve unambiguous communication. We show that, depending on how strictly linguistic utterances are interpreted, coordination of the individuals' categories is not always a prerequisite for successful communication.

Our computational models specifically focus on how language can have a beneficial impact on the process of category acquisition. The impact of language on cognition in its broadest sense is known as linguistic relativism (or the Sapir-Whorf hypothesis, Carrol 1956) and has recently received renewed attention, both in cognitive science (e.g. Gumperz and Levinson, 1996; Gentner and Boroditsky, 2001) and in computational modelling (e.g. Steels and Belpaeme, 2005; Luypan, 2005).

As a case study for our model we will take colour: we will study how colour categories can be acquired and how language can affect this process. In this respect, linguistic relativism has received quite some attention. Brown and Lenneberg (1954) were among the first to suggest that language affects colour perception, and many others have since confirmed these findings (for recent results see Davidoff et al., 1999; Roberson, 2005). Gilbert et al. (2006) noted how subjects tend to react faster in a discrimination task for colours across the green-blue boundary, but only when the target, which had to be discriminated from distractor colours, appeared in the *right* visual field. As the right visual field is projected onto the left hemisphere, and as language is predominantly processed in the left hemisphere, Gilbert et al. concluded that linguistic relativity for colour is clearly demonstrated, but that it is subject to hemispheric lateralisation.

All these results interestingly contrast with the evidence for the universal character of colour categories. Berlin and Kay (1969) noted that there is a remarkable cross-cultural similarity between the referents of basic colour terms. English has 11 basic colour terms (black, white, red, green, blue, yellow, orange, purple, pink, brown, and grey) and similar linguistic colour categories are found in other non-industrialised cultures. In the World Color Survey (Kay et al., 1997) the linguistic colour categories of a large sample of cultures across the world were collected. A statistical study of the data confirmed that colour categories are indeed universal (Kay and Regier, 2003; Regier et al., 2005). This could suggest that a strong genetic component is at work, an idea that has been entertained by many (among others Berlin and Kay, 1969; Kay and McDaniel, 1978; Shepard, 1992). Recently, Franklin et al. (2005a,b) reported that pre-linguistic infants react in an adult-like way to colour discrimination tasks, and that colour categories are not influenced by linguistic colour terms.

However, there are a number of alternative hypotheses which try to explain the universal nature of colour categories without primarily resorting to innate constraints (for a short survey see Kay and Regier, 2006). One is that colour categories might be the product of a learning process which optimises the categories to encode the chromatic structure of the world. Another hypothesis is that colour categories are culturally transmitted with its main vector being language. This latter hypothesis will be at the basis of the computational models presented here.

Another issue that will be highlighted is the amount of coordination needed between the categories of agents in order to successfully communicate. It is generally accepted that some sort of coordination is needed, one extreme being that all categories of all individuals are identical. However, this does not seem to be the case in humans, as for example observed in the World Color Survey where inter-individual variations in a single culture are quite pronounced (Webster and Kay, 2005). A certain amount of dissimilarity between the categories is tolerated, but how far this stretches is not known. We try to shed light on how much coordination is required, and show —maybe surprisingly— that for *perceptual* categories little coordination is needed to allow for successful communication.

18.2. Related Work in Computational Modelling

Computational modelling of linguistic phenomena has received quite some attention recently (for an overview see Christiansen and Kirby, 2003; Steels, 2003). In computational modelling the agent-based approach, in which individual language users can be represented as autonomous software agents, has been popular. Studying macroscopic effects of the interactions between the agents can suggest how similar mechanisms might be at work in human language and cognition.

With regard to learning form-meaning mappings a number of agent-based models exist. Many of these models focus on how a population of agents can agree without central control on which word corresponds to which meaning (e.g. Oliphant, 1996; Steels, 1996; Barr, 2004; De Vylder and Tuyls, 2006). In these models, the meanings are fixed and do not change while the associations between forms and meanings are learnt. Other models focus on how language and meaning can be learned simultaneously (Steels and Kaplan, 1999; Smith, 2003; Vogt, 2003),. Typically a meaning is some abstract representation not justified by psychological insights on categorisation or conceptualisation. For example, *discrimination trees* (Steels, 1997) are often used to represent meaning: an agent perceives features of objects and each perceptual feature is divided in a number hierarchically ordered ranges. A concept is then a set of ranges for different features. However, there is no psychological justification for the use of discrimination trees, and therefore simulations using discrimination trees do not lend themselves to draw conclusions on the interaction between language and cognition. Our models use a representation that captures a number of properties of perceptual categories, and specifically of the *prototype theory* of perceptual categories (Rosch, 1973).

With regard to colour categories and colour terms there have been a number of computational models trying to explain the typology of colour categories. Yendrikhovskij (2001) used unsupervised clustering of images and observed how the clusters tend to correspond to English colour categories. These results support an empiricist view: colour categories are the product of an individual learning process, and the main influence on the nature of colour categories are (1) the perception of colour and (2) the chromatic content of the world[1]. Dowman (2006) uses an expression-induction model, in which one agent expresses a colour with a linguistic term and another agent induces the meaning of the term. Dowman's model assumes that red, yellow, green and blue have a special status by making these colours easier to remember for the agents. The model reproduces most of the colour category systems proposed by Kay and Maffi (1999), showing how a learning bias acting over a period of time can explain the typology of colour categories.

18.3. Computational Model

In order to investigate the influence of language on category acquisition, we have constructed two models. In the first one, language has a direct influence on the category formation: both categories and their forms are learned in one stage; in the second model learning is divided into stages: in the first stage the agents

---

[1] But see (Steels and Belpaeme, 2005) for a critical note.

induce their categories individually from the environment and in the second stage they learn the forms to communicate about these categories without further changing their category repertoires.

18.3.1. Internal Structure of the Agents

Each agent is endowed with identical internal mechanisms which allows it to perceive the environment and map it onto an internal representation space. The agents also categorize the stimuli in the environment using prototypical categories and lexicalise these categories.

Perception Although the perceptual system can handle data in an unlimited number of continuous dimensions, we serve RGB colours to the agent in this specific experiment. Because this colour representation is a rather technical one, designed to be used to recreate colour on display devices, it is a poor model of how humans perceive colour. In order to make our experiments more realistic, the agents use the CIE $L^*a^*b^*$ colour appearance model as internal representation space. The L^*-dimension corresponds to the lightness of the colour, the a^* and b^*-dimension to the red-green and the blue-yellow dimension respectively[2]. The CIE $L^*a^*b^*$ colour space is a *perceptually equidistant* colour space: the Euclidean distance between two colours in this colour space is equal to their psychological dissimilarity (Fairchild, 1998).

Categorization For categorisation we have chosen to implement prototypical categories as introduced by Rosch (1973, 1975). In this theory, for each category there exists a stimulus which is the best representative for that category. The membership function decays gradually as the distance between the stimulus and the prototypical member increases. Mapping this theory to our model, each category is represented by its prototype: a single point in the internal representation space. To calculate the membership function for a stimulus, we take the inverse Euclidean distance between the prototype and the stimulus.

Each agent maintains its own category repertoire. When categorizing a stimulus, the category which has the highest output value (hence whose prototype is closest to the stimulus) is selected. One can think of a category repertoire as a Voronoi diagram in the internal representation space: each category categorizes all points in the internal representation space for which no other category has a prototype which is closer to the stimulus.

This theory is very suitable for working with colour categories as it has been shown that colour categories fit well in the framework of prototypical categories. Our model covers the main features observed in this kind of categories: colour categories are sensitive to only one connected region in perceptual space

---

[2] See (Belpaeme and Bleys, 2005) for exact details on the conversion between RGB and CIE $L^*a^*b^*$.

and categorical perception (Harnad, 1990) is implemented through the use of the distance function[3].

Lexicalisation and Communication Each agent maintains its own lexicon which contains associations between categories and terms. Each association is represented by its *strength*: a scalar between 0 and unity denoting respectively a minimal and maximal association. Each category can be associated with multiple terms, allowing for homonymy, and each term can be associated with multiple categories, allowing for synonymy. The lexicon of an agent can be represented as a matrix with all known terms in one dimension and the known categories in the other. Each element (i, j) represents the strength of the association between category i and term j. An example of an association matrix is given in eq. 1.

$$
\begin{array}{c}
\\
c_1 \\
c_2 \\
\vdots \\
c_n
\end{array}
\begin{array}{cccc}
t_1 & t_2 & \ldots & t_m \\
\end{array}
\left(
\begin{array}{cccc}
0.1 & 0.7 & \ldots & 0.0 \\
0.0 & 0.1 & \ldots & 1.0 \\
\vdots & \vdots & s_{ij} & \vdots \\
0.1 & 0.0 & \ldots & 0.1
\end{array}
\right)
\tag{1}
$$

Selecting a form to express a category and vice versa, is implemented as a winner-takes-all competition. For selecting the best word for expressing category c_i, the agents select the association which has the highest strength in row i for that category and uses the associated term for communication. When an agent has to interpret a term t_j it selects the association which has the highest strength in column j and selects the associated category.

18.3.2. Interactions

The behaviour of the agents is implemented in terms of two interaction scenarios. The first, also known as the *discrimination game* is at the level of an individual agent and serves to let the agent develop a category repertoire sufficient to discriminate a stimulus from its context. The second type of interaction, the *guessing game*, is played at the population level. Its main goal is to develop a lexicon which is sufficiently shared in the population to allow communication through language.

Discrimination game During a *discrimination game*, a single agent is presented a context S which contains n stimuli. One stimulus s_t is selected to be the topic of this game. Each stimulus is converted to its internal representation which is classified using the categories in the agent's repertoire. The *discrimination game* is a success when the category c_t used to classify the topic is not used

---

[3] Previous models, like for instance (Steels and Belpaeme, 2005), have used Radial Basis Network Functions for representing categories. These representations were complex and allowed non-symmetric and non-convex category memberships. However, they also allowed categories to cover multiple unconnected regions in the internal representation space, which is somewhat controversial in any theory of categorisation.

for classifying any other stimulus in the context. A detailed scenario for the *discrimination game* is presented in algorithm 1.

Algorithm 1 discrimination game *(A, S)*

1: Agent A chooses a topic s_t from the context $S = \{s_1, \ldots, s_n\}$
2: Agent A perceives each stimulus in the context by constructing an internal representation for it: $\{s_1, \ldots, s_n\} \rightarrow \{r_1, \ldots, r_n\}$
3: For each internal representation r_i, the best matching category is found. This is the category which has the highest output for r_i of all the categories available in the category repertoire of A and which we will denote by c_i: $\{r_1, \ldots, r_n\} \rightarrow \{c_1, \ldots, c_n\}$
4: If the best matching category for the topic is unique: $\mathrm{count}(c_t, \{c_1, \ldots, c_n\}) = 1$, the game succeeded, otherwise it has failed.
5: If the game failed, the agent adds a new category or adapts the best matching category c_t (see text).

This scenario can fail in several ways to which the agent can react either by adding a category to its repertoire or by adapting a category to represent the topic better. The choice between these two actions depends on a number of conditions. When the category repertoire of the agent is empty, the agent adds a new category which has the internal representation r_t of the topic as prototype to its repertoire. When the category c_t is also used for other stimuli in the context, the agent chooses depending on its current *discriminative success* (see section 18.3.4): if it is below a certain threshold $\theta_{adapt} = .9$ the agent chooses to add a new category; otherwise it adapts c_t using eq. 2. This results in moving the prototype of that category towards the internal representation of the topic r_t with a certain rate $\alpha = .7$.

$$c_t \leftarrow c_t + \alpha(r_t - c_t) \tag{2}$$

Guessing game A *guessing game* is played between two agents, randomly selected from the population. One acts as the *speaker* and the other as the *hearer*. A context S containing n stimuli is presented to both agents. The speaker selects a topic s_H from the context and plays a *discrimination game* which yields a discriminating category c_S. The speaker looks into its lexicon and finds the best term t associated with category c_S which it then utters. The hearer finds the category c_H which is associated with this term. Next it selects a topic s_H from the context using category c_S. Two selection-procedures are implemented:

lenient interpretation: the hearer chooses the stimulus which has the highest output value for category c_H
strict interpretation: identical to lenient interpretation but additionally category c_H needs to be discriminative for the selected topic; this is implemented through a *discrimination game* on s_H which has to result in a discriminating category equal to c_H

Algorithm 2 *guessing game (A_S, A_H, s)*

speaker A_S		hearer A_H
chooses topic s_S		
plays DG for s_S		
DG succeeds and returns c_S		
finds term t for c_S		
utters t	$\rightarrow t \rightarrow$	hears t
		finds category c_H for t_H
		finds s_H using c_H
sees s_H	$\leftarrow s_H \leftarrow$ points to s_H	
$s_S = s_H$		
updates (c_S, t) using eq. 3		
points to s_S	$\rightarrow s_S \rightarrow$	sees s_S
		updates (c_H, t) using eq. 3
		adapts category c_H to r_S using eq. 2

If s_H is identical to c_S, the game succeeds; otherwise it fails. A script for this scenario is listed in algorithm 2. A *guessing game* can fail in many ways. Each failure is an opportunity for the agents to learn:

- the speaker couldn't discriminate topic s_S: the *guessing game* fails but the *speaker* has adapted its category repertoire through the *discrimination game* it played
- the speaker does not have a term to describe c_S: the speaker invents a new word and the game continues
- the hearer does not know the term t: the hearer is not able to point to a stimulus in the context and the speaker reveals the actual topic s_H; the hearer plays a *discrimination game* using s_H as topic and adds the new word to its lexicon associating it with the resulting discriminating category; both speaker and hearer decrease the strength of the association they used using eq. 4.
- the category c_H is not discriminative for s_H: (only applies when using strict interpretation); the hearer switches to lenient interpretation but notifies the speaker it is doing so; the normal update rules apply but the game itself is considered as a failure
- the hearer pointed to the wrong stimulus: both speaker and hearer update their lexicons using eq. 4.

The update rules used for the lexicon are as follows. When the *guessing game* was successful the strengths in their lexicon are updated using *lateral inhibition*: the strength of the used association is increased by a value $\delta = 0.1$ and competing associations are decreased by δ. Competing associations are those that either use

the same form or the same category (eq. 3). When the game failed, the strengths
of the used associations are decreased (as in eq. 4).

$$
\begin{cases}
s_{ij} = \min\left(s_{ij} + \delta, 1\right) \\
s_{kl} = \max\left(s_{kl} - \delta, 0\right) \quad \text{in row i and column j with } k \neq i, l \neq j
\end{cases} \tag{3}
$$

$$
s_{ij} = \max\left(s_{ij} - \delta, 0\right) \tag{4}
$$

18.3.3. Two Models

Now we have defined the internal structure of our agents and the two different
scenarios by which they interact with their environment and each other, we
can define two models to study the interaction between language and category
acquisition. The main difference between both models is that in the first,
language has a direct influence on the acquisition of categories whereas in the
second these processes are independent.

Model 1: Language influences category acquisition In this model the agents
interact through *guessing games* (Belpaeme and Bleys, 2005). This allows
them to learn both their repertoire of categories and the forms to express these
categories at the same time through social communicative interactions. Previous
research has shown that this kind of model results in a category system which
is coordinated within a population (Steels and Belpaeme, 2005).

Model 2: Language does not influence category acquisition In this second
model the process of learning the categories and the forms for these categories
are separated. In a first stage the agents develop their ontologies individually
by playing *discrimination games*. In a second stage, only the forms to express
these categories are learned through *guessing games*. The category repertoires
are not allowed to change.

18.3.4. Measures

In order to evaluate the performance of our models we have defined several
measures. The *average number of categories* and *forms* are self-explanatory.
Discriminative and *communicative success* keep track of how successful the
population of agents has been in playing *discrimination* and *guessing games* respectively. It is computed by taking the average of the success rate, the average
percentage of successful games of the last $n = 20$ games it was involved in, of each
agent in the population.

18.4. Experimental Results

We have tested both models in a batch of 10 runs using a population of 10 agents.
Each run of model 1 consisted of 30000 guessing games; each run of the model 2
consisted of 30000 discrimination games followed by 30000 guessing games.

18.4.1. Input Stimuli

As input stimuli for our experiments, we have created a dataset containing 25000 colours uniformly distributed in the $CIEL^*a^*b^*$ colour space. For each point in the set a L^*, a^* and b^* value was picked in the range $L^* = [0, 100]$, $a^* = [-152, 152]$ and $b^* = [-127, 140]$; as these range values specify a cube, this would allow for some unrealistic CIE $L^*a^*b^*$ triplets. To avoid this, each stimulus was checked to be within the Munsell colour solid (see for example Hardin and Maffi, 1997), if it was not, it was discarded.

18.4.2. Coordination of Category Repertoires through Language

The experiments confirm earlier results (Belpaeme, 2001; Steels and Belpaeme, 2005): cultural acquisition of categories under the influence of language results in category repertoires which are coordinated among all agents in a population. Figure 18.1 shows the prototypes of each category of all agents of a population at the end of a simulation projected on the a^*b^*-plane. Model 1 results in categories which are clustered; model 2 results in colour categories which are scattered randomly across the colour space. This shows clearly that the coordination of the categories should be credited to the cultural influence on the acquisition process.

18.4.3. Measures

The graphs of the different measures for model 1 and model 2 are shown in Figure 18.2 and 18.3 respectively. In model 1 the average number of categories is lower than in model 2; the overshoot in the average number of words is

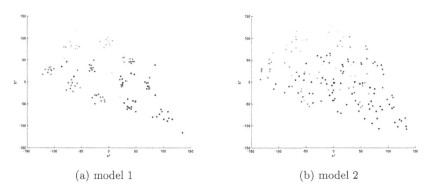

(a) model 1   (b) model 2

FIGURE 18.1. Resulting categories of all agents in the population at the end of a simulation for each model. When language has an influence on category acquisition (a), the categories of agents tend to cluster. If agents acquire their categories individually, without communication (b), the categories are spread out in perceptual space.

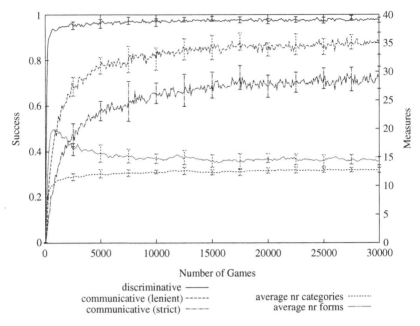

FIGURE 18.2. Results for model 1 (language influences category acquisition); results are averaged over 10 simulations.

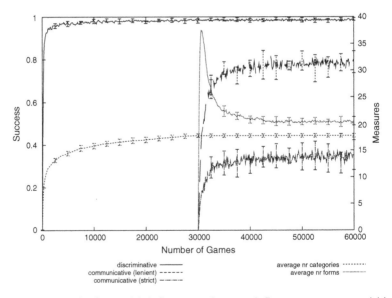

FIGURE 18.3. Results for model 2 (language does not influence category acquisition); results are averaged over 10 simulations.

higher in model 2; these results suggest that the cultural influence of language helps to limit the number of required categories and facilitates the learning of corresponding forms.

The discriminative success for both models is close to 100%. The communicative success using lenient interpretation of both models are similar. However, the coordination of the category repertoires shows its real value when agents use strict interpretation: the communicative success of model 1 is still reasonably good whereas the communicative success of model 2 drops below 40%.

18.5. Discussion

If language has an influence on cognition, and specifically on category acquisition, we might expect to find evidence of this in humans. There is quite some evidence available for colour categories, and for other cognitive representation, such as numerical reasoning (Gumperz and Levinson, 1997) or time (Boroditsky, 2001). However, it is not always clear on what level language has an influence. With regards to colour, having a linguistic form for a category can help in memorising and recognising colour (Rosch-Heider, 1972; Davidoff et al., 1999; Roberson et al., 2000), or it can influence similarity judgements between colours (Brown and Lenneberg, 1954; Kay and Kempton, 1984), or it can influence reaction time in spotting colours (Gilbert et al., 2006). However, although it has been assumed by many, it still remains to be shown how language can aid in coordinating conceptual representations. Our model operationalises the hypothesis that the use of linguistic forms and feedback —implicit or explicit— received on the use of these forms can steer the individuals' categories. The categories are changed so that (a) future linguistic interactions will have a higher probability of being successful and (b) the categories of all agents in the population become coordinated. The latter, the coordination —or self-organisation— of categories in a population, happens without central control. The coordination of categories is an emergent property of the category acquisition of each individual. The underlying system responsible for this is the positive feedback loop between linguistic forms, the categories and the referents to which agents have access (Steels and Belpaeme, 2005).

Our model seems tolerant to the degree the categories are coordinated between agents. Even if the categories are not at all coordinated, as is the case in the model where categories are acquired without the influence of language, the agents still manage to acquire a term-category mapping which allows for good communication, provided the interpretation by the hearer is not strict. This can be understood when considering the categories of agents: as these categories are models of perceptual categories, and have properties of prototypical categories, they have a *continuous* membership function. The membership of a perceived stimulus can be expressed as a continuous function. This implies that there is always a referent in the context which can be associated with a category. If you hear "red", but can only select between orange and green to interpret "red", you will still take orange and the communication will succeed. However, if categories do not have a continuous membership function but a membership function that is discrete (such as discrimination trees in Steels 1997) then communication will more often fail if both agents' categories are not coordinated. For example, if you hear "square", but you only see a triangle and a pentagon, there is no way of disambiguating "square". The reason is that categories of geometrical figures are discrete: because of their categorization according to the number of corners, there is no continuous membership, and a square cannot in some way be a triangle or a pentagon. On the other hand, orange can be interpreted as either yellow or red, depending on how tolerant the interpreting agent is willing to be and depending on the context in which the word needs to be interpreted.

The degree to which the model is tolerant to uncoordinated categories depends on how strict the hearer interprets forms. If it interprets a form by selecting the closest referent in the context, then coordination is not required to have unambiguous communication. However, if the hearer interprets a form by relating it to only one referent, then communication breaks down if categories are not coordinated. This might be related to the mutual exclusivity principle (Markman, 1989), in which category terms are assumed to be associated with only one object in the context: a single object cannot be chair and table at the same time. If humans, and especially, if children during language acquisition rely on the mutual exclusivity principle, then their perceptual categories should be coordinated in order to allow unambiguous communication.

18.6. Conclusion

Building a computational model capturing something as complex as human category acquisition and the influence of language on the process is complicated and our model is only what it is: a model. So drawing conclusions on human cognition from a model might seem outright presumptuous. Still, simple models of language and cognition, even if their explanatory power is limited, might suggest a number of new directions of thought. One suggestion would be to test if humans do need identical, or even similar, perceptual categories to be able to communicate well. Our model suggests that perceptual categories can be rather different without hampering linguistic communication (or maybe even without hampering reasoning with these categories). The reason for this is that the membership to a perceptual category decays gradually and continuously, making the mapping of a referent in the world onto a category tolerant to differences in individuals' categories. Webster and Kay (2005) seem to have observed this in colour categories, but our model suggests that this might be case for other any perceptual categories, or indeed any categories with a continuous membership.

Bibliography

Barr, D. (2004). Establishing conventional communication systems: Is common knowledge necessary? *Cognitive Science*, 28:937–962.

Belpaeme, T. (2001). Simulating the formation of color categories. In Nebel, B., editor, *Proceedings of the International Joint Conference on Artificial Intelligence (IJCAI'01)*, Seattle, WA, pages 393–398, San Francisco, CA. Morgan Kaufmann.

Belpaeme, T. and Bleys, J. (2005). Explaining universal colour categories through a constrained acquisition process. *Adaptive Behavior*, 13(4):293–310.

Berlin, B. and Kay, P. (1969). *Basic Color Terms: Their Universality and Evolution*. University of California Press, Berkeley, CA.

Boroditsky, L. (2001). Does language shape thought? English and Mandarin speakers' conceptions of time. *Cognitive Psychology*, 43:1–22.

Brown, R. W. and Lenneberg, E. H. (1954). A study in language and cognition. *Journal of Abnormal and Social Psychology*, 54:454–462.

Carrol, J. (1956). *Language, Thought and Reality: selected writings of Benjamin Lee Whorf*. The MIT Press, Cambridge, MA.

Christiansen, M. H. and Kirby, S. (2003). Language evolution: consensus and controversies. *Trends in Cognitive Sciences*, 7(1):300–307.

Davidoff, J., Davies, I., and Roberson, D. (1999). Colour categories in a stone-age tribe. *Nature*, 398:203–204.

De Vylder, B. and Tuyls, K. (2006). How to reach linguistic consensus: A proof of convergence for the naming game. *Journal of Theoretical Biology*. In press.

Dowman, M. (2006). Explaining color term typology with an evolutionary model. *Cognitive Science*. In press.

Fairchild, M. D. (1998). *Color Appearance Models*. Addison-Wesley, Reading, MA.

Franklin, A., Clifford, A., Williamson, E., and Davies, I. (2005a). Color term knowledge does not affect categorical perception of color in toddlers. *Journal of Experimental Child Psychology*, 90(2):114–141.

Franklin, A., Pilling, M., and Davies, I. (2005b). The nature of infant color categorization: Evidence from eye movements on a target detection task. *Journal of Experimental Child Psychology*, 91:227–248.

Gentner, D. and Boroditsky, L. (2001). Individuation, relational relativity and early word learning. In Bowerman, M. and Levinson, S., editors, *Language acquisition and conceptual development*. Cambridge University Press, Cambridge, England.

Gilbert, A., Regier, T., Kay, P., and Ivry, R. (2006). Whorf's hypothesis is supported in the right visual field but not the left. *Proceedings of the National Academy of Sciences*, 103(2):489–494.

Gumperz, J. and Levinson, S. (1997). Rethinking linguistic relativity. *Current Anthropology*, 32:613–623.

Gumperz, J. J. and Levinson, S. C. (1996). *Rethinking Linguistic Relativity*. Studies in the Social and Cultural Foundations of Language 17. Cambridge University Press, Cambridge.

Hardin, C. and Maffi, L., editors (1997). *Color categories in thought and language*. Cambridge University Press, Cambridge.

Harnad, S. (1990). The symbol grounding problem. *Physica D*, 42:335–346.

Kay, P., Berlin, B., Maffi, L., and Merrifield, W. (1997). Color naming across languages. In Hardin, C. and Maffi, L., editors, *Color Categories in Thought and Language*. Cambridge University Press, Cambridge.

Kay, P. and Kempton, W. (1984). What is the Sapir-Whorf hypothesis? *American Anthropologist*, 86(1):65–79.

Kay, P. and Maffi, L. (1999). Color appearance and the emergence and evolution of basic color lexicons. *American Anthropologist*, 101(4):743–760.

Kay, P. and McDaniel, C. (1978). The linguistic significance of the meanings of basic color terms. *Language*, 54(3):610–646.

Kay, P. and Regier, T. (2003). Resolving the question of color naming universals. *Proceedings of the National Academy of Sciences*, 100(15):9085–9089.

Kay, P. and Regier, T. (2006). Language, thought and color: recent developments. *Trends in Cognitive Science*, 10(2):51–54.

Luypan, G. (2005). Carving nature at its joints and carving joints into nature: How labels augment category representations. In Cangelosi, A., Bugmann, G., and Borisyuk, R., editors, *Modelling Language, Cognition and Action: Proceedings of the 9th Neural Computation and Psychology Workshop*, Singapore. World Scientific.

Markman, E. M. (1989). *Categorization and naming in children: problems of induction*. The MIT Press, Cambridge, MA.

Oliphant, M. (1996). The dilemma of Saussurean communication. *BioSystems*, 37(1-2):31–38.

Regier, T., Kay, P., and Cook, R. S. (2005). Focal colors are universal after all. *Proceedings of the National Academy of Science*, 102(23):8386–8391.

Roberson, D. (2005). Color categories are culturally diverse in cognition as well as in language. *Cross-Cultural Research*, 39:56–71.

Roberson, D., Davies, I., and Davidoff, J. (2000). Colour categories are not universal: Replications and new evidence from a Stone-age culture. *Journal of Experimental Psychology: General*, 129:369–398.

Rosch, E. (1973). Natural categories. *Cognitive Psychology*, 4:328–350.

Rosch, E. (1975). Universals and cultural specifics in human categorisation. In Brislin, R., Bochner, S., and Lonner, W., editors, *Cross-cultural perspectives on learning: The interface between culture and learning*. Halstead Press, New York.

Rosch-Heider, E. (1972). Universals in color naming and memory. *Journal of Experimental Psychology*, 93:10–20.

Shepard, R. N. (1992). The perceptual organization of colors: An adaptation to regularities of the terrestrial world? In Barkow, J., Cosmides, L., and Tooby, J., editors, *Adapted Mind*, pages 495–532. Oxford University Press, Oxford.

Smith, A. D. M. (2003). Intelligent meaning creation in a clumpy world helps communication. *Artificial Life*, 9(2):175–190.

Steels, L. (1996). Self-organizing vocabularies. In Langton, C. and Shimohara, T., editors, *Proceedings of the Conference on Artificial Life V (Alife V) (Nara, Japan)*, Cambridge, MA. The MIT Press.

Steels, L. (1997). Construction and sharing perceptual distinctions. In van Someren, M. and Widmer, G., editors, *Proceedings of the European Conference on Machine Learning*, Berlin. Springer Verlag.

Steels, L. (2003). Evolving grounded communication for robots. *Trends in Cognitive Science*, 7(7):308–312.

Steels, L. and Belpaeme, T. (2005). Coordinating perceptually grounded categories through language. A case study for colour. *Behavioral and Brain Sciences*, 24(8):469–529.

Steels, L. and Kaplan, F. (1999). Bootstrapping grounded word semantics. In Briscoe, T., editor, *Linguistic evolution through language acquisition: formal and computational models*. Cambridge University Press, Cambridge.

Vogt, P. (2003). Anchoring of semiotic symbols. *Robotics and Autonomous Systems*, 43(2):109–120.

Webster, M. A. and Kay, P. (2005). Variations in color naming within and across populations. *Behavioral and Brain Sciences*, 28(4):512–513.

Yendrikhovskij, S. N. (2001). Computing color categories from statistics of natural images. *Journal of Imaging Science and Technology*, 45(5):409–417.

Part 3
Insights from Animal Communication

19
Emergence of Linguistic Communication: Studies on Grey Parrots

Irene M. Pepperberg

19.1. Introduction

Most studies on the evolution of communication systems concentrate on the primate lineage, ignoring the concept of parallel lines of evolution. Although phylogenetically remote from humans, some birds—particularly Grey parrots—share many cognitive and communicative abilities with humans. On certain tasks, they demonstrate processing abilities comparable to 5-6 year-old humans; they learn very simple vocal syntactic patterns and referential elements of human communication, but only through social interaction and in a manner that proceeds in ways similar to those of humans. Given this knowledge of vocal learning in birds, of the effects of social interaction on such learning, and of birds' complex cognitive abilities, we should not ignore the avian line if we wish to determine the evolutionary pressures that purportedly affected the evolution of complex communication systems—particularly vocal systems—and develop theories and models that can be tested.

Twenty-first century scientists are not alone in having an interest in the evolution and emergence of language and communication. Throughout the ages, humans have attempted to explain how their unique communication system came into being; earlier civilizations and non-Western societies often proposed various creation stories for this purpose. Among the many myths concerning the origins of human language, that of the Bwiti tribe has a certain personal appeal. These denizens of western equatorial Africa claim that Grey parrots brought language to humans as a gift from the gods (Fernandez, 1982). Such stories may actually lead to plausible explanations, for example, arguments for language developing out of song, maybe the first songs being based on vocalizations of sympatric animals. Although some modern Western researchers have pursued this path (Dunbar, 2004; Liska, 1993; Richman, 1993), most prefer not to base theories on such beliefs, and have instead engaged in different forms of investigation and debate to find scientific explanations of language creation (e.g., Hurford et al., 1998; MacNeilage and Davis, 2005; Oller and Griebel, 2004; Wray and Gonzalez, 2002). After almost 30 years of involvement in this field, I nevertheless sometimes wonder if we have not substituted one set of "just-so" stories for another. Research on language evolution, although vibrant and maximally interdisciplinary, still seems trapped in a web of primate-centric theories. A common ancestor for nonhuman primates and humans is undeniable, as are many neurological, anatomical, and resultant behavioral parallels (e.g., Deacon, 1997), particularly with respect to brain function and mirror neurons[1] (see Arbib, 2005: Corballis, 2003; Fogassi and Gallese, 2002), but an exclusively primate-centric model overlooks the likelihood that, through evolutionary pressures and the exploitation of different ecological niches, similar communicative abilities may evolve in somewhat different ways in different species, and that birds can also provide intriguing models for the evolution of communication and possibly even language. Even what once seemed to be obviously different neuroanatomical structures subserving vocal behavior in birds and humans are now considered to be likely homologues, with researchers arguing for avian brain evolution from the same pallial structures as occurred in mammals (Jarvis et al., 2005). Thus, given my knowledge of the vocal abilities of birds, particularly with respect to their learning of human communication patterns (Pepperberg, 1999), I suggest that focus on the relevance of avian subjects, particularly concerning how they learn and use various vocal systems, will shed considerable light on the evolution of linguistic communication. But first, some background that explains why birds would be good model systems.

19.1.1. A Focus on Vocal Learning

Because birds, like humans (but few other mammals) *learn* their vocal communication systems, the study of birds allows us to focus both on learning and vocal behavior. Few theses concerning the origins of language focus on the evolution of *learning* as the basis for communicative skills, probably for two reasons: First, evidence for the full range of such human-based behavior (i.e., learning *of* vocal patterns and not only how to use them) is absent or at least limited in even our closest primate relatives, the great apes (e.g., Deacon, 2000). Although some form of vocal learning probably occurred in the so-called 'missing links' between modern humans and our ancestral lineage, most researchers do not discuss the details of this part of the evolutionary continuum (but see Arbib, 2005; Corballis, 2003). Second, the nativist perspective concerning language acquisition still has strong adherents (e.g., Crain and Pietroski, 2001); even those who accept a role for limited environmental experience—for example, as being necessary to trigger innate core knowledge for language development

---

[1] Mirror neurons respond to observed actions as if the observer had executed the actions him/herself. Other neurons in the spinal cord act to inhibit the individual from executing the observed action spontaneously.

(see review in Cowie, 1999; also Sakai, 2005)—do not express much interest in an evolutionary theory that involves a strong component of learning in the development of communicative competence. I take the evolution of learning to communicate as a given: I believe that we can construct a hypothetical phylogeny of communicative learning by examining the avian line and proposing parallel forms for primates (Pepperberg, in prep). Remember, communication that is unlearned is rote, inflexible, unable to adapt to changing environmental situations, and thus unlikely to be usefully employed in transferring anything but limited forms of information. In contrast, learning opens the communicative process to innovation and improvisation, to transfer across contexts, to expansion in depth and complexity.

Furthermore, vocal learning is important not only because humans communicate primarily in the vocal mode, but also because it is one of the most transparent of modes for study (Pepperberg, 1999, in prep). Possibly communicative competence was an evolutionary outcome not only of good memory and a need for flexibility, but also of learning to choose what to ignore as well as what to process based at least in part on social interaction (including joint attention with respect to context: objects and others)—and the *vocal* mode provides a window on such decisions. Social primates must actively engage in behavioral choice; an animal that could not form a hierarchy of information would be unable to act. But in animals, only in birds can we clearly see, by what is vocally reproduced and what is not, the outcome of such choices in the communicative domain. Specifically, many birds have the capacity to learn large numbers of different vocalizations, yet they generally choose to learn a specific subset or a few subsets, whether of conspecific or of allospecific sympatric species, and the choices and the reasons for their choices can provide models for human behavior (Neapolitan et al., 1988). Too, parrots seem able to parse phonological space in ways that are similar to those of humans (Patterson and Pepperberg, 1994, 1998) and nonhuman mammals (Kuhl, 1981), thus giving credence to suggestions that the phonology of speech evolved so as to make use of existent auditory sensitivities basic not just to humans or even mammals, but at least to vertebrates (e.g., Dent et al., 1997, but see Locke, 1997). I'll discuss many of these similarities between birds and humans in some depth below to emphasize evolutionary parallels.

19.1.2. Additional Rationale for Birds as Evolutionary Models

We still have on this planet bird species (nonoscines) whose communicative behavior is primarily (though not exclusively) genetically determined (e.g., De Kort and ten Cate, 2001), other species (sub-oscines) whose relatively simple vocalizations are not learned but who must learn how the context in which they use these vocalizations alters meaning (Smith and Smith, 1992, 1996), birds (oscines) who learn both their vocalizations and the appropriate context for use from the environment (Kroodsma, 1988), often including social interactions with one another (Pepperberg, 1985) and even species that seem to span the divide between the last two categories (Kroodsma, 2005). Maybe by examining these creatures we can develop valid hypotheses about how our ancestors branched from the great apes. An argument can be made, for example, that flycatchers (suboscines) who alter the number of repetitions of their single song or alter flight patterns or body postures while singing in order to signal different levels of aggression (i.e., engage in a very simple combinatory syntax; Smith and Smith, 1992, 1996) are living models of our ancestors whose mixtures of grunts and gestures may have served a similar purpose (cf. Bickerton, 2003). If such parallels seem a bit far-fetched, note that earlier studies of parallels between human bilingualism and a related form of avian song acquisition (Neapolitan et al., 1998; Pepperberg and Schinke-Llano, 1991) have demonstrated how birds can indeed be used as models for human behavior (for details, see Pepperberg, in prep).

Moreover, as noted above, these evolutionary hypotheses include aspects of neurobiology. The different forms of avian communication described above are reflected in different neuroanatomical systems (Jarvis and Mello, 2000; Jarvis et al., 2005; Kroodsma and Konishi, 1991; Nottebohm, 1980), with the nonoscines and suboscines lacking those parts of the brain that have been implicated in vocal learning; too, some evidence exists to explain how the more "advanced" brains evolved from the more "primitive" ones, that is, how the fully-developed song system evolved as a specialization from pre-existing motor pathways (e.g., Farries, 2001; Perkel, 2004), via paths such as the addition and subtraction of certain projections between brain nuclei (e.g., Farries, 2004). At the very least, by teasing apart those developing communicative patterns that we once assumed were fully innate in birds (Kroodsma, 2005) and examining their neurological correlates, we might achieve an essential understanding of processes some researchers likewise now assume are innate in humans (Pepperberg, in prep). Specifically, in both songbirds and humans we see the evolution of brain and other anatomical features that enable both the production and processing of rapid sound sequences (Carr and Soares, 2002; Liberman, 1991; Stevens, 1998; Williams, 1989) that, even in birds, require some level of rule-governed behavior (i.e., a simplistic form of syntax (Pepperberg and Schinke-Llano, 1991)). Margoliash (2003) argues that the organization of auditory information (in terms of internal representations and issues of timing) may also reflect similar physical constraints that are expressed in related biological solutions. Birds, for example, have neurons that uniquely respond to their own individual vocalizations (Dave and Margoliash, 2000) that seem to assist in vocal learning; given recent studies on mirror neurons (Fadiga and Craighero, 2003), humans are likely to have a related system, although no experimental data yet exists. Thus birds might provide intriguing models for studying these issues; quite possibly the areas that were co-opted in mammals for the evolution of language have parallels in avian brain areas that were co-opted for the evolution of song learning and song decoding: If communication structures in humans can be said to have evolved from the reptilian brain (Lieberman, 2000), certainly so did those of birds (Medina and Reiner, 2000).

In the following pages, I present the specific data on which I base my argument for using birds as evolutionary models. I begin by describing parallels I have found between Grey parrots and humans with respect to both learning and use of a human-based communication system. I then briefly examine relevant work on songbirds and mirror neurons, and conclude by suggesting specific areas of interest for future study.

19.2. Grey Parrot Cognitive and Communicative Capacities: Parallels with Young Children

Although phylogenetically remote from one another, Grey parrots and humans share certain cognitive and communicative abilities. Greys learn simple vocal syntactic patterns and referential elements of human communication; on certain tasks (e.g., label acquisition, categorization, numerical competence, relative size, conjunction, recursion) their processing abilities and learning strategies may parallel those of young human children (Pepperberg, 1981, 1994, 1996, 1999, 2006a,b; Pepperberg and Gordon, 2005; Pepperberg and Shive, 2001; Pepperberg and Wilcox, 2000) despite their walnut-sized brains that are organized somewhat differently from those of primates and even songbirds (Jarvis and Mello, 2000; Jarvis et al., 2005; Striedter, 1994). Like children, Grey parrots use sound play (phonetic 'babbling' and recombination, Pepperberg et al., 1991) to produce new speech patterns from existent ones (Pepperberg, 1990b), implying that they acoustically represent labels as do humans and develop phonetic categories. Greys may use anticipatory coarticulation—separate specific phonemes from speech flow *and* produce these sounds to facilitate production of upcoming phonemes (Patterson and Pepperberg, 1998)—which along with sound play is consistent with *top-down* processing (Ladefoged, 1982). Greys recombine at least a few labels in novel ways to respond to novel situations and transfer such use across contexts (Pepperberg and Brezinsky, 1991). They can learn from each other in the laboratory (Pepperberg et al., 2000); and, if their natural behavior resembles that of other parrots (Gnam, 1988; Levinson, 1980; Nottebohm, 1970; Wright, 1996; Wright and Dorin, 2001; Yamashita, 1987), they establish strong pair-bonds, recognize specific individuals, have vocal sentinel behavior, complex pair-bond duets, dialects, and likely alter calls when changing dialect areas. Long-lived, they reside in large groups whose social complexity may match that of primates.

19.2.1. Brief Summary of Labeling and Simple Combinatory Abilities

For almost 30 years, I have trained Grey parrots to use the elements of English speech to communicate referentially with humans, and have then used this communication code to examine these birds' cognitive processes (e.g., Pepperberg, 1999). My oldest Grey parrot subject, Alex, now 30, labels more than 50 different objects, seven colors, five shapes, quantity up to and including 6, three categories (material/color/shape); he uses *no, come here, wanna go X, want Y* (where X and Y are, respectively, appropriate location or item labels). He combines labels to identify, classify, request, or refuse approximately 100 items and to alter his environment, and he comprehends these labels. This combinatory ability, although limited and far from true human syntax (Bickerton, 2003), resembles children's early use of sentence frames (de Villiers and de Villiers, 1979) in which there is a simplified knowledge of order (i.e., a rule-governed behavior, such as *qualifier + object label*, or a general request pattern; see Tomasello, 2003).

Alex also answers questions and demonstrates other forms of label use. He processes queries to judge category, relative size, quantity, presence or absence of similarity and difference in attributes. He, like some other 'language-trained' subjects, can use symbols dispassionately, that is, to separate identification of an object from a request for that item (Pepperberg, 1988; i.e., he separates illocutionary force from prepositional content; see Oller, 2004, for the implications of such behavior). Alex's label use resembles that of similarly trained apes (e.g., Gardner and Gardner, 1978; Savage-Rumbaugh et al., 2003); that is, he can use a label as a symbol not only for a specific item but also for a type of object (e.g., for all bananas) or action (e.g., request), and can use different labels as symbols for categories that subsume the specific objects (e.g., material) or actions. Moreover, these labels are used not only to refer to what is currently in view: Apes and parrots, like humans, request absent objects or an action not currently being performed, and accept that object or action and no other (Pepperberg, 1999; see Hockett's (1959) concept of displacement). As do the apes, Alex generally demonstrates both label comprehension and production: If given the label of a specific object, he can indicate the label's referent within a collection of many items by stating something unique about it (review in Pepperberg, 1999). Alex use labels to refer to similar but non-identical items without additional training, for example, to identify the material of any colored or shaped piece of rawhide as "hide". Similarly, Alex understand the hierarchical nature of labels for objects and labels for categories, that is, that the label "yellow" refers to the concept "yellowness"—to corn as well as to training objects—and how the arbitrary label "yellow" is subsumed into a category whose arbitrary label is "color" (Pepperberg, 1996, 2004a). Alex also has numerical concepts comparable to those of young children (labeling of quantities, including those in heterogeneous sets; he understands limited forms of addition and ordinality; he has a restricted concept of zero (Pepperberg, 1999, 2006, 2006c; Pepperberg and Gordon, 2005)). He can reply to questions that involve simple forms of recursion and conjunction; that is, given a tray of seven objects of various colors, shapes, and materials, he can answer any of the three possible questions "What object is color X and shape Y?", "What color is material Z and shape Y?", or "What shape is color X and material Z?" (Pepperberg, 1992, but note Hauser et al., 2002).

Alex also questions his trainers about various objects; using the same phrases as do his trainers (e.g., "What color?", "What shape?", "How many?"). He learned the label for a carrot by asking what we were eating, and the color *orange* by asking its color. Such behavior also suggests parallels with children (e.g., Brown's (1973) naming game).

Details of this research have been summarized elsewhere (Pepperberg, 1999, 2004a). Suffice it to say that such abilities were once presumed limited to humans or apes (Premack, 1978), and that Alex is not unique; other Greys are replicating some of his results (Pepperberg, 1999, 2004a; Pepperberg and Shive, 2001; Pepperberg and Wilcox, 2000; Pepperberg et al., 2000). Thus Greys qualify as good models for the evolution of complex communication skills. Moreover, Greys are also good models for the *acquisition* of such skills. Complex skills must be learned, and evolution also exerts pressures on learning processes.

19.2.2. How Greys Learn a Human-Based Code

My Greys' learning sometimes parallels human processes, suggesting a long evolutionary history for the acquisition of complex communication (Pepperberg, 2004a). Like young children (e.g., Hollich et al., 2000), parrots acquire communication skills most effectively when input is referential, demonstrates functionality (i.e., shows contextual applicability), and is socially rich (Pepperberg, 1997; Pepperberg et al., 1998, 1999, 2000). The primary training technique, the Model/Rival (M/R) procedure, has been described in detail many times (e.g., Pepperberg, 1999) and will be reviewed here only briefly; basically, it involves threeway *social* interactions among two humans and a parrot.

Typically, a parrot observes two humans talking about one or more items in which it has already shown interest: The trainer presents, and queries a another human about, the item(s) (e.g., "What's here?", "What color?") and gives praise and the object(s) so as to reward correct answers *referentially*. Incorrect responses (like those birds may make) are punished by scolding and temporarily removing item(s) from sight. Thus the second human is a model for the parrot's responses, its rival for the trainer's attention, and illustrates effects of an error: S/he tries again or talks more clearly after a (deliberately) incorrect or garbled response, thereby demonstrating corrective feedback, as well as the reason for learning the specific sounds of the label. The bird is included in the interactions and is rewarded for successive approximations to a correct response; training is thereby adjusted to its level. We also reverse roles of human trainer and model to emphasize that one being is not always the questioner and the other the respondent. M/R training thus involves (a) reference: a one-to-one correspondence between the label to be learned and the item to be obtained; (b) functionality: a bird learns the label initially as a way to obtain the item; (c) social interaction: considerable turn-taking and interactive, vocal behavior; and (d) modeling: a means to demonstrate exactly what is to be learned.

What is of particular interest is that Grey parrots do not learn if any of these four elements of training are absent. Studies with four other parrots, Kyaaro, Alo,

Griffin, and Arthur, that used techniques lacking one or more elements failed to demonstrate any significant label acquisition (Pepperberg and Wilkes, 2004; see review Pepperberg, 2004a). My students and I exposed these birds to audiotapes of Alex's M/R sessions (omitting all four elements of input), to videotapes of Alex's sessions (with no social interaction or various levels of social interaction and/or automatized rewards); we tried using live video feed from Alex's sessions and an LCD computer screen to avoid possible problems with, respectively, habituation and flicker-fusion effects; we tried using a single trainer who either avoided or maintained joint attention with the bird and the targeted object. Only our standard M/R training was successful. Interestingly, the M/R technique has also been shown to engender interactive, referential communication in children diagnosed as having autism spectrum disorders who did not respond to more traditional forms of therapy (Pepperberg and Sherman 2000, 2002).

Also of interest is that for both our parrots and for children, first labels are qualitatively different from later labels (Pepperberg, 2001). First labels may be acoustically biased by and based on prenatal (DeCasper and Spence, 1986; Querleu et al., 1981) or prehatching exposure to sounds (e.g., Gottlieb, 1982), and have a clear, probably evolutionarily based, predisposition to refer to whole objects. To err on the side of caution, a 'hawk' alarm call for juvenile birds and monkeys initially doesn't necessarily refer to the specific predator or some aspect of a bird, but simply some big object overhead with a general type of shape that could be a threat (e.g., Cheney and Seyfarth, 1990). These first labels are often mimetic, occasionally are indexical in that they may refer to a specific item rather than a class, and may sometimes lack true meaning and communicative intent (de Villiers and de Villiers, 1979). Nevertheless, at least for humans—and I suspect for my parrots—first labels are still not based on simple associations (Pepperberg, 2001). If that were true, children could be as easily trained to use tones rather than speech-based labels to refer to objects (Colunga and Smith, 2000), or to void the whole-object assumption (that labels generally refer to whole objects rather than to some feature of the object)—and they can't (Macnamara, 1982; Markman and Wachtel, 1988). And my birds easily transfer their label use from training exemplars to related objects—without training, the oldest labeled an old-fashioned huge sheet of computer output as "paper", although he had exclusively experienced various pieces of index cards as the original exemplars (Pepperberg, 1981). Acquisition of my parrots' later labels, as we will see, is qualitatively different, is generally more rapid, more broadly applied, and is often limited only by the need to learn how to structure their vocal apparatus. To understand their acquisition more fully, let's concentrate for a moment on the effects of input and the whole-object concept.

19.2.3. Mutual Exclusivity

One of our studies (Pepperberg and Wilcox, 2000) on the effect of input on Grey parrot's label learning focused on the whole-object concept and specifically demonstrated parallels with children's data on mutual exclusivity

(ME). ME refers to many children's brief assumption during early word acquisition that each object has one, and only one, label (e.g., Liittschwager and Markman, 1991; cf Merriman, 1991). Along with the whole-object assumption (Macnamara, 1982; Markman and Wachtel, 1988), ME supposedly guides children in initial label acquisition. Using these assumptions, a child shown a familiar and an unfamiliar object and given a novel label will likely associate the new label with the new object, deducing that the familiar object already has its own particular label and thus, by exclusion, the meaning of the novel label. ME may also help children interpret novel words as feature labels (i.e., overcome the whole-object assumption, e.g., "If I know these are both 'cups' and I also know this one is 'red', then 'glorp' must refer to this weird new color", Markman, 1990), but very young children may find second labels for items initially more difficult to acquire than the first, because the second label may be viewed as an alternative object name and not immediately as a feature (Liittschwager and Markman, 1994); that is, they can't yet overcome the whole-object assumption. Input, however, affects ME: Children (Gottfried and Tonks, 1996) and parrots like Alex, who receive explicit or even implicit *inclusivity* data (X is a kind of Y; such that, for example, color names are taught as additional, not alternative, labels, i.e., "Here's a key; it's a green key"), generally accept multiple labels for items and form hierarchical relations more readily. Thus, shown a wooden block, Alex answers "What color?", "What shape?", "What matter?" *and* "What toy?" (Pepperberg, 1990a). However, parrots given colors or shapes as alternative labels (e.g., first told "Here's key" and later told merely "It's green"), like children, exhibit ME. My parrot Griffin, given the latter input, answered "What color?" with a previously learned object label in over 50 training sessions on color; only then did he begin to provide a color label on some trials. Similarly, while learning an object label—*cup*—for an item whose color he knew, he answered "What toy?" with colors and had difficulty acquiring "cup" (Pepperberg and Wilcox, 2000). Thus even small input differences affect label acquisition in parrots much as they do for young children.

19.2.4. Practice and Monologue Speech

Parallels also exist in the ways that birds and children learn to produce the sounds that make up their vocalizations. Both birds and humans engage various types of practice, including that in private. For now I'll emphasize the various aspects of solitary practice that precede the production of different types of utterances; later, I'll discuss the phonology, that is, how the parrots babble, using the elements of human speech sounds.

All birds that learn their vocalizations practice before achieving adult competence: Even laboratory-raised, isolate oscines being tutored with songs from audiotapes engage in solitary vocal practice (monologue-like routines) before developing adult forms (Hultsch, 1990; Marler and Peters, 1982). These birds, like their wild compatriots, may practice order of notes in songs, order of songs if they have a repertoire, recombine elements from different tutors if given multiple input sources, and practice different songs in different contexts (e.g., under different lighting conditions; Kroodsma, 1988). If raised in the laboratory but not as isolates, they may change the type of song they practice, emphasizing some song types and dropping others after noting how different songs affect various other individuals (Hultsch, 1990; King et al., 1996; Kroodsma and Pickert, 1984; Lemon, 1975; Margoliash et al., 1994; Nelson, 1992; Nordby et al., 2001; Smith et al., 2000). Note that some songbird species have also been documented as producing what appear to be monologues in a social context, in ways similar to that of human children. Juvenile white-crowned sparrows (*Zonotrichia leucophyrs*) and Bewick's wrens (*Thryomanes bewickii*), for example, may produce adult versions of song in the presence of adult conspecifics before adult functions of these songs could reasonably be used (Baptista, 1983; Kroodsma, 1974), much as some children use certain adult speech forms (Fuson, 1979; Kuczaj and Bean, 1982).

Parrots behave similarly in captivity when learning natural vocalizations (Nottebohm, 1970) or mimetic speech (Baldwin, 1914; Pepperberg et al., 1991; Todt, 1975). How parrots might use this behavior in nature is unknown, but given the complexity of their learned vocalizations (May, 2004), their behavior might parallel human children's practice of syntax, semantics, and pragmatics (West and King, 1985), that is, both children's early babbling and their later monologue speech. Such monologue speech, although not essential for human language acquisition, has been observed for most children (Kuczaj, 1983; Nelson, 1989) and has two components: *private speech* produced in solitude, and *social-context speech* produced in the presence of potential receivers but without obvious communicative purpose (e.g., undirected commentary while playing with toys; Fuson, 1979; Kuczaj and Bean, 1982). Interestingly, in our laboratory Alex demonstrated certain parallels with children's practice of both types of monologue speech (Pepperberg, 1999).

Over a designated period, my students and I taped and transcribed evidence (Pepperberg et al., 1991) showing that Alex practiced his labels in private, often (though not always) for several weeks before he uttered them in public. He would generally start with sounds already in his repertoire, then recombine and vary them until he hit upon something that resembled the targeted pattern that he heard during training.[2] He also occasionally reproduced sets of questions and answers, reconstructing and reinventing scenarios not involved in formal training. Monologues included utterances from daily routines (e.g., "you go gym", "want some water") and strings involving often-heard patterns (e.g., "you be good, gonna go eat lunch, I'll be back tomorrow"). Question-answer dialogues (e.g., "snap, snap, snap," "How many?" "Three") also emerged. Such performance may be integral to development and, because it occurs across many species, suggests an evolutionary theory of language play (Kuczaj, 1998).

---

[2] So, for example, when the target was "none", he would practice "nnnn....one" (Pepperberg et al., 1991).

19.2.5. Referential Mapping and Regarding Humans as Sources of Information

As noted above, Alex sometimes produced new potential labels (ones we were not training) by combining parts of existing utterances. Parallels may exist with young children's phonemic (re)-combinations: Children, including those that may have some form of language impairment, are more likely to spontaneously produce utterances that combine existent rather than new phonemes (Baddeley et al., 1998; Leonard et al., 1983; review in Pepperberg, 1999), even if they are trying to match a novel label that contains new phonemes. Alex's spontaneous novel phonemic combinations often occurred socially outside of testing and training (Pepperberg, 1990b), and our juvenile Greys behave similarly (e.g., Neal, 1996). Such utterances thus appear in contexts reminiscent of children's vocal play. These vocalizations were rarely, if ever, used by trainers but resembled both existing labels and separate human vocalizations— for example, "grain" from "grey" (Pepperberg, 1999). After hearing "grain", trainers gave Alex seed (not normally available), talked about and identified "grain" for one another; later we substituted sprouted legumes. Alex received a ring of paper clips for his innovation of "chain", the appropriate fruit for "grape"[3] and wire mesh (later a nutmeg grater) for trimming his beak after he uttered "grate". "Cup" (from "up") was mapped to metal cups and plastic mugs, "copper" (first produced as "cupper") to pennies, and "block" to cubical wooden beads. "Chalk" (from "talk") was mapped to variously colored blackboard chalk; "truck" to toy cars and trucks. Thus, when we *referentially mapped* objects onto his spontaneous utterances, Alex rapidly integrated these labels into his repertoire, using them routinely to identify or request appropriate items. We ignored certain combinations, such as "cane", "shane", and "cheenut"; he later abandoned these utterances (Pepperberg, 1990b).

Such behavior also reflects the parrots' emerging understanding of humans as sources of information. I cannot definitely argue that Alex's (and subsequently that of other parrots) vocal play in our presence as described above was (or is) an intentional behavior to elicit referents, but other data suggest that our parrots do begin to test out the possibility that humans are good information sources for the reference for novel labels and for new uses of familiar labels (i.e., transfer of label use from one situation to another; Pepperberg, 2001). They see humans in this context during training; they then take the situation a step further: In many instances, they not only play with sounds that constitute a known label, but also take a label they have seen used in a very specific context, such as "wool" for a woolen pompon, and, for example, pull at a trainer's sweater while uttering that label. The probability of such action happening by chance is slim; at that stage a bird usually has at least 3 and usually 4 other labels, and has other means of getting a trainer's attention, if that were the only goal. The birds—like children

---

[3] He probably had heard "grape" from his human trainers, but not any of the other mapped utterances.

(Brown, 1973)—seem to be testing the situation; possibly even directing the attention of the trainer in a manner seen in children but not in nonhuman primates (Tomasello, 1997).[4] Can the sweater's material be categorized as "wool"? Can the label "wool" be extended to this new item with a similar texture? Can humans help with these questions? And our responses—of high affect and excitement, which stimulate the birds further—show them the power of their utterances, reinforce their early attempts at label extension and object categorization, and reward their interactive, triadic behavior (Pepperberg, 2001). Even if birds err in initial categorizations or usage, they still get positive reinforcement, in that we provide a correct, new label for something; for example, we tell them an almond isn't a "cork", but suggest the term "cork nut" (Pepperberg, 1999).

Importantly, Alex always combined label pieces in ways suggesting that he abstracted rules for utterances' beginnings and endings. After analyzing over 22000 English vocalizations, we never observed 'backwards' combinations (e.g., "percup" rather than "cupper" (Pepperberg et al., 1991) although our transcriptions are subjective). Such behavior thus implied (but could not prove) that he parsed human sound streams in human-like ways, acoustically represented labels as do humans, had similar phonetic categories (Patterson and Pepperberg, 1994, 1998), and that his behavior is consistent with top-down processing like that of humans (Ladefoged, 1982; Lieberman, 2002). Such behavior is unlikely to have arisen from instruction, suggesting a cognitive architecture analogous to that of humans. Moreover, I next discuss newer data that provides even stronger evidence for phonological parallels with children's behavior (Pepperberg, 2004b, 2006b).

19.2.6. Label Recombination and Phonological Awareness

Of particular interest was a specific recombination that Alex formed in an attempt to produce a novel label, "spool"; the process appeared to involve vocal segmentation and phonological awareness (Pepperberg, 2004b, 2006b). Demonstrating segmentation by a Grey parrot would be an important milestone in comparing animal and human cognitive and communicative abilities. Only limited evidence exists that parrots, or any animal taught a human communication code, can indeed segment the human code, that is, recombine existing labels intentionally either to describe novel situations or, for example, to produce a phrase to request novel items—rather than simply produce several referential labels that, by chance, appropriately apply to the situation (Fouts and Rigby, 1977; Pepperberg, 1999; Savage-Rumbaugh et al., 1993). Such intentional creativity is, in contrast, common in the earliest stages of normal human language acquisition (de Boysson-Bardies, 1999; Green-field, 1991; Marschark et al., 1987; Tomasello, 2003). Another form of segmentation, the intentional recombination of existing phonemes (parts of words) or

---

[4] Remember that Alex questioned trainers directly; such behavior in the juveniles is therefore not unexpected.

their approximations to create or reproduce what is for the subject a novel targeted utterance (Greenfield, 1991; Peperkamp, 2003), has not previously been reported in animals; it is not only considered basic to human language development (Carroll et al., 2003), but also a uniquely human trait.

Such phonetic awareness, which requires understanding that words are made up of a finite number of sounds that can be recombined into an almost infinite number of patterns (limited only by the constraints of a given language)—the parsing of a complex entity into pieces that are then integrated into a new schema that represents the imitated act (Arbib, 2002)—has additionally been considered a trait that is acquired over time. Children, for example, apparently shift from recognizing and producing words holistically (a simple form of imitation; Corballis, 2003; Studdert-Kennedy, 2002) to recognizing words as being constructed via a rule-based phonology sometime around three years of age or later (Carroll et al., 2003; Vihman, 1996), although the exact time-line appears to vary depending on the languages the child is hearing (review in Anthony and Francis, 2005). Furthermore, manipulation of individual parts of words is presumed to require development of an internal representation of phonological structure (Byrne and Liberman, 1999). That is, in order to sound out—i.e., to imitate, rather than mimic—a novel label, the child must segment the stream of sound into discrete elements, recognize a match between those elements and elements (or close approximations) that exist in its own repertoire, and then recombine these elements in an appropriate sequence (see Corballis, 2003; Gathercole and Baddeley, 1990; Treiman, 1995). Moreover, children's ability to focus on the sounds of words and sound elements of words rather than solely on word meaning appears to be assisted by training in sound-letter associations (Anthony and Francis, 2005; Carroll et al., 2003; Mann and Foy, 2003). Most animals, lacking speech, are never exposed to, nor trained nor tested on, such issues of phonological awareness or imitation, nor are they expected to have internal representations of phonemes (Pepperberg, 2006b).[5]

Note that a student and I had already demonstrated that Alex's human utterances were not the result of interference of pure tones that merely sounded like human vowels and consonants, as some researchers had expected (Lieberman, 2000), but rather contained human-like formants (Patterson and Pepperberg, 1994, 1998). Comparisons of Alex's vowel parameters with those of mine (Patterson and Pepperberg, 1994) demonstrated both differences (e.g., absolute values of first formant frequencies) and similarities (e.g., general values of second formant frequencies, separation of vowels into back and front categories with respect to tongue placement) in acoustic properties of avian and human speech. We also found similarities and differences in articulatory mechanisms: Parrots, for example, use their tongues in some but not all ways used by humans to produce vowels. Nevertheless, Alex's sonagrams resemble

---

[5] Nonhuman primates have been trained and tested on their ability to segment human speech sounds (e.g., Newport, Hauser, Spaepen, G., Aslin, R.N., 2004), but not on sound-letter associations or on productive recombination of speech elements.

those of humans. He uses a two-tube system and frequency modulation like humans, but exactly reproduces neither human articulatory motions nor acoustic idiosyncracies; his articulatory/acoustic constructs derive from his anatomy. Alex's consonants also resemble those of humans, which require teeth and lips. Patterson and Pepperberg (1998) found similarities (category distinctions) and differences (predictive power of measures related to F_1 and F_2; coherence of voicing/place subcategories) in Alex's and human speech. For consonants, his F_2 varies somewhat more than ours; he may use his esophagus to produce /p/ and /b/. His stops, however, exhibit voiced/voiceless, labial, alveolar, and velar groupings; thus such distinctions are basic to vertebrates, not mammals. Alex, moreover, is not unique; our conclusions are supported by recent data from researchers who are teaching their Grey parrots to produce Italian words and phrases (Masin et al., 2005).

Alex's acquisition of *spool*, however, did not follow the usual pattern observed during training of earlier labels (Pepperberg, 2006b). During the usual course of training, Alex's labels most often appear initially as rudimentary patterns— first a vocal contour, then with vowels, finally with consonants (Patterson and Pepperberg, 1994, 1998)—although completely-formed new labels sometimes materialize after minimal training and without overt practice (Pepperberg, 1983). In these latter cases (e.g., production of "carrot", or of the novel label "banerry" to refer to an apple), the label generally contained sounds already in the repertoire (e.g., for "carrot", the /k/ from *key*, the remainder from *parrot*; "banerry" was derived from "banana"-"cherry"), that is, were created from phonotactically probable sequences involving beginnings and ends of existent labels (see Storkel, 2001). Because such utterances appeared with immediacy and no overt practice (Pepperberg, 1999), however, neither my students nor I could ever convincingly argue that Alex had deliberately parsed labels in his repertoire to form the novel vocalizations. That is, we could not claim that he acoustically represented labels as do humans with respect to phonetic categories and understood that his labels are made of individual elements that can be recombined in various ways to produce new ones. Possibly this behavior was potentiated by his already being able to manipulate his vocal tract to produce such sounds or, in the case of "banerry", by semantic relations. Even data (Patterson and Pepperberg, 1994, 1998) demonstrating that he (a) recognizes small phonetic differences ("tea" versus "pea") as meaningful, (b) produces initial phonemes differently depending upon subsequent ones (anticipatory co-articulation, e.g., the /k/ in "key" versus that in "cork"), and (c) consistently recombines parts of labels according to their order in existent labels (e.g., combines only beginnings of one label with the ends of others; (Pepperberg et al., 1991) merely suggested but did not prove that he engages in such *top-down* processing (Ladefoged, 1982).

The present data for Alex were obtained after our youngest subject, Arthur, had acquired the label *spool* to refer to a wooden bobbin (Pepperberg, 2006b). Arthur learned the label via standard M/R training (Pepperberg, 1999), and his production followed the customary acquisition pattern, that is, beginning with /u/ ("ooo") and ending with a fully-formed "spool" (Suppl. 1, Figure 19.1,

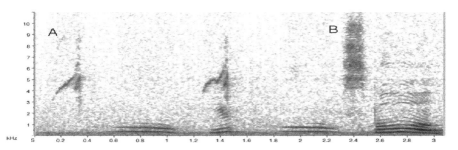

FIGURE 19.1. Sonagram of (A) Arthurs's "spool" (twice); (B) Pepperberg's "spool".

Pepperberg, 2006b). Although Arthur occasionally mis-identified the object as "wool" or "wood" (some of his other labels at the time with "wood" being a correct response for the object's material and "wool" being a reasonable phonological error; Pepperberg and Wilkes, 2004), he did not consistently use such labels during training. Note that Arthur's production contained a whistle-like form for the /sp/ that, as Lieberman (2000) had predicted, did not contain human formants, although the other parts of the label did contain formants, and somewhat resembled mine (Pepperberg, 2006b).

After Arthur's training, Alex began to show interest in the object. When given the item, he would chew it apart or roll it around his play stand. We therefore decided to initiate M/R training on the object for Alex.

Unlike Arthur, and unlike his usual form of acquisition, Alex immediately began using a combination of existing phonemes and labels to identify the object: /s/ (trained independently in conjunction with the Arabic letter, S) and *wool*, to form "s" (pause) "wool" ("s-wool"; Suppl. 2, Figure 19.2, Pepperberg, 2006b).

Note that no labels existed in his repertoire that contained /sp/, nor did he have the label "pool"; he did have labels such as "paper" "peach", "parrot", "pick",

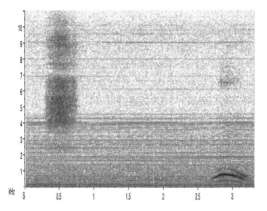

FIGURE 19.2. Sonagram of Alex's "s-wool".

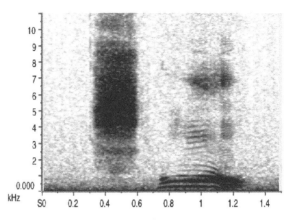

FIGURE 19.3. Sonagram of Alex's "spool"

etc. (Pepperberg, 1999). He retained this "s-wool" formulation for almost a year of M/R training, although normally only about 25 M/R sessions (at most, several weeks of training) are sufficient for learning a new label (Pepperberg, 1999). At the end of this year-long period, he spontaneously produced "spool", perfectly formed, when I rewarded Arthur with the object for producing the label (Suppl. 3, Figure 19.3, Pepperberg, 2006b).

Note, too, that Alex's and Arthur's productions differ significantly in their sonagraphic patterns (Figs. 19.1A, 19.3), so that Alex did not simply learn to mimic Arthur's production. Instead, his vocal pattern more closely resembles mine, complete with appropriate formants (Fig. 19.1B), even though I did less than one-tenth of the M/R training (Pepperberg, 2006b). I had, however, done the majority of training on *wool* almost 20 years earlier (Pepperberg, 1999).

Even the two closest behavior patterns reported above that suggest some form of label parsing (Pepperberg, 1990b; Pepperberg et al., 1991), which both involve forms of sound play, differ significantly from the process described here. In one earlier behavior, for example, Alex produced strings such as *mail chail benail* in private practice before producing the targeted, trained label *nail* (Pepperberg et al. 1991). The *nail* situation differs from the current process in that the combinations of phonemes leading toward *nail* did not seem to be a deliberate attempt to create a new label from specific sound patterns that resembled the target, but, as noted above, rather to be deliberate play within a range of existent patterns in an attempt to hit on a correct pairing that matched some remembered template.[6] In a second earlier behavior described above (Pepperberg, 1990b), Alex babbled derivative utterances such as *grape, grain, chain* in the absence of specific objects. Although these labels could quickly be referentially mapped

---

[6] Such rhyme awareness is considered closely aligned to children's language skills, but is separate from phoneme awareness (see Mann and Foy, 2003; cf. Anthony and Francis, 2005).

onto physical objects, we had no reason to believe that production of such babbled strings was intentional, other than to gain the attention of trainers.

With respect to acquisition of *spool*, another aspect of Alex's behavior addresses the issue of whether he has simply shown a sensitivity to sound similarity (Pepperberg, 2006b). Because of the difficulty of producing /p/ (i.e., the need to use esophageal speech), Alex may have used "s-pause-wool" as a way of initiating the vocalization such that two known utterances provided the overall structure and the pause was a place filler, somewhat like that occasionally used by young children, until he could learn how to insert the /p/ and adapt the vowel. Specifically, Peters (2001) suggests that children use certain sounds as fillers (a "holding tank") to preserve the number of syllables or the prosodic rhythm of the target vocalization until the standard form is learned (note also Leonard, 2001). Even though Alex used a pause, rather than another phoneme, his behaviour suggests (but, of course, does not prove), that he had an awareness of the need for something additional and somewhat different to complete the vocalization. Simply omitting or closing the gap—and responding on the basis of sound similarity—would have produced /swUl/ ("swull"), not /swul/ ("swooool").

The current data, when taken in combination with previous evidence, suggests that at least one parrot understands, much like a child, that sounds such as "car" and "pet" can be recombined for use in identifying a totally distinct object— *carpet*—whose label has no referential correlation to the original utterances. That is, Alex seemed to attempt to form the closest match based on onset + nucleus + rhyme (Storkel, 2002). Arguably, the data presented here could be considered stronger if Alex had had the label *pool* in his repertoire and had initially produced "s-pool". I believe, however, that his production of "s-wool" is actually more important, because he took the closest sounds in his repertoire, rather than exact matches, to form the initial attempts at a novel vocalization. For children, manipulation of individual parts of a word implies the existence of internal representations of words as divisible units. I suggest that Alex's training on both referential labeling and sound-letter association has engendered comparable phonological awareness (Pepperberg, 2006b).

19.2.7. Other Combinatorial Behavior

Some parallels may exist between birds and humans (as well as with nonhuman primates) in terms of *developmental stages* in communicative competence (Pepperberg and Shive, 2001). Such findings were quite unexpected in terms of what had been known and assumed in the literature, as a review of such material makes clear.

In very young children, development of early combinations, both of physical objects (e.g., spoon-into-cup) and phonological/grammatical elements (e.g., "more + X") are temporally related (Greenfield et al., 1972). Greenfield (1991) posited that control of such parallel development initially resides in a single neural structure (roughly Broca's area) that differentiates as a child matures. After reviewing comparable data on combinatorial behavior, both physical and grammatical, on nonhuman primates that had received training in a human-based code (e.g., Greenfield and Savage-Rumbaugh, 1991), and also detailed research on neural substrates (cited from Deacon, 1992), Greenfield (1991) also proposed that a homologous structure to that in humans was responsible for the initial, similar—if more limited—development in nonhuman primates, and that the responsible brain structure predated the evolutionary divergence of apes and hominids. In order to estimate when in evolution the responsible brain structure might have emerged, she and colleagues also studied *Cebus* monkeys (Johnson-Pynn et al., 1999). Experiments on these animals showed that they could be *trained* to combine objects in hierarchical order (behavior that spontaneously emerges in chimpanzees and children); research on their natural vocal and physical behavior provided evidence for some combinatorial processes but ones more limited than those of chimpanzees in both modalities. Add to that information some well-known proposals (e.g., Hewes, 1973) that spoken language derived from gestural forms without major neural restructuring (see below for a detailed discussion of this point), and one might conclude that parallel development of communicative/physical combinatorial acts controlled by a purported single neural center is not unique to humans, but possibly is unique to primate evolutionary lines.

Such a primate-centered thesis was abetted by the fact that few investigations of spontaneous object manipulation at the time included birds (but see Huber et al., 1997), and none compared avian vocal and physical hierarchical combinatorial abilities or discussed their co-occurrence. A developmental study on one of my Grey parrots, Griffin, however, documented behavior similar to that of primates. Our project began after we observed spontaneous physical two-object combinatory activity by Griffin at the time he was routinely combining two human vocal labels. As noted above, my parrots are comparable to very young children with respect to the earliest processes of label acquisition; they move through analogous initial stages of sound and label production and combination (Patterson and Pepperberg, 1998; Pepperberg, 1983; Pepperberg and Wilcox, 2000; Pepperberg et al., 1991). Thus, whatever neural structures are involved, the simplest (two-item) parallel physical and vocal combinatory behavior was clearly not limited to primates. Moreover, a review arguing that certain avian and mammalian brain structures are homologous rather than analogous (Medina and Reiner, 2000; see also Jarvis et al., 2005) suggested the possibility that brain areas responsible for combinatory actions might be even older than the primate line. Thus we began a formal study involving larger numbers of objects and labels.

Griffin showed comparable limited, parallel combinatorial development of three-item and three-label combinations (Pepperberg and Shive, 2001). Percentages of physical and vocal combinations were roughly equal; despite months of training, vocal three-label combinations emerged only when he more frequently initiated three-objects combinations (within about 10 days); vocal combinations were generally not those trained; and physical combinations were performed with his beak, not feet. (Remember, for birds, a beak plays a major role in object manipulation; it is the avian equivalent of forelimbs.) Moreover, unlike Johnson-Pynn et al.'s (1999) *Cebus*, Griffin was not trained on physical tasks and we limited training on three-label combinations (to *2,5-corner wood/paper*) to see if spontaneous manipulative behavior developed in parallel with vocal complexity. Of note was that our data (Pepperberg and Shive, 2001) showed that a trained phrase was only one of Griffin's 14 recorded three-label utterances once he began producing these longer phrases.

Although Griffin's behavior—or that of our most advanced subject, Alex (e.g., Pepperberg, 1999)—is fully equivalent neither to human language nor 2-3 yr old humans' combinatory actions, we suggest that our Greys' behavior patterns match some of nonhuman primates, that parallel combinatory development is not limited to primates, and that a particular mammalian brain structure is not uniquely responsible for such behavior (Pepperberg and Shive, 2001). Responsible substrates are likely analogous, if not homologous, arising independently under similar evolutionary pressures (see Jarvis et al., 2005; Medina and Reiner, 2000), and searches for and arguments concerning responsible substrates and common behavior should not be restricted to primates.

19.2.8. Summary of Parallels between Parrot and Child Behavior

In sum, Grey parrots have demonstrated several behavior patterns once thought to be the exclusive domain of primates and, in many cases, humans. Clearly, humans evolved from the *Homo* line, parrots did not, and thus one can argue for only a parallel evolution of avian vocal behavior. But it is this parallel evolution that I believe holds some extremely important clues for understanding the evolution of human communication. To understand these clues, we need now to look at passerine birds—the suboscines that do not learn their song, the oscines that do, and a few intriguing birds classified as suboscines but that do appear to learn. We also must revisit those mirror neurons (MNs) that I mentioned briefly above.

19.3. Birds and Mirror Neurons, and Gestural Theories

As mentioned above, gestural (or motor) theories of language evolution have been proposed by researchers trying to explain how vocal communication evolved in the primate line (Hewes, 1973), and a similar proposal exists for birds (Williams and Nottebohm, 1985). The idea of a gestural origin for language has been around for quite some time; Fogassi and Ferrari (2004) and Vauclair (2004) present cogent review articles. Briefly, Hewes (1973) was one of the earliest (although not the first; see Condillac, 1746) to suggest that gestural communication—initially, voluntary use of various manual signals—arose fairly early in the hominid line and that only later was it subsumed by a vocal communication system. In this view, manual gestures became associated with non-speech movements of parts of the body used for cries and calls, sucking and feeding; these non-speech movements were precursors of what were, when adapted for communicative intent, then termed *articulatory gestures* (e.g., reviewed in Fogassi and Ferrari, 2004; Studdert-Kennedy, 2005)—the *hidden* constrictions and releases of different parts of the vocal tract. Part of what was missing in all these accounts, at least until recently, was just how the brain transferred voluntary control from manual to vocal gestures. One idea, refined by Corballis (1989, 1991, 2003), was that the left hemisphere took over control of manual communicative gestures that were voluntary (e.g., pointing actions), and that this laterality (and presumably the voluntary nature of the behavior) was preserved when facial motions connected with manual gestures. But that hypothesis did not explain another part of the motor theory, which involves the idea that an individual understands vocal communication by representing the speech that is heard as motor articulatory behavior (note Liberman and Mattingly, 1985; Vihman, 1993); such representation would be assisted if, for example, your articulatory system responded to my voice as if you were talking. But because some MNs are involved in exactly that kind of parity (e.g., Arbib, 2005), the discovery of the MN system tied up many confusing loose ends. Too, because MNs have an inhibitory component, allowing you not to repeat my utterance if you so chose (Baldissera et al., 2001), they do not preclude voluntary choice. The specific connection to language is that MNs are found in Broca's area in humans—one of the 'language centers'—and in the Broca's homologue in monkeys, an area designated as F5; the monkey's system reacts to grasping and related actions (e.g., Fadiga et al., 1995). According to a hypothesis presented by Rizzolatti and Arbib (1998), the development of vocal from manual communication involves the evolution of Broca's area from the F5: the mirror system is likely the neural "missing link" between the communication abilities of our nonhuman ancestors and modern human language. Specifically, instead of a major evolutionary brain reorganization to go from the proposed voluntary control of manual to articulatory gestures in the hominid line—that is, adding voluntary control to vocalizations—all that needed to be posited was a shift in (or evolution of) the existent MN system (see Arbib, 2005). For birds, a similar evolutionary scenario could be proposed, including lateralization (Williams and Nottebohm, 1985), concerning all but the manual gestures (remember, the beak is the avian equivalent of forelimbs; moreover, motor control of the beak resides in areas separate from, but near to, the neural song system; Wild et al., 1985); note, too, that use of the tongue/beak system could easily be adapted from feeding to singing (Homberger, 1986), and that many songbirds use their beaks and tongues in specific patterns for building nests, suggesting that ordering of these gestures is part of their biology.

   But we still have to understand how to get from voluntary control of vocalizations to learning the vocalizations, in both humans and birds (Pepperberg, in prep). Even if the MN system is involved in voluntary control of communication, stating that a vocal behavior is under voluntary control does not necessarily imply that it is learned; what can be learned is merely the context of use rather than the form of production, such as the alarm calls of the vervet monkey (Cheney and Seyfarth, 1990) or chicken (Evans and Marler, 1992). Thus we need to understand the connections among learning, voluntary control, and MNs, which takes us to another aspect of the MN system: its involvement in imitation. Imitation is, of course, a form of learning... and one that is involved in certain aspects of language and song acquisition. Initially, researchers proposed that the MN system enabled its owner to recognize an action through resonance and, because such recognition is one of the first steps in being able to imitate the actions, these researchers also suggested that MNs were the basis for imitation (reviews in Fogassi and Ferrari, 2004; Vauclair, 2004); that is, upon seeing a novel action (whether manual or vocal), individuals somehow know how to configure their own body parts so as to replicate (even if in rough form at first) the action, and this 'knowledge' resides in the MN system. But monkeys, in which MNs were first discovered, don't imitate (Visalberghi and Fragaszy, 1990, 2002). In fact, data showed that MNs in monkeys respond only when the observed action is already in their repertoire, not when they observe a novel action (Chaminade et al., 2001; Rizzolatti et al., 2001). What human MNs seem to do, however, is to recognize a novel behavior as a combination of novel actions that can be *approximated* by variants of actions already in the repertoire (see Arbib, 2005), thus assisting in the imitation of the behavior. But what does this mean for the evolution of imitation and thus learning?

The key seems to be that various levels of imitation exist, and, I propose, so do various types of MNs that relate to these various levels of imitation (Pepperberg, 2005a,b),[7] both for different species and along the evolutionary pathway. Without going into the detail that has been and is being presented elsewhere (Pepperberg, 2005a,b, in prep), let me review some literature and then propose a possible model. Let's first accept that, as is implied by others (e.g., Arbib, 2005), some intermediate form of MN system existed in our human ancestors, somewhat between that of present humans and nonhuman primates, that enabled imitative learning of a simple vocal system. Let me also argue that, given that avian brain structures are now thought to be derived from the same pallial structures as the brains of mammals, and that many birds (particularly parrots) are thus thought to have large cortical-like structures (Jarvis et al., 2005), it does not seem unreasonable to propose that some form of MN system is likely also to exist in birds that learn their vocalizations (the oscines). Where such a system exists, of course is problematic, as one cannot argue for direct correlations to Broca's area in birds as one can for F5 in monkeys. Possibly the bits of brain corresponding to specific mammalian language-articulatory gesture centers are apportioned across several centers in the avian brain (Reiner, pers.

---

[7] Note that Fogassi and Ferrari (2004) suggest how the MNS might have evolved from monkeys to humans and thus also argue for various forms of MNs relating to various forms of imitation. I did not have access to their material when I wrote the original version of what is in this chapter, in Fall, 2002, after attending a conference on mirror neuron studies.

comm., April, 2005). Nevertheless, the parallels between avian and human vocal learning would lead us to believe in the existence of an avian MN system that responds in ways similar to that of primates.

Now, remember the bit of information at the beginning of this chapter mentioning differences in brains of birds that do and don't learn their songs. The former, the oscines and the parrots, are the ones whose brains have been shown to have striking similarities to those of humans, which I am assuming includes some kind of MN system that approaches that of humans. The latter, the subsocines, birds like flycatchers, appear to lack any vocal learning center, although they are still likely to engage in some level of learning; that is, they learn, from interactions, how the context in which a song is produced affects its meaning (Smith and Smith, 1992, 1996; see also Leger, 2005), and, of course, they have brain nuclei that control the physical production of song (Kroodsma and Konishi, 1991). Might subosines then have some monkey-like form of MN system? If, as has been argued (Smith, 1997), communication involves parity for both sender and receiver, and a MN system is what allows a brain to process this parity (e.g., Arbib, 2005), some form of MN system is likely. Crucial to my model, however, are two subosines, one of which is the three-wattled bellbird (*Procnias tricarunculata*), that do not quite fit into the current picture of oscine versus subosine classification. Supposedly, the three-wattled bellbird *is* a subosine, but even in the 1970s, Snow (1973) suggested that this bird, a close relative of flycatchers, learned its songs, and more recent reports (Kroodsma, 2005) provide some evidence that males have dialects, can be bilingual with respect to these dialects (at least for several years), and that a related bellbird, the bare-throated bellbird (*P. nudicollis*), can learn the songs of other species. Although the critical experiments have not been performed (raising a baby bellbird in social isolation, or removing its cochlea, as was done with phoebes (Kroodsma and Konishi, 1991), or even collection of DNA samples to determine if the different dialects come from different species),[8] these facts along with the knowledge that some bellbirds don't begin to sound like (or even look like) adults until they are four or five years old (Kroodsma, 2005) suggest something radically different from what is expected of a subosine. Even oscines that are open-ended learners usually have a recognizable song in their first year as an adult. And, although bellbirds supposedly don't change their overall dialects in adulthood, the birds seem to shift frequency over the years;[9] the suggestion is that the older males shift, forcing the younger ones to shift as well

---

[8] Note that these experiments are critical in the sense that they would confirm what has already been demonstrated. Even a single bellbird that has learned the vocalizations of another species provides fairly strong evidence that learning occurs in the species, but many researchers would want these experiments carried out because the notion of learning by a bird that is supposedly a subosine and incapable of such behavior is almost heretical.

[9] Other features of the song have also changed over the years (Kroodsma, pers. comm., September 2005), but the change in frequency has been emphasized because it is the most obvious (Kroodsma, 2005).

or lose status (and possibly mating chances) within the group (Kroodsma, 2005). Their learning seems to be more oscine-like, except for the extraordinarily long juvenile stage and the fact that they are classified as suboscines. Do they have specific areas in the brain devoted to song learning like oscines? No one yet knows. Is their prolonged babbling stage a consequence of a brain that is "differently" equipped for learning? If so, might they have a primitive MN system that is slow to mature, slow to take it beyond the babbling stage?

I'm going to suggest that we look to the behavior—and the brain—of the bellbirds as a model for what kind of communication existed for the early hominids, that is, as a model for the kind of MN system that existed in the species (or multiple species) that likely bridged the gap between *Homo sapiens* and our nonhuman primate ancestors. Such a model should help us to determine what is innate and what is learned—and the likelihood of there being a continuum, rather than a sharp break, between innate and learned. Might the same evolutionary pressures that led from the innate, relatively simple song of the true suboscines to the fairly simple but slowly learned song of the bellbird to the amazing complexity of a bird such as the brown thrasher's hundreds of songs similarly have been exerted on the nonhuman-to-hominid line? Could these evolutionary pressures have been exerted on a MN system, such that the complexity of the MN system and the complexity of the behavior involved evolve in parallel, synergistically supporting the next evolutionary stage? The existence of articulatory gestures grounded in feeding behavior and contact calls/cries that can be co-opted for other uses is not likely limited to primates; possibly a MN system could conceivably shift in the same manner in birds as in primates. And, although I've switched from parrots to songbirds, what is relevant for the latter is relevant for the former, given that both parrot and songbird brains evolved from the same brain areas (Farries, 2001, 2004).

I admit that I have not included all the necessary, detailed arguments to support my proposal in this chapter (for many details, see Pepperberg, in prep), but the bare bones presented here should at least provide food for thought. At the very least, I hope the material will engender detailed experimentation.

19.4. Overall Discussion

In sum, whether avian and human abilities evolved convergently—whether similar adaptive responses independently evolved in association with similar environmental pressures—is unclear, but a common core of skills likely underlies complex cognitive and communicative behavior across species, even if specific skills manifest differently. We thus should examine many species for information on evolutionary pressures that helped shape existent systems (Pepperberg, 1999, 2004a, in prep). Such pressures were exerted not only on primates; hence the existence of analogous avian complex communication systems and their bases in what likely are homologous neural architectures. Although we no longer have access to the precursor neuroanatomy that gave rise to current human language abilities, the parallels between the acquisition, development, and use of current human communication and some avian systems (for details, see Neapolitan and Pepperberg, 1988; Pepperberg, in prep, Pepperberg and Schinke-Llano, 1991) suggest that parallels likely existed in their evolutionary history. Possibly species such as the bellbird could be a model for the missing human precursor. If the overall goal of research is to increase our knowledge concerning the evolution and development of linguistic communication, the specific manner of approach is less important than an openness to develop numerous theories and the appropriate design of experiments to test these various theories

Acknowledgements. Preparation of this manuscript was supported by donors to *The Alex Foundation*, with special thanks to The Pearl Family Foundation, Dr. Janice Boyd, and Team Alex. Sonograms were prepared by Drs. Donald Kroodsma and Diana Reiss.

References

Anthony, J.L., Francis, D.J.: Development of phonological awareness. Curr. Dir. Psychol. Sci. 14 (2005) 255–259

Arbib, M.A.: The mirror system, imitation, and the evolution of language. In: Dautenhahn, K., Nehaniv, C.L. (eds.): Imitation in Animals and Artifacts. MIT Press, Cambridge, MA (2002) 229–279

Arbib, M.A.: From monkey-like action recognition to human language: An evolutionary framework for neurolinguistics. Behav. Brain Sci. 28 (2005) 105–167

Baddeley, A., Gathercole, S., Papagno, C.: The phonological loop as a language learning device. Psych. Rev. 105 (1998) 158–173

Baldissera, F., Cavallari, P., Craighero, L., Fadiga, L.: Modulation of spinal excitability during observation of hand actions in humans. Eur. J. Neurosci. 13 (2001) 190–194

Baldwin, J.M.: Deferred imitation in West African Grey parrots. IXth Int'l Cong. Zool., (1914) 536

Baptista, L.F.: Song learning. In: Brush, A.H., Clark, G.A. Jr. (eds.): Perspectives in Ornithology. Cambridge University Press, Cambridge UK (1983) 500–506

Bickerton, D.: Symbol and structure: A comprehensive framework for language evolution. In: Christiansen, M.H., Kirby, S. (eds.): Language Evolution. Oxford University Press, Oxford, UK (2003) 77–93

Brown, R.: A First Language: the Early Stages. Harvard University Press, Cambridge, MA (1973)

Byrne, B., Liberman, A.M.: Meaninglessness, productivity and reading: Some observations about the relation between the alphabet and speech. In: Oakhill, J., Beard, R. (eds.): Reading Development and the Teaching of Reading. Blackwell, Oxford, UK (1999) 157–174

Carr, C.E., Soares, D.: Evolutionary convergence and shared computational principles in the auditory system. Brain Behav. Evol. 59 (2002) 294–311

Carroll, J.M., Snowling, M.J., Hulme, C., Stevenson, J.: The development of phonological awareness in preschool children. Dev. Psychol. 39 (2003) 913–923

Chaminade, T., Meary, D., Orliaguet, J-P., Decety, J.: Is perceptual anticipation a motor simulation? A PET study. Brain Imag. 12 (2001) 3669–3674

Cheney, D.L., Seyfarth, R.M.: How Monkeys See the World. University of Chicago Press, Chicago (1990)

Colunga, E., Smith, L.B.: *Learning what is a word*. Paper presented at the 25th Annual Boston University Conference on Language Development, November (2000)

Condillac, E.B. de: Essai sur l'origine des connaissances humaines, ouvage ou l'on réduit à un seul principe tout ce concerne l'entendenment (1746). In *Oeuvres Philosophiquede Condillac*, Paris: George Leroy (1947)

Corballis, M.C.: Laterality and human evolution. Psych. Rev. 96 (1989) 492–505

Corballis, M.C.: The Lopsided Ape: Evolution of the Generative mind. Oxford University Press, Oxford, UK (1991)

Corballis, M.C.: From mouth to hand: Gesture, speech, and the evolution of right-handedness. Behav. Brain Sci. 26 (2003) 199–260

Cowie, F.: What's Within: Nativism Reconsidered. Oxford University Press, Oxford (1999)

Crain, S., Pietroski, P.: Nature, nurture, and universal grammar. Linguist. Philos. 24 (2001) 139–186

Dave, A.S., Margoliash, D.: Song replay during sleep and computational rules for senso-rimotor vocal learning. Science 290 (2000) 812–816

Deacon, T.W.: Brain-language coevolution. In: Hawkins, J.A., Gell-Mann, M. (eds.): The Evolution of Human Languages, Vol. 10. Addison-Wesley, Redwood City, CA (1992) 49–83

Deacon, T.W.: The Symbolic Species: Co-Evolution of Language and the Brain. Norton, New York (1997)

Deacon, T.W.: Evolutionary perspectives on language and brain plasticity. J. Commun. Disord. 33 (2000) 273–291

de Boysson-Bardies, B.: How Language Comes to Children. MIT Press, Cambridge, MA (1999)

DeCasper, A.J., Spence, M.J.: Prenatal maternal speech influences newborn's perception of speech sounds. Infant Behav. Devel. 9 (1986) 133–150

De Kort, S.R., ten Cate, C.: Response to interspecific vocalizations is affected by degree of phylogenetic relatedness in *Streptopelia* doves. Anim. Behav. 61 (2001) 239–247

Dent, M.L., Brittan-Powell, E.F., Dooling, R.J., Pierce, A.: Perception of synthetic /ba/-/wa/ speech continuum by budgerigars (*Melopsittacus undulatus*). J. Acoust. Soc. Am. 102, (1997) 1891–1897

de Villiers, P.A., de Villiers J.G.: Early Language. Harvard University Press, Cambridge, MA (1979)

Dunbar, R.I.M.: Language, music, and laughter in evolutionary perspective. In: Oller, D.K., Griebel, U. (eds.): Evolution of Communication Systems: A Comparative Approach. MIT Press, Cambridge, MA (2004) 257–273

Evans, C.S., Marler, P.: Female appearance as a factor in the responsiveness of male chickens during anti-predator behaviour and courtship. Anim. Behav. 43 (1992) 137–145

Fadiga, L., Craighero, L.: New insights on sensorimotor integration: From hand action to speech perception. Brain Cognition 53 (2003) 514–524

Fadiga, L., Fogassi, L., Pavesi, G., Rizzolatti, G.: Motor facilitation during action obser-vation: a magnetic simulation study. J. Neurophysiol. 73 (1995) 2608–2611

Farries, M.A.: The oscine song system considered in the context of the avian brain: Lessons learned from comparative neurobiology. Brain Behav. Evol. 58 (2001) 80–100

Farries, M.A.: The avian song system in comparative perspective. Ann. N.Y. Acad. Sci. 1016 (2004) 61–76

Fernandez, J.W.: Bwiti: An Ethnography of the Religious Imagination in Africa. Princeton University Press, Princeton (1982)

Fogassi, L., Ferrari, P.F.: Mirror neurons, gestures, and language evolution. Interact. Stud. 5 (2004) 345–363

Fogassi, L., Gallese, V.: The Neural Correlates of Action Understanding in Non-Human Primates. In: Stamenov, M.I., Gallese, V. (eds.): Mirror Neurons and the Evolution of Brain and Language, John Benjamins, Philadelphia, PA (2002) 21–43

Fouts, R., Rigby, R.: Man-chimpanzee communication. In: Sebeok, T. (ed.): How Animals Communicate. Indiana University Press, Bloomington, IN (1977) 1034–1054

Fuson, K.C.: The development of self regulating aspects of speech: A review. In: Zivin, G. (ed.): Development of Self Regulation through Private Speech. Wiley, New York (1979) 135–217

Gardner, R.A., Gardner, B.T.: Comparative psychology and language acquisition. Ann. N.Y. Acad. Sci. 309 (1978) 37–76

Gathercole, S.E., Baddeley, A.D.: The role of phonological memory in vocabulary acquisition: A study of young children learning new names. Brit. J. Psychol. 81 (1990) 439–454

Gnam, R.: Preliminary results on the breeding biology of Bahama amazon. Parrot Let. 1 (1988) 23–26

Gottfried, G.M., Tonks, J.M.: Specifying the relation between novel and known: Input affects the acquisition of novel color terms. Child Devel. 67 (1996) 850–866

Gottlieb, G.: Development of species identification in ducklings: IX. The necessity of experiencing normal variations in embryonic auditory stimulation. Dev. Psychobiol. 15 (1982) 507–517

Greenfield, P.: Language, tools and brain: The ontogeny and phylogeny of hierarchically organized sequential behavior. Behav. Brain Sci. 14 (1991) 531–595

Greenfield, P.M., Nelson, K., Salzman, E.: The development of rulebound strategies for manipulating seriated nesting cups: A parallel between action and grammar. Cog. Psychol. 3 (1972) 291–310

Greenfield, P.M., Savage-Rumbaugh, E.S.: Imitation, grammatical development, and the invention of protogrammar by an ape. In: Krasnegor, N.A., Rumbaugh, D.M., Schiefelbusch, R.L., Studdert-Kennedy, M. (eds.): Biological and Behavioral Determinants of Language Development. Erlbaum, Hillsdale, NJ (1991) 235–258

Hauser, M.D., Chomsky, N., Fitch, W.T.: The faculty of language: What is it, who has it, and how did it evolve? Science 298 (2002) 1569–1579

Hewes, G.W.: Primate communication and the gestural origin of language. Cur. Anthropol. 33 (1973) 65–84

Hockett, C.: Animal "languages" and human language. Hum. Biol. 31 (1959) 32–39

Hollich, G.J., Hirsh-Pasek, K., Golinkoff, R.M.: Breaking the language barrier: an emergentist coalition model for the origins of word learning. SRCD Monog. 262 (2000) 1–138

Homberger, D.G.: The Lingual Apparatus of the African Grey Parrot, Psittacus erithacus Linne (Aves: Psittacidae) Description and Theoretical Mechanical Analysis. Ornithological Monographs, No. 39. The American Ornithologists' Union, Washington, DC (1986)

Huber, L., Voelkl, B., Rechberger, S.: New methods of analysing the copying fidelity of socially learning animals. Paper presented at the XXVth Int'l Etholog. Cong., Vienna, August (1997)

Hultsch, H.: Recombination of acquired songs as a correlate of package formation. In: Elsner, N., Roth, G. (eds.): Brain-Perception-Cognition. Thieme Verlag, Stuttgart (1990) 433

Hurford, J.R., Studdert-Kennedy, M., Knight, C. (eds.): Approaches to the Evolution of Language. Cambridge University Press, Cambridge, UK (1998)

Jarvis, E.D., Güntürkün, O., Bruce, L., Csillag, A., Karten, H., Kuenzel, W., Medina, L.,Paxinos, G., Perkel, D.J., Shimizu, T., Striedter, G., Wild, J.M., Ball, G.F., Dugas-Ford, J., Durand, S.E., Hough, G.E., Husband, S., Kubikova, L., Lee, D.W., Mello, C.V., Powers, A., Siang, C., Smulders, T.V., Wada, K., White, S.A., Yamamoto, K., Yu, J., Reiner, A., Butler, A.B. (2005). Avian brains and a new understanding of vertebrate evolution. Nature Rev. Neurosci. 6 (2005) 151–159

Jarvis, E.D., Mello, C.V.: Molecular mapping of brain areas involved in parrot vocal communication. J. Comp. Neurol. 419 (2000) 1–31

Johnson Pynn, J., Fragaszy, D.M., Hirsh, E.M., Brakke, K.E., Greenfield P.M.: Strategies used to combine seriated cups by chimpanzees (*Pan troglodytes*), bonobos (*Pan paniscus*), and capuchins (*Cebus apella*). J. Comp. Psychol. 113 (1999)137–48

King, A.S., Freeberg, T.M., West, M.J.: Social experience affects the process and outcome of vocal ontogeny in two populations of cowbirds (*Molothrus ater*). J. Comp. Psychol. 110 (1996) 276–285

Kroodsma, D.E.: Song learning, dialects, and dispersal in the Bewick's wren. Z. Tierpsychol. 35 (1974) 352–380

Kroodsma, D.E.: Song types and their use: Developmental flexibility of the male blue-winged warbler. Ethology 79 (1988) 235–247

Kroodsma, D.E.: The Singing Life of Birds. Houghton-Mifflin, Boston, New York (2005)

Kroodsma, D.E., Konishi, M.: A suboscine bird (Eastern phoebe, *Sayornis phoebe*) develops normal song without auditory feedback. Anim. Behav. 42 (1991) 477–487

Kroodsma, D.E., Pickert, R.: Sensitive phases for song learning: Effects of social inter-action and individual variation. Anim. Behav. 32 (1984) 389–394

Kuczaj, S.A., Bean. A.: The development of non communicative speech systems. In: Kuczaj, S.A. (ed.): Language Development: Language, Thought, and Culture. Erlbaum, Hillsdale, NJ (1982) 279–300

Kuczaj, S.A.: Crib Speech and Language Play. Springer Verlag, New York (1983)

Kuczaj, S.A.: Is an evolutionary theory of language play possible? Cah. Psychol. Cogn. 17 (1998) 135–154

Kuhl, P.K.: Discrimination of speech by nonhuman animals: Basic auditory sensitivies conducive to the perception of speech-sound categories. J. Acoust. Soc. Am. 70 (1981) 340–349

Ladefoged, P.: A Course in Phonetics. Harcourt Brace Jovanovitch, San Diego, CA (1982)

Leger, D.W.: First documentation of combinatorial song syntax in a suboscine passerine species. Condor 107 (2005) 765–774

Lemon, R.E.: How birds develop song dialects. Condor 77 (1975) 385–406

Leonard, L.B.: Fillers across languages and language abilities. J. Child Lang. 28 (2001) 257–261

Leonard, L., Chapman, K., Rowan, L., Weiss, A. Three hypotheses concerning young children's imitations of lexical items. Dev. Psychol. 19 (1983) 591–601

Levinson, S.T.: The social behavior of the White-fronted Amazon (*Amazona albifrons*). In: Pasquier, R.F. (ed.): Conservation of New World Parrots. ICBP Technical Publication No. 1, Washington, DC (1980) 403–417

Liberman, A., Mattingly, I.: The motor theory of speech perception revisited. Cognition 21 (1985) 1–36

Lieberman, P.: Preadaptation, natural selection, and function. Lang. Commun. 11 (1991) 63–65

Lieberman, P.: Human Language and Our Reptilian Brain. Harvard, Cambridge, MA (2000)

Lieberman, P.: On the nature and evolution of the neural bases of human language. Yearb. Phys. Anthropol. 45 (2002) 36–62

Liittschwager, J.C., Markman, E.M.: *Mutual exclusivity as a default assumption in second label learning*. Paper presented at the biennial convention, SRCD, Seattle, April (1991)

Liittschwager, J.C., Markman, E.M.: Sixteen- and 24-month olds' use of mutual exclusivity as a default assumption in second-label learning. Dev. Psychol. 30 (1994) 955–968

Liska, J.: Bee dances, bird songs, monkey calls, and cetacean sonar: Is speech unique? Western J. Comm. 57 (1993) 1–26

Locke, J.L.: A theory of neurolinguistic development. Brain Lang. 58 (1997) 265–326.

Macnamara, J.: Names for Things: A Study of Human Learning. MIT Press, Cambridge, MA (1982)

MacNeilage, P.F., Davis, B.L.: The Evolution of Language. In: Buss, D.M. (ed.): The Handbook of Evolutionary Psychology. John Wiley & Sons, New York (2005) 698–723

Mann, V.A., Foy, J.G.: Phonological awareness, speech development, and letter knowledge in preschool children. Ann. Dyslexia 53 (2003) 149–173

Margoliash, D.: Offline learning and the role of autogenous speech: New suggestions from birdsong research. Speech Commun. 41 (2003) 165–178

Margoliash, D., Staicer, C.A., Inoue, S.A.: Stereotyped and plastic song in adult indigo buntings, *Passerina cyanea*. Anim. Behav. 42 (1994) 367–388

Markman, E.M.: Constraints children place on word meaning. Cog. Sci. 14 (1990) 57–77

Markman, E.M., Wachtel, G.F.: Children's use of mutual exclusivity to constrain the meanings of words. Cog. Psychol. 20 (1988) 121–157

Marler, P., Peters, S.: Subsong and plastic song: their role in the vocal learning process. In: Kroodsma, D.E., Miller, E.H. (eds.): Acoustic Communication in Birds, Vol. 2: Song Learning and its Consequences. Academic, New York (1982) 25–50

Marschark, M., Everhart, V.S., Martin, J., West, S.A.: Identifying linguistic creativity in deaf and hearing children. Metaphor Symb. Act. 2 (1987) 281–306

Masin, S., Lenti Boero, D., Massa, R,, Bottoni, L. *Acoustic characteristics of vowel-like sounds of an African Grey parrot (Psittacus erithacus)*. Poster presented at the Avian Brain Conference, XXIXth Int'l Etholog. Cong., August (2005)

May, D.: Unpublished PhD Thesis, University of Arizona, 2004

Medina, L., Reiner, A.: Do birds possess homologues of mammalian primary visual, somatosensory and motor cortices? TiNS 23 (2000) 1–12

Merriman, W.E.: The mutual exclusivity bias in children's word learning: A reply to Woodward and Markman. Dev. Rev. 11 (1991) 164–191

Neal, K.B.: The development of a vocalization in an African Grey parrot (*Psittacus erithacus*). Unpublished senior thesis, University of Arizona, Tucson (1996)

Neapolitan, D.M., Pepperberg, I.M., Schinke Llano, L.: An avian model for studies on second language acquisition. Stud. Second Lang. Acq. 10 (1988) 1–11

Nelson, D.E.: Song overproduction and selective attrition lead to song sharing in the field sparrow. Behav. Ecol. Sociobiol. 30 (1992) 415–424

Nelson, K.: Monologues in the crib. In: Nelson, K. (ed.): Narratives from the Crib. Harvard University Press, Cambridge, MA (1989) 1–23

Nordby, J.C., Campbell, S.E., Beecher, M.D.: Late song learning in song sparrows. Anim. Behav. 61 (2001) 835–846

Nottebohm, F.: Ontogeny of bird song. Science 167 (1970) 950–956

Nottebohm, F.: Brain pathways for vocal learning in birds: a review of the first ten years. Progr. Psychobiol. Physiolog. Psychol. 9 (1980) 85–124

Oller, D.K.: Underpinnings for a theory of communicative evolution. In: Oller, D.K., Griebel, U. (eds.): Evolution of Communication Systems: A Comparative Approach. MIT Press, Cambridge, MA (2004) 49–65

Oller, D.K, Griebel, U. (eds.): Evolution of Communication Systems: A Comparative Approach. MIT Press, Cambridge, MA (2004)

Patterson, D.K., Pepperberg, I.M.: A comparative study of human and parrot phonation: I. Acoustic and articulatory correlates of vowels. J. Acoust. Soc. Am. 96 (1994) 634–648

Patterson, D.K. and Pepperberg, I.M.: A comparative study of human and Grey parrot phonation: Acoustic and articulatory correlates of stop consonants. J. Acoust. Soc. Am. 103, (1998) 2197–2213

Peperkamp, S.: Phonological acquisition: Recent attainments and new challenges. Lang. Speech 46 (2003) 87–113

Pepperberg, I.M.: Functional vocalizations by an African Grey parrot (*Psittacus erithacus*). Z. Tierpsychol. 55 (1981) 139–160

Pepperberg, I.M.: Cognition in the African Grey parrot: Preliminary evidence for auditory/vocal comprehension of the class concept. Anim. Learn. Behav. 11 (1983) 179–185

Pepperberg, I.M.: Social modeling theory: A possible framework for avian vocal learning. Auk 102 (1985) 854–864

Pepperberg, I.M.: An interactive modeling technique for acquisition of communication skills: separation of 'labeling' and 'requesting' in a psittacine subject. Appl. Psycholing. 9 (1988) 59–76

Pepperberg, I.M.: Cognition in an African Grey parrot (*Psittacus erithacus*): Further evidence for comprehension of categories and labels. J. Comp. Psychol. 104 (1990a) 42–51

Pepperberg, I.M.: Referential mapping: attaching functional significance to the innovative utterances of an African Grey parrot (*Psittacus erithacus*). Appl. Psycholing. 11 (1990b) 23–44

Pepperberg, I.M.: Proficient performance of a conjunctive, recursive task by an African Grey parrot (*Psittacus erithacus*). J. Comp. Psychol. 106 (1992) 295–305

Pepperberg, I.M.: Evidence for numerical competence in an African Grey parrot (*Psittacus erithacus*). J. Comp. Psychol. 108 (1994) 36–44

Pepperberg, I.M.: Categorical class formation by an African Grey parrot (*Psittacus erithacus*). In Zentall, T.R., Smeets, P.R. (eds.): Stimulus Class Formation in Humans and Animals, Elsevier, Amsterdam (1996) 71–90

Pepperberg, I.M.: Social influences on the acquisition of human-based codes in parrots and nonhuman primates. In: Snowdon, C.T., Hausberger, M. (eds.): Social Influences on Vocal Development. Cambridge University Press, Cambridge, UK (1997) 157–177

Pepperberg, I.M.: The Alex Studies: Cognitive and Communicative Abilities of Grey Parrots. Harvard University Press, Cambridge, MA (1999)

Pepperberg, I.M.: Lessons from cognitive ethology: Animal models for ethological computing. Proceedings of the First Conference on Epigenetic Robotics. In: Balkenius, C., Zlatev, J., Kozima, H., Dautenhahn, K., Breazeal, C. (eds.): Lund University Cognitive Science Series No. 85, Lund, Sweden, http://www.lucs.lu.se/Abstracts/LUCS_Studies/LUCS85.html (2001)

Pepperberg, I.M.: Evolution of communication from an avian perspective. In: Oller, D.K., Griebel, U. (eds.): Evolution of Communication Systems: A Comparative Approach. MIT Press, Cambridge, MA (2004a) 171–192

Pepperberg, I.M.: Grey parrots do not always 'parrot': Phonological awareness and the creation of new labels from existing vocalizations. Keynote address, Third International Symposium on Imitation in Animals and Artifacts, Hatfield UK, April (2004b)

Pepperberg, I.M. An avian perspective on language evolution: implications of simultaneous development of vocal and physical object combinations by a Grey parrot (*Psittacus erithacus*). In: Tallerman, M. (ed.): Language Origins: Perspectives on Evolution. Oxford University Press, Oxford, UK (2005a) 239–261

Pepperberg, I.M. Insights into vocal imitation in African Grey parrots (*Psittacus erithacus*). In: Hurley, S., Chater, N. (eds.): Perspectives on Imtation: From Neuroscience to Social Science. MIT Press, Cambridge, MA (2005b) 243–262

Pepperberg, I.M.: Grey Parrot (*Psittacus erithacus*) numerical abilities: addition and further experiments on a zero-like concept. J. Comp. Psychol. 120 (2006a) 1–11

Pepperberg, I.M.: Grey parrots do not always parrot: roles of imitation and phonological awareness in the creation of new labels from existing vocalizations. Lang. Sci. 28 (2006b)

Pepperberg, I.M.: Ordinality and inferential abilities of a Grey Parrot (*Psittacus erithacus*). J. Comp. Psychol. 120 (2006c) 205–216

Pepperberg, I.M.: Learning to Communicate. Harvard University Press, Cambridge, MA (in prep)

Pepperberg, I.M., Gordon, J.D.: Numerical comprehension by a Grey Parrot (*Psittacus erithacus*), including a zero-like concept. J. Comp. Psychol. 119 (2005) 197–209

Pepperberg, I.M., Schinke Llano, L. Language acquisition and use in a bilingual environment: A framework for studying birdsong in zones of sympatry. Ethology 89 (1991) 1–28

Pepperberg, I.M., Sherman, D.V.: A two-trainer modeling system to engender social skills in children with disabilities. Int'l J. Comp. Psychol. 15 (2002) 138–153

Pepperberg, I.M., Shive, H.A.: Simultaneous development of vocal and physical object combinations by a Grey Parrot (*Psittacus erithacus*): Bottle caps, lids, and labels. J. Comp. Psychol. 115 (2001) 376–384

Pepperberg, I.M. Wilcox, S.E.: Evidence for a form of mutual exclusivity during label acquisition by Grey parrots (*Psittacus erithacus*)? J. Comp. Psychol. 114 (2000) 219–231

Pepperberg, I.M., Wilkes, S.R.: Lack of referential vocal learning from LCD video by Grey Parrots (*Psittacus erithacus*). Interaction Stud. 5 (2004) 75–97

Pepperberg, I.M., Brese, K.J., Harris, B.J.: Solitary sound play during acquisition of English vocalizations by an African Grey parrot (*Psittacus erithacus*): Possible parallels with children's monologue speech. Appl. Psycholing. 12 (1991) 151–177

Pepperberg, I.M., Gardiner, L.I., Luttrell, L.J.: Limited contextual vocal learning in the Grey parrot (*Psittacus erithacus*): the effect of co-viewers on videotaped instruction. J. Comp. Psychol. 113 (1999) 158–172

Pepperberg, I.M., Naughton, J.R., Banta, P.A.: Allospecific vocal learning by Grey parrots (*Psittacus erithacus*): A failure of videotaped instruction under certain conditions. Behav. Process. 42 (1998) 139–158

Pepperberg, I.M., Sandefer, R.M., Noel, D., Ellsworth, C.P.: Vocal learning in the Grey Parrot (*Psittacus erithacus*): Effect of species identity and number of trainers. J. Comp. Psychol. 114 (2000) 371–380

Pepperberg, I.M., Brezinsky, M.V.: Relational learning by an African Grey parrot (*Psittacus erithacus*): Discriminations based on relative size. J. Comp. Psychol. 105 (1991) 286–294

Perkel, D.J.: Origin of the anterior forebrain pathway. Ann. N.Y. Acad. Sci. 1016 (2004) 736–748

Peters, A.N.: Filler syllables: What is their status in emerging grammar? J. Child Lang. 28 (2001) 229–242

Premack D.: On the abstractness of human concepts: Why is would be difficult to talk to a pigeon. In: Hulse, S.H., Fowler, H., Honig, W.K. (eds.): Cognitive Processes in Animal Behavior. Erlbaum, Hillsdale, NJ (1978) 421–451

Querleu, D., Renard, X., Versyp. F.: Les perceptions auditives du foetus humain. Méd. Hygiène 39 (1981) 2101–2110

Reiner, A.: pers. comm., April 19, 2005

Richman, B.: On the evolution of speech: Singing as the middle term. Cur. Anthropol. 34 (1993) 721–722

Rizzolatti, G., Arbib, M.: Language within our grasp. TiNS 21 (1998) 188–194

Rizzolatti, G., Fogassi, L., Gallese, V.: Neurophysiological mechanisms underlying the understanding and imitation of actions. Nature Rev. Neurol. 2 (2001) 661–670

Sakai, K.L.: Language acquisition and brain development. Science 310 (2005) 815–819.

Savage-Rumbaugh, E.S., Murphy, J., Sevcik, R.A., Brakke, K.E., Williams, S.L., Rumbaugh, D.M. Language comprehension in ape and child. SRCD Monog. 233 (1993) 1–258

Smith, W.J.: The behavior of communicating, after twenty years. In: Owings, D.H., Beecher, M.D., Thompson, N.S. (eds.): Perspectives in Ethology, Vol. 12, Plenum Press, New York (1997) 7–53

Smith, W.J., Smith, A.M.: Behavioral information provided by two song forms of the Eastern kingbird, *T. tyrannus*. Behaviour 120 (1992) 90–102

Smith, W.J., Smith, A.M.: Information about behavior provided by Louisiana waterthrush, *Seurus motacilla* (Parulinae), songs. Anim. Behav. 51 (1996) 785–799

Smith, V.A., King, A.P., West, M.J.: A role of her own: Female cowbirds, *Molothrus ater*, influence the development and outcome of song learning. Anim. Behav. 60 (2000) 599–609

Snow, D.W.: Distribution, ecology, and evolution of the bellbirds (*Procnias*, Cotingidae). Bull. Brit. Mus. Nat. Hist. 25 (1973) 369–391

Stevens, K.N.: Acoustic Phonetics. MIT Press, Cambridge, MA (1998)

Storkel, H.: Learning new words II: Phonotactic probability in verb learning. J. Speech Lang. Hearing Res. 44 (2001) 1312–1323

Storkel, H.: Restructuring of similarity neighbourhoods in the developing mental lexicon. J. Child Lang. 29 (2002) 251–274

Striedter, G.: The vocal control pathways in budgerigars differ from those in songbirds. J. Comp. Neurol. 343 (1994) 35–56

Studdert-Kennedy, M.: Mirror neurons, vocal imitation, and the evolution of particulate speech. In: Stamenov, M.I., Gallese, V. (eds.): Mirror Neurons and The Evolution of

Brain and Language. John Benjamins, Amsterdam, Netherlands (2002) 207–227

Studdert-Kennedy, M.: How did language go discrete? In: Tallerman, M. (ed.): Language Origins. Oxford, UK: Oxford University Press (2005) 48–67

Todt, D.: Spontaneous recombinations of vocal patterns in parrots. Naturwissen. 62 (1975) 399–400

Tomasello, M.: Constructing a Language. Harvard University Press, Cambridge, MA (2003)

Tomasello, M., Call, J.: Primate Cognition. Oxford University Press, Oxford, UK (1997).

Treiman, R.: Errors in short-term memory for speech: A developmental study. J. Expt'l Psychol.: Learn. Mem. Cogn. 21 (1995) 1197–1208

Vauclair, J.: Lateralization of communicative signals in nonhuman primates and the hypothesis of the gestural origin of language. Interact. Stud. 5 (2004) 365–386

Vihman, M.M.: Vocal motor schemes, variation, and the production-perception link. J. Phonet. 21 (1993) 163–169

Vihman, M.M.: Phonological Development: The Origins of Language in the Child. Blackwell, Malden, MA (1996)

Visalberghi, E., Fragaszy, D.M.: Do monkeys ape? In: Parker, S.T., Gibson, K.R. (eds.): "Language" and Intelligence in Monkeys and Apes. Cambridge University Press, Cambridge, UK (1990) 247–273

Visalberghi, E., Fragaszy, D.M.: "Do monkeys ape?" Ten years after. In: Dautenhahn, K., Nehaniv, C.L. (eds.): Imitation in Animals and Artifacts. MIT Press, Cambridge, MA (2002) 471–499

West, M.J., King, A.P.: Social guidance of vocal learning by female cowbirds: validating its functional significance. Z. Tierpsychol. 70 (1985) 225–235

Wild, J.M. Arends, J.J.A., Zeigler, H.P.: Telencephalic connections of the trigeminal system in the pigeon (*Columba livia*): a trigeminal sensorimotor circuit. J. Comp. Neurol. 234 (1985) 441–464

Williams, H.: Multiple representations and auditory-motor interactions in the avian song system. Ann. N. Y. Acad. Sci. 563 (1989) 148–164

Williams, H., Nottebohm, F.: Auditory responses in avian vocal motor neurons: A motor theory for song perception in birds. Science 229 (1985) 279–282

Wray, A., Gonzalez, R.C. (eds.): The Transition to Language. Oxford University Press, Oxford, UK (2002)

Wright, T.F.: Regional dialects in the contact calls of a parrot. Proc. Roy. Soc. Lon. B 263 (1996) 867–872

Wright, T.F., Dorin, M.: Pair duets in the yellow-naped Amazon (Psittaciformes: *Amazona auropalliata*): Responses to playbacks of different dialects. Ethology 107 (2001) 111–124

Yamashita, C.: Field observations and comments on the Indigo macaw (*Anodorhynchus leari*), a highly endangered species from northeastern Brazil. Wilson Bull. 99 (1987) 280–282

20
A Possible Role for Selective Masking in the Evolution of Complex, Learned Communication Systems

Graham R. S. Ritchie and Simon Kirby

20.1. Introduction

The human capacity for language is one of our most distinctive characteristics. While communication systems abound in the natural world, human language distinguishes itself in terms of its communicative power, flexibility and complexity. One of the most unusual features of human language, when compared to the communication systems of other species, is the degree to which it involves learning. Just how much of language is innate and how much is learned is an ongoing controversy, but it is undeniable that the specific details of any particular language must be learned anew every generation. We do, of course, bring a great deal of innate resources to bear on our language learning process, and the results these innate biases have on the development of languages may explain a great deal about the structure of the languages we see today. But still every child in every new generation must go through a lengthy process of language acquisition if they are to become normal language users.

Once in place, this inter-generational process of language acquisition and use, or *iterated learning* (Kirby and Hurford, 2002) can give rise to cultural evolution, which studies have shown may explain many prominent phenomena of human language, including the emergence of dialects and, by extension, separate languages (Livingstone, 2002), regular and irregular word forms (Kirby, 2001) and compositional syntax, (e.g. Brighton, 2002).

The emergence of learning can therefore be seen as a major transition in the evolution of language and we would like to better understand the evolutionary pressures and factors which caused this transition. A natural point at which to start such an investigation is to look at the communication systems of other animals to see if there are any parallels which might illuminate the relevant ecological factors. Much comparative research has been carried out with the non-human primates, but despite some fascinating results, it seems that their natural communication systems are very different to language, including the fact that learning plays a much less prominent role. In fact it appears that vocal learning systems have evolved in only three groups of mammals: humans, bats and cetaceans, and three groups of birds: songbirds, hummingbirds, and parrots (Jarvis, 2004) (though there is initial evidence of vocal learning in other species, including some elephants and seals.)

In this paper we concentrate on bird song as it has many striking parallels with language, particularly the way in which it is learned, as Darwin noted in *The Descent of Man*:

The sounds uttered by birds offer in several respects the nearest analogy to language, for all the members of the same species utter the same instinctive cries expressive of their emotions; and all the kinds that sing, exert their power instinctively; but the actual song, and even the call notes, are learnt from their parents or foster-parents. (Darwin, 1879)

Since Darwin's day much research has been carried out into bird song and, to take Tinbergen's four perspectives of ethology, we now know a great deal about its mechanism, development, function and evolution. However, despite much research, in general the evolutionary function of song learning remains unclear (Slater, 2003). The parallels between bird song and human language have also been further elaborated as modern techniques have allowed us to establish the neural mechanisms of both song and language (Doupe and Kuhl, 1999).

In this chapter we present a computational model of the evolutionary history of the Bengalese finch which demonstrates how an increase in song complexity (in some sense) and increased influence from early learning could evolve spontaneously as a result of domestication acting to mask the natural selection pressure on song behaviour. We argue that this may provide an insight into how increased reliance on vocal learning could evolve in other communication systems, including human language.

20.2. A Case Study

Recent studies by Kazuo Okanoya of a domesticated species of finch, the Bengalese finch (*Lonchura striata* var. *domestica*), and its feral ancestor, the white-backed munia (*Lonchura striata*) which still lives in the wild throughout Asia, provide an interesting case study of the interaction of learning and evolution in bird song. The Bengalese finch sings a song with complex[1] finite state syntax which is heavily influenced by early auditory experience. Surprisingly, the munia sings a strikingly simpler, more linear song which is less influenced by early

---

[1] Okanoya defines song complexity as the song linearity, i.e. the total number of unique song notes divided by the number of unique note-to-note transitions. We are not entirely satisfied with this as a measure of complexity, as discussed in section 4.2, but we use the term in Okanoya's sense throughout this paper.

learning. In other words, in a relatively short period of domestication, there have been radical changes in song behaviour. This has happened even though the domesticated species has been artificially bred for plumage rather than song.

Okanoya (2004) has identified the neural mechanism underlying this difference in behaviour and has shown that while Bengalese chicks are able to learn the songs of munia tutors, munia chicks are not able to learn all aspects of the more complex Bengalese song, demonstrating that there is a physiological, as opposed to cultural, basis for this difference.

20.2.1. Okanoya's Hypothesis

As experiments have shown that both female munias and female Bengalese finches prefer the more complex song, Okanoya (2002) argues that it is sexual selection which drove the increase in complexity. He argues that domestication freed the Bengalese finch from the pressure of predation and other pressures associated with life in the wild which had previously held song complexity in check. According to Okanoya, the more complex song of the Bengalese finch may therefore be seen as an honest signal of fitness (Zahavi, 1975); a fitter bird can afford a more complex song. Sasahara and Ikegami (2004) show with a computational model of the finch data that, under some assumptions about female preferences and perception, song complexity could indeed increase as a result of sexual selection.

20.2.2. Deacon's Hypothesis

Reviewing the same data, Deacon (p.c.) agrees that domestication masked the natural selection pressure keeping the munia's song simple, but argues that the increase in complexity happened *without* direct selection on the trait. Essentially, he posits that domestication shielded the trait from selection which allowed random genetic drift to erode innate song biases in the munia. This allows previously minor influences, such as mnemonic biases and early auditory experience, to have more of an effect on song structure and learning, which results in the various neural modules involved in song production and learning becoming increasingly *de-differentiated*. Deacon goes on to argue that this process of masking and subsequent de-differentiation is a potential explanation for the evolution of complex functional synergies such as the neural mechanisms for song production now present in the Bengalese finch, and, he argues, in the human capacity for language.

The concept of selective masking and its effect on the evolution of language are explored in more detail in (Deacon, 2003). Wiles et al. (2005) demonstrate with a computational model how this kind of masking (and later unmasking) effect may have played a role in the functional integration of groups of genes underlying complex traits, e.g. the mammalian colour vision system.

20.3. A Computational Model

In order to evaluate Deacon's hypothesis and to try to establish if such behaviour could evolve spontaneously as a result of domestication, we have developed a computational model of the finch data. The model is designed to be reasonably biologically plausible, and also general enough that it could be extended to other species. The model works with an evolving population of agents, or birds, and the main stages in the simulation are listed here, details of each stage are given below:

Birth The bird's song filter is built up from its genotype as described in section 3.1.

Development The bird is exposed to *e* songs from its environment, and, using its filter, selects *t* songs from which it will learn (its training set) as described in section 3.2. The bird then uses the learning algorithm described in section 3.3 to learn the song grammar it will use to sing throughout its life.

Adulthood The bird is tested in *f* fitness trials, as described in section 3.4 to see how many times, using its filter, is can correctly recognise a bird of its own species and how many times it is correctly recognised by a bird of its own species. These values are added to give a bird's fitness score.

Reproduction Parents of the same species are selected probabilistically according to their fitness score and their chromosomes are crossed over using one-point crossover with probability pCO (set to 0.7 for all results provided here), to give a new child. Individual genes are mutated with probability $pMut$ (set to 0.05 for all results provided here, lower values have qualitatively similar results but the simulations take considerably longer to show the same effects). The mutation operator used is the 'Reflect' operator described in (Bullock, 1999).

Death Each bird in the population is sampled *s* times and the resulting songs are stored for the next generation to learn from. All of the current birds in the population are removed and their children become the new population.

20.3.1. The Song Filter

A bird is modelled as having a genetically coded note[2] transition matrix, which specifies a transition probability from each note to every other note used in the simulation, including a probability for the first and final notes. The total number of notes is a parameter of the simulation, *numNotes*, but in all results provided here this was set to 8, i.e. the notes from *a* alphabetically through to *h*, this value was chosen as it appears to be the number of unique notes identifiable

---

[2] It should be noted that while we use the term 'note' throughout this chapter, this is not intended to refer to a particular acoustic note, rather we simply use it to denote an atomic song element that can be reliably differentiated from other elements which appear in the song.

in both the Bengalese finch and munia's songs (Okanoya, 2002). The matrix is coded for by a chromosome which has one real valued locus for each entry in the matrix which can vary between 0 and 1. This chromosome will thus have $(numNotes + 1)^2$ loci, the 1 is added to include the transitions at the beginning and end of the song. To construct a matrix from the chromosome we take each $numNotes + 1$ loci of the chromosome in turn, and normalise the values to give a probability distribution for each row of the matrix (i.e. we sum the values of each $numNotes + 1$ loci and then divide each value by this sum to give a probability). An example matrix, and the chromosome that codes for it is shown in table 20.1.

The transition matrix serves one main purpose; to establish the probability that a given song is one of the bird's own species song. This is done by establishing the average probability of each note transition in the song, as shown in equation 1 which defines the preference a given matrix m_x has for a particular song s_y, in this equation n is the number of note transitions in s_y and $m_x(t_i)$ is the entry in m_x for the ith transition of s_y. For example the preference value the matrix in table 1 gives for the song cab, which has the transitions S-c, c-a, a-b and b-E, is $\frac{0.62+0.82+0.89+0.45}{4} = 0.695$, while the preference for the song acb is 0.043. Note that we always include the transition to the first note and from the last note, so the empty song '' has a single transition S-E, for which this matrix has a preference value of 0.15.

$$preference(m_x, s_y) = \frac{\sum_{i=1}^{n} m_x(t_i)}{n} \tag{1}$$

The matrix can be thought of as a song 'filter'. A song with a high probability will be more likely to pass though the filter than one with a lower probability, in our example cab would be much more likely to pass through the filter than acb. If the matrix has a single high probability transition for each note this can be thought of as a strong filter, as it will only accept songs which contain these

TABLE 20.1. An example note transition matrix and the chromosome that codes for it. $numNotes$ here is set to 3 meaning that the chromosome will have $(3+1)^2 = 16$ loci (we used 8 notes in our simulations, and hence chromosomes with 81 loci). The S indicates the start of the song, and the E indicates the end of the song.

	a	b	c	E
S	0.08	0.15	0.62	0.15
a	0.11	0.89	0.00	0.00
b	0.05	0.10	0.40	0.45
c	0.82	0.09	0.00	0.09

0.1	0.2	0.8	0.2	0.1	0.8	0.0	0.0	0.1	0.2	0.8	0.9	0.9	0.1	0.0	0.1

transitions. If the matrix has even probabilities for each transition it is considered a weak filter as it accepts all songs equally.

We can measure the strength of the filter explicitly by calculating the entropy for each transition distribution (i.e. each row in the matrix), using Shannon (1948)'s measure. This will result in a value which ranges from 0 to $log_2(nValues)$, where $nValues$ is the number of probabilities in row r_x (i.e. the number of columns in the matrix). We then normalise this value into the range 0 to 1, as shown in in equation 2, which defines the normalised entropy for a given row r_x, in this equation p_i is the probability of the ith transition in r_x. The overall strength of a matrix m_x is then calculated as the average entropy of each row r in the matrix, as shown in equation 3. A filter strength of 0 means that the filter will only accept one song while a strength of 1 means that the filter will accept all songs equally. As an example, the matrix in table 20.1 has a strength value of 0.56.

$$entropy(r_x) = \frac{-\sum_{i=1}^{nValues} p_i \; log \; (p_i)}{log(nValues)} \tag{2}$$

$$strength(m_x) = \frac{\sum_{i=1}^{nRows} entropy(r_i)}{nRows} \tag{3}$$

This filter is intended to model the preferences many songbirds have for their species specific song (Catchpole and Slater, 1995). In the model a bird uses its filter for two purposes:

1. To select its training set (the songs it will later use to learn from) from the songs it is exposed to during infancy.
2. To judge whether another bird is a member of the same species for mating or territorial defense.

In this respect, this model is similar to those used in Lachlan's models of the 'cultural trap' in bird song (Lachlan and Slater, 1999; Lachlan and Feldman, 2003). This seems a reasonably plausible assumption, as it is known that some songbirds do have an innate preference for conspecific song both when learning songs as a nestling and also for later mate selection (Catchpole and Slater, 1995).

20.3.2. Selecting the Training Set

The infant bird is exposed to e environmental songs to select its t training songs from, both e and t are parameters of the simulation, but were set to 50 and 5 respectively for all results provided here. 5 seems a rather low value of t, but the learning algorithm is very computationally intensive and so a low value is used to speed up the simulation. The e environmental songs are randomly selected from the songs sampled from the previous generation, to compose this set each bird is sampled s times, another parameter which is set to 5 here, so for a population size $popSize$ of 100, as used here, this will contain 500 songs.

The infant bird is exposed to each of the e songs in turn and uses its filter to compute the probability it will be accepted. During experimental runs it was determined that checking that the song is accepted once did not impose enough of a pressure for the bird to correctly select conspecific song and so a song is only added if it is accepted by the filter twice successively. If the bird has not picked t songs after being exposed to all e songs, the process is repeated until t songs have been selected. The training songs are then fed into the learning algorithm described below.

20.3.3. Song Learning

Song learning is modelled as minimum description length (MDL) induction of a probabilistic finite state machine (PFSM), closely following the algorithm described in (Teal and Taylor, 2000). Induction of finite-state machines was chosen to model learning as Okanoya (2002) argues that the songs of both munias and Bengalese finches can be usefully described by a finite-state syntax. The algorithm works by firstly establishing the maximal PFSM that explicitly represents each song in the training set, the prefix tree. The algorithm then searches for nodes which can be merged which will reduce the MDL of the overall machine, whilst also ensuring that the PFSM remains deterministic. The MDL measure takes into account the amount of information (measured by the number of bits) required to code for the machine itself, and also to code for each of the training songs in terms of the machine. Essentially the algorithm searches for the most parsimonious machine in terms of the data. This approach allows a bird to generalise from its training set, whilst also always being able to reproduce each of the songs it learned from. The reader is referred to (Teal and Taylor, 2000) for a more detailed description of the algorithm used. The only difference between Teal and Taylor's and our approach is that we also take into account the probability of each note transition, given the probabilities of each transition in the training set.

20.3.4. Calculating a Bird's Fitness

To establish a bird's fitness we want to check both that its filter allows it to correctly identify its own species, and that its song is correctly identified by other birds of its species. This seems a reasonable model of the pressures acting on song in the wild (Catchpole and Slater, 1995).

To calculate an individual bird b_i's fitness we perform f fitness trials, a parameter set to 250 for the results provided here. In each fitness trial we get b_i to produce a song and we then randomly select another member of the population, b_j and check that b_j correctly recognises the song using its filter. We also get b_j to produce a song and check that b_i correctly recognises the song with its filter.

Every correct recognition means that b_i's fitness is incremented by 1. With f set to 250, this means that the maximum fitness achievable is 500, or generally $2f$.

20.3.5. Modelling the Finch Data

This is a fairly general model of bird song, and so we need to set it up to match the data available on the Bengalese finch and the munia as closely as possible. The simulation passes through 3 main phases, each of which runs for 500 generations. The phases are described below.

Phase 1 We know that the white-backed munia has a very stereotyped song and that it seems to only be able to learn songs that match its species-specific song fairly closely (a munia cross-fostered with Bengalese parents is not able to learn all aspects of its tutor's song). In our model this corresponds to the munia having a strong filter. To simulate this state we seed the environmental songs with a single song type, e.g. *abcdef*. We then run the simulation for 500 generations using the fitness function and learning algorithm described above. As the environment songs are entirely identical the songs that any bird will learn from are always the same, and so they will always induce the same PFSM. This is not meant to be biologically plausible, we simply want the population to develop strong filters for a particular simple song type.

Phase 2 At the end of phase 1 we have a population of birds who sing a stereotypical song and produce offspring with a strong genetic bias to learn that song. To test if the filter can indeed help young birds recognise the appropriate song to learn from in the second phase of the run we start introducing random songs into the bird's environment, this is intended to model hetero-specific song in the environment. We model this by replacing 10% of the s sampled songs with randomly generated songs which use the same notes as the current population and which are constrained to within the same length. We realise that hetero-specific songs are unlikely to be truly 'random' in a real environment and so this may be an unrealistic modelling decision, but we simply want to model some degree of noise in the acoustic environment which the population should be able to filter out. This seems reasonable to us as if a population of birds really had a completely reliable set of songs to learn from every generation we would expect them to have lost any bias to conspecific song as this would be unnecessary, every song they heard would be conspecific, but this doesn't match the biological data. An alternative strategy that we have experimented with (but not used here) is to randomly 'mutate' notes from the songs sampled at the end of each generation with some low probability, and tests show that this produces qualitatively similar results to those provided here, but runs take much longer to show the same effects.

Phase 3 We model domestication of the population simply by ceasing to calculate fitness, but we continue to perform the crossover and mutation operations. The seems a reasonable model of domestication, as in captivity the birds no longer have to recognise their own species to successfully mate or defend their territory as the mating is now controlled by humans and they are kept in aviaries. Domestication can thus be seen to *mask* the selection pressure on these functions. We continue to introduce 10% of random songs into the environment each generation, as it seems a reasonable assumption that the birds will still be exposed to hetero-specific song, or at least other extraneous sounds, in captivity. Experimental results of this setup are described in the next section.

20.4. Results

The graphs in figure 20.1 shows several measures taken over the course of each of the three phases described above.

The first graph shows the change in the average population fitness plotted against the change in filter strengths through the three phases. Fitness values are not calculated for the population in phase 3. The filter strength is calculated as described in equation 3.

The second graph shows our various complexity measures plotted against each other over the entire run, the first of these the average grammar encoding length (GEL) of the population's PFSMs, this is a measure of the size, in bits, it would take to encode a PFSM using the measure defined in (Teal and Taylor, 2000). The second measure is the average song linearity of the population's songs (Okanoya's definition of complexity), defined as the number of unique notes in each song divided by the number of unique note to note transitions. The final measure is the average linearity of the population's PFSMs calculated simply as the number of states divided by the number of transitions. A completely linear PFSM would thus have a linearity of 1, while a maximally non-linear PFSM would have a linearity equal to 1 over the number of transitions in the PFSM.

Two example PFSMs taken from the population at the end of phase 2 are shown in figure 20.2, and two PFSMs from the end of phase 3 are shown figure 20.3. The GEL and PFSM linearity values for each machine is also given.

20.4.1. Analysis

The results in the first graph demonstrate that the strong filters built up in phase 1, as shown by the increase in filter strength[3], enable the birds to filter out the hetero-specific songs introduced in phase 2 without any fitness decrease. We see that all 5 measures stay roughly the same throughout this phase, indicating that this is a fairly stable state. When we 'domesticate' the population in phase 3

---

[3] Recall that the strongest filter would give a value of 0, and the weakest 1.

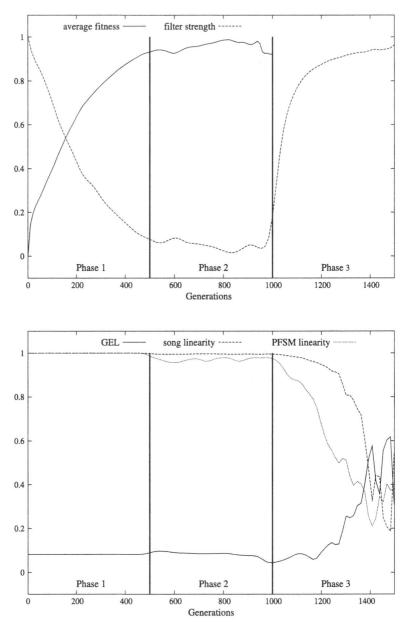

FIGURE 20.1. These results are averages taken over 10 separate runs of the simulation with a different random number generator seed for each run. It should be noted that all these measures have been normalised into the range $0-1$. These graphs therefore only shows the relative change in each of the measures over the course of a run, not the absolute values of each measure. We have also smoothed the lines in the graph to better allow us to see the overall trends. More detailed results are available upon request. (PFSM is a probabilistic finite state machine, and GEL is the grammer encoding length of a PFSM.)

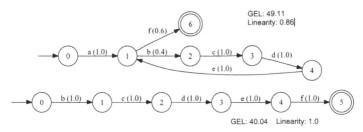

FIGURE 20.2. Two example PFSMs from the population at the end of phase 2.

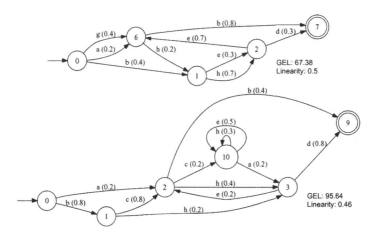

FIGURE 20.3. Two example PFSMs from the population at the end of phase 3.

we see a significant change in its behaviour. Immediately we see that the filters begin to weaken, and we see that the average GEL rises steadily throughout the phase indicating that the population's PFSMs are getting larger and the birds have a more varied song repertoire. At the same time we see both the song, and underlying PFSM linearity drop, indicating that the songs a bird will sing have comparatively more varied note transitions, i.e. a more 'complex' song in Okanoya's sense.

This behaviour seems to be a result of the fact that the strength of the population's filters is no longer being selectively maintained, that is they have been *masked* from selection. This allows mutations to accumulate and for the filters to become steadily weaker. This allows some of the hetero-specific songs to pass though the filter when a bird is selecting its training set, which results in the bird inducing a more varied PFSM. Essentially the domesticated population is able to learn from much more varied sources and so early auditory experience has much more of an effect on adult song behaviour.

These results are comparable to the masking phase described by Wiles et al. (2005). Their model, however, goes further than ours and shows that if the selection pressure were later *un*masked this could result in a selection pressure for any other abilities able to help the organism survive in the new environment (e.g. colour vision). It would be interesting to investigate what might happen to the Bengalese finch's song if its environment changed substantially again, e.g. if a population was released back into the wild.

20.4.2. Song Complexity?

Okanoya (2002) argues that the Bengalese finch has a much more 'complex' song than the munia. As mentioned earlier, his measure of complexity is the song linearity. He finds that the average song linearity of the munia is around 0.8 while the Bengalese finch song has a value of around 0.4. We provide results for this measure over the course of our simulations in the graph above, but on average we also see a higher value, around 0.95, for the ancestral population and a lower value, around 0.6, for the domesticated population at the end of our run.

While this measure seems a reasonably intuitive measure of song complexity (the more varied a song is, the more complex it is), it should be noted that this measure will classify an entirely random song as maximally complex. We do not want to equate randomness with complexity, but we find it hard to define a measure that can differentiate between the two. Any standard measure of the information content of a song will not be able to do so; a random song is maximally informative in information-theoretic terms. However we consider that two measures, the GEL of a bird's PFSM taken together with the linearity of the PFSM provide a reasonable estimate of the complexity of a song. A PFSM with a very small GEL and a low linearity is likely to produce more random songs, as it approaches a one state PFSM with multiple transitions back to the same state. A PFSM with a large GEL, but a very high linearity (as we see in the ancestral population in the model) will produce an entirely linear song. A PFSM with a large GEL and a relatively low linearity will produce songs that we are more happy to refer to as complex, as the GEL indicates that it has many states, and so different notes will be used in different contexts, but each state also has several transitions which means that different transitions can be made from each context. Our results demonstrate that the domesticated population does have a higher GEL and a lower PFSM linearity than the wild population and so we are tentatively happy to agree that domestication has caused an increase in song complexity. However, we are still working on developing a more satisfactory measure of song complexity.

20.4.3. Comparison with the Biological Data

Comparing these results with the data available for the Bengalese finch we find that the model does seem to capture some of the phenomena involved. Okanoya has shown that a munia chick which is not exposed to conspecific song will not sing a normal song, which seems to fit with the model. He has also shown that while Bengalese chicks can readily learn munia songs, munia chicks cannot learn the more complex Bengalese songs. In the model this difference is attributable to their different filters. The difference in the values for the song linearity in the ancestral and domesticated populations also seem to match fairly well.

As it stands though, the model does not explain why the female munia prefers the Bengalese song. We would argue that a bias for complex song may have been latent in the munia, and the fact that the munia females prefer the more complex song does not prove that this was the driving force for the change in song behaviour, although introducing such a preference into the model may help to tease these pressures apart. Okanoya (2004) demonstrates that the NIf region of the Bengalese finch's brain is necessary for it to be able to sing the more complex song; when surgically lesioned a Bengalese finch with previously complex song will sing a simpler, more munia-like song. We would argue that the model remains neutral to this datum, as it is possible that the munia does have this pathway present in its brain but, because it only ever learns a simpler song, does not use it.

20.5. Discussion

Our results demonstrate that, as Deacon initially proposed, an increase in song complexity (in some sense) and increased influence from early learning can arise *without* direct selection on either trait, simply through the process of domestication, but what is the significance of this result for the study of human language? Can studying the evolution of learning and complexity in bird song inform our study of the origins of complex language in our species? We believe that understanding the mechanisms behind the emergence of the Bengalese finch's song, and indeed the evolution of bird song in general, is valuable for evolutionary linguistics in two ways.

Firstly, it has been argued that iterated learning is a key mechanism for the origins of syntax in human language (Kirby and Hurford, 2002). It is striking that human language differs from most other communication systems both in being transmitted through iterated learning and in having complex syntactic structure. We say "most" here but not "all". We appear to be in a very exclusive club with songbirds possibly as another member. Of course, there are important differences between iterated learning in humans and birds. For example, in the former a central constraint on transmitted languages is that they be *expressive*, in that strings must convey complex information. Bird song does not seem to carry 'meaning' in the same way, although a diversity of songs may play a role as a sexual display (Catchpole and Slater, 1995). Nevertheless the co-occurrence of iterated learning and signal complexity in both songbirds and humans combined with the rarity of either anywhere else in nature cannot be ignored.

Secondly, and more specifically, by uncovering the crucial role of selective *masking* in the case of the Bengalese Finch, we provide some support for Deacon's hypothesis and in doing so bring a new mechanism to the table for discussions of the origins of human syntax (though see also the discussion in Deacon (2003)). It is quite possible that we should not be looking for selective advantages of a culturally transmitted syntactic language, but rather asking what selective forces may have been shielded in our recent evolutionary past. The lifting of selection pressure, and the subsequent diversification of behaviour could have been the necessary precursors of a system of iterated learning for language. What remains to be understood is exactly what more is required for any subsequent modification and synergistic reorganisation of the neural mechanisms underlying these new behaviours.

We feel that computational modelling of the vocal behaviour of birds, humans and perhaps of other vocal learning species, may provide valuable insights to this question.

Acknowledgments. We would like to thank Kazuo Okanoya and Terry Deacon for very useful discussion on this work. We would also like to thank the members of the Language Evolution and Computation Research Unit at the University of Edinburgh for helpful comments and feedback. The first author is supported by an EPSRC studentship.

References

Brighton, H. (2002). Compositional syntax from cultural transmission. *Artificial Life*, 8(1):25–54.

Bullock, S. (1999). Are artificial mutation biases unnatural? In Floreano, D., Nicoud, J.-D., and Mondada, F., editors, *Fifth European Conference on Artificial Life (ECAL99)*, pages 64–73. Springer-Verlag.

Catchpole, C. K. and Slater, P. J. B. (1995). *Bird Song: Biological themes and variations*. Cambridge University Press.

Darwin, C. (1879). *The Descent of Man, and Selection in Relation to Sex*. John Murray, London, 2nd edition. Reprinted in 2004 by Penguin.

Deacon, T. (2003). Multilevel selection in a complex adaptive system: the problem of language origins. In Weber, B. and Depew, D., editors, *Evolution and Learning: the Baldwin Effect Reconsidered*, pages 81–106. MIT Press, Cambridge, MA.

Doupe, A. J. and Kuhl, P. K. (1999). Birdsong and human speech: Common themes and mechanisms. *Annual Reviews of Neuroscience*, 22:567–631.

Jarvis, E. D. (2004). Learned birdsong and the neurobiology of human language. *Annals of the New York Academy of Sciences*, 1016:749–777.

Kirby, S. and Hurford, J. R. (2002). The emergence of linguistic structure: An overview of the iterated learning model. In Cangelosi, A. and Parisi, D., editors, *Simulating the Evolution of Language*. Springer Verlag, London.

Kirby, S. (2001). Spontaneous evolution of linguistic structure: an iterated learning model of the emergence of regularity and irregularity. *IEEE Journal of Evolutionary Computation*, 5(2):102–110.

Lachlan, R. F. and Feldman, M. W. (2003). Evolution of cultural communication systems: the coevolution of cultural signals and genes encoding learning preferences. *Journal of Evolutionary Biology*, 16:1084–1095.

Lachlan, R. F. and Slater, P. J. B. (1999). The maintenance of vocal learning by gene-culture interaction: the cultural trap hypothesis. *Proceedings of the Royal Society of London. B*, 266:701–706.

Livingstone, D. (2002). The evolution of dialect diversity. In Cangelosi, A. and Parisi, D., editors, *Simulating the Evolution of Language*, chapter 5, pages 99–118. Springer Verlag, London.

Okanoya, K. (2002). Sexual display as a syntactic vehicle: The evolution of syntax in birdsong and human language through sexual selection. In Wray, A., editor, *The Transition to Language*, chapter 3. Oxford University Press, Oxford.

Okanoya, K. (2004). The bengalese finch: A window on the behavioral neurobiology of birdsong syntax. *Annals of the New York Academy of Sciences*, 1016:724–735.

Sasahara, K. and Ikegami, T. (2004). Song grammars as complex sexual displays. In *Artificial Life 9*.

Shannon, C. E. (1948). A mathematical theory of communication. *Bell Systems Technical Journal*, 27:379–423 and 623–656. Reprinted in "Shannon Collected Papers", ed. Sloane & Wyner, 1993, IEEE Press.

Slater, P. J. B. (2003). Fifty years of bird song research: a case study in animal behaviour. *Animal Behaviour*, 65:633–639.

Teal, T. K. and Taylor, C. E. (2000). Effects of compression on language evolution. *Artificial Life*, 6:129–143.

Wiles, J., Watson, J., Tonkes, B., and Deacon, T. W. (2005). Transient phenomena in learning and evolution: Genetic assimilation and genetic redistribution. *Artificial Life*, (11):177–188.

Zahavi, A. (1975). Mate selection – a selection for a handicap. *Journal of Theoretical Biology*, 53:205–214.

21
The Natural History of Human Language: Bridging the Gaps without Magic

Bjorn Merker and Kazuo Okanoya

21.1. Introduction

Human languages are quintessentially historical phenomena. Every known aspect of linguistic form and content is subject to change in historical time (Lehmann, 1995; Bybee, 2004). Many facts of language, syntactic no less than semantic, find their explanation in the historical processes that generated them. If adpositions were once verbs, then the fact that they tend to occur on the same side of their arguments as do verbs ("cross-category harmony": Hawkins, 1983) is a matter of historical contingency rather than a reflection of inherent structural constraints on human language (Delancey, 1993).

We are beginning to get an inkling of the shaping power of non-genetic cultural mechanisms not only from progress in historical linguistics, but in the outcome of more schematic modelling of such processes by computer simulation of multigeneration populations of learning agents (see Hurford, 2002, for an overview with comparisons and contrasts of the principal approaches). From these it emerges that the process of intergenerational transmission itself, without any natural selection or differential reinforcement of outcomes, can transform an initial state in which nonsense-strings are randomly paired with meanings on an individual basis to a state of shared semantic and syntactic organization exhibiting compositionality, lexical categories, constituent order, frequency-dependent coexistence of regular and irregular forms, and recursion (Batali, 1998, 2002; Kirby, 1998, 2000, 2001, 2002).

The key to this apparent magic is the obligatory dependence of the process of intergenerational transmission on the sparse sampling available to the language learner of the linguistic output of the population of language users. The process through which utterances are filtered though this "learner bottleneck" creates competition among inchoate linguistic forms for access to subsequent generations. In this competition simple statistics of intergenerational transmission lead more general forms to outlast less general ones in the population over time, eventually assuring convergence on a stable and efficient grammar (see Kirby, 2000 for details). That is, an aspect of the so called "poverty of the stimulus" employed in arguments for the necessity of innate syntactic structure (Chomsky, 1980) turns out to be a key factor in the emergence of syntax from syntax-free string labels by learning alone, given sufficiently many generations and without intervention of natural selection or differential reinforcement (Smith, 2003).

Processes such as these must have been operative throughout language history, and this opens new possibilities regarding the reconstruction of language origins. In fact, it may allow us to turn from the so far intractable problem of equipping our forebears with an innate universal grammar by natural selection (Pinker and Bloom, 1990) to an exploration of the biological prerequisites for arriving at the initial conditions necessary for the historical process to begin, and a search for plausible biological sources of the particular traits its agents must possess in order to sustain it. As we shall see, even these issues are far from trivial or unproblematic from a biological point of view. The remainder of this chapter will accordingly be devoted to outlining the obstacle course they place between nature and language, along with a sketch of how one sole species of animal nevertheless managed to wind its way through it to language.

21.2. The Problem of Initial Conditions, or How to Get Language History Started in Nature Rather than in a Computer

Two facets of a structure-generating history of the kind modelled by Kirby and proposed on linguistic grounds by Wray (1998) are already now susceptible to scrutiny from a biological point of view. One is the source of the medium of observable language assumed in these proposals, namely the holistic "strings" destined to act as carriers of meaning in the historical process (Hurford, 2000). The other is the question of how these strings achieve their pairing with meanings. These questions are particularly acute in the initial stage of history, a stage at which learning agents as yet cannot be said to have language. As a starting point for a computer simulation it is an admirably conservative strategy to equip agents with a tendency to produce random strings to stand for meanings they wish to communicate, but such a tendency is hardly a trait we can expect to find in a biological creature as yet lacking language. Whence then the strings and their meanings?

We note first of all that what we are looking for are vocal strings. In principle any expressive modality – manual, postural or vocal – might implement the historical process. However, the strings must be learned from models, and for this the vocal modality has an advantage over others. It allows more complete monitoring (by ear) of self-produced output for purposes of comparison with model patterns than other expressive modalities (Thorpe, 1961, p. 79), and this may account for the prevalence of vocal imitation over other forms in nature (Fitch, 2000). It is, in any case, only in the vocal sphere that nature presents us with robust examples of strings of the requisite kind, and human language, moreover, is expressed vocally in speech. Between these two constraints, no reason remains to go beyond the vocal domain for present purposes.

What constitutes "strings of the requisite kind"? They are sequences of distinct elements drawn from a finite set of such elements – in the computer simulations initially at random – with a string as a whole destined for arbitrary meaning assignment. The longer and more numerous these concatenations of elements are from the outset the richer the potential outcome in the end, other things being equal. They should also combine sequence variation with redundancy in their patterning. Moreover, since the historical process proceeds via changes in the order of sequential grouping of elements in strings, there must be no innate constraints on string structure or use. Given these desiderata, it should be clear that the greater part of animal vocalizations, namely the ubiquitous and robust category of animal calls, is eliminated from consideration as a source of the kind of vocal behavior needed to feed the historical process.

Animal call systems have an innate basis (even when refined and differentiated by learning, as occurs in vervet alarm calls: Seyfarth and Cheney, 1980) and they typically feature a pair-wise and species-specific mapping between call type and its emotional significance or functional reference (Marler et al., 1992; Marler, 2004). Though calls are easily repeated when the evoking mood or situation persists, their form is typically unitary in the sense of consisting of a single ("monosyllabic") sound gesture (Marler, 2004). Even when this is not the case, as in the loud and complex pair-duets of gibbons (whose different call elements make up a larger cycle) the form of these elements as well as their global sequential organization obey species-and-sex-specific innate constraints (Geissmann, 2000). All of these characteristics, well suited to efficient signalling, prevent animal call systems from supplying the raw materials for a learned (initially arbitrary) system of meaning assignments as required by the historical process. We must accordingly look elsewhere for vocal strings of the arbitrary and composite nature we require.

21.3. The Cornucopia of Animal Song

All vocal animals have calls, but some species of animals in addition are equipped with a very different modality of vocal production, which they exercise in addition to and independently of their call system, in some manner reminiscent of the way in which humans exercise vocal language in addition to their nonverbal vocal expressiveness. That modality is animal song, whose structural complexity and special ontogenetic and neurobiological mechanisms have led biologists to distinguish song from calls. The suggestion that animal song somehow might bear on the origin of human language has been made repeatedly, not only by modern students of bird song (Marler, 1970; Nottebohm, 1975; Doupé and

Kuhl, 1999; Okanoya, 2002), but by the Danish linguist Jespersen (1922), and before him by Darwin (1871).

In animal song we find the "strings" of distinct elements that are so conspicuously absent from animal calls, and along with the strings the mechanisms for their learned duplication and inter-generational transmission through vocal learning (Marler, 2000). The song-bouts of many birds and a very few mammals abound in sequence complexity achieved by the patterning of a finite set of song elements or phrases. The sedge warbler, for example, varies the *sequencing* of the members of its stock of some 50 different song elements, producing song patterns which essentially never repeat (Catchpole, 1976). In the case of Bengalese finches the nature of their endlessly varying non-deterministic song sequences has been formally worked out: it conforms to the output of a finite state grammar (Okanoya, 2002), and may even require a context free grammar to be fully described (Okanoya, unpublished observations). In the case of the humpback whale, one of the few mammals with complex learned song, the patterns that result from song learning are also socially shared. Individual males introduce innovations in their song, and the novelty spreads through the group by copying (Payne, 2000; Okanoya, unpublished observations). The resulting repertoire is a socially shared set of complex and syntactically structured vocal strings specific for a given group and time which gradually turns over through innovation.

Even the few examples just given indicate that the specifics of song vary widely from species to species, and this is also true of the extent to which there are innate constraints on the learnability of song patterns (Williams, 2004). This varies widely, but species that copy eclectically from other species, as do for example mocking birds (Baylis, 1982), obviously cannot be constrained by a species-specific template. In the learned and culturally transmitted songstrings of such songbirds and those of the humpback whales as well, we have an existence proof that nature actually produces the kinds of strings that are needed as raw material for the historical process. As such they are in fact ideal, because unlike calls, the patterns of animal song are not used to convey different determinate meanings.[1] Rather, song is a display by which an animal gives proof of its mastery of the act of singing itself, as a means of *impressing* upon potential mates and rivals.

The use of song displays for this purpose is predicated on the general principle that signals will be used to manipulate recipients when the interests of signaller and receiver differ (Enquist et al., 2002; Wachtmeister, 2001). An elaborate display which is costly on account of its loudness, length or complexity may

---

[1] The claim that song is without meaning does not imply that it is without purpose, nor that song characteristics do not convey information. Factors such as proficiency and complexity serve to impress, and different exemplars of song are bound to vary in the extent to which they do so, and thus they do carry information in this sense. But that is something altogether different from the way in which sentence structure is linked to propositional meaning in human language, a feature entirely absent from animal song.

persuade a potential mate to become an actual mate by giving proof of the displaying animal's quality, fitness or command of resources (the so called "handicap principle", Zahavi and Zahavi, 1997). By engaging in an activity that lacks utility in survival terms, the animal demonstrates that it has a corresponding margin in resource terms beyond what is required for simply "getting by". The costlier and the more wasteful the display, the more definitive its demonstration of that margin. In the case of learned song (which is all we are concerned with here) this logic extends to the learning capacity needed to acquire the patterns of the song culture into which the animal is born as well as to the various resources needed to sustain the protracted period of practice needed to achieve proficiency. This includes early nutritional status (Hasselquist et al., 1996; Nowicki et al., 2002; Johnson and Whitney, 2005; Soma et al., 2005) as well as foraging capacity (see Merker, 2005, for further details). All of this is later summed up in a proficient song-bout, and broadcast to potential mates and rivals. Song is thus classifiable alongside the peacocks magnificent tail rather than the peacock's vocal call from a functional point of view. The evolution of such displays is generally attributed to sexual selection (Darwin, 1871), though a number of instances require the more general theory of manipulative signal use already referred to (see Wachtmeister, 2001).

It is the fact that animal song – unlike animal calls – serves purposes other than those of conveying differential meanings that makes its structural richness available as a starting point for the historical process. Its patterns are unencumbered by differential meaning assignments of their own, and can therefore become subject to such assignment through the historical process if, that is, a way can be found for songstrings to enter it as raw materials.

21.4. Vocal Learning: Key to String-Transmission and Beyond

With every word we know how to pronounce and with every song we know how to sing we are reproducing with our voice a pattern of sound originally received through the ear. If this capacity seems unremarkable to us, it is only because we have it. Yet in phylogenetic perspective it is rare. Mammals excel in their capacity to learn, yet *vocal* learning – which is the technical term for the learned duplication of an auditory model by voice – is a rarity among them (see review by Janik and Slater, 1997). No dog has ever been heard to imitate a cat or a crow, and human-reared chimpanzees have failed to acquire spoken words despite heroic efforts to teach them (Kellog and Kellog, 1933; Hayes and Hayes, 1951; see also Snowdon and Elowson, 1992; Janik and Slater, 1997).

There should be nothing surprising about this inability on the part of chimpanzees: the capacity to reproduce by voice a heard pattern of sound has few uses in nature. By far the most common one is song learning, and chimpanzees of course do not sing. Regarding other potential uses, such as the shaping of distinctive individual identifying signals (mother offspring recognition in certain bats; "signature whistles" in dolphins) these tend to be complex sound gestures rather than the concatenated strings with which we are concerned. Even given the completely generalized vocal imitative capacity of a parrot or a mynah bird, we would still have to find a source or motive for concentrating its use to strings of recombinable elements (as featured in the song displays of many bird species). We therefore consider only vocal learning for song in this chapter. Another chapter in this volume (Pepperberg) considers non-song avian communication.

Beginning with the pioneering studies of Thorpe (1961) half a century of intensive study of vocal learning for song in birds has uncovered a wealth of detail regarding its ontogeny, behavioral stages, and neural mechanisms, including intriguing parallels to the "babbling stage" of human language acquisition (Marler, 1970; Doupé and Kuhl, 1999; Goldstein et al., 2003). There is no standard ontogenetic trajectory for a hatchling's path to competence in its song culture that is independent of species, sex, or individual (Devoogd, 2004; Williams, 2004) or of environmental and social context (Freeberg, 2000; King and West, 2002), and the interested reader is referred to the recent summary of the state of the art edited by Ziegler and Marler (2004) for details. Whatever the ontogenetic details, adult competence is acquired through a protracted process stretching over weeks and months to cover a good part of the bird's first year of life. An intricate neural system of "song nuclei" is dedicated to the feats of sensorimotor learning that issue in adult song (see Ziegler and Marler, 2004, for recent reviews). The process is a neurally demanding one: a variable like the average size of the song repertoire is reflected volumetrically in the size of component song nuclei across species (Devoogd et al., 1993).

In fact, there is evidence to suggest that vocal learning for song may drive telencephalization in birds (Iwaniuk et al., 2005; Johnson and Whitney, 2005). A nonsinging bird like the pigeon devotes 38 percent of its total brain volume to telencephalic tissue, which is comparable to that of the rat (Swanson, 1995), while in the zebra finch, a vocal learner, the telencephalon occupies 64 percent of its total brain volume (Johnson and Whitney, 2005). This is impressive, since the comparable figure for humans is 81 percent, again based on Swanson. There are fundamental reasons for believing that vocal learning specifically should act as a powerful promoter of encephalization. Not only are the nuclei of the song system all located in the forebrain, but the fact that they of necessity involve *both* sensory (model acquisition) *and* motor (vocal skill) learning, and that these must be coupled, may play a special role in this regard. In accordance with the analysis of brain expansion in mammals performed by Finlay and Darlington (1995), the expansion of a single telencephalic nucleus or area might be accommodated within the bounds of variability underlying the regression of a given brain compartment on total brain size across species (i.e. by a local expansion). The typical pattern, however, is that the whole brain is expanded in order to enlarge a local compartment. But this means that when there is a need for *conjoint* expansion of both a sensory and a motor area – areas located in very different parts of the telencephalon – this would constitute a particularly powerful pressure for whole-brain expansion (always quantitatively led by the telencephalon), as described by Finlay and Darlington for mammals.

There is no reason to believe that the brains of birds obey a different logic than mammals with regard to encephalization (Emery and Clayton, 2005). Should the suggestion of a relationship between vocal learning and telencephalization in birds be confirmed by further systematic comparative surveys, then it would seem likely that the human capacity for vocal learning – lacking in chimpanzees and accordingly acquired since we shared common ancestry with them – may have played a role in the spectacular trajectory of human encephalization as well (Merker, 2000, p. 321). That such a development should involve higher-order auditory areas in the temporal lobe for storing song memory stands to reason, and it hardly strains credulity to invoke what was to become Broca's area, as well as the basal ganglia and primary motor cortex, for the sequencing, segmentation, and vocal control requirements on the motor side of vocal learning (see Jarvis, 2004; and Okanoya and Merker, this volume).

Encephalization is thus added to a set of potential physical markers for a human turn to song and vocal learning, markers which heretofore have been discussed with almost exclusive reference to speech and language. As pointed out by Sundberg (1987), song is more demanding than speech when quantitatively assessed by measures such as tidal volume, range of subglottal pressure, and associated muscular control of respiration. This means that potential physical correlates of vocal functions, such as the relative size of the thoracic vertebral lumen (MacLarnon and Hewitt, 1999) or the hypoglossal canal (Kay et al., 1998; DeGusta et al., 1999; Jungers et al., 2003) cease to bear on evolutionary adaptations for speech unless the possibility of a prior adaptation for singing has been eliminated (cf. Fitch, 2006). Perhaps an analysis that observes the song/speech distinction, and combines every fossilizing potential marker for vocal behavior, including encephalization, may yet succeed in providing evidence regarding the manner and timing of the evolutionary transition to vocal learning on the part of our ancestors.

Other anatomical correlates of speech often cited in relation to the evolution of language, such as the detailed anatomy of the human vocal tract (Lieberman, 1975), are essentially rendered irrelevant by the presence of vocal learning in humans. As pointed out by Nottebohm (1976), an Amazonian parrot, whose vocal apparatus differs radically from the human in every respect including the physical principle of its phonatory source, is capable of pronouncing human words and phrases with perfect diction. It will do this with such fidelity that it fools the human ear despite the actual acoustic differences between its production and ours that are revealed in the details of a sonagram. It can do so by guiding its vocal practice by auditory monitoring of its own vocal output, so as to shape that output to the human input received through its sense of hearing. Only a vocal learner is capable of such feats.

This is also how we ourselves acquire the ability to pronounce the words of our language. Vocal learning shapes the infant's articulatory output according to the standards of its natal speech community. Not only the basic ability to learn to articulate words in the first place, but the massive imprint of the nuances of dialectal detail on the child's developing speech attests to the acute operation of vocal learning in us no less than in the Amazonian parrot. If as already suggested, we acquired this novelty as an adaptation for song display, it is hardly surprising that every song we have learned how to sing depends upon it as well. It is worth noting, moreover, that outside of song and speech there are few uses for this major piece of neural equipment which is so rare among mammals generally that we are the only primate known to possess it.

Since the historical path to human language requires strings as its input, and the capacity to produce strings of the requisite kind exists in nature in species with learned song, it seems plausible to suggest that we evolved our capacity for vocal learning for the purpose of song, and that vocal learning for song in turn launched us on the historical path to language. To do so, songstrings somehow had to acquire meaning on entry to the historical process, and we turn next to the problem of endowing songstrings with meaning.

21.5. Endowing Songstrings with Meaning Without Meaning to do so

Some songbird repertoires such as those of the already mentioned mockingbird are large, containing hundreds of songtypes characterized by both pattern variety and redundancy (Baylis, 1982). The current record holder is the brown thrasher whose repertoire has been estimated to contain 1800 distinct songtypes (Kroodsma and Parker, 1979). Such large repertoires are built up by ubiquitous copying, re-arrangement, and innovation through processes that presuppose an emancipation of vocal learning from constraints imposed by innate templates. This also appears to be true of the large and group-specific repertoires of humpback whales (Payne, 2000). If a way could be found to differentiate such large string repertoires by behavioral or environmental context, so that certain parts of the repertoire were sung in one context while other parts of it were sung each in their own contexts, we would be well on our way to the kind of semantization of the string repertoire we require. Let us borrow the innovative and socially shared song traditions of humpback whales for a thought experiment regarding a plausible biological setting in which such a process might get under way and sustain itself.

Assume that elaborate learned song of the kind possessed by whales occurred in a group-living mammal which unlike whales did not have a seasonally defined breeding period (even that of humpbacks may not be as sharply defined as once thought: see Clark and Clapham, 2004). As already indicated, let the handicap principle ensure that the string repertoire is large and that song display is lengthy (the longest single humpback songbout so far observed spanned 21 hours of continuous singing; see Payne, 2000). The absence of a well defined breeding season in our hypothetical species would make it advantageous to engage in song display throughout the year, in a variety of places and times and under circumstances featuring a variety of social settings and behaviors. In short, song displays would be spread out over the full range of the group's life circumstances, initially in haphazard fashion. Learners would therefore encounter songstrings in different life contexts, and considering the nature of mammalian learning, it would be difficult to prevent individual learners from associating the songstring with the context in which they experienced it. In fact, strings would not be stored in memory separately from its context, but as part of it. Note that *no observational learning of song display meant to communicate meaning* is involved in such instances of memory storage, that is, no observational learning of communicative acts proper is involved. What is stored is simply meaningless songstrings in context.

Over generations of transmission under such circumstances, the by now familiar learner bottleneck statistics would ensure a gradual assortative segregation of songstrings by context, certain parts of the large repertoire tending to be sung (and thus also to be heard) in certain environmental, behavioral or social contexts, other parts of the repertoire in others. The process would benefit, moreover, by the fact that a given context would remind an individual of the strings encountered in that context before, making strings from that part of the larger repertoire more likely to be chosen and produced when the individual subsequently encountered that context. But that means that we are done, because the string-meaning pairing we were intent on establishing is now a fact: the meaning of a string is simply the context in which it is habitually sung.

Note that the process of assortment will go on generation after generation, unsupported and undisturbed by any need to use the pairings in order to actually *communicate* meanings, or to gain any advantage from them at all. String production, in this scenario, is driven by the need to *display* (for mate attraction and fending off rivals), and not by the need to communicate meanings. Generated as statistical "artefacts" of the learner bottleneck, the string-meaning pairings are implicit only, embodied in a string's associations with learning-context, perhaps unbeknownst to the singers themselves. They are simply trying to impress and please one another by singing demanding and resource-consuming songs, in conformity with the handicap principle. After many generations of passing through the learner bottlenecks of the population, the display behavior simply happens to take place in such a way that certain strings are sung in certain contexts (adding, in a sense, to the handicap by making memory for proper context part of the display).

After this first round of multigenerational differentiation by context of the string-repertoire as a whole, the same bottleneck dynamic would simply continue to *further* differentiate the now context-specific strings or string-sets according to the logic disclosed by the computer simulations of Kirby and colleagues (see chapter in this volume). One crucial result disclosed by the modelling work is that substrings that happen to be shared between strings attached to different contexts will tend to get attached to aspects or features that happen to be shared by the contexts with which the strings are associated. The principle, independently proposed on linguistic grounds by Wray (1998), causes the historical process to work its way downwards from holistic strings through their progressive segmentation in accordance with shared aspects of the original contexts. Thus, if one or more particular substrings that occur in songstrings used during *group* foraging also happen to occur in songs sung while the *group* gathers for the night's rest, then these substrings will increase in frequency in the singing that takes place during *other group activities* as well (generalization by the bottleneck mechanism). The meaning of the affected strings in this particular example might then be glossed as "done together" (see Figure 22.1, this volume). Continued long enough – and the pressure to display will ensure that it is continued indefinitely – the process will arrive at what we know as words with their meanings, as shown by the simulations.

The entirety of the results regarding a basis for syntactic structuring of strings will follow by the logic of the bottleneck principle uncovered by the simulation work (Batali, 1998, 2002; Kirby, 1998, 2000, 2001, 2002). The final shaping of string structure (syntax) to contextual variables (semantics) will proceed according to the principles uncovered by historical linguistics, because the hypothetical species we just characterized as a group-living mammal without sharply defined breeding season is, needless to say, one of the species along the evolutionary trajectory of *Homo*. Our kind does not exhibit a seasonally defined breeding period: human females remain sexually receptive throughout the year (Alexander, 1990; Geary, 2000). We are, moreover, vocal learners and not only a talking but a singing species (as noted already by von Humboldt, 1836). If, as we have proposed, our capacity for vocal learning evolved for song in accordance with the display principle, the essential requirements of our hypothetical sketch of an entry into the syntax-generating dynamics of language history are fulfilled.

It might appear that our use of whales as our point of departure leads to the counter-factual prediction that only human males should sing and talk, but there are alternatives. Extravagant display by both sexes occurs in many monogamous species (review by Wachtmeister, 2001). In such species display activity typically extends beyond pair formation and is featured throughout the shared life of the partners, a point not without interest in the present context. A number of birds with vocal learning engage in duetting between male and female (Farabaugh, 1982). Moreover, in all primates that sing, both males and females do so (Geissmann, 2000), and most of these species engage in duetting (albeit unlearned). As in birds, there is an association between duetting and pairbonding in primates (Haimoff, 1986). The application of these circumstances to the human past is complicated by the pattern of multimale group sociality among our ancestors, yet some form of pairbond appears to have arisen in this setting as a means of recruiting male parental investment to the demands as well as benefits of infant care and childrearing as encephalization progressed (see Alexander, 1990; MacDonald, 1997; Geary, 2000; Geary and Flinn 2001, and references therein). If human encephalization was at least in part promoted by selection for vocal learning, as we have suggested, then a pleasing temporal coincidence between that crucial development and a behavioral framework for duetting arises.

We also note that Finlay and Darlington's (1995) demonstration that mammalian encephalization proceeds through whole-brain expansion means that encephalization driven by a selection pressure for vocal learning would have expanded all forebrain compartments, even those unrelated to vocal learning. This would have made spare cognitive capacity available as a by-product of the step to vocal learning. Needless to say, potential uses for such spare capacity in the setting of incipient language history are not far to seek.

Much, then, hinges on the crucial question of how and why we evolved vocal learning, an issue that lies beyond the scope of our present remarks. As Nottebohm cautioned some 30 years ago, "you might find it much harder to explain this first step, vocal learning, than the latter acquisition of language" (Nottebohm, 1976, p. 645). For now we rest content, therefore, with proposing that if our capacity for vocal learning evolved for elaborate song used for display purposes then language may have arisen as a direct sequel to vocal learning through the historical dynamics of a multigenerational bottleneck mechanism, as schematically modelled in the computer simulations we have referred to.

21.6. Conclusions: Taken Unawares by Language

It should be noted that what we have outlined in the foregoing is a process by which our forebears might have arrived at a state in which the learned vocal strings they employed in order to impress upon potential mates and rivals acquired not only context-specific use, but syntactic structure. Assuming only the prior existence of vocal learning unconstrained by a species-specific template this outcome is obtainable as the purely historical product of intergenerational transmission through filtering through repeated learner bottlenecks. No natural selection or differential reinforcement or even communicative utility for informational purposes beyond the original non-referential one of display was invoked to achieve this outcome. Nevertheless, the strings in the end possess reference through their intimate matching to the epistemic space of the displaying agents, embodied in a hierarchically organized fit between string syntax and the structure of the agents' contextually organized knowledge of their world (for the latter, see Merker, 2004). This, however, is an entirely inadvertent consequence of the historical process in our conjectural account. It was not intended by the agents themselves at any point of their progress, nor did any use of that fit for purposes of communicating instrumentally useful information play any role on their path to their new cognitive organization, as we have described it. We conclude that they can be said to possess language without knowing it.

Once such an outcome becomes thinkable, it helps us understand that in many ways this is still true of our unselfconscious use of language as it exists among us today. Until our first encounter with a foreign language, a grammar teacher, or a linguist, many of us may not be aware that we have a language separate from life as we live it: we simply talk the talk fitting the context in which we find ourselves, and the motive to do so in order to please or impress rather than to convey veridical or useful information is still with us (cf. Dessalles, 1998, p. 141). In fact, that motive may be the predominant one in our use of language in everyday, non-technical circumstances (cf. Miller, 1997, 2000). That said, it stands to reason that the instrumental uses of the contextual embeddedness of our string-structures is unlikely to have remained undiscovered for long by a large-brained primate like ourselves. Just as a given context serves to remind us of strings appropriate to that context, so a given string can be used to remind our audience of its context (Richman, 2000, p. 306). This opens to us the possibility of exercising instrumental control over the cognitive deployment of the focus of attention of our audience, and it would be strange indeed if that power of language were not to be exploited by us as we go through our daily lives. It is salutary, however, to remind ourselves that a lie can serve such a purpose no less than a truth, and language itself remains entirely neutral between them. There is nothing, in other words, in the account of language given in the foregoing that would suggest that an essential function of language is to communicate useful information – to transfer a resource – between individuals, though nothing prevents it from being put to such use.

To remove any possibility of misunderstanding: By no means should this characterization of human language be taken to imply that human language somehow is a low-cost mode of signalling removed from the functional domain of the handicap principle or manipulative signal use more generally (cf. Knight, 1998; Zahavi, 1993). On the contrary, it exists because of its costliness, but this costliness does not pertain to the energetics of its real-time production, which are decidedly economical (Sundberg, 1987), nor to its structural characteristics as such, but rather to the process of its acquisition. As in elaborate learned birdsong, these costs include the infant's and child's *capacity* (neural resources included) to perceive, discriminative, attend to, learn, memorize, and practice the requisite information and skills, its *effort* devoted to these ends, and the huge amounts of developmental *time* consumed in the process. But far more is involved, because all of this is dependent upon a *massive parental investment* of time and resources in that process by adults providing the infant and child with the support, stimulation and opportunities required for its successful completion. The ontogenetic trajectory of this resource-intensive acquisition of language spans until puberty, and in some cultures even beyond it into young adulthood (see Locke and Bogin, forthcoming).

All of these early investments into the developing individual's facility with language have consequences for adult competence, and have a number of corre-lates in adult accomplishment, reproductive ones included (Alexander, 1990; Geary and Flinn, 2001; MacDonald, 1997; Locke and Bogin, forthcoming). The ontogenetic investment is summed up in the fluency, vocabulary size, and general facility of the resulting adult's use of language, whose facility with language accordingly becomes a marker for the quality of the developmental process that issued in such competence. It serves as such a marker quite independently of the specific content that is conveyed. Idle talk about the weather will do just fine as an opportunity for such display. Our account of human language is thus related to the framework somewhat infelicitously referred to as the "nutritional stress hypothesis" developed to relate developmental factors including brain size to the function of learned song in birds (Hasselquist et al., 1996; Nowicki et al., 2002; Johnson and Whitney, 2005; Soma et al., 2005).

As we have described the process by which language structure originally may have emerged through the multigenerational process of language history starting from songstrings, the conventional meaning and referential content of language strings are inadvertent byproducts of signalling. They are features which did not in themselves drive the processes through which language emerged. Once there, however, these inadvertent characteristics of string-displays could be put to use for actual transmission and exchange of useful information among kin, and extended beyond kin through the practice of reciprocity, but these are issues beyond the scope of the present chapter.

Finally, let us note that the path to language sketched in this chapter may help us understand one of the signal facts about language that has to be accounted for by any theory of its origin that means to be taken seriously, the fact namely that only one lone species among more than 4300 species of mammals, in fact one lone species in the entire history of life on earth, has developed language. This means that general advantages and robust selection pressures are the wrong kinds of agencies to invoke in theories of language origins, or we are left with the puzzle of why only a single species on earth has found its way to it.

Considering its many uses once it is in hand, something must keep language from evolving. An attractive way out of this dilemma would be to find that its emergence depends on a whole set of biological circumstances, each of which is necessary, and at the same time rare, though nevertheless instantiated in nature. The joint fulfillment of such a set of rare possibilities is subject to the shrinking arithmetic of multiplicative probabilities. But that is just what the path to language we have proposed is subject to: vocal learning is rare in mammals, and to this we have added the further requirements of a large song repertoire unconstrained by a species-specific template, group living, absence of determinate breeding season, and some form of pair-bonding or other factor. On multiplying each of these diminutive probabilities together, a single species may indeed be all that we expect to be left with in the end. Whether our ancestors did in fact traverse the path we have sketched is for the future to decide. For now we rest content with having suggested a possible natural history of human language without resorting to biological magic.

Acknowledgments. We thank Tecumseh Fitch and Simon Kirby for valuable discussions relevant to the contents of this chapter.

References

Alexander, R. D. (1990). How Did Humans Evolve? Reflections on the Uniquely Unique Species. *University of Michigan Museum of Zoology Special Publication, 1*, 1–38.

Batali, J. (1998). Computational simulations of the emergence of grammar. In J. R. Hurford, M. Studdert-Kennedy and C. Knight (Eds.), *Approaches to the evolution of language: Social and cognitive bases*, pp. 405–426. Cambridge: Cambridge University Press.

Batali, J. (2002). The negotiation and acquisition of recursive grammars as a result of competition among exemplars. In T. Briscoe (Ed.), *Linguistic Evolution through Language Acquisition: Formal and Computational Models*, pp. 111–172. Cambridge: Cambridge University Press.

Baylis, J. R. (1982). Avian vocal mimicry: Its function and evolution. In D.E. Kroodsma and E.H. Miller (Eds.), *Acoustic communication in birds*, pp. 51–83. Academic Press, New York.

Bybee, Joan (2004). Mechanisms of change as universals of language. Article to appear in Spanish, English version available for download at http://www.unm.edu/~jbybee/

Catchpole, C. K. (1976). Temporal and sequential organization of song in the sedge warbler (Acrocephalus schoenobaenus). *Behaviour, 59*, 226–246.

Chomsky, N. (1980). *Rules and representations.* New York: Columbia University Press.

Clark, C. W. and Clapham, P. J. (2004). Acoustic monitoring on a humpback whale (*Megaptera novaeangliae*) feeding ground shows continual singing into late spring. *Proceedings of the Royal Society of London B, 271*, 1051–1057.

Darwin, C. (1871). *The descent of man and selection in relation to sex.* D. Appleton & Company, New York.

DeGusta, D., Gilbert, W. H. and Turner, S. P. (1999). Hypoglossal canal size and hominid speech. *Proceedings of the National Academy of Sciences (USA), 96*, 1800–1804.

DeLancey, Scott (1993). Grammaticalization and Linguistic Theory. In J. Gomez de Garcia and D. Rood (Eds.), *Proceedings of the 1993 Mid-America Linguistics Conference*, pp. 1–22. Department of Linguistics, University of Colorado.

Dessalles, J. -L. (1998). Altruism, status, and the origin of relevance. In J. R. Hurford, M. Studdert-Kennedy and C. Knight (Eds.), *Approaches to the evolution of language. Social and cognitive bases*, pp. 130–148. Cambridge: Cambridge University Press.

Devoogd, T. J., Krebs, J. R., Healy, S. D. and Purvis, A. (1993). Relations between song repertoire size and the volume of brain nuclei related to song: comparative evolutionary analysis amongst oscine birds. *Proceedings of the Royal Society, London, B254*, 75–82.

Devoogd, T. J. 2004. Where is the bird? In H. P. Ziegler and P. Marler (Eds.), The Behavioral Neurobiology of Birdsong, pp. 778–786. *Annals of the New York Academy of Sciences*, 1016.

Doupé, A. J. and Kuhl, P. K. (1999). Birdsong and human speech: Common themes and mechanisms. *Annual Review of Neuroscience, 22*, 567–631.

Enquist, M., Arak, A., Ghirlanda, S. and Wachtmeister, C. -A. (2002). Spectacular phenomena and limits to rationality in genetic and cultural evolution. *Transactions of the Royal Society of London, B357*, 1585–1594.

Emery, N. J. and Clayton, N.S. (2005). Evolution of the avian brain and intelligence. *Current Biology, 15*, R946–950.

Farabaugh, S. M. (1982). The ecological and social significance of duetting. In D. E. Kroodsma, E. H. Miller and H. Ouellet (Eds.), *Acoustic communication in birds*, pp. 84–124. New York: Academic Press.

Finlay, B. L. and Darlington, R. B. (1995). Linked regularities in the development and evolution of mammalian brains. *Science, 268,* 1578–1584.

Fitch, W. T. (2000). The evolution of speech: a comparative review. *Trends in Cognitive Sciences, 4,* 258–267.

Fitch, W. T. (2006). The biology and evolution of music: A comparative perspective. *Cognition, 100,* 173–215.

Freeberg, T. M. (2000). Culture and courtship in vertebrates: a review of social learning and transmission of courtship systems and mating patterns. *Behavioural Processes, 51,* 177–192.

Geary, D. C. (2000). Evolution and proximate expression of human paternal investment. *Psychological Bulletin, 126,* 55–77.

Geary, D. C. and Flinn, M. V. (2001). Evolution of Human Parental Behavior and the Human Family. *Parenting: Science and Practice, 1,* 5–61.

Geissmann, T. (2000). Gibbon song and human music from an evolutionary perspective. In NL Wallin, B Merker and S Brown, eds. *The origins of music,* pp. 103–123. The MIT Press, Cambridge, MA.

Goldstein, M. H., King, A. P. and West, M. J. (2003). Social interaction shapes babbling: testing parallels between birdsong and speech. *Proceedings of the National Academy of Sciences, USA, 100,* 8050–8055.

Haimoff, E. H. (1986). Convergence in the duetting of monogamous Old World primates. *Journal of Human Evolution, 15,* 51–59.

Hasselquist, D., Bensch, S. and von Schantz, T. (1996). Correlation between song repertoire, extra-pair paternity and offspring survival in the great reed warbler. *Naure,* 381, 229–232.

Hawkins, J. A. (1983). *Word order universals.* Academic Press, New York.

Hayes, K. J. and Hayes, C. H. (1951). The intellectual development of a home-raised chimpanzee. *Proceedings of the American Philosophical Society, 95,* 105–109.

Humboldt, W. von (1836/1988). *On language: The diversity of human language structure and its influence on the mental development of mankind.* Cambridge University Press.

Hurford, J. R. (2000). The emergence of syntax. Editorial introduction to the section on syntax in C. Knight, M. Studdert-Kennedy and J. Hurford (Eds.), *The Evolutionary Emergence of Language: Social function and the origins of linguistic form,* pp. 219–230. Cambridge: Cambridge University Press.

Hurford, J. (2002) Expression/induction models of language evolution: dimensions and issues. In T. Briscoe (Ed.), *Linguistic Evolution through Language Acquisition: Formal and Computational Models.* Cambridge University Press.

Iwaniuk, A. N., Dean, K. M. and Nelson J. E. (2005). Interspecific Allometry of the Brain and Brain Regions in Parrots (Psittaciformes): Comparisons with Other Birds and Primates. *Brain, Behavior and Evolution, 65,* 40–59.

Janik, V. M. and Slater, P. J. B. (1997). Vocal learning in mammals. *Advances in the Study of Behavior, 26,* 59–99.

Jarvis, E. D. (2004). Learned birdsong and the neurobiology of human language. In H.P. Ziegler and P. Marler (Eds.), Behavioral Neurobiology of Birdsong, pp. 749–777. *Annals of the New York Academy of Sciences, 1016.*

Jespersen, O. (1922). *Language, its nature, development and origin.* London: Allen and Unwin.

Johnson, F. and Whitney, O. (2005). Singing-driven gene expression in the developing songbird brain. *Physiology and Behavior, 86,* 390–398.

Jungers, W. L., Pokempner, A. A., Kay, R. F. and Cartmill, M. (2003). Hypoglossal Canal Size in Living Hominoids and the Evolution of Human Speech. *Human Biology*, 75, 473–184.

Kay, R. F., Cartmill, M. and Balow, M. (1998). The hypoglossal canal and the origin of human vocal behavior. *Proceedings of the National Academy of Sciences, USA*, 95, 5417–5419.

Kellogg, W. N. and Kellogg, L. A. (1933). *The Ape and the Child*. New York: McGraw Hill.

King, A. P. and West, M. J. (2002). The ontogeny of competence. In D.J. Lewkcowicz and R. Lickliter (Eds.), *Conceptions of Development*, pp. 77–104. Psychology Press. Philadelphia.

Kirby, S. (1998). Language evolution without natural selection: From vocabulary to syntax in a population of learners. Technical Report, *Edinburgh Occasional Papers in Linguistics, 98–1*, Department of Linguistics, University of Edinburgh.

Kirby, S. (2000). Syntax without Natural Selection: How compositionality emerges from vocabulary in a population of learners. In C. Knight, M. Studdert-Kennedy and J. Hurford (Eds.), *The Evolutionary Emergence of Language: Social function and the origins of linguistic form*, pp. 303–323. Cambridge: Cambridge University Press.

Kirby, S. (2001). Spontaneous evolution of linguistic structure: an iterated learning model of the emergence of regularity and irregularity. *IEEE Transactions on Evolutionary Computation, 5*, 102–110.

Kirby, S. (2002) Learning, bottlenecks and the evolution of recursive syntax. In T. Briscoe (Ed.), *Linguistic Evolution through Language Acquisition: Formal and Computational Models*, pp 173–204. Cambridge: Cambridge University Press.

Knight, C. (1998). Ritual/speech coevolution: a solution tio the problem of deception. In J. R. Hurford, M. Studdert-Kennedy and C. Knight (Eds.), *Approaches to the evolution of language: Social and cognitive bases*, pp. 68–91. Cambridge: Cambridge University Press.

Kroodsma, D. E. and Parker, L. D. (1977). Vocal virtuosity in the brown thrasher. *Auk, 94*, 783–785.

Lehmann, C. (1995). *Thoughts on Grammaticalization*. Second, revised edition. München: LINCOM Europa.

Lieberman, P. (1975). *On the Origins of Language: An Introduction to the Evolution of Human Speech*. New York: Macmillan.

Locke, J. L. and Bogin, B. (in press). Language and life history: A new perspective on the development and evolution of human language. *Behavioral and Brain Sciences*, forthcoming.

MacDonald, K. (1997). Life history theory and human reproductive behavior: Environmental/contextual influences and heritable variation. *Human Nature, 8*, 327–359.

MacLarnon, A. and Hewitt, G. (1999). The evolution of human speech: The role of enhanced breathing control. *American Journal of Physical Anthropology, 109*, 341–363.

Marler, P. (1970). Bird song and speech development: could there be parallels? *American Scientist, 58*, 669–673.

Marler, P. (2000). Origins of music and speech: Insights from animals. In N. L. Wallin, B. Merker & S. Brown (Eds.), *The origins of music*, (pp. 31–48). Cambridge, MA: MIT Press.

Marler, P. (2004). Bird calls: Their potential for behavioral biology. In HP Ziegler and P Marler, eds. The behavioral neurobiology of birdsong, pp. 31–44. *Annals of the New York Academy of Sciences, 1016*.

Marler, P., Evans, C. S., and Hauser, M. D. (1992). Animal signals. Reference, motivation or both? In H. Papousek, U. Jürgens, and M. Papousek (Eds.) *Nonverbal vocal communication: Comparative and developmental approaches* (pp. 66–86). Cambridge University Press.

Merker, B. (2000). Synchronous chorusing and human origins. In N. L. Wallin, B. Merker and S. Brown (Eds.), *The origins of music*, pp. 315–327. Cambridge, MA: MIT Press.

Merker, B. (2004). Cortex, countercurrent context, and dimensional integration of lifetime memory. *Cortex, 40*, 559–576.

Merker, B. (2005). The conformal motive in birdsong, music and language. *Annals of the New York Academy of Sciences, 1060*, 17–28.

Miller, G. F. (1997). Protean primates: The evolution of adaptive unpredictability in competition and courtship. In A. Whiten and R. W. Byrne (Eds.), *Machiavellian Intelligence II*, pp. 312–340. Cambridge University Press.

Miller, G. F. (2000). *The mating mind: how sexual choice shaped the evolution of human nature*. New York: Doubleday.

Nottebohm, F. (1975). A zoologist's view of some language phenomena, with particular emphasis on vocal learning. In E. H. Lenneberg, & E. Lenneberg (Eds.), *Foundations of language development*, pp. 61–103. New York: Academic Press.

Nottebohm F (1976). Discussion paper. Vocal tract and brain: A search for evolutionary bottlenecks. In S.R. Harnad, H.D. Steklis and J. Lancaster (Eds.), Origins and evolution of language and speech, pp. 643–649. *Annals of the New York Academy of Sciences, 280*.

Nowicki, S., Searcy, W. A. and Peters, S. (2002). Brain development, song learning and mate choice in birds: a review and experimental test of the "nutritional stress hypothesis". *Journal of Comparative Physiology A: Sensory, Neural, and Behavioral Physiology*, 188, 1003–1004.

Okanoya, K. (2002). Sexual Display as a Syntactic Vehicle: The Evolution of Syntax in Birdsong and Human Language through Sexual Selection. In A. Wray (Ed.), *The transition to language*, pp. 44–64. Oxford: Oxford University Press.

Payne, K. (2000). The progressively changing songs of humpback whales: A window on the creative process in a wild animal. In N.L. Wallin, B. Merker, & S. Brown (Eds.), *The Origins of Music*, pp. 135–150. Cambridge, MA: The MIT Press.

Pinker, S. and Bloom, P. (1990). Natural Language and Natural Selection. *Behavioral and Brain Sciences, 13*, 707–784.

Richman, B. (2000). How music fixed "nonsense" into significant formulas: On rhythm, repetition, and meaning. In N. L. Wallin, B. Merker and S. Brown (Eds.), *The origins of music*, pp. 301–314. Cambridge, Mass.: The Mit Press.

Seyfarth R. M. and Cheney D. L. (1980). The ontogeny of vervet monkey alarm-calling behavior: A preliminary report. *Zeitschrift für Tierpsychologie, 54*, 37–56.

Snowdon, C. T. and Elowson, A. M. (1992). Ontogeny of primate vocal communication. *In Topics in Primatology, Vol. 1, Human Origins*. T. Nishida, F.B. M. de Waal, W. McGrew, P. Marler and M. Pickford (Eds.), pp. 279–290. Tokyo University Press. Tokyo.

Soma, M., Hasegawa, T. and Okanoya, K. (2005). The evolution of song learning: A review from a biological perspective. *Cognitive Studies*, 12, 166–176.

Smith, K. (2003). Learning biases and language evolution. In S. Kirby (Ed.) *Language Evolution and Computation* (pp. 22–31). Proceedings of the Workshop on Language Evolution and Computation, 15th European Summer School on Logic, Language and Information, Vienna.

Sundberg, J. (1987). *The Science of the Singing Voice*. Dekalb, Illinois: Northern Illinois University Press.

Swanson, L. W. (1995). Mapping the human brain: past, present, and future. *Trends in Neurosciences, 18*, 471–474.

Thorpe, W. H. (1961). *Bird-Song*. Cambridge University Press.

Wachtmeister, C. -A. (2001). Display in monogamous pairs: A review of empirical data and evolutionary explanations. *Animal Behavior, 61*, 861–868.

Williams, H. (2004). Birdsong and singing behavior. In H.P. Ziegler and P. Marler (Eds.), Behavioral Neurobiology of Birdsong, pp. 1–30. *Annals of the New York Academy of Sciences, 1016*.

Wray, A. (1998). Protolanguage as a holistic system for social interaction. *Language and Communication, 18*, 47–67.

Zeigler, H. P. & Marler, P. (Eds.) (2004). Behavioral Neurobiology of Birdsong. *Annals of the New York Academy of Sciences, 1016*.

Zahavi, A. (1993). The fallacy of conventional signaling. *Philosophical Transactions of the Royal Society of London, 340*, 227–230.

Zahavi, A. and Zahavi, A. (1997). *The handicap principle: A missing piece of Darwin's puzzle*. Oxford University Press, Oxford.

22
Neural Substrates for String-Context Mutual Segmentation: A Path to Human Language

Kazuo Okanoya and Bjorn Merker

22.1. Introduction

Linguistic structures are products of biological prerequisites and historical processes. Here we consider a number of neural, behavioral, and learning mechanisms that serve necessary or facilitating roles in the initiation of historical processes. We hypothesize that if mutual segmentation of strings and contexts is promoted by particular biological adaptations and ecological pressures, this could initiate a subsequent historical process of linguistic elaboration. To enable this mutual segmentation, three biological sub-faculties are indispensable: vocal learning, string segmentation, and contextual segmentation. Vocal learning enabled intentional control of vocal output via the direct connection between face motor cortex and medullary vocal nuclei. String segmentation became possible by bottom-up statistical learning by basal ganglia and top-down rule extraction by the prefrontal cortex. Contextual segmentation was implemented also by bottom-up induction of situational correlations at hippocampal and related limbic structures and top-down segmentation of perceived states by the prefrontal cortex. Taken together, we propose that string-context mutual segmentation got its start through the interaction of the prefrontal-hippocampal and prefrontal-striatal parallel loops.

22.1.1. String-Context Mutual Segmentation

In the previous chapter we presented a hypothesis (first suggested by Darwin) for the possible origin of human language. Briefly, we assume our ancestor was a singing ape. Song display was an honest indicator of the singer's fitness. Through the handicap principle, song displays became complex and lengthy (Zahavi & Zahavi, 1996) and included many vocal tokens that were shared with the group members through imitation. Song was initially used for attracting mates and repelling rivals, but gradually different variations of songs were used in different behavioral context. Since songs were learned and song elements were shared within society, a fixed sub-part of these songs appeared in several situation-specific songs. These sub-strings began to be associated with the sub-commonality in the situations within which songs were sung. As processes were repeated and transmitted through generations, linguistic structures would emerge as historical consequences (Figure 22.1).

We divided the requirements for linguistic structures into biological prerequisites and the historical process and then defined what are required as biological preparations to initiate the historical process of linguistic elaboration. The historical process may simply be stated as the process of string-context mutual segmentation: song strings and behavioral contexts are mutually segmented during social interactions. Over generations, this would lead to the emergence of linguistic structure. The natural history up until the historical process was initiated has been described in detail in the previous chapter. The aim of the present chapter is thus to provide neural substrates for the biological prerequisites required to start the process of mutual segmentation.

22.1.2. Sub-Faculties for Mutual Segmentation

Sub-faculties we consider here are vocal learning, string segmentation, and context segmentation (Figure 22.2). Vocal learning is strictly defined as a postnatal acquisition of a novel motor pattern for a novel vocal performance (Jarvis, 2004). A mere modification of innate vocal patterns, which is often seen in vocal animals, should be referred to as vocal plasticity rather than vocal learning. Vocal learning should not be confused with auditory learning that refers to an acquisition of the association between a specific auditory stimulus and a specific behavior: auditory learning is a form of general associative learning with stimuli being auditory, but vocal learning is a specific imitative learning that requires dense vocal-auditory interactions.

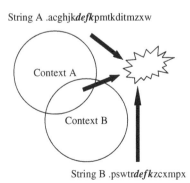

String A .acghjk*defk*pmtkditmzxw

Context A

Context B

String B .pswtr*defk*zcxmpx

FIGURE 22.1. The string-context mutual segmentation hypothesis.

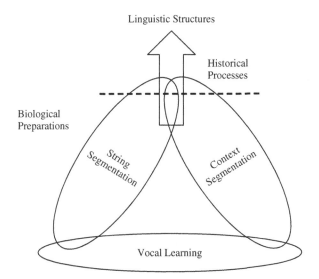

FIGURE 22.2. Biological preparations for mutual segmentation.

String segmentation is an ability to divide a continuous stream of sensory stimuli into smaller functional units. Strings can be mediated by any sensory modalities including visual, auditory, olfactory and tactile, but we specifically deal with auditory segmentation in this chapter, since the primary mode of both song and language is auditory, although language could be expressed in other domains. Auditory segmentation could possibly be based on several cues such as pauses between auditory tokens, sudden discontinuities or transitions in pitch or intensity continua, and probabilistic relations between auditory tokens. In first language acquisition, infants can use any of these cues to segment words from the continuous speech stream (Gomez & Gerken, 2000). This is a first step towards acquiring the syntax.

Context segmentation is an ability to divide a continuous contextual/cognitive space into smaller (functional) units. Contextual space here is loosely defined as a multivariate space whose dimensions might include sensory modalities, internal states including memory, and reinforcement contingencies. Animals explicitly or implicitly can learn and discriminate complex context and learn to select adaptive behavior accordingly. Undoubtedly, this form of learning is widespread among vertebrates. This is the very first step in acquiring semantics.

22.2. Vocal Learning

22.2.1. Species with Vocal Learning

Although auditory learning is widespread among animals possessing an auditory system, vocal learning is scarce. Among primates, we humans are the only species that show vocal learning. There is evidence of vocal plasticity in non-human primates (Hihara et al., 2003), but these exemplify the degree of plasticity that cannot be classified as an acquisition of novel vocal patterns (Janik and Slater, 1997). In mammals, only three phylogenic lines of animals show vocal learning. These are primates (only humans), bats (Boughman, 1998), and cetaceans (Payne, 2000). Coincidently, also in birds, only three classes of animals show vocal learning; passerines (songbirds), psittacines (parrots), and swifts (humming birds) (Jarvis, 2004). It is important to note that these classes of animals are only distantly related when considering evolutionary origins of vocal learning.

This observation provides three possibilities as to the evolution of vocal learning. First, vocal learning independently evolved in these animals. Thus, neural substrates for vocal learning are different among animals with vocal learning. Second, vocal learning independently disappeared from many classes of animals and vocal learning was actually widespread in the past. In this case, vocal learning was present in a common ancestor of birds and mammals and we should consider examining some existing reptiles for vocal learning. Also, in this case, neural substrates utilized for vocal learning should be common among mammals and birds. This is unlikely considering the vast divergence of telencephalic architecture between mammals and birds.

Third, and most likely, vocal learning evolved independently, but out of common plans of brain circuitry under similar selection pressures. A general plan for intentional motor execution and a general plan for sensory-motor interface were probably precursors for vocal learning. In fact, Jarvis (2000) observed similar topography and connectivity as well as the pattern of gene expression in the forebrain nuclei responsible for vocal learning in three lines of avian vocal learners. If vocal learning evolved independently out of common sensory-motor systems, under common selection pressures, we need to consider the neural substrates and pre-adaptations for vocal learning.

22.2.2. Neural Substrates for Vocal Learning

Are there any specific anatomical substrates that correlate with the faculty of vocal learning? One candidate substrate would be the direct cortical-medullary pathway for articulation and breathing. In humans, a part of the motor cortex directly projects to the nucleus retro-ambiguous of the medulla (Kuypers, 1958). This projection is absent in the squirrel monkey and chimpanzee and Jurgens (2002) thus assumes that this projection exists only in humans among primates. Similarly, there is the same direct cortical-medullary pathway for articulation and breathing in the zebra finch, a species of songbirds, but a similar projection in pigeons does not exist and all of pigeon vocalizations are innate (Wild, 1993; Wild et al., 1997). Considering this evidence, we can hypothesize that this projection exists in those species that show vocal learning while it is absent in the species without vocal learning (Okanoya et al., 2004).

While this projection exists only in a limited number of species, there is still a possibility that a very faint projection of this kind is nevertheless present in most species. Deacon (1997) introduced the anecdotal story of an orphaned harbor seal that learned to mimic the speech of the fisherman who raised the seal in his home. This animal had a brain inflammation when young and Deacon suggested that during the process of recovery the cortical medullar projection might have been reinforced in this particular animal. If so, the possibility arises that animals trained to perform spontaneous vocalizations while young might have this pathway reinforced, thus inducing vocal learning in a species that would not ordinarily possess this capacity.

22.2.3. Pre-Adaptations for Vocal Learning

Among vocal learners, birds, bats, and whales seem to have reasonable pre-adaptation for vocal learning. Birds and bats have to control their breathing while they are flying and this requirement was probably the pre-adaptation for intentional vocal control. Similarly, whales need to control breathing while they are submerged and this led to intentional vocal control (Janik & Slater, 2000). The issue of the origin of vocal learning in humans is a major unsolved issue, as noted in our previous chapter (this volume). Here too, intentional control of respiration may have played a significant role, and that in the context of the special circumstances surrounding the immaturity of the human neonate and its need for parental care (Okanoya et al., 2002).

Human babies are conspicuous among primates in that they emit high-intensity, long-lasting cries right after birth. Such cries are obviously maladaptive in wild animals in that it could easily attract predators. We suggest therefore that the infant cry must be a behavior obtained after ancestral humans acquired social and cultural skills to protect themselves from predation pressure. The first cry after the birth has a function to eliminate amniotic fluid, but crying continues long after that. Likewise, nidicolous species of birds emit very loud begging calls and isolation calls that recruit parental behavior including feeding and protection of the hatchlings. Begging calls are so loud that they easily can attract predators. Therefore, parents have to engage in strong parental behavior to avoid predation of hatchlings and themselves (cf. Trivers, 1974). Chicks can thus manipulate parents because they acquire cortical control of breathing to adapt for flying. In this regard, the fact that humans and nidicolous songbirds share helplessness in infancy may also be related to this pre-adaptation (Alexander, 1990).

We analyzed syntactical and phonological developmental changes in the baby cry to show how the pattern becomes complex as the baby grows (Okanoya et al., 2002). At least three stages of cry development could be identified; each may be associated with respective anatomical changes. Baby cries begin as a regular repetition of a stereotyped vocal unit. At this stage, the cry probably is controlled by the midbrain vocal center only. This type of vocalization continues for two post-natal weeks after which cries begin to be more irregular, showing variable patterns of phonology and rhythmic patterns. At this stage, limbic influences are presumably gradually growing stronger. Mothers often can identify what babies want based on the pattern of their cries. During the interaction with mothers, the cry probably became more adaptive by allowing cortical control so that mothers can be more precisely governed by the baby's crying. Infant cries thus may function to train cortical-midbrain connections necessary for more intentional vocal output that eventually results in speech competence.

22.3. String Segmentation

22.3.1. Behavioral Evidence for String Segmentation

It is essential for our sensory systems to segment continuous streams of stimuli into functional units. Especially, the very beginning of language acquisition involves segmentation of words out of a continuous speech stream. Among several cues available for string segmentation, let us examine the statistical cue. Learning of sequence statistics or "statistical learning" has attracted a great deal of attention in recent years (Gomez & Gerken, 2000). When a nonsense auditory stream consisting of 6 tri-syllable "words" were continuously presented, the transitional probability within a "word" was always 1 but that between "words" was 1/6. Without knowing each word and without knowing the structure of the stimulus, we only hear a nonsense stream of syllables but gradually begin to appreciate word boundaries because of statistical learning. When asked the familiarity of the stimulus "word" that was presented in the task versus a "pseudo word" that was never presented, we can usually identify which was more familiar.

As early as at eight months after birth, babies can detect transitional probabilities between on-going speech syllables and use those statistics to find word boundaries, as shown by a habituation paradigm (Saffran et al., 1996). The same "word boundary" detection was possible with non-linguistic stimuli of pure tones (Saffran et al., 1999). Similar procedures were used to examine statistical learning in a New World monkey, the cotton-top Tamarin (Hauser et al., 2001) showing that this ability is not specific to humans. These were taken as evidence that word segmentation learning may not require any special language device but rather is made possible by a domain general ability of statistical learning (Bates & Elman, 1996).

22.3.2. String Segmentation in Birdsong

Songbirds learn courtship songs from adult males (reviewed in Catchpole & Slater, 1995; Zeigler & Marler, 2004). Their songs consist of temporally isolated song elements and their elements are arranged in a fixed order or in accordance with a specific syntactical rule. Most of these song elements are learned from their fathers and conspecific neighbors. When song learning occurs in a multi-tutor environment, learners often splice parts of songs that are sung by different males based on prosodic cues such as silent intervals between song notes, changes in element types, or at the point of interruption (Williams & Staples, 1992). In a species with more complex song syntax, birds also use statistical information in conspecific songs: chunking of song notes often occurs at junctions of lower transition probability (Takahasi & Okanoya, unpublished data). Thus, string segmentation occurs in songbirds during song learning and song production.

When perceiving speech streams, a phrase structure is processed as a perceptual unit in humans. When a sentence like "I love you" is presented into one ear and a click is presented into the other in a temporal position that overlaps with the word "love", the perceptual position of the click is likely to shift in between "I" and "love." That is, the perceptual position of an embedded click moves outside of the phrase structure (Fodor & Bever, 1965). We examined whether a similar phenomenon could be observed in songbirds. We trained Bengalese finches, a species of songbirds with complex song syntax, in a click-detection experiment. Birds were trained to peck a key when they heard a click in an operant conditioning task with food reinforcement. When a background of his own song was played in the test box, the reaction time of the subject bird to detect the click was longer than without the background song or with the background song played in reverse: detection of clicks is postponed until a chunk of song notes is processed. Thus, chunks of birdsong, like chunks of linguistic elements, are processed as a cognitive unit (Suge & Okanoya, under revision).

These data suggest that one essential prerequisite for the type of historical structural transformation dealt with in our previous chapter – namely the capacity for segmentation (cf. Hurford, 2000) – is already present in the vocal learning of some singing species. The capacity for segmentation might also lead to the hierarchical nature of songs in some species (Okanoya, 2004).

22.3.3. Neural Substrates for String Segmentation

If statistical learning is possible with domain-general brain mechanisms, language areas in the brain may not be required for such processes. However, brain imaging studies on learning of sequential rules in music have shown the contrary: Broca's area was active during such tasks (Maess et al., 2001; Patel, 2003). More directly, we have used a similar statistical stimulus and the stimulus with the same token but without statistical rules to compare brain activation by near-infrared optic spectroscopy and found that Broca's area was active only during statistical stimulation (Abla & Okanoya, in preparation). Thus, statistical learning probably utilizes Broca's areas but it is also possible without such specialized areas as shown in the new world monkey, tamarins. Perhaps, results of statistical learning is expressed in Broca's area in humans, but computation of statistical information could be processed by some other systems as well.

Here again, results from birdsongs may be suggestive (Okanoya, 2004). Most neural substrates for song learning, song maintenance, and song performance have been identified in the bird brain (Zeigler & Marler, 2004). Briefly, birdsong is controlled by two major forebrain pathways: anterior pathway and posterior pathway. Auditory information is conveyed up to a part of the forebrain equivalent to the primary auditory cortex, Field L (a part of the primary auditory cortex). From there, processing for more specific information occurs in NCM (nidopallium code-laterale, a part of the secondary auditory cortex) and cHV (caudal Hyperpallium ventrale, a part of the secondary auditory cortex). Programming for song motor patterns occurs in a region of the face motor cortex equivalent, the RA (robustus archipallium, a part of the primary motor cortex), which directly projects to the medullary respiratory and motor centers, or via the midbrain vocal area, the DM (dorsal medial nucleus of the midbrain), which is equivalent to the periaquadactal gray in mammals. The auditory information is fed into NIf (nucleus interfacialis, a part of the association cortex) and then to HVC (hyperpallium ventrale pars caudalis, a part of the association cortex). HVC has direct projection to RA and also to Area X, which is a part of basal ganglia. Area X then projects to a thalamic nucleus DLM and from there, projection comes back to a telencephalic nucleus LMAN (lateral magnocellular nucleus of the nidopallium, a part of the sensory/motor cortex). LMAN then projects to RA, completing the indirect connection between HVC and RA. The HVC-RA-medullar connection is called the posterior motor pathway and the HVC-Area X-DLM-LMAN-RA connection is called the anterior pathway.

Thus, when an analogy between human language and birdsong is considered, we can propose the followings: NIf may be comparable with Wernicke's area and HVC may be comparable with Broca's area, because NIf receives higher auditory information and sends to HVC that controls the face-motor cortex equivalent, the RA. Also, LMAN may be comparable with the anterior cingulate cortex, because LMAN receives projection from the basal ganglia and also sends projection to RA, the motor cortex equivalent (Figure 22.3).

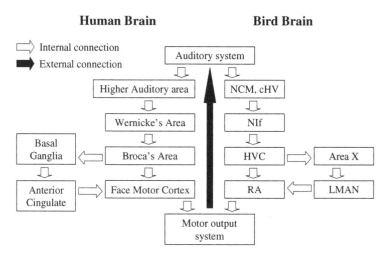

FIGURE 22.3. Analogy for string segmentation by human brain and by bird brain.

In an ERP study with human subjects, we found that string segmentation was associated with a negative brain potential that was strongest at an electrode placed near the anterior cingulate cortex (Abla et al., in preparation). When a source estimation algorithm was applied on the same data recorded from 32 channels, the basal ganglia was the source of the signal. With the data from the near infrared spectroscopy stated earlier, these data suggest that the prefrontal cortex – basal ganglia loop maybe responsible for statistical segmentation of the continuous auditory stream. The same loop may be responsible for controlling complex serial behavior involving string segmentation of a continuous stream, such as piano playing or type writing (Parsons et al., 2005).

The same loop is also known to be used in birdsong learning and maintenance. When LMAN was lesioned in juvenile zebra finches, their songs became stereotyped without further elaboration (Bottjer et al., 1984). On the other hand, when Area X was lesioned in adult Bengalese finches, segmental structure of the song was impaired by causing stuttering (Kobayashi et al., 2001). Furthermore, when pharmacological manipulation was made to suppress neural activities in LMAN, variations in juvenile song disappeared but it recovered as the drug effect waned (Ölveczky et al., 2005). Thus, segmentation of birdsong strings may also be governed by the cortex-basal ganglia pathway.

Both HVC in songbirds and Broca's area in humans are song- or language-specific organs in the sense that these could not be identified in the brains of related species (i.e., non-songbirds or non-human primates) without vocal learning. In both humans and birds, these structures appeared on the motor side of the sensory-motor junction in the forebrain. These structures may be a specialized form of prefrontal structures that promote statistical learning and rule learning. In this regard, it may be interesting to examine the efficiency of statistical learning in animals with and without these specialized structures. The controversy between the nativist and the empiricist could partially reside in how the modularity and domain specificity of these structures are seen. Are they structures specially evolved for that specific purpose or are they simply a specialization of existing structures? This is an essential question to be solved by comparative neuroethological investigations in birds and humans.

22.4. Context Segmentation

We routinely segment behavioral context based on multiple environmental and internal cues and this would be a rudimentary form of semantics. A somewhat simpler example is spatial navigation. The idea that the hippocampus may function as a spatial map was first presented by O'Keefe and Dostrovsky in 1971 with some experimental evidence. When a rat navigates a novel environment freely, a particular neuron in the hippocampus fires when the rat is exploiting a particular part of the environment. This finding was later expanded to include modeling research. In general, it was shown that with Hebbian learning and lateral inhibition, a network of suitably interconnected neurons begins to fire when a specific class of inputs is present. Such a network can establish attractor dynamics and several attractors can specify specific locations of the environment. Not only that, since the hippocampus receives sensory, emotional, and reinforcement information from different brain areas, this structure is suitable for segmenting a multi-dimensional behavioral context (Gluck & Myers, 1993).

In fact, a recent experiment by O'Keefe's group showed that these cells not only respond to specific locations, but also begin to behave as attractors for specific environmental shapes (Wills et al., 2005). This is in good agreement with our current hypothesis that the hippocampus could function as a bottom-up categorizer for behavioral context in general. In common with many other learning networks, such a categorizing network will show the capacity for generalization (Ghirlanda & Enquist, 2003), supplying the other essential prerequisite for the type of historical structural transformation dealt with in our previous chapter (cf. Hurford, 2000).

While the hippocampus functions as a bottom-up categorizer, top-down effects are probably governed by the prefrontal cortex. While the learning rate of the neocortex is slow, the hippocampus learns rapidly based on concurrent, local, and time-limited information (O'Reilly & Rudy, 2000; O'Reilly & Norman, 2002). Thus, the hippocampus can segment contextual parameters quickly, and the result of segmentation is tested by statistical or rule-based prediction by the prefrontal cortex. This is similar to the case of string segmentation in which basal ganglia give rise to short term statistics of on-going stimuli, the prefrontal cortex is more likely to function at a slower rate with a longer time constant.

22.5. Putting them Together

22.5.1. Mutual Categorization of Vocalizations and Behavioral Contexts: A Rudimentary Step

It is not easy to show the process of string-context mutual segmentation experimentally since it is a historical process. But even in the short run, similar processes might occur. Precedents for a rudimentary form of acquired "naming" achieved through association between behavioral contexts and particular behavioral tokens exists in several animals. When this process is enhanced by the ability to learn new behavioral tokens and combine them freely, that is, for example, by vocal learning, we are almost at the stage to begin the string-context mutual segmentation.

We observed that when trained to use a rake to retrieve distant food, monkeys spontaneously began to vocalize "coo" calls. They did so especially when the preparation of the rake tool by the experimenter was delayed (Hihara et al., 2003).

To further investigate this phenomenon, we systematically manipulated behavioral contexts by presenting the tool or food whenever the monkey made a vocalization *irrespective of the type of call emitted*. In one experimental situation, the experimenter placed a food morsel at a distance when the monkey produced a coo call (Call occasion A). By the second coo call (Call occasion B) the experimenter gave a rake tool to the monkey. The monkey could retrieve the food by the rake. In another, the experimenter gave the rake to the monkey beforehand. A piece of food was placed at a distance when the monkey vocalized a coo call (Call occasion C). Again, no attempt was made to differentiate the calls by type in these situations (A, B, and C). After 5 sessions of trainings, the monkeys eventually used acoustically distinct types of calls when they asked for the tool (Call B) or food (Call A and C). The calls used to ask for the tool was longer and higher pitched than the ones used to ask for the food. Calls had become correlated with context without being differentially reinforced to this end. We note the relevance of this finding to the process of segregation of song-strings by context discussed in our previous chapter.

As a possible explanation for this finding we suggest that the different reward conditions (food or tool) set up different emotional contexts for the monkeys. Different emotional contexts, in turn, affected the production of coo calls differently for the tool or food situations. Since the tool training can be assumed to activate the neocortex very highly, the calls were associated with different behavioral contexts. Thus, the calls became categorized and emotionally differentiated calls gradually became categorical vocalizations. Through this process, we suspect the emotional coo calls changed into categorical labels denoting the behavioral situation. We speculate that this categorization of vocal tokens may be related to highly specified behavioral situations. Such specified behavioral situations would evoke specific emotional content in the limbic system including amygdala and hippocampus. States of excitation in the limbic system may thus be labeled by the emotional vocalizations associated with the situations.

Naturally, our macaque example is limited to a contextual association between *call* types and context, but the principle is no less applicable to the association of contexts with full songstrings produced by a singing animal, as discussed in the previous chapter.

22.6. Conclusion

Taking these speculations together, we propose that longer strings are segmented by the action of the cortex-basal ganglia pathway and each part-string is represented by a mnemonic. In either case, the parallel, complex behavioral contexts are segmented by the prefrontal- hippocampal loop and each part-context may also be represented by a different mnemonic. These two sets of mnemonics can interact together to represent both part-string and part-context. Alternatively, if the process advanced slowly, the two sets of mnemonics may not be necessary and string and context segmentation would proceed with one common mnemonic.

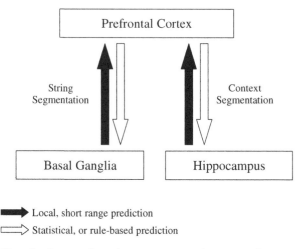

FIGURE 22.4. Neural substrates for string-context mutual segmentation

In any case, the parallel operation of these two systems would then enable mutual segmentation and matching of behavioral context and song strings, a process tantamount to an incipient language system (Merker & Okanoya, 2005).

In this regard, language may be possible without assuming a special "recursion" device suggested by Hauser, Chomsky and Fitch (2002). The recursive function might arise secondarily from the interaction between the prefrontal-basal ganglia loop and the prefrontal-hippocampus loop (Figure 22.4); that is, although the recursive function reflects the formal aspect of language, it may actually be the outcome of syntax-semantics interaction. Once a system of mutual segmentation is in place, the historical process itself may generate the remaining formal linguistic devices and structures. As shown by Kirby (2002) even recursion can emerge from the historical process, given "predicates that can take other predicates as arguments."

References

Alexander, R. D. (1990). How Did Humans Evolve? Reflections on the Uniquely Unique Species. *University of Michigan Museum of Zoology Special Publication, 1*, 1–38.

Bates, E. & Elman, J. (1996) Learning rediscovered. *Science*, 274, 1849–1850.

Bottjer, S. W., Miesner, E. A. & Arnold, A. P. (1984). Forebrain lesions disrupt development but not maintenance of song in passerine birds. *Science*, 224, 901–3.

Boughman, J. W. (1998). Vocal learning by greater spear-nosed bats. *Proc. R. Soc. Lond.B*, 265, 227–233.

Catchpole, C. K., & Slater, P. J. B. (1995). *Bird song: Biological themes and variations.* Cambridge, UK: Cambridge University Press.

Deacon, T. W. (1997). *The symbolic species.* Norton & Company, New York.

Fodor, J, & Bever, T (1965). The psychological reality of linguistic segments. *J verbal learn verbal behav* 4, 414–420.

Ghirlanda, S. and Enquist, M. (2003). A century of generalization. *Animal Behaviour*, 66, 15–36.

Gluck, M. A., Myers, C. E. (1993). Hippocampal mediation of stimulus representation: a computational theory. *Hippocampus*, 3, 491–516.

Gomez, R. L. & Gerken, L. (2000). Infant artificial language learning and language acquisition. *Trends in Cognitive Sciences*, 4, 178–186.

Hauser, M. D., Newport, E. L. & Aslin, R. N. (2001). Segmentation of the speech stream in a nonhuman primate: statistical learning in cotton-top tamarins. *Cognition*, 78, B53–B64.

Hauser, M., Chomsky, N. & Fitch, T. (2002). The faculty of language: what is it, who has it, and how did it evolve? *Science*, 298, 1569–1579.

Hihara S, Yamada H, Iriki A, Okanoya K. (2003). Spontaneous vocal differentiation of coo-calls for tools and food in Japanese monkeys. *Neurosci Res*. 45, 383–9.

Hosino, T. & Oknanoya, K. (2000). Lesion of a higher order song nucleus disrupts phrase level complexity in Bengalese finches. *NeuroReport*, 11, 2091–2095.

Hurford, J. R. (2000). The emergence of syntax. Editorial introduction to the section on syntax in C. Knight, M. Studdert-Kennedy and J. Hurford (Eds.), *The Evolutionary Emergence of Language: Social function and the origins of linguistic form*, pp. 219–230. Cambridge: Cambridge University Press.

Janik, V. M. and Slater, P. J. B. (1997). Vocal learning in mammals. *Advances in the Study of Behavior, 26*, 59–99.

Jarvis, E. D. et al. (2000). Behaviourally driven gene expression reveals song nuclei in hummingbird brain. *Nature*, 406, 628–632.

Jarvis ED (2004). Learned birdsong and the neurobiology of human language. In HP Ziegler and P Marler, eds. *Behavioral Neurobiology of Birdsong*, pp. 749–777. *Annals of the New York Academy of Sciences*, 1016.

Jurgens U. (2002). A study of the central control of vocalization using the squirrel monkey. Med. Eng. Phys., 7-8, 473–477.

Kirby, S. (2002). Learning, bottlenecks, and the evolution of recursive syntax. In T. Briscoe (Ed.), *Linguistic Evolution through Language Acquisition: Formal and Computational Models*, pp. 173–204. Cambridge University Press.

Kobayashi, K., Uno, H. & Okanoya, K. (2001). Partial lesions in the anterior forebrain pathway affect song production in adult Bengalese finches. *NeuroReport*, 12, 353–358.

Kuypers, H. G. J. M. (1958). Corticobulbar connection to the pons and lower brain-stem in man. Brain, 81, 364–88.

Maess, B., Koelsch, S., Gunter, T. C. & Friederici, A. D. (2001). Musical syntax is processed in Broca's area: an MEG study. Nature Neuroscience 4, 540–545.

Merker, B. & Okanoya, K. (2005). Contextual semanticization of song strings syntax: a possible path to human language. *Proceedings of Second International Symposium on the Emergence and Evolution of Linguistic Communication*, Universisty of Hertfordshire, April 2005, pp. 72–75.

Okanoya, K. (2002). Sexual Display as a Syntactic Vehicle: The Evolution of Syntax in Birdsong and Human Language through Sexual Selection. In A. Wray (Ed.), *The transition to language*, pp. 44–64. Oxford: Oxford University Press.

Okanoya, K. (2004). Song syntax in Bengalese finches: proximate and ultimate analyses. Advances in the study of behaviour, 34, 297–345.

Okanoya, K., Ichii, H., Ushijima, H. (2002). Baby cry as a pre-adaptation to language. *Proceedings of Fourth International Conference on the Evolution of Language*, Harvard, March 2002, pp. 86.

Okanoya, K., Hihara, S., Tokimoto, N., Tobari, Y. & Iriki, A. (2004). Complex vocal behaviour and cortical-medullar projection. *Proceedings of First International Symposium on the Emergence and Evolution of Linguistic Communication*, Kanazawa, Japan, May 2004, pp. 65–69.

O'Keefe, J. & Dostrovsky, J. (1971). The hippocampus as a spatial map. Preliminary evidence from unit activity in the freely-moving rat. *Brain Research*, 34, 171–175.

Ölveczky, B. P., Andalman, A. S. & Fee, M. S. (2005). Vocal experimentation in the juvenile songbird requires a basal ganglia circuit. *PLoS Biol.* 3, e153.

O'Reilly, R. C. & Rudy, J. W. (2000). Computational principles of learning in the neocortex and hippocampus. *Hippocampus*, 10, 389–397.

O'Reilly, R. C. & Norman, K. (2002). Hippocampal and neocortical contributions to memory: advances in the complementary learning systems framework. *Trends in Cognitive Science*, 505–510.

Parsons, L. M., Sergent, J., Hodges, D. A. & Fox, P. T. (2005). The brain basis of piano performance. *Neuropsychologia*, 43, 199–215.

Patel, A. D. (2003). Language, music, syntax and the brain. *Nature Neuroscience*, 6, 674– 681.

Pepperberg, I. (1999). The Alex studies: cognitive and communicative abilities of grey parrots. Harvard University Press, Cambridge.

Payne, K. (2000). The progressively changing songs of humpback whales: A window on the creative process in a wild animal. In N.L. Wallin, B. Merker, & S. Brown (Eds.), *The Origins of Music,* pp. 135–150. Cambridge, MA: The MIT Press.

Saffran, J. R., Aslin, R. N., & Newport, E. L. (1996). Statistical Learning by 8-Month-Old Infants. *Science*, 274, 1926–1928.

Saffran, J.R. et al. (1999). Statistical learning of tonal structure by adults and infants. *Cognition*, 70, 27–52

Suge, R. & Okanoya, K. (under revision). Perceptual chunking in self-produced song by Bengalese finches. *Animal Cognition.*

Trivers, R. L. (1974). Parent-offspring conflict. *Americal Zoologist*, 14, 249–264.

Wild, J. M. (1993). Descending projections of the songbird nucleus robustus archistriatalis. *J. Comp. Neurol.* 338, 225–241.

Wild, J. M., Li, D. & Eagleton, C. (1997). Projections of the dorsomedial nucleus of the intercollicular complex (DM) in relation to respiratory – vocal nuclei in the brainstem of pigeon and zebra finch. *J. Comp. Neurol.* 377, 392–413.

Williams, H. & Staples, K. (1992). Syllable chunking in zebra finch (Taeniopygia guttata) song. *Journal of Comparative Psychology*, 106, 278–286.

Wills, T. J., Lever, C., Cacucci, F., Burgess, N. & O'Keefe, J. (2005). Attractor dynamics in the hippocampal representation of the local environment. *Science*, 308, 873–876.

Zahavi, A. and Zahavi, A. (1997). The handicap principle: A missing piece of Darwin's puzzle. Oxford University Press, Oxford.

Zeigler, H. P. & Marler, P. (Eds.) (2004). Behavioral Neurobiology of Birdsong. *Annals of the New York Academy of Sciences, 1016.*

INDEX